THE
DOLPHIN
READER

THE
DOLPHIN
READER

FOURTH EDITION

DOUGLAS HUNT
University of Missouri

CAROLYN PERRY
Westminster College

HOUGHTON MIFFLIN COMPANY   BOSTON   TORONTO
GENEVA, ILLINOIS   PALO ALTO
PRINCETON, NEW JERSEY

Senior Sponsoring Editor: Dean Johnson
Editorial Assistant: Mary Furlong
Senior Project Editor: Susan Westendorf
Senior Production/Design Coordinator: Jill Haber
Senior Manufacturing Coordinator: Priscilla Bailey
Marketing Manager: Charles Caveliere

ACKNOWLEDGMENTS

DIANE ACKERMAN: From *The Moon by Whale Light* by Diane Ackerman. Copyright © 1991 by Diane Ackerman. Reprinted by permission of Random House, Inc.

SHERWOOD ANDERSON: "Discovery of a Father" by Sherwood Anderson. Reprinted by permission of Harold Ober Associates Incorporated. Copyright 1939 by The Reader's Digest Association, Inc. Renewed © 1966 by Eleanor Copenhver Anderson.

Acknowledgments continue following Author/Title Index.

COVER DESIGNER: Clifford Stoltze, Stoltze Design
COVER IMAGE: computer graphics by Clifford Stoltze

Printed in the U.S.A.

Library of Congress Catalog Card Number: 95-76951

ISBN: 0-395-73343-X

Examination Copy ISBN: 0-395-76557-9

123456789-QM-98   97   96   95

CONTENTS

Note: An asterisk denotes fiction or drama. Annotated Contents may be found in the Previews that begin each unit.

PREFACE

Just as a physician's first responsibility is "to do no harm," a reviser's first responsibility may be to avoid throwing the baby out with the bath water. Let's begin, therefore, by mentioning two features that have remained constant from the first edition of *The Dolphin Reader* to the present edition. The first is *connectedness*. The readings cluster around questions central to the lives of students and central to the disciplines they study:

> How are we initiated into our culture?
> How do we define what is masculine and what is feminine?
> How does the community we live in shape our individual identities?
> How do we deal with social differences within the community?
> Do we view ourselves as a part of nature or apart from nature?
> When is technological change progress, and when is it folly?
> How do the media shape our perceptions of life?
> What is the difference between mere learning and real understanding?

Though each of the eight units in this edition "specializes" in one of these questions, each question is such a powerful magnet for ideas that, as one user reports, they "saturate" the book and create "crossovers": Daniel Boorstin's "Technology and Democracy" is placed in "Progress," but can be a powerful supplement to "Communities" or to "Nature"; Carol Bly's "Growing Up Expressive" could contribute to *any* unit in the book. All this is to say that we took our questions seriously, knowing that each would lead eventually to all and that a ball put up by one essay would land resoundingly in several other essays.

The second baby in the bath water is *variety in tone and style*. If every edition of *The Dolphin Reader* has taken ideas seriously, every edition has likewise avoided the stuffiness of some "great ideas" readers by balancing major essays with others that are shorter, lighter, more contemporary, and (frankly) more transient. We think that the major essays are crucial: they contain what Malcolmn X called "intellectual vitamins," and no student should leave college without learning to deal with a "hard" reading. But, as Samuel Johnson once said, every reader eventually wants to escape the schoolmaster and turn to a friend. The shorter and lighter essays deal with the central ideas in forms that many students are more likely to warm to and perhaps more likely to emulate.

Twenty-one of the seventy essays in this edition are new, enough to add fresh insights without robbing loyal users of too many favorites. We have also added two new short stories and—for the first time—have included a poem in each unit. We had considered including poems in previous editions, but a qualm about shackling them to themes held us back. At last we had to laugh at this qualm: it seemed like refusing to use an umbrella for fear it would get wet. Also new to this edition are "lead off" essays for each unit with marginal annotations and questions intended to alert students to the issues that will arise in subsequent essays. The opening essay is not the heaviest hitter in the line-up: ordinarily it is a fairly short piece that can be read and discussed in a single class period, perhaps as a way of getting a new unit started on a day when students hand in papers that are connected to a previous unit.

In the third edition we had added two features that some instructors have found particularly useful, and these have been retained: *paper topics* and *style lessons*. The sixteen paper topics collected in Appendix A, many of which call for comparative reading of selections in *The Dolphin Reader*, should yield substantial pieces of writing, ranging from the auto-biographical to the historical. Appendix B contains a sampler of 18 style lessons drawn from essays in the text. These lessons may provide students an opportunity to imitate the author's way of styling a sentence or dovetailing a paragraph or managing some of the other technical skills that might otherwise go unnoticed and unused. In the *Instructor's Resource Manual*, instuctors will find additional style lessons to accompany most of the essays in the reader.

The *Instructor's Resource Manual* is certainly one of the most thorough available, containing "work-ups" of each reading, including background for the instructor, style lessons, questions for class discussion or writing, and a teacher-to-teacher discussion of how these questions may play out in class. For her excellent work on the *Instructor's Resource Manual*, we offer special thanks to Melody Richardson Daily.

Thanks go also to our supportive editors at Houghton Mifflin, especially to Dean Johnson, whose steady hand on the tiller reassured us. We are indebted to dozens of teachers who have made suggestions in person, by phone, and by mail, and especially to the following colleagues for their reviews:

James K. Bell, College of San Mateo, CA
Frank Fennell, Loyola University, Chicago, IL
Ronald Johnson, Northern Michigan University
Joseph Powell, Central Washington University
Linda Pritchett, University of Texas, San Antonio
Lynda Swanson, South Puget Sound Community College, WA

DOUG HUNT

CAROLYN PERRY

THE
DOLPHIN
READER

Introduction: About the Essay

DOUGLAS HUNT

UNDERSTANDING AT THREE LEVELS

When I was about ten, I used to watch a television show called "Learn to Draw" with Jon Gnagy. Gnagy told his viewers that anyone could draw well who began by mastering the four basic shapes: ball, cone, cube, and cylinder. Once you could visualize these shapes and sketch them, you would recognize them—bent and stretched, highlighted and shaded—as the building blocks of every object, every scene. The method worked. After a few weeks you began to see, for example, the human nose as a cone (base down, point tilted back between the eyes) embedded in the elongated ball of the head, which rested on the cylinder of the neck, and so forth down to the toes (cylinder, cylinder, ball). Once you saw things this way, drawing became not easy, but possible. And as you drew, you improved your eye for the underlying shapes of everything you looked at, in nature or the cityscape or the art museum. Years later in a college art history class, I learned that the great French painter Cézanne had recommended to a young painter a system even leaner than Gnagy's: "You must see in nature the cylinder, the sphere, the cone, all put into perspective."

To identify the underlying "shapes" or elements seems a promising step toward mastering writing as well as drawing, but people disagree about what these elements are. My seventh-grade teacher was convinced that what counted were the patterns of sentences, and she taught us to recognize all the basic types: subject–verb, subject–verb–object, subject–verb–object–indirect object, and so on. My eleventh-grade teacher said that the thesis, the supporting details, and the transitions were the elements that mattered. What I learned from these two teachers benefits me every day. I owe them kind words, but I can't say that I learned to write essays from them. What I learned to write were "papers" that self-consciously used the various sentence types and that were organized with an almost military precision—shells, really, into which we all hoped somehow, someday, an essay could be poured. Systems that deal with the surfaces of writing tell us very little about what gives an essay weight and interest.

More fruitful for helping us see what goes on in an essay is Aristotle's statement that the persuasive speech reaches the audience through three "appeals": the logical, the ethical, and the emotional. Aristotle's system, however, focuses on the sort of rhetoric we find in the courtroom or legislature. Let's adapt it to the very broad range of things we call essays (including many types of articles, letters, and re-

1

ports) by assuming that the crucial elements of an essay are its three levels of meaning: the logical, the social, and the visceral levels.

The logical level involves statements that require proof: proof that the defendant is guilty as charged, proof that a design flaw caused the bridge to collapse, proof that the plays attributed to Shakespeare were actually written by the Earl of Oxford. Proofs can take many different forms, but the most basic is *generalization and specification*. This may sound like two processes, but logically the two are inseparable, like breathing in and breathing out.

A clear example of the relation between generalization and specification comes from Nazi Germany, where Hitler's propaganda machine made sweeping statements about the superiority of the Aryan race and the threat posed to it by Jews and Judaism. The reaction of many intelligent and well-educated Germans was to examine the logic of these claims. For every generalization, they reasoned, there ought to be specification. To justify the generalization that the Jews were conspiring to undermine the Aryan race, the Nazis should offer specific evidence, specific examples. A historian tells me that the call for "specification" (in German, *Spezifizierung*) became so closely identified with resistance to the Nazi "big lie" that Hitler's agents would sit in bars, restaurants, and other public places, listening for the word *Spezifizierung* and prepared to arrest and interrogate those who said it too loudly or too often. That no questionable generalization should stand without adequate specification is one of the rules of the road in the logical level of an essay.

When the generalization is new or controversial, logical people will usually want the writer to provide several examples. Take, for example, the way Daniel Boorstin supports his generalization that technology has produced a "removal of distinctions" in our ordinary experience:

> One of the consequences of our success in technology, of our wealth, of our energy and our imagination, has been the removal of distinctions, not just between people but between everything and everything else, between every place and every other place, between every time and every other time. For example, television removes the distinction between being here and being there. And the same kind of process, of thinning out, of removing distinctions, has appeared in one area after another of our lives.
>
> For instance, in the seasons. One of the great unheralded achievements of American civilization was the rise of transportation and refrigeration, the development of techniques of canning and preserving meat, vegetables, and fruits in such a way that it became possible to enjoy strawberries in winter, to enjoy fresh meat at seasons when the meat was not slaughtered, to thin out the difference between the diet of winter and the diet of summer.

Boorstin's essay goes on to talk about central heating and air conditioning (which thin the distinction between summer and winter), plate

glass windows (which lessen the difference between indoors and outdoors), and easy-to-use cameras (which mix the past into the present).
The generalization that technology "thins" our experience by removing
distinctions may never have occurred to us before, but Boorstin's specification makes it relatively clear and convincing.

Of course, *disputing* generalizations is as much a logical action as
proposing them. Couldn't we write a short essay challenging Boorstin's
generalization by offering a few counter-examples of our own? We
could point out that when a family flies from Minneapolis to southern
Florida for a midwinter vacation, the contrast between winter and summer is not diminished for them, but sharpened. Or we could argue that
in our own experience, sitting snug by a window during a thunderstorm
doesn't diminish our awareness of the difference between being outdoors and indoors, but heightens it.

That Boorstin's generalization can be disputed does not weaken
Boorstin's essay; in fact it adds spice. Readers are more likely to be
engaged by the logic of the essay if there is a real chance of dispute, a
real need to show a connection between generalization and specifics.
Offer the generalization that "Goldfish are easy pets to keep" and few
readers will wait, breathless, to hear the predictable specifics about water temperature, food, and aeration.

There are occasions when the generalization seems to be uncontro-
versial, and the spice lies in connecting a specific case to it. In our
society, for example, the general definition of murder is fairly well settled, but there can still be hot controversy about whether the actions
of Dr. Kavorkian, inventor of the suicide machine, fit the definition of
murder. Deciding the specific case, of course, will shift the general definition of murder slightly, if only by clarifying it.

Much more, of course, could be said about the logical aspect of
writing, but for now we can conclude that it involves making connections between generalizations and specific cases. The writer who offers
a sweeping generalization without specifics has done nothing at the
logical level; the writer who offers a list of details unconnected to any
general idea has done nothing. We should also say, however, that the
logical level of an essay is not the only one; in some fine essays, it is
far from the most important. Developing the logical level alone is acting
as if we were severed heads, kept alive by tubes and machines and
interacting with society only by analyzing data. The essayist remembers
that we are alive from the neck down and that we have an almost
inexhaustible interest in the lives of those around us.

Let's leave logic behind for now and move to the social level of our
lives and of the essay. I'll begin indelicately by putting you in my shoes
on the day I composed this page, and putting those shoes into a stall
in the men's rest room of the public library. To our left is another stall,

occupied by a man wearing a pair of brown Kangaroos who is puffing noisily as he hauls himself to his feet and slowly walks out. As he opens the stall door, we hear him say, "They ought to make these stalls wider; you can hardly turn around in there." Into the newly vacated stall walks a pair of Adidas, and as the outer door closes behind the Kangaroos, the man in the Adidas says, apparently to us, "That guy ought to lose some weight."

The scene reminds us that humans are a gossipy, judgmental race, always ready to give and take opinions about the proper management of society ("*They* ought to make these stalls wider") or about the proper management of the individual life ("*That guy* ought to lose some weight"). As Aristotle said, we are all creatures of the *polis* (the community), and one of our life's great projects is to contribute to the community's consensus on what behavior is good or bad, noble or base, cool or uncool. You may remember reading a children's magazine that contained a comic strip called "Gufus and Gallant." Week after week, the cartoonist would produce a scenario in which Gufus would show us how not to behave and Gallant would behave with a shining nobility. From childhood forward, we think incessantly about what behavior is Gufus and what is Gallant.

Among the earliest surviving essays are thirty short sketches by Theophrastus, Aristotle's pupil. These "characters," as he called them, explore the social side of life as directly as "Gufus and Gallant" did. Here, for instance, is a Gufus piece usually called "The Faultfinder":

> Faultfinding is being unreasonably critical of your portion in life. For example, a friend sends over a serving of the main dinner course with his compliments: the faultfinder is the kind who says to the messenger, "You can go tell your master I said that he didn't want me to have a taste of his soup and his third-rate wine—that's why he wouldn't give me a dinner invitation." And even while his mistress is kissing him he will complain, "I wonder if you really love me the way you say you do." He gets angry at the weather, too, not because it rained but because it didn't rain soon enough.
>
> If he comes on a wallet in the street, his comment is "Always this—never a real find!" Let him get a slave at bargain prices, moreover, after begging and pleading, and what does he say but, "I really wonder if the fellow can be in sound shape, seeing that he was so cheap." Or supposing somebody announces, "You've got a baby boy!" He meets this good news with: "You might as well have told me half my estate's down the drain—that's what it really means." What's more, he can win a case with every single ballot in his favor; he will still claim that his lawyer passed over a lot of sound arguments. And when friends have raised a loan to help him out and one of them asks him, "Aren't you pleased?" his answer is "How can I be, when I have to pay everybody back and then act grateful besides?"

This essay makes the modest logical claim that there exists in society (or at least there existed in ancient Athens) a recognizable category of people who can be called faultfinders. The point, however, is less to show that the group exists than to remind us that we don't want to belong to it. For a day or two after reading "The Faultfinder," we may be less likely to complain about the food someone cooks for us, less likely to be critical of the present a friend gives us.

Other essays are less direct in presenting standards of good or bad behavior. In an essay on medical school education, for example, Perri Klass discusses the jargon used by medical students and doctors working in a teaching hospital.

> I picked up not only the specific expressions but also the patterns of speech and the grammatical conventions; for example, you never say that a patient's blood pressure fell or that his cardiac enzymes rose. Instead, the patient is always the subject of the verb: "He dropped his pressure." "He bumped his enzymes." This sort of construction probably reflects the profound irritation of the intern when the nurses come in the middle of the night to say that Mr. Dickinson has disturbingly low blood pressure. "Oh, he's gonna hurt me bad tonight," the intern might say, inevitably angry at Mr. Dickinson for dropping his pressure and creating a problem.
>
> When chemotherapy fails to cure Mrs. Bacon's cancer, what we say is, "Mrs. Bacon failed chemotherapy."

This passage is well developed at the logical level; it offers a novel generalization about the way doctors talk about their patients and supports the generalization with a number of specific examples. The effect of the passage is less logical than social, however. Klass, writing an article for *The New York Times Magazine*, knows that her readers will identify with the patients and will react to the doctors' talk with a sharp disapproval that has nothing to do with logic and everything to do with our notion of good behavior. Doctors *ought to* think about and talk about their parents with more sympathy.

Ought to is the password to the social level, and our behavior toward one another is the subject. Directly or indirectly, the best essayists go beyond cold logic and try to shape their readers into a community with a shared vision of morals, manners, and style.

Of course, writing is itself a bit of behavior, good or bad. Readers may approve or disapprove of the way the essayist talks just as they may approve or disapprove of the way doctors talk. Listen, for example, to E. B. White's discussion of the "breezy style."

> The breezy style is often the work of an egocentric, the person who imagines that everything that pops into his head is of general interest and that uninhibited prose creates high spirits and carries the day. Open any alumni magazine, turn to the class notes, and you are quite likely to encounter old Spontaneous Me at work—an aging collegian who writes something like this:

> Well, chums, here I am again with my bagful of dirt about your disor-
> derly classmates, after spending a helluva weekend in N'Yawk trying to
> view the Columbia game from behind two bumbershoots and a glazed
> cornea. And speaking of news, howzabout tossing a few chirce nuggets
> my way?

This is an extreme example, but the same wind blows, at lesser velocities,
across vast expanses of journalistic prose. The author in this case has managed in two sentences to commit most of the unpardonable sins: he obviously has nothing to say, he is showing off and directing the attention of
the reader to himself, he is using slang with neither provocation nor ingenuity, he adopts a patronizing air by throwing in the word *chirce*, he is
tasteless, humorless (though full of fun), dull, and empty. He has not done
his work.[1]

You may feel that White is being too hard on the "aging collegian,"
but the severity of his attack should remind us that to the essayist *tone*
is a serious issue. How we say something may be as important socially
as what we say.

Our educational system does less to alert us to the visceral (bodily)
level of writing than to the logical or social levels, perhaps because
teachers tend to see the body as a natural enemy. Let me introduce the
visceral level by telling you about my baby daughter Kate and her first
word, *kitty*. She learned the word early because her baby sitter Nancy
used to lure a neighbor's cat onto the porch on summer days to pet it.
After winter set in, we would show Kate a photograph and ask her
where the kitty was, and she would smile, coo, and wiggle all over as
she pointed to the cat and said "kitty." For her, the word must have
been the key that unlocked a number of bodily experiences. It probably
summoned up memories of summer days on the porch, the silky feel
of the fur, the purring, the comfort of being held on Nancy's lap. As
the rhetorician Kenneth Burke put it, the word "glowed" for her; it
had emotional and physical associations no dictionary maker records.
She reacted to these associations as a whole creature, not merely as a
logical or social being.

This creaturely reaction to words, phrases, and images may become
dulled as we grow older—it may be overlayered by the development
of our logical and social responses to what we read—but it never goes
away. My reaction to words like *lake, sandpaper,* and *baby* is not as
dramatic as Kate's response to *kitty* (I can read them and sit still), but
it is not different in kind. And, of course, it is not just words, but phrases
and whole sentences that may have a bodily impact on us. The other
day, in the midst of an abstract discussion of social policy, I heard one
speaker quote the Buddhist proverb, "You can't water a tree by water-

---

1. *The Elements of Style* (Macmillan, 1959), pp. 59–60.

ing each individual leaf." The escape from this dry discussion of hard issues to the familiar and tangible world of trees and water had great appeal to me, for reasons my body probably understood better than my mind ever will.

The writer of a scientific paper or a mathematical proof may ignore the body's "reasoning," but the skillful writer of essays doesn't. Take, for example, the first sentence of George Orwell's "Marrakech": "As the corpse went past, the flies left the restaurant table in a cloud and rushed after it, but they came back a few minutes later." The sentence might have no effect on an android with a stainless steel gut, but it is enough to make a human's skin crawl. It probably *does* make our skins crawl, as a clever physiologist with a galvanometer might demonstrate. Or consider this paragraph from Carol Bly's "Getting Tired":

> The second day I was promoted from elevating corncobs at the corn pile to actual plowing. Hour after hour I sat up there on the old Alice, as she was called (an Allis-Chalmers WC that looked rusted from the Flood). You have to sit twisted part way around, checking that the plowshares are scouring clean, turning over and dropping the dead crop and soil, not clogging. For the first two hours I was very political. I thought about what would be good for American farming—stronger marketing organizations, or maybe a law like the Norwegian Odal law, preventing the breaking up of small farms or selling them to business interests. Then the sun got high, and each time I reached the headlands area at the field's end I dumped off something else, now my cap, next my jacket, finally my sweater.

Few of us, these days, have plowed with an open tractor, but our muscles have probably been in the twisted posture Bly describes, and we probably remember stripping off layers of clothing on days that start out cold and then heat with the rising sun. These bodily memories are evoked, however briefly, as we read. Those who have been around farms may associate Bly's language—*plowshares, scouring, headlands*—with the sights and sounds and solid objects they remember, objects that carry with them memories and emotions, pleasant or unpleasant. Writing that points us to objects and sensations—to tastes, textures, smells, temperatures, sounds, colors, shapes, motions—will ordinarily involve us more deeply than writing that is merely logical or merely social.

I don't want to leave the impression that our visceral responses depend entirely on the relation between words and past physical experience. Language is also, itself, a *present* physical experience. Perhaps half a dozen times in the last decade I have passed through a room where Martin Luther King, Jr.'s "I Have a Dream" speech was playing on radio or television. It has always stopped me cold. Listen to the following passage, a series of sentences that are rhythmically perfect in them-

selves and that are joined rhythmically by the repetition of "I have a
dream":

> I say to you today, my friends, that in spite of the difficulties and frustra-
> tions of the moment I still have a dream tonight. It is a dream deeply
> rooted in the American dream.
>
> I have a dream that one day this nation will rise up and live out the true
> meaning of its creed: "We hold these truths to be self-evident, that all men
> are created equal."
>
> I have a dream that one day on the red hills of Georgia the sons of
> former slaves and the sons of former slaveowners will be able to sit down
> together at the table of brotherhood.
>
> I have a dream that one day even the state of Mississippi, a desert state
> sweltering with the heat of injustice and oppression, will be transformed
> into an oasis of freedom and justice.
>
> I have a dream that my four little children will one day live in a nation
> where they will not be judged by the color of their skin but by the content
> of their character.

Listen to the beat of the *k* sounds in that last sentence (*color, skin,
content, character*) and think how much would be lost if King had said,
"where they will be judged by their character, rather than their skin
tone." The speech moves us partly because of the way the language
moves. Essays are not speeches, but when we read closely we register
the sounds in our mental ear and even (researchers tell us) subcon-
sciously form them with our vocal cords. Rhythm, assonance, allitera-
tion, onomatopoeia—the whole palette of verbal sound effects—create
visceral responses.

Sound and physical details work together to create the visceral effect of beekeeper Sue Hubbell's description of a swarm.

> I was near a slender post oak sapling, and the bees began to light on one
> of its lower limbs right next to my elbow. They came flying in, swirling as
> they descended, spiraling around me and the post oak until I was envel-
> oped by the swarm, the air moving gently from the beat of their wings. I
> am not sure how long I stood there. I lost all sense of time and felt only
> elation, a kind of human emotional counterpart of the springlike, optimis-
> tic, burgeoning, state that the bees were in.

The sense of the bees' motion comes through strongly when Hubbell
mentions "the air moving gently from the beat of their wings," a reminder of spring breezes on our cheeks, perhaps, but also a reminder
of the panic most of us feel when even a single bee approaches *this*
close. And, of course, we aren't talking about single bees. The passage
strengthens our response to the sheer number of bees by building it
incrementally. First the bees begin to "light" on the sapling, a detail
that may call up from our memories the sight of individual bees. Then
the bees are "swirling" and "spiraling," no longer individual bees but

a cloud[2] of them. Then Hubbell is "enveloped" in the cloud of bees so dense that the beating of their wings creates a breeze. The impression of mass motion is also created by the form of the sentences, particularly the second one:

> They came flying in,
>> swirling as they descended,
>> spiraling around me and the post oak
>>> until I was enveloped by the swarm,
>>>> the air moving gently from the beat of their wings.

All those present participles (*flying, swirling, spiraling, moving*) keep the sentence in motion in a way that seems to imitate the swarming of the bees, and Hubbell has carefully arranged her sentence so that the motion comes closer to her (psychologically, to us) in each phrase.

What difference does it make if we read essays with increased consciousness that they work on three levels? If my experience is typical, we begin to *see* essays more clearly, to become more consciously aware of what essayists have accomplished. When I graduated from high school as part of a post-*Sputnik*, scientifically oriented generation of students, I was fixated on the logical level of writing and simply missed the other two in most of what I read. I was like an artist attempting to see all objects as balls, and so dismissing cones, cylinders, and cubes as balls that failed the test of roundness. Eventually I broadened my range and learned to recognize that writing could be excellent because it engaged us socially and viscerally. And eventually I learned to recognize a type of excellence I had not suspected, the excellence of balance achieved when an essay works on all three levels and so appeals to mind, body, and character at once.

Have we exhausted the truth about the essay when we recognize that it has three levels? Certainly not. The harder we look, the more levels we are likely to see: four, six, ten, who can say? The well-written essay, like a ray of clear light, contains a whole spectrum of colors. The important thing is to recognize both its complexity and its unity.

THE THREE LEVELS AND REVISION

Being aware as we write that an essay can develop at three levels is both a blessing and a challenge. It is a blessing because it gives us three channels through which to reach the reader. It is a challenge

---

2. What actually comes to my mind are the huge galactic clouds that "swirled" and "spiraled" in my junior high science books.

because we must now

1. Think what the subject means logically. (How can its details be connected to generalizations or generalizations to details?)
2. Think what the subject means socially. (How can it be related to a standard for admirable or dishonorable behavior?)
3. Think what the subject means viscerally. (How can it be connected to the senses and the emotions that are evoked by the senses?)

The struggle to work at three levels is part of the hidden drama behind drafting and revision.

Those who have written very little are generally surprised at the amount of revision experienced writers do. The economist John Kenneth Galbraith, equally famous for the subtlety of his theories and for the clarity of his prose, puts it this way:

> There may be inspired writers for whom the first draft is just right. But anyone who is not certifiably a Milton had better assume that the first draft is a very primitive thing. The reason is simple: writing is very difficult work. . . . Thinking, as Voltaire avowed, is also a very tedious process which men and women will do anything to avoid. So all first drafts are deeply flawed by the need to combine composition with thought. Each later one is less demanding in this regard; hence the writing can be better.

Galbraith tells us that on bad days he writes so poorly that "no fewer than five revisions are required. However, when I'm greatly inspired, only four are needed before, as I've often said, I put in that note of spontaneity which even my meanest critics concede."[3]

Great writers rarely preserve the four or five (or more) drafts that led them to a finished product. By good fortune, however, we do have access to six drafts of a *New Yorker* "comment" by E. B. White, one of the best American essayists of this century. In this section we will take a short tour through three of White's drafts, watching the way that he develops the logical, social, and visceral levels. I am not, of course, saying that White wrote with these levels consciously in his mind (any more than a bicyclist consciously thinks about balance, velocity, and centrifugal force as she rounds a corner), but I think we can see their presence in the decisions White makes.

First, a word about the nature of the writing and the writer. "Comments" are unsigned essays in miniature; in *The New Yorker* they have traditionally been written using the "editorial *we*," a practice that irritated White because it tends to make the writer sound like a Siamese twin. White began writing comments in 1927, and so had more than

---

3. "Writing, Typing, and Economics," *The Atlantic Monthly* (March 1978), p. 103.

forty years of experience with them by 1969, when the magazine asked him to comment on *Apollo 11*'s landing on the moon.

The deadline pressure on White was more intense than usual. Neil Armstrong took his historic "small step" to the lunar surface at 10:56 P.M. on July 20, and the television broadcast of the moon walk lasted until 1:00 A.M.; White, who lived on a farm in Maine, had to cable his comment to New York in time for it to go to press at noon.

The visceral level, for this writer and this subject, posed a problem. White's best writing generally evoked the places and activities he loved best—ball games, circuses, zoos, farming, camping, canoeing. He was by disposition and habit an outdoorsman, capable of describing barns, pigs, and spiders affectionately (as you will know if you have read *Charlotte's Web*) and passionate about the sights, sounds, and smells of sailing. A few years before he wrote the moon-landing comment, he wrote these sentences in "The Sea and the Wind That Blows":

> My first encounter with the sea was a case of hate at first sight. I was taken, at the age of four, to a bathing beach in New Rochelle. Everything about the experience frightened and repelled me: the taste of salt in my mouth, the foul chill of the wooden bathhouse, the littered sand, the stench of the tide flats. I came away hating and fearing the sea. Later, I found that what I had hated and feared, I now feared and loved.

In the wide outdoors world, White could certainly find the keys that unlock visceral responses, the connections between the senses and the emotions. Now, however, he was being asked to write about what is to the senses a much narrower world—the images and sounds produced by his television set. This situation presented him with a handicap that, as we will see, he had difficulty overcoming.

The logical level presented White with another sort of difficulty. Here there was generalization to connect the event with, but the nature of the connection wasn't clear. World War II had convinced White that in a world of electronic communication, long-range bombers, and nuclear weaponry, nationalism was irrational and dangerous.

> Whether we wish it or not, we may soon have to make a clear choice between the special nation to which we pledge our allegiance and the broad humanity of which we are born a part. The choice is implicit in the world to come. We have a little time in which we can make that choice intelligently. Failing that, the choice will be made for us in the confusion of war, from which the world will emerge unified—the unity of total desolation.

Logic taught White that nationalism was a thing of the past, and (as we will see) this generalization shaped his view of the particular event he witnessed.

At the social level, the moon landing presented White the familiar struggle between pride and modesty, between boasting about our accomplishments and keeping them in perspective. In this struggle, White consistently favored modesty. Much of the humor in his writing comes from his tendency to find himself slightly ridiculous, and many of his essays aim to "keep Man in a mood of decent humility," particularly when people are crowing about their conquest of nature. "I am pessimistic about the human race," he once said, "because it is too ingenious for its own good. Our approach to nature is to beat it into submission." To the degree that the moon landing became an occasion for crowing and strutting, therefore, it went against the grain of White's character.

If we look at White's very rough first draft, we can see his struggle to make one coherent statement that combines his visceral, logical, and social responses to the event.

> Planning a trip to the moon differs in no essential respect from planning a trip to the beach. You have to decide what to take along, what to leave behind. Should the thermos jug go? The child's rubber horse? The dill pickles? These are the sometimes fateful decisions on which the success or failure of the whole outing turns. Something goes along that spoils everything because it is always in the way. Something gets left behind that is desperately needed for comfort or safety. The men who had to decide what to take along to the moon must have pondered long and hard, drawn up many a list. We're not sure they planned well, when they included the little telescoped flagpole and the American flag, artificially stiffened so that it would fly to the breeze that didn't blow. As we watched the Stars and Stripes planted on the surface of the moon, we experienced the same sensations of pride that must have filled the hearts of millions of Americans. But the emotion soon turned to   This was our great chance, and we muffed it. The men who stepped out onto the surface of the moon are in a class by themselves—pioneers of what is universal. They saw the earth whole—just as it is, a round ball in   But they colored the moon red, white, and blue—good colors all—but out of place in that setting. The moon still influences the tides, and the tides lap on every shore, right around the globe. The moon still belongs to lovers, and lovers are everywhere—not just in America. What a pity we couldn't have planted some emblem that precisely expressed this unique, this incredible occasion, even if it were nothing more than a white banner, with the legend: "At last!"

White clearly didn't intend this to be a final draft: he twice began sentences that he couldn't end. *What* exactly did our emotions turn to? A round ball in *what*? Having no adequate answers, he left spaces and went on. His aim was to discover the general shape of the comment, to see what he had to say.

I mentioned before that the subject was difficult for White because it offered so little visceral interest, and he knew that he needed to engage his own senses and emotions if he wanted to engage his readers'. In this draft, you can see three attempts to overcome the difficulty. One comes directly from the television screen: "the American flag, artificially stiffened so that it would fly to the breeze that didn't blow." Here is a visual image most of White's readers would have remembered, one that jars us a little by reminding us that there is no *air* up there. Another attempt is the analogy with the beach trip. This analogy gives White access to objects and sense impressions: a thermos jug (with its suggestion of hot liquid), a rubber horse (an interesting item for those who think about the feel of it), and dill pickles (a pungent taste). The third attempt is the mention of the moon's effects here on earth, on the tides and on lovers. Here we have some footholds for visceral reactions.

Of course, the flag is related to White's key logical concern: the outdated nature of nationalism. The astronauts are "pioneers of what is universal"; they can see "the earth whole"; they are standing on the moon, creator of tides that "lap on every shore." In this draft, White wants us to see that for them to plant a *national* flag is a case of invoking antiquated patriotism in an international age.

The most serious difficulty in the draft is social. White is clearly uneasy about the amount of boasting and strutting associated with the moon landing, but he can't seem to find the right alternative posture. The opening sentences seem determined to take the whole occasion lightly. Later, he criticizes the planners harshly: "We're not sure they planned well. . . . This was our great chance, and we muffed it." In these passages he sounds like a scold, a spoilsport. On the other hand, he sometimes bends over backward to sound like a patriot and enthusiast: "As we watched the Stars and Stripes planted on the surface of the moon, we experienced the same sensations of pride that must have filled the hearts of millions of Americans. . . . red, white, and blue— good colors all. . . . this unique, this incredible occasion." It would be hard for readers to trust (or even understand) a man who seems to have three sides to his mouth and seems to talk out of all three in a single paragraph.

The changes White made in the next two drafts show him working at the social level, trying to find the proper tone. Since some of the changes are slight, we'll find them easier to detect if we look at drafts one and three side by side, section by section. The first section in both drafts presents the analogy to the beach trip.

DRAFT ONE	DRAFT THREE
Planning a trip to the moon differs in no essential respect from planning a trip to the beach. You have to decide what to take along, what to leave behind. Should the thermos jug go? The child's rubber horse? The dill pickles? These	Planning a trip to the moon differs in no essential respect from planning a trip to the beach. You have to decide what to take along, what to leave behind. Should the thermos jug go? The child's rubber horse? The dill pickles? These

are the sometimes fateful decisions on which the success or
failure of the whole outing
turns. Something goes along
that spoils everything because
it is always in the way. Something gets left behind that is
desperately needed for comfort
or safety. The men who had to
decide what to take along to
the moon must have pondered
long and hard, drawn up many
a list.

are the sometimes fateful decisions on which the success or
failure of the whole outing
turns. Something goes along
that spoils everything because
it is always in the way; something gets left behind that is
desperately needed for comfort
or for safety. The men who
drew up the moon list for the
astronauts planned long and
hard and well. (Should the vacuum cleaner go to suck up
moondust?)

"Do not adjust your set," as they say on television. The two columns
are nearly identical until we get to the last sentence or two. There we
get some changes that soften White's scolding tone. Now the planners
don't just work "long" and "hard"; they work "well." The parentheti-
cal sentence about the vacuum cleaner is apparently intended as an
example of the sort of planning they did well, though it seems a lame
joke. (In draft two it had been lamer still: "Should they take along a
vacuum cleaner to suck up moondust and save the world?") Notice,
too, that White separates the astronauts from the planners. This distinction will be useful to him as he continues to rewrite and rethink.

In the middle section, the complaint about the presence of the flag,
the drafts differ more sharply.

DRAFT ONE

We're not sure they planned
well, when they included the
little telescoped flagpole and
the American flag, artificially
stiffened so that it would fly
to the breeze that didn't blow.
As we watched the Stars and
Stripes planted on the surface
of the moon, we experienced
the same sensations of pride
that must have filled the hearts
of millions of Americans. But
the emotion soon turned to
          This was our great
chance, and we muffed it. The
men who stepped out onto the
surface of the moon are in a
class by themselves—pioneers
of what is universal. They saw

DRAFT THREE

Among the items they sent
along, of course, was the little
jointed flag that could be stiffened to the breeze that did not
blow. (It is traditional for explorers to plant the flag.) Yet
the two men who stepped out
on the surface of the moon
were in a class by them-
selves and should have been
equipped accordingly; they
were of the new breed of men,
those who had seen the earth
whole. When, following instructions, they colored the
moon red, white, and blue,
they were fumbling with the
past—or so it seemed to us
who watched, trembling with

the earth whole—just as it is, a round ball in But they colored the moon red, white, and blue—good colors all—but out of place in that setting.

awe and admiration and pride. This was the last chapter in the long book of nationalism, one that could well have been omitted.

Most of the changes affect White's tone, bringing out a less cantankerous, more sympathetic side of his character. In the first draft, White directly challenged NASA's decision to plant the flag ("We're not sure they planned well"). Now he is understanding: the planners send along the flag "of course," since it is "traditional" for explorers to plant one. White has been more generous toward the astronauts, especially. In draft one, they were lumped with the planners who had "muffed" our "great chance." Anyone who has played Little League baseball knows the sting of being told that you have "muffed it." In draft three, they are "following instructions" and "fumbling with the past" (a ball too large for anyone to catch neatly). Notice that in the last sentence of this section, White states his logical point more clearly than ever before: "This was the last chapter in the long book of nationalism, one that could well have been omitted." The relation between White's logical position and his social posture is now considerably clearer. This draft says, "Look, I am convinced that nationalism is outdated, and I don't intend to hide my conviction, but I don't intend to be a spoilsport either. It was a shining moment, and I felt its wonder, though I wish we could have used it for a better purpose."

The final section in both drafts reminds us that the moon is international property and argues that the right "flag" to plant would have been one that represented the entire world. White has reworked the passage considerably by the time he gets to draft three.

DRAFT ONE

The moon still influences the tides, and the tides lap on every shore, right around the globe. The moon still belongs to lovers, and lovers are everywhere—not just in America. What a pity we couldn't have planted some emblem that precisely expressed this unique, this incredible occasion, even if it were nothing more than a white banner, with the legend: "At last!"

DRAFT THREE

But the moon still holds the key to madness, which is universal, still controls the tides that lap on shores everywhere, and guards lovers that kiss in every land, under no banner but the sky. What a pity we couldn't have forsworn our little Iwo Jima scene and planted instead a banner acceptable to all—a simple white handkerchief, perhaps, symbol of the common cold, which, like the moon, affects us all.

Partly because of the forceful verbs, the first sentence in the new draft has more visceral effect than the old version:

> But the moon
> > still *holds* the key to madness,
> > > which is universal,
> > still *controls* the tides that lap on shores everywhere,
> > and *guards* lovers that kiss in every land,
> > > under no banner but the sky.

The moon sounds like a strong ruler here, stronger than any mere superpower. A more dramatic change happens in the final sentence of the new draft. By mentioning Iwo Jima, White conjures up memories of the most famous photograph of World War II, an object that "glows" with associations. And in contrast to this image of embattled marines planting a flag on a conquered hilltop, White offers a white handkerchief, "symbol of the common cold, which . . . affects us all." Again we have an object that "glows" with visceral associations, but very different ones. Rather than encouraging stiff-necked pride, the handkerchief "keeps Man in a mood of decent humility." White has brought the visceral level and the social level together.

By common standards, this third draft seems a finished product; White telegraphed it to *The New Yorker*, but when the heat of composition began to cool, he saw there was more work to be done at both the social and logical levels. By beginning with the beach comparison and ending with the handkerchief, White had trivialized the moon landing, and he now saw that this trivializing was unfair and shoddy (it sounds like the cheap breeziness of Spontaneous Me). By hinging his essay on the generalization that nationalism was out of date, he had demanded that his readers accept an enormous assumption without any reasoning or evidence. Time was very short, but White took the paragraph through three more drafts before telegraphing *The New Yorker* that the comment was "no good as is" and offering to dictate over the phone "a shorter one on the same theme but different in tone." Here, for comparison, are draft three and draft six, the one that appeared on page one of the magazine:

DRAFT THREE

Planning a trip to the moon differs in no essential respect from planning a trip to the beach. You have to decide what to take along, what to leave behind. Should the thermos jug go? The child's rubber horse? The dill pickles? These are the sometimes fateful deci-

DRAFT SIX

The moon, it turns out, is a great place for men. One-sixth gravity must be a lot of fun, and when Armstrong and Aldrin went into their bouncy little dance, like two happy children, it was a moment not only of triumph, but of gaiety.

sions on which the success or failure of the whole outing turns. Something goes along that spoils everything because it is always in the way; something gets left behind that is desperately needed for comfort or for safety. The men who drew up the moon list for the astronauts planned long and hard and well. (Should the vacuum cleaner go to suck up moondust?)

Among the items they sent along, of course, was the little jointed flag that could be stiffened to the breeze that did not blow. (It is traditional for explorers to plant the flag.) Yet the two men who stepped out on the surface of the moon were in a class by themselves and should have been equipped accordingly; they were of the new breed of men, those who had seen the earth whole. When, following instructions, they colored the moon red, white, and blue, they were fumbling with the past—or so it seemed to us who watched, trembling with awe and admiration and pride. This was the last chapter in the long book of nationalism, one that could well have been omitted.

The moon, on the other hand, is a poor place for flags. Ours looked stiff and awkward, trying to float on the breeze that does not blow. (There must be a lesson here somewhere.) It is traditional, of course, for explorers to plant the flag, but it struck us, as we watched with awe and admiration and pride, that our two fellows were universal men, not national men, and should have been equipped accordingly.

But the moon still holds the key to madness, which is universal, still controls the tides that lap on shores everywhere, and guards lovers that kiss in every land, under no banner but the sky. What a pity we couldn't have forsworn out little Iwo Jima scene and planted instead a banner acceptable to

Like every great river and every great sea, the moon belongs to none and belongs to all. It still holds the key to madness, still controls the tides that lap on shores everywhere, still guards the lovers that kiss in every land under no banner but the sky. What a pity in our moment of triumph we

all—a simple white handkerchief, perhaps, symbol of the
common cold, which, like the
moon, affects us all.

couldn't have forsworn the
familiar Iwo Jima scene and
planted instead a device acceptable to all: a limp white handkerchief, perhaps, symbol of
the common cold, which, like
the moon, affects us all, unites
us all.

What has happened here? Socially, White has stopped being a kill-
joy, stopped being the one person at the party who intends to spend
the evening complaining. Once he gets the chip off his shoulder, he is
able to recall a detail that appeals to all of us on the visceral level—the
"bouncy little dance" of the astronauts.

He is also able to clarify and strengthen his logical point. Rather
than insist on the controversial generalization that nationalism is anach-
ronistic, he builds on the widely acceptable generalization that some
things belong to all humankind: "Like every great river and every great
sea, the moon belongs to none and belongs to all." If the high seas are
regarded as beyond nationalism, how much more so the moon, which
"still holds the key to madness, still controls the tides that lap on shores
everywhere"? And with the little addition of "unites us all" at the
very end, White brings the three dimensions of the essay together.
The visceral things that affect us all—tides, kisses, the common cold,
the moon—also unite us all, as logic should tell us; as social creatures
we should behave accordingly. No flags for the moon, no sniping in
the essay. White has come to terms with his subject.

You will find many more changes in White's drafts than I have
mentioned: of the 305 words in the first draft, only 15 remain to the
end, a survival rate lower than we find in most airline crashes. But the
small changes in the essay are less important than the changes of mind
that go with them. An essay is not just a finished product. For the
writer, it is a process that leads to changes, not only on paper, but in
the logical, social, and visceral levels of the self.

Our word *essay*, any dictionary will tell you, is derived from the
French word *essai*, "a trial, an attempt, a test." The attempt begins with
the blank page and ends when the writer declares some draft final. In
this sense, we don't see a living essay in a book, any more than we see
a living butterfly in the collector's case. To read well, we have to bring
the essay back to life. We have to enter the writer's mind far enough
to understand what his or her "attempt" was and against what resis-
tances it made its way forward. Even if we finally disagree with the
writer, we should use our intelligence and imagination to see the distance traveled since the page was blank.

As writers, we travel the same road in the other direction. Faced with the blank sheet, we must feel the pull of the completed essay, which is partly the pull of all the essays we have read, understood, and admired. When E. B. White was nearly fifty, his brother gave him a box of white typing paper. Writing back his thanks, White said, "I'm glad to report that even now, at this late day, a blank sheet of paper holds the greatest excitement there is for me—more promising than a silver cloud, prettier than a little red wagon. It holds all the hope there is, all fears." To learn what our own blank sheets may hold is one of the reasons to read.

CHILDHOOD AND CHILDHOOD'S END

We find ourselves growing up in a grown-up world.

Childhood and Childhood's End: Preview

I am 16 now, still not old enough to vote. . . . While I am grateful that I have the right to speak my mind, I believe that it is a grave injustice to deny young people the most effective tool they could have to bring about change in a democracy.

Adults were coming apart, but they neither noticed nor minded. . . . Our beauty was a mere absence of decrepitude; their beauty, when they had it, was not passive but earned; it was grandeur; it was a party to power, and to artifice, even, and to knowledge.

She stood another whole song through and then opened the screen door to look down on me crying in rage. She looked until I looked up. Her face was a brown moon that shone on me. She was beautiful. Something had happened out there, which I couldn't completely understand, but I could see that she was happy.

It was a feeling of closeness. It was something strange. It was as though there were only we two in the world. It was as though I had been jerked suddenly out of myself, out of my world of the schoolboy, out of a world in which I was ashamed of my father.

A month shy of my fifteenth birthday, I felt I had died and gone to heaven. . . . We drank ideas and ate controversy. Is God dead? we asked. Can you love two people at the same time? I feasted on the idea of learning about the world and being a citizen of it. And yet my sense of this citizenship would be jeopardized not long after I arrived.

The fear of appearing ridiculous first entered my life, as a governing motive, during my second year in the convent. Up to then, a desire for prominence had decided many of my actions. . . . But in the eighth grade, I became aware of mockery and perceived that I could not seek prominence without attracting laughter.

Most people who believe in the institution of childhood as we know it see it as a kind of walled garden in which children, being small and weak, are protected from the harshness of the world outside. . . . But I believe that most young people, and at earlier and earlier ages, begin to experience childhood not as a garden but as a prison.

It's not really that I want her to be a little girl forever. It's just that it would be nice if she were a child during her childhood. Instead, she's been bathed in the fantasy of bodies and beauty that marinates our entire culture. The result is an insidious form of premature sexual awakening that is stealing our kids' youth.

I invented games for us to play, and after it stopped raining we stood outside, even though it was cold, so that we could watch for the headlights of our parents' car as it turned in to the motel. When our parents finally came, I was so relieved that I didn't feel angry until later. . . . I felt as though I'd been tricked.

My mother drops the dirty clothes in an exaggerated gesture of defeat. She almost—almost—throws them on the floor. The way she holds her hands accentuates their emptiness. "If you're not going to go to school," she says, "the least you can do is clean your room."

Then it was dusk in Illinois, the small boy
After an afternoon of carting dung
Hung on the rail fence, a sapped thing
Weary to crying.

Overview and Ideas for Writing

The division of our lives into childhood and adulthood, though it is agonizing for many sixteen-year-olds, seems inevitable to most Americans today. By nine o'clock in the morning most families scatter: the adults to jobs children know nothing about, the children to schools where they slowly learn to be adults. Since the publication of Philip Aries's *Centuries of Childhood* in 1962, however, it has been clear that this way of organizing life has slowly developed over several centuries and that it has little to do with physical maturation. In the Middle Ages, for instance, people seemed to view the eight-year-old and the twenty-eight-year-old as essentially equal. Both could talk fluently, both could work long hours in the fields or in the house. There seemed no reason to see the two as living in separate conditions.

But for various reasons our society has erected a wall between the adult world, which children must inevitably inherit, and the child's world, where they play and learn. Three of the essays in this unit deal specifically with that wall. Fifty-year-old educator John Holt and six-teen-year-old violinist Vita Wallace challenge it and suggest that for many children the institution of childhood is not so much a "walled garden" as a prison in which capable and restless people are forced to serve their time. Joy Overbeck, however, approves of the wall, fearing that without it children are thrown into an overly sexualized world in which they not only lose the innocence of childhood too quickly but may also be threatened with physical harm.

Most of the essays and stories in the unit, however, are less concerned with the wisdom of building a wall around childhood than with the experience of individuals living inside the garden or opening the gate to leave it. We begin with Annie Dillard's very early memory of discovering that, unlike children, adults are "loose in their skins." In memoirs by Maya Angelou and Sherwood Anderson, we see children attempting to penetrate the mysterious behavior of parents and grand-parents, while in his memoir, Henry Louis Gates, Jr., recalls a transitional moment when he learned about his position in a large and distant world. And while Galway Kinnell captures a young boy poised between two worlds, Judy Troy and Peter Cameron deal with moments of sorrow when children enter the adult world they will soon inhabit.

Childhood is a fertile subject for writers. If you are interested in its history and prepared to write a research paper, you may want to examine such books as *Centuries of Childhood*, Lloyd deMause's *The History of Childhood*, Neil Postman's *The Disappearance of Childhood*, and Michael Mitterauer's *A History of Youth*. If you want to try your hand at social criticism, you might enter the debate between those who favor a long, protected childhood and those who would "free the child," using your own knowledge and memories of growing up. If you find the memoirs and stories collected here interesting, you may want to write your own memoir showing how you began to understand the world you would enter as an adult.

VITA WALLACE

Give Children the Vote

Vita Wallace (1975–   ) is the youngest and most obscure of the authors included in *The Dolphin Reader*. At the time she wrote this essay, Wallace was a writer and violinist living in Philadelphia. "Give Children the Vote" was first published in *The Nation* in October 1991.

Wallace's proposal calls for all children—regardless of age—to be given the right to vote when they see fit. Does her proposal strike you as outrageous or sensible? Consider other issues concerning children's rights as well: should children be allowed to manage their own money? move away from home whenever they choose? file lawsuits against their parents?

I first became interested in children's rights two years ago, when I learned that several states had passed laws prohibiting high school dropouts from getting driver's licenses. I was outraged, because I believe that children should not be forced to go to school or be penalized if they choose not to, a choice that is certainly the most sensible course for some people.

I am what is called a home schooler. I have never been to school, having always learned at home and in the world around me. Home schooling is absolutely legal, yet as a home schooler, I have had to defend what I consider to be my right to be educated in the ways that make the most sense to me, and so all along I have felt sympathy with people who insist on making choices about how they want to be educated, even if that means choosing not to finish high school. Now this choice is in jeopardy.

Like Joy Overbeck, Wallace presents arguments about the public good by combining personal experience and public sources. How effectively does she balance personal and public evidence? Try comparing Wallace's use of evidence with Overbeck's.

Since first learning about the discriminatory laws preventing high school dropouts from getting driver's licenses that have been passed by some state legislatures, I have done a lot of constitutional and historical research that has convinced me that children of all ages must be given the same power to elect their representatives that adults have, or they will continue to be unfairly treated and punished for exercising the few legal options they now have, such as dropping out of high school.

Here Wallace raises the issue of control, which is also suggested by Overbeck. To what extent should children be controlled by parents or law?

Most people, including children themselves, probably don't realize that children are the most regulated people in the United States. In addition to all the laws affecting adults, including tax laws, children must comply with school attendance laws, child labor laws, and alcohol and cigarette laws. They are denied driver's licenses because of their age, regardless of the dropout issue; they are victims of widespread child abuse; and they are blatantly discriminated against everywhere they go, in libraries, restaurants and movie theaters. They have no way to protect themselves: Usually they cannot hire lawyers or bring cases to court without a guardian, and they are not allowed to vote.

The child labor and compulsory schooling laws 5 were passed by well-meaning people to protect children from exploitation. Child labor laws keep children from being forced to work, and compulsory schooling allows all children to get an education.

Why might Wallace have included historical information here? Is this move effective?

But the abolition of slavery in 1865 didn't end the exploitation of black people. They needed the right to vote and the ability to bring lawsuits against their employers. Children need those rights too. Without them, laws that force children to go to school and generally do not allow them to work may be necessary to prevent exploitation, but they also take away children's rights as citizens to life, liberty and the pursuit of happiness. In my case, the compulsory education laws severely limited my right to pursue the work that is important to me (which is surely what "the pursuit of happiness" referred to in the Declaration of Independence).

I am 16 now, still not old enough to vote. Like all children, then, 6 the only way I can fight for children's rights is by using my freedom of speech to try to convince adults to fight with me. While I am grateful that I have the right to speak my mind, I believe that it is a grave injustice to deny young people the most effective tool they could have to bring about change in a democracy. For this reason, I suggest that the right of citizens under 18 to vote not be denied or abridged on account of age.

Many people argue that it would be dangerous 7 to let loose on society a large group of new voters who might not vote sensibly. They mean that children might not vote for the right candidates. The essence of democracy, however, is letting people vote for the wrong candidates. Democratic society has its risks, but we must gamble on the reasonableness of all our citizens, because it is less dangerous than gambling on the reasonableness of a few.

Notice how in the next several paragraphs Wallace presents opposing views and then refutes them. Are these the arguments you would have chosen to discuss? Are they valid ones? The best ones?

That is why we chose to be a democracy instead of a dictatorship in the first place.

As it is, only 36 to 40 percent of adults who are eligible to vote 8 actually vote in nonpresidential years, and about 25 percent of the population is under 18. As you can see, our representatives are elected by a very small percentage of our citizens. That means that although they are responsible *for* all of us, they are responsible *to* only a few of us. Politicians usually do all they can to keep that few happy, because both voters and politicians are selfish, and a politician's re-election depends on the well-being of the voters. Large segments of society that are not likely or not allowed to vote are either ignored or treated badly because of this system. It would be too much to expect the few always to vote in the interests of the many. Under these circumstances, surely the more people who vote the better, especially if they are of both sexes and of all races, classes and ages.

People also claim that children are irresponsible. Most of the teenagers who act irresponsibly do so simply because they are not allowed to solve their problems in any way that would be considered responsible—through the courts or legislature. They fall back on sabotage of the system because they are not allowed to work within it. [9]

Here Wallace presents a common theme in this unit: the problem of being trapped in childhood or somewhere in between childhood and adulthood. Have you ever felt trapped? Compare your experiences not only with Wallace's, but also with those of Peter Cameron's protagonist in "Homework."

How convincing is Wallace's use of analogy in this paragraph? Look for other analogies in the essay. Are they more or less effective?

Some people believe that children would vote the way their parents tell them to, which would, in effect, give parents more votes. Similarly, when the Nineteenth Amendment was passed in 1920, giving women the vote, many people thought women would vote the way their husbands did. Now women are so independent that the idea of women voting on command seems absurd. The Nineteenth Amendment was a large part of the process that produced their independence. I think a similar and equally desirable result would follow if children were allowed to vote. They are naturally curious, and most are interested in the electoral process and the results of the elections even though they are not allowed to vote. Lacking world-weary cynicism, they see, perhaps even more clearly than their elders, what is going on in their neighborhoods and what is in the news. [10]

Suffragist Belle Case La Follette's comment that if women were allowed to vote there would be a lot more dinner-table discussion of politics is as true of children today. More debate would take place not only in the home but among children and adults everywhere. Adults would also benefit if politics were talked about in libraries, churches, stores, laundromats and other places where children gather. [11]

People may argue that politicians would pander to children if they could vote, promising for instance that free ice cream would be distributed every day. But if kids were duped, they would not be duped for long. Children don't like to be treated condescendingly. [12]

Even now, adults try to manipulate children
all the time in glitzy TV ads or, for example, in
the supposedly educational pamphlets that nuclear
power advocates pass out in school science classes.
Political candidates speak at schools, addressing
auditoriums full of captive students. In fact, schools
should be no more or less political than work-
places. Children are already exposed to many different opinions, and they would likely be exposed
to even more if they could vote. The point is that with the vote, they
would be better able to fight such manipulation, not only because they
would have the power to do so but because they would have added
reason to educate themselves on the issues.

> Concern about the power of
> the media connects Wal-
> lace's essay to Overbeck's
> and to many of the essays in
> the "Media" unit.

What I suggest is that children be allowed to
grow into their own right to vote at whatever rate
suits them individually. They should not be forced
to vote, as adults are not, but neither should they
be hindered from voting if they believe themselves
capable, as old people are not hindered.

> Finally, Wallace turns to her
> own proposal. Do you think
> her choice to delay so long
> was a wise one?

As for the ability to read and write, that should
never be used as a criterion for eligibility, since we
have already learned from painful past experience
that literacy tests can be manipulated to insure discrimination. In any case, very few illiterate adults
vote, and probably very few children would want
to vote as long as they couldn't read or write. But
I firmly believe that, whether they are literate or
not, the vast majority of children would not attempt to vote before they are ready. Interest follows hand in hand with readiness, something that
is easy to see as a home schooler but that is perhaps not so clear to
many people in this society where, ironically, children are continually
taught things when they are not ready, and so are not interested. Yet
when they are interested, as in the case of voting, they're told they are
not yet ready. I think I would not have voted until I was 8 or 9, but
perhaps if I had known I could vote I would have taken an interest
sooner.

> Do you know to what liter-
> acy tests Wallace refers? Is it
> fair for her to assume her au-
> dience will know? Look for
> other references with which
> a general audience may or
> may not be familiar. How
> does Wallace handle these
> references?

Legally, it would be possible to drop the voting-age requirements.
In the Constitution, the states are given all powers to set qualifications
for voters except as they defy the equal protection clause of the Fourteenth Amendment, in which case Congress has the power to enforce
it. If it were proved that age requirements "abridge the privileges or
immunities of citizens of the United States" (which in my opinion they
do, since people born in the United States or to U.S. citizens are citizens
from the moment they are born), and if the states could not come up

with a "compelling interest" argument to justify a limit at a particular age, which Justices Potter Stewart, Warren Burger and Harry Blackmun agreed they could not in *Oregon v. Mitchell* (the Supreme Court case challenging the 1970 amendment to the Voting Rights Act that gave 18-year-olds the vote), then age requirements would be unconstitutional. But it is not necessary that they be unconstitutional for the states to drop them. It is within the power of the states to do that, and I believe that we must start this movement at the state level. According to *Oregon v. Mitchell,* Congress cannot change the qualifications for voting in state elections except by constitutional amendment, which is why the Twenty-sixth Amendment setting the voting age at 18 was necessary. It is very unlikely that an amendment would pass unless several states had tried eliminating the age requirement and had good results. The experience of Georgia and Kentucky, which lowered their age limits to 18, helped to pass the Twenty-sixth Amendment in 1971.

Wallace ends on a note of hope: that younger people will persuade older people to accept and act on their views. As you study other essays in this unit, consider the likelihood of adults presented being persuaded to accept the ideas of the children. Given the time span of these essays, can you see changes that occurred over the past century?

Already in our country's history several oppressed groups have been able to convince the unoppressed to free them. Children, who do not have the power to change their situation, must now convince the adults who do to allow them that power.

17

ANNIE DILLARD

Skin

Annie Dillard (1945–   ) grew up in Pittsburgh, Pennsylvania, with two sisters, a mother who fretted in her role as housewife like "Samson in chains," and a father who was such an avid reader of Mark Twain that he quit his job to float downriver to New Orleans. Dillard herself, at about the same time (1955), discovered *The Field Book of Ponds and Streams* in her neighborhood library and embarked on a lifetime of discoveries about the natural world (see "The Fixed," page 344), many of which are recorded in her Pulitzer Prize–winning *Pilgrim at Tinker Creek.* Dillard's natural curiosity was not limited to the world of wildflowers and praying mantises, however. In 1987 she published *An American Childhood,* an account of her early years that re-creates "a child's interior life" by articulating "what it feels like to be alive from the inside." As Dillard explains, "Childhood is when

you first notice you're alive. So I wrote about childhood and consciousness." "Skin," a chapter from this book, recounts one of her
earliest memories of the adult world. Like many of her best essays, it
combines minute observation with subtle exploration of the nature of
our lives.

Our parents and grandparents, and all their friends, seemed insensi-   1
ble to their own prominent defect, their limp, coarse skin.

We children had, for instance, proper hands; our fluid, pliant fin-   2
gers joined their skin. Adults had misshapen, knuckly hands loose in
their skin like bones in bags; it was a wonder they could open jars.
They were loose in their skins all over, except at the wrists and ankles,
like rabbits.

We were whole, we were pleasing to ourselves. Our crystalline   3
eyes shone from firm, smooth sockets; we spoke in pure, piping voices
through dark, tidy lips. Adults were coming apart, but they neither
noticed nor minded. My revulsion was rude, so I hid it. Besides, we
could never rise to the absolute figural splendor they alone could on
occasion achieve. Our beauty was a mere absence of decrepitude; their
beauty, when they had it, was not passive but earned; it was grandeur;
it was a party to power, and to artifice, even, and to knowledge. Our
beauty was, in the long run, merely elfin. We could not, finally, dis-
count the fact that in some sense they owned us, and they owned the
world.

Mother let me play with one of her hands. She laid it flat on a   4
living-room end table beside her chair. I picked up a transverse pinch
of skin over the knuckle of her index finger and let it drop. The pinch
didn't snap back; it lay dead across her knuckle in a yellowish ridge. I
poked it; it slid over intact. I left it there as an experiment and shifted
to another finger. Mother was reading *Time* magazine.

Carefully, lifting it by the tip, I raised her middle finger an inch and   5
released it. It snapped back to the tabletop. Her insides, at least, were
alive. I tried all the fingers. They all worked. Some I could lift higher
than others.

"That's getting boring."   6

"Sorry, Mama."   7

I refashioned the ridge on her index-finger knuckle; I made the   8
ridge as long as I could, using both my hands. Moving quickly, I made
parallel ridges on her other fingers—a real mountain chain, the Alleghenies; Indians crept along just below the ridgetops, eyeing the frozen
lakes below them through the trees.

Skin was earth; it was soil. I could see, even on my own skin, the   9
joined trapezoids of dust specks God had wetted and stuck with his spit
the morning he made Adam from dirt. Now, all these generations later,

we people could still see on our skin the inherited prints of the dust specks of Eden.

I loved this thought, and repeated it for myself often. I don't know where I got it; my parents cited Adam and Eve only in jokes. Someday I would count the trapezoids, with the aid of a mirror, and learn precisely how many dust specks Adam comprised—one single handful God wetted, shaped, blew into, and set firmly into motion and left to wander about in the fabulous garden bewildered.

The skin of my mother's face was smooth, fair, and tender; it took impressions readily. She napped on her side on the couch. Her face skin pooled on the low side; it piled up in the low corners of her deep-set eyes and drew down her lips and cheeks. How flexible was it? I pushed at a puddle of it by her nose.

She stirred and opened her eyes. I jumped back.

She reminded me not to touch her face while she was sleeping. Anybody's face.

When she sat up, her cheek and brow bone bore a deep red gash, the mark of a cushion's welting. It was textured inside precisely with the upholstery's weave and brocade.

Another day, after a similar nap, I spoke up about this gash. I told her she had a mark on her face where she'd been sleeping.

"Do I?" she said; she ran her fingers through her hair. Her hair was short, blond, and wavy. She wore it swept back from her high, curved forehead. The skin on her forehead was both tight and soft. It would only barely shift when I tried to move it. She went to the kitchen. She was not interested in the hideous mark on her face. "It'll go away," I said. "What?" she called.

I noticed the hair on my father's arms and legs; each hair sprang from a dark dot on his skin. I lifted a hair and studied the puckered tepee of skin it pulled with it. Those hairs were in there tight. The greater the strain I put on the hair, the more puckered the tepee became, and shrunken within, concave. I could point it every which way.

"Ouch! Enough of that."

"Sorry, Daddy."

At the beach I felt my parents' shinbones. The bones were flat and curved, like the slats in a Venetian blind. The long edges were sharp as swords. But they had unexplained and, I thought, possibly diseased irregularities: nicks, bumps, small hard balls, shallow ridges, and soft spots. I was lying between my parents on an enormous towel through which I could feel the hot sand.

Loose under their shinbones, as in a hammock, hung the relaxed flesh of their calves. You could push and swing this like a baby in a sling. Their heels were dry and hard, sharp at the curved edge. The bottoms of their toes had flattened, holding the imprint of life's smooth floors even when they were lying down. I would not let this happen to me. Under certain conditions, the long bones of their feet showed under their skin. The bones rose up long and miserably thin in skeletal rays on the slopes of their feet. This terrible sight they ignored also.

In fact, they were young. Mother was twenty-two when I was born, and Father twenty-nine; both appeared to other adults much younger than they were. They were a handsome couple. I felt it overwhelmingly when they dressed for occasions. I never lost a wondering awe at the transformation of an everyday, tender, nap-creased mother into an exalted and dazzling beauty who chatted with me as she dressed.

Her blue eyes shone and caught the light, and so did the platinum waves in her hair and the pearls at her ears and throat. She was wearing a black dress. The smooth skin on her breastbone rent my heart, it was so familiar and beloved; the black silk bodice and the simple necklace set off its human fineness. Mother was perhaps a bit vain of her long and perfect legs, but not too vain for me; despite her excited pleasure, she did not share my view of her beauty.

"Look at your father," she said. We were all in the dressing room. I found him in one of the long mirrors, where he waggled his outthrust chin over the last push of his tie knot. For me he made his big ears jiggle on his skull. It was a wonder he could ever hear anything; his head was loose inside him.

Father's enormousness was an everyday, stunning fact; he was taller than everyone else. He was neither thin nor stout; his torso was supple, his long legs nimble. Before the dressing-room mirror he produced an anticipatory soft-shoe, and checked to see that his cuffs stayed down.

Now they were off. I hoped they knocked them dead; I hoped their friends knew how witty they were, and how splendid. Their parties at home did not seem very entertaining, although they laughed loudly and often fetched the one-man percussion band from the basement, or an old trumpet, or a snare drum. We children could have shown them how to have a better time. Kick the Can, for instance, never palled. A private game called Spider Cow, played by the Spencer children, also had possibilities: The spider cow hid and flung a wet washcloth at whoever found it, and erupted from hiding and chased him running all over the house.

But implicitly and emphatically, my parents and their friends were not interested. They never ran. They did not choose to run. It went with being old, apparently, and having their skin half off.

MAYA ANGELOU

Momma

Maya Angelou (1928–   ), poet, dancer, actress, civil rights organizer, film director, and now Reynolds Professor of American Studies
at Wake Forest University, is best known for her five volumes of autobiography, beginning with *I Know Why the Caged Bird Sings* (1970).
This book chronicles Angelou's childhood in the rigidly segregated
town of Stamps, Arkansas. There she was raised by her grandmother,
known to her as Momma, who owned a store and a large amount of
land, much of which she rented to whites. Despite her grandmother's
prominence in the black community of Stamps, Angelou's early years
were marred by poverty, discrimination, and abuse, all of which she
presents with frankness and honesty when she writes about her life.
These hardships gave her a sharp sense of everyone's struggle to become adult with pride and dignity: "Most people don't grow up," she
once said. "It's too damn difficult." "Momma," excerpted from *I Know
Why the Caged Bird Sings*, recalls one of Angelou's first glimpses into
what true maturity might mean.

"Thou shall not be dirty" and "Thou shall not be impudent" were   1
the two commandments of Grandmother Henderson upon which hung
our total salvation.

Each night in the bitterest winter we were forced to wash faces,   2
arms, necks, legs and feet before going to bed. She used to add, with a
smirk that unprofane people can't control when venturing into profan-
ity, "and wash as far as possible, then wash possible."

We would go to the well and wash in the ice-cold, clear water,   3
grease our legs with the equally cold stiff Vaseline, then tiptoe into the
house. We wiped the dust from our toes and settled down for school-
work, cornbread, clabbered milk, prayers and bed, always in that order.
Momma was famous for pulling the quilts off after we had fallen asleep
to examine our feet. If they weren't clean enough for her, she took the
switch (she kept one behind the bedroom door for emergencies) and
woke up the offender with a few aptly placed burning reminders.

The area around the well at night was dark and slick, and boys told   4
about how snakes love water, so that anyone who had to draw water
at night and then stand there alone and wash knew that moccasins and
rattlers, puff adders and boa constrictors were winding their way to the
well and would arrive just as the person washing got soap in her eyes.
But Momma convinced us that not only was cleanliness next to Godliness, dirtiness was the inventor of misery.

The impudent child was detested by God and a shame to its parents   5 and could bring destruction to its house and line. All adults had to be addressed as Mister, Missus, Miss, Auntie, Cousin, Unk, Uncle, Buhbah, Sister, Brother and a thousand other appellations indicating familial relationship and the lowliness of the addressor.

Everyone I knew respected these customary laws, except for the powhitetrash children. 6

Some families of powhitetrash lived on Momma's farm land behind the school. Sometimes a gaggle of them came to the Store, filling the whole room, chasing out the air and even changing the well-known scents. The children crawled over the shelves and into the potato and onion bins, twanging all the time in their sharp voices like cigar-box guitars. They took liberties in my Store that I would never dare. Since Momma told us that the less you say to whitefolks (or even powhitetrash) the better, Bailey and I would stand, solemn, quiet, in the displaced air. But if one of the playful apparitions got close to us, I pinched it. Partly out of angry frustration and partly because I didn't believe in its flesh reality. 7

They called my uncle by his first name and ordered him around the Store. He, to my crying shame, obeyed them in his limping dip-straight-dip fashion. 8

My grandmother, too, followed their orders, except that she didn't seem to be servile because she anticipated their needs. 9

"Here's sugar, Miz Potter, and here's baking powder. You didn't buy soda last month, you'll probably be needing some." 10

Momma always directed her statements to the adults, but sometimes, Oh painful sometimes, the grimy, snotty-nosed girls would answer her. 11

"Naw, Annie . . ."—to Momma? Who owned the land they lived on? Who forgot more than they would ever learn? If there was any justice in the world, God should strike them dumb at once!—"Just give us some extry sody crackers, and some more mackerel." 12

At least they never looked in her face, or I never caught them doing so. Nobody with a smidgen of training, not even the worst roustabout, would look right in a grown person's face. It meant the person was trying to take the words out before they were formed. The dirty little children didn't do that, but they threw their orders around the Store like lashes from a cat-o'-nine-tails. 13

When I was around ten years old, those scruffy children caused me the most painful and confusing experience I had ever had with my grandmother. 14

One summer morning, after I had swept the dirt yard of leaves, spearmint-gum wrappers and Vienna-sausage labels, I raked the yellow-red dirt, and made half-moons carefully, so that the design stood out clearly and mask-like. I put the rake behind the Store and came through the back of the house to find Grandmother on the front porch 15 in her big, wide white apron. The apron was so stiff by virtue of the starch that it could have stood alone. Momma was admiring the yard, so I joined her. It truly looked like a flat redhead that had been raked with a big-toothed comb. Momma didn't say anything but I knew she liked it. She looked over toward the school principal's house and to the right at Mr. McElroy's. She was hoping one of those community pillars would see the design before the day's business wiped it out. Then she looked upward to the school. My head had swung with hers, so at just about the same time we saw a troop of the powhitetrash kids marching over the hill and down by the side of the school.

I looked to Momma for direction. She did an excellent job of sagging from her waist down, but from the waist up she seemed to be pulling for the top of the oak tree across the road. Then she began to moan a hymn. Maybe not to moan, but the tune was so slow and the meter so strange that she could have been moaning. She didn't look at me again. When the children reached halfway down the hill, halfway to the Store, she said without turning,"Sister, go on inside." 16

I wanted to beg her, "Momma, don't wait for them. Come on inside with me. If they come in the Store, you go to the bedroom and let me wait on them. They only frighten me if you're around. Alone I know how to handle them." But of course I couldn't say anything, so I went in and stood behind the screen door. 17

Before the girls got to the porch I heard their laughter crackling and popping like pine logs in a cooking stove. I suppose my lifelong paranoia was born in those cold, molasses-slow minutes. They came finally to stand on the ground in front of Momma. At first they pretended seriousness. Then one of them wrapped her right arm in the crook of her left, pushed out her mouth and started to hum. I realized that she was aping my grandmother. Another said, "Naw, Helen, you ain't standing like her. This here's it." Then she lifted her chest, folded her arms and mocked that strange carriage that was Annie Henderson. Another laughed, "Naw, you can't do it. You mouth ain't pooched out enough. It's like this." 18

I thought about the rifle behind the door, but I knew I'd never be able to hold it straight, and the .410, our sawed-off shotgun, which stayed loaded and was fired every New Year's night, was locked in the trunk and Uncle Willie had the key on his chain. Through the fly-specked screen-door, I could see that the arms of Momma's apron jiggled from the vibrations of her humming. But her knees seem to have locked as if they would never bend again. 19

She sang on. No louder than before, but no softer either. No slower or faster. 20

The dirt of the girls' cotton dresses continued on their legs, feet, arms and faces to make them all of a piece. Their greasy uncolored hair hung down, uncombed, with a grim finality. I knelt to see them better, 21 to remember them for all time. The tears that had slipped down my dress left unsurprising dark spots, and made the front yard blurry and even more unreal. The world had taken a deep breath and was having doubts about continuing to revolve.

The girls had tired of mocking Momma and turned to other means   22 of agitation. One crossed her eyes, stuck her thumbs in both sides of her mouth and said, "Look here, Annie." Grandmother hummed on and the apron strings trembled. I wanted to throw a handful of black pepper in their faces, to throw lye on them, to scream that they were dirty, scummy peckerwoods, but I knew I was as clearly imprisoned behind the scene as the actors outside were confined to their roles.

One of the smaller girls did a kind of puppet dance while her fellow   23 clowns laughed at her. But the tall one, who was almost a woman, said something very quickly, which I couldn't hear. They all moved backward from the porch, still watching Momma. For an awful second I thought they were going to throw a rock at Momma, who seemed (except for the apron strings) to have turned into stone herself. But the big girl turned her back, bent down and put her hands flat on the ground—she didn't pick up anything. She simply shifted her weight and did a hand stand.

Her dirty bare feet and long legs went straight for the sky. Her dress   24 fell down around her shoulders, and she had on no drawers. The slick pubic hair made a brown triangle where her legs came together. She hung in the vacuum of that lifeless morning for only a few seconds, then wavered and tumbled. The other girls clapped her on the back and slapped their hands.

Momma changed her song to "Bread of Heaven, bread of Heaven,   25 feed me till I want no more."

I found that I was praying too. How long could Momma hold out?   26 What new indignity would they think of to subject her to? Would I be able to stay out of it? What would Momma really like me to do?

Then they were moving out of the yard, on their way to town.   27 They bobbed their heads and shook their slack behinds and turned, one at a time:

" 'Bye, Annie."   28
" 'Bye, Annie."   29
" 'Bye, Annie."   30

Momma never turned her head or unfolded her arms, but she   31 stopped singing and said, " 'Bye, Miz Helen, 'bye, Miz Ruth, 'bye, Miz Eloise."

I burst. A firecracker July-the-Fourth burst. How could Momma   32 call them Miz? The mean nasty things. Why couldn't she have come inside the sweet, cool store when we saw them breasting the hill? What did she prove? And then if they were dirty, mean and impudent, why did Momma have to call them Miz?

She stood another whole song through and then opened the screen 33
door to look down on me crying in rage. She looked until I looked up.
Her face was a brown moon that shone on me. She was beautiful.
Something had happened out there, which I couldn't completely understand, but I could see that she was happy. Then she bent down and
touched me as mothers of the church "lay hands on the sick and afflicted" and I quieted.

"Go wash your face, Sister." And she went behind the candy 34
counter, and hummed, "Glory, glory, hallelujah, when I lay my burden
down."

I threw the well water on my face and used the weekday handker- 35
chief to blow my nose. Whatever the contest had been out front, I knew
Momma had won.

I took the rake back to the front yard. The smudged footprints were 36
easy to erase. I worked for a long time on my new design and laid the
rake behind the wash pot. When I came back in the Store, I took
Momma's hand and we both walked outside to look at the pattern.

It was a large heart with lots of hearts growing smaller inside, and 37
piercing from the outside rim to the smallest heart was an arrow.
Momma said, "Sister, that's right pretty." Then she turned back to the
Store and resumed, "Glory, glory, hallelujah, when I lay my burden
down."

SHERWOOD ANDERSON

Discovery of a Father

Sherwood Anderson (1876–1941) spent his childhood in and out of
school and was largely self-educated. Growing up in Camden, Ohio,
Anderson experienced some difficult early years, particularly after his
mother died when he was fourteen. Working to support himself, he
was first a newsboy and later a farm laborer, soldier, and advertising
copywriter. In 1912, then the manager of an Ohio paint factory, he
suffered a breakdown brought on by the demands of his family and
work, left his wife, and moved to Chicago to begin writing. Inspired
by Carl Sandburg and Gertrude Stein, Anderson completed his first
novel, *Windy McPherson's Son*, in 1916. His literary career was established just three years later with the publication of *Winesburg, Ohio*, a
collection of related stories that together create a portrait of life in a
typical Midwestern town. Anderson often wrote about his own childhood, through autobiography and fiction. *Tar: A Midwest Childhood*
(1926), a novel, draws almost entirely on his own experience. "Dis-

covery of a Father" was first published in *Reader's Digest* in 1939, then
reprinted as part of his *Memoirs* (1942).

One of the strangest relationships in the world is that between   1
father and son. I know it now from having sons of my own.

A boy wants something very special from his father. You hear it   2
said that fathers want their sons to be what they feel they cannot themselves be, but I tell you it also works the other way. I know that as a
small boy I wanted my father to be a certain thing he was not. I wanted
him to be a proud, silent, dignified father. When I was with other boys
and he passed along the street, I wanted to feel a glow of pride: "There
he is. That is my father."

But he wasn't such a one. He couldn't be. It seemed to me then   3
that he was always showing off. Let's say someone in our town had
got up a show. They were always doing it. The druggist would be in it,
the shoe-store clerk, the horse doctor, and a lot of women and girls.
My father would manage to get the chief comedy part. It was, let's say,
a Civil War play and he was a comic Irish soldier. He had to do the
most absurd things. They thought he was funny, but I didn't.

I thought he was terrible. I didn't see how Mother could stand it.   4
She even laughed with the others. Maybe I would have laughed if it
hadn't been my father.

Or there was a parade, the Fourth of July or Decoration Day. He'd   5
be in that, too, right at the front of it, as Grand Marshal or something,
on a white horse hired from a livery stable.

He couldn't ride for shucks. He fell off the horse and everyone   6
hooted with laughter, but he didn't care. He even seemed to like it. I
remember once when he had done something ridiculous, and right out
on Main Street, too. I was with some other boys and they were laughing
and shouting at him and he was shouting back and having as good a
time as they were. I ran down an alley back of some stores and there
in the Presbyterian Church sheds I had a good long cry.

Or I would be in bed at night and Father would come home a little   7
lit up and bring some men with him. He was a man who was never
alone. Before he went broke, running a harness shop, there were always
a lot of men loafing in the shop. He went broke, of course, because he
gave too much credit. He couldn't refuse it and I thought he was a fool.
I had got to hating him.

There'd be men I didn't think would want to be fooling around   8
with him. There might even be the superintendent of our schools and
a quiet man who ran the hardware store. Once I remember there was
a white-haired man who was a cashier of the bank. It was a wonder
to me they'd want to be seen with such a windbag. That's what I
thought he was. I know now what it was that attracted them. It was

because life in our town, as in all small towns, was at times pretty dull and he livened it up. He made them laugh. He could tell stories. He'd even get them to singing.

If they didn't come to our house they'd go off, say at night, to where there was a grassy place by a creek. They'd cook food there and drink beer and sit about listening to his stories.

He was always telling stories about himself. He'd say this or that wonderful thing had happened to him. It might be something that made him look like a fool. He didn't care.

If an Irishman came to our house, right away Father would say he was Irish. He'd tell what county in Ireland he was born in. He'd tell things that happened there when he was a boy. He'd make it seem so real that, if I hadn't known he was born in southern Ohio, I'd have believed him myself.

If it was a Scotchman the same thing happened. He'd get a burr into his speech. Or he was a German or a Swede. He'd be anything the other man was. I think they all knew he was lying, but they seemed to like him just the same. As a boy that was what I couldn't understand.

And there was Mother. How could she stand it? I wanted to ask but never did. She was not the kind you asked such questions.

I'd be upstairs in my bed, in my room above the porch, and Father would be telling some of his tales. A lot of Father's stories were about the Civil War. To hear him tell it he'd been in about every battle. He'd known Grant, Sherman, Sheridan[1] and I don't know how many others. He'd been particularly intimate with General Grant so that when Grant went East, to take charge of all the armies, he took Father along.

"I was an orderly at headquarters and Sam Grant said to me, 'Irve,' he said, 'I'm going to take you along with me.' "

It seems he and Grant used to slip off sometimes and have a quiet drink together. That's what my father said. He'd tell about the day Lee surrendered and how, when the great moment came, they couldn't find Grant.

"You know," my father said, "about General Grant's book, his memoirs. You've read of how he said he had a headache and how, when he got word that Lee was ready to call it quits, he was suddenly and miraculously cured.

"Huh," said Father. "He was in the woods with me.

"I was in there with my back against a tree. I was pretty well corned. I had got hold of a bottle of pretty good stuff.

"They were looking for Grant. He had got off his horse and come into the woods. He found me. He was covered with mud.

1. Ulysses S. Grant (1822–1885), William Tecumseh Sherman (1820–1891), and Philip Henry Sheridan (1831–1888) were all Union generals during the Civil War.

"I had the bottle in my hand. What'd I care? The war was over. I   21
knew we had them licked."

My father said that he was the one who told Grant about Lee. An   22
orderly riding by had told him, because the orderly knew how thick he
was with Grant. Grant was embarrassed.

"But, Irve, look at me. I'm all covered with mud," he said to Father.   23

And then, my father said, he and Grant decided to have a drink   24
together. They took a couple of shots and then, because he didn't want
Grant to show up potted before the immaculate Lee, he smashed the
bottle against the tree.

"Sam Grant's dead now and I wouldn't want it to get out on him,"   25
my father said.

That's just one of the kind of things he'd tell. Of course the men   26
knew he was lying, but they seemed to like it just the same.

When we got broke, down and out, do you think he ever brought   27
anything home? Not he. If there wasn't anything to eat in the house,
he'd go off visiting around at farm houses. They all wanted him. Sometimes he'd stay away for weeks, Mother working to keep us fed, and
then home he'd come bringing, let's say, a ham. He'd got it from some
farmer friend. He'd slap it on the table in the kitchen. "You bet I'm
going to see that my kids have something to eat," he'd say, and Mother
would just stand smiling at him. She'd never say a word about all the
weeks and months he'd been away, not leaving us a cent for food.
Once I heard her speaking to a woman in our street. Maybe the woman
had dared to sympathize with her. "Oh," she said, "it's all right. He
isn't ever dull like most of the men in this street. Life is never dull when
my man is about."

But often I was filled with bitterness, and sometimes I wished he   28
wasn't my father. I'd even invent another man as my father. To protect
my mother I'd make up stories of a secret marriage that for some strange
reason never got known. As though some man, say the president of a
railroad company or maybe a Congressman, had married my mother,
thinking his wife was dead and then it turned out she wasn't.

So they had to hush it up but I got born just the same. I wasn't   29
really the son of my father. Somewhere in the world there was a very
dignified, quite wonderful man who was really my father. I even made
myself half believe these fancies.

And then there came a certain night. Mother was away from home.   30
Maybe there was church that night. Father came in. He'd been off
somewhere for two or three weeks. He found me alone in the house,
reading by the kitchen table.

It had been raining and he was very wet. He sat and looked at me   31
for a long time, not saying a word. I was startled, for there was on his
face the saddest look I had ever seen. He sat for a time, his clothes
dripping. Then he got up.

"Come on with me," he said.   32

I got up and went with him out of the house. I was filled with   33
wonder but I wasn't afraid. We went along a dirt road that led down
into a valley, about a mile out of town, where there was a pond. We
walked in silence. The man who was always talking had stopped his
talking.

I didn't know what was up and had the queer feeling that I was   34
with a stranger. I don't know whether my father intended it so. I don't
think he did.

The pond was quite large. It was still raining hard and there were   35
flashes of lightning followed by thunder. We were on a grassy bank at
the pond's edge when my father spoke, and in the darkness and rain
his voice sounded strange.

"Take off your clothes," he said. Still filled with wonder, I began   36
to undress. There was a flash of lightning and I saw that he was already
naked.

Naked, we went into the pond. Taking my hand he pulled me in.   37
It may be that I was too frightened, too full of a feeling of strangeness,
to speak. Before that night my father had never seemed to pay any
attention to me.

"And what is he up to now?" I kept asking myself. I did not swim   38
very well, but he put my hand on his shoulder and struck out into the
darkness.

He was a man with big shoulders, a powerful swimmer. In the   39
darkness I could feel the movement of his muscles. We swam to the
far edge of the pond and then back to where we had left our clothes.
The rain continued and the wind blew. Sometimes my father swam on
his back and when he did he took my hand in his large powerful one
and moved it over so that it rested always on his shoulder. Sometimes
there would be a flash of lightning and I could see his face quite clearly.

It was as it was earlier, in the kitchen, a face filled with sadness.   40
There would be the momentary glimpse of his face and then again the
darkness, the wind and the rain. In me there was a feeling I had never
known before.

It was a feeling of closeness. It was something strange. It was as   41
though there were only we two in the world. It was as though I had
been jerked suddenly out of myself, out of my world of the schoolboy,
out of a world in which I was ashamed of my father.

He had become blood of my blood; he the strong swimmer and I   42
the boy clinging to him in the darkness. We swam in silence and in
silence we dressed in our wet clothes, and went home.

There was a lamp lighted in the kitchen and when we came in, the   43
water dripping from us, there was my mother. She smiled at us. I
remember that she called us "boys." "What have you boys been up
to?" she asked, but my father did not answer. As he had begun the

evening's experience with me in silence, so he ended it. He turned and looked at me. Then he went, I thought, with a new and strange dignity, out of the room.

I climbed the stairs to my own room, undressed in darkness and   44
got into bed. I couldn't sleep and did not want to sleep. For the first time I knew that I was the son of my father. He was a storyteller as I was to be. It may be that I even laughed a little softly there in the darkness. If I did, I laughed knowing that I would never again be wanting another father.

HENRY LOUIS GATES, JR.

Living Under Grace

Henry Louis Gates, Jr. (1950–   ), grew up in the small town of Piedmont, West Virginia, and is now Director of the Afro-American Studies Department and W.E.B. Du Bois Professor of Humanities at Harvard. As a student at Yale in the late 1960s, Gates received fellowships that allowed him to spend a year in East Africa, working as a general anesthetist for the Anglican Mission Hospital in Tanzania. After graduating from Yale in 1973, Gates entered Cambridge University, where, in 1979, he became the first African-American to receive a Ph.D. Although he had gone to Cambridge to study medicine, after studying literature there under Nobel laureate Wole Soyinka, Gates decided to pursue degrees in English. He held teaching positions at Yale, Cornell, and Duke before accepting the position at Harvard in 1991. Gates has edited several works on African-American writers, including the thirty-volume *Schomburg Library of Nineteenth-Century Black Women Writers* and collections of essays on Wole Soyinka and Frederick Douglass. His studies of literary criticism include *Black Literature and Literary Theory* (1984) and *The Signifying Monkey: Towards a Theory of Afro-American Literary Criticism* (1988). In sharp contrast to his scholarly writing is Gates's *Colored People* (1994), the story of his coming-of-age during the 1950s and 1960s. In writing this memoir, Gates worked deliberately to simplify his writing, wishing to regain the child's perspective on small-town life. "Living Under Grace" is excerpted from this work.

It was at Peterkin, an Episcopal church camp in West Virginia that   1
I attended that summer—the summer of 1965—and the two summers following, that I was given an opportunity to explore the contours of my new faith, and the world beyond Piedmont.

Spending two weeks at Peterkin, made possible by a scholarship,   2 was like stepping into a dream world. It was populated by well over a hundred seemingly self-confident, generous-spirited teenagers, their ages ranging from fifteen to eighteen; they were rebellious, worldly, questioning, cosmopolitan, articulate, bold, and smart. I learned so much at that camp, I don't even know where to begin.

Following a regular regime of breakfast, morning prayers in the   3 chapel, cleanup, seminars, then lunch, we'd sit for long hours in the afternoon, playing hands of bridge, which I was learning as I went along. We'd play on the front porch of the main house, which used to be an elegant hunting lodge, complete with a huge stone fireplace. I had beginner's luck: a couple of small slams, a grand slam, hands with lots of points. We'd play, the four of us—Tandy Tully and her boyfriend, Peter Roberts, Andrea Strader and I—all afternoon sometimes, watching the other campers come and go, and we'd talk about this and that and everything, books and ideas, people and concepts. The war in Vietnam. Smoking. The existence of God.

Andrea was smart and well-read, intuitive and analytical. She was   4 also beautiful, cocoa-colored, with a wide plum-purple mouth that tasted delicious. It was Andrea who told me early on that I should go to prep school, and then to the Ivy League. (What's a prep school? I asked her.) That I should travel and read this and that. She was petite and elegant, and she sang like an angel. Every night we'd have a camp-fire, and every night I'd sit next to her, trying to learn the words of the traditional gospel songs and the camp songs, listening to my past and future through Andrea's lovely voice. She had large black eyes and long, straightened hair that was soft to the touch. I couldn't believe that she even existed or that she would want to be with me.

The third black camper at Peterkin was Eddie James—Edward Lawrence James, The Third, thank you very much. Eddie was rich. His   5 grandfather had founded a produce business in Charleston at the turn of the century, and it had prospered. Everybody in Charleston knew and respected the Jameses, he let us know. All the Democratic politicians kissed Mr. James II's black behind. Money can't erase color, Andrea would explain to me, but sometimes it can help you blend a bit better. The Jameses were proof of that. Eddie was dating a white girl at camp, which was giving the director, Mary Jo Fitts, fits. She chain-smoked so much that her teeth looked like yellow fangs, and her personality matched her teeth.

Sex was everywhere at Peterkin—everywhere but in my bed.   6 Maybe it could have been there, but I didn't know it, and I didn't know how to put it there. I was fond of making all sorts of lofty pronouncements, like: I'm naturally high, or I'll wait to do it until I get married. I was the walking, talking equivalent of those wall plaques that you can buy in Woolworth's that attest to such sentiments as "M Is for the Many Things She Gave Me" or "Lord, Help Us to Accept the Things

We Cannot Change." I wonder how people could stand me. But I was being honest, in the same way that people who collect paintings on black velvet are being honest. I thought I was thinking the right things, remaining pure of heart. I was terribly earnest: the Pentheus[1] of Peterkin. Meantime, everybody else was getting down with somebody or other. You could feel the sexual energy flowing. There was a charge in the air.

A month shy of my fifteenth birthday, I felt I had died and gone to   7 Heaven. I was living in a kingdom, one of the princes. We drank ideas and ate controversy. Is God dead? we asked. Can you love two people at the same time? I feasted on the idea of learning about the world and being a citizen of it.

And yet my sense of this citizenship would be jeopardized not long   8 after I arrived. After a solid week of complete isolation, a deliveryman bringing milk and bread to the camp told the head counselor that "all hell has broken loose in Los Angeles" and the "colored people have gone crazy." He handed him a Sunday paper, which screamed the news about Negroes rioting in some place called Watts. Andrea had overheard and was the one to tell me. Your soul brothers have gone totally crazy, she said. Rioting and shit. I stared at the headline: NEGROES RIOT IN WATTS.[2] We were all trying to understand what was really happening, forced to judge from one screaming headline.

I was bewildered. I didn't understand what a riot was. Were colored   9 people being killed by white people, or were they killing white people? Watching myself being watched by all the white campers, I experienced that strange combination of power and powerlessness that you feel when the actions of another black person affect your own life, simply because you both are black. I realized that the actions of people I did not know had become my responsibility as surely as if the black folk in Watts had been my relatives in Piedmont, just twenty or so miles away.

Sensing my mixture of pride and discomfiture, a priest handed me   10 a book later that day. From the cover, the wide-spaced eyes of a black man transfixed me. *Notes of a Native Son*, the book was called, by James Baldwin.[3] Was this man the *author*, I wondered, this man with a closely

---

1. Pentheus: In Euripides' play *The Bacchae*, Pentheus attempts to suppress the followers of Dionysus, god of wine, drunkenness, and fertility, to his own demise—he is torn apart by the Bacchae, a group of frenzied women.
2. Watts: a southwestern district of Los Angeles; from August 11–16, 1965, in the face of insurmountable racial problems, thousands of African-Americans rioted, resulting in thirty-four deaths and more than a thousand injuries.
3. Baldwin: One of the most distinguished essayists and novelists of the twentieth century, James Baldwin (1924–1987) published his earliest essays in *Notes of a Native Son* in 1955.

cropped "natural," with brown skin, splayed nostrils, and wide lips, so very Negro, so seemingly comfortable to be so?

From the book's first few sentences, I was caught up thoroughly in 11 the sensibility of another person—a black person. It was the first time I had heard a voice capturing the terrible exhilaration and anxiety of being a person of African descent in this country. The book performed for me the Adamic function of naming the complex racial dynamic of the American cultural imagination. I could not put it down.

It became all the more urgent to deal with the upheaval I had felt 12 when I read that headline.

We were pioneers, people my age, in cross-race relations, able to 13 get to know each other across cultures and classes in a way that was unthinkable in our parents' generation. Honest hatreds, genuine friend-ships, rivalries bred from contiguity rather than from the imagination. Love and competition. In school, I had been raised with white kids, from first grade. To speak to white people was just to speak. Period. No artificial tones, no hypercorrectness. And yet I have known so many Negroes who were separated from white people by an abyss of fear. Whenever one of my uncles would speak to a white person, his head would bow, his eyes would widen, and the smile he would force on his lips said: I won't hurt you, boss, an' I'm your faithful friend. Just come here and let ole me help you. Laughing much too loud and too long at their jokes, he assumed the same position with his head and his body as when he was telling a lie.

But there, at Peterkin, on that day especially, we were all trying to 14 understand what had just happened and what it might mean for our lives, and to do so with a measure of honesty.

What the news of the riots did for us was to remind everybody in 15 one fell swoop that there was a racial context outside Peterkin that affected relations between white and black Americans; we had suddenly to remember that our roles were scripted by that larger context. We had for a blissful week been functioning outside these stereotypes of each other—functioning as best we could, that is—when all of a sudden the context had come crashing down upon us once again. I hated that newspaper. But we overcame it: with difficulty, with perseverance, we pushed away the racial context and could interact not as allegories but as people. It felt like something of an achievement.

I didn't want to leave. I cried when I had to go . . . but then 16 everybody cried. When I got home, my wonderful room full of books and records looked like Cinderella's hovel must have, when she re-turned from the ball at half-past midnight. My beautiful mountain val-ley on the banks of the mighty Potomac looked like a dirty, smelly mill town, full of people who cared more about basketball and baseball and eating than anything else. Somehow, between the six weeks of the hospital[4] and the two weeks of Peterkin, some evil blight had stricken my magical kingdom. It made me heartsick, especially the once or twice I was foolhardy enough to try to explain all this to Linda Hoffman or to Johnny DiPilato.[5] There are *lots* of nice church camps, was all that Hoffman said.

MARY McCARTHY

Names

Mary McCarthy (1912–1989) grew up in Seattle and Minneapolis, raised by her relatives and in parochial boarding schools after being orphaned at six. She recounts her early life in *Memoirs of a Catholic Girlhood* (1957), from which "Names" is taken. McCarthy graduated from Vassar in 1933 and began writing book reviews for *The New Republic* and *The Nation*, making a reputation for herself because of her unflinching frankness. Known also for her keen political and social criticism, McCarthy established her literary career with a collection of satiric short stories, *The Company She Keeps* (1942). She taught at Sarah Lawrence College and Bard College during the 1940s, but, urged to continue writing by her second husband, critic Edmund Wilson, McCarthy also worked as an editor and drama critic for *Partisan Review*. McCarthy later published an autobiographical novel, *The Group* (1963), as well as several volumes of nonfiction, including *Vietnam* (1967), *The Writing on the Wall* (1970), and *How I Grew* (1987). McCarthy spent the final years of her life teaching at Bard, attaining the Stevenson Chair in Literature in 1986.

Anna Lyons, Mary Louise Lyons, Mary von Phul, Emilie von Phul,   1
Eugenia McLellan, Marjorie McPhail, Marie-Louise L'Abbé, Mary Danz,
Julia Dodge, Mary Fordyce Blake, Janet Preston—these were the names
(I can still tell them over like a rosary) of some of the older girls in the
convent: the Virtues and Graces. The virtuous ones wore wide blue or
green moire good-conduct ribbons, bandoleer-style, across their blue
serge uniforms; the beautiful ones wore rouge and powder or at least
were reputed to do so. Our class, the eighth grade, wore pink ribbons
(I never got one myself) and had names like Patricia ("Pat") Sullivan,

---

4. hospital: Earlier in *Colored People*, Gates describes a prolonged hospital stay after intensive surgery to correct a slipped epithesis, which had resulted from a touch-football knee injury.
5. Linda Hoffman, Johnny DiPilato: two of Gates's white friends.

Eileen Donohoe, and Joan Kane. We were inelegant even in this re-
spect; the best name we could show, among us, was Phyllis ("Phil")
Chatham, who boasted that her father's name, Ralph, was pronounced
"Rafe" as in England.

Names had a great importance for us in the convent, and foreign   2
names, French, German, or plain English (which, to us, were foreign,
because of their Protestant sound), bloomed like prize roses among a
collection of spuds. Irish names were too common in the school to have
any prestige either as surnames (Gallagher, Sheehan, Finn, Sullivan,
McCarthy) or as Christian names (Kathleen, Eileen). Anything exotic
had value: an "olive" complexion, for example. The pet girl of the
convent was a fragile Jewish girl named Susie Lowenstein, who had
pale red-gold hair and an exquisite retroussé nose, which, if we had
had it, might have been called "pug." We liked her name too and the
name of a child in the primary grades: Abbie Stuart Baillargeon. My
favorite name, on the whole, though, was Emilie von Phul (pronounced
"Pool"); her oldest sister, recently graduated, was called Celeste. Another name that appealed to me was Genevieve Albers, Saint Genevieve
being the patron saint of Paris who turned back Attila from the gates
of the city.

All these names reflected the still-pioneer character of the Pacific   3
Northwest. I had never heard their like in the parochial school in Minneapolis, where "foreign" extraction, in any case, was something to be
ashamed of, the whole drive being toward Americanization of first
name and surname alike. The exceptions to this were the Irish, who
could vaunt such names as Catherine O'Dea and the name of my second
cousin, Mary Catherine Anne Rose Violet McCarthy, while an unfortunate German boy named Manfred was made to suffer for his. But that
was Minneapolis. In Seattle, and especially in the convent of the Ladies
of the Sacred Heart, foreign names suggested not immigration but emi-
gration—distinguished exile. Minneapolis was a granary; Seattle was a
port, which had attracted a veritable Foreign Legion of adventurers—
soldiers of fortune, younger sons, gamblers, traders, drawn by the fortunes to be made in virgin timber and shipping and by the Alaska gold
rush. Wars and revolutions had sent the defeated out to Puget Sound,
to start a new life; the latest had been the Russian Revolution, which
had shipped us, via Harbin, a Russian colony, complete with restaurant,
on Queen Anne Hill. The English names in the convent, when they did
not testify to direct English origin, as in the case of "Rafe" Chatham,
had come to us from the South and represented a kind of internal exile;
such girls as Mary Fordyce Blake and Mary McQueen Street (a class
ahead of me; her sister was named Francesca) bore their double-
barreled first names like titles of aristocracy from the ante-bellum South.
Not all our girls, by any means, were Catholic; some of the very prettiest
ones—Julia Dodge and Janet Preston, if I remember rightly—were

Protestants. The nuns had taught us to behave with special courtesy to these strangers in our midst, and the whole effect was of some superior hostel for refugees of all the lost causes of the past hundred years. Money could not count for much in such an atmosphere; the fathers and grandfathers of many of our "best" girls were ruined men.

Names, often, were freakish in the Pacific Northwest, particularly 4 girls' names. In the Episcopal boarding school I went to later, in Tacoma, there was a girl called De Vere Utter, and there was a girl called Rocena and another called Hermoine. Was Rocena a mistake for Rowena and Hermoine for Hermione? And was Vere, as we called her, Lady Clara Vere de Vere? Probably. You do not hear names like those often, in any case, east of the Cascade Mountains; they belong to the frontier, where books and libraries were few and memory seems to have been oral, as in the time of Homer.

Names have more significance for Catholics than they do for other 5 people; Christian names are chosen for the spiritual qualities of the saints they are taken from; Protestants used to name their children out of the Old Testament and now they name them out of novels and plays, whose heroes and heroines are perhaps the new patron saints of a secular age. But with Catholics it is different. The saint a child is named for is supposed to serve, literally, as a model or pattern to imitate; your name is your fortune and it tells you what you are or must be. Catholic children ponder their names for a mystic meaning, like birthstones; my own, I learned, besides belonging to the Virgin and Saint Mary of Egypt, originally meant "bitter" or "star of the sea." My second name, Therese, could dedicate me either to Saint Theresa or to the saint called the Little Flower, Soeur Thérèse of Lisieux, on whom God was supposed to have descended in the form of a shower of roses. At Confirmation, I had added a third name (for Catholics then rename themselves, as most nuns do, yet another time, when they take orders); on the advice of a nun, I had taken "Clementina," after Saint Clement, an early pope—a step I soon regretted on account of "My Darling Clementine" and her number nine shoes. By the time I was in the convent, I would no longer tell anyone what my Confirmation name was. The name I had nearly picked was "Agnes," after a little Roman virgin martyr, always shown with a lamb, because of her purity. But Agnes would have been just as bad, I recognized in Forest Ridge Convent—not only because of the possibility of "Aggie," but because it was subtly, indefinably *wrong*, in itself. Agnes would have made me look like an ass.

The fear of appearing ridiculous first entered my life, as a governing 6 motive, during my second year in the convent. Up to then, a desire for prominence had decided many of my actions and, in fact, still persisted. But in the eighth grade, I became aware of mockery and perceived that I could not seek prominence without attracting laughter. Other people could, but I couldn't. This laughter was proceeding, not from my classmates, but from the girls of the class just above me, in particular from two boon companions, Elinor Heffernan and Mary Harty, a clownish pair—oddly assorted in size and shape, as teams of clowns generally are, one short, plump, and baby-faced, the other tall, lean, and owlish—who entertained the high-school department by calling attention to the oddities of the younger girls. Nearly every school has such a pair of satirists, whose marks are generally low and who are tolerated just because of their laziness and non-conformity; one of them (in this case, Mary Harty, the plump one) usually appears to be half asleep. Because of their low standing, their indifference to appearances, the sad state of their uniforms, their clowning is taken to be harmless, which, on the whole, it is, their object being not to wound but to divert; such girls are bored in school. We in the eighth grade sat directly in front of the two wits in study hall, so that they had us under close observation; yet at first I was not afraid of them, wanting, if anything, to identify myself with their laughter, to be initiated into the joke. One of their specialties was giving people nicknames, and it was considered an honor to be the first in the eighth grade to be let in by Elinor and Mary on their latest invention. This often happened to me; they would tell me, on the playground, and I would tell the others. As their intermediary, I felt myself almost their friend and it did not occur to me that I might be next on their list.

I had achieved prominence not long before by publicly losing my 7 faith and regaining it at the end of a retreat. I believe Elinor and Mary questioned me about this on the playground, during recess, and listened with serious, respectful faces while I told them about my conversations with the Jesuits. Those serious faces ought to have been an omen, but if the two girls used what I had revealed to make fun of me, it must have been behind my back. I never heard any more of it, and yet just at this time I began to feel something, like a cold breath on the nape of my neck, that made me wonder whether the new position I had won for myself in the convent was as secure as I imagined. I would turn around in study hall and find the two girls looking at me with speculation in their eyes.

It was just at this time, too, that I found myself in a perfectly absurd 8 situation, a very private one, which made me live, from month to month, in horror of discovery. I had waked up one morning, in my convent room, to find a few small spots of blood on my sheet; I had somehow scratched a trifling cut on one of my legs and opened it during the night. I wondered what to do about this, for the nuns were fussy about bedmaking, as they were about our white collars and cuffs, and if we had an inspection those spots might count against me. It was best, I decided, to ask the nun on dormitory duty, tall, stout Mother Slattery, for a clean bottom sheet, even though she might scold me for having scratched my leg in my sleep and order me to cut my toenails. You

never know what you might be blamed for. But Mother Slattery, when
she bustled in to look at the sheet, did not scold me at all; indeed, she
hardly seemed to be listening as I explained to her about the cut. She
told me to sit down: she would be back in a minute. "You can be
excused from athletics today," she added, closing the door. As I waited,
I considered this remark, which seemed to me strangely munificent, in
view of the unimportance of the cut. In a moment, she returned, but
without the sheet. Instead, she produced out of her big pocket a sort of
cloth girdle and a peculiar flannel object which I first took to be a
bandage, and I began to protest that I did not need or want a bandage;
all I needed was a bottom sheet. "The sheet can wait," said Mother
Slattery, succinctly, handing me two large safety pins. It was the pins
that abruptly enlightened me; I saw Mother Slattery's mistake, even as
she was instructing me as to how this flannel article, which I now
understood to be a sanitary napkin, was to be put on.

"Oh, no, Mother," I said, feeling somewhat embarrassed. "You 9
don't understand. It's just a little cut, on my leg." But Mother, again,
was not listening; she appeared to have grown deaf, as the nuns had a
habit of doing when what you were saying did not fit in with their
ideas. And now that I knew what was in her mind, I was conscious of
a funny constraint; I did not feel it proper to name a natural process,
in so many words, to a nun. It was like trying not to think of their
going to the bathroom or trying not to see the straggling iron-grey hair
coming out of their coifs (the common notion that they shaved their
heads was false). On the whole, it seemed better just to show her my
cut. But when I offered to do so and unfastened my black stocking, she
only glanced at my leg, cursorily. "That's only a scratch, dear," she
said. "Now hurry up and put this on or you'll be late for chapel. Have
you any pain?" "No, no, Mother!" I cried, "You don't understand!"
"Yes, yes, I understand," she replied soothingly, "and you will too, a
little later. Mother Superior will tell you about it some time during the
morning. There's nothing to be afraid of. You have become a woman."

"I know all about that," I persisted. "Mother, please listen. I just 10
cut my leg. On the athletic field. Yesterday afternoon." But the more
excited I grew, the more soothing, and yet firm, Mother Slattery became. There seemed to be nothing for it but to give up and do as I was
bid. I was in the grip of a higher authority, which almost had the power
to persuade me that it was right and I was wrong. But of course I was
not wrong; that would have been too good to be true. While Mother
Slattery waited, just outside my door, I miserably donned the equipment she had given me, for there was no place to hide it, on account
of drawer inspection. She led me down the hall to where there was a
chute and explained how I was to dispose of the flannel thing, by
dropping it down the chute into the laundry. (The convent arrange-

ments were very old-fashioned, dating back, no doubt, to the days of Louis Philippe.)

The Mother Superior, Madame MacIllvra, was a sensible woman, 11 and all through my early morning classes, I was on pins and needles, chafing for the promised interview with her which I trusted would clear things up. *"Ma Mère,"* I would begin, "Mother Slattery thinks . . ." Then I would tell her about the cut and the athletic field. But precisely the same impasse confronted me when I was summoned to her office at recess-time. *I* talked about my cut, and *she* talked about becoming a woman. It was rather like a round, in which she was singing "Scotland's burning, Scotland's burning," and I was singing "Pour on water, pour on water." Neither of us could hear the other, or, rather, I could hear her, but she could not hear me. Owing to our different positions in the convent, she was free to interrupt me, whereas I was expected to remain silent until she had finished speaking. When I kept breaking in, she hushed me, gently, and took me on her lap. Exactly like Mother Slattery, she attributed all my references to the cut to a blind fear of this new, unexpected reality that had supposedly entered my life. Many young girls, she reassured me, were frightened if they had not been prepared. "And you, Mary, have lost your dear mother, who could have made this easier for you." Rocked on Madame MacIllvra's lap, I felt paralysis overtake me and I lay, mutely listening, against her bosom, my face being tickled by her white, starched, fluted wimple, while she explained to me how babies were born, all of which I had heard before.

There was no use fighting the convent. I had to pretend to have 12 become a woman, just as, not long before, I had had to pretend to get my faith back—for the sake of peace. This pretense was decidedly awkward. For fear of being found out by the lay sisters downstairs in the laundry (no doubt an imaginary contingency, but the convent was so very thorough), I reopened the cut on my leg, so as to draw a little blood to stain the napkins, which were issued me regularly, not only on this occasion, but every twenty-eight days thereafter. Eventually, I abandoned this bloodletting, for fear of lockjaw, and trusted to fate. Yet I was in awful dread of detection; my only hope, as I saw it, was either to be released from the convent or to become a woman in reality, which might take a year, at least, since I was only twelve. Getting out of athletics once a month was not sufficient compensation for the farce I was going through. It was not my fault; they had forced me into it; nevertheless, it was I who would look silly—worse than silly; half mad—if the truth ever came to light.

I was burdened with this guilt and shame when the nickname 13 finally found me out. "Found me out," in a general sense, for no one ever did learn the particular secret I bore about with me, pinned to the linen band. "We've got a name for you," Elinor and Mary called out to me, one day on the playground. "What is it?" I asked, half hoping, half fearing, since not all their sobriquets were unfavorable. "Cye," they answered, looking at each other and laughing. " 'Si'?" I repeated, supposing that it was based on Simple Simon. Did they regard me as a hick? "C.Y.E.," they elucidated, spelling it out in chorus. "The letters stand for something. Can you guess?" I could not and I cannot now. The closest I could come to it in the convent was "Clean Your Ears." Perhaps that was it, though in later life I have wondered whether it did not stand, simply, for "Clever Young Egg" or "Champion Young Eccentric." But in the convent I was certain that it stood for something horrible, something even worse than dirty ears (as far as I knew, my ears were clean), something I could never guess because it represented some aspect of myself that the world could see and I couldn't, like a sign pinned on my back. Everyone in the convent must have known what the letters stood for, but no one would tell me. Elinor and Mary had made them promise. It was like halitosis; not even my best friend, my deskmate, Louise, would tell me, no matter how much I pleaded. Yet everyone assured me that it was "very good," that is, very apt. And it made everyone laugh.

This name reduced all my pretensions and solidified my sense of *wrongness*. Just as I felt I was beginning to belong to the convent, it turned me into an outsider, since I was the only pupil who was not in the know. I liked the convent, but it did not like me, as people say of certain foods that disagree with them. By this, I do not mean that I was actively unpopular, either with the pupils or with the nuns. The Mother Superior cried when I left and predicted that I would be a novelist, which surprised me. And I had finally made friends; even Emilie von Phul smiled upon me softly out of her bright blue eyes from the far end of the study hall. It was just that I did not fit into the convent pattern; the simplest thing I did, like asking for a clean sheet, entrapped me in consequences that I never could have predicted. I was not bad; I did not consciously break the rules; and yet I could never, not even for a week, get a pink ribbon, and this was something I could not understand, because I was trying as hard as I could. It was the same case as with the hated name; the nuns, evidently, saw something about me that was invisible to me.

The oddest part was all that pretending. There I was, a walking mass of lies, pretending to be a Catholic and going to confession while really I had lost my faith, and pretending to have monthly periods by cutting myself with nail scissors; yet all this had come about without my volition and even contrary to it. But the basest pretense I was driven to was the acceptance of the nickname. Yet what else could I do? In the convent, I could not live it down. To all those girls, I had become "Cye McCarthy." That was who I was. That was how I had to identify myself when telephoning my friends during vacations to ask them to the movies: "Hello, this is Cye." I loathed myself when I said it, and yet I succumbed to the name totally, making myself over into a sort of hearty to go with it—the kind of girl I hated. "Cye" was my new patron saint. This false personality stuck to me, like the name, when I entered public high school, the next fall, as a freshman, having finally persuaded my grandparents to take me out of the convent, although they could never get to the bottom of my reasons, since, as I admitted, the nuns were kind, and I had made many nice new friends. What I wanted was a fresh start, a chance to begin life over again, but the first thing I heard in the corridors of the public high school was that name called out to me, like the warmest of welcomes: "Hi, there, Si!" That was the way they thought it was spelled. But this time I was resolute. After the first weeks, I dropped the hearties who called me "Si" and I never heard it again. I got my own name back and sloughed off Clementina and even Therese—the names that did not seem to me any more to be mine but to have been imposed on me by others. And I preferred to think that Mary meant "bitter" rather than "star of the sea."

JOHN HOLT

The Institution of Childhood

John Holt (1923–1985) spent much of his career teaching elementary and high school English, French, and mathematics, yet he never studied education formally. In fact, Holt once stated that most of what he knew he did not learn in school or in "learning situations," and after years of teaching young people he concluded that our schools do more to hinder learning than to encourage it. Disillusioned with school reform, Holt turned to writing books about children and education. His first, *How Children Fail* (1964), immediately caught the public's eye, as did the many books that followed. One critic commented that "respect for and trust in children became Holt's constant theme in the eleven books he wrote." For Holt, this respect in part meant that we must let children decide for themselves what they want to learn, an idea he promoted in *Growing Without Schooling*, a magazine that encouraged parents to turn the responsibility for learning over to their children through home schooling. In *Escape from Childhood* (1974), Holt argues that "in many respects our power to protect becomes the power to abuse"; one critic has claimed, conversely, that Holt's surrendering of power only produces "amoral, ignorant monsters." The following chapter is from *Escape from Childhood*.

Of course, in one sense childhood is not an institution but a fact of human life. At birth we depend for our lives on others to take care of us, feed us, keep us warm and clean, and protect us from harm. In this we are like other animals. But unlike most animals, we do not outgrow our helplessness and dependency in a few months—it takes years. This is the fact of childhood, a fact as old as mankind. But it is also a fact that as we grow older we do continue to get more able to take care of ourselves.

When I was first teaching school in Colorado there came to the school for a while twin boys from Italy. An American who lived up the valley from the school had some years before heard about these boys when traveling in Italy and had made himself their foster parent. When they were very small, at most four or five years old, during World War II, their parents had disappeared—killed or taken prisoner. Somehow these two small boys had managed to live and survive for several years, in a large city, in a country terribly torn and dislocated by war, in the midst of great poverty and privation—*all by themselves.* They had apparently found or made some sort of shelter for themselves in a grave-yard and lived by begging and stealing what they needed. Only after several years of this life were they discovered and brought under the wing of the state. They were living in an orphan asylum when the American first heard of them and began to take an interest in their growing up and their education. He sent them to our school for a while because he thought it would be useful for them to know some English and hoped that they might learn it there.

I don't want to be understood as saying that I think it is good for small children to live alone in graveyards, or even that the response of these two boys to this experience was typical. But the fact remains that they did not seem to have been deeply or permanently hurt by that experience. Though smaller for their age than most Americans, they were exceedingly quick, strong, and well coordinated, by far the best soccer players in the school. Also, though they were not very good students and not much interested in learning English—what good would it do them back in Bologna?—they were friendly, lively, curious, enthusiastic, and, in spite of the language barrier, much liked by all who knew them at school. Clearly it may be possible for us to outgrow our physical helplessness and dependency much sooner or faster than most people think.

We might think of human life as a sort of curve, starting at birth, rising to various peaks of physical, mental, and social power, continuing for some time on a kind of plateau, and then slowly declining to old age and death. This curve of life is different for all human beings. Sometimes it is cut abruptly short by death. But for every human being that curve is a single curve, a wholeness. It is of course a curve of continual growth and change. To some degree we are different every day from what we were the day before. But this growth and change are continuous. There are no breaks or gaps in it. We do not, like some insects, suddenly turn from one kind of creature into another that is very different.

Here the fact of childhood ends and the institution of childhood begins. Childhood as we now know it has divided that curve of life, that wholeness, into two parts—one called Childhood, the other called Adulthood, or Maturity. It has made a Great Divide in human life, and made us think that the people on opposite sides of this divide, the Children and the Adults, are very different. Thus we *act* as if the differences between any sixteen-year-old and any twenty-two-year-old were far greater and more important than the differences between someone aged two and someone aged sixteen, or between someone aged twenty-two and someone aged seventy. For with respect to the kind of control he has over his own life, the ability to make important choices, the sixteen-year-old is much closer to the two-year-old than he is to someone of twenty-two.

In short, by the institution of childhood I mean all those attitudes and feelings, and also customs and laws, that put a great gulf or barrier between the young and their elders, and the world of their elders; that make it difficult or impossible for young people to make contact with the larger society around them, and, even more, to play any kind of active, responsible, useful part in it; that lock the young into eighteen years or more of subserviency and dependency, and make of them, as I said before, a mixture of expensive nuisance, fragile treasure, slave, and super-pet.

For a while I thought of calling this book *The Prison of Childhood* or, as other friends suggested, using the word "Liberation" in the title. But one friend objected that *The Prison of Childhood* made it sound as if everyone who supported the present institution of childhood did so because he disliked children and wanted to keep them in some sort of prison. This, she insisted, is not so. Many people who believe in our present ways of raising children, and who will therefore deeply dislike many or most of the ideas in this book, are people who like children and want to do what they think is best for them.

I agreed and gave up both "Prison" and "Liberation," both of which imply letting children out of a bad place that bad people have locked them into. The word "escape" need not imply this. If we are in a house that catches fire, or on a boat that begins to sink, we want to escape—but this does not mean that we think someone lured or put us into that house or boat. Also, "escape" is a word of action. To escape from a danger, you must first decide that it *is* a danger and then act to get away from it. I want to leave to the young the right to make that decision and to choose and take that action.

Most people who believe in the institution of childhood as we know it see it as a kind of walled garden in which children, being small and weak, are protected from the harshness of the world outside until they become strong and clever enough to cope with it. Some children experience childhood in just that way. I do not want to destroy their garden or kick them out of it. If they like it, by all means let them stay in it. But I believe that most young people, and at earlier and earlier ages, begin to experience childhood not as a garden but as a prison. What I want to do is put a gate, or gates, into the wall of the garden, so that those who find it no longer protective or helpful, but instead confining and humiliating, can move out of it and for a while try living in a larger space. If that proves too much for them, they can always come back into the garden. Indeed, perhaps we all ought to have walled gardens to take refuge in when we feel we must.

I am not saying that childhood is bad for all children all the time.   10
But Childhood, as in Happy, Safe, Protected, Innocent Childhood, does not exist for many children. For many other children, however good it may be, childhood goes on far too long, and there is no gradual, sensible, and painless way to grow out of it or leave it.

Some children have no families. Their parents are dead or have   11
abandoned them. Or the law may have taken them from their parents, perhaps because they brutalized or neglected them, perhaps because the state did not approve of their parents' politics or morals or style of life. Most children who lose their families remain wards of the state—*i.e.*, they are prisoners. That is the choice the law now offers. If you can't (or won't) be a child, you must be a convict, in some kind of jail, guarded by people whose chief concern is to keep you from running away.

Many children live seemingly normal lives in seemingly normal   12
families. But their childhood, if in some respects safe, is by no means happy, protected, or innocent. On the contrary, they may be in many ways exploited, bullied, humiliated, and mistreated by their families. But even in such families life might not be so painful and destructive for the young if they could now and then get away for a while from parents, or rival brothers and sisters.

For many children, childhood, happy and ideal though it may be,   13
simply goes on too long. Among families that I know well, many children who for years have been living happily with their parents have suddenly found them intolerable and have become intolerable to them. The happier was their previous life together, the more painful will this be for the parents, and perhaps for the young person as well. "We used to get along so well." "He used to be so happy." "I don't know what's gotten into him." "We must have done something wrong, but we can't imagine what it is." Many times, too, I have heard a young person, usually in late teens or early twenties, say, "I love my parents, we've

always gotten along very well, but now they want me to do this, or that, and I don't want to do it, I want to do something else, which they don't like. I feel so guilty and confused, I don't know what to do. I don't want to hurt them but I have to live my own life." The end of childhood seems often most painful for those whose childhood was most happy.

It goes on too long, and there is too seldom any sensible and gradual   14
way to move out of it and into a different life, a different relationship with the parents. When the child can find no way to untie the bonds to his parents, the only thing left for him is to break them. The stronger the bonds, the harder and more desperate must be the pull required to break them. This can cause terrible, almost unforgettable bad feelings, injury, and pain. It is as if, having no other way to get out of the nest, the young had no choice but to blow it up.

A sign in a Boston subway says NO ONE EVER RUNS AWAY FROM A HAPPY   15
HOME. But the happiest homes may give to the children just that extra confidence, curiosity, and energy that makes them want to test their strength and skill against a larger world. If they are then not allowed to do it—that's when the unhappiness starts.

Not long ago I was asked to speak at a number of meetings in   16
schools in a lower-middle-class near-suburb of a midwestern city. Almost everyone worked either as fairly well paid union labor in large industries or in lower-level white collar jobs. Most of the adults were the children or grandchildren of immigrants and wanted very much for their children to go to college and establish themselves firmly in the middle class. By conventional standards the politics of the district are well over to the right.

It had been arranged that during the afternoon, in one of the junior   17
high schools, I was to spend a class period in a joint meeting of two ninth grade English classes, discussing with the students whatever they and I wanted to talk about. It had also been agreed that at this meeting I would be the only adult in the group, but for some reason a number of the school officials who had been showing me around followed me into the classroom. The appearance of these well-known authority figures ended our chances for any very free or candid discussion. A few students, either fearless by nature, or so successful that they did not have to worry about getting in trouble, or in so much trouble already that they did not have to worry about getting into any more, did almost all of what little talking was done.

I had been talking about schools and school reform. In the closing   18
minutes of the period, it occurred to me to try to find out what some of these young people thought about the institution of childhood. And let me stress again, these were not radical or even liberal young people. The local high school had only just modified, and very slightly, its dress

code. In this junior high school, the boys had to wear coats and ties; the girls, dresses or skirts. They were running a tight ship in this school, and most of the top brass was right there in the room.

I asked three questions, for a show-of-hands response. The first 19 was, "If you could legally vote in political elections, how many of you think that at least some of the time you would vote?" About two-thirds of the students raised their hands, many of them slowly and thought-fully. The second was, "If you could legally work for money, how many of you think that at least some of the time you would work?" Again, about two-thirds raised their hands. One boy in the front row, who had not spoken during the discussion, said, "Hey, we're going to have to spend the rest of our lives working, what's the big hurry to start?" People laughed, but the hands stayed up. Finally, almost as an after-thought, not expecting any particular response, I asked the third ques-tion: "If you could legally live away from home, how many of you think that at least some of the time you would do so?" Every hand shot into the air, so quickly and violently that I half expected shoulders to pop out of joint. Faces came alive. Clearly, I had touched a magic button. I thought to myself, "If only I had thought to ask that sooner, how much I might have learned." But the period was at an end. I thanked the students, wished them luck, and they filed out of the room. My hosts and I continued our tour of the schools. No one mentioned that last response, and I thought it better to let it drop.

Some might say that the young people only wanted to get away 20 from home and the nay-saying parents so that they could enjoy forbid-den adult pleasures—smoking, drinking, sex—but though this may be part of what those young people were saying, I think that they were also saying that they want to live, at least for a while, among other people who might see them and deal with them as people, not as children.

JOY OVERBECK

Sex, Kids and the Slut Look

Joy Overbeck (1950–   ), born in Park Ridge, Illinois, was educated at DePauw University and the University of Illinois. Having desired "to make a career out of words" since she was a child, Overbeck began taking her writing seriously in college, when, in the era of "new journalism," she wrote for her college newspaper and graduated with a degree in English. Her first writing job was in San Francisco, where she wrote window signs (and eventually advertisements) for a large department store. After moving to Denver, Overbeck expanded her writing career, doing investigative work for *The Denver Magazine,* and also got married and started a family. While pregnant with her daughter, Overbeck wrote *The Whole Birth Catalogue* (1986), a collection of over one hundred outrageous, not-available-anywhere products for pregnancy and child rearing, which landed her and her new baby a feature in *People* magazine. After her divorce, she wrote another satirical book *Love Stinks: The Romantic's Guide to Breaking Up Without Breaking Down* (1990), which was published in several languages. Overbeck hosts a three-hour radio talk show on parenting issues for a Denver station and writes for several magazines, including *Redbook, Newsweek, New Woman, Parents,* and *Family Fun.* As she explains, "Ideas wake me up in the middle of the night and won't let me rest until I put them on paper." "Sex, Kids and the Slut Look" was published in *Newsweek* in 1993.

The other day my 10-year-old daughter and I breached the prurient wilds of the Junior Fashion Department. Nothing in what she sneeringly calls the "little kid" department seems to fit anymore. She's tall for her age and at that awkward fashion stage between Little Red Riding Hood and Amy Fisher.[1] She patrolled the racks, hunting the preteen imperative—a pair of leg-strangling white tights culminating in several inches of white lace. Everywhere were see-through dresses made out of little-flower-print fabric, lacy leggings, transparent tops and miniature bustiers for females unlikely to own busts. Many were garments that Cher[2] would have rejected as far too obvious. 1

Lace leggings? When I went to grade school, you were sent home if you wore even normal pants. The closest we got to leggings were our Pillsbury Doughboy snow pants, mummy-padding we pulled on under our dresses and clumped around in as we braved the frigid blasts of winter. Today's high-school girls have long dressed like street-corner pros; but since when did elementary school become a Frederick's of Hollywood[3] showroom? 2

Grousing that her dumb clothes compromised her popularity, the offspring had herded me to fashion's outer limits. She appeared to be the only 10-year-old in the area; the rest were 14 or so, unaccompanied by their mothers. She pranced up, holding out a hanger on which dangled a crocheted skirt the size of a personals ad and a top whose deep V-neck yawned like the jaws of hell. 3

"Isn't this great! I want this!" she yodeled, sunshine beaming from 4

1. Amy Fisher: teenager who was convicted in 1992 of shooting Mary Jo Buttafuco, the wife of her 36-year-old lover.
2. Cher (1946–   ): singer, entertainer, and actress notorious for her immodest and eccentric costumes.
3. Frederick's of Hollywood: franchise marketer of risqué women's lingerie.

her sweet face once more. "You're 10 years old," I said. "Shhh," she hissed, whipping her head around in frantic oh-God-did-anybody-hear mode. Then she accused me of not wanting her to grow up. She's 10 years old and the kid talks like a radio shrink.

It's not really that I want her to be a little girl forever. It's just that   5
it would be nice if she were a child during her childhood. Instead, she's been bathed in the fantasy of bodies and beauty that marinates our entire culture. The result is an insidious form of premature sexual awakening that is stealing our kids' youth.

Meredith was 8 and we were in the car, singing along to some   6
heartbroken musical lament on the radio, when she said, "Mom, why is everything in the world about sex?" I laughed and asked where she got that idea. But then, listening as she knowledgeably recited examples from music, movies, MTV and advertising, it hit me that she was right. The message of our popular culture for any observant 8-year-old is: *sex rules*. Otherwise, why would it deserve all this air time, all this agony and ecstasy, all this breathless attention?

Kids pick up on the sexual laser focus of our society, then mimic   7
what they see as the ruling adult craze, adding their own bizarre kid twist. Recently, I read that the authors of "The Janus Report on Sexual Behavior" were shocked to find how many had sex at 10, 11 and 12. Too young to know how to handle it, kids mix sex with the brutal competitiveness they learn in the two worlds they know best: sports and the streets. Sex is grafted onto their *real* consuming passion—to be the most radical dude or dudette in their crowd. Peer pressure—what I'm seeing now in my 10-year-old's wardrobe angst—takes over. The result is competitive sex: California gangs vying for the record in number of girls bedded; teenage boys raping girls my daughter's age in a heartless sexual all-star game where all that counts is the points you rack up. In Colorado Springs, not far from where I live, gangs are demanding that kids as young as 10 have sex as a form of initiation. It's the old "chicken" game in "Rebel Without a Cause,"[4] played with young bodies instead of cars.

The adult reaction to all of this is outrage. But why should we be   8
shocked? Children learn by example. Sex is omnipresent. What do we expect when we allow fashion designers to dress us, grown women, in garments so sheer that any passing stranger can see us nearly naked for the price of a casual glance?

Or look at Madonna[5] on the cover of Vanity Fair[6] wearing only a   9

4. Rebel: In the 1955 classic, two teenagers play a fatal game of "chicken,"· driving stolen cars at high speed toward a cliff, the winner being the last to jump from his vehicle.
5. Madonna (1958–   ): singer and actress who has made a career of her sexual frankness.
6. Vanity Fair: a popular and glossy magazine whose covers feature more cleavage than information.

pink inner tube and hair done up in cutesy '50s pigtails. Here's a 34-year-old heroine to little girls—the core of her fandom is about 14—posing as innocent jailbait. Inside, she romps on a playground in baby-doll nighties, toying with big, stuffed duckies and polar bears. This is a blatant child molester's fantasy-in-the-flesh. Does kiddie porn encourage sex crimes against children? Who cares!

Rudimentary good sense must tell us that sexualizing children not only sullies their early years, but also exposes them to real danger from human predators. What our culture needs is a little reality check: in an era when sexual violence against children is heartbreakingly common—a recent study estimates that about one quarter of women have been victims of childhood sexual abuse—anything that eroticizes our children is irresponsible, at best.   10

It's up to adults to explode the kids-are-sexy equation. Our kids need us to give them their childhood back. But this summer, the eroticization of our girl children proceeds apace. The crop tops! The tight little spandex shorts! (Our moms wore them under their clothes and called them girdles.) My daughter's right, everybody struts her stuff. I've seen 5-year-old Pretty Babies.[7]   11

As for me, I don't care anymore if my kid has a hissy fit in the junior department. She's not wearing the Slut Look. Let her rant that I'm a hopelessly pathological mom who wants to keep her in pacifiers and pinafores forever. Let her do amateur psychoanalysis on me in public until my ears fry—I've shaken the guilt heebie-jeebies and drawn the line. So you can put those white lace spandex leggings back on the rack, young lady.   12

JUDY TROY

The Way Things Will Be

Judy Troy (1951–   ) was born in northwest Indiana. She started writing at ten or eleven but didn't consider writing as a career until she found herself, some fifteen years later, "writing stories no matter what [she] was supposed to be doing instead." Troy graduated from the University of Chicago before receiving her M.A. in creative writing from the University of Indiana in 1981. Her first collection of short

7. Pretty Babies: an allusion to *Pretty Baby,* the controversial 1978 film about a 12-year-old who grows up in a New Orleans brothel in the early 20th century.

stories, *Mourning Doves* (1993), includes eleven stories first published in *The New Yorker*; within this collection is "The Way Things Will Be," the first of a sequence of four stories about the same family. Although the facts of the story are fictitious, Troy claims the emotional content stems from experiences in her own childhood. Troy is now completing a novel, *Small Rain*. She has taught creative writing at Indiana University and the University of Missouri and now teaches at Auburn University.

On our way to Florida in the winter of 1965, Eddie, the older of my two brothers, had an appendicitis attack and was operated on in a hospital in Nashville. My parents didn't have much money—we were moving from South Bend, Indiana, to Key West, where my aunt and uncle owned a motel. My father's idea was for us to live in one of the units while he and my uncle started a fishing business. My father had been a car salesman in South Bend, and before that he had worked in a dairy, and before that he had sold suits in a department store. He said that people he worked for didn't like him. He said that he was the kind of person who should have his own business, because he was independent-minded and good at making decisions. My mother said she thought it took a lot of money to start a business of your own, but my father said no, it just took courage and intelligence, and a family that was willing to stand behind you. 1

In Nashville, while Eddie was being operated on, my other brother, Lee, and I slept on couches in the lobby. We had been up all night in the car. Eddie had been crying, and my parents had been arguing about what to do. My father had wanted to wait until morning to see if Eddie felt better, and my mother wanted to find a hospital immediately. In the middle of the night, as they were shouting at one another, my father took his hand off the steering wheel and slapped her. There was suddenly silence. As far as my brothers and I knew, my father had never hit her before, and he seemed as shocked as anyone. As soon as he could, he stopped at a gas station and got out of the car. He walked to the edge of the pavement, which bordered a field. His shoulders were hunched over, and he was looking down at his feet. He was standing just outside the circle of light that separated the gas station from the darkness. 2

My mother got out of the car, too. "If it weren't for Eddie I wouldn't get back in," she said, loudly enough for him to hear. "I'd find a bus and go back to South Bend." Lee started to cry. He was seven, and Eddie was ten, and I was twelve. My mother got in the back seat with us, and after a few minutes my father came over to the car and put his hands on the hood, as though he didn't want the car ever to move again. My mother told him to drive to a hospital. 3

After Eddie's operation was over, my father drove Lee and me to 4 a motel on the outskirts of the city, because it was cheaper, and he gave us money to buy hamburgers at a restaurant next door. He said that he would be back before too long. "I'm putting you in charge, Jean," he said. "Take care of Lee." I made Lee take a bath, and I took a bath, and I unpacked clean clothes for us. It was raining, and we ran to the restaurant, which was a diner on a road that ran parallel to the highway. It was noon, and the restaurant was crowded with truckers. I ate my hamburger quickly and wrapped up Lee's to take with us. He had brought a toy car with him, and instead of eating his lunch he pushed the car back and forth across the table, crashing it into the sugar bowl.

At the motel, Lee fell asleep and I lay down next to him and imag- 5 ined shapes of faces in the patterns that the streaks of rain were making on the window. There wasn't a TV in the room, and most of our books and games were in the car. There wasn't even a clock, and I couldn't tell how much time was going by until it began to get dark outside, late in the afternoon, and then I became really frightened. Lee was up by then, and he kept asking me when our parents were coming back. He didn't cry, but when I put my arms around him I could feel him shaking. I tried to make my voice sound normal. I invented games for us to play, and after it stopped raining we stood outside, even though it was cold, so that we could watch for the headlights of our parents' car as it turned in to the motel. When our parents finally came, I was so relieved that I didn't feel angry until later, when I was in bed, trying to fall asleep. I thought about how scared I'd been all afternoon, and how happy I'd acted to see them, and I felt as though I'd been tricked.

They weren't speaking to one another—at least my mother wasn't 6 speaking to my father. It seemed that he hadn't shown up at the hospital for a long time after he'd left us; he had stopped for a beer and got into a conversation with someone. My father liked talking to strangers. That morning, just before he'd driven Lee and me to the motel, he'd had a conversation with a nurse in the hospital lobby. "She thought we lived here in Nashville," he said cheerfully on the way to the motel, which made the motel seem even shabbier and lonelier than it was when we pulled up in front.

My mother sat on one of the beds with me and Lee. She told us 7 what Eddie had said after he woke up, and what his roommate was like, and what she had eaten at the hospital cafeteria. My father was unpacking his clothes, but all of his attention was focussed on her. Even when he wasn't looking at her I felt that he was listening unusually hard, that he was waiting for her to say something especially meant for him. She didn't, though. She sent him out to bring us back some dinner, and later slept in bed with me.

In the morning, my parents took us to the hospital with them—they 8 didn't have enough money to stay in the motel again. We brought our

Monopoly game in with us and set it up on a table in the lobby. My father was in charge of the bank. Each time Lee or I asked for anything he would say, "I'm not sure. What have you done to deserve it?" He tried to joke this way once with my mother and she took the money out of his hand without saying a word. After that we played the game as seriously as if the outcome of it would change our lives. I hadn't wanted to go to Florida to begin with, but now I felt as though I would do anything to get there, so that we could at least stay in one place. I started to think, This is the way things will be from now on—nothing planned.

After lunch, my father took Lee and me for a walk. We passed a   9 pawnshop and a liquor store and a big vacant lot. It was winter weather, but warm compared to South Bend. The wind was pushing dry leaves and scraps of paper down the street, and dark clouds were flying across the sky. We could hear thunder in the distance. "Are we going to live here?" Lee asked. He was holding my father's hand.

"We're going to live in Florida," my father said. "You'll see the   10 ocean every day, and it will always be warm outside. It will never snow."

"Why not?" Lee asked.   11

"Because it's too far south," my father told him. "It's where the   12 birds in Indiana fly to in the winter."

He bought us ice-cream bars at a candy store and we walked back   13 to the hospital. When my mother saw us, the expression on her face changed from serious to happy. My father put his arm around her and she didn't pull away, and we sat down on a couch in the lobby. They discussed what we were going to do. Eddie had to stay in the hospital three more days, and if we stayed in a motel again we wouldn't have enough money to get to Florida, and my parents didn't know how they were going to pay the hospital bill. My father didn't seem worried now that my mother had stopped being angry with him. "I think you should call your dad," he said to her. "He can wire us money, and when things are going well for us in Florida we can pay him back."

My mother said no at first, but changed her mind. As a result,   14 late that afternoon we checked into a nicer motel—with TV. It was in downtown Nashville, across the street from a park. We ate dinner in the coffee shop, and afterward my parents decided to go to the motel bar, which had a band and dancing. My mother pushed back the curtains in our room and showed us where it was—in front of the motel, just across the parking lot. It was a small, low building with red lights around the windows and a flashing neon sign. "Dad and I will sit next to the window and keep an eye on you, so you don't have to worry," my mother said. "And if you need us for any reason, just come out and get us. But watch out for cars."

"O.K.," we said. Lee was watching TV, but when our parents left   15 he went to the window and watched them walk across the parking lot and disappear into the bar. "We could go over there now and ask them to come back," I told him. He shook his head; his eyes were on the TV again.

At nine o'clock we both got ready for bed and I made Lee lie down. 16 I turned out the light and went into the bathroom and sat on the floor to read "Black Beauty." I had probably read it twenty times before. I was reading the part where Black Beauty is made to gallop with one shoe missing when I heard my parents' voices. I went outside in my nightgown. The stormy weather had ended, and now it was colder and there was a bright moon. Because my mind was still on my book, I was feeling waves of pity for both Black Beauty and myself. I had been crying, and my mother noticed the tears on my face. "I'm sorry we didn't come back sooner, honey," she said. She gave my father an angry look and walked me inside. My father hesitated in the doorway. Just in front of where he was standing the door to the bathroom was open, and the light was on. He picked up "Black Beauty" without looking at it and put it on top of a luggage rack in the open closet.

"Go back over to the bar if you want," my mother told him. 17

"Why should I?" he said. He closed the door. "Why should I do 18 something I don't want to do?"

My mother helped me into bed, next to Lee. "I was reading a sad 19 part of 'Black Beauty,'" I told her. "That's why I was crying."

"We're back now," my mother said. "Go to sleep. Everything's 20 fine." I closed my eyes and listened to my parents undressing.

"May," my father whispered a little later. 21

"I don't want to talk now," my mother whispered back. I opened 22 my eyes and saw that they were lying just at the edges of the bed, as far apart as if I had been lying in the middle between them.

"May, just put your arms around me," I heard my father say. After 23 a few minutes my mother moved closer to him. "Things will be better when we get to Florida," my father whispered.

"You're always looking on the bright side," my mother said. 24

The next morning, my father took Lee and me to the park while 25 my mother slept; we had woken up early. It was cold outside, and there were high white clouds drifting across the sky. We had Eddie's football with us, which we passed around—my father to Lee to me to my father. About every five minutes Lee would try to tackle one of us. We were the only people in the park. But gradually more traffic appeared in the streets and buses began delivering people to work. My father seemed depressed all of a sudden. "Let's get Mom," he said. We walked across the street to the motel.

My mother was already awake and dressed. "I was watching you 26 from here," she said. "I was spying on you."

We all went out to the car; we were going to have breakfast at the 27
hospital cafeteria. "We have a flat," my mother said. She was standing
next to the front passenger door, looking at the tire. She squatted down
in her high heels and touched it.

My father came around the car. He rested his hand on my mother's 28
shoulder. "We have nothing but bad luck," he said. "We don't have a
spare."

My mother stood up. "How can you tell me something like that 29
now?" she said.

"Can't we buy a tire or get it fixed?" I asked. Neither of them paid 30
attention to me. They were looking at each other. They were having a
conversation without words. I took Lee's hand and walked across the
parking lot, and then across the street to the park. I was careful and
crossed at the light, but I knew my parents would be nervous watching
us cross a street this busy. By the time they called us back, though, we
were halfway across. "It's O.K.," I told Lee. "They won't be mad at
us."

We sat on a bench in the sun. After a few minutes, Lee got up to 31
look at something shiny in the grass which turned out to be a dime. I
watched my parents standing next to the car, arguing. I wasn't afraid
that my father would hit my mother. I didn't think that would happen
again unless, as in a "Twilight Zone"[1] episode, we had to relive that
night in the car all over again, just as it took place the first time. But I
could see now that my parents were not going to be any happier in
Florida.

I called to Lee, and he looked up at me. "Come over here and sit 32
still for five minutes," I told him.

By this time, our parents were crossing the street. But they got 33
caught in the middle by a yellow light and were stranded together on
the concrete strip that separated the lanes of traffic. From where we
were sitting we could hardly see the concrete strip—just their heads,
which looked as small as flowers, above a steady stream of cars. "They
shouldn't be standing there," Lee said.

"They'll be all right," I told him. The light changed, and they 34
crossed the street without looking at anything except us.

---

1. Twilight Zone: CBS television series running from 1959–1964, featuring tales of the
supernatural.

PETER CAMERON

Homework

Peter Cameron (1959–   ) grew up in Pompton Plains, New Jersey. After graduating from Hamilton College in 1982, he began writing while doing clerical work for St. Martin's Press and for New York City's Trust for Public Land. His early stories were an instant success, particularly "Homework," which was included in *Prize Stories: O. Henry Awards* for 1985. By 1986, Cameron had published his first collection of stories, *One Way or Another*. One critic remarked that these stories reflect a sense of anger directed at families that, "rather than providing havens, are themselves the fulcrums of the most sweeping upheavals." While an assistant professor at Oberlin College in 1987, Cameron worked on his first novel, *Leap Year*, which was published in 1989 and depicts a year in the life of young New Yorkers. His second collection of short stories, *Far Flung* (1991), continues to explore the difficulty, particularly for young people, of connecting emotionally with others, and his second novel, *The Weekend* (1994), has been compared to the works of E. M. Forster and Virginia Woolf. "Homework," like many of Cameron's other stories, depicts a young man "indelicately balanced between adolescence and adulthood." Cameron continues to publish short stories in *The New Yorker* and in *The Paris Review*.

My dog, Keds, was sitting outside of the A. & P. last Thursday when   1
he got smashed by some kid pushing a shopping cart. At first we thought he just had a broken leg, but later we found out he was bleeding inside. Every time he opened his mouth, blood would seep out like dull red words in a bad silent dream.

Every night before my sister goes to her job she washes her hair in   2
the kitchen sink with beer and mayonnaise and eggs. Sometimes I sit at the table and watch the mixture dribble down her white back. She boils a pot of water on the stove at the same time; when she is finished with her hair, she steams her face. She wants so badly to be beautiful.

I am trying to solve complicated algebraic problems I have set for   3
myself. Since I started cutting school last Friday, the one thing I miss is homework. Find the value for *n*. Will it be a whole number? It is never a whole number. It is always a fraction.

"Will you get me a towel?" my sister asks. She turns her face   4
toward me and clutches her hair to the top of her head. The sprayer hose slithers into its hole next to the faucet.

I hand her a dish towel. "No," she says. "A bath towel. Don't be   5
stupid."

In the bathroom, my mother is watering her plants. She has ar-   6 ranged them in the tub and turned the shower on. She sits on the toilet lid and watches. It smells like outdoors in the bathroom.

I hand my sister the towel and watch her wrap it round her head. [7] She takes the cover off the pot of boiling water and drops lemon slices in. Then she lowers her face into the steam.

This is the problem I have set for myself: [8]

$$\frac{245\,(n + 17)}{34} = 396\,(n - 45)$$

$n =$

Wednesday, I stand outside the high-school gym doors. Inside, stu- [9] dents are lined up doing calisthenics. It's snowing, and prematurely dark, and I can watch without being seen.

"Well," my father says when I get home. He is standing in the [10] garage testing the automatic door. Every time a plane flies overhead, the door opens or closes, so my father is trying to fix it. "Have you changed your mind about school?" he asks me.

I lock my bicycle to a pole. This infuriates my father, who doesn't [11] believe in locking things up in his own house. He pretends not to notice. I wipe the thin stripe of snow off the fenders with my middle finger. It is hard to ride a bike in the snow. This afternoon on my way home from the high school I fell off, and I lay in the snowy road with my bike on top of me. It felt warm.

"We're going to get another dog," my father says. [12]

"It's not that," I say. I wish everyone would stop talking about [13] dogs. I can't tell how sad I really am about Keds versus how sad I am in general. If I don't keep these things separate, I feel as if I'm betraying Keds.

"Then what is it?" my father says. [14]

"It's nothing," I say. [15]

My father nods. He is very good about bringing things up and then [16] letting them drop. A lot gets dropped. He presses the button on the automatic control. The door slides down its oiled tracks and falls shut. It's dark in the garage. My father presses the button again and the door opens, and we both look outside at the snow falling in the driveway, as if in those few seconds the world might have changed.

My mother has forgotten to call me for dinner, and when I confront [17] her with this she tells me that she did, but that I was sleeping. She is loading the dishwasher. My sister is standing at the counter, listening, and separating eggs for her shampoo.

"What can I get you?" my mother asks. "Would you like a meatloaf [18] sandwich?"

"No," I say. I open the refrigerator and survey its illuminated con- [19] tents. "Could I have some scrambled eggs?"

"O.K.," says my mother. She comes and stands beside me and puts   20
her hand on top of mine on the door handle. There are no eggs in the
refrigerator. "Oh," my mother says; then, "Julie?"

"What?" my sister says.   21

"Did you take the last eggs?"   22

"I guess so," my sister says. "I don't know."   23

"Forget it," I say. "I won't have eggs."   24

"No," my mother says. "Julie doesn't need them in her shampoo.   25
That's not what I bought them for."

"I do," my sister says. "It's a formula. It doesn't work without the   26
eggs. I need the protein."

"I don't want eggs," I say. "I don't want anything." I go into my   27
bedroom.

My mother comes in and stands looking out the window. The snow   28
has turned to rain. "You're not the only one who is unhappy about
this," she says.

"About what?" I say. I am sitting on my unmade bed. If I pick up   29
my room, my mother will make my bed: that's the deal. I didn't pick
up my room this morning.

"About Keds," she says. "I'm unhappy too. But it doesn't stop me   30
from going to school."

"You don't go to school," I say.   31

"You know what I mean," my mother says. She turns around and   32
looks at my room, and begins to pick things off the floor.

"Don't do that," I say. "Stop."   33

My mother drops the dirty clothes in an exaggerated gesture of   34
defeat. She almost—almost—throws them on the floor. The way she
holds her hands accentuates their emptiness. "If you're not going to go
to school," she says, "the least you can do is clean your room."

In the algebra word problems, a boat sails down a river while a   35
jeep drives along the bank. Which will reach the capital first? If a plane
flies at a certain speed from Boulder to Oklahoma City and then at a
different speed from Oklahoma City to Detroit, how many cups of coffee
can the stewardess serve, assuming she is unable to serve during the
first and last ten minutes of each flight? How many times can a man
ride the elevator to the top of the Empire State Building while his wife
climbs the stairs, given that the woman travels one stair slower each
flight? And if the man jumps up while the elevator is going down,
which is moving—the man, the woman, the elevator, or the snow
falling outside?

The next Monday I get up and make preparations for going to   36
school. I can tell at the breakfast table that my mother is afraid to
acknowledge them for fear it won't be true. I haven't gotten up before
ten o'clock in a week. My mother makes me French toast. I sit at the

table and write the note excusing me for my absence. I am eighteen, an adult, and thus able to excuse myself from school. This is what my note says:

> Dear Mr. Kelly [my homeroom teacher]:
>   Please excuse my absence February 17–24. I was unhappy and did not feel able to attend school.
>
> Sincerely,
Michael Pechetti

This is the exact format my mother used when she wrote my notes,   37
only she always said, "Michael was home with a sore throat," or "Michael was home with a bad cold." The colds that prevented me from going to school were always bad colds.

My mother watches me write the note but doesn't ask to see it. I   38
leave it on the kitchen table when I go to the bathroom, and when I come back to get it I know she has read it. She is washing the bowl she dipped the French toast into. Before, she would let Keds lick it clean. He liked eggs.

In Spanish class we are seeing a film on flamenco dancers. The   39
screen wouldn't pull down, so it is being projected on the blackboard, which is green and cloudy with erased chalk. It looks a little as if the women are sick, and dancing in Heaven. Suddenly the little phone on the wall buzzes.

Mrs. Smitts, the teacher, gets up to answer it, and then walks over   40
to me. She puts her hand on my shoulder and leans her face close to mine. It is dark in the room. "Miguel," Mrs. Smitts whispers, *"Tienes que ir a la oficina de* guidance."

"What?" I say.   41

She leans closer, and her hair blocks the dancers. Despite the click-   42
ing castanets and the roomful of students, there is something intimate about this moment. *"Tienes que ir a la oficina de* guidance," she repeats slowly. Then, "You must go to the guidance office. Now. *Vaya.*"

My guidance counsellor, Mrs. Dietrich, used to be a history teacher,   43
but she couldn't take it anymore, so she was moved into guidance. On her immaculate desk is a calendar blotter with "lunch" written across the middle of every box, including Saturday and Sunday. The only other things on the desk are an empty photo cube and my letter to Mr. Kelly. I sit down, and she shows me the letter as if I haven't yet read it. I reread it.

"Did you write this?" she asks.   44

I nod affirmatively. I can tell Mrs. Dietrich is especially nervous   45
about this interview. Our meetings are always charged with tension. At the last one, when I was selecting my second-semester courses, she

started to laugh hysterically when I said I wanted to take Boys' Home Ec. Now every time I see her in the halls she stops me and asks me how I'm doing in Boys' Home Ec. It's the only course of mine she remembers.

I hand the note back to her and say, "I wrote it this morning," as if this clarified things.   46

"This morning?"   47

"At breakfast," I say.   48

"Do you think this is an acceptable excuse?" Mrs. Dietrich asks. "For missing more than a week of school?"   49

"I'm sure it isn't," I say.   50

"Then why did you write it?"   51

Because it is the truth, I start to say. It is. But somehow I know that saying this will make me more unhappy. It might make me cry. "I've been doing algebra at home," I say.   52

"That's fine," Mrs. Dietrich says, "but it's not the point. The point is, to graduate you have to attend school for a hundred and eighty days, or have legitimate excuses for the days you've missed. That's the point. Do you want to graduate?"   53

"Yes," I say.   54

"Of course you do," Mrs. Dietrich says.   55

She crumples my note and tries to throw it into the wastepaper basket but misses. We both look for a second at the note lying on the floor, and then I get up and throw it away. The only other thing in her wastepaper basket is a banana peel. I can picture her eating a banana in her tiny office. This, too, makes me sad.   56

"Sit down," Mrs. Dietrich says.   57

I sit down.   58

"I understand your dog died. Do you want to talk about that?"   59

"No," I say.   60

"Is that what you're so unhappy about?" she says. "Or is there something else?"   61

I almost mention the banana peel in her wastebasket, but I don't. "No," I say. "It's just my dog."   62

Mrs. Dietrich thinks for a moment. I can tell she is embarrassed to be talking about a dead dog. She would be more comfortable if it were a parent or a sibling.   63

"I don't want to talk about it," I repeat.   64

She opens her desk drawer and takes out a pad of hall passes. She begins to write one out for me. She has beautiful handwriting. I think of her learning to write beautifully as a child and then growing up to be a guidance counsellor, and this makes me unhappy.   65

"Mr. Neuman is willing to overlook this matter," she says. Mr. Neuman is the principal. "Of course, you will have to make up all the work you've missed. Can you do that?"   66

"Yes," I say.   67

Mrs. Dietrich tears the pass from the pad and hands it to me. Our   68
hands touch. "You'll get over this," she says. "Believe me, you will."

My sister works until midnight at the Photo-Matica. It's a tiny booth   69
in the middle of the A. & P. parking lot. People drive up and leave their
film and come back the next day for pictures. My sister wears a uniform
that makes her look like a counterperson in a fast-food restaurant.
Sometimes at night when I'm sick of being at home I walk downtown
and sit in the booth with her.

There's a machine in the booth that looks like a printing press,   70
only snapshots ride down a conveyor belt and fall into a bin and then
disappear. The machine gives the illusion that your photographs are
being developed on the spot. It's a fake. The same fifty photographs roll
through over and over, and my sister says nobody notices, because
everyone in town is taking the same pictures. She opens up the enve-
lopes and looks at them.

Before I go into the booth, I buy cigarettes in the A. & P. It is open   71
twenty-four hours a day, and I love it late at night. It is big and bright
and empty. The checkout girl sits on her counter swinging her legs. The
Muzak plays "If Ever I Would Leave You." Before I buy the cigarettes,
I walk up and down the aisles. Everything looks good to eat, and the
things that aren't edible look good in their own way. The detergent
aisle is colorful and clean-smelling.

My sister is listening to the radio and polishing her nails when I   72
get to the booth. It is almost time to close.

"I hear you went to school today," she says.   73

"Yeah."   74

"How was it?" she asks. She looks at her nails, which are so long   75
it's frightening.

"It was O.K.," I say. "We made chili dogs in Home Ec."   76

"So are you over it all?"   77

I look at the pictures riding down the conveyor belt. I know the   78
order practically by heart: graduation, graduation, birthday, mountains,
baby, baby, new car, bride, bride and groom, house . . . "I guess so,"
I say.

"Good," says my sister. "It was getting to be a little much." She   79
puts her tiny brush back in the bottle, capping it. She shows me her
nails. They're an odd brown shade. "Cinnamon," she says. "It's an
earth color." She looks out at the parking lot. A boy is collecting the
abandoned shopping carts, forming a long silver train, which he noses
back toward the store. I can tell he is singing by the way his mouth
moves.

"That's where we found Keds," my sister says, pointing to the   80
Salvation Army bin.

When I went out to buy cigarettes, Keds would follow me. I hung 81
out down here at night before he died. I was unhappy then, too. That's
what no one understands. I named him Keds because he was all white
with big black feet and it looked as if he had high-top sneakers on. My
mother wanted to name him Bootie. Bootie is a cat's name. It's a dumb
name for a dog.

"It's a good thing you weren't here when we found him," my sister 82
says. "You would have gone crazy."

I'm not really listening. It's all nonsense. I'm working on a new 83
problem: Find the value for n such that n plus everything else in your
life makes you feel all right. What would n equal? Solve for n.

GALWAY KINNELL

First Song

Galway Kinnell (1927–   ) was born in Rhode Island and began
studying poetry as a teenager. He is now a translator and author of
more than a dozen books of poetry; "First Song" is the lead poem in
his first book, *What a Kingdom It Was* (1960). Kinnell's poetry is best
known for its concreteness and intensity of observation, which tends
to focus on the wildness of nature and the fragility of civilization or
the relationship between life and death. Other notable works of poetry
include *The Avenue Bearing the Initial of Christ into the New World: Poems
1946–1964* (1974) and *Body Rags* (1968); his translations include Henri
Lehmann's *Pre-Columbian Ceramics* and *The Poems of François Villon*. In
1983 Kinnell received the American Book Award for poetry and the
Pulitzer Prize for *Selected Poems*; from 1989 to 1993 he served as the
State Poet of Vermont. Kinnell has taught in France, Iran, Spain, and
Australia and is now a professor of English at New York University.
He holds several honorary degrees, including ones from Kalamazoo
College, Holy Cross College, Providence College, Hofstra University,
and Southern Vermont College. Kinnell continues to publish poetry,
particularly in *The New Yorker, Hudson Review, The Nation,* and
Harper's.

Then it was dusk in Illinois, the small boy   1
After an afternoon of carting dung
Hung on the rail fence, a sapped thing
Weary to crying. Dark was growing tall
And he began to hear the pond frogs all
Calling on his ear with what seemed their joy.

Soon their sound was pleasant for a boy   2
Listening in the smoky dusk and the nightfall
Of Illinois, and from the fields two small
Boys came bearing cornstalk violins
And they rubbed the cornstalk bows with resins
And the three sat there scraping of their joy.

It was now fine music the frogs and the boys   3
Did in the towering Illinois twilight make
And into dark in spite of a shoulder's ache
A boy's hunched body loved out of a stalk
The first song of his happiness, and the song woke
His heart to the darkness and into the sadness of joy.

FEMININITY AND MASCULINITY

We find ourselves confronting a fork in the road.

Femininity and Masculinity: Preview

The instant Grady shot from the pool, shaking water from his orange hair,
freckled shoulders shining, my attraction to members of my own sex became
a matter I could no longer suppress or rationalize.

It was "masculine" to think the blots looked like man-made objects, and
"feminine" to think they looked like natural objects. It was masculine to
think they looked like things capable of causing harm, and feminine to think
of innocent things.

I've always wanted to be one of these guys: a lone wolf, austere and
independent, a secular saint of the wilderness. As a teen-ager, sporting
glasses, braces, global acne and Lee's "Husky" jeans, I found it consoling to
think of myself in years to come as a solitary wanderer. . . .

The word *girl* had formerly seemed to me innocent and unburdened, like
the word *child;* now it appeared that it was no such thing. A girl was not,
as I had supposed, simply what I was; it was what I had to become.

He tore out a reed, the great god Pan . . .
And hacked and hewed as a great god can,
With his hard bleak steel at the patient reed,
Till there was not a sign of the leaf indeed
    To prove it fresh from the river.

Overview and Ideas for Writing

Even in our time, when the roles of men and women are defined
with a flexibility that would have astonished our ancestors, sexual identity provides one of the great forks in the road of everyone's life. We
may no longer see men as strong oaks and women as clinging vines,
men as brutes and women as sweet civilizers. Nonetheless, we grow
up with strong signals about what our society considers feminine (or
effeminate) and what it considers masculine (or mannish). In school-
yards you can still hear children repeat the rhyme that little girls are

made of "sugar and spice and everything nice" and boys are made of "nails and snails and puppy-dog tails." Most men can remember being told that some kind of behavior might be acceptable in a *girl,* but not in a boy, and most women can remember getting the mirror image of the same talk. How do such messages affect our view of ourselves? That is the underlying question of this unit.

Some writers in this unit answer the question with a good deal of humor, others with considerable seriousness. Dave Barry answers with an observation about his own behavior: "Men are still basically scum when it comes to helping out in the kitchen," and Stephen Harrigan reports ruefully on his inability to be a "lone wolf." Lois Gould tells us a fable: "Once upon a time, a Baby named X was born. It was named X so that nobody could tell whether it was a boy or a girl." Alice Munro, on the other hand, offers a sensitive portrayal of a young girl's first glimpse of how her life must ultimately differ from her brother's. Other writers remind us that encounters with the model society presents to us can be bruising, whether the model is a "he-man" (Noel Perrin, Bernard Cooper) or an "Angel in the House" (Virginia Woolf). Naomi Wolf, writing sixty years after Woolf, argues that, despite the tremendous advances women have made in this century, they are still fighting the angel and subjecting themselves to standards of femininity prescribed by men. Wolf questions how far we have come from the age of Victoria and Elizabeth Barrett Browning, when such mandates were more overtly imposed.

The essays by Jennifer Brice and Scott Russell Sanders complicate the picture by reminding us that the sex roles many people now see as confining can also provide avenues for growth and discovery. Taking what may be viewed as an odd twist on recent feminism, Brice "discovers herself" through the birth of her daughter, which brings her into touch with her own body as well as with her mother and grandmother. Also interested in the physical nature of gender-definition, Sanders explores how the world of "masculine" sports, passed father to son, may teach lessons deeper than athletic skill.

The changing of sex roles over time can be a fascinating area of research. You might develop an interesting paper by interviewing older relatives, for instance, and contrasting their views of masculinity and femininity with the ideas that are fashionable today. Or you might scrutinize magazines from fifty years ago, from twenty-five years ago, and from this month, looking at the articles, stories, and advertisements for clues about changing roles for men and women. Or you might examine a nineteenth-century novel—*Pride and Prejudice, Huckleberry Finn,* or *Jane Eyre,* for example—to see how much the meaning of male and female has changed over a longer stretch of time.

Introspection and memory, however, can provide you with material for excellent essays. Defining masculine and feminine roles is in some ways a public business, involving religious bodies, the media, and even the courts. But it is also very much an individual business. Each of us has a story to tell about how we learned what society expected of us and how we dealt with that expectation. Each thoughtfully told story contributes to our understanding of the mysterious relationships among femininity, masculinity, and humanity.

DAVE BARRY

Lost in the Kitchen

Dave Barry (1947–   ) is a nationally syndicated columnist for the *Miami Herald* and the 1988 winner of the Pulitzer Prize for Commentary. After being honored as Class Clown at New York's Pleasantville High School, Barry went on to take his B.A. in English from Haverford College. He then worked as a small-town newspaper reporter in Pennsylvania and as a consultant on effective writing for various businesses. In 1983 humor became his full-time job. Besides writing his weekly column, he has been a guest on Garrison Keillor's "Radio Company of the Air" and has written several books, including *Taming the Screw: Several Million Homeowners' Problems* (1983), *Stay Fit Until You're Dead* (1985), *Dave Barry Turns 40* (1990), *Dave Barry Talks Back* (1991), and *Dave Barry's Guide to Guys* (1995). Recently Barry's humor has landed him on a wide variety of talk shows and his life has been commemorated through a highly rated TV sitcom, *Dave's World*. "Lost in the Kitchen" appeared in the *Miami Herald* and other newspapers in May 1986.

> If you were writing an essay about sexual equality, would your teacher let you begin with Barry's introductory paragraph? What is its relationship to the rest of the essay? Why might Barry have started his essay with it?

Men are still basically scum when it comes to helping out in the kitchen. This is one of two insights I had last Thanksgiving, the other one being that Thanksgiving night must be the slowest night of the year in terms of human sexual activity. Nobody wants to engage in human sexual activity with somebody who smells vaguely like yams and is covered with a thin layer of turkey grease, which describes pretty much everybody in the United States on Thanksgiving except the Detroit Lions, who traditionally play football that day and would therefore be too tired.

But that, as far as I can tell, is not my point. My point is that despite all that has been said in the past 20 years or so about sexual equality, most men make themselves as useful around the kitchen as ill-trained Labrador retrievers. This is not just my opinion: It is a scientific finding based on an exhaustive study of what happened last Thanksgiving when my family had dinner at the home of friends named Arlene and Gene.

Barry's descriptions of the dog and the children are obviously exaggerated. Where else do you find Barry using overstatements? Try replacing his inflated phrases with common language in order to decide why he chose his.

Why did Barry include the fact that Arlene is a prosecuting attorney? Compare his approach to equality between the sexes to that found in the essays by Woolf or Wolf.

In these two paragraphs, Barry implies that there are basic differences between men and women. What is he saying? Consider how Noel Perrin might respond to Barry's assumption that men are "bumbling scum" when it comes to domestic affairs (see Perrin, paragraphs 11 and 13).

Who are Ozzie and Harriet? What is Barry assuming about his audience by including such a reference? Can you find other references that an audience may not be familiar with?

Picture a typical Thanksgiving scene: On the floor, three small children and a dog who long ago had her brain eaten by fleas are running as fast as they can directly into things, trying to injure themselves. On the television, the Detroit Lions are doing pretty much the same thing. 3

In the kitchen, Arlene, a prosecuting attorney responsible for a large staff, is doing something with those repulsive organs that are placed in little surprise packets inside turkeys, apparently as a joke. Surrounding Arlene are thousands of steaming cooking containers. I would no more enter that kitchen than I would attempt to park a nuclear aircraft carrier, but my wife, who runs her own business, glides in very casually and picks up EX-ACTLY the right kitchen implement and starts doing EXACTLY the right thing without receiving any instructions whatsoever. She quickly becomes enshrouded in steam. 4

So Gene and I, feeling like the scum we are, finally bumble over and ask what we can do to help, and from behind the steam comes Arlene's patient voice asking us to please keep an eye on the children. Which we try to do. 5

But there is a famous law of physics that goes: "You cannot watch small children and the Detroit Lions at the same time, and let's face it, the Detroit Lions are more interesting." So we would start out watching the children, and then one of us would sneak a peek at the TV and say, "Hey! Look at this tackle!" And then we'd have to watch for a while to see the replay and find out whether the tackled person was dead or just permanently disabled. By then the children would have succeeded in injuring themselves or the dog, and this voice from behind the kitchen steam would call, VERY patiently, "Gene, PLEASE watch the children." 6

I realize this is awful. I realize this sounds just like Ozzie and Harriet. I also realize that there are some males out there, with hyphenated last names, who have advanced much farther than Gene and I have, who are not afraid to stay home full time and get coated with baby vomit while their wives work as test pilots, and who go into the kitchen on a daily basis to prepare food for other people, as opposed to going in there to get a beer and 7 maybe some peanut butter on a spoon. But I think Gene and I are fairly typical. I think most males rarely prepare food for others, and when they do, they have their one specialty dish (spaghetti, in my case) that they prepare maybe twice a year in a very elaborate production, for which they expect to be praised as if they had developed, right there in the kitchen, a cure for heart disease.

In defense of men, let me say this: Women do not make it easy to   8
learn. Let's say a woman is in the kitchen, working away after having been at her job all day, and the man, feeling guilty, finally shuffles in and offers to help. So the woman says something like: "Well, you can cut up the turnips." Now to the WOMAN, who had all this sexist Home Economics training back in the pre-feminism era, this is a very simple instruction. It is the absolute simplest thing she can think of.

How does Barry's conclu-
sion relate to the rest of the
essay? How effective is it?

I asked my wife to read this and tell me   9
what she thought. This is what she said: She said before Women's Liberation, men took care of the cars and women took care of the kitchen, whereas now that we have Women's Liberation, men no longer feel obligated to take care of the cars. This seemed pretty accurate to me, so I thought I'd just tack it on to the end here, while she makes waffles.

Compare Barry's use of humor to that of Lois Gould or
Stephen Harrigan and de-
cide which writer most effectively presents serious ideas
by using humor.

LOIS GOULD

X

Lois Gould (1938?–   ), a full-time writer of journalism, fiction, and social commentary, has devoted much of her career to writing about gender issues. As executive editor and columnist for *Ladies' Home Journal* and a contributor to *The New York Times* "Hers" column, Gould has made her opinions, often controversial, known to a wide audience. Because of her iconoclastic handling of women's issues, Gould has been labeled an antifeminist by feminists and an archfeminist by antifeminists. Some critics labeled her first novel, *Such Good Friends* (1970), pornographic, while others praised its impact on the women's movement; one commentator called it an "important, awful, believable book." *A Sea-Change* (1976), an allegory in which a woman becomes a man ("exploitee-turning-exploiter," as one reviewer said), was no less controversial. *X*, first published in *Ms.* magazine in 1972, was later expanded into Gould's third novel, *X: A Fabulous Child's Story* (1978), a book praised for its insight into gender stereotyping but also harshly criticized for being too authoritarian and middle-class. Her most recent novel, *Medusa's Gift,* was published in 1991.

Once upon a time, a Baby named X was born. It was named X so   1
that nobody could tell whether it was a boy or a girl.

Its parents could tell, of course, but they couldn't tell anybody else.   2
They couldn't even tell Baby X—at least not until much, much later.

You see, it was all part of a very important Secret Scientific Xperi-   3
ment, known officially as Project Baby X.

This Xperiment was going to cost Xactly 23 billion dollars and 72   4
cents. Which might seem like a lot for one Baby, even if it was an important Secret Scientific Xperimental Baby.

But when you remember the cost of strained carrots, stuffed bun-   5
nies, booster shots, 28 shiny quarters from the tooth fairy . . . you begin to see how it adds up.

Long before Baby X was born, the smartest scientists had to work   6
out the secret details of the Xperiment, and to write the *Official Instruction Manual,* in secret code, for Baby X's parents, whoever they were.

These parents had to be selected very carefully. Thousands of peo-   7
ple volunteered to take thousands of tests, with thousands of tricky questions.

Almost everybody failed because, it turned out, almost everybody   8
wanted a boy or a girl, and not a Baby X at all.

Also, almost everybody thought a Baby X would be more trouble   9
than a boy or a girl. (They were right, too.)

There were families with grandparents named Milton and Agatha,   10
who wanted the baby named Milton or Agatha instead of X, even if it *was* an X.

There were aunts who wanted to knit tiny dresses and uncles who   11
wanted to send tiny baseball mitts.

Worst of all, there were families with other children who couldn't   12
be trusted to keep a Secret. Not if they knew the Secret was worth 23 billion dollars and 72 cents—and all you had to do was take one little peek at Baby X in the bathtub to know what it was.

Finally, the scientists found the Joneses, who really wanted to raise   13
an X more than any other kind of baby—no matter how much trouble it was.

The Joneses promised to take turns holding X, feeding X, and sing-   14
ing X to sleep.

And they promised never to hire any baby-sitters. The scientists   15
knew that a baby-sitter would probably peek at X in the bathtub, too.

The day the Joneses brought their baby home, lots of friends and   16 relatives came to see it. And the first thing they asked was what kind of a baby X was.

When the Joneses said, "It's an X!" nobody knew what to say.   17

They couldn't say, "Look at her cute little dimples!"   18

On the other hand, they couldn't say, "Look at his husky little   19
biceps!"

And they didn't feel right about saying just plain "kitchy-coo."   20

The relatives all felt embarrassed about having an X in the family.   21

"People will think there's something wrong with it!" they whis-   22
pered.

"Nonsense!" the Joneses said cheerfully. "What could possibly be   23
wrong with this perfectly adorable X?"

Clearly, nothing at all was wrong. Nevertheless, the cousins who   24
had sent a tiny football helmet would not come and visit any more.
And the neighbors who sent a pink-flowered romper suit pulled their
shades down when the Joneses passed their house.

The *Official Instruction Manual* had warned the new parents that this   25
would happen, so they didn't fret about it. Besides, they were too busy
learning how to bring up Baby X.

Ms. and Mr. Jones had to be Xtra careful. If they kept bouncing it   26
up in the air and saying how *strong* and *active* it was, they'd be treating
it more like a boy than an X. But if all they did was cuddle it and kiss
it and tell it how *sweet* and *dainty* it was, they'd be treating it more like
a girl than an X.

On page 1654 of the *Official Instruction Manual*, the scientists pre-   27
scribed: "plenty of bouncing and plenty of cuddling, *both*. X ought to
be strong and sweet and active. Forget about *dainty* altogether."

There were other problems, too. Toys, for instance. And clothes.   28
On his first shopping trip, Mr. Jones told the store clerk, "I need some
things for a new baby." The clerk smiled and said, "Well, now, is it a
boy or a girl?" "It's an X," Mr. Jones said, smiling back. But the clerk
got all red in the face and said huffily, "In *that* case, I'm afraid I can't
help you, sir."

Mr. Jones wandered the aisles trying to find what X needed. But   29
everything was in sections marked BOYS or GIRLS: "Boys' Pajamas"
and "Girls' Underwear" and "Boys' Fire Engines" and "Girls
Housekeeping Sets." Mr. Jones went home without buying anything
for X.

That night he and Ms. Jones consulted page 2326 of the *Official*   30
Instruction Manual. It said firmly: "Buy plenty of everything!"

So they bought all kinds of toys. A boy doll that made pee-pee and   31
cried "Pa-Pa." And a girl doll that talked in three languages and said,
"I am the Pres-i-dent of Gen-er-al Mo-tors."

They bought a storybook about a brave princess who rescued a   32 handsome prince from his tower, and another one about a sister and brother who grew up to be a baseball star and a ballet star, and you had to guess which.

The head scientists of Project Baby X checked all their purchases 33 and told them to keep up the good work. They also reminded the Joneses to see page 4629 of the *Manual,* where it said, "Never make Baby X feel *embarrassed* or *ashamed* about what it wants to play with. And if X gets dirty climbing rocks, never say, 'Nice little Xes don't get dirty climbing rocks.' "

Likewise, it said, "If X falls down and cries, never say, 'Brave little 34 Xes don't cry.' Because, of course, nice little Xes *do* get dirty, and brave little Xes *do* cry. No matter how dirty X gets, or how hard it cries, don't worry. It's all part of the Xperiment."

Whenever the Joneses pushed Baby X's stroller in the park, smiling 35 strangers would come over and coo: "Is that a boy or a girl?" The Joneses would smile back and say, "It's an X." The strangers would stop smiling then and often snarl something nasty—as if the Joneses had said something nasty to *them.*

Once a little girl grabbed X's shovel in the sandbox, and zonked X 36 on the head with it. "Now, now, Tracy," the mother began to scold, "little girls mustn't hit little—" and she turned to ask X, "Are you a little boy or a little girl, dear?"

Mr. Jones, who was sitting near the sandbox, held his breath and 37 crossed his fingers.

X smiled politely, even though X's head had never been zonked so 38 hard in its life. "I'm a little X," said X.

"You're a *what*?" the lady exclaimed angrily. "You're a little b-r-a-t, 39 you mean!"

"But little girls mustn't hit little Xes, either!" said X, retrieving the 40 shovel with another polite smile. "What good's hitting, anyway?"

X's father finally X-haled, uncrossed his fingers, and grinned. 41

And at their next secret Project Baby X meeting, the scientists 42 grinned, too. Baby X was doing fine.

But then it was time for X to start school. The Joneses were really 43 worried about this, because school was even more full of rules for boys and girls, and there were no rules for Xes.

Teachers would tell boys to form a line, and girls to form another 44 line.

There would be boys' games and girls' games, and boys' secrets and 45 girls' secrets.

The school library would have a list of recommended books for 46 girls, and a different list for boys.

There would even be a bathroom marked BOYS and another one 47 marked GIRLS.

Pretty soon boys and girls would hardly talk to each other. What   48
would happen to poor little X?

The Joneses spent weeks consulting their *Instruction Manual*.   49

There were 249 and one-half pages of advice under "First Day   50
of School." Then they were all summoned to an Urgent Xtra Special
Conference with the smart scientists of Project Baby X.

The scientists had to make sure that X's mother had taught X how   51
to throw and catch a ball properly, and that X's father had been sure
to teach X what to serve at a doll's tea party.

X had to know how to shoot marbles and jump rope and, most of   52
all, what to say when the Other Children asked whether X was a Boy
or a Girl.

Finally, X was ready.   53

X's teacher had promised that the class could line up alphabetically,   54
instead of forming separate lines for boys and girls. And X had permission to use the principal's bathroom, because it wasn't marked anything
except BATHROOM. But nobody could help X with the biggest problem
of all—Other Children.

Nobody in X's class had ever known an X. Nobody had even heard   55
grown-ups say, "Some of my best friends are Xes."

What would other children think? Would they make Xist jokes?   56
Or would they make friends?

You couldn't tell what X was by its clothes. Overalls don't even   57
button right to left, like girls clothes, or left to right, like boys' clothes.

And did X have a girl's short haircut or a boy's long haircut?   58

As for the games X liked, either X played ball very well for a girl,   59
or else played house very well for a boy.

The children tried to find out by asking X tricky questions, like,   60
"Who's your favorite sports star?" X had two favorite sports stars: a
girl jockey named Robyn Smith and a boy archery champion named
Robin Hood.

Then they asked, "What's your favorite TV show?" And X said: 61
"Lassie," which stars a girl dog played by a boy dog.

When X said its favorite toy was a doll, everyone decided that X   62
must be a girl. But then X said the doll was really a robot, and that X
had computerized it, and that it was programmed to bake fudge and
then clean up the kitchen.

After X told them that, they gave up guessing what X was. All they   63
knew was they'd sure like to see X's doll.

After school, X wanted to play with the other children. "How about   64
shooting baskets in the gym?" X asked the girls. But all they did was
make faces and giggle behind X's back.

"Boy, is *he* weird," whispered Jim to Joe.   65

"How about weaving some baskets in the arts and crafts room?"   66

X asked the boys. But they all made faces and giggled behind X's back, too.

"Boy, is *she* weird," whispered Susie to Peggy. 67

That night, Ms. and Mr. Jones asked X how things had gone at 68 school. X tried to smile, but there were two big tears in its eyes. "The lessons are okay," X began, "but . . ."

"But?" said Ms. Jones. 69

"The Other Children hate me," X whispered. 70

"Hate you?" said Mr. Jones. 71

X nodded, which made the two big tears roll down and splash on 72 its overalls.

Once more, the Joneses reached for their *Instruction Manual.* Under 73 "Other Children," it said:

"What did you Xpect? Other Children have to obey silly boy-girl 74 rules, because their parents taught them to. Lucky X—you don't have rules at all! All you have to do is be yourself.

"P.S. We're not saying it'll be easy." 75

X liked being itself. But X cried a lot that night. So X's father held 76 X tight, and cried a little, too. X's mother cheered them up with an Xciting story about an enchanted prince called Sleeping Handsome, who woke up when Princess Charming kissed him.

The next morning, they all felt much better, and little X went back 77 to school with a brave smile and a clean pair of red and white checked overalls.

There was a seven-letter-word spelling bee in class that day. And 78 a seven-lap boys' relay race in the gym. And a seven-layer-cake baking contest in the girls' kitchen corner.

X won the spelling bee. X also won the relay race. 79

And X almost won the baking contest, Xcept it forgot to light the 80 oven. (Remember, nobody's perfect.)

One of the Other Children noticed something else, too. He said: "X 81 doesn't care about winning. X just thinks it's fun playing boys' stuff *and* girls' stuff."

"Come to think of it," said another one of the Other Children, "X 82 is having twice as much fun as we are!"

After school that day, the girl who beat X in the baking contest 83 gave X a big slice of her winning cake.

And the boy X beat in the relay race asked X to race him home. 84

From then on, some really funny things began to happen. 85

Susie, who sat next to X, refused to wear pink dresses to school 86 any more. She wanted red and white checked overalls—just like X's.

Overalls, she told her parents, were better for climbing monkey 87 bars.

Then Jim, the class football nut, started wheeling his little sister's 88 doll carriage around the football field.

He'd put on his entire football uniform, except for the helmet.   89

Then he'd put the helmet *in* the carriage, lovingly tucked under an   90
old set of shoulder pads.

Then he'd jog around the field, pushing the carriage and singing   91
"Rockabye Baby" to his helmet.

He said X did the same thing, so it must be okay. After all, X was   92
now the team's star quarterback.

Susie's parents were horrified by her behavior, and Jim's parents   93
were worried sick about his.

But the worst came when the twins, Joe and Peggy, decided to   94
share everything with each other.

Peggy used Joe's hockey skates, and his microscope, and took half   95
his newspaper route.

Joe used Peggy's needlepoint kit, and her cookbooks, and took two   96
of her three baby-sitting jobs.

Peggy ran the lawn mower, and Joe ran the vacuum cleaner.   97

Their parents weren't one bit pleased with Peggy's science experi-   98
ments, or with Joe's terrific needlepoint pillows.

They didn't care that Peggy mowed the lawn better, and that Joe   99
vacuumed the carpet better.

In fact, they were furious. It's all that little X's fault, they agreed.   100
X doesn't know what it is, or what it's supposed to be! So X wants to
mix everybody *else* up, too!

Peggy and Joe were forbidden to play with X any more. So was   101
Susie, and then Jim, and then *all* the Other Children.

But it was too late: the Other Children stayed mixed-up and happy   102
and free, and refused to go back to the way they'd been before X.

Finally, the parents held an emergency meeting to discuss "The X   103
Problem."

They sent a report to the principal stating that X was a "bad influ-   104
ence," and demanding immediate action.

The Joneses, they said, should be *forced* to tell whether X was a boy   105
or a girl. And X should be *forced* to behave like whichever it was.

If the Joneses refused to tell, the parents said, then X must take an   106
Xamination. An Impartial Team of Xperts would Xtract the secret. Then
X would start obeying all the old rules. Or else.

And if X turned out to be some kind of mixed-up misfit, then X   107
must be Xpelled from school. Immediately! So that no little Xes would
ever come to school again.

The principal was very upset. X, a bad influence? A mixed-up mis-   108
fit? But X was a Xcellent student! X set a fine Xample! X was Xtra-
ordinary!

X was president of the student council. X had won first prize in the   109
art show, honorable mention in the science fair, and six events on field
day, including the potato race.

Nevertheless, insisted the parents, X is a Problem Child. X is the 110 Biggest Problem Child we have ever seen!

So the principal reluctantly notified X's parents and the Joneses 111 reported this to the Project X scientists, who referred them to page 85769 of the *Instruction Manual.* "Sooner or later," it said, "X will have to be Xamined by an Impartial Team of Xperts.

"This may be the only way any of us will know for sure whether 112 X is mixed up—or everyone else is."

At Xactly 9 o'clock the next day, X reported to the school health 113 office. The principal, along with a committee from the Parents' Association, X's teacher, X's classmates, and Ms. and Mr. Jones, waited in the hall outside.

Inside, the Xperts had set up their famous testing machine: the 114 Superpsychiamedicossocioculturometer.

Nobody knew Xactly how the machine worked, but everybody 115 knew that this examination would reveal Xactly what everyone wanted to know about X, but were afraid to ask.

It was terribly quiet in the hall. Almost spooky. They could hear 116 very strange noises from the room.

There were buzzes. 117

And a beep or two. 118

And several bells. 119

An occasional light flashed under the door. Was it an X ray? 120

Through it all, you could hear the Xperts' voices, asking questions, 121 and X's voice, answering answers.

I wouldn't like to be in X's overalls right now, the children thought. 122

At last, the door opened. Everyone crowded around to hear the 123 results. X didn't look any different; in fact, X was smiling. But the Impartial Team of Xperts looked terrible. They looked as if they were crying!

"What happened?" everyone began shouting. 124

"*Sssh,*" ssshed the principal. "The Xperts are trying to speak." 125

Wiping his eyes and clearing his throat, one Xpert began: "In our 126 opinion," he whispered—you could tell he must be very upset—"in our opinion, young X here—"

"Yes? Yes?" shouted a parent. 127

"Young X," said the other Xpert, frowning, "is just about the *least* 128 mixed-up child we've ever Xamined!" Behind the closed door, the Superpsychiamedicossocioculturometer made a noise like a contented hum.

"Yay for X!" yelled one of the children. And then the others began 129 yelling, too. Clapping and cheering and jumping up and down.

"*SSSH!*" SSShed the principal, but nobody did. 130

The Parents' Committee was angry and bewildered. How *could* X 131 have passed the whole Xamination?

Didn't X have an *identity* problem? Wasn't X mixed up at *all?* [132]
Wasn't X any kind of a misfit?

How could it *not* be, when it didn't even *know* what it was? [133]

"Don't you see?" asked the Xperts. "X isn't one bit mixed up! As [134]
for being a misfit—ridiculous! X knows perfectly well what it is! Don't
you, X?" The Xperts winked. X winked back.

"But what *is* X?" shrieked Peggy and Joe's parents. "*We* still want [135]
to know what it is!"

"Ah, yes," said the Xperts, winking again. "Well, don't worry. [136]
You'll all know one of these days. And you won't need us to tell you."

"What? What do they mean?" Jim's parents grumbled suspiciously. [137]

Susie and Peggy and Joe all answered at once. "They mean that by [138]
the time it matters which sex X is, it won't be a secret any more!"

With that, the Xperts reached out to hug Ms. and Mr. Jones. "If [139]
we ever have an X of our own," they whispered, "we sure hope you'll
lend us your instruction manual."

Needless to say, the Joneses were very happy. The Project Baby X [140]
scientists were rather pleased, too. So were Susie, Jim, Peggy, Joe, and
all the Other Children. Even the parents promised not to make any
trouble.

Later that day, all X's friends put on their red and white checked [141]
overalls and went over to see X.

They found X in the backyard, playing with a very tiny baby that [142]
none of them had ever seen before.

The baby was wearing very tiny red and white checked overalls. [143]

"How do you like our new baby?" X asked the Other Children [144]
proudly.

"It's got cute dimples," said Jim. "It's got husky biceps, too," said [145]
Susie.

"What kind of baby is it?" asked Joe and Peggy. [146]

X frowned at them. "Can't you tell?" Then X broke into a big, [147]
mischievous grin. "*It's a Y!*"

VIRGINIA WOOLF

Professions for Women

Virginia Woolf (1882–1941), the daughter of a distinguished Victorian
biographer, was denied formal education because women could not
take degrees from British universities until 1920. Nonetheless, she became one of the first women in British history to be a literary professional, supporting herself by writing and by operating (with her husband, Leonard) a successful publishing firm, the Hogarth Press. The

disadvantages under which she labored were considerable, and they showed her that English women, however they might be pampered and honored, were a political underclass. Out of this awareness grew *A Room of One's Own* (1929), a book based on addresses given to women's societies in 1928. "Professions for Women" was a talk delivered to the Women's Service League about 1930.

When your secretary invited me to come here, she told me that   1
your Society is concerned with the employment of women and she suggested that I might tell you something about my own professional experiences. It is true I am a woman; it is true I am employed; but what professional experiences have I had? It is difficult to say. My profession is literature; and in that profession there are fewer experiences for women than in any other, with the exception of the stage— fewer, I mean, that are peculiar to women. For the road was cut many years ago—by Fanny Burney, by Aphra Behn, by Harriet Martineau, by Jane Austen, by George Eliot—many famous women, and many more unknown and forgotten, have been before me, making the path smooth, and regulating my steps. Thus, when I came to write, there were very few material obstacles in my way. Writing was a reputable and harmless occupation. The family peace was not broken by the scratching of a pen. No demand was made upon the family purse. For ten and sixpence one can buy paper enough to write all the plays of Shakespeare—if one has a mind that way. Pianos and models, Paris, Vienna and Berlin, masters and mistresses, are not needed by a writer. The cheapness of writing paper is, of course, the reason why women have succeeded as writers before they have succeeded in the other professions.

But to tell you my story—it is a simple one. You have only got to   2
figure to yourselves a girl in a bedroom with a pen in her hand. She had only to move that pen from left to right—from ten o'clock to one. Then it occurred to her to do what is simple and cheap enough after all—to slip a few of those pages into an envelope, fix a penny stamp in the corner, and drop the envelope into the red box at the corner. It was thus that I became a journalist; and my effort was rewarded on the first day of the following month—a very glorious day it was for me—by a letter from an editor containing a cheque for one pound ten shillings and sixpence. But to show you how little I deserve to be called a professional woman, how little I know of the struggles and difficulties of such lives, I have to admit that instead of spending that sum upon bread and butter, rent, shoes and stockings, or butcher's bills, I went out and bought a cat—a beautiful cat, a Persian cat, which very soon involved me in bitter disputes with my neighbours.

What could be easier than to write articles and to buy Persian cats   3
with the profits? But wait a moment. Articles have to be about some-

thing. Mine, I seem to remember, was about a novel by a famous man. And while I was writing this review, I discovered that if I were going to review books I should need to do battle with a certain phantom. And the phantom was a woman, and when I came to know her better I called her after the heroine of a famous poem, The Angel in the House. It was she who used to come between me and my paper when I was writing reviews. It was she who bothered me and wasted my time and so tormented me that at last I killed her. You who come of a younger and happier generation may not have heard of her—you may not know what I mean by the Angel in the House. I will describe her as shortly as I can. She was intensely sympathetic. She was immensely charming. She was utterly unselfish. She excelled in the difficult arts of family life. She sacrificed herself daily. If there was a chicken, she took the leg; if there was a draught she sat in it—in short she was so constituted that she never had a mind or a wish of her own, but preferred to sympathize always with the minds and wishes of others. Above all—I need not say it—she was pure. Her purity was supposed to be her chief beauty—her blushes, her great grace. In those days—the last of Queen Victoria— every house had its Angel. And when I came to write I encountered her with the very first words. The shadow of her wings fell on my page; I heard the rustling of her skirts in the room. Directly, that is to say, I took my pen in hand to review that novel by a famous man, she slipped behind me and whispered: "My dear, you are a young woman. You are writing about a book that has been written by a man. Be sympathetic; be tender; flatter; deceive; use all the arts and wiles of our sex. Never let anybody guess that you have a mind of your own. Above all, be pure." And she made as if to guide my pen. I now record the one act for which I take some credit to myself, though the credit rightly belongs to some excellent ancestors of mine who left me a certain sum of money—shall we say five hundred pounds a year?—so that it was not necessary for me to depend solely on charm for my living. I turned upon her and caught her by the throat. I did my best to kill her. My excuse, if I were to be had up in a court of law, would be that I acted in self-defence. Had I not killed her she would have killed me. She would have plucked the heart out of my writing. For, as I found, directly I put pen to paper, you cannot review even a novel without having a mind of your own, without expressing what you think to be the truth about human relations, morality, sex. And all these questions, according to the Angel in the House, cannot be dealt with freely and openly by women; they must charm, they must conciliate, they must—to put it bluntly—tell lies if they are to succeed. Thus, whenever I felt the shadow of her wing or the radiance of her halo upon my page, I took up the inkpot and flung it at her. She died hard. Her fictitious nature was of great assistance to her. It is far harder to kill a phantom than a reality. She was always creeping back when I thought I had despatched

her. Though I flatter myself that I killed her in the end, the struggle
was severe; it took much time that had better have been spent upon
learning Greek grammar; or in roaming the world in search of adventures. But it was a real experience; it was an experience that was bound
to befall all women writers at that time. Killing the Angel in the House
was part of the occupation of a woman writer.

But to continue my story. The Angel was dead; what then re-   4
mained? You may say that what remained was a simple and common
object—a young woman in a bedroom with an inkpot. In other words,
now that she had rid herself of falsehood, that young woman had only
to be herself. Ah, but what is "herself"? I mean, what is a woman? I
assure you, I do not know. I do not believe that you know. I do not
believe that anybody can know until she has expressed herself in all
the arts and professions open to human skill. That indeed is one of the
reasons why I have come here—out of respect for you, who are in
process of showing us by your experiments what a woman is, who are
in process of providing us, by your failures and successes, with that
extremely important piece of information.

But to continue the story of my professional experiences. I made   5
one pound ten and six by my first review; and I bought a Persian cat
with the proceeds. Then I grew ambitious. A Persian cat is all very well,
I said; but a Persian cat is not enough. I must have a motor car. And
it was thus that I became a novelist—for it is a very strange thing that
people will give you a motor car if you will tell them a story. It is a still
stranger thing that there is nothing so delightful in the world as telling
stories. It is far pleasanter than writing reviews of famous novels. And
yet, if I am to obey your secretary and tell you my professional experiences as a novelist, I must tell you about a very strange experience that
befell me as a novelist. And to understand it you must try first to imagine a novelist's state of mind. I hope I am not giving away professional
secrets if I say that a novelist's chief desire is to be as unconscious as
possible. He has to induce in himself a state of perpetual lethargy. He
wants life to proceed with the utmost quiet and regularity. He wants to
see the same faces, to read the same books, to do the same things day
after day, month after month, while he is writing, so that nothing may
break the illusion in which he is living—so that nothing may disturb
or disquiet the mysterious nosings about, feelings round, darts, dashes
and sudden discoveries of that very shy and illusive spirit, the imagination. I suspect that this state is the same both for men and women. Be
that as it may, I want you to imagine me writing a novel in a state of
trance. I want you to figure to yourselves a girl sitting with a pen in
her hand, which for minutes, and indeed for hours, she never dips into
the inkpot. The image that comes to my mind when I think of this girl
is the image of a fisherman lying sunk in dreams on the verge of a deep
lake with a rod held out over the water. She was letting her imagination

sweep unchecked round every rock and cranny of the world that lies submerged in the depths of our unconscious being. Now came the experience, the experience that I believe to be far commoner with women writers than with men. The line raced through the girl's fingers. Her imagination had rushed away. It had sought the pools, the depths, the dark places where the largest fish slumber. And then there was a smash. There was an explosion. There was foam and confusion. The imagination had dashed itself against something hard. The girl was roused from her dream. She was indeed in a state of the most acute and difficult distress. To speak without figure she had thought of something, something about the body, about the passions which it was unfitting for her as a woman to say. Men, her reason told her, would be shocked. The consciousness of what men will say of a woman who speaks the truth about her passions had roused her from her artist's state of unconsciousness. She could write no more. The trance was over. Her imagination could work no longer. This I believe to be a very common experience with women writers—they are impeded by the extreme conventionality of the other sex. For though men sensibly allow themselves great freedom in these respects, I doubt that they realize or can control the extreme severity with which they condemn such freedom in women.

These then were two very genuine experiences of my own. These 6
were two of the adventures of my professional life. The first—killing the Angel in the House—I think I solved. She died. But the second, telling the truth about my own experiences as a body, I do not think I solved. I doubt that any woman has solved it yet. The obstacles against her are still immensely powerful—and yet they are very difficult to define. Outwardly, what is simpler than to write books? Outwardly, what obstacles are there for a woman rather than for a man? Inwardly, I think, the case is very different; she has still many ghosts to fight, many prejudices to overcome. Indeed it will be a long time still, I think, before a woman can sit down to write a book without finding a phantom to be slain, a rock to be dashed against. And if this is so in literature, the freest of all professions for women, how is it in the new professions which you are now for the first time entering?

Those are the questions that I should like, had I time, to ask you. 7
And indeed, if I have laid stress upon these professional experiences of mine, it is because I believe that they are, though in different forms, yours also. Even when the path is nominally open—when there is nothing to prevent a woman from being a doctor, a lawyer, a civil servant—there are many phantoms and obstacles, as I believe, looming in her way. To discuss and define them is I think of great value and importance; for thus only can the labour be shared, the difficulties be solved. But besides this, it is necessary also to discuss the ends and the aims for which we are fighting, for which we are doing battle with these formidable obstacles. Those aims cannot be taken for granted;

they must be perpetually questioned and examined. The whole position, as I see it—here in this hall surrounded by women practising for the first time in history I know not how many different professions—is one of extraordinary interest and importance. You have won rooms of your own in the house hitherto exclusively owned by men. You are able, though not without great labour and effort, to pay the rent. You are earning your five hundred pounds a year. But this freedom is only a beginning; the room is your own, but it is still bare. It has to be furnished; it has to be decorated; it has to be shared. How are you going to furnish it, how are you going to decorate it? With whom are you going to share it, and upon what terms? These, I think, are questions of the utmost importance and interest. For the first time in history you are able to ask them; for the first time you are able to decide for yourselves what the answers should be. Willingly would I stay and discuss those questions and answers—but not tonight. My time is up; and I must cease.

NAOMI WOLF

The Rites of Sisterhood

Naomi Wolf (1962–   ), born in San Francisco, has become a leading spokesperson for the latest wave of feminism. Wolf gives credit to her grandmother, a professor and a first-generation feminist, for shaping her thinking as a young girl. Growing up in the midst of progressive ideas, however, did not save Wolf from the pressures of femininity: Although she always thought of herself as a feminist, Wolf nearly died of anorexia as a teenager. After graduating from Yale in 1984, Wolf went to Oxford University as a Rhodes scholar, and there her thesis on the ideals of beauty in nineteenth- and twentieth-century writing paved the way for her first book, the controversial *The Beauty Myth: How Images of Beauty Are Used Against Women* (1990). Wolf argues that as long as Western thought continues to impose standards of beauty on women that force them to put looks before health and self-esteem, women will not attain political power equal to that of men. In addition to publishing a second book, *Fire with Fire: The New Female Power and How It Will Change the Twenty-first Century* (1993), Wolf has been published in several magazines, including *Glamour* and *Ms.*, and twice won the Academy of American Poet's prize for her poetry. In 1993 she married magazine editor David Shipley, and in her spare time she enjoys roller blading and country music. The following essay is adapted from a commencement speech she delivered in 1992 at Scripps College in Claremont, California.

Guillotine joke: 1

Once there was a revolution. Three revolutionaries were charged with   2
treason—two men and a woman. The first revolutionary was taken to the
guillotine. He was asked, "Do you want to die facing up or down?" "I'll
face down." The headsman pulls the string—nothing happens. The crowd
says, "It's a miracle! Set him free!" The second man approaches the block
and, given the same choice, he opts to face the ground. Again when the
headsman pulls the string, nothing happens and the crowd cheers to set
him free. The third revolutionary replies, "I'll face up." Headsman pulls
string—nothing happens! She points upward and says, "I think I see what
the problem is."

Even the best of revolutions can go awry when we begin to inter-   3
nalize the attitudes that we are fighting. During the past twenty years
women have gained legal and reproductive rights as never before, have
entered new jobs and professions. At the same time, anorexia and bulimia became epidemic; sexual assaults against women are at a record
high, up 59 percent from last year; *Roe* v. *Wade*[1] is about to be reconsidered in the Supreme Court; the weight of fashion models and Miss
Americas plummeted, from 8 percent below the weight of the average
American woman to 23 percent below. And the Blonde joke is enjoying
a renaissance.

You are graduating in the midst of a violent backlash against the   4
advances women have made over the last twenty years. This backlash
is taking many forms, from the sudden relevance of quotes from *The
Exorcist*[2] in Senate hearing rooms to beer commercials with the Swedish
bikini team. What I want to give you today is a survival kit for the
backlash into which you are about to graduate, a sort of five-step program to keep the dragons from taking up residence inside your own
heads.

First, let me tell you why it's so important for me to have been   5
asked here today. My own graduation was the Commencement from
Hell, an exercise in female disempowerment. I graduated eight years
ago from Yale. The speaker was Dick Cavett,[3] for little more reason
than that he had been the college president's brother in an all-male
secret society when they were both undergraduates. While the president

---

1. Roe v. Wade: 1973 Supreme Court decision legalizing abortion in the first trimester
of pregnancy.
2. Senate Hearings: During 1991 Senate Judiciary Committee hearings, law professor
Anita Hill accused Supreme Court nominee Clarence Thomas of having sexually harassed
her—one allegation being that he talked bizarrely about the presence of a pubic hair in
her Coke. Defenders of Thomas accused Hill of having taken this incident not from life,
but from the pages of *The Exorcist*, a popular thriller.
3. Dick Cavett (1936–   ): Comedian and host of a late night talk show at his prime
in the 1970s, widely admired for his intelligence and liberal views.

was withdrawing college funds from South African investment, he was blind to the gender apartheid that he was endorsing on his own well-tended lawns.

Cavett took the microphone and seemed visibly to pale at the sight of two thousand female about-to-be Yale graduates. "When I was an undergraduate," he said, "there were no women here. The women went to Vassar. At Vassar," he said, "they had nude photographs taken of the women to check their posture in gym class. One year some of the photos were stolen, and they showed up for sale in New Haven's red-light district." His punch line? "The photos found no buyers."

I will never forget that moment. There were our parents and grand-parents, many of whom had come long distances at great expense to be with us on our special day. There were we, silent in our black gowns, our tassels, our new shoes. We did not dare break the silence with boos or hisses, out of respect for our families who had given so much to make that day a success; and they in turn kept silent out of the same concern for us. Whether or not it was conscious, Cavett at that moment was using the beauty myth as it is often used in the backlash: whenever women get too close to masculine power, someone will draw critical attention to their bodies. Confronted with two thousand women who were about to become just as qualified as he himself was, his subtext was clear: you may be Elis,[4] but you still wouldn't make pornography worth the buying.

That day, three thousand men were confirmed in the power of a powerful institution. But many of the two thousand women felt the shame of the powerless; the choking on silence, the complicity, the helplessness. We were orphaned from our institution at that moment—or rather, that moment laid bare the way in which the sons were truly sons all along, but the daughters were there on sufferance, intellectual and spiritual foster children whose membership in the family depended on self-effacement.

Commencement should be a rite of passage that makes you feel the opposite of how my graduation made me feel. My graduation did not celebrate in any way my wisdom and maturation as a woman; rather, it was a condescending pat on the head for having managed to "pass" for four years, in intellectual terms, as one of the boys.

So I want to give you the commencement talk I was denied. Since I'm only eight years older than you and still figuring things out myself, I don't feel comfortable using the second-person imperative in a way that would pretend that I have all the answers for your life. What I do when I say "you" is send a message back to my twenty-one-year-old

4. Eli: nickname for a graduate of Yale, from Elihu Yale (1649–1721), whose donation in 1718 helped found the school.

self with the information I wish I had had then. As Gloria Steinem[5] says, "we teach what we need to learn."

MESSAGE #1: The first message in your survival kit is to *cherish a* 11 *new definition of what it means to "become a woman."* Today, you have ended your apprenticeship into the state of adult womanhood; today, you have "become women."

But that sounds terribly odd in ordinary usage, doesn't it? What 12 is usually meant by the phrase "You're a real woman now"? Most connotations are biological: you "become a woman" when you menstruate for the first time, or when you lose your virginity, when you have a child. Sometimes people say "a real woman" to suggest decorativeness—a real woman wears a DD-cup bra—or a state of matrimony: a man can make a "real" or "honest" woman out of someone by marrying her.

These merely endocrinological definitions of becoming a woman 13 are very different from how we say boys become men. Someone "becomes a man" when he undertakes responsibility or successfully completes a dangerous quest. Let us make a new definition of "becoming a woman" that includes the fact that you, too, no less and in some ways more than your brothers and male friends graduating today, have not moved from childhood to adulthood by biological maturation alone but through your own successful completion of a struggle with new responsibilities—a difficult, ultimately solitary quest for the adult self.

But we have no archetypes for the questing young woman, her 14 separation from home and family, her trials by fire. We lack words for how you become a woman through the chrysalis of education, the difficult passage from one book, one idea, to the next. My commencement pitted my scholarship and my gender against each other. We need a definition of "becoming a woman" in which a scholar learns womanhood and a woman learns scholarship, each term informing the other; Plato and Hegel, Djuna Barnes[6] and particle physics, mediated to their own enrichment through the eyes and brain of the female body with its wisdoms and its gifts.

When I say that you have already showed courage in earning your 15 B.A.'s and passing through the forest, I am not talking about the demons of footnotes and poststructuralism. I'm talking about the extra lessons you had outside the classroom as well as in. Many of you graduate today in spite of the posttraumatic stress syndrome that follows

5. Steinem (1934–   ): Editor, writer, lecturer, and leader of the feminist movement who founded *Ms.* magazine in 1972. See "Sex, Lies, and Advertising," pp. 493–510.
6. Plato, Hegel, Barnes: Wolf's list ranges from an ancient Greek philosopher (*ca.* 428–348) to a 19th-century German philosopher (1770–1831) to a 20th-century American writer and artist (1892–1982).

acquaintance rape, which on campuses across America one-fourth of female undergraduates undergo. Many of you earned your credits while surviving on eight hundred calories a day, weak from ketosis and so faint from the anorexia that strikes one undergraduate woman in ten that it took every last ounce of your will to get your work in. Up to five times that number graduate today in spite of the crushing shame of bulimia, which consumes enormous energy and destroys self-esteem. You managed to stay focused on political theory and Greek while negotiating private lives through a minefield of new strains of VD, a 30 percent chlamydia rate among U.S. undergraduates, and the ascending shadow of HIV and AIDS. You had the force of imagination to believe that Emily Dickinson and Jane Austen still had something to say to you while your airwaves flickered with ever more baroque and ingenious forms of glamorized violence against women.

Not to mention the more mundane trials of undergraduate life. You [16] fell in love, fell in love with the wrong person, fell out of love, and survived love triangles, intrigues, betrayals, and jealousies. You took false starts in finding your life's work. Perhaps you questioned your religious assumptions, lost spiritual faith, found it again in forms that might alarm your grandparents, and lost it again to find it elsewhere anew. You lived through cliques, gossip, friends who borrowed your clothes and ruined them, dates from the Black Lagoon, money worries, second jobs, college loans, wardrobe angst, a Gulf war, earthquakes, and the way you break out magically just when you have an important job interview.

You made friends with people much richer or much poorer than [17] your own families, and I trust that made you question how fairly this country distributes its wealth. You made friends with people of other racial and religious backgrounds and sexual affiliations than yourself, which I trust made you face the racism and homophobia that this culture embeds in all of our subconsciouses.

In earning your B.A.'s while fighting these battles so often labeled [18] trivial, you have already proven that you are the triumphant survivors you will continue to have to be as you make your way through the backlash landscape outside this community. You have "become women," and as women, your commencement is not just a beginning but a confirmation of achievement. I applaud you.

MESSAGE #2 in your kit is the ultimate taboo subject for women. It [19] makes grown women blush and fidget, and no, it's not sex. It's money. *Ask for money in your lives.* Expect it. Own it. Learn to use it. One of the most disempowering lessons we learn as little girls is the fear of money—that it's not nice, or feminine, to ensure that we are paid fairly for honest work. Meanwhile, women make fifty-nine cents for every male dollar and half of marriages end in divorce, at which point women's standard of living drops 43 percent. To cling to ignorance about money is to be gender illiterate.

Of course you must never choose a profession for material or status reasons, unless you want to guarantee your unhappiness. But, for God's sake, whatever field your heart chooses, get the highest, most specialized training in it you can and hold out hard for just compensation. You owe it to your daughters to fight a system that is happy to assign you to the class of highly competent, grossly underpaid women who run the show while others get the cash and the credit. Once you get your hands on every resource that is due to you, organize with other women for a better deal for the supports women need in the workplace—the parental leave and child care that European women take for granted, and that we need if we are to be what almost every man assumes he can be: both a parent and a worker.

Get the highest salary you can not out of selfish greed but so that you can tithe your income to women's political organizations, shelters, crisis lines, cultural events, and universities. Ten percent is a good guideline that I use myself. When you have equity, you have influence as sponsors, shareholders, trustees, and alumnae to force institutions into positive change. Male-dominated or racist institutions won't give up power if we are sweet and patient; the only language the status quo understands is money, votes, and public embarrassment. Use your clout to open opportunities to the women of all colors and classes who deserve the education and the training you had. As a women, your B.A. and the income it represents don't belong to you alone, just as, in the Native American tradition, the earth doesn't belong to its present occupants alone. Your education was lent to you by women of the past who made it possible for you to have it; and it is your job to give some back to living women, as well as to your unborn daughters seven generations from now.

MESSAGE #3: *Never cook for or sleep with anyone who routinely puts you down.*

MESSAGE #4: *Honor your foremothers,* literal and metaphorical. Ask your mom or grandmother about her own life story, her own quest as she defines it. Read biographies of women of the past that you admire. Knowing how hard women worked because they believed in you will remind you, in dark moments, just how precious your freedom—and hence you—really are.

MESSAGE #5: *Give yourself the gift of speech;* become goddesses of disobedience. Sixty years ago Virginia Woolf[7] wrote that we need to

7. Woolf and Angel: See Woolf's essay "Professions for Women" (pp. 93–98).

slay the Angel in the House, the self-sacrificing, compliant impulse in our own minds. It's still true. Across America, I meet young women who tell me stories of profound injustice: rape cover-ups on campus, blatant sexism in the classroom, discriminatory hiring and admission policies. When I suggest proven strategies to confront the injustice—like holding a press conference about campus crimes if the administration is unwilling to listen—they freeze at the suggestion, paralyzed into niceness. Their eyes take on a distant look, half longing, half petrified. If only! They laugh nervously. They would, but . . . people would get mad at them, they'd be called aggressive, the dean would hate their guts, the trustees might disapprove.

We are taught that the very worst thing we can do is cause conflict,   25
even in the service of doing what is right. Antigone,[8] you will remember, is imprisoned; Joan of Arc[9] burns at the stake; and someone might call us unfeminine! Outrage, which we would not hesitate to express on behalf of a child, we are terrified of showing on behalf of ourselves, or other women.

This fear of not being liked is a big dragon in my own life. I saw   26
the depths of my own paralysis by niceness when I wrote a book that caused controversy. *The Beauty Myth* argues that rigid ideals of beauty are part of the backlash against feminism, designed to lower women's self-esteem for a political purpose. While I meant every word I said, and while enormous positive changes followed, from heightened awareness about eating disorders to an FDA crackdown on breast implants, all of that would dwindle into insignificance when someone yelled at me—as plastic surgeons, for instance, often did on television. I would sob on my boyfriend's shoulder, People are mad at me! (Of course they were mad; a three-hundred-million-dollar industry was at stake.)

Halfway through the slings and arrows, I read something by Afri-   27
can-American poet Audre Lorde that set me free to speak truth to power without blaming myself when power got a little annoyed.

Lorde was diagnosed with breast cancer. "I was going to die,'' she   28
wrote, "sooner or later, whether or not I had ever *spoken* myself. My silences had not protected me. Your silence will not protect you. But for every real word spoken, I had made contact with other women while we examined words to fit a world in which we all believed . . . What are the words you do not yet have? What are the tyrannies you swallow day by day and attempt to make your own, until you will sicken

8. Antigone: in Greek mythology, heroine whose devotion to family over the law led her to perform funereal rites over her brother's body in defiance of the king, her uncle. She was buried alive for doing so.
9. Joan of Arc (1412–1431): French heroine and military leader, she was condemned for witchcraft and burned at the stake for heresy. She was canonized in 1920.

and die of them, still in silence? We have been socialized to respect fear more than our own need for language."

So I began to ask, at every skirmish: "What's the worst that could happen to me if I tell this truth?" The fact is that the backlash greatly exaggerates the consequences of our speaking. Unlike women in other countries, our breaking silence is unlikely to land us in jail and tortured, or beaten with firehoses, or "disappeared," or run off the road at midnight. Our speaking out will make some people irritated, disrupt some dinner parties (and doubtless make them livelier), get us called names and ridiculed. And then our speaking out will permit other women to speak, and others, until laws are changed and lives are saved and the world is altered forever.   29

So I wish upon you the ability to distinguish between silencings. Some are real: if you will lose your livelihood or get the life beat out of you. You will respect the necessity of the circumstance at that moment and then organize like hell so you are not faced with it again. But then there are the other 90 percent, the petty, day-to-day silencings, like when you are being hassled by some drunken guests in a hotel and, rather than confronting them, the front desk tells you to lock yourself in your room. Or when your male classmates make sexist jokes. You know when you last swallowed your words.   30

Next time, ask yourself: What's the worst that will happen? So you might get called a bitch, or aggressive, or a slut, or the hostess will try to change the subject, or you might have to have a long talk with your male friends. Then, each time you are silenced, push yourself a little further than you think you dare to go. It will get easier and easier.   31

Then, once you are not immobilized with niceness, you know what? People *will* yell at you. They *will* interrupt, put you down, try to make you feel small, and suggest it's a personal problem. And the world won't end. And you will grow stronger by the day and find you have fallen in love with your own vision of the world, which you may never have known you had, because you were trying so hard not to know what you knew. And you will lose some friends and some lovers, and find you don't miss them; and new ones will find you. And you will still go dancing all night, still flirt and dress up and party, because as Emma Goldman[10] said, "If I can't dance, it's not my revolution." And as time goes on you will know with surpassing certainty that there is only one thing more dangerous and frightening and harmful to your well-being than speaking your truth. And that is the certain psychic death of not speaking.   32

10. Emma Goldman (1869–1940): Russian socialist, anarchist, feminist, and author who lived much of her life in the United States crusading for freedom of speech and birth control.

JENNIFER BRICE

My Mother's Body

Jennifer Brice (1963–   ) was born in Fairbanks, Alaska, and has
spent most of her life there. After graduating from Smith College, she
began her writing career by composing obituaries. After five years of
newspaper work, Brice received a Jacob K. Javits Fellowship in the
Humanities, which has supported her through graduate school in creative writing at the University of Alaska. To complete a collection of
essays for her M.A. thesis, Brice has spent the past three years traveling
through the Alaskan interior with a photographer, interviewing families on remote home sites; the hybrid of documentary photography,
reportage, and memoir looks at the arbitrary nature of the borders
between nature and civilization. Brice divides her time between writing and raising her two-year-old daughter, trying to fit in as much
skiing and solitude as possible between the two. In writing "My
Mother's Body," Brice explains, she came to see "the conflict between
many aspects of the self as constructive rather than destructive" and
that generations of women in her family, in every family, have wres-
tled with the same issues. "My Mother's Body" was published in the
Sierra Club collection *American Nature Writing* (1994). Brice has also
published essays in *Permafrost, Manoa, Critique,* and in an anthology
from Graywolf Press, *The Island's Edge.*

Winter solstice. Festive and frail like the orange globe of a Chinese   1
lantern, the sun hangs on the horizon where it seems to absorb rather
than radiate heat. Outside the window of the spare bedroom in my
mother's house, where I dress for my sister's wedding, ice fog wisps
around the frost-filigreed branches of birch trees, and glittering snow car-
apaces the ground. With a lamp at my back, the window is a mirror into
which I lean, struggling with the old-fashioned clasp on my pearl necklace. I see my reflection—a slender, dark-haired woman in green velvet—
and next to it, my sister-in-law, eight months pregnant. She tugs the lace
bertha of the bridesmaid's dress up over her shoulders and steps back,
cradling her ponderous belly in both hands. "I was crazy to say yes when
Hannah asked me to be in this wedding," she says. "I look obscene." I
tell her she's beautiful and mean it, but she shrugs. Then I turn sideways
to the window and slide flattened hands over my collarbones, breasts,
stomach, hips. My fingers meet at the center of my body where they probe
gently for something smaller than the mole above my right breast, something more mysterious than the black spots on the sun. I have never been
good at secrets. "Can you see my baby yet?" I ask.

The wedding is by candlelight in the same log-cabin Episcopal   2
church where my husband and I made our vows eighteen months ear-

lier. It was June then, summer solstice, and the church doors were flung open. Baskets of roses and peonies flanked the steps to the nave. Purcell's trumpet voluntary shattered dust motes hanging in shafts of sunlight. Tonight, however, the earth pitches away from the sun. After the service the guests shrug into furs and parkas against the thirty-five-below night. After the church empties out, the wedding photographer shapes my family into a V headed by Helenka, my grandmother, in her sequined evening gown and fluffy bedroom slippers. The slippers catch me unawares. They remind me how everything living is dying: this is likely to be Grandma's last wedding.

When my grandfather died in 1987, he left her eighty acres, a farm, and a construction business. Grandma hired a landscaper to fill in the swimming pool with dirt and she planted a rose garden there with as many bushes as grandchildren. Greenhouse owners laughed at her. "You might as well try growing cacti in Antarctica," they said. But Grandma fertilizes her rose bushes with backbone. They bloom only for her. Whenever one of her grandchildren is ill, she sends a crystal bowl of fragrant roses instead of chicken soup. In the winter when her bushes sleep, their colors tumble off her tongue, incantatory, like Abraham's[1] descendants in the book of Genesis: Sterling Silver, Sunflare, Summer Fashion, Summer Sunshine, Allspice, American Pride, Touch of Class, Tropicana, Mr. Lincoln, Legend, Prince Charles, Fountain Square, White Lightning, Double Delight, Sheer Bliss, and Peace. "Jennifer's color is American Beauty," she declared once. Deeper than pink and shallower than red, it is a rare shade. I see it in the northern lights that stain the sky on my sister's wedding night.

Surrounded by her children and grandchildren, Helenka perches like a plump, bright-eyed chickadee on a barstool in the old-timey saloon the bride and groom rented for their reception. I tell my grandmother I'm pregnant. She has a knack for planting familiar words in unfamiliar gardens, so I'm not surprised when she says, serenely, "I loved making my babies." The way she uses "make" emphasizes the "-creation" end of "procreation," as though a baby were a bowl crafted from clay on a pottery wheel and glazed for strength and beauty, or a seed pressed into the womb of the earth and nourished with food and water until it is strong enough to bend in the wind. I've never been good with my hands, never thrown a pot, never painted a still life with fruit, never even grown a Mother's Day geranium from a seed planted in a Styrofoam cup. But my body is making a baby.

Vernal equinox. The myth of Demeter and Persephone[2] was at the

1. Abraham: traditional progenitor of the Hebrew people.
2. Demeter and Persephone: In Greek mythology, after being abducted by Hades, Persephone became both queen of the underworld and goddess of vegetation; her release from the underworld each spring to spend several months with her mother, Demeter, is reflected in the cycle of the seasons.

heart of The Eleusinian Mysteries, the rites of spiritual renewal celebrated in Greece for more than 2,000 years. The myth encompasses the
cycle of the seasons, death and reincarnation, rending and healing, loss
and joy, but it centers on the relationship between mother and daughter. Adrienne Rich, in *Of Woman Born*, writes extensively about the
relevance of the myth to modern mother-daughter bonds. In my own
life, the biggest complication in my relationship with my mother has
always been my relationship with my grandmother, who, serendipi-
tously, is the mother of my father. In *Our Mothers/Our Selves*, Nancy
Friday says every household reverberates with the voices of three
women: mother, daughter, and grandmother. My mother's voice was
reverent when she unveiled the mysteries of cycles, Kotex and garter
belts. Everything was in place, waiting in the special drawer in the
bathroom for the special moment when I shed the chrysalis of childhood. I got my first period on a trip with my grandmother. When I told
her in the airport, she asked, offhandedly, "Do you need anything?"
Yes, I told her, everything. She bought me a box of OB tampons, and
nothing more was ever said.

Spring is late this year. Torn between mother and lover, Persephone   6
tarries in the Underworld. Jealous Demeter stirs up blizzards in May.
No one is able to coax Helenka's rose bushes, dull green sticks bran-
dishing thorns, into bloom. Melting snow and mud puddles paint a
landscape in charcoal grays and dingy browns on the day of her funeral.
I wear pearls again, and my first maternity dress. Last week in the ultra-
sound lab at the hospital I watched my healthy baby girl somersault in
her amniotic sac of fluid and blood. Now it is early morning and the
family has gathered, some seventy-strong, to pray with Episcopal restraint and to spread Grandma's ashes over the farm. With our coffee
and croissants we mill about as helplessly as geese without a leader. I
want to writhe on the wet grass and gouge at the soil. Today, my baby's
cells multiply by the million; my grandmother's ashes fertilize her rose
bushes. In *The Lives of a Cell*, Lewis Thomas writes: "Everything that
comes alive seems to be in trade for something that dies, cell for cell.
There might be some comfort in . . . synchrony." There may be some
comfort in synchrony, but it is not great.

I never thought of my mother as beautiful. Evenings when I was   7
growing up, I used to nudge open the bathroom door and roost on the
edge of her tub, soaking my feet in the steaming, scented water. "Tell
me about your day," Mom would say. As we talked, I studied surreptitiously the landscape of her body. Blue-black varicose veins, like tangled rivers and their tributaries, roped their way up to the sparse triangle
between her legs. Scarlet moles punctuated a stomach puckered and
seamed by surgeries, including the hysterectomy that had proscribed
her motherhood. One side of her belly was as firm as a ripe pomegran-
ate; the other hemisphere, molded by scar tissue, collapsed in folds of

flab. Illness and childbirth had buffeted her body in ways that I, with the vanity of youth, vowed they would never touch me.

Pregnant, I find myself back on the edge of my mother's bathtub   8 where I now study the landscape of possibility while we design flower gardens in our heads. "You know the gravel pit off Peger Road?" she asks. "I saw wild iris growing there last week." For us, garden talk is a code: "Plant perennials instead of annuals so you won't have to work so hard next summer, with the baby." The only roses in my mother's garden are portulaca, moss roses, whose silver-dollar-size blooms quilt the sandy soil of her wildflower garden in pastel patches. From Memorial Day until Labor Day, Mom lets spiders spin webs in her basement and dust bunnies collect under the beds. Wearing a terry-cloth sun suit, she kneels outside in the dirt from eight in the morning until seven at night, digging troughs in the topsoil, planting seeds one at a time, sprinkling mounds with fertilized rainwater. She weeds a little every day and coaxes more blooms by snipping off deadheads. By the time July rolls around, the plants are so profuse it can be difficult to find my mother in her garden. Fiddlehead ferns, delphinium, tiger lilies, snapdragons, geraniums, daisies, begonias, pansies, lobelia, Johnny-jump-ups, creeping Jenny, forget-me-nots, lettuce, tomatoes, peas, carrots, radishes, squash and pumpkins: my mother's garden is both hymn to the regenerative power of earth and drunken orgy under the midnight sun.

Summer solstice. Two years ago Mom flew to Anchorage for what   9 the doctors expected to be routine gallbladder surgery. Instead she developed complications and nearly died. Her garden withered while she lay in a hospital bed on life-support machines. Watching my mother weaken and realizing she might die kindled a deep existential fear in me. I was working in Fairbanks from Monday through Friday and flying to Anchorage on the weekends; for the first time in my life, I was afraid of dying in a plane crash. Strangely, I felt safe on takeoff and landing, but once airborne, I dreaded elements beyond human control—turbulence, wind shear, electrical storms—that might tear the jet apart in mid-air. I left the pressurized cabin of the jet for the silent, gray, temperature-controlled corridors of Humana Hospital. The tinted windows in my mother's room watered down harsh sunlight and drained the landscape of color. Mom shrunk daily into a chaos of plastic umbilical cords. Intellectually, I knew it was the natural order of things for my mother to die before me. But not in her 50s, not before she taught me how to be a mother, not until I had come to terms with the fact of my own mortality. My mother's illness taught me this: my strongest identification is not as someone's friend, sister, granddaughter or wife but as my mother's daughter. She is my road map; without her, I would be completely lost.

Mom is nearly her old self again now. Working in her garden,   10 squeezing dirt between her fingers, she grows stronger daily. Unlike her, I lack the patience to let things grow. I over-fertilize in a fit of solicitousness or forget to weed in a fit of laziness. This summer of my pregnancy, for the first time in my life, I crave the physicality of gardening. Mornings Mom and I visit local greenhouses. She discourages me from temperamental species; I yearn toward hothouse roses. Every afternoon I lug baskets onto the back porch, fill them with dirt, dig shallow holes with a trowel or my fingers, pop the seedlings out of their six-packs, and set them in their new nests. Mosquitos buzz around my head. Hugely pregnant in a denim jumper, I make trip after trip to the kitchen sink for jugs of water mixed with pink fish fertilizer. The front yard is a typical Alaska lawn, which is to say no lawn at all, just a few spruce trees, willow bushes, a delphinium here and there, and a ground covering of ferns, wild roses and cranberry bushes. If I cannot have long-stemmed roses then I want wildness. I strew wildflower seeds everywhere. By mid-summer, daisies overflow a rusting wheelbarrow, impatiens spring from the hollows of rotting stumps, and nasturtiums cascade off the roof of the doghouse. One of the reasons I never liked gardening before was the waste: all that money and energy expended on something that was going to die anyway. Recently a couple of friends stopped by on bicycles and stayed to help me plant a lilac bush. Afterward, over ice cream, one of them asked, "How can you justify bringing a child into this over-populated world full of wars and famine and acid rain and ozone holes?" I replied, "Because I still hope." Lewis Thomas finds comfort, not despair, in the knowledge that everything living is also dying. Cultivating a garden that will surely die in September can be seen as an act of senseless futility or one of consummate hope. So can having a baby. After all, everything dying is also living.

On the Fourth of July, friends invite Craig and me to float the Chena River with them. The river is a shallow, slow-moving artery that winds through town, binding three-story houses with gazebos to houses with chain-link fences and yapping dogs to houses that are really lean-tos. A radio announcer says it's 75 degrees but a cooling breeze riffles the leaves of birch trees on shore. We paddle the stretch of water below the city power plant because the water there never freezes in winter, not even at 50 below. Now we rest our paddles on our knees and float, trading insults and banter between canoes. I gasp when the first bucket of river water slaps me in the back of the head. I see the second bucket coming and lean to the right. Quicker than regret, the canoe spills all 165 pounds of me into the river. Panicked, I grab for the overturned boat, but my lifejacket rides up over my belly, hampers my arms. Lisa mimics me—"The baby, oh God, the baby"—and, laughing, my friends tug me ashore like a harpooned whale.

Back on the river, I think about how this baby fills up space inside me that used to be wilderness unexplored by anyone, least of all me. Hugh Brody, the anthropologist and author, has spoken of finding the center at the edge, in the most remote hut in the most remote village in the most remote region of the country farthest from home. I have found certain truths at the edge but, for me, the center is at the center: in my family, in my flower boxes, in my womb. For the rest of the afternoon I ride in the middle of the canoe with hands cupped over the mound of my tummy.

My due date is still six weeks away, but I feel like one of those 13 ancient stone fertility figures whose images flashed on the screen of the darkened art history auditorium during college. I drive the half-mile to my mother's house instead of walking. She lays down her trowel and fixes us sandwiches of turkey breast, garden lettuce and tomatoes. Afterward we work on Sunday's *New York Times* crossword puzzle. Deeply afraid of giving birth, I yearn for the only solace my mother cannot—or will not—give. Casually, while she looks up a four-letter word for an African gazelle, I ask about labor. She tells me stories about water breaking in the middle of the night, evenly spaced contractions, the urge to push, a swaddled baby drowsing in her arms. She never uses the word "pain." During our Lamaze class, my husband and I watched three films of women having babies: an "easy" labor, an "average" labor, and a "hard" labor. One friend says it's like bad menstrual cramps. Another friend, the one who cuts my hair, laid down her scissors when I told her I was pregnant. She spun my chair around until her face was right up against mine, and she placed a hand on either side of my head to hold it still. Then she said: "Don't let anyone ever tell you having a baby doesn't hurt. There is no worse pain in the world." What I want to ask my mother is this: how bad is the pain when a woman's lips turn white? But she will not look in my eyes. My mother knows. My garden grows. There is mystery as well as synchrony. Some comfort.

The first contraction tears through me at midnight on August thirty- 14 first. It feels less like a menstrual cramp than a hot poker. Earlier, I had made a pact with my doctor to try to get by without drugs. Now I want a talisman against pain. My mother walks into the hospital room at 7:30 in the morning, pale but crisp in a madras jumpsuit, carrying a pile of books and newspapers against her chest. Insulation against my wildness, her helplessness. For a while we tell jokes between contractions. My mother and Craig take turns walking the corridors with me, pushing the IV tree with its bag of sap-like fluid. Only water and electrolytes at this point, but the doctor predicts a long, exhausting labor, and she wants to be able to administer drugs quickly, if necessary. We stop in front of the nursery windows. I look at the newborns and think, "Soon. Soon." My water has not yet broken. The nurse swabs the inside of my cervix and looks at the cells under a microscope. If the sac of amniotic fluid had broken, she would see a fern-like pattern. "No ferns," she tells me, shaking her head.

My contractions are severe but irregular. The doctor uses an instru- 15 ment like a crochet hook to reach inside me and puncture the bag of waters. It feels as though someone broke a ten-gallon hot water bottle over my stomach. The distance between pains narrows a little, but daylight is waning outside my window. On the doctor's orders, the nurse adds pitocin, a labor-intensifying drug, to my IV line. Within minutes, my body travels to a place inhabited by insatiable pain, a place where language can never go, a place where I am no longer someone's daughter and not yet someone's mother. The nurse grabs the backs of my hands, spreads my fingers in front of my clenched eyelids. "Jennifer, listen to me. *Listen* to me. Open your eyes. Don't go inside the pain. You'll only make it worse." What is she talking about? There is no inside or outside to this pain. The plate tectonics of childbirth remold the peaks and valleys of my body. The bones of my mother's hand feel as frail as a fledgling's skeleton. It is extraordinary to me that the process of bringing forth life should bring women to the brink of death. For a baby, the violent, bruising passage through the birth canal must be like expulsion from paradise. Before, amniotic bliss; after, cold and hunger and hands. As the mother's pain ends, the daughter's begins.

Autumnal equinox. Last night, the temperature dipped below freez- 16 ing. In Alaska, the cusp seasons of spring and fall can be figments of the calendar's imagination. So reluctant to be dragged from the earth's womb last spring, Persephone seems eager to return this fall. The birch trees have barely begun to shed their chattering leaves when the first snow falls in big, wet clumps. In a defiant blaze of color, the blossoms in my garden faced death, their stems and leaves collapsing around them like tattered seaweed. Turbulent post-partum depression runs in my family but still it blindsides me. Grief for my grandmother, who will never name a rose for my daughter, Kinzea Grace, is a subterranean place into which I burrow every night. My mother probably will not live to see another generation grow up. As for me, creating life has forced me to confront my own mortality as never before. In the Eskimo culture, babies were traditionally granted the same title and respect as a recently deceased elder. I could find comfort in calling Kinzea "Grandmother."

I left the hospital after the baby was born without seeing her naked. 17 I was so tired, the nurses so smoothly efficient. Now, as she wriggles and coos in the bathtub, I study her body for the first time: the parallel lines beneath her lips, the pearls of dirt that collect under her chin, her nearly invisible nipples, bracelets of fat at wrists and ankles, a tulip-shaped birthmark on her left buttock, the arch of a tiny foot. Her fifth toes are shriveled like mine, with nails the size of carrot seeds. Our feet foretell a time when the descendants of homo sapiens will balance on eight toes instead of ten.

I sit behind Kinzea in the tub, cradling her body between thighs 18 gone flaccid from lack of exercise. My belly slides back and forth in the moving water like a Jell-O mold at a church picnic. Violet stretch marks form a complex root system spreading upward from the fork of my legs where the baby's head rests. My breasts are laden with milk. Looking down, I recognize my mother's body, my grandmother's body, my great-grandmother's body. Flawed but familiar. Living and dying at the same time. There is some comfort—even grace—in synchrony, in being the daughter of a mother and the mother of a daughter. Somewhere, I read that a child needs the care of someone for whom she is a miracle. Mother love, I think, is born of wonder at that miracle.

SCOTT RUSSELL SANDERS

Reasons of the Body

Scott Russell Sanders (1945–   ), a native of Tennessee, received his Ph.D. from Cambridge University and is currently a professor of English at Indiana University. Although he has written in a variety of genres, including science fiction, folktales, children's stories, and historical novels, he has concentrated in recent years on essays and autobiography. Sanders is well acquainted with the rugged side of American culture, which he explores in *Wilderness Plots: Tales About the Settlement of the American Land* (1983) and in *Paradise of Bombs* (1987), a collection of personal essays about violence in contemporary culture. "Reasons of the Body" was published in *Georgia Review* in 1990 and is collected in *Secrets of the Universe* (1991), Sanders's recollections of his Midwestern childhood. His most recent collection of essays, *Staying Put: Making a Home in a Restless World,* was published in 1993. Sanders has also begun writing children's books, such as *Here Comes the Mystery Man* (1993) and *The Floating House* (1995).

My son has never met a sport he did not like. I have met a few   1 that left an ugly tingle—boxing and rodeo and pistol shooting, among others—but, then, I have been meeting them for forty-four years, Jesse only for twelve. Our ages are relevant to the discussion, because, on the hill of the sporting life, Jesse is midway up the slope and climbing rapidly, while I am over the crest and digging in my heels as I slip down.

"You still get around pretty well for an old guy," he told me last   2 night after we had played catch in the park.

The catch we play has changed subtly in recent months, a change   3
that dramatizes a shift in the force field binding father and son. Early
on, when I was a decade younger and Jesse a toddler, I was the agile
one, leaping to snare his wild throws. The ball we tossed in those days
was rubbery and light, a bubble of air as big around as a soup bowl,
easy for small hands to grab. By the time he started school, we were
using a tennis ball, then we graduated to a softball, then to gloves and
a baseball. His repertoire of catches and throws increased along with
his vocabulary.

Over the years, as Jesse put on inches and pounds and grace, I still   4
had to be careful how far and hard I threw, to avoid bruising his ribs
or his pride. But this spring, when we began limbering up our arms,
his throws came whistling at me with a force that hurt my hand, and
he caught effortlessly anything I could hurl back at him. It was as
though the food he wolfed down all winter had turned into spring steel.
I no longer needed to hold back. Now Jesse is the one, when he is
feeling charitable, who pulls his pitches.

Yesterday in the park, he was feeling frisky rather than charitable.   5
We looped the ball lazily back and forth awhile. Then he started backing
away, backing away, until my shoulder twinged from the length of
throws. Unsatisfied, he yelled, "Make me run for it!" So I flung the ball
high and deep, low and wide, driving him over the grass, yet he loped
easily wherever it flew, gathered it in, then whipped it back to me with
stinging speed.

"Come on," he yelled, "put it where I can't reach it." I tried, ignor-   6
ing the ache in my arm, and still he ran under the ball. He might have
been gliding on a cushion of air, he moved so lightly. I was feeling
heavy, and felt heavier by the minute as his return throws, grown
suddenly and unaccountably wild, forced me to hustle back and forth,
jump and dive.

"Hey," I yelled, waving my glove at him, "look where I'm   7
standing!"

"Standing is right," he yelled back. "Let's see those legs move!"   8
His next throw sailed over my head, and the ones after that sailed
farther still, now left now right, out of my range, until I gave up even
trying for them, and the ball thudded accusingly to the ground. By the
time we quit, I was sucking air, my knees were stiffening, and a fire
was blazing in my arm. Jesse trotted up, his T-shirt dry, his breathing
casual. This was the moment he chose to clap me on the back and say,
"You still get around pretty well for an old guy."

It was a line I might have delivered, as a cocky teenager, to my   9
own father. He would have laughed, and then challenged me to a round
of golf or a bout of arm-wrestling, contests he could still easily have
won.

Whatever else these games may be, they are always contests. For   10 many a boy, a playing field, court, or gym is the first arena in which he can outstrip his old man. For me, the arena was a concrete driveway, where I played basketball against my father, shooting at a rusty hoop that was mounted over the garage. He had taught me how to dribble, how to time my jump, how to follow through on my shots. To begin with, I could barely heave the ball to the basket, and he would applaud if I so much as banged the rim. I banged away, year by year, my bones lengthening, muscles thickening. I shuffled over the concrete to the jazz of birdsong and the opera of thunderstorms. I practiced fervently, as though my life depended on putting the ball through the hoop, practiced when the driveway was dusted with pollen and when it was drifted with snow. From first light to twilight, while the chimney swifts spiraled out to feed on mosquitoes and the mosquitoes fed on me, I kept shooting, hour after hour. Many of those hours, Father was tinkering in the garage, which reverberated with the slap of my feet and the slam of the ball. There came a day when I realized that I could outleap him, outhustle and outshoot him. I began to notice his terrible breathing—terrible because I had not realized he could run short of air. I had not realized he could run short of anything. When he bent over and grabbed his knees, huffing, "You're too much for me," I felt at once triumphant and dismayed.

I still have to hold back when playing basketball with Jesse. But 11 the day will come, and soon, when he'll grow taller and stronger, and he will be the one to show mercy. The only dessert I will be able to eat, if I am to avoid growing fat, will be humble pie. Even now my shots appear old-fashioned to him, as my father's arching two-handed heaves seemed antique to me. "Show me some of those Neanderthal moves," Jesse cries, as we shoot around at a basket in the park, "show me how they did it in the Stone Age!" I do show him, clowning and hot-dogging, wishing by turns to amuse and impress him. As I fake and spin, I am simultaneously father and son, playing games forward and backward in time.

The game of catch, like other sports where body faces body, is a 12 dialogue carried on with muscle and bone. One body speaks by throwing a ball or a punch, by lunging with a foil, smashing a backhand, sinking a putt, rolling a strike, kicking a shot toward the corner of the net; the other replies by swinging, leaping, dodging, tackling, parrying, balancing. As in lovemaking, this exchange may be a struggle for power or a sharing of pleasure. The call and response may be in the spirit of antiphonal singing, a making of music that neither person could have achieved alone, or it may be in the spirit of insults bellowed across a table.

When a father and son play sports, especially a game the son has 13 learned from the father, every motive from bitter rivalry to mutual

delight may enter in. At first eagerly, then grudgingly, and at last unconsciously, the son watches how his father grips the ball, handles the
glove, swings the bat. In just the same way, the son has watched how
the father swings a hammer, how the father walks, jokes, digs, starts a
car, gentles a horse, pays a bill, shakes hands, shaves. There is a season
in one's growing up, beginning at about the age Jesse is now, when a
son comes to feel his old man's example as a smothering weight. You
must shrug free of it, or die. And so, if your father carries himself soldier
straight, you begin to slouch; if he strides along with a swagger, you
slink; if he talks in joshing Mississippi accents to anybody with ears,
you shun strangers and swallow your drawl. With luck and time, you
may come to accept that you bear in your own voice overtones of your
father's. You may come to rejoice that your own least motion—kissing
a baby or opening a jar—is informed by memories of how your father
would have done it. Between the early delight and the late reconciliation, however, you must pass through that season of rivalry, the son
striving to undo or outdo his father's example, the father chewing on
the bitter rind of rejection.

Why do I speak only of boys and men? Because, while there are   14
females aplenty who relish any sport you can name, I have never shared
a roof with one. In her seventies, my mother still dances and swims,
even leads classes in aerobics, but she's never had much use for games
played with balls, and neither has my wife Ruth or our daughter. When
Ruth was a child, a bout of rheumatic fever confined her to bed and
then to a wheelchair for several years. Until she was old enough for
university, a heart rendered tricky by the illness kept her from doing
anything that would raise her pulse, and by then she had invested her
energies elsewhere, in music and science. To this day, Ruth sees no
point in moving faster than a walk, or in defying gravity with exuberant
leaps, or in puzzling over the trajectory of a ball.

And what of our firstborn, sprightly Eva? Surely I could have   15
brought her up to become a partner for catch? Let me assure you that
I tried. I put a sponge ball in her crib, as Father had put a baseball in
mine. (I was going to follow tradition exactly and teethe her on a
baseball, but Ruth, sensible of a baby's delicacy, said nothing doing.)
From the moment in the hospital when the nurse handed me Eva, a
quivering bundle, ours to keep, I coached my spunky girl, I coaxed and
exhorted her, but she would not be persuaded that throwing or shooting
or kicking a ball was a sensible way to spend an hour or an afternoon.
After seventeen years of all the encouragement that love can buy, the
one sport she will deign to play with me is volleyball, in which she
hurtles over the grass, leaping and cavorting, as only a dancer could.

A gymnast and ballerina, Eva has always been on good terms with   16
her body, and yet, along with her mother and my mother, she rolls her

eyes when Jesse and I begin rummaging in the battered box on the porch for a baseball, basketball, or soccer ball. "So Dad," she calls, "it's off to recover past glories, is it? You show 'em, tiger. But don't break any bones."

Eva's amusement has made the opinion of the women in my life 17 unanimous. Their baffled indulgence, bordering at times on mockery, has given to sports a tang of the mildly illicit.

Like many other women (not all, not all), those in my family take 18 even less interest in talking about sports than in playing them. They pride themselves on being above such idle gab. They shake their heads when my son and I check the scores in the newspaper. They are astounded that we can spend longer rehashing a game than we spent in playing it. When Jesse and I compare aches after a session on field or court, the women observe mildly that it sounds as though we had been mugged. Surely we would not inflict such damage on ourselves? Perhaps we have gotten banged up from wrestling bears? We kid along and say, "Yes, we ran into the Chicago Bears," and my daughter or mother or wife will reply, "You mean the hockey team?"

In many households and offices, gossip about games and athletes 19 breaks down along gender lines, the men indulging in it and the women scoffing. Those on each side of the line may exaggerate their feelings, the men pumping up their enthusiasm, the women their indifference, until sport becomes a male mystery. No locker room, no sweat lodge is needed to shut women out; mere talk will do it. Men are capable of muttering about wins and losses, batting averages and slam dunks, until the flowers on the wallpaper begin to wilt and every woman in the vicinity begins to yearn for a supply of gags. A woman friend of mine, an executive in a computing firm, has been driven in self-defense to scan the headlines of the sports pages before going to work, so that she can toss out references to the day's contests and stars, like chunks of meat, to feed the appetites of her male colleagues. After gnawing on this bait, the men may consent to speak with her of things more in keeping with her taste, such as books, birds, and the human condition.

My daughter has never allowed me to buy her a single item of 20 sports paraphernalia. My son, on the other hand, has never declined such an offer. Day and night, visions of athletic gear dance in his head. With religious zeal, he pores over magazine ads for sneakers, examining the stripes and insignia as if they were hieroglyphs of ultimate truth. Between us, Jesse and I are responsible for the hoard of equipment on our back porch, which contains at present the following items: one bicycle helmet and two bicycles; a volleyball set, badminton set, and a bag of golf clubs; three racquets for tennis, two for squash, one for paddle ball; roller skates and ice skates, together with a pair of hockey sticks; goalie gloves, batting gloves, three baseball gloves and one catcher's mitt; numerous yo-yos; ten pairs of cleated or waffle-soled shoes; a drying rack festooned with shorts and socks and shirts and sweatsuits; and a cardboard box heaped with (I counted) forty-nine balls, including those for all the sports implicated above, as well as for ping-pong, lacrosse, juggling, and jacks.

Excavated by some future archaeologist, this porch full of gear   21 would tell as much about how we passed our lives as would the shells and seeds and bones of a kitchen midden. An excavation of the word *sport* also yields evidence of breaks, bruises, and ambiguities. A sport is a game, an orderly zone marked off from the prevailing disorder, but it can also be a mutation, a violation of rules. To be good at sports is to be a winner, and yet a good sport is one who loses amiably, a bad sport one who kicks and screams at every setback. A flashy dresser might be called a sport, and so might a gambler, an idler, an easygoing companion, one who dines high on the hog of pleasure. But the same label may be attached to one who is the butt of jokes, a laughingstock, a goat. As a verb, to sport can mean to wear jewelry or clothes in a showy manner, to poke fun, to trifle, to roll promiscuously in the hay. It is a word spiced with unsavory meanings, rather tacky and cheap, with hints of brothels, speakeasies, and malodorous dives. And yet it bears also the wholesome flavor of fairness, vigor, and ease.

The lore of sports may be all that some fathers have to pass down   22 to their sons in place of lore about hunting animals, planting seeds, killing enemies, or placating the gods. Instead of telling him how to shoot a buffalo, the father whispers in the son's ear how to shoot a lay-up. Instead of consulting the stars or the entrails of birds, father and son consult the smudged print of newspapers to see how their chosen spirits are faring. They fiddle with the dials of radios, hoping to catch the oracular murmur of a distant game. The father recounts heroic deeds, not from the field of battle, but from the field of play. The seasons about which he speaks lead not to harvests but to championships. No longer intimate with the wilderness, no longer familiar even with the tamed land of farms, we create artificial landscapes bounded by lines of paint or lime. Within those boundaries, as within the frame of a chessboard or painting, life achieves a memorable, seductive clarity. The lore of sports is a step down from that of nature, perhaps even a tragic step, but it is lore nonetheless, with its own demigods and demons, magic and myths.

The sporting legends I carry from my father are private rather than   23 public. I am haunted by scenes that no journalist recorded, no camera filmed. Father is playing a solo round of golf, for example, early one morning in April. The fairways glisten with dew. Crows rasp and fluster in the pines that border the course. Father lofts a shot toward a par-three hole, and the white ball arcs over the pond, over the sand trap, over the shaggy apron of grass onto the green, where it bounces, settles down, then rolls toward the flag, rolls unerringly, inevitably, until it falls with a scarcely audible click into the hole. The only eyes within sight besides his own are the crows'. For once, the ball has obeyed him perfectly, harmonizing wind and gravity and the revolution of the spheres, one shot has gone where all are meant to go, and there is nobody else to watch. He stands on the tee, gazing at the distant hole, knowing what he has done and that he will never do it again. The privacy of this moment appeals to me more than all the clamor and fame of a shot heard round the world.

Here is another story I live by: The man who will become my father is twenty-two, a catcher for a bush-league baseball team in Tennessee. He will never make it to the majors, but on weekends he earns a few dollars for squatting behind the plate and nailing runners foolish enough to try stealing second base. From all those bus rides, all those red-dirt diamonds, the event he will describe for his son with deepest emotion is an exhibition game. Father's team of whites, most of them fresh from two-mule farms, is playing a touring black team, a rare event for that day and place. To make it even rarer, and the sides fairer, the coaches agree to mix the teams. And so my father, son of a Mississippi cotton farmer, bruised with racial notions that will take a lifetime to heal, crouches behind the plate and for nine innings catches fastballs and curves, change-ups and screwballs from a whirling, muttering wizard of the Negro Baseball League, one Leroy Robert Paige, known to the world as Satchel. Afterward, Satchel Paige tells the farm boy, "You catch a good game," and the farm boy answers, "You've got the stuff, mister." And for the rest of my father's life, this man's pitching serves as a measure of mastery.

And here is a third myth I carry: One evening when the boy who will become my father is eighteen, he walks into the Black Cat Saloon in Tupelo, Mississippi. He is looking for a fight. Weary of plowing, sick of red dirt, baffled by his own turbulent energy, he often picks fights. This evening the man he picks on is a stranger who occupies a nearby stool at the bar, a husky man in his thirties, wearing a snap-brim hat, dark suit with wide lapels, narrow tie, and infuriatingly white shirt. The stranger is slow to anger. The red-headed Sanders boy keeps at him, keeps at him, mocking the Yankee accent, the hat worn indoors, the monkey suit, the starched shirt, until at last the man stands up and backs away from the bar, fists raised. The Sanders boy lands three punches, he remembers that much, but the next thing he remembers is waking up on the sidewalk, the stranger bending over him to ask if he is all right, and to ask, besides, if he would like a boxing scholarship to Mississippi State. The man is headed there to become the new coach. The boy who will become my father goes to Mississippi State for two years, loses some bouts and wins more, then quits to pursue a Golden

Gloves title, and when he fails at that he keeps on fighting in bars and streets, and at last he quits boxing, his nose broken so many times there is no bone left in it, only a bulb of flesh which a boy sitting in his lap will later squeeze and mash like dough. From all those bouts, the one he will describe to his son with the greatest passion is that brawl from the Black Cat Saloon, when the stranger in the white shirt, a good judge of fighters, found him worthy.

Father tried, with scant success, to make a boxer of me. Not for a   26
career in the ring, he explained, but for defense against the roughs and rowdies who would cross my path in life. If I ran into a mean customer, I told him, I could always get off the path. No, Father said, a man never backs away. A man stands his ground and fights. This advice ran against my grain, which inclined toward quickness of wits rather than fists, yet for years I strove to become the tough guy he envisioned. Without looking for fights, I stumbled into them at every turn, in schoolyard and backyard and in the shadows of barns. Even at my most belligerent, I still tried cajolery and oratory first. Only when that failed did I dig in my heels and start swinging. I gave bruises and received them, gave and received bloody noses, leading with my left, as Father had taught me, protecting my head with forearms, keeping my thumbs outside my balled fists to avoid breaking them when I landed a punch.

Some bullies saw my feistiness as a red flag. One boy who kept   27
hounding me was Olaf Magnuson, a neighbor whose surname I would later translate with my primitive Latin as Son of Big. The name was appropriate, for Olaf was two years older and a foot taller and forty pounds heavier than I was. He pestered me, cursed me, irked and insulted me. When I stood my ground, he pounded me into it. One evening in my twelfth summer, after I had staggered home several times from these frays bloodied and bowed, Father decided it was time for serious boxing lessons. We would train for two months, he told me, then challenge Olaf Magnuson to a fight, complete with gloves and ropes and bell. This did not sound like a healthy idea to me; but Father insisted. "Do you want to keep getting pushed around," he demanded, "or are you going to lick the tar out of him?"

Every day for two months I ran, skipped rope, did chin-ups and   28
push-ups. Father hung his old punching bag from a rafter in the basement, and I flailed at it until my arms filled with sand. He wrapped an old mattress around a tree and told me to imagine Olaf Magnuson's belly as I pounded the cotton ticking. I sparred with my grizzly old man, who showed me how to jab and hook, duck and weave, how to keep my balance and work out of corners. Even though his feet had slowed, his hands were still so quick that I sometimes dropped my own gloves to watch him, dazzled. "Keep us those dukes," he warned.

"Never lower your guard." For two months I trained as though I had a boxer's heart.

Father issued our challenge by way of Olaf Magnuson's father, a strapping man with a voice like a roar in a barrel. "Hell yes, my boy'll fight," the elder Magnuson boomed.

On the morning appointed for our bout, Father strung rope from tree to tree in the yard, fashioning a ring that was shaped like a lozenge. My mother, who had been kept in the dark about the grudge match until that morning, raised Cain for a while; failing to make us see what fools we were, disgusted with the ways of men, she drove off to buy groceries. My sister carried word through the neighborhood, and within minutes a gaggle of kids and a scattering of bemused adults pressed against the ropes.

"You're going to make that lunkhead bawl in front of the whole world," Father told me in the kitchen while lacing my gloves. "You're going to make him call for his mama. Before you're done with him, he's going to swallow so many teeth that he'll never mess with you again."

So long as Father was talking, I believed him. I was a mean hombre. I was bad news, one fist of iron and the other one steel. When he finished his pep talk, however, and we stepped out into the sunshine, and I saw the crowd buzzing against the ropes, and I spied enormous Olaf slouching from his own kitchen door, my confidence hissed away like water on a hot griddle. In the seconds it took me to reach the ring, I ceased to feel like the bringer of bad news and began to feel like the imminent victim. I danced in my corner, eyeing Olaf. His torso, hulking above jeans and clodhopper boots, made my own scrawny frame look like a preliminary sketch for a body. I glanced down at my ropy arms, at my twiggy legs exposed below red gym shorts, at my hightopped basketball shoes, at the grass.

"He'll be slow," Father growled in my ear, "slow and clumsy. Keep moving. Bob and weave. Give him that left jab, watch for an opening, and then *bam*, unload with the right."

Not trusting my voice, I nodded, and kept shuffling my sneakers to hide the shivers.

Father put his palms to my cheeks and drew my face close to his and looked hard at me. Above that smushed, boneless nose, his brown eyes were as dark and shiny as those of a deer. "You okay, big guy?" he asked. "You ready for this?" I nodded again. "Then go get him," he said, turning me around and giving me a light shove toward the center of the ring.

I met Olaf there for instructions from the referee, a welder who lived down the road from us, a wiry man with scorched forearms who had just fixed our trailer hitch. I lifted my eyes reluctantly from Olaf's boots, along the trunks of his jean-clad legs, over the expanse of brawny chest and palooka jaw to his ice-blue eyes. They seemed less angry than amused.

A cowbell clattered. Olaf and I touched gloves, backed apart and lifted our mitts. The crowd sizzled against the ropes. Blood banged in my ears, yet I could hear Father yelling. I hear him still. And in memory I follow his advice. I bob, I weave, I guard my face with curled gloves, I feint and jab within the roped diamond, I begin to believe in myself, I circle my lummoxy rival and pepper him with punches, I feel a grin rising to my lips, and then Olaf tires of the game and rears back and knocks me flat. He also knocks me out. He also breaks my nose, which will remain crooked forever after. 37

That ended my boxing career. Olaf quit bullying me, perhaps because my blackout had given him a scare, perhaps because he had proved whatever he needed to prove. What I had shown my father was less clear. He may have seen weakness, may have seen a doomed and reckless bravery, may have seen a clown's pratfall. In any case, he never again urged me to clear the path with my fists. 38

And I have not offered boxing lessons to my son. Instead, I offered him the story of my defeat. When Jesse would still fit in my lap, I cuddled him there and told of my fight with Olaf, and he ran his delicate finger against the crook in my nose, as I had fingered the boneless pulp of Father's nose. I told Jesse about learning to play catch, the ball passing back and forth like a thread between my father and me, stitching us together. I told him about the time one of my pitches sailed over Father's head and shattered the windshield of our 1956 Ford, a car just three days old, and Father only shook his head and said, "Shoot, boy, you get that fastball down, and the batters won't see a thing but smoke." And I told Jesse about sitting on a feather tick in a Mississippi farmhouse, wedged between my father and grandfather, shaking with their excitement while before us on a tiny black-and-white television two boxers slammed and hugged each other. Cradling my boy, I felt how difficult it is for men to embrace without the liquor of violence, the tonic of pain. 39

Why do we play these games so avidly? All sports, viewed dispassionately, are dumb. The rules are arbitrary, the behaviors absurd. For boxing and running, perhaps, you could figure out evolutionary advantages. But what earthly use is it to become expert at swatting a ball with a length of wood or at lugging an inflated pigskin through a mob? Freudians might say that in playing with balls we men are simply toying with the prize portion of our anatomies. Darwinians might claim that we are competing for the attention of females, like so many preening peacocks or head-butting rams. Physicians might attribute the sporting frenzy to testosterone, economists might point to our dreams of profes- 40 sional paychecks, feminists might appeal to our machismo, philosophers to our fear of death.

No doubt all of those explanations, like buckets put out in the rain, 41 catch some of the truth. But none of them catches all of the truth. None of them explains, for example, what moves a boy to bang a rubber ball against a wall for hours, for entire summers, as my father did in his youth, as I did in mine, as Jesse still does. That boy, throwing and catching in the lee of garage or barn, dwells for a time wholly in his body, and that is reward enough. He aims the ball at a knothole, at a crack, then leaps to snag the rebound, mastering a skill, working himself into a trance. How different is his rapture from the dancing and drumming of a young brave? How different is his solitude from that of any boy seeking visions?

The less use we have for our bodies, the more we need reminding 42 that the body possesses its own way of knowing. To steal a line from Pascal: The body has its reasons that reason knows nothing of. Although we struggle lifelong to dwell in the flesh without rancor, without division between act and desire, we succeed only for moments at a time. We treasure whatever brings us those moments, whether it be playing cello or playing pool, making love or making baskets, kneading bread or nursing a baby or kicking a ball. Whoever teaches us an art or skill, whoever shows us a path to momentary wholeness, deserves our love.

I am conscious of my father's example whenever I teach a game to 43 my son. Demonstrating a stroke in tennis or golf, I amplify my gestures, like a ham actor playing to the balcony. My pleasure in the part is increased by the knowledge that others, and especially Father, have played it before me. What I know about hitting a curve or shooting a hook shot or throwing a left jab, I know less by words than by feel. When I take Jesse's hand and curl his fingers over the baseball's red stitches, explaining how to make it deviously spin, I feel my father's hands slip over mine like gloves. Move like so, like so. I feel the same ghostly guidance when I hammer nails or fix a faucet or pluck a banjo. Working on the house or garden or car, I find myself wearing more than my father's hands, find myself clad entirely in his skin.

One blistering afternoon when I was a year younger than Jesse is 44 now, a flyball arched toward me in center field. I ran under it, lifted my face and glove, and lost the ball in the sun. The ball found me, however, crashing into my eye. In the split second before blacking out I saw nothing but light. We need not go hunting pain, for pain will find us. It hurts me more to see Jesse ache than to break one of my own bones. I cry out as the ground ball bangs into his throat. I wince as he comes down crookedly with a rebound and turns his ankle. I wish to spare him injury as I wish to spare him defeat, but I could not do so even if I had never lobbed him that first fat pitch.

As Jesse nears thirteen, his estimate of my knowledge and my ₄₅ power declines rapidly. If I were a potter, say, or a carpenter, my skills would outreach his for decades to come. But where speed and stamina are the essence, a father in his forties will be overtaken by a son in his teens. Training for soccer, Jesse carries a stopwatch as he jogs around the park. I am not training for anything, only knocking rust from my joints and beguiling my heart, but I run along with him, puffing to keep up. I know that his times will keep going down, while I will never run faster than I do now. This is as it should be, for his turn has come. Slow as I am, and doomed to be slower, I relish his company.

In the game of catch, this dialogue of throw and grab we have been ₄₆ carrying on since he was old enough to crawl, Jesse has finally begun to put questions that I cannot answer. I know the answers; I can see how my back should twist, my legs should pump; but legs and back will no longer match my vision. This faltering is the condition of our lives, of course, a condition that will grow more acute with each passing year. I mean to live the present year before rushing off to any future ones. I mean to keep playing games with my son, so long as flesh will permit, as my father played games with me well past his own physical prime. Now that sports have begun to give me lessons in mortality, I realize they have also been giving me, all the while, lessons in immortality. These games, these contests, these grunting conversations of body to body, father to son, are not substitutes for some other way of being alive. They are the sweet and sweaty thing itself.

BERNARD COOPER

A Clack of Tiny Sparks:
Remembrances of a Gay Boyhood

Bernard Cooper (1951–   ) was born in Los Angeles and educated at the California Institute of the Arts, where he received both B.F.A. and M.F.A. degrees. He has been an instructor in creative writing at the Otis School of Art and Design in Los Angeles and at the Southern California Institute of Architecture. His first book, *Maps to Anywhere* (1990), is a collection of autobiographical essays, many of which explore his relationship with his father. His most recent book, *A Year of Rhymes* (1993), while largely about the sexual awakening of a teenager in the 1960s, is also somewhat autobiographical in that Cooper draws on his experience of coming to terms with the deaths of his three brothers. Cooper continues to publish essays and poems, most notably in *Grand Street, Harper's, Yale Review,* and *Kenyon Review.* "A Clack of Tiny Sparks" was first published in *Harper's* in January 1991.

Theresa Sanchez sat behind me in ninth-grade algebra. When Mr. 1 Hubbley faced the blackboard, I'd turn around to see what she was reading; each week a new book was wedged inside her copy of *Today's Equations.* The deception worked; from Mr. Hubbley's point of view, Theresa was engrossed in the value of *X*, but I knew otherwise. One week she perused *The Wisdom of the Orient,* and I could tell from Theresa's contemplative expression that the book contained exotic thoughts, guidelines handed down from high. Another week it was a paperback novel whose title, *Let Me Live My Life,* appeared in bold print atop every page, and whose cover, a gauzy photograph of a woman biting a strand of pearls, head thrown back in an attitude of ecstasy, confirmed my suspicion that Theresa Sanchez was mature beyond her years. She was the tallest girl in school. Her bouffant hairdo, streaked with blond, was higher than the flaccid bouffants of other girls. Her smooth skin, plucked eyebrows, and painted fingernails suggested hours of pampering, a worldly and sensual vanity that placed her within the domain of adults. Smiling dimly, steeped in daydreams, Theresa moved through the crowded halls with a languid, self-satisfied indifference to those around her. "You are merely children," her posture seemed to say. "I can't be bothered." The week Theresa hid *101 Ways to Cook Hamburger* behind her algebra book, I could stand it no longer and, after the bell rang, ventured a question.

"Because I'm having a dinner party," said Theresa. "Just a couple 2 of intimate friends."

No fourteen-year-old I knew had ever given a dinner party, let 3 alone used the word "intimate" in conversation. "Don't you have a mother?" I asked.

Theresa sighed a weary sigh, suffered my strange inquiry. "Don't 4 be so naive," she said. "Everyone has a mother." She waved her hand to indicate the brick school buildings outside the window. "A higher education should have taught you that." Theresa draped an angora sweater over her shoulders, scooped her books from the graffiti-covered desk, and just as she was about to walk away, she turned and asked me, "Are you a fag?"

There wasn't the slightest hint of rancor or condescension in her 5 voice. The tone was direct, casual. Still I was stunned, giving a sidelong glance to make sure no one had heard. "No," I said. Blurted really, with too much defensiveness, too much transparent fear in my response. Octaves lower than usual, I tried a "Why?"

Theresa shrugged. "Oh, I don't know. I have lots of friends who 6 are fags. You remind me of them." Seeing me bristle, Theresa added,

"It was just a guess." I watched her erect, angora back as she sauntered out the classroom door.

She had made an incisive and timely guess. Only days before, I'd   7
invited Grady Rogers to my house after school to go swimming. The instant Grady shot from the pool, shaking water from his orange hair, freckled shoulders shining, my attraction to members of my own sex became a matter I could no longer suppress or rationalize. Sturdy and boisterous and gap-toothed, Grady was an inveterate backslapper, a formidable arm wrestler, a wizard at basketball. Grady was a boy at home in his body.

My body was a marvel I hadn't gotten used to; my arms and legs   8
would sometimes act of their own accord, knocking over a glass at dinner or flinching at an oncoming pitch. I was never singled out as a sissy, but I could have been just as easily as Bobby Keagan, a gentle, intelligent, and introverted boy reviled by my classmates. And although I had always been aware of a tacit rapport with Bobby, a suspicion that I might find with him a rich friendship, I stayed away. Instead, I emulated Grady in the belief that being seen with him, being like him, would somehow vanquish my self-doubt, would make me normal by association.

Apart from his athletic prowess, Grady had been gifted with all the   9
trappings of what I imagined to be a charmed life: a fastidious, aproned mother who radiated calm, maternal concern; a ruddy, stoic father with a knack for home repairs. Even the Rogerses' small suburban house in Hollywood, with its spindly Colonial furniture and chintz curtains, was a testament to normalcy.

Grady and his family bore little resemblance to my clan of Eastern   10
European Jews, a dark and vociferous people who ate with abandon—matzo and halvah and gefilte fish; foods the goyim[1] couldn't pronounce—who cajoled one another during endless games of canasta, making the simplest remark about the weather into a lengthy philosophical discourse on the sun and the seasons and the passage of time. My mother was a chain-smoker, a dervish in a frowsy housedress. She showed her love in the most peculiar and obsessive ways, like spending hours extracting every seed from a watermelon before she served it in perfectly bite-sized, geometric pieces. Preoccupied and perpetually frantic, my mother succumbed to bouts of absentmindedness so profound she'd forget what she was saying midsentence, smile and blush and walk away. A divorce attorney, my father wore roomy, iridescent suits, and the intricacies, the deceits inherent in his profession, had the effect of making him forever tense and vigilant. He was "all wound up," as my mother put it. But when he relaxed, his laughter was explosive, his disposition prankish: "Walk this way," a waitress would say,

1. goyim: Gentile.

leading us to our table, and my father would mimic the way she walked, arms akimbo, hips liquid, while my mother and I were wracked with laughter. Buoyant or brooding, my parents' moods were unpredictable, and in a household fraught with extravagant emotion it was odd and awful to keep my longing secret.

One day I made the mistake of asking my mother what a "fag"   11
was. I knew exactly what Theresa had meant but hoped against hope it was not what I thought; maybe "fag" was some French word, a harmless term like "naive." My mother turned from the stove, flew at me, and grabbed me by the shoulders. "Did someone call you that?" she cried.

"Not me," I said. "Bobby Keagan."   12

"Oh," she said, loosening her grip. She was visibly relieved. And   13
didn't answer. The answer was unthinkable.

For weeks after, I shook with the reverberations from that afternoon   14
in the kitchen with my mother, pained by the memory of her shocked expression and, most of all, her silence. My longing was wrong in the eyes of my mother, whose hazel eyes were the eyes of the world, and if that longing continued unchecked, the unwieldy shape of my fate would be cast, and I'd be subjected to a lifetime of scorn.

During the remainder of the semester, I became the scientist of my   15
own desire, plotting ways to change my yearning for boys into a yearning for girls. I had enough evidence to believe that any habit, regardless of how compulsive, how deeply ingrained, could be broken once and for all: The plastic cigarette my mother purchased at the Thrifty pharmacy—one end was red to approximate an ember, the other tan like a filtered tip—was designed to wean her from the real thing. To change a behavior required self-analysis, cold resolve, and the substitution of one thing for another: plastic, say, for tobacco. Could I also find a substitute for Grady? What I needed to do, I figured, was kiss a girl and learn to like it.

This conclusion was affirmed one Sunday morning when my father,   16
seeing me wrinkle my nose at the pink slabs of lox he layered on a bagel, tried to convince me of its salty appeal. "You should try some," he said. "You don't know what you're missing."

"It's loaded with protein," added my mother, slapping a platter of   17
sliced onions onto the dinette table. She hovered above us, cinching her housedress, eyes wet from onion fumes, the mock cigarette dangling from her lips.

My father sat there chomping with gusto, emitting a couple of   18
hearty grunts to dramatize his satisfaction. And still I was not convinced. After a loud and labored swallow, he told me I may not be fond of lox today, but sooner or later I'd learn to like it. One's tastes, he assured me, are destined to change.

"Live," shouted my mother over the rumble of the Mixmaster. 19
"Expand your horizons. Try new things." And the room grew fragrant
with the batter of a spice cake.

The opportunity to put their advice into practice, and try out my 20
plan to adapt to girls, came the following week when Debbie Coburn,
a member of Mr. Hubbley's algebra class, invited me to a party. She
cornered me in the hall, furtive as a spy, telling me her parents would
be gone for the evening and slipping into my palm a wrinkled sheet of
notebook paper. On it were her address and telephone number, the
lavender ink in a tidy cursive. "Wear cologne," she advised, wary eyes
darting back and forth. "It's a make-out party. Anything can happen."

The Santa Ana wind blew relentlessly the night of Debbie's party, 21
careening down the slopes of the Hollywood hills, shaking the road
signs and stoplights in its path. As I walked down Beachwood Avenue,
trees thrashed, surrendered their leaves, and carob pods bombarded the
pavement. The sky was a deep but luminous blue, the air hot, abrasive,
electric. I had to squint in order to check the number of the Coburns'
apartment, a three-story building with glitter embedded in its stucco
walls. Above the honeycombed balconies was a sign that read
BEACHWOOD TERRACE in lavender script resembling Debbie's.

From down the hall, I could hear the plaintive strains of Little 22
Anthony's[2] "I Think I'm Going Out of My Head." Debbie answered the
door bedecked in an Empire dress, the bodice blue and orange polka
dots, the rest a sheath of black and white stripes. "Op art,"[3] proclaimed
Debbie. She turned in a circle, then proudly announced that she'd rolled
her hair in orange juice cans. She patted the huge unmoving curls and
dragged me inside. Reflections from the swimming pool in the court-
yard, its surface ruffled by wind, shuddered over the ceiling and walls.
A dozen of my classmates were seated on the sofa or huddled together
in corners, their whispers full of excited imminence, their bodies barely
discernible in the dim light. Drapes flanking the sliding glass doors
bowed out with every gust of wind, and it seemed that the room might
lurch from its foundations and sail with its cargo of silhouettes into the
hot October night.

Grady was the last to arrive. He tossed a six-pack of beer into 23
Debbie's arms, barreled toward me, and slapped my back. His hair was
slicked back with Vitalis, lacquered furrows left by the comb. The wind
hadn't shifted a single hair. "Ya ready?" he asked, flashing the gap
between his front teeth and leering into the darkened room. "You bet,"
I lied.

Once the beers had been passed around, Debbie provoked every- 24
one's attention by flicking on the overhead light. "Okay," she called.

2. Little Anthony: soul singer during the 1950s and 1960s.
3. Op art: optical art, mid-20th century geometric art that deals with optical illusions.

"Find a partner." This was the blunt command of a hostess determined to have her guests aroused in an orderly fashion. Everyone blinked, shuffled about, and grabbed a member of the opposite sex. Sheila Garabedian landed beside me—entirely at random, though I wanted to believe she was driven by passion—her timid smile giving way to plain fear as the light went out. Nothing for a moment but the heave of the wind and the distant banter of dogs. I caught a whiff of Sheila's perfume, tangy and sweet as Hawaiian Punch. I probed her face with my own, grazing the small scallop of an ear, a velvety temple, and though Sheila's trembling made me want to stop, I persisted with my mission until I found her lips, tightly sealed as a private letter. I held my mouth over hers and gathered her shoulders closer, resigned to the possibility that, no matter how long we stood there, Sheila would be too scared to kiss me back. Still, she exhaled through her nose, and I listened to the squeak of every breath as though it were a sigh of inordinate pleasure. Diving within myself, I monitored my heartbeat and respiration, trying to will stimulation into being, and all the while an image intruded, an image of Grady erupting from our pool, rivulets of water sliding down his chest. "Change," shouted Debbie, switching on the light. Sheila thanked me, pulled away, and continued her routine of gracious terror with every boy throughout the evening. It didn't matter whom I held—Margaret Sims, Betty Vernon, Elizabeth Lee—my experiment was a failure; I continued to picture Grady's wet chest, and Debbie would bellow "change" with such fervor, it could have been my own voice, my own incessant reprimand.

Our hostess commandeered the light switch for nearly half an hour. 25 Whenever the light came on, I watched Grady pivot his head toward the newest prospect, his eyebrows arched in expectation, his neck blooming with hickeys, his hair, at last, in disarray. All that shuffling across the carpet charged everyone's arms and lips with static, and eventually, between low moans and soft osculations, I could hear the clack of tiny sparks and see them flare here and there in the dark like meager, short-lived stars.

I saw Theresa, sultry and aloof as ever, read three more books— 26 *North American Reptiles*, *Bonjour Tristesse*, and *MGM: A Pictorial History*— before she vanished early in December. Rumors of her fate abounded. Debbie Coburn swore that Theresa had been "knocked up" by an older man, a traffic cop, she thought, or a grocer. Nearly quivering with relish, Debbie told me and Grady about the home for unwed mothers in the San Fernando Valley, a compound teeming with pregnant girls who had nothing to do but touch their stomachs and contemplate their mistake. Even Bobby Keagan, who took Theresa's place behind me in algebra, had a theory regarding her disappearance colored by his own wish for escape; he imagined that Theresa, disillusioned with society, booked passage to a tropical island, there to live out the rest of her days without restrictions or ridicule. "No wonder she flunked out of school," I overheard Mr. Hubbley tell a fellow teacher one afternoon. "Her head was always in a book."

Along with Theresa went my secret, or at least the dread that she   27 might divulge it, and I felt, for a while, exempt from suspicion. I was, however, to run across Theresa one last time. It happened during a period of torrential rain that, according to reports on the six o'clock news, washed houses from the hillsides and flooded the downtown streets. The halls of Joseph Le Conte Junior High were festooned with Christmas decorations: crepe-paper garlands, wreaths studded with plastic berries, and one requisite Star of David twirling above the atten-dance desk. In Arts and Crafts, our teacher, Gerald (he was the only teacher who allowed us—*required* us—to call him by his first name), handed out blocks of balsa wood and instructed us to carve them into bugs. We would paint eyes and antennae with tempera and hang them on a Christmas tree he'd made the previous night. "Voilà," he crooned, unveiling his creation from a burlap sack. Before us sat a tortured scrub, a wardrobe-worth of wire hangers that were bent like branches and soldered together. Gerald credited his inspiration to a Charles Addams[4] cartoon he'd seen in which Morticia, grimly preparing for the holidays, hangs vampire bats on a withered pine. "All that red and green," said Gerald. "So predictable. So *boring.*"

As I chiseled a beetle and listened to rain pummel the earth, Gerald   28 handed me an envelope and asked me to take it to Mr. Kendrick, the drama teacher. I would have thought nothing of his request if I hadn't seen Theresa on my way down the hall. She was cleaning out her locker, blithely dropping the sum of its contents—pens and textbooks and mimeographs—into a trash can. "Have a nice life," she sang as I passed. I mustered the courage to ask her what had happened. We stood alone in the silent hall, the reflections of wreaths and garlands submerged in brown linoleum.

"I transferred to another school. They don't have grades or bells,   29 and you get to study whatever you want." Theresa was quick to sense my incredulity. "Honest," she said. "The school is progressive." She gazed into a glass cabinet that held the trophies of track meets and intramural spelling bees. "God," she sighed, "this place is so . . . bar-baric." I was still trying to decide whether or not to believe her story when she asked me where I was headed. "Dear," she said, her exclama-tion pooling in the silence, "that's no ordinary note, if you catch my drift." The envelope was blank and white; I looked up at Theresa, baffled. "Don't be so naive," she muttered, tossing an empty bottle of

4. Charles Addams: 20th-century cartoonist whose work, as he says, "specializes in making the fantastic and absurd seem entirely commonplace."

nail polish into the trash can. It struck bottom with a resolute thud. "Well," she said, closing her locker and breathing deeply, "bon voyage." Theresa swept through the double doors and in seconds her figure was obscured by rain.

As I walked toward Mr. Kendrick's room, I could feel Theresa's 30 insinuation burrow in. I stood for a moment and watched Mr. Kendrick through the pane in the door. He paced intently in front of the class, handsome in his shirt and tie, reading from a thick book. Chalked on the blackboard behind him was THE ODYSSEY BY HOMER. I have no recollection of how Mr. Kendrick reacted to the note, whether he accepted it with pleasure or embarrassment, slipped it into his desk drawer or the pocket of his shirt. I have scavenged that day in retrospect, trying to see Mr. Kendrick's expression, wondering if he acknowledged me in any way as his liaison. All I recall is the sight of his mime through a pane of glass, a lone man mouthing an epic, his gestures ardent in empty air.

Had I delivered a declaration of love? I was haunted by the need 31 to know. In fantasy, a kettle shot steam, the glue released its grip, and I read the letter with impunity. But how would such a letter begin? Did the common endearments apply? This was a message between two men, a message for which I had no precedent, and when I tried to envision the contents, apart from a hasty, impassioned scrawl, my imagination faltered.

Once or twice I witnessed Gerald and Mr. Kendrick walk together 32 into the faculty lounge or say hello at the water fountain, but there was nothing especially clandestine or flirtatious in their manner. Besides, no matter how acute my scrutiny, I wasn't sure, short of a kiss, exactly what to look for—what semaphore of gesture, what encoded word. I suspected there were signs, covert signs that would give them away, just as I'd unwittingly given myself away to Theresa.

In the school library, a *Webster's* unabridged dictionary lay on a 33 wooden podium, and I padded toward it with apprehension; along with clues to the bond between my teachers, I risked discovering information that might incriminate me as well. I had decided to consult the dictionary during lunch period, when most of the students would be on the playground. I clutched my notebook, moving in such a way as to appear both studious and nonchalant, actually believing that, unless I took precautions, someone would see me and guess what I was up to. The closer I came to the podium, the more obvious, I thought, was my endeavor; I felt like the model of The Visible Man in our science class, my heart's undulations, my overwrought nerves legible through transparent skin. A couple of kids riffled through the card catalogue. The librarian, a skinny woman whose perpetual whisper and rubber-soled shoes caused her to drift through the room like a phantom, didn't seem to register my presence. Though I'd looked up dozens of words before, the pages felt strange beneath my fingers. *Homer* was the first word I saw. *Hominid. Homogenize.* I feigned interest and skirted other words before I found the word I was after. Under the heading HO · MO · SEX · U · AL was the terse definition: *adj. Pertaining to, characteristic of, or exhibiting homosexuality.—n. A homosexual person.* I read the definition again and again, hoping the words would yield more than they could. I shut the dictionary, swallowed hard, and, none the wiser, hurried away.

As for Gerald and Mr. Kendrick, I never discovered evidence to prove or dispute Theresa's claim. By the following summer, however, I had overheard from my peers a confounding amount about homosexuals: They wore green on Thursday, couldn't whistle, hypnotized boys with a piercing glance. To this lore, Grady added a surefire test to ferret them out.

"A test?" I said.

"You ask a guy to look at his fingernails, and if he looks at them like this"—Grady closed his fingers into a fist and examined his nails with manly detachment—"then he's okay. But if he does this"—he held out his hands at arm's length, splayed his fingers, and coyly cocked his head—"you'd better watch out." Once he'd completed his demonstration, Grady peeled off his shirt and plunged into our pool. I dove in after. It was early June, the sky immense, glassy, placid. My father was cooking spareribs on the barbecue, an artist with a basting brush. His apron bore the caricature of a frazzled French chef. Mother curled on a chaise longue, plumes of smoke wafting from her nostrils. In a stupor of contentment she took another drag, closed her eyes, and arched her face toward the sun.

Grady dog-paddled through the deep end, spouting a fountain of chlorinated water. Despite shame and confusion, my longing for him hadn't diminished; it continued to thrive without air and light, like a luminous fish in the dregs of the sea. In the name of play, I swam up behind him, encircled his shoulders, astonished by his taut flesh. The two of us flailed, pretended to drown. Beneath the heavy press of water, Grady's orange hair wavered, a flame that couldn't be doused.

I've lived with a man for seven years. Some nights, when I'm half-asleep and the room is suffused with blue light, I reach out to touch the expanse of his back, and it seems as if my fingers sink into his skin, and I feel the pleasure a diver feels the instant he enters a body of water.

I have few regrets. But one is that I hadn't said to Theresa, "Of course I'm a fag." Maybe I'd have met her friends. Or become friends with her. Imagine the meals we might have concocted: hamburger Stroganoff, Swedish meatballs in a sweet translucent sauce, steaming slabs of Salisbury steak.

NOEL PERRIN

The Androgynous Man

Noel Perrin (1927–   ) teaches English and Environmental Studies
at Dartmouth College, farms, and writes essays, which are collected
in *A Passport Secretly Green* (1961), *First Person Rural* (1978), *Second
Person Rural* (1980), *Third Person Rural* (1983), and *Last Person Rural*
(1991). He also takes a lively interest in literature that lies somewhat
off the beaten path. His *Dr. Bowdler's Legacy* (1970) is a history of
expurgated books, and *A Reader's Delight* (1988) contains essays on
meritorious works so unfamiliar that many of them are out of print.
Recently Perrin has focused his attention on the environment. In response to a student who made note of his driving to work in a "gas-
guzzling pickup," Perrin bought an electric car; a book resulted, *Solo:
Life with an Electric Car* (1993), which has been the subject of numerous
reviews in environmental, literary, and automobile magazines. "The
Androgynous Man" appeared in the "About Men" column of *The New
York Times Magazine* on February 5, 1984.

The summer I was 16, I took a train from New York to Steamboat   1
Springs, Colo., where I was going to be assistant horse wrangler at a
camp. The trip took three days, and since I was much too shy to talk
to strangers, I had quite a lot of time for reading. I read all of *Gone with
the Wind*. I read all the interesting articles in a couple of magazines I
had, and then I went back and read all the dull stuff. I also took all the
quizzes, a thing of which magazines were even fuller then than now.

The one that held my undivided attention was called "How Mascu-   2
line/Feminine Are You?" It consisted of a large number of inkblots.
The reader was supposed to decide which of four objects each blot most
resembled. The choices might be a cloud, a steam engine, a caterpillar
and a sofa.

When I finished the test, I was shocked to find that I was barely   3
masculine at all. On a scale of 1 to 10, I was about 1.2. Me, the horse
wrangler? (And not just wrangler, either. That summer, I had to skin
a couple of horses that died—the camp owner wanted the hides.)

The results of that test were so terrifying to me that for the first   4
time in my life I did a piece of original analysis. Having unlimited time
on the train, I looked at the "masculine" answers over and over, trying
to find what it was that distinguished real men from people like me—
and eventually I discovered two very simple patterns. It was "masculine" to think the blots looked like man-made objects, and "feminine"
to think they looked like natural objects. It was masculine to think they
looked like things capable of causing harm, and feminine to think of
innocent things.

Even at 16, I had the sense to see that the compilers of the test were using rather limited criteria—maleness and femaleness are both more complicated than *that*—and I breathed a huge sigh of relief. I wasn't necessarily a wimp, after all.

That the test did reveal something other than the superficiality of its makers I realized only many years later. What it revealed was that there is a large class of men and women both, to which I belong, who are essentially androgynous. That doesn't mean we're gay, or low in the appropriate hormones, or uncomfortable performing the jobs traditionally assigned our sexes. (A few years after that summer, I was leading troops in combat and, unfashionable as it now is to admit this, having a very good time. War is exciting. What a pity the 20th century went and spoiled it with high-tech weapons.)

What it does mean to be spiritually androgynous is a kind of freedom. Men who are all-male, or he-man, or 100 percent red-blooded Americans, have a little biological set that causes them to be attracted to physical power, and probably also to dominance. Maybe even to watching football. I don't say this to criticize them. Completely masculine men are quite often wonderful people: good husbands, good (though sometimes overwhelming) fathers, good members of society. Furthermore, they are often so unself-consciously at ease in the world that other men seek to imitate them. They just aren't as free as us androgynes. They pretty nearly have to be what they are; we have a range of choices open.

The sad part is that many of us never discover that. Men who are not 100 percent red-blooded Americans—say, those who are only 75 percent red-blooded—often fail to notice their freedom. They are too busy trying to copy the he-men ever to realize that men, like women, come in a wide variety of acceptable types. Why this frantic imitation? My answer is mere speculation, but not casual. I have speculated on this for a long time.

Partly they're just envious of the he-man's unconscious ease. Mostly they're terrified of finding that there may be something wrong with them deep down, some weakness at the heart. To avoid discovering that, they spend their lives acting out the role that the he-man naturally lives. Sad.

One thing that men owe to the women's movement is that this kind of failure is less common than it used to be. In releasing themselves from the single ideal of the dependent woman, women have more or less incidentally released a lot of men from the single ideal of the dominant male. The one mistake the feminists have made, I think, is in supposing that *all* men need this release, or that the world would be a better place if all men achieved it. It wouldn't. It would just be duller.

So far I have been pretty vague about just what the freedom of the androgynous man is. Obviously it varies with the case. In the case I

know best, my own, I can be quite specific. It has freed me most as a
parent. I am, among other things, a fairly good natural mother. I like
the nurturing role. It makes me feel good to see a child eat—and it
turns me to mush to see a 4-year-old holding a glass with both small
hands, in order to drink. I even enjoyed sewing patches on the knees
of my daughter Amy's Dr. Dentons when she was at the crawling stage.
All that pleasure I would have lost if I had made myself stick to the
notion of the paternal role that I started with.

Or take a smaller and rather ridiculous example. I feel free to kiss   12
cats. Until recently it never occurred to me that I would want to, though
my daughters have been doing it all their lives. But my elder daughter
is now 22, and in London. Of course, I get to look after her cat while
she is gone. He's a big, handsome farm cat named Petrushka, very
unsentimental, though used from kittenhood to being kissed on the top
of the head by Elizabeth. I've gotten very fond of him (he's the adventurous kind of cat who likes to climb hills with you), and one night I
simply felt like kissing him on the top of the head, and did. Why did
no one tell me sooner how silky cat fur is?

Then there's my relation to cars. I am completely unembarrassed   13
by my inability to diagnose even minor problems in whatever object I
happen to be driving, and don't have to make some insider's remark to
mechanics to try to establish that I, too, am a "Man With His Machine."

The same ease extends to household maintenance. I do it, of course.   14
Service people are expensive. But for the last decade my house has functioned better than it used to because I've had the aid of a volume called
"Home Repairs Any Woman Can Do," which is pitched just right for people at my technical level. As a youth, I'd as soon have touched such a book
as I would have become a transvestite. Even though common sense says
there is really nothing sexual whatsoever about fixing sinks.

Or take public emotion. All my life I have easily been moved by   15
certain kinds of voices. The actress Siobhan McKenna's, to take a notable case. Give her an emotional scene in a play, and within 10 words
my eyes are full of tears. In boyhood, my great dread was that someone
might notice. I struggled manfully, you might say, to suppress this
weakness. Now, of course, I don't see it as a weakness at all, but as a
kind of fulfillment. I even suspect that the true he-men feel the same
way, or one kind of them does, at least, and it's only the poor imitators
who have to struggle to repress themselves.

Let me come back to the inkblots, with their assumption that mas-   16
culine equates with machinery and science, and feminine with art and
nature. I have no idea whether the right pronoun for God is He, She,
or It. But this I'm pretty sure of. If God could somehow be induced to
take that test, God would not come out macho, and not feminismo,
either, but right in the middle. Fellow androgynes, it's a nice thought.

Answering the Howl

Stephen Harrigan (1948–   ) grew up in Texas, graduated from the
University of Texas in 1970, and works today in Austin as a senior
editor at *Texas Monthly*, a position he has held since 1983. His first
publication, fittingly, was the introduction to *Contemporary Texas: A
Photographic Portrait*, but he went on to publish several articles in *The
Atlantic Monthly, Esquire*, and *The New York Times Magazine*, as well as
three books. His novel *Aransas* (1980) was well received because of
its realism, particularly in its descriptions of the lives of dolphins. *A
Natural State* appeared in 1988, and *Water and Light*, a history of the
Caribbean coral reef, in 1992. Recently Harrigan has made a name for
himself as a travel writer, reporting on his mountain climbing and
underwater adventures for such magazines as *Travel Holiday, Life* magazine, *The New Yorker*, and *Audubon*. "Answering the Howl" was published in *The New York Times Magazine* on April 14, 1991.

He comes down from three months alone in the mountains, his   1
eyes wary and haunted, his nerves already jangly from the prospect of
city life. Though he does not speak of it, he had a rough time up there
in the tundra. He may yet lose a toe to frostbite, and his famous dog
with the eerie, colorless eyes—Denali—has disappeared in a lightning
storm.

His hands are frightful: the thick nails opaque as parchment, the   2
knuckles swollen and scraped, the span of the fingers unnaturally wide
from gripping perilous handholds on the cliff face. He chipped a front
tooth in a fall down a scree slope, and when you try to engage him in
conversation he has a distracting habit of sucking air against the exposed nerve just to feel the pain. He is courteous but skittish, full of
bitter wisdom and secret thoughts. His first night back in the city, unable
to sleep, he walks out into the yard at 3 in the morning, lies down in
the cold grass and weeps for his lost dog.

Now that's my idea of a man.   3

I've always wanted to be one of these guys: a lone wolf, austere and   4
independent, a secular saint of the wilderness. As a teen-ager, sporting
glasses, braces, global acne and Lee's "Husky" jeans, I found it consoling to think of myself in years to come as a solitary wanderer, impatient
with civilization, indifferent to comfort, lulled by the sounds of howling
beasts.

And yet, here you find me: lining up a putt on the tricky Tyranno-   5
saurus Rex hole at Peter Pan Golf; sitting out in the backyard chucking
PupPeroni snacks to an overstimulated and mentally deficient dog; set-

ting aside "Walden" to read a newspaper article about Ted Danson's
hairpiece.

The fact is, I was never really lone-wolf material, though I tried   6
hard to cultivate an air of lofty solitude. When I was in my early 20's,
I told one and all that I would be leaving any day for the Big Thicket.
The Big Thicket! I wasn't exactly sure what this place was—knowing
only that it was a dense swath of primeval forest in East Texas—but
the name excited my lone-wolf imagination. I would melt into the Big
Thicket for six months, eight months, a year, and then emerge from it
as skittish as a panther, my soul on fire and my mind full of hard-won
lore.

But I kept putting off the moment of departure, thinking of all the   7
upcoming movies I would miss and starting to wonder what exactly I
would be doing out there in the woods all day by myself. "You're still
here?" friends would exclaim when they saw me. "I heard you were
living in the Big Thicket!"

Finally, to save face, I went. It was August, the worst time to set   8
foot in a steaming East Texas forest. For two days I tramped around
the sloughs and baygalls, ate beef jerky and cookies and mopped the
sweat out of my eyes with a dish towel. The woods were gloomy and
dark, filled with undifferentiated trees and odious fungi. I had no interest in them. I had thought I would teach myself the names and habits
of every woodland creature, but I just sat there in my tent, crestfallen,
counting the hours till it might be respectable for me to return home.
The awful truth assaulted me: I was not a lone wolf after all. I was a
lonely wolf.

I have known this about myself for quite a few years now, but have   9
never lost my fascination with this role I was never destined to play.
The other day I was reading a biography of John Muir, the great naturalist who was, for my money, the ultimate lone wolf. Muir was a
brilliant, passionate, crotchety man, his handsome features obscured by
a beard as wild and scraggly as a bird's nest. His great love was Yosemite
Valley, with which he was locked in a lifelong spiritual embrace that
made his human-to-human relationships a mere afterthought. He was
famous for climbing a Douglas spruce in the middle of a violent lightning storm high in the mountains, where he swayed back and forth in
the topmost branches and howled in crazy happiness. He filled his pen
with sequoia sap and wrote rapturous letters to his friends—"Ink cannot tell the glow that lights me at this moment. . . . Hotels and human
impurity will be far below. I will fuse in spirit skies." Once, a beautiful
French writer came to Yosemite, hired Muir as her guide, made him
the main character in a novel and chased after him for months, but
Muir would not submit. "His all-consuming passion for the wilderness," writes a biographer, "lay like a sword between himself and love
for any woman."

Few lone wolves have ever been as kinkily celibate as Muir ("The   10
King tree and I have sworn eternal love . . ."), but when it comes to
women you will find most lone wolves on the wary end of the scale.
They are caught between the desire to be a lusty animal and the fear
of becoming a caged beast. At every moment they are nervously reckoning the potential limits to their freedom. Usually they are not secretive
about this apprehension, which they refer to chivalrously as "a weakness" or "a problem I seem to have." However—since they are walking
advertisements of domestic catastrophe—they do not really regard it
as their fault that women find their remoteness, their ethereal self-
absorption so alluring. In fact, I think, they *are* blameless. Lone wolves
are not, after all, ski bums. The true lone wolf is selfish but pure. He
sees a woman not as a conquest but as a source of temporary consolation, someone who will give him strength as he trudges along on his
epic spiritual errand.

What is that errand exactly? Lone wolves are often articulate—and   11
can be good talkers once you break through their many layers of shyness and reserve—but chances are they can't tell you what they're
looking for. Let's give them the benefit of the doubt and say that they
are not running away from responsibility but heading incrementally
toward salvation. They paddle their sea kayaks through the islands of
British Columbia. They rappel precipitous rock walls to monitor the
welfare of peregrine-falcon chicks. They set up their tepees in the cottonwoods, eat a button or two of peyote and wait for their spirit animals
to pay them a visit. They are not fooling around. Their lives are mis-
sions. Nature has spoken their names and called them into her embrace.

I've noticed that lone wolves, in the ripeness of their years, often   12
settle down finally and make adorable husbands. (It even happened to
John Muir.) Maybe for an armchair lone wolf like me the process works
in reverse. Every now and then, faintly, I think I hear my name being
called again. And why not? Maybe one day I will grow intolerably
restless and, as if in a trance, get down my backpack from the attic and
slip out of the house, leaving a note stuck to the refrigerator with
a Bart Simpson magnet—"Gone to the Brooks Range. Back whenever."
From time to time I will send home pressed Alpine flowers and surprisingly adequate sketches of marmots. "You should never have married
that jerk," my wife's friends will tell her. "Yeah," she'll say, "but it's
my own fault. I knew the first time I laid eyes on him that he was a
real lone wolf."

ALICE MUNRO

Boys and Girls

Alice Munro (1931–   ) is a Canadian-born writer who began producing stories at age twelve while growing up on her father's fox farm.
Re-creating the world of her childhood, Munro's works often examine
the lives of women in small-town Ontario. She began writing short
stories partly because raising three children left her too little time to
undertake a novel but also because the short story genre allows her
to present "intense, but not connected, moments of experience." Her
works include *Lives of Girls and Women* (1971), *Something I've Been
Meaning to Tell You* (1974), *The Beggar Maid* (1984), and *The Progress
of Love* (1986). Her eighth book of short stories, *Open Secrets,* was
published in 1994. Winner of three Canadian Governor General's
Awards, Munro is also popular in the United States, where she is a
frequent contributor to such magazines as *The New Yorker* and *The
Atlantic Monthly.* "Boys and Girls" was first collected in *Dance of the
Happy Shades* (1968). Munro continues to live near her childhood
home in Ontario, where, in addition to writing, she has recently taken
up an amateur acting career.

My father was a fox farmer. That is, he raised silver foxes, in pens;   1
and in the fall and early winter, when their fur was prime, he killed
them and skinned them and sold their pelts to the Hudson's Bay Company or the Montreal Fur Traders. These companies supplied us with
heroic calendars to hang, one on each side of the kitchen door. Against
a background of cold blue sky and black pine forests and treacherous
northern rivers, plumed adventurers planted the flags of England or of
France; magnificent savages bent their backs to the portage.

For several weeks before Christmas, my father worked after supper   2
in the cellar of our house. The cellar was whitewashed, and lit by a
hundred-watt bulb over the worktable. My brother Laird and I sat on
the top step and watched. My father removed the pelt inside-out from
the body of the fox, which looked surprisingly small, mean and rat-like,
deprived of its arrogant weight of fur. The naked, slippery bodies were
collected in a sack and buried at the dump. One time the hired man,
Henry Bailey, had taken a swipe at me with his sack saying, "Christmas
present!" My mother thought that was not funny. In fact she disliked
the whole pelting operation—that was what the killing, skinning, and
preparation of the furs was called—and wished it did not have to
take place in the house. There was the smell. After the pelt had been
stretched inside-out on a long board my father scraped away delicately,
removing the little clotted webs of blood vessels, the bubbles of fat; the
smell of blood and animal fat, with the strong primitive odour of the

fox itself, penetrated all parts of the house. I found it reassuringly seasonal, like the smell of oranges and pine needles.

Henry Bailey suffered from bronchial troubles. He would cough   3
and cough until his narrow face turned scarlet, and his light blue, derisive eyes filled up with tears; then he took the lid off the stove, and,
standing well back, shot out a great clot of phlegm—hsss—straight into
the heart of the flames. We admired him for this performance and for
his ability to make his stomach growl at will, and for his laughter,
which was full of high whistlings and gurglings and involved the whole
faulty machinery of his chest. It was sometimes hard to tell what he
was laughing at, and always possible that it might be us.

After we had been sent to bed we could still smell fox and still hear   4
Henry's laugh, but these things, reminders of the warm, safe, brightly
lit downstairs world, seemed lost and diminished, floating on the stale
cold air upstairs. We were afraid at night in the winter. We were not
afraid of *outside* though this was the time of year when snowdrifts curled
around our house like sleeping whales and the wind harassed us all
night, coming up from the buried fields, the frozen swamp, with its old
bugbear chorus of threats and misery. We were afraid of *inside*, the
room where we slept. At this time the upstairs of our house was not
finished. A brick chimney went up one wall. In the middle of the floor
was a square hole, with a wooden railing around it; that was where
the stairs came up. On the other side of the stairwell were the things
that nobody had any use for any more—a soldiery roll of linoleum,
standing on end, a wicker baby carriage, a fern basket, china jugs and
basins with cracks in them, a picture of the Battle of Balaclava, very
sad to look at. I had told Laird, as soon as he was old enough to
understand such things, that bats and skeletons lived over there; whenever a man escaped from the county jail, twenty miles away, I imagined
that he had somehow let himself in the window and was hiding behind
the linoleum. But we had rules to keep us safe. When the light was on,
we were safe as long as we did not step off the square of worn carpet
which defined our bedroom-space; when the light was off no place was
safe but the beds themselves. I had to turn out the light kneeling on
the end of my bed, and stretching as far as I could to reach the cord.

In the dark we lay on our beds, our narrow life rafts, and fixed our   5
eyes on the faint light coming up the stairwell, and sang songs. Laird
sang "Jingle Bells," which he would sing any time, whether it was
Christmas or not, and I sang "Danny Boy." I loved the sound of my
own voice, frail and supplicating, rising in the dark. We could make
out the tall frosted shapes of the windows now, gloomy and white.
When I came to the part, *When I am dead, as dead I well may be*—a fit
of shivering caused not by the cold sheets but by pleasurable emotion
almost silenced me. *You'll kneel and say, an Ave there above me*— What
was an Ave? Every day I forgot to find out.

Laird went straight from singing to sleep. I could hear his long, ₆
satisfied, bubbly breaths. Now for the time that remained to me, the
most perfectly private and perhaps the best time of the whole day, I
arranged myself tightly under the covers and went on with one of the
stories I was telling myself from night to night. These stories were about
myself, when I had grown a little older; they took place in a world that
was recognizably mine, yet one that presented opportunities for courage, boldness and self-sacrifice, as mine never did. I rescued people
from a bombed building (it discouraged me that the real war had gone
on so far away from Jubilee). I shot two rabid wolves who were menac-
ing the schoolyard (the teachers cowered terrified at my back). I rode
a fine horse spiritedly down the main street of Jubilee, acknowledging the townspeople's gratitude for some yet-to-be-worked-out piece
of heroism (nobody ever rode a horse there, except King Billy in the
Orangemen's Day parade).[1] There was always riding and shooting in
these stories, though I had only been on a horse twice—bareback because we did not own a saddle—and the second time I had slid right
around and dropped under the horse's feet; it had stepped placidly
over me. I really was learning to shoot, but I could not hit anything
yet, not even tin cans on fence posts.

Alive, the foxes inhabited a world my father made for them. It was ₇
surrounded by a high guard fence, like a medieval town, with a gate
that was padlocked at night. Along the streets of this town were ranged
large, sturdy pens. Each of them had a real door that a man could go
through, a wooden ramp along the wire, for the foxes to run up and
down on, and a kennel—something like a clothes chest with airholes—
where they slept and stayed in winter and had their young. There were
feeding and watering dishes attached to the wire in such a way that
they could be emptied and cleaned from the outside. The dishes were
made of old tin cans, and the ramps and kennels of odds and ends of
old lumber. Everything was tidy and ingenious; my father was tirelessly
inventive and his favourite book in the world was Robinson Crusoe.
He had fitted a tin drum on a wheelbarrow, for bringing water down
to the pens. This was my job in summer, when the foxes had to have
water twice a day. Between nine and ten o'clock in the morning, and
again after supper, I filled the drum at the pump and trundled it down
through the barnyard to the pens, where I parked it, and filled my
watering can and went along the streets. Laird came too, with his little
cream and green gardening can, filled too full and knocking against his

1. King Billy: William III of Great Britain, also known as the Prince of Orange, whose
coronation in 1689 ensured that Britain would become a Protestant nation and a parlia-
mentary democracy.

legs and slopping water on his canvas shoes. I had the real watering can, my father's, though I could only carry it three-quarters full.

The foxes all had names, which were printed on a tin plate and hung beside their doors. They were not named when they were born, but when they survived the first year's pelting and were added to the breeding stock. Those my father had named were called names like Prince, Bob, Wally and Betty. Those I had named were called Star or Turk, or Maureen or Diana. Laird named one Maud after a hired girl we had when he was little, one Harold after a boy at school, and one Mexico, he did not say why.

Naming them did not make pets out of them, or anything like it. Nobody but my father ever went into the pens, and he had twice had blood-poisoning from bites. When I was bringing them their water they prowled up and down on the paths they had made inside their pens, barking seldom—they saved that for nighttime, when they might get up a chorus of community frenzy—but always watching me, their eyes burning, clear gold, in their pointed, malevolent faces. They were beautiful for their delicate legs and heavy, aristocratic tails and the bright fur sprinkled on dark down their backs—which gave them their name—but especially for their faces, drawn exquisitely sharp in pure hostility, and their golden eyes.

Besides carrying water I helped my father when he cut the long grass, and the lamb's quarter and flowering money-musk, that grew between the pens. He cut with the scythe and I raked into piles. Then he took a pitchfork and threw fresh-cut grass all over the top of the pens, to keep the foxes cooler and shade their coats, which were browned by too much sun. My father did not talk to me unless it was about the job we were doing. In this he was quite different from my mother, who, if she was feeling cheerful, would tell me all sorts of things—the name of a dog she had had when she was a little girl, the names of boys she had gone out with later on when she was grown up, and what certain dresses of hers had looked like—she could not imagine now what had become of them. Whatever thoughts and stories my father had were private, and I was shy of him and would never ask him questions. Nevertheless I worked willingly under his eyes, and with a feeling of pride. One time a feed salesman came down into the pens to talk to him and my father said, "Like to have you meet my new hired man." I turned away and raked furiously, red in the face with pleasure.

"Could of fooled me," said the salesman. "I thought it was only a girl."

After the grass was cut, it seemed suddenly much later in the year. I walked on stubble in the earlier evening, aware of the reddening skies, the entering silences, of fall. When I wheeled the tank out of the gate and put the padlock on, it was almost dark. One night at this time I saw my mother and father standing talking on the little rise of ground we called the gangway, in front of the barn. My father had just come from the meathouse; he had his stiff bloody apron on, and a pail of cut-up meat in his hand.

It was an odd thing to see my mother down at the barn. She did not often come out of the house unless it was to do something—hang out the wash or dig potatoes in the garden. She looked out of place, with her bare lumpy legs, not touched by the sun, her apron still on and damp across the stomach from the supper dishes. Her hair was tied up in a kerchief, wisps of it falling out. She would tie her hair up like this in the morning, saying she did not have time to do it properly, and it would stay tied up all day. It was true, too; she really did not have time. These days our back porch was piled with baskets of peaches and grapes and pears, bought in town, and onions and tomatoes and cucumbers grown at home, all waiting to be made into jelly and jam and preserves, pickles and chili sauce. In the kitchen there was a fire in the stove all day, jars clinked in boiling water, sometimes a cheese-cloth bag was strung on a pole between two chairs, straining blue-black grape pulp for jelly. I was given jobs to do and I would sit at the table peeling peaches that had been soaked in the hot water, or cutting up onions, my eyes smarting and streaming. As soon as I was done I ran out of the house, trying to get out of earshot before my mother thought of what she wanted me to do next. I hated the hot dark kitchen in summer, the green blinds and the flypapers, the same old oilcloth table and wavy mirror and bumpy linoleum. My mother was too tired and preoccupied to talk to me, she had no heart to tell about the Normal School Graduation Dance; sweat trickled over her face and she was always counting under her breath, pointing at jars, dumping cups of sugar. It seemed to me that work in the house was endless, dreary and peculiarly depressing; work done out of doors, and in my father's serv-ice, was ritualistically important. 13

I wheeled the tank up to the barn, where it was kept, and I heard my mother saying, "Wait till Laird gets a little bigger, then you'll have a real help." 14

What my father said I did not hear. I was pleased by the way he stood listening, politely as he would to a salesman or a stranger, but with an air of wanting to get on with his real work. I felt my mother had no business down here and I wanted him to feel the same way. What did she mean about Laird? He was no help to anybody. Where was he now? Swinging himself sick on the swing, going around in circles, or trying to catch caterpillars. He never once stayed with me till I was finished. 15

"And then I can use her more in the house," I heard my mother 16 say. She had a dead-quiet, regretful way of talking about me that always made me uneasy. "I just get my back turned and she runs off. It's not like I had a girl in the family at all."

I went and sat on a feedbag in the corner of the barn, not wanting   17
to appear when this conversation was going on. My mother, I felt, was not to be trusted. She was kinder than my father and more easily fooled, but you could not depend on her, and the real reasons for the things she said and did were not to be known. She loved me, and she sat up late at night making a dress of the difficult style I wanted, for me to wear when school started, but she was also my enemy. She was always plotting. She was plotting now to get me to stay in the house more, although she knew I hated it (*because* she knew I hated it) and keep me from working for my father. It seemed to me she would do this simply out of perversity, and to try her power. It did not occur to me that she could be lonely, or jealous. No grown-up could be; they were too fortunate. I sat and kicked my heels monotonously against a feedbag, raising dust, and did not come out till she was gone.

At any rate, I did not expect my father to pay any attention to what   18
she said. Who could imagine Laird doing my work—Laird remembering the padlock and cleaning out the watering-dishes with a leaf on the end of a stick, or even wheeling the tank without it tumbling over? It showed how little my mother knew about the way things really were.

I have forgotten to say what the foxes were fed. My father's bloody   19
apron reminded me. They were fed horsemeat. At this time most farmers still kept horses, and when a horse got too old to work, or broke a leg or got down and would not get up, as they sometimes did, the owner would call my father, and he and Henry went out to the farm in the truck. Usually they shot and butchered the horse there, paying the farmer from five to twelve dollars. If they had already too much meat on hand, they would bring the horse back alive, and keep it for a few days or weeks in our stable, until the meat was needed. After the war the farmers were buying tractors and gradually getting rid of horses altogether, so it sometimes happened that we got a good healthy horse, that there was just no use for any more. If this happened in the winter we might keep the horse in our stable till spring, for we had plenty of hay and if there was a lot of snow—and the plow did not always get our road cleared—it was convenient to be able to go to town with a horse and cutter.

The winter I was eleven years old we had two horses in the stable.   20
We did not know what names they had before, so we called them Mack and Flora. Mack was an old black workhorse, sooty and indifferent. Flora was a sorrel mare, a driver. We took them both out in the cutter. Mack was slow and easy to handle. Flora was given to fits of violent alarm, veering at cars and even at other horses, but we loved her speed

and high-stepping, her general air of gallantry and abandon. On Saturdays we went down to the stable and as soon as we opened the door on its cosy, animal-smelling darkness Flora threw up her head, rolled her eyes, whinnied despairingly and pulled herself through a crisis of nerves on the spot. It was not safe to go into her stall; she would kick.

This winter also I began to hear a great deal more on the theme my mother had sounded when she had been talking in front of the barn. I no longer felt safe. It seemed that in the minds of the people around me there was a steady undercurrent of thought, not to be deflected, on this one subject. The word *girl* had formerly seemed to me innocent and unburdened, like the word *child;* now it appeared that it was no such thing. A girl was not, as I had supposed, simply what I was; it was what I had to become. It was a definition, always touched with emphasis, with reproach and disappointment. Also it was a joke on me. Once Laird and I were fighting, and for the first time ever I had to use all my strength against him; even so, he caught and pinned my arm for a moment, really hurting me. Henry saw this, and laughed, saying, "Oh, that there Laird's gonna show you, one of these days!" Laird was getting a lot bigger. But I was getting bigger too. **21**

My grandmother came to stay with us for a few weeks and I heard other things. "Girls don't slam doors like that." "Girls keep their knees together when they sit down." And worse still, when I asked some questions, "That's none of girls' business." I continued to slam the doors and sit as awkwardly as possible, thinking that by such measures I kept myself free. **22**

When spring came, the horses were let out in the barnyard. Mack stood against the barn wall trying to scratch his neck and haunches, but Flora trotted up and down and reared at the fences, clattering her hooves against the rails. Snow drifts dwindled quickly, revealing the hard grey and brown earth, the familiar rise and fall of the ground, plain and bare after the fantastic landscape of winter. There was a great feeling of opening-out, of release. We just wore rubbers now, over our shoes; our feet felt ridiculously light. One Saturday we went out to the stable and found all the doors open, letting in the unaccustomed sunlight and fresh air. Henry was there, just idling around looking at his collection of calendars which were tacked up behind the stalls in a part of the stable my mother had probably never seen. **23**

"Come to say goodbye to your old friend Mack?" Henry said. "Here, you give him a taste of oats." He poured some oats into Laird's cupped hands and Laird went to feed Mack. Mack's teeth were in bad shape. He ate very slowly, patiently shifting the oats around in his mouth, trying to find a stump of a molar to grind it on. "Poor old Mack," said Henry mournfully. "When a horse's teeth's gone, he's gone. That's about the way." **24**

"Are you going to shoot him today?" I said. Mack and Flora had **25**

been in the stable so long I had almost forgotten they were going to be
shot.

Henry didn't answer me. Instead he started to sing in a high, trem- 26
bly, mocking-sorrowful voice, *Oh, there's no more work, for poor Uncle
Ned, he's gone where the good darkies go.* Mack's thick, blackish tongue
worked diligently at Laird's hand. I went out before the song was ended
and sat down on the gangway.

I had never seen them shoot a horse, but I knew where it was 27
done. Last summer Laird and I had come upon a horse's entrails before
they were buried. We had thought it was a big black snake, coiled up
in the sun. That was around in the field that ran up beside the barn. I
thought that if we went inside the barn, and found a wide crack or
knothole to look through, we would be able to see them do it. It was
not something I wanted to see; just the same, if a thing really happened,
it was better to see it, and know.

My father came down from the house, carrying the gun. 28

"What are you doing here?" he said. 29

"Nothing." 30

"Go on up and play around the house." 31

He sent Laird out of the stable. I said to Laird, "Do you want to 32
see them shoot Mack?" and without waiting for an answer led him
around to the front door of the barn, opened it carefully, and went in.
"Be quiet or they'll hear us," I said. We could hear Henry and my
father talking in the stable, then the heavy, shuffling steps of Mack
being backed out of his stall.

In the loft it was cold and dark. Thin, crisscrossed beams of sunlight 33
fell through the cracks. The hay was low. It was a rolling country, hills
and hollows, slipping under our feet. About four feet up was a beam
going around the walls. We piled hay up in one corner and I boosted
Laird up and hoisted myself. The beam was not very wide; we crept
along it with our hands flat on the barn walls. There were plenty of
knotholes, and I found one that gave me the view I wanted—a corner
of the barnyard, the gate, part of the field. Laird did not have a knothole
and began to complain.

I showed him a widened crack between two boards. "Be quiet and 34
wait. If they hear you you'll get us in trouble."

My father came in sight carrying the gun. Henry was leading Mack 35
by the halter. He dropped it and took out his cigarette papers and
tobacco; he rolled cigarettes for my father and himself. While this was
going on Mack nosed around in the old, dead grass along the fence.
Then my father opened the gate and they took Mack through. Henry
led Mack away from the path to a patch of ground and they talked
together, not loud enough for us to hear. Mack again began searching
for a mouthful of fresh grass, which was not to be found. My father
walked away in a straight line, and stopped short at a distance which

seemed to suit him. Henry was walking away from Mack too, but sideways, still negligently holding on to the halter. My father raised the
gun and Mack looked up as if he had noticed something and my father
shot him.

Mack did not collapse at once but swayed, lurched sideways and   36
fell, first on his side; then he rolled over on his back and, amazingly,
kicked his legs for a few seconds in the air. At this Henry laughed, as
if Mack had done a trick for him. Laird, who had drawn a long, groaning breath of surprise when the shot was fired, said out loud, "He's not
dead." And it seemed to me it might be true. But his legs stopped, he
rolled on his side again, his muscles quivered and sank. The two men
walked over and looked at him in a businesslike way; they bent down
and examined his forehead where the bullet had gone in, and now I
saw his blood on the brown grass.

"Now they just skin him and cut him up," I said. "Let's go." My   37
legs were a little shaky and I jumped gratefully down into the hay.
"Now you've seen how they shoot a horse," I said in a congratulatory
way, as if I had seen it many times before. "Let's see if any barn cat's
had kittens in the hay." Laird jumped. He seemed young and obedient
again. Suddenly I remembered how, when he was little, I had brought
him into the barn and told him to climb the ladder to the top beam.
That was in the spring, too, when the hay was low. I had done it out
of a need for excitement, a desire for something to happen so that I
could tell about it. He was wearing a little bulky brown and white
checked coat, made down from one of mine. He went all the way up,
just as I told him, and sat down on the top beam with the hay far below
him on one side, and the barn floor and some old machinery on the
other. Then I ran screaming to my father, "Laird's up on the top beam!"
My father came, my mother came, my father went up the ladder talking
very quietly and brought Laird down under his arm, at which my
mother leaned against the ladder and began to cry. They said to me,
"Why weren't you watching him?" but nobody ever knew the truth.
Laird did not know enough to tell. But whenever I saw the brown and
white checked coat hanging in the closet, or at the bottom of the rag
bag, which was where it ended up, I felt a weight in my stomach, the
sadness of unexorcized guilt.

I looked at Laird who did not even remember this, and I did not   38
like the look on this thin, winter-pale face. His expression was not
frightened or upset, but remote, concentrating. "Listen," I said, in an
unusually bright and friendly voice, "you aren't going to tell, are you?"

"No," he said absently.   39

"Promise."   40

"Promise," he said. I grabbed the hand behind his back to make   41
sure he was not crossing his fingers. Even so, he might have a nightmare; it might come out that way. I decided I had better work hard to

get all thoughts of what he had seen out of his mind—which, it seemed to me, could not hold very many things at a time. I got some money I had saved and that afternoon we went into Jubilee and saw a show, with Judy Canova, at which we both laughed a great deal. After that I thought it would be all right.

Two weeks later I knew they were going to shoot Flora. I knew   42
from the night before, when I heard my mother ask if the hay was holding out all right, and my father said, "Well, after to-morrow there'll just be the cow, and we should be able to put her out to grass in another week." So I knew it was Flora's turn in the morning.

This time I didn't think of watching it. That was something to see   43
just one time. I had not thought about it very often since, but sometimes when I was busy, working at school, or standing in front of the mirror combing my hair and wondering if I would be pretty when I grew up, the whole scene would flash into my mind: I would see the easy, practised way my father raised the gun, and hear Henry laughing when Mack kicked his legs in the air. I did not have any great feeling of horror and opposition, such as a city child might have had; I was too used to seeing the death of animals as a necessity by which we lived. Yet I felt a little ashamed, and there was a new wariness, a sense of holding-off, in my attitude to my father and his work.

It was a fine day, and we were going around the yard picking up   44
tree branches that had been torn off in winter storms. This was something we had been told to do, and also we wanted to use them to make a teepee. We heard Flora whinny, and then my father's voice and Henry's shouting, and we ran down to the barnyard to see what was going on.

The stable door was open. Henry had just brought Flora out, and   45
she had broken away from him. She was running free in the barnyard, from one end to the other. We climbed up on the fence. It was exciting to see her running, whinnying, going up on her hind legs, prancing and threatening like a horse in a Western movie, an unbroken ranch horse, though she was just an old driver, an old sorrel mare. My father and Henry ran after her and tried to grab the dangling halter. They tried to work her into a corner, and they had almost succeeded when she made a run between them, wild-eyed, and disappeared around the corner of the barn. We heard the rails clatter down as she got over the fence, and Henry yelled, "She's into the field now!"

That meant she was in the long L-shaped field that ran up by the   46
house. If she got around the center, heading towards the lane, the gate was open; the truck had been driven into the field this morning. My father shouted to me, because I was on the other side of the fence, nearest the lane, "Go shut the gate!"

I could run very fast. I ran across the garden, past the tree where   47
our swing was hung, and jumped across a ditch into the lane. There

was the open gate. She had not got out, I could not see her up on the
road; she must have run to the other end of the field. The gate was
heavy. I lifted it out of the gravel and carried it across the roadway. I
had it half-way across when she came in sight, galloping straight towards me. There was just time to get the chain on. Laird came scrambling through the ditch to help me.

Instead of shutting the gate, I opened it as wide as I could. I did   48
not make any decision to do this; it was just what I did. Flora never
slowed down; she galloped straight past me, and Laird jumped up and
down, yelling, "Shut it, shut it!" even after it was too late. My father
and Henry appeared in the field a moment too late to see what I had
done. They only saw Flora heading for the township road. They would
think I had not got there in time.

They did not waste any time asking about it. They went back to   49
the barn and got the gun and knives they used, and put these in the
truck; then they turned the truck around and came bouncing up the
field toward us. Laird called to them, "Let me go too, let me go too!"
and Henry stopped the truck and they took him in. I shut the gate after
they were all gone.

I supposed Laird would tell. I wondered what would happen to   50
me. I had never disobeyed my father before, and I could not understand
why I had done it. Flora would not really get away. They would catch
up with her in the truck. Or if they did not catch her this morning
somebody would see her and telephone us this afternoon or tomorrow.
There was no wild country here for her to run to, only farms. What
was more, my father had paid for her, we needed the meat to feed the
foxes, we needed the foxes to make our living. All I had done was
make more work for my father who worked hard enough already. And
when my father found out about it he was not going to trust me any
more; he would know that I was not entirely on his side. I was on
Flora's side, and that made me no use to anybody, not even to her.
Just the same, I did not regret it; when she came running at me and I
held the gate open, that was the only thing I could do.

I went back to the house, and my mother said, "What's all the   51
commotion?" I told her that Flora had kicked down the fence and got
away. "Your poor father," she said, "now he'll have to go chasing over
the countryside. Well, there isn't any use planning dinner before one."
She put up the ironing board. I wanted to tell her, but thought better
of it and went upstairs and sat on my bed.

Lately I had been trying to make my part of the room fancy, spread-   52
ing the bed with old lace curtains, and fixing myself a dressing-table
with some leftovers of cretonne for a skirt. I planned to put up some
kind of barricade between my bed and Laird's, to keep my section
separate from his. In the sunlight, the lace curtains were just dusty rags.
We did not sing at night any more. One night when I was singing Laird

said, "You sound silly," and I went right on but the next night I did not start. There was not so much need to anyway, we were no longer afraid. We knew it was just old furniture over there, old jumble and confusion. We did not keep to the rules. I still stayed awake after Laird was asleep and told myself stories, but even in these stories something different was happening, mysterious alterations took place. A story might start off in the old way, with a spectacular danger, a fire or wild animals, and for a while I might rescue people; then things would change around, and instead, somebody would be rescuing me. It might be a boy from our class at school, or even Mr. Campbell, our teacher, who tickled girls under the arms. And at this point the story concerned itself at great length what what I looked like—how long my hair was, and what kind of dress I had on; by the time I had these details worked out the real excitement of the story was lost.

It was later than one o'clock when the truck came back. The tarpau- 53
lin was over the back, which meant there was meat in it. My mother had to heat dinner up all over again. Henry and my father had changed from their bloody overalls into ordinary working overalls in the barn, and they washed their arms and necks and faces at the sink, and splashed water on their hair and combed it. Laird lifted his arm to show off a streak of blood. "We shot old Flora," he said, "and cut her up in fifty pieces."

"Well I don't want to hear about it," my mother said. "And don't 54
come to my table like that."

My father made him go and wash the blood off. 55

We sat down and my father said grace and Henry pasted his chew- 56
ing-gum on the end of his fork, the way he always did; when he took it off he would have us admire the pattern. We began to pass the bowls of steaming, overcooked vegetables. Laird looked across the table at me and said proudly, distinctly, "Anyway it was her fault Flora got away."

"What?" my father said. 57

"She could of shut the gate and she didn't. She just open' it up and 58
Flora run out."

"Is that right?" my father said. 59

Everybody at the table was looking at me. I nodded, swallowing 60
food with great difficulty. To my shame, tears flooded my eyes.

My father made a curt sound of disgust. "What did you do that 61
for?"

I did not answer. I put down my fork and waited to be sent from 62
the table, still not looking up.

But this did not happen. For some time nobody said anything, then 63
Laird said matter-of-factly, "She's crying."

"Never mind," my father said. He spoke with resignation, even 64
good humour, the words which absolved and dismissed me for good. "She's only a girl," he said.

I didn't protest that, even in my heart. Maybe it was true. 65

ELIZABETH BARRETT BROWNING

A Musical Instrument

Elizabeth Barrett Browning (1806–1861) was probably the most popular female poet in England during the nineteenth century, far more
famous than her husband, Robert Browning, during her lifetime. Subjected to poor health and an overly protective father, Elizabeth Barrett
lived much of her life as an invalid. At the age of forty, she eloped
with Browning, and the two lived in Italy for several years. There
Barrett Browning regained her health, became involved in Italian politics, produced a large volume of poetry, and raised their son. For many
years, Barrett Browning was best known for her love poems, collected
in *Sonnets from the Portuguese* (1850) and praised for their moral integrity. More recently, however, critics have turned their attention to
poems such as *Aurora Leigh* (1857), a lengthy narrative poem that
portrays an artist as a young woman, refusing marriage to pursue her
own career. Barrett Browning was not an outspoken advocate for
women's rights, but twentieth-century critics are finding in poems
like *Aurora Leigh* and "A Musical Instrument" (1860) evidence of her
concern for each woman's right to choose and shape her own identity.

> What was he doing, the great god Pan,[1]   1
>   Down in the reeds by the river?
> Spreading ruin and scattering ban,
> Splashing and paddling with hoofs of a goat,
> And breaking the golden lilies afloat
>   With the dragon-fly on the river.
>
> He tore out a reed, the great god Pan,   2
>   From the deep cool bed of the river:
> The limpid water turbidly ran,
> And the broken lilies a-dying lay,
> And the dragon-fly had fled away,
>   Ere he brought it out of the river.
>
> High on the shore sat the great god Pan   3
>   While turbidly flowed the river;
> And hacked and hewed as a great god can,
> With his hard bleak steel at the patient reed,
> Till there was not a sign of the leaf indeed
>   To prove it fresh from the river.

---

1. Pan: In Greek mythology, god of fields and flocks, who is represented as half-man,
half-goat; pursued by Pan, the nymph Syrinx was changed into a reed, from which Pan
made his famous musical pipe.

He cut it short, did the great god Pan,　　　　　　　　4
　　(How tall it stood in the river!)
Then drew the pith, like the heart of a man,
Steadily from the outside ring,
And notched the poor dry empty thing
　　In holes, as he sat by the river.

"This is the way," laughed the great god Pan　　　　　5
　　(Laughed while he sat by the river),
"The only way, since gods began
To make sweet music, they could succeed."
Then, dropping his mouth to a hole in the reed,
　　He blew in power by the river.

Sweet, sweet, sweet, O Pan!　　　　　　　　　　　6
　　Piercing sweet by the river!
Blinding sweet, O great god Pan!
The sun on the hill forgot to die,
And the lilies revived, and the dragon-fly
　　Came back to dream on the river.

Yet half a beast is the great god Pan,　　　　　　　7
　　To laugh as he sits by the river,
Making a poet out of a man:
The true gods sigh for the cost and pain,—
For the reed which grows nevermore again
　　As a reed with the reeds in the river.

COMMUNITIES

We find ourselves in a place we call home.

Communities: Preview

Has a philosopher like you failed to discover that our country is more to be valued and higher and holier far than mother or father or any ancestor, and more to be regarded in the eyes of the gods and of men of understanding?

It was a rough place to get along in, the center, but my mother said that I needed to be be'd with and she needed to not be with me, so I went. . . . I looked into one of those not-quite-white folders and saw that I was from a deviant family in a deviant neighborhood.

He is all pine and I am apple orchard.
My apple trees will never get across
And eat the cones under his pines, I tell him.
He only says, 'Good fences make good neighbors.'

Overview and Ideas for Writing

There is no such thing as an independent ant. The caste distinctions in the colony are so strict that the specialists in reproduction—the blimplike queens and feeble males—would perish without the aid of the female workers and soldiers. But there is more to it than feeding and breeding. Take a worker out of the nest and put her in a separate jar with food and water and dirt to dig in. Sheer loneliness will make her disorganized and lazy. Her productivity (which entomologists have measured in volume of dirt moved) will drop to a fraction of what it had been. Whether kept alone or with only half a dozen others, she will pine away for the bustle of the community and will die prematurely.

Humans are not ants, of course, but we too are tribal creatures, dependent for health and happiness on the family and community even when we are most eager to assert our independence. Aristotle saw this interdependence 2,500 years ago and declared that "man is a political animal," a creature designed to live in the *polis,* the community. "The person who by nature, not by accident, does not belong to a *polis* is either a wild animal or a god."

In this unit are eight essays, a story, and a poem, all concerned with the connections between individuals and the communities to which they are attached by birth or by choice. Three of the essayists—Karla Holloway, Scott Momaday, and Barry Lopez—remember their childhood homes. Two—Meredith Maran and Gretel Ehrlich—describe the places they have chosen to live their adult lives. David Guterson takes a more detached view of a place he would clearly prefer *not* to call home. Like the personal essays in the unit, Toni Cade Bambara's short story "The Hammer Man" gives us a "close-in" view of the social and emotional life of a particular neighborhood, while Robert Frost's poem "Mending Wall" provides both a snapshot of life in rural New England and an opportunity to consider the edge where neighborliness and independence meet.

The most philosophical selections in the unit are about the ancient Greek notion of community. H. D. F. Kitto's chapter on the Greek polis and Plato's *Crito* give us an opportunity to compare our own feelings about our city or town with the robust civic spirit that convinced Socrates that it was better to die as an Athenian than live as an exile.

You will have had your own experiences living in communities, and you should have your own thoughts about how these communities functioned, how they helped define who you are. These personal experiences and reflections could become the basis of a first-person essay that casts a light on some of the questions raised in this unit: How do we separate ourselves from our homes and neighborhoods? How do we rebuild the bridges we have burned in the process? How do we make a new community our home? Or you may want to go beyond your personal experience to discuss these issues more broadly, examining how the American ant (by reputation a rugged individualist) is connected to her colony.

Mean Streets

Meredith Maran (1951–   ), expelled from Bronx High School of Science in 1968 for editing an underground newspaper, never attended college. After raising goats and corn in New Mexico, she moved to Berkeley, California, where, she reports, "I shaved my armpits and went off to organize the proletariat" in Bay Area factories. A move to the Silicon Valley to organize high-tech workers and write magazine stories ended unhappily: Her marriage "was shattered by the stress of raising two babies in the utter isolation of the San Jose suburbs." In 1987 she became the editor of the Banana Republic catalogue and "got hooked on a new recipe for changing the world: progressive business." Since then she has worked with such socially responsible companies as Working Assets, Smith & Hawken, and Ben & Jerry's. Her first book, *How Would You Feel If Your Dad Was Gay?* (1991), was coauthored with her lover, Ann Heron; her second, *What It's Like to Live Now* (1995), includes the following essay, first published in *The Utne Reader*, March-April 1993.

This is how it usually starts: I see a headline in the paper or one of 1 our cars gets broken into or I'm in bed overhearing an argument on the street and wondering whether or when to call 911. Then my throat constricts and the thought erupts: "I want to move away from here."

This is how it started this morning: The kids 2 and I walked together to the Ashby Bay Area Rapid Transit (BART) station, they to take the Concord train to their junior high school; I to board the San Francisco train to work. Inside the station, two BART cops are talking to a boy 12 or 13, about the age of my oldest son, Peter. The boy is crying and covering one eye with his hand. I glance at my kids. They've both got that

> Maran's style depends heavily on rhythms created by repetition, as in the repeated phrase that opens this paragraph. Where else do you see her using this technique?

studied "shit happens" look on their downy little faces. How could this be? I moved to California to raise my kids so they wouldn't grow up to be crime-glazed New Yorkers. Now they're more jaded than I am.

"He got beat up," Peter says flatly, slicing through my denial of 3 that same thought.

"At 8:00 in the *morning*," I mutter, and immediately regret my words. 4 Peter exhales loudly, shakes his flat-topped head, and gives me a long-suffering, eternally patient frown. "Mom," he begins, and I know I'm in for it. "People get beat up here all the time. Teenagers hang around in the parking lot and wait for white kids to beat up. We're used to it. Why do you make such a big deal out of every little thing?"

This is how it starts, the self-berating that builds on its own momen- 5
tum. I can't believe I'm raising my kids like this. How can I call myself
a mother when I can't even keep my kids safe? How can they turn out
to be sweet, sensitive men when the life I've given them requires such
callousness, such denial, such smooth, detached responses to daily fear
and horror? How did I let this happen—to them, to me?

Moments later I embark on the San Francisco train, alone. 6

The morning newspaper headline says "7 murders in 24 hours jolt 7
Oakland." Oakland, I remind myself needlessly, is where I have
entrenched myself—where I own a house and pay
taxes and send my children to school. I imagine
my richer, wiser, and infinitely more fortunate
friends in more exclusive neighborhoods, reading
that headline and wondering what the hell Meredith's problem is, anyway. When will she ever get
over that outdated commitment to raising her kids
in a "mixed" (meaning mostly black and poor)
neighborhood and move somewhere *safe*, already?

Here a voice other than
Maran's enters the essay.
How would you describe
the owner of this voice?
How many other voices, in
quotation marks or out, do
you detect in the essay?

The train pulls into the West Oakland station, which is outdoors 8
and elevated, providing me with a sweeping view
of what the 1989 earthquake left behind after it
compressed 45 people into bone and blood on the
Cypress freeway: two cement platforms suspended
100 feet above the ground, neatly sliced off by the
demolition crews that cleared the crushed cars and
people from the shattered interchange.

The earthquake is a natural
disaster, unrelated to urban
culture. Should Maran have
included it in the essay?

Since the earthquake, every moment of stillness has felt to me like 9
a warning, a gathering of the forces of disaster preparing for the next
strike—a brief cease-fire between the sounds of
overpowered, undermuffled cars screaming
through the streets with cop cars in hot pursuit;
between diagnoses of AIDS and cancer in people I
count on for my happiness; between dark rainy
nights when my kids come home a few minutes
late to find me shaking with terror and rage.

Compare this cityscape with
that in Barry Lopez's "Manhattan, 1976."

This is how it goes on from here: "I've got to get away from Oak- 10
land, get safe. I'll put the kids in private school, move to New Mexico,
Vermont, Marin County. . . ."

Eight years ago I divorced my husband and 11
uprooted my children from suburban San Jose,
where we never locked our doors and a car
break-in was a gossipworthy neighborhood event.
I wanted to raise my kids in what I then referred
to as "the real world." I wanted them to know
people who weren't white. I wanted neighbors
who didn't wear bras.

Notice the transition here,
signaling a flashback to an
earlier time. Would it have
been better for Maran to
present her material in
straight chronological order,
beginning with the divorce?

And so, after five years in the stucco tracts of San Jose, I put my $10,000 divorce settlement down on an $80,000 cottage near the Berkeley-Oakland city line and hurtled myself and my kids into the closest thing to a '60s life I could construct. 12

I put Peter and Jesse into an Oakland public school and went to endless meetings to make sure their education was politically, if not academically, correct. I rode my bicycle to the market and rode home with my backpack full of exotic lettuces and basil-garlic baguettes. I helped organize our neighborhood watch association. I took my kids to puppet shows about Nicaragua at the neighborhood community center whose walls were papered with fliers announcing solidarity marches, multicultural day-care centers, and incest-survivor support groups. 13

I got to know my neighbors, the mix I'd dreamed of: long-haired carpenter guys and short-haired carpenter women, friendly Southern black men whose grandchildren played double-Dutch on the sidewalk, a coven of pagans who danced with flutes in their adjoining backyards, a couple of lesbian chiropractors—and never mind about the crack house up the block or the speed freaks across the street, or the unemployed young man next door who rattled both our houses and our brains with pounding rap music all day while I sat at my computer trying to earn a living as a writer. 14

I slept with a crowbar next to my bed for the first few months and then installed a burglar alarm in my house. But for the first time since I'd moved away from Haight-Ashbury in 1972 and embarked on a course that led me, eventually, to 10 years of union organizing and living among white working-class people who'd never met a Jew, let alone a communist, I felt again that I was living among my people. 15

Five years later I sold the first house for $185,000—an inadvertent beneficiary of the Bay Area real estate boom—and bought a three-story Victorian a few blocks away, big enough so that after six years together my lover, Ann, and I could live under the same roof, and Peter and Jesse would each have his own door to shut. 16

Now, I find myself considering another move, one that must honestly be called white flight. 17

As my parents did, and as I scorned them for doing. I find myself yearning for the good and safe old days. "Just" a few years ago I never leashed my dog, locked my car, hesitated to take a walk alone at night. 18

Compare the activities that build a community in Karla Holloway's "The Thursday Ladies."

What is Maran's attitude toward her earlier self? How does it show?

This sentence is 101 words long. Can you write a comparable 100-word sentence describing a neighborhood you think (or once thought) ideal? Try patterning your sentence on Maran's phrase by phrase.

See David Guterson's "No Place Like Home" for a picture of the kind of community Maran might find herself in.

As my parents did, and as I came of age swearing I would never 19
do, I find myself worrying about who my children's role models and
friends are, and why my children choose them, and what these strangers might teach or convince my children to do.

As my parents did, and as I never could imag- 20
ine myself doing, I find myself turning to money as

Is it self-evident why the
12-year-olds are wearing
beepers? Why doesn't
Maran explain?
---

the balm for my fears. I resolve to earn or somehow
acquire more of it: money to move into a neighborhood—or, better yet, a town—in which beepers
are worn by pediatricians, not 12-year-olds; in
which the silence of night is not shattered by explosions of gunfire or the rattling of shopping carts filled with rags and
bottles being pushed down the street; in which bicycles are left un-
chained outside shops that do not have cast-iron bars on their windows,
and teenagers speak politely to each other's parents on the telephone.

As my parents did, I have uttered aloud on several occasions the 21
two words I swore I'd never say—"private school." My politically correct commitment to "fighting to make the public schools work" has
been replaced by the indignation of a taxpayer at the failure of the
schools to make their own damn selves work.

How have I come to this? 22

Is it that, despite all I'd sworn would never happen to me, the 23
upper-middle-class values I ingested along with baby formula from sterilized bottles have curdled and congealed in my nearly middle-aged
soul?

See H. D. F. Kitto's "The Polis" for a suggestion that life
in a big city has been seen
as intolerable for 2,500
years.

Is it that life in the city—any city, but most 24
certainly the one I live in—has simply gotten expo-
nentially worse (along with my fears) since I
moved here eight years ago?

And whatever the source of these fears—not 25
just the risks in my life but the death of all I've
believed in—what can I do about it now?

What *should* I do about it now? 26

At whom are these ques-
tions directed? What is their
tone? Are they effective?

Would I be happier, would I feel like a better 27
mother, would I *be* a better mother if I sent my kids
off on mountain bikes to the very nearly all-white
school I used to pass every morning on my way to
work in wealthy, suburban Mill Valley?

Would my kids be happier? 28

Driving through a small California town one 29
night on our way to a weekend in the moun-

Compare Jesse's version of
country life with that of
Gretel Ehrlich in "Wy-
oming."
---

tains, I dreamily ask Peter and Jesse, "Wouldn't
you love to move to the country? Where people
are friendly and we wouldn't have to be afraid all
the time?" "Yeah, right, Mom," answers Jesse,

rolling his eyes in the rearview mirror. "Then we could hang out in the 7-Eleven parking lot every Friday night and smoke cigarettes. Sounds really great."

"But what's so much better about living where we live?" I persist. 30
"What do you do on Friday nights that's so exciting?"

"I couldn't live without Telegraph," says 31
Jesse of the famous avenue in Berkeley on

Why does Maran include so much explanation of what Telegraph Avenue is and was?

which many anti-war demonstrations were held, where his father was shot while throwing tear gas grenades back at the National Guardsmen who'd fired them at him, where today homeless panhandlers extend their begging cups from sleeping bags stretched across the sidewalk, and Jesse is regularly threatened and occasionally robbed by the boys he beats at video games.

During a family trip to New York last summer, Peter overheard me 32
muttering to myself that I could have chosen a worse place than Oakland to raise my kids. "I'm

Is Peter right?

glad I grew up in Oakland, Mom," he said. "Now I'm prepared for anything. If I decide I want to live in New York someday, I know I'll be able to handle myself."

I'm anchored now in the city I chose, the 33
life I chose all those years and decisions ago,

How strong is this anchor? Compare the anchor in Scott Momaday's "The Way to Rainy Mountain."

because it's not just me, not just my lover and me, who live in it. This is the place and the life, the streets and the people my children know and therefore the place and the life they want to be in, and they are old enough to say that they don't want to be wrenched away from.

I remember the night a year ago when Peter, at age 12, requested 34
(and was denied) the right to carry a knife, for self-protection, to junior high school. "I didn't raise you guys to believe in violence," I declared.

"Make up your mind, Mom," replied my 35
clear-eyed son. "If you didn't want us to grow up this way, you shouldn't have raised us in this

Compare Peter's attitude with that of the narrator in Toni Cade Bambara's "The Hammer Man."

neighborhood."

Make up my mind, indeed. 36

Backed into a '90s corner by my '60s poli- 37
tics, I am forced to admit that my greatest motivator is no longer militant anger, but fear—the fear that is the truest mark of the privileged class and culture into which I was born, the fear that screams self-righteously, "But I'm entitled to better!"

And I must admit that what I am desperately seeking is no longer   38
the most effective way to fight and overcome what is wrong in my
world, or anyone else's. Now, like the generals in the latter days of the
Vietnam War, I'm looking for nothing more noble than an honorable
escape.

DAVID GUTERSON

No Place Like Home
On the manicured streets of a master-planned community

David Guterson (1951–   ), who lives on Bainbridge Island near
Seattle, seems intensely interested in the ways people inhabit their
environments, natural or artificial. He has written about fishing in
Clear Lake (the crater of Mount Saint Helens) for *Sports Illustrated* and
on shopping in Minneapolis's Mall of America for *Harper's*. In 1989
he published a collection of short stories titled, significantly, *The Country Ahead of Us, the Country Behind Us*. Despite being a teacher in a
public high school, he believes that home is the right environment for
his four children to learn in, and in 1993 he explained his reasons in
Family Matters: Why Homeschooling Makes Sense. *Snow Falling on Cedars*,
a novel set in Washington's San Juan Islands, followed the next year.
Travel writer Pico Iyer praised the novel for presenting "one fully
researched scene after another—gill netters at work, an autopsy, digging for geoduck clams." The same curiosity about the details of a
community's life show in the following essay from *Harper's*, November
1991.

To the casual eye, Green Valley, Nevada, a corporate master-   1
planned community just south of Las Vegas, would appear to be a
pleasant place to live. On a Sunday last April—a week before the riots
in Los Angeles and related disturbances in Las Vegas—the golf carts
were lined up three abreast at the upscale "Legacy" course; people in
golf outfits on the clubhouse veranda were eating three-cheese omelets
and strawberry waffles and looking out over the palm trees and fairways, talking business and reading Sunday newspapers. In nearby Park-
side Village, one of Green Valley's thirty-five developments, a few
homeowners washed cars or boats or pulled up weeds in the sun. Cars

wound slowly over clean broad streets, ferrying children to swimming pools and backyard barbecues and Cineplex matinees. At the Silver Springs tennis courts, a well-tanned teenage boy in tennis togs pummeled his sweating father. Two twelve-year-old daredevils on expensive mountain bikes, decked out in Chicago Bulls caps and matching tank tops, watched and ate chocolate candies.

Green Valley is as much a verb as a noun, a place in the process of becoming what it purports to be. Everywhere on the fringes of its 8,400 acres one finds homes going up, developments going in (another twenty-one developments are under way), the desert in the throes of being transformed in accordance with the master plan of Green Valley's designer and builder, the American Nevada Corporation. The colors of its homes are muted in the Southwest manner: beiges, tans, dun browns, burnt reds, olive grays, rusts, and cinnamons. Its graceful, palm-lined boulevards and parkways are conspicuously devoid of gas stations, convenience stores, and fast-food restaurants, presenting instead a seamless facade of interminable, well-manicured developments punctuated only by golf courses and an occasional shopping plaza done in stucco. Within the high walls lining Green Valley's expansive parkways lie homes so similar they appear as uncanny mirror reflections of one another—and, as it turns out, they are. In most neighborhoods a prospective homeowner must choose from among a limited set of models with names like "Greenbriar," "Innisbrook," and "Tammaron" (or, absurdly, in a development called Heartland, "Beginnings," "Memories," and "Reflections"), each of which is merely a variation on a theme: Spanish, Moorish, Mexican, Territorial, Mediterranean, Italian Country, Mission. Each development inhabits a planned socio-economic niche—$99,000, $113,900, $260,000 homes, and on into the stratosphere for custom models if a wealthy buyer desires. Neighborhoods are labyrinthine, confusing in their sameness; each block looks eerily like the next. On a spring evening after eight o'clock it is possible to drive through miles of them without seeing a single human being. Corners are marked with signs a visitor finds more than a little disconcerting: WARNING, they read, NEIGHBORHOOD WATCH PROGRAM IN FORCE. WE IMMEDIATELY REPORT ALL SUSPICIOUS PERSONS AND ACTIVITIES TO OUR POLICE DEPARTMENT. The signs on garages don't make me feel any better. WARNING, they read, YOUR NEIGHBORS ARE WATCHING.

I'd come to Green Valley because I was curious to meet the citizens of a community in which everything is designed, orchestrated, and executed by a corporation. More and more Americans, millions of them—singles, families, retirees—are living in such places. Often proximate to beltway interchanges and self-contained office parks of boxy glass buildings, these communities are everywhere now, although far more common in the West than elsewhere: its vast terrain, apparently, still lends itself to dreamers with grand designs. Irvine, California—the master-planned product of the Irvine Company, populated by 110,000 people and one of the fastest-growing *cities* in America—is widely considered a prototype, as are Reston, Virginia, and Columbia, Maryland, two early East Coast versions. Fairfield Communities, Inc., owns fourteen "Fairfield Communities": Fairfield in the Foothills, Fairfield's La Cholla, Fairfield's River Farm, and so forth. The Walt Disney Co. has its entry—Celebration—under way not far from Florida's Disney World. Las Colinas, Inc., invented Las Colinas, Texas, "America's Premier Master Planned Community," "America's Premier Development," and "America's Corporate Headquarters." The proliferation of planned communities is most visible in areas of rapid growth, which would certainly include the Las Vegas valley, the population of which has nearly doubled, to 799,381, since 1982.

That Sunday afternoon I made my way along peaceful boulevards   4
to Green Valley's civic center, presumably a place where people congregate. A promotional brochure describes its plaza as "the perfect size for public gatherings and all types of social events," but on that balmy day, the desert in bloom just a few miles off, no one had, in fact, gathered here. The plaza had the desultory ambience of an architectural mistake—deserted, useless, and irrelevant to Green Valley's citizens, who had, however, gathered in large numbers at stucco shopping centers not far off—at Spotlight Video, Wallpaper World, Record City, and Bicycle Depot, Rapunzel's Den Hair Salon, Enzo's Pizza and Ristorante, A Basket of Joy, and K-Mart.

Above the civic center, one after another, flew airplanes only sec-   5
onds from touching down at nearby McCarran International Airport, which services Las Vegas casinogoers. Low enough that the rivets in their wings could be discerned, the planes descended at sixty-second intervals, ferrying fresh loads of gamblers into port. To the northeast, beyond a billboard put up by a developer—WATCH US BUILD THE NEW LAS VEGAS—lay a rectangle of desert as yet not built upon but useful as a dumping ground: scraps of plastic, bits of stucco, heaps of wire mesh and lumber ends were all scattered in among low creosote bush. The corporate master plan, I later learned, calls for hauling these things away and replacing them with, among other things, cinemas, a complex of swimming pools, restaurants, and substantially more places to shop.

Inside the civic center were plenty of potted palms, walls of black   6
glass, and red marble floors, but again, no congregating citizens. Instead, I found the offices of the Americana Group Realtors; Lawyer's Title of Nevada, Inc.; RANPAC Engineering Corporation; and Coleman Homes, a developer. A few real estate agents were gearing up for Sunday home tours, dressed to kill and shuffling manila folders, their BMWs parked outside. Kirk Warren, a marketing specialist with the Americana Group, listened patiently to my explanation: I came to the

civic center to talk to people; I wanted to know what brought them to a corporate-planned community and why they decided to stay.

"It's safe here," Warren explained, handing me a business card [7] with his photograph on it. "And clean. And nice. The schools are good and the crime rate low. It's what buyers are looking for."

Outside the building, in the forlorn-looking plaza, six concrete [8] benches had been fixed astride lawns, offering citizens twenty-four seats. Teenagers had scrawled their graffiti on the pavement (DARREN WAS HERE, JASON IS AWESOME), and a footlight beneath a miniature obelisk had been smashed by someone devoted to its destruction. Someone had recently driven past on a motorcycle, leaving telltale skid marks.

The history of suburbia is a history of gradual dysfunction, says [9] Brian Greenspun, whose family owns the American Nevada Corporation (ANC), the entity that created Green Valley. Americans, he explains, moved to the suburbs in search of escape from the more undesirable aspects of the city and from undesirable people in particular. Time passed and undesirables showed up anyway; suburbia had no means to prevent this. But in the end, that was all right, Greenspun points out, because master planners recognized the problem as an enormously lucrative market opportunity and began building places like Green Valley.

Rutgers history professor Robert Fishman, author of *Bourgeois Uto-* [10] *pias: The Rise and Fall of Suburbia,* would agree that suburbia hasn't worked. Suburbia, he argues, appeared in America in the middle of the nineteenth century, offering escape from the squalor and stench of the new industrial cities. The history of suburbia reached a climax, he says, with the rise of Los Angeles as a city that is in fact one enormous suburb. Today, writes Fishman, "the original concept of suburbia as an unspoiled synthesis of city and countryside has lost its meaning." Suburbia "has become what even the greatest advocates of suburban growth never desired—a new form of city." These new suburb-cities have, of course, inevitably developed the kinds of problems— congestion, crime, pollution, tawdriness—that the middle class left cities to avoid. Now, in the Nineties, developers and corporate master planners, recognizing an opportunity, have stepped in to supply the middle class, once again, with the promise of a bourgeois utopia.

As a product of the American Nevada Corporation, Green Valley is [11] a community with its own marketing logo: the letters G and V intertwined quite cleverly to create a fanciful optical illusion—two leaves and a truncated plant stem. It is also a community with an advertising slogan: ALL THAT A COMMUNITY CAN BE. Like other master-planned communities in America, it is designed to embody a corporate ideal not only of streets and houses but of image and feeling. Green Valley's crisp lawns, culs-de-sac, and stucco walls suggest an amiable suburban existence where, as an advertising brochure tells us, people can enjoy life *more than they ever did before*. And, apparently, they do enjoy it. Thirty-four thousand people have filled Green Valley's homes in a mere fourteen years—the place is literally a boomtown. . . .

On weekday mornings, familiar yellow buses amble through Green Valley toward public schools built on acreage set aside in a 1971 land-sale agreement between ANC and Henderson, a blue-collar town just south of Vegas that was initially hostile to its new upscale neighbor but that now willingly participates in Green Valley's prosperity. Many parents prefer to drive their children to these schools before moving on to jobs, shopping, tennis, or aerobics classes. (Most Green Valley residents work in Las Vegas, commuting downtown in under twenty minutes.) The characteristic Green Valley family—a married couple with two children under twelve—has an average annual income of $55,000; about one in five are members of the Green Valley Athletic Club, described by master planners as "the focal point of the community" (family initiation fee: $1,000). The club's lavish swimming pools and air-conditioned tennis courts are, I was told, especially popular in summer, when Green Valley temperatures can reach 115 degrees and when whole caravans of Porsches and BMWs make their way toward its shimmering parking lots. 12

Inside is a state-of-the-art body-sculpting palace with Gravitron Upper Body Systems in its weight room, $3.99 protein drinks at its Health Bar, complimentary mouthwash in its locker rooms (swilled liberally by well-preserved tennis aficionados primping their thinning hair at mirrors before heading upstairs to Café Brigette Deux), and employees trained "to create an experience that brings a smile to every Member at every opportunity." I was given a tour by Jill Johnson, a Membership Service Representative, who showed me the Cybex systems in the weight room, the Life-Circuit computerized resistance equipment, the aerobics studio, and the day-care center. 13

Upstairs, the bartender mixed an "Arnold Schwarzenegger" for an adolescent boy with a crisp haircut and a tennis racket: yogurt, banana, and weight-gain powder. Later, in the weight room, I met a man I'll call Phil Anderson, an accountant, who introduced me to his wife, Marie, and to his children, Jason and Sarah. Phil was ruddy, overweight, and sweat-soaked, and had a towel draped over his shoulders. Marie was trim, dressed for tennis; the kids looked bored. Phil had been playing racquetball that evening while Marie took lessons to improve her serve and the children watched television in the kids' lounge. Like most of the people I met in Green Valley, the Andersons were reluctant to have their real names used ("We don't want the reaction," was how some residents explained it, including Marie and Phil). I coaxed them 14 by promising to protect their true identities, and the Andersons began to chat.

"We moved here because Jase was getting on toward junior high age," Marie explained between sets on a machine designed to strengthen her triceps. "And in San Diego, where we lived before, there were these . . . *forces,* if you know what I mean. There were too many things we couldn't control. Drugs and stuff. It wasn't healthy for our kids."   15

"I had a job offer," Phil said. "We looked for a house. Green Valley was . . . the obvious place—just sort of obvious, really. Our real estate agent sized us up and brought us out here right away."   16

"We found a house in Silver Springs," Marie said. "You can go ahead and put that in your notes. It's a big development. No one will figure it out."   17

"But just don't use our names, okay?" Phil pleaded. "I would really appreciate that."   18

"We don't need problems," Marie added.   19

Master planners have a penchant not just for slogans but for predictable advertising strategies. Their pamphlets, packets, and brochures wax reverent about venerable founding fathers of passionate vision, men of foresight who long ago—usually in the Fifties—dreamed of building cities in their own image. Next comes a text promising an upscale pastoral: golf courses, blissful shoppers, kindly security guards, pleasant walkways, goodly physicians, yeomanly fire fighters, proficient teachers. Finally—invariably—there is culture in paradise: an annual arts and crafts festival, a sculpture, a gallery, Shakespeare in the park. In Las Colinas's Williams Square, for example, a herd of bronze mustangs runs pell-mell across a plaza, symbolizing, a brochure explains, a "heritage of freedom in a free land." Perhaps in the interstices of some sophisticated market analysis, these unfettered mustangs make perfectly good sense; in the context of a community whose dominant feature is walls, however, they make no sense whatsoever.   20

Walls are everywhere in Green Valley too; they're the first thing a visitor notices. Their message is subliminal and at the same time explicit; controlled access is as much metaphor as reality. Controlled access is also a two-way affair—both "ingress" and "egress" are influenced by it; both coming and going are made difficult. The gates at the thresholds of Green Valley's posher neighborhoods open with a macabre, mechanical slowness; their guards speak firmly and authoritatively to strangers and never smile in the manner of official greeters. One of them told me to take no pictures and to go directly to my destination "without stopping to look at anything." Another said that in an eight-hour shift he felt constantly nervous about going to the bathroom and feared that in   21 abandoning his post to relieve himself he risked losing his job. A girl at the Taco Bell on nearby Sunset Road complained about Clark County's ten o'clock teen curfew—and about the guard at her neighborhood's gate who felt it was his duty to remind her of it. A ten-year-old pointed out that his friends beyond the wall couldn't join him inside without a telephone call to "security," which meant "the policeman in the guardhouse." Security, of course, can be achieved in many ways, but one implication of it, every time, is that security has insidious psychological consequences for those who contrive to feel secure.

"Before I built a wall," wrote Robert Frost, "I'd ask to know what I was walling in or walling out, and to whom I was like to give offense."[1] The master planners have answers that are unassailably prosaic: "lot owners shall not change said walls in any manner"; "perimeter walls are required around all single family residential projects"; "side yard walls shall conform to the Guidelines for intersecting rear property walls." Their master plan weighs in with ponderous wall specifics, none of them in any way actionable: location, size, material, color, piers, pillars, openings. "Perimeter Project Walls," for example, "shall be made of gray colored, split face concrete masonry units, 8" by 16" by 6" in size, with a 4" high gray, split face, concrete block. . . . The block will be laid in a running bond pattern. . . . No openings are allowed from individual back yard lots into adjoining areas."

All of Green Valley is defined in this manner, by CC&Rs, as the planners call them—covenants, conditions, and restrictions embedded in deeds. Every community has some restrictions on matters such as the proper placement of septic tanks and the minimum distance allowed between homes, but in Green Valley the restrictions are detailed and pervasive, insuring the absence of individuality and suppressing the natural mess of humanity. Clotheslines and Winnebagos are not permitted, for example; no fowl, reptile, fish, or insect may be raised; there are to be no exterior speakers, horns, whistles, or bells. No debris of any kind, no open fires, no noise. Entries, signs, lights, mailboxes, sidewalks, driveways, rear yards, side yards, carports, sheds—the planners have had their say about each. All CC&Rs are inscribed into books of law that vary only slightly from development to development: the number of dogs and cats you can own (until recently, one master-planned community in Newport Beach, California, even limited the *weight* of dogs) as well as the placement of garbage cans, barbecue pits, satellite dishes, and utility boxes. The color of your home, the number of stories, the materials used, its accents and trim. The interior of your garage, the way to park your truck, the plants in your yard, the angle of your flagpole, the size of your address numbers, the placement of mirrored

22

23

---

1. See "Mending Wall," p. 225.

glass balls and birdbaths, the grade of your lawn's slope, and the size of your FOR SALE sign should you decide you want to leave.

"These things," explained Brad Nelson, an ANC vice president, "are 24 set up to protect property values." ANC owner Greenspun put it another way: "The public interest and ANC's interest are one." . . .

As a journalist, I may have preferred a telling answer to my most 25 frequent question—Why do you live here?—but the people of Green Valley, with disconcerting uniformity, were almost never entirely forthcoming. ("I moved here because of my job," they would say, or "I moved here because we found a nice house in Heartland.") Many had never heard of the American Nevada Corporation; one man took me for a representative of it and asked me what I was selling. Most had only a vague awareness of the existence of a corporate master plan for every detail of their community. The covenants, conditions, and restrictions of their lives were background matters of which they were cognizant but about which they were yawningly unconcerned. It did not seem strange to anyone I spoke with that a corporation should have final say about their mailboxes. When I explained that there were CC&Rs for nearly everything, most people merely shrugged and pointed out in return that it seemed a great way to protect property values. A woman in a grocery store checkout line explained that she'd come here from southern California because "even the good neighborhoods there aren't good anymore. You don't feel safe in L.A."

What the people of Green Valley want, explained a planner, is 26 safety from threats both real and imagined and control over who moves in beside them. In this they are no different from the generation that preceded them in search of the suburban dream. The difference this time is that nothing has been left to chance and that everything has been left to the American Nevada Corporation, which gives Green Valley its contemporary twist: to achieve at least the illusion of safety, residents must buy in to an enormous measure of corporate domination. Suburbia in the Nineties has a logo.

But even Eden—planned by God—had serpents, and so, appar- 27 ently, does Green Valley. Last year a rapist ran loose in its neighborhoods; police suspected the man was a resident and responsible for three rapes and five robberies. George Hennard, killer of twenty-three people in a Killeen, Texas, cafeteria in October 1991, was a resident of Green Valley only months before his rampage and bought two of his murder weapons here in a private transaction. Joseph Weldon Smith, featured on the television series *Unsolved Mysteries,* strangled to death his wife and two stepdaughters in a posh Green Valley development called The Fountains.

The list of utopia's outrages also includes a November 1991 heist 28 in which two armed robbers took a handcuffed hostage and more than

$100,000 from a Green Valley bank, then fled and fired military-assault-rifle rounds at officers in hot pursuit. The same week police arrested a suspected child molester who had been playing football with Green Valley children and allegedly touching their genitals.

"You can run but you can't hide," one Green Valley resident told   29
me when I mentioned a few of these incidents. "People are coming here from all over the place and bringing their problems with them." Perhaps she was referring to the gangs frequenting a Sunset Road fast-food restaurant—Sunset Road forms one fringe of Green Valley—where in the summer of 1991, according to the restaurant's manager, "the dining room was set on fire and there were fights every weekend." Perhaps she had talked to the teenagers who told me that LSD and crystal meth are the narcotics of choice at Green Valley High School, or to the doctor who simply rolled his eyes when I asked if he thought AIDS had arrived here.

Walls might separate paradise from heavy industry, but the protec-   30
tion they provide is an illusion. In May 1991 a leak at the nearby Pioneer Chlor Alkali plant spread a blanket of chlorine gas over Green Valley; nearly a hundred area residents were treated at hospitals for respiratory problems. The leak came three years after another nearby plant—this one producing rocket-fuel oxidizer for the space shuttle and nuclear missiles—exploded powerfully enough to register on earthquake seismographs 200 miles away. Two people were killed, 210 injured. Schools were closed and extra police officers called in to discourage the looting of area homes with doors and windows blown out.

And, finally, there is black comedy in utopia: a few days after   31
Christmas last year, police arrested the Green Valley Community Association president for allegedly burglarizing a model home. Stolen items included pictures, cushions, bedspreads, and a gaudy brass figurine—a collection with no internal logic. A local newspaper described the civic leader running from the scene, dropping his loot piece by piece in his wake as he was chased by police to his residence. At home he hid temporarily in his attic but ultimately to no avail. The plaster cracked and he fell through a panel into the midst of the arresting officers.

Is it a coincidence that the one truly anomalous soul I met roams   32
furtively the last unpaved place in Green Valley, a short stretch of desert called Pittman Wash?

Pittman Wash winds through quiet subdivisions, undeveloped   33
chiefly because it is useful for drainage and unbuildable anyway. Lesser washes have been filled in, built on, and forgotten, but Pittman remains full of sand and desert hollyhock, a few tamarisks, some clumps of creosote bush. Children prefer it to the manicured squares of park grass provided for them by the master planners; teenagers drink beer here

and write graffiti on the storm-drain access pillars buried in the wash's channel: FUCK HENDERSON PK. DSTC., and the like. Used condoms, rusting oil filters, a wind-whipped old sleeping bag, a rock wren, a yellow swallowtail butterfly.

Here I met nine-year-old Jim Collins, whose name has been changed—at his fervent request—on the off chance his mother reads these words and punishes him for playing in Pittman Wash again. Jim struck me as a lonesome, Huck Finn sort, brown-skinned and soft-spoken, with grit beneath his nails and sun-bleached hair. I found him down on his dirty knees, lazily poking a stick into a hole.

"Lizards," he explained. "I'm looking for lizards. There's rattlers, chipmunks, coyote, mountain lion, black widows, and scorpions too." He regaled me with stories of parents in high dudgeon over creatures of the wash brought home. Then, unsolicited, he suddenly declared that "most of the time I'm bored out of my guts . . . the desert's all covered up with houses—that sucks."

He insisted, inexplicably, on showing me his backyard, which he described as "just like the desert." So we trudged out of the wash and walked the concrete trail the master planners have placed here. Jim climbed the border wall and ran along its four-inch top with the unconscious facility of a mountain goat. We looked at his yard, which had not yet been landscaped, a rectangle of cracked desert caliche. Next door three children dressed fashionably in sporting attire shot baskets on a Michael Jordan Air Attack hoop. "We don't get along," Jim said. He didn't want me to go away in the end, and as I left he was still chattering hopefully. "My favorite store is Wild Kingdom of Pets," he called. "If you go there you can see Tasha the wildcat."

Some might call Green Valley a simulacrum of a real place, Disneyland's Main Street done in Mediterranean hues, a city of haciendas with cardboard souls, a valley of the polished, packaged, and perfected, an empyrean of emptiness, a sanitized wasteland. They will note the Southwest's pastel palette coloring a community devoid of improvisation, of caprice, spontaneity, effusiveness, or the charm of error—a place where the process of commodification has at last leached life of the accidental and ecstatic, the divine, reckless, and enraged.

Still, many now reside in this corporate domain, driven here by insatiable fears. No class warfare here, no burning city. Green Valley beckons the American middle class like a fabulous and eternal dream. In the wake of our contemporary trembling and discontent, its pilgrims have sought out a corporate castle where in exchange for false security they pay with personal freedoms; where the corporation that does the job of walling others out also walls residents in. The principle, once political, is now economic. Just call your real estate agent.

The Thursday Ladies

Karla F. C. Holloway (1949–   ), daughter of a public school superintendent and an English teacher, was educated at Talladega College
in Talladega, Alabama, and at Michigan State University. She is presently a professor of English and African-American Literature at Duke
University. Even in her academic writings on linguistic and literary
theory, her prose carries the ease and the drama of a spoken voice.
"If there are passages in my books or essays that read with some
difficulty," she reports, "I often suggest that my readers read them
aloud. It is often a cadence that's missing: something only the spoken
voice can supply. I hear this voice as I write." Listen for the sound of
Holloway's voice as you read the following essay, written for *Double
Stitch: Black Women Write About Mothers and Daughters* (1991).

for Gloria and her memory

I wasn't coaxed awake that morning. My sister didn't nudge me   1
off her side of the bed. Mama didn't call, quietly expecting no answer,
or louder, getting irritated. No summer morning breeze blew through
our window, rattling the shell chimes I'd made on the back porch.
Nothing Sunday woke me up—no vaseline-shined shoes waiting to be
worn or church waiting to be filled. Nothing but the intermittent squeak
of the back screen door, followed by muffled good mornings ". . . them
sweeties still sleep?" constantly echoing through the house woke me.
I knew it was Thursday after the fourth or fifth squeak . . . and so I
punched Shirley in the back and told her "Get up—those ladies are
back."

We called them the Thursday ladies. But they could have been the   2
summer ladies or weekday ladies or servant ladies. They were all of
those things. In our small Michigan town ours was one of the few Black
families. We lived apart from the town's center. I never knew the reason
we lived past the main highway, almost to the church we shared with
the next town's Black Baptist congregation. I wasn't sure whether it
was to be close to the church where we spent so much of our family
time or to be distant from the town that had only grudgingly admitted
us into the outskirts of its community. It was the town where my Papa
brought Mama after they'd married and left Sedalia, and he'd made a
living for all of us there. Mama, me, my sister Shirley, and my three
brothers. My brothers were gone now, army, college, dead (hit by a car
in the town my mama avoided) and only me and Shirley were home.

Mama was obviously proud that her family had made it—even into the fringes of that community where we lived. So she accepted the town because it grounded our family. But Shirl and me thought she must have hated it some too by the way she never went to town unless it was to shop (on Wednesday) or to school to see about us.

Those ladies were the most constant event in our lives. They con- 3
nected the time before our brother Junior (we called him June Bug) died and the time after. They'd always been coming on Thursday, and they were always the same.

I don't mean that they were all softly warm brown. Some were 4
night-dark, deep black women with loving, caring eyes. Some were high-yellow. Like Mama. Some were so slender that I wondered how they took care of all those children they always talked about. They were too fragile, I thought. Some were large and big-boned, and their gentleness was marked in their smiles and the weariness in their eyes. They carried pocketbooks when they came to see us; they all wore the same shoes—"nurse's shoes" Shirl and I called them—and they never acknowledged that they knew. Shirl and I would sneak down the hall when we heard them coming, hide behind the stove closet (where Mama kept cooking stuff), and spend most of Thursday listening to the strange community that entered our kitchen.

They didn't talk like us—me, or Shirl or Mama. They sounded like 5
M'dear, our grandmama back in Sedalia. They kissed (when we came out to grab a biscuit or bacon) like those ladies in M'dear's church. Their voices were soft and their feelings were loud. And Mama smiled more on those summer Thursdays than on any other day.

Their community was well-established. They had ritualized those 6
mornings spent in Mama's kitchen, the evenings on our porch. All of the ladies worked for white families who had come to Michigan to escape the summer heat of places like Charleston or Natchez or New Orleans. They brought their "girls" with them to take care of the children (and them) while they vacationed in our Lake Michigan town. These ladies weren't on vacation—except on Thursday. That was their day off and the day when they gathered in the home of one of the only Black families in town and relieved themselves of the burdens of working for white folks. So Shirl and I knew to come to the kitchen without coaxing that morning, and to be there while they were coming, slowly filling in the spaces around our kitchen table, leaning up against the cupboard, standing duty near the ice box in case someone wanted something, or helping Mama roll biscuits. Shirl and I knew they'd talk first about their "people" and we didn't want to miss any of the ritual. "Girl, you should'a seen . . ." or "She didn't have no better sense than to . . ." or "Well, what chu do when they . . . ?" We'd listen in on the fascinating world of Southern white women who didn't seem to want

to see their children all day (except after their naps, or after they'd been fed, or after they were dressed for bed). That would intrigue us, but even more compelling was the aura of the community of these Black women who talked like M'dear and who were absolutely out of place in our sophisticated preadolescent vision of the world. I think now that we kind of resented the woman our mother became on Thursdays because on those days she was happy in ways that we never could make her and she laughed at things we didn't think were funny, and she seemed a part of them instead of us.

So most Thursdays, we'd pick on these ladies like they picked at 7 the white folks they worked for. "Girl, did you see those ankles on that lady by the window?" We'd exaggerate their dialect and ridicule the country manners that caused the younger ladies to call our Mama "Ma'am." "Yes, chile!" I'd pitch my voice real high to sound thin and reed-like like the cocoa-brown lady who'd just joined the group this summer. "Lawd knows my feet cain't take much more of runnin after these chillun." I rubbed my feet like I had seen her do. "Mah Jesus— mah ankles so swole I speck they'll bust!"

"Do Jesus!" Shirl would roll her eyes up and then we'd hit the 8 floor, laughing at our laughing at them. But we'd make sure to get down the hall before the talk about their people was done and shifted to the talk about what they were going to do on their day off.

Our house was the base for Thursday breakfast, supper, late night 9 talk and a kind of gathering of spirit that I didn't understand then, but respected (or feared, or envied) for the strength that was obviously a part of these women's meetings.

On that Thursday Mamie, the new lady, announced she was going 10 to the movie house in town. The other ladies just glanced at her, a smiling acknowledgement of her intent and went on back to their conversations. They were talking about men . . . and that was the ritual talk (after breakfast and before the late afternoon lethargy when a lot of them napped on the porch swing or on the davenport in the living room) that Shirl and I had to be really quiet and careful listeners for, because we reviewed it in our beds Thursday nights. So we didn't pay much attention when Mamie put her bag on her left arm, pulled on her gloves (like she was going to church, Shirl said later) and straightened that black triangle hat she always wore. She went out the front door. We heard it bang shut, but our attention quickly went back to their conversation—certain we'd hear something new about men, something that demanded review, or experimentation or a conference with some of our older girl friends from church. So we sat, our backs firmly pressed against the hall wall, munching peaches and collecting the seeds for planting in our backyard spot that we always forgot the location of.

We did hear Mamie come back. The door's slam punctuated a point   11
that one of the older ladies made: ". . . ain't that just like them mens."
And the noise broke our concentration, because it was too early. By
the time the movie let out, we should have been back in the kitchen,
cutting up tomatoes for supper or heating the frying pan in the oven
for the corn bread being stirred on the table. But she was too early for
that evening kitchen time. And so Shirl and I looked at each other,
then at her, sure we would see some indication of why Mamie had
returned too early from the movie house.

But she just smiled—and said, "Scuse me, y'all," in that high   12
squeaky voice of hers and shyly (we agreed later her moves weren't
sneaky, just shy) made her way through the living room, past us in the
hall and down the passage to the bathroom. She closed the door and
turned the water on. We could hear her tinkling into the toilet and the
flush even though the water was running. Then she came back out,
smiled that "scuse me, y'all" smile and the front door slammed behind
her. We jumped up and ran back to the kitchen window where we
could see her making her way back down the road to town—back to
the movie house.

We looked at each other for just a moment until the truth hit us   13
and then we burst into hysterical, derisive laughter. "She came back
just to use the bathroom!" Shirl shouted.

"Countre-e-e-e-e!" I giggled. "Maybe she thought the toilet was   14
outside the movie house and she just kept on walking till she got back
here!"

"Maybe the girl on the 'Ladies' sign didn't look enough like her so   15
she didn't think she could go in!" Shirl's voice was broken by the
hilarity that had descended on us both.

I yelled back, "Maybe she couldn't read!"   16

We were both just about overcome with her obvious ignorance and   17
our own delightful sophistication when Mama appeared in the kitchen
doorway. She spoke to us in a voice that controlled her rage but could
not suppress her unhappiness. Later we both said that we thought she
was going to cry instead of talk, but she did talk and it seemed to come
out of a memory. Shirl said later that it felt like she hadn't even been
in the kitchen with us.

"Maybe," Mama said quietly "maybe in that little country town in   18
Mississippi that's so funny and so foreign to you two, where Mamie
works her life away in a home that will never be hers and for a family
that will never love her back . . . maybe the bathrooms in movie houses
there say something that hurts her so bad she wishes she couldn't read."

And she looked at us like she knew we didn't know what she   19
meant and went back to the room and to her community of Thursday
ladies who lived the memory Mama had left in Sedalia.

N. SCOTT MOMADAY

The Way to Rainy Mountain

N(avarre) Scott Momaday (1934–   ) is the son of a Kiowa father and a mother of mixed white and Cherokee ancestry. He spent his earliest years among Kiowas on a family farm in Oklahoma. Later he moved with his parents to New Mexico, where they taught in reservation schools. Momaday took a B.A. in English from the University of New Mexico and an M.A. and Ph.D. from Stanford University, and he has been a professor of English at the University of Arizona since 1982. Like his father, he is an accomplished artist, and, like his mother, he is a skilled writer. Among his best-known works are *House Made of Dawn* (1968), a Pulitzer Prize–winning novel; *The Gourd Dancer* (1976), a book of poems he also illustrated; and *The Way to Rainy Mountain* (1969), a collection of traditional Kiowa stories. Many of the stories in *Rainy Mountain* were told to Momaday by his father (who illustrated the book), his grandmother, and several of his grandmother's friends, "who were in close touch with the oral tradition of the tribe." Its introduction, first published as a separate essay in *The Reporter* (1967), gives a sense of what Momaday values in his Kiowa heritage and what he sees threatened by the dominance of white civilization. Momaday's latest projects include *In the Presence of the Sun: Stories and Poems 1961–1991* (1992) and *Circle of Wonder: A Native American Christmas Story* (1993). He has also narrated a PBS documentary, *Winds of Change*, focusing on contemporary Native American experiences.

A single knoll rises out of the plain in Oklahoma, north and west   1
of the Wichita Range. For my people, the Kiowas, it is an old landmark, and they gave it the name Rainy Mountain. The hardest weather in the world is there. Winter brings blizzards, hot tornadic winds arise in the spring, and in the summer the prairie is an anvil's edge. The grass turns brittle and brown, and it cracks beneath your feet. There are green belts along the rivers and creeks, linear groves of hickory and pecan, willow, and witch hazel. At a distance in July or August the steaming foliage seems almost to writhe in fire. Great green-and-yellow grasshoppers are everywhere in the tall grass, popping up like corn to sting the flesh, and tortoises crawl about on the red earth, going nowhere in the plenty of time. Loneliness is an aspect of the land. All things in the plain are isolate; there is no confusion of objects in the eye, but *one* hill or *one* tree or *one* man. To look upon that landscape in the early morning, with the sun at your back, is to lose the sense of proportion. Your imagination comes to life, and this, you think, is where Creation was begun.

I returned to Rainy Mountain in July. My grandmother had died 2
in the spring, and I wanted to be at her grave. She had lived to be very
old and at last infirm. Her only living daughter was with her when she
died, and I was told that in death her face was that of a child.

I like to think of her as a child. When she was born, the Kiowas 3
were living that last great moment of their history. For more than a
hundred years they had controlled the open range from the Smoky Hill
River to the Red, from the headwaters of the Canadian to the fork of
the Arkansas and Cimarron. In alliance with the Comanches, they had
ruled the whole of the southern Plains. War was their sacred business,
and they were among the finest horsemen the world has ever known.
But warfare for the Kiowas was preeminently a matter of disposition
rather than of survival, and they never understood the grim, unrelenting
advance of the U.S. Cavalry. When at last, divided and ill-provisioned,
they were driven onto the Staked Plains in the cold rains of autumn,
they fell into panic. In Palo Duro Canyon they abandoned their crucial
stores to pillage and had nothing then but their lives. In order to save
themselves, they surrendered to the soldiers at Fort Sill and were imprisoned in the old stone corral that now stands as a military museum. My
grandmother was spared the humiliation of those high gray walls by
eight or ten years, but she must have known from birth the affliction
of defeat, the dark brooding of old warriors.

Her name was Aho, and she belonged to the last culture to evolve 4
in North America. Her forebears came down from the high country in
western Montana nearly three centuries ago. They were a mountain
people, a mysterious tribe of hunters whose language has never been
positively classified in any major group. In the late seventeenth century
they began a long migration to the south and east. It was a long journey
toward the dawn, and it led to a golden age. Along the way the Kiowas
were befriended by the Crows, who gave them the culture and religion
of the Plains. They acquired horses, and their ancient nomadic spirit
was suddenly free of the ground. They acquired Tai-me, the sacred Sun
Dance doll, from that moment the object and symbol of their worship,
and so shared in the divinity of the sun. Not least, they acquired the
sense of destiny, therefore courage and pride. When they entered upon
the southern Plains, they had been transformed. No longer were they
slaves to the simple necessity of survival; they were a lordly and dangerous society of fighters and thieves, hunters and priests of the sun. According to their origin myth, they entered the world through a hollow
log. From one point of view, their migration was the fruit of an old
prophecy, for indeed they emerged from a sunless world.

Although my grandmother lived out her long life in the shadow of 5
Rainy Mountain, the immense landscape of the continental interior lay
like memory in her blood. She could tell of the Crows, whom she had
never seen, and of the Black Hills, where she had never been. I wanted

to see in reality what she had seen more perfectly in the mind's eye, and traveled fifteen hundred miles to begin my pilgrimage.

Yellowstone, it seemed to me, was the top of the world, a region 6 of deep lakes and dark timber, canyons and waterfalls. But, beautiful as it is, one might have the sense of confinement there. The skyline in all directions is close at hand, the high wall of the woods and deep cleavages of shade. There is a perfect freedom in the mountains, but it belongs to the eagle and the elk, the badger and the bear. The Kiowas reckoned their stature by the distance they could see, and they were bent and blind in the wilderness.

Descending eastward, the highland meadows are a stairway to the 7 plain. In July the inland slope of the Rockies is luxuriant with flax and buckwheat, stonecrop and larkspur. The earth unfolds and the limit of the land recedes. Clusters of trees and animals grazing far in the distance cause the vision to reach away and wonder to build upon the mind. The sun follows a longer course in the day, and the sky is immense beyond all comparison. The great billowing clouds that sail upon it are shadows that move upon the grain like water, dividing light. Farther down, in the land of the Crows and Blackfeet, the plain is yellow. Sweet clover takes hold of the hills and bends upon itself to cover and seal the soil. There the Kiowas paused on their way; they had come to the place where they must change their lives. The sun is at home on the plains. Precisely there does it have the certain character of a god. When the Kiowas came to the land of the Crows, they could see the dark lees of the hill at dawn across the Bighorn River, the profusion of light on the grain shelves, the oldest deity ranging after the solstices. Not yet would they veer southward to the caldron of the land that lay below; they must wean their blood from the northern winter and hold the mountains a while longer in their view. They bore Tai-me in procession to the east.

A dark mist lay over the Black Hills, and the land was like iron. At 8 the top of a ridge I caught sight of Devil's Tower upthrust against the gray sky as if in the birth of time the core of the earth had broken through its crust and the motion of the world was begun. There are things in nature that engender an awful quiet in the heart of man; Devil's Tower is one of them. Two centuries ago, because they could not do otherwise, the Kiowas made a legend at the base of the rock. My grandmother said:

> Eight children were there at play, seven sisters and their brother. Suddenly the boy was struck dumb; he trembled and began to run upon his hands and feet. His fingers became claws, and his body was covered with fur. Directly there was a bear where the boy had been. The sisters were terrified; they ran, and the bear after them. They came to the stump of a great tree, and the tree spoke to them. It bade them climb upon it and as they did so, it began to rise into the air. The bear came to kill them, but they were just

beyond its reach. It reared against the tree and scored the bark all around with its claws. The seven sisters were borne into the sky, and they became the stars of the Big Dipper.

From that moment, and so long as the legend lives, the Kiowas have kinsmen in the night sky. Whatever they were in the mountains, they could be no more. However tenuous their well-being, however much they had suffered and would suffer again, they had found a way out of the wilderness.

My grandmother had a reverence for the sun, a holy regard that 9 now is all but gone out of mankind. There was a wariness in her and an ancient awe. She was a Christian in her later years, but she had come a long way about, and she never forgot her birthright. As a child she had been to the Sun Dances; she had taken part in those annual rites, and by them she had learned the restoration of her people in the presence of Tai-me. She was about seven when the last Kiowa Sun Dance was held in 1887 on the Washita River above Rainy Mountain Creek. The buffalo were gone. In order to consummate the ancient sacrifice—to impale the head of a buffalo bull upon the medicine tree—a delegation of old men journeyed into Texas, there to beg and barter for an animal from the Goodnight herd. She was ten when the Kiowas came together for the last time as a living Sun Dance culture. They could find no buffalo; they had to hang an old hide from the sacred tree. Before the dance could begin, a company of soldiers rode out from Fort Sill under orders to disperse the tribe. Forbidden without cause the essential act of their faith, having seen the wild herds slaughtered and left to rot upon the ground, the Kiowas backed away forever from the medicine tree. That was July 20, 1890, at the great bend of the Washita. My grandmother was there. Without bitterness, and for as long as she lived, she bore a vision of deicide.

Now that I can have her only in memory, I see my grandmother 10 in the several postures that were peculiar to her: standing at the wood stove on a winter morning and turning meat in a great iron skillet; sitting at the south window, bent above her beadwork, and afterwards, when her vision had failed, looking down for a long time into the fold of her hands; going out upon a cane, very slowly as she did when the weight of age came upon her; praying. I remember her most often at prayer. She made long, rambling prayers out of suffering and hope, having seen many things. I was never sure that I had the right to hear, so exclusive were they of all mere custom and company. The last time I saw her she prayed standing by the side of her bed at night, naked to the waist, the light of a kerosene lamp moving upon her dark skin. Her long, black hair, always drawn and braided in the day, lay upon her shoulders and against her breasts like a shawl. I do not speak Kiowa, and I never understood her prayers, but there was something inherently sad in the sound, some merest hesitation upon the syllables of sorrow.

She began in a high and descending pitch, exhausting her breath to silence; then again and again—and always the same intensity of effort, of something that is, and is not, like urgency in the human voice. Transported so in the dancing light among the shadows of her room, she seemed beyond the reach of time. But that was illusion; I think I knew then that I should not see her again.

Houses are like sentinels in the plain, old keepers of the weather watch. There, in a very little while, wood takes on the appearance of great age. All colors wear soon away in the wind and rain, and then the wood is burned gray and the grain appears and the nails turn red with rust. The windowpanes are black and opaque; you imagine there is nothing within, and indeed there are many ghosts, bones given up to the land. They stand here and there against the sky, and you approach them for a longer time than you expect. They belong in the distance; it is their domain. 11

Once there was a lot of sound in my grandmother's house, a lot of coming and going, feasting and talk. The summers there were full of excitement and reunion. The Kiowas are a summer people; they abide the cold and keep to themselves; but when the season turns and the land becomes warm and vital, they cannot hold still; an old love of going returns upon them. The aged visitors who came to my grandmother's house when I was a child were made of lean and leather, and they bore themselves upright. They wore great black hats and bright ample shirts that shook in the wind. They rubbed fat upon their hair and wound their braids with strips of colored cloth. Some of them painted their faces and carried the scars of old and cherished enmities. They were an old council of warlords, come to remind and be reminded of who they were. Their wives and daughters served them well. The women might indulge themselves; gossip was at once the mark and compensation of their servitude. They made loud and elaborate talk among themselves, full of jest and gesture, fright and false alarm. They went abroad in fringed and flowered shawls, bright beadwork, and German silver. They were at home in the kitchen, and they prepared meals that were banquets. 12

There were frequent prayer meetings, and great nocturnal feasts. When I was a child, I played with my cousins outside, where the lamplight fell upon the ground and the singing of the old people rose up around us and carried away into the darkness. There were a lot of good things to eat, a lot of laughter and surprise. And afterwards, when the quiet returned, I lay down with my grandmother and could hear the frogs away by the river and feel the motion of the air. 13

Now there is a funeral silence in the rooms, the endless wake of some final word. The walls have closed in upon my grandmother's house. When I returned to it in mourning, I saw for the first time in my life how small it was. It was late at night, and there was a white 14 moon, nearly full. I sat for a long time on the stone steps by the kitchen door. From there I could see out across the land; I could see the long row of trees by the creek, the low light upon the rolling plains, and the stars of the Big Dipper. Once I looked at the moon and caught sight of a strange thing. A cricket had perched upon the handrail, only a few inches away from me. My line of vision was such that the creature filled the moon like a fossil. It had gone there, I thought, to live and die, for there of all places, was its small definition made whole and eternal. A warm wind rose up and purled like the longing within me.

The next morning I awoke at dawn and went out on the dirt road   15
to Rainy Mountain. It was already hot, and the grasshoppers began to fill the air. Still, it was early in the morning, and the birds sang out of the shadows. The long yellow grass on the mountain shone in the bright light, and a scissortail hied above the land. There, where it ought to be, at the end of a long and legendary way, was my grandmother's grave. Here and there on the dark stones were ancestral names. Looking back once, I saw the mountain and came away.

BARRY LOPEZ

Manhattan, 1976

Barry Lopez (1945–   ), born in New York City, spent most of his early life in Southern California, where he developed an emotional attachment to the West Coast and its natural history (he currently lives in Oregon, near the McKenzie River). His first major book, *Of Wolves and Men* (1979), revealed his deep interest in the way humans think and feel about animals, an interest that shows in almost all of his writing. A self-described "writer who travels," Lopez is alarmed that "we don't have a spiritual relationship with the landscape," which for him includes people, animals, weather, and topography. He also writes about the prejudices and intolerances that stand in the way of loving human relationships. *Arctic Dreams: Imagination and Desire in a Northern Landscape* won Lopez a National Book Award in 1986. The following section from a longer essay published in *Georgia Review* (Spring 1993) shows Lopez's ability to represent a cityscape with the same physical and spiritual alertness he has so often devoted to the natural landscape.

The hours of coolness in the morning just before my mother died   1
I remember for their relief. It was July and it had been warm and humid in New York City for several days, temperatures in the high eighties, the air motionless and heavy with the threat of rain.

I awoke early that morning. It was also my wife's thirtieth birthday,   2
but our celebration would be wan. My mother was in her last days,
and the lives of all of us in the family were contorted by grief and
tension—and by a flaring of anger at her cancer. We were exhausted.

I felt the coolness of the air immediately when I awoke. I walked   3
the length of the fourth-floor apartment, opened one side of a tall case-
ment window in the living room, and looked at the sky. Cumulus
clouds, moving to the southeast on a steady wind. Ten degrees cooler
than yesterday's dawn, by the small tin thermometer. I leaned forward
to rest my arms on the sill and began taking in details of movement in
the street's pale light, the city's stirring.

In the six years I had lived in this apartment as a boy, from 1956   4
until 1962, I had spent cumulative months at this window. At the time,
the Murray Hill section of Manhattan was mostly a neighborhood of
decorous living and brownstone row houses, many of them not yet
converted to apartments. East 35th Street for me, a child newly arrived
from California, presented an enchanting pattern of human life. Foot-
beat policemen began their regular patrol at eight. The delivery of residential mail occurred around nine and was followed about ten by the
emergence of women on shopping errands. Young men came and went
the whole day on three-wheel grocery cart bikes, either struggling with
a full load up the moderate rise of Murray Hill from Gristede's[1] down
on Third Avenue, or hurtling back the other way, driving no-hands
against light traffic, cartons of empty bottles clattering explosively as
the bike's solid tires nicked potholes.

In the afternoon a dozen young girls in private-school uniforms   5
swirled in glee and posed with exaggerated emotion across the street,
waiting to be taken home. By dinnertime the street was almost empty of
people; then, around eleven, it was briefly animated again with couples
returning from the theater or some other entertainment. Until dawn,
the pattern of glinting chrome and color in the two rows of curbed
automobiles remained unchanged. And from night to night that pattern
hardly varied.

Overlaying the street's regular, diurnal rhythm was a more chaotic   6
pattern of events, an unpredictability I would watch with unquenchable
fascination for hours at a time. (A jog in the wall of The Advertising
Club of New York next door made it impossible for me to see very far
to the west on 35th Street. But if I leaned out as far as I dared, I could
see all the way to the East River in the other direction.) I would study
the flow of vehicles below: an aggressive insinuation of yellow taxis,
the casual slalom of a motorcycle through lines of stalled traffic, the
obstreperous lumbering of large trucks. The sidewalks, with an occa-

1. Gristede's: New York City supermarket chain.

sional imposing stoop jutting out, were rarely crowded, for there were neither shops nor businesses here, and few tourists. But with Yeshiva University down at the corner of Lexington, the 34th Street Armory a block away, a Swedenborgian church midblock, and 34th Precinct police headquarters just up from Third Avenue, I still saw a fair array of dress and captivating expressions of human bearing. The tortoise pace of elderly women in drab hats paralleled the peeved ambling of a middle-aged man anxious to locate a cab. A naïf, loose-jointed in trajectory down the sidewalk, with wide-flung strides. A buttonhooking young woman, intently scanning door lintels and surreptitiously watching a building superintendent leaning sullenly against a service entrance. Two men in vested suits in conversation on the corner where, rotund and oblivious, they were a disruption, like a boulder in a creek. A boy running through red-lighted traffic with a large bouquet in his hand, held forth like a bowsprit.

All these gaits together with their kindred modulations seemed 7 mysteriously revealing to me. Lingering couples embraced, separated with resolve, then embraced once more. People halted and turned toward each other in hilarious laughter. I watched as though I would never see such things again—screaming arguments, the other-worldly navigations of the deranged, and the haughty stride of single men dressed meticulously in evening clothes.

This pattern of traffic and people, an overlay of personality and 8 idiosyncrasy on the day's fixed events, fed me in a wordless way. My eyes would drift up from these patterns to follow the sky over lower Manhattan, a flock of house sparrows, scudding clouds, a distant airplane approaching La Guardia or Idlewild with impossible slowness.

Another sort of animation drew me regularly to this window: 9 weather. The sound of thunder. Or a rising hiss over the sound of automobiles that meant the streets were wet from a silent rain. The barely audible rattle of dozens of panes of glass in the window's leadwork—a freshening wind. A sudden dimming of sunshine in the living room. Whatever I was doing, these signals would pull me away. At night, in the isolating light cone of a streetlamp, I could see the slant, the density, and sometimes the exact size of raindrops. (None of this could I learn with my bare hands outstretched, in the penumbral dark under the building's cornices.) I watched rainwater course east in sheets down the calico-patched street in the wake of a storm; and cascades of snow, floating and wind-driven, as varied in their character as falls of rain, pile up in the streets. I watched the darkness between buildings burst with lightning, and I studied intently the rattle-drum of hail on car roofs.

The weather I watched from this window, no matter how wild, 10 was always comforting. My back was to rooms secured by family life. East and west, the room shared its walls with people I imagined little different from myself. And from this window I could see a marvel as imbued with meaning for me then as a minaret—the Empire State Building. The high windows of its east wall gleamed imperially in the first rays of dawn, before the light flared down 35th Street, glinting in bits of mica in the façades of brownstones. Beneath the hammer of winter storms, the building seemed courageous and adamantine.

The morning that my mother would die I rested my forearms on   11
the sill of the window, glad for the change of weather. I could see more of the wind, moving gray clouds, than I could feel; but I knew the walk to the subway later that morning, and the short walk up 77th Street to Lennox Hill Hospital, would be cooler.

I had been daydreaming at the window for perhaps an hour when   12
my father came downstairs. The faint odors in the street's air—the dampness of basements, the acrid fragrance of ailanthus trees, the aromatics in roof tar—had drawn me off into a dozen memories. My father paused, speechless, at the foot of the stairs by the dining table. As determined as he was to lead a normal life around Mother's last days, he was at the beck and call of her disease almost as much as she was. With a high salute of his right hand, meant to demonstrate confidence, and an ironic grimace, he went out the door. Downstairs he would meet my brother, who worked with him, and together they would take a cab up to the hospital. My brother, three years younger, was worn out by these marathon days but uncomplaining, almost always calm. He and my father would eat breakfast together at the hospital and sit with Mother until Sandra and I arrived, then leave for work.

I wanted an undisturbed morning, the luxury of that kind of time,   13
in which to give Sandra her birthday presents, to have a conversation not shrouded by death. I made breakfast and took it into the bedroom. While we sipped coffee I offered her what I had gotten. Among other things, a fossil trilobite, symbol of longevity. But we could not break the rind of oppression this terminal disease had created.

While Sandra showered, I dressed and returned to the window. I   14
stood there with my hands in my pockets staring at the weathered surface of the window's wood frame, with its peeling black paint. I took in details in the pitted surface of the sandstone ledge and at its boundary, where the ledge met the color of buildings across the street. I saw the stillness of the ledge against the sluggish flow of early morning traffic and a stream of pedestrians in summer clothing below. The air above the street was a little warmer now. The wind continued to blow steadily, briskly moving cloud banks out over Brooklyn.

I felt a great affection for the city, for its tight Joseph's coat[2] of   15

---

2. Joseph's coat: The "coat of many colors" roused the jealousy of Joseph's brothers in Genesis, chapter 37.

buildings, the vitality of its people, the enduring grace of its plane trees, and the layers of its history, all of it washed by a great tide of weather under maritime skies. Standing at the window I felt the insistence and the assurance of the city, and how I was woven in here through memory and affection.

Sandra touched my shoulder. It was time we were gone, uptown. 16 But something stayed me. I leaned out, bracing my left palm against the window's mullion. The color I saw in people's clothes was now muted. Traffic and pedestrians, the start-up of myriad businesses, had stirred the night's dust. The air was more rank with exhaust. A flock of pigeons came down the corridor of the street toward me, piebald, dove gray, white, brindled ginger, ash black—thirty or more of them. They were turning the bottom of a long parabolic arc, from which they shot up suddenly, out over Park Avenue. They reached a high, stalling apex, rolled over it, and fell off to the south, where they were cut from view by a building. A few moments later they emerged much smaller, wings pounding over brownstones below 34th Street, on a course parallel to the wind's.

I left, leaving the window open. 17

When Sandra and I emerged a half-hour later from the hospital 18 elevator, my brother was waiting to meet us. I could see by the high, wistful cast of his face that she was gone.

GRETEL EHRLICH

Wyoming: The Solace of Open Spaces

Gretel Ehrlich (1946–   ) was raised in Santa Barbara, California, so close to the beach that on quiet nights she "could hear the seals barking on the channel islands." Educated at Bennington College in Vermont and UCLA, she worked briefly in New York as a film editor, and it was to make a documentary film that she went to Wyoming in 1976. She quickly fell in love with what she saw there, and today she is a rancher near Shell. She says that if she rode a horse north, it would take her three days to reach the nearest fence and that in three directions she has an unobstructed horizon for a hundred miles. In addition to miscellaneous essays, Ehrlich has published three books of poetry, a novel, and a collection of essays about her ranch life, *The Solace of Open Spaces* (1985), from which the following essay comes. Her latest work, *A Match to the Heart* (1994), tells the story of her being struck by lightning near her ranch. The writer's love of nature was, perhaps surprisingly, a support for her during her recovery.

It's May, and I've just awakened from a nap, curled against sagebrush the way my dog taught me to sleep—sheltered from wind. A
front is pulling the huge sky over me, and from the dark a hailstone
has hit me on the head. I'm trailing a band of 2000 sheep across a
stretch of Wyoming badland, a fifty-mile trip that takes five days because sheep shade up in hot sun and won't budge until it cools.
Bunched together now, and excited into a run by the storm, they drift
across dry land, tumbling into draws like water and surging out again
onto the rugged, choppy plateaus that are the building blocks of this
state.

The name Wyoming comes from an Indian word meaning "at the   2
great plains," but the plains are really valleys, great arid valleys, 1600
square miles, with the horizon bending up on all sides into mountain
ranges. This gives the vastness a sheltering look.

Winter lasts six months here. Prevailing winds spill snowdrifts to   3
the east, and new storms from the northwest replenish them. This white
bulk is sometimes dizzying, even nauseating, to look at. At twenty,
thirty, and forty degrees below zero, not only does your car not work
but neither do your mind and body. The landscape hardens into a
dungeon of space. During the winter, while I was riding to find a new
calf, my legs froze to the saddle, and in the silence that such cold creates
I felt like the first person on earth, or the last.

Today the sun is out—only a few clouds billowing. In the east,   4
where the sheep have started off without me, the benchland tilts up in
a series of red-earthed, eroded mesas, planed flat on top by a million
years of water; behind them, a bold line of muscular scarps rears up
10,000 feet to become the Big Horn Mountains. A tidal pattern is engraved into the ground, as if left by the sea that once covered this
state. Canyons curve down like galaxies to meet the oncoming rush of
flat land.

To live and work in this kind of open country, with its hundred-   5
mile views, is to lose the distinction between background and foreground. When I asked an older ranch hand to describe Wyoming's
openness, he said, "It's all a bunch of nothing—wind and rattle-
snakes—and so much of it you can't tell where you're going or where
you've been and it don't make much difference." John, a sheepman I
know, is tall and handsome and has an explosive temperament. He has
a perfect intuition about people and sheep. They call him "Highpock-
ets," because he's so long-legged; his graceful stride matches the distance he has to cover. He says, "Open space hasn't affected me at all.
It's all the people moving in on it." The huge ranch he was born on
takes up much of one county and spreads into another state; to put
100,000 miles on his pickup in three years and never leave home is
not unusual. A friend of mine has an aunt who ranched on Powder

River and didn't go off her place for eleven years. When her husband died, she quickly moved to town, bought a car, and drove around the States to see what she'd been missing.

Most people tell me they've simply driven through Wyoming, as if there were nothing to stop for. Or else they've skied in Jackson Hole, a place Wyomingites acknowledge uncomfortably, because its green beauty and chic affluence are mismatched with the rest of the state. Most of Wyoming has a "lean-to" look. Instead of big, roomy barns and Victorian houses, there are dugouts, low sheds, log cabins, sheep camps, and fence lines that look like driftwood blown haphazardly into place. People here still feel pride because they live in such a harsh place, part of the glamorous cowboy past, and they are determined not to be the victims of a mining-dominated future. ⁶

Most characteristic of the state's landscape is what a developer euphemistically describes as "indigenous growth right up to your front door"—a reference to waterless stands of salt sage, snakes, jackrabbits, deerflies, red dust, a brief respite of wildflowers, dry washes, and no trees. In the Great Plains, the vistas look like music, like kyries of grass, but Wyoming seems to be the doing of a mad architect—tumbled and twisted, ribboned with faded, deathbed colors, thrust up and pulled down as if the place had been startled out of a deep sleep and thrown into a pure light. ⁷

I came here four years ago. I had not planned to stay, but I couldn't make myself leave. John, the sheepman, put me to work immediately. It was spring, and shearing time. For fourteen days of fourteen hours each, we moved thousands of sheep through sorting corrals to be sheared, branded, and deloused. I suspect that my original motive for coming here was to "lose myself" in new and unpopulated territory. Instead of producing the numbness I thought I wanted, life on the sheep ranch woke me up. The vitality of the people I was working with flushed out what had become a hallucinatory rawness inside me. I threw away my clothes and bought new ones; I cut my hair. The arid country was a clean slate. Its absolute indifference steadied me. ⁸

Sagebrush covers 58,000 square miles of Wyoming. The biggest city has a population of 50,000, and there are only five settlements that could be called cities in the whole state. The rest are towns, scattered across the expanse with as much as sixty miles between them, their populations 2000, fifty, or ten. They are fugitive-looking, perched on a barren, windblown bench, or tagged onto a river or a railroad, or laid out straight in a farming valley with implement stores and a block-long Mormon church. In the eastern part of the state, which slides down into the Great Plains, the new mining settlements are boomtowns, trailer cities, metal knots on flat land. ⁹

Despite the desolate look, there's a coziness to living in this state. ¹⁰

There are so few people (only 470,000) that ranchers who buy and sell
cattle know each other statewide; the kids who choose to go to college
usually go to the state's one university, in Laramie; hired hands work
their way around Wyoming in a lifetime of hirings and firings. And,
despite the physical separation, people stay in touch, often driving two
or three hours to another ranch for dinner.

Seventy-five years ago, when travel was by buckboard or horse-   11
back, cowboys who were temporarily out of work rode the grub line—
drifting from ranch to ranch, mending fences or milking cows, and
receiving in exchange a bed and meals. Gossip and messages traveled
this slow circuit with them, creating an intimacy between ranchers who
were three and four weeks' ride apart. One old-time couple I know,
whose turn-of-the-century homestead was used by an outlaw gang as
a relay station for stolen horses, recall that if you were traveling, des-
perado or not, any lighted ranch house was a welcome sign. Even
now, for someone who lives in a remote spot, arriving at a ranch or
coming to town for supplies is cause for celebration. To emerge from
isolation can be disorienting. Everything looks bright, new, vivid. After
I had been herding sheep for only three days, the sound of the camp-
tender's pickup flustered me. Longing for human company, I felt a
foolish grin take over my face, yet I had to resist an urgent temptation
to run and hide.

Things happen suddenly in Wyoming: the change of seasons and   12
weather; for people, the violent swings in and out of isolation. But
goodnaturedness is concomitant with severity. Friendliness is a tradition. Strangers passing on the road wave hello. A common sight is two
pickups stopped side by side far out on a range, on a dirt track winding
through the sage. The drivers will share a cigarette, uncap their thermos
bottles, and pass a battered cup, steaming with coffee, between windows. These meetings summon up the details of several generations,
because in Wyoming, private histories are largely public knowledge.

Because ranch work is a physical and, these days, economic strain,   13
being "at home on the range" is a matter of vigor, self-reliance, and
common sense. A person's life is not a series of dramatic events for
which he or she is applauded or exiled but a slow accumulation of
days, seasons, years, fleshed out by the generational weight of one's
family and anchored by a land-bound sense of place.

In most parts of Wyoming, the human population is visibly out-   14
numbered by the animal. Not far from my town of fifty, I rode into a
narrow valley and startled a herd of 200 elk. Eagles look like small
people as they eat car-killed deer by the road. Antelope, moving in
small, graceful bands, travel at 60 miles an hour, their mouths open as
if drinking in the space.

The solitude in which westerners live makes them quiet. They tele-   15

graph thoughts and feelings by the way they tilt their heads and listen;
pulling their Stetsons into a steep dive over their eyes, or pigeon-toeing
one boot over the other, they lean against a fence with a fat wedge of
snoose beneath their lower lips and take the whole scene in. These
detached looks of quiet amusement are sometimes cynical, but they can
also come from a dry-eyed humility as lucid as the air is clear.

Conversation goes on in what sounds like a private code; a few   16
phrases imply a complex of meanings. Asking directions, you get a
curious list of details. While trailing sheep, I was told to "ride up to
that kinda upturned rock, follow the pink wash, turn left at the dump,
and then you'll see the waterhole." One friend told his wife on roundup
to "turn at the salt lick and the dead cow," which turned out to be a
scattering of bones and no salt lick at all.

Sentence structure is shortened to the skin and bones of a thought.   17
Descriptive words are dropped, even verbs; a cowboy looking over a
corral full of horses will say to a wrangler, "Which one needs rode?"
People hold back their thoughts in what seems to be a dumbfounded
silence, then erupt with an excoriating, perceptive remark. Language,
so compressed, becomes metaphorical. A rancher ended a relationship
with one remark: "You're a bad check," meaning bouncing in and out
was intolerable, and even coming back would be no good.

What's behind this laconic style is shyness. There is no vocabulary   18
for the subject of feelings. It's not a hangdog shyness, or anything coy—
always there's a robust spirit in evidence behind the restraint, as if the
earth-dredging wind that pulls across Wyoming had carried its people's
voices away but everything else in them had shouldered confidently
into the breeze.

I've spent hours riding to sheep camp at dawn in a pickup when   19
nothing was said; eaten meals in the cookhouse when the only words
spoken were a mumbled "Thank you, ma'am" at the end of dinner.
The silence is profound. Instead of talking, we seem to share one eye.
Keenly observed, the world is transformed. The landscape is engorged
with detail, every movement on it chillingly sharp. The air between
people is charged. Days unfold, bathed in their own music. Nights become hallucinatory; dreams, prescient.

Spring weather is capricious and mean. It snows, then blisters with   20
heat. There have been tornadoes. They lay their elephant trunks out in
the sage until they find houses, then slurp everything up and leave. I've
noticed that melting snowbanks hiss and rot, viperous, then drip into
calm pools where ducklings hatch and livestock, being trailed to summer range, drink. With the ice cover gone, rivers churn a milkshake
brown, taking culverts and small bridges with them. Water in such an
arid place (the average annual rainfall where I live is less than eight
inches) is like blood. It festoons drab land with green veins: a line of

cottonwoods following a stream; a strip of alfalfa; and on ditchbanks, wild asparagus growing.

I've moved to a small cattle ranch owned by friends. It's at the foot 21 of the Big Horn Mountains. A few weeks ago, I helped them deliver a calf who was stuck halfway out of his mother's body. By the time he was freed, we could see a heartbeat, but he was straining against a swollen tongue for air. Mary and I held him upside down by his back feet, while Stan, on his hands and knees in the blood, gave the calf mouth-to-mouth resuscitation. I have a vague memory of being pneumonia-choked as a child, my mother giving me her air, which may account for my romance with this windswept state.

If anything is endemic to Wyoming, it is wind. This big room of 22 space is swept out daily, leaving a boneyard of fossils, agates, and carcasses in every stage of decay. Though it was water that initially shaped the state, wind is the meticulous gardener, raising dust and pruning the sage.

I try to imagine a world of uncharted land, in which one could 23 look over an uncompleted map and ride a horse past where all the lines have stopped. There is no wilderness left; wilderness, yes, but true wilderness has been gone on this continent since the time of Lewis and Clark's overland journey.

Two hundred years ago, the Crow, Shoshone, Arapaho, Cheyenne, 24 and Sioux roamed the intermountain West, orchestrating their movements according to hunger, season, and warfare. Once they acquired horses, they traversed the spines of all the big Wyoming ranges—the Absarokas, the Wind Rivers, the Tetons, the Big Horns—and wintered on the unprotected plains that fan out from them. Space was life. The world was their home.

What was life-giving to native Americans was often nightmarish to 25 sodbusters who arrived encumbered with families and ethnic pasts to be transplanted in nearly uninhabitable land. The great distances, the shortage of water and trees, and the loneliness created unexpected hardships for them. In her book *O Pioneers!*, Willa Cather gives a settler's version of the bleak landscape:

> The little town behind them had vanished as if it had never been, had fallen behind the swell of the prairie, and the stern frozen country received them into its bosom. The homesteads were few and far apart; here and there a windmill gaunt against the sky, a sod house crouching in a hollow.

The emptiness of the West was for others a geography of possibility. 26 Men and women who amassed great chunks of land and struggled to preserve unfenced empires were, despite their self-serving motives, unwitting geographers. They understood the lay of the land. But by the 1850s, the Oregon and Mormon trails sported bumper-to-bumper traffic. Wealthy landowners, many of them aristocratic absentee landlords, known as remittance men because they were paid to come West and get out of their families' hair, overstocked the range with more than a million head of cattle. By 1885, the feed and water were desperately short, and the winter of 1886 laid out the gaunt bodies of dead animals so closely together that when the thaw came, one rancher from Kaycee claimed to have walked on cowhide all the way to Crazy Woman Creek, twenty miles away.

Territorial Wyoming was a boy's world. The land was generous with everything but water. At first there was room enough, food enough, for everyone. And, as with all beginnings, an expansive mood set in. The young cowboys, drifters, shopkeepers, schoolteachers, were heroic, lawless, generous, rowdy, and tenacious. The individualism and optimism generated during those times have endured. 27

John Tisdale rode north with the trail herds from Texas. He was a college-educated man with enough money to buy a small outfit near the Powder River. While driving home from the town of Buffalo with a buckboard full of Christmas toys for his family and a winter's supply of food, he was shot in the back by an agent of the cattle barons who resented the encroachment of small-time stockmen like him. The wealthy cattlemen tried to control all the public grazing land by restricting membership in the Wyoming Stock Growers Association, as if it were a country club. They ostracized from roundups and brandings cowboys and ranchers who were not members, then denounced them as rustlers. Tisdale's death, the second such cold-blooded murder, kicked off the Johnson County cattle war, which was no simple good-guy-bad-guy shootout but a complicated class struggle between landed gentry and less affluent settlers—a shocking reminder that the West was not an egalitarian sanctuary after all. 28

Fencing ultimately enforced boundaries, but barbed wire abrogated space. It was stretched across the beautiful valleys, into the mountains, over desert badlands, through buffalo grass. The "anything is possible" fever—the lure of any new place—was constricted. The integrity of the land as a geographic body, and the freedom to ride anywhere on it, was lost. 29

I punched cows with a young man named Martin, who is the great-grandson of John Tisdale. His inheritance is not the open land that Tisdale knew and prematurely lost but a rage against restraint. 30

Wyoming tips down as you head northeast; the highest ground—the Laramie Plains—is on the Colorado border. Up where I live, the Big Horn River leaks into difficult, arid terrain. In the basin here it's dammed, sandhill cranes gather and, with delicate legwork, slice through the stilled water. I was driving by with a rancher one morning when he commented that cranes are "old-fashioned." When I asked 31 why, he said, "Because they mate for life." Then he looked at me with a twinkle in his eyes, as if to say he really did believe in such things but also understood why we break our own rules.

In all this open space, values crystallize quickly. People are strong on scruples but tenderhearted about quirky behavior. A friend and I found one ranch hand, who's "not quite right in the head," sitting in front of the badly decayed carcass of a cow, shaking his finger and saying, "Now, I don't want you to do this ever again!" When I asked what was wrong with him, I was told, "He's goofier than hell, just like the rest of us." Perhaps because the West is historically new, conventional morality is still felt to be less important than rock-bottom truths. Though there's always a lot of teasing and sparring around, people are blunt with each other, sometimes even cruel, believing honesty is stronger medicine than sympathy, which may console but often conceals. 32

The formality that goes hand in hand with the rowdiness is known as "the Western Code." It's a list of practical dos and don'ts, faithfully observed. A friend, Cliff, who runs a trapline in the winter, cut off half his foot while axing a hole in the ice. Alone, he dragged himself to his pickup and headed for town, stopping to open the ranch gate as he left, and getting out to close it again, thus losing, in his observance of rules, precious time and blood. Later, he commented, "How would it look, them having to come to the hospital to tell me their cows had gotten out?" 33

Accustomed to emergencies, my friends doctor each other from the vet's bag with relish. When one old-timer suffered a heart attack in hunting camp, his partner quickly stirred up a brew of red horse liniment and hot water and made the half-conscious victim drink it, then tied him onto a horse and led him twenty miles to town. He regained consciousness and lived. 34

The roominess of the state has affected political attitudes as well. Ranchers keep up with world politics and the convulsions of the economy but are basically isolationists. Being used to running their own small empires of land and livestock, they're suspicious of big government. It's a "don't fence me in" holdover from a century ago. They still want the elbow room their grandfathers had, so they're strongly conservative, but with a populist twist. 35

Summer is the season when we get our "cowboy tans"—on the lower parts of our faces and on three fourths of our arms. Excessive heat, in the nineties and higher, sends us outside with the mosquitoes. In winter, we're tucked inside our houses, and the white wasteland outside appears to be expanding, but in summer, all the greenery abridges space. Summer is a go-ahead season. Every living thing is off 36 the block and in the race: battalions of bugs in flight and biting; bats swinging around my log cabin as if the bases were loaded and someone had hit a home run. Some of summer's high-speed growth is ominous: larkspur, death camas, and green greasewood can kill sheep—an ironic idea, dying in this desert from eating what is too verdant. With sixteen hours of daylight, farmers and ranchers irrigate feverishly. There are first, second, and third cuttings of hay, some crews averaging only four hours of sleep a night for weeks. And, like the cowboys who in summer ride the night rodeo circuit, nighthawks make daredevil dives at dusk with an eerie whirring that sounds like a plane going down on the shimmering horizon.

In the town where I live, they've had to board up the dance-hall windows because there have been so many fights. There's so little to do except work that people wind up in a state of idle agitation that becomes fatalistic, as if there were nothing to be done about all this untapped energy. So the dark side to the grandeur of these spaces is the small-mindedness that seals people in. Men become hermits; women go mad. Cabin fever explodes into suicides, or into grudges and lifelong family feuds. Two sisters in my area inherited a ranch but found they couldn't get along. They fenced the place in half. When one's cows got out and mixed with the other's, the women went at each other with shovels. They ended up in the same hospital room, but never spoke a word to each other for the rest of their lives. 37

Eccentricity ritualizes behavior. It's a shortcut through unmanage-able emotions and strict social conventions. I knew a sheepherder named Fred who, at seventy-eight, still had a handsome face, which he kept smooth by plastering it each day with bag balm and Vaseline. He was curious, well-read, and had a fact-keeping mind to go along with his penchant for hoarding. His reliquary of gunnysacks, fence wire, wood, canned food, unopened Christmas presents, and magazines matched his odd collages of meals: sardines with maple syrup; vegetable soup garnished with Fig Newtons. His wagon was so overloaded that he had to sleep sitting up because there was no room on the bed. Despite his love of up-to-date information, Fred died from gangrene when an old-timer's remedy of fresh sheep manure, applied as a poul-tice to a bad cut, failed to save him. 38

After the brief lushness of summer, the sun moves south. The range grass is brown. Livestock has been trailed back down from the moun-tains. Waterholes begin to frost over at night. Last fall Martin asked me to accompany him on a pack trip. With five horses, we followed a river into the mountains behind the tiny Wyoming town of Meeteetse. Groves of aspen, red and orange, gave off a light that made us look toasted. Our hunting camp was so high that clouds skidded across our 39 foreheads, then slowed to sail out across the warm valleys. Except for a bull moose who wandered into our camp and mistook our black gelding for a rival, we shot at nothing.

One of our evening entertainments was to watch the night sky. My   40 dog, who also came on the trip, a dingo bred to herd sheep, is so used to the silence and empty skies that when an airplane flies over he always looks up and eyes the distant intruder quizzically. The sky, lately, seems to be much more crowded than it used to be. Satellites make their silent passes in the dark with great regularity. We counted eighteen in one hour's viewing. How odd to think that while they circumnavigated the planet, Martin and I had moved only six miles into our local wilderness, and had seen no other human for the two weeks we stayed there.

At night, by moonlight, the land is whittled to slivers—a ridge, a   41 river, a strip of grassland stretching to the mountains, then the huge sky. One morning a full moon was setting in the west just as the sun was rising. I felt precariously balanced between the two as I loped across a meadow. For a moment, I could believe that the stars, which were still visible, work like cooper's bands, holding everything above Wyoming together.

Space has a spiritual equivalent, and can heal what is divided and   42 burdensome in us. My grandchildren will probably use space shuttles for a honeymoon trip or to recover from heart attacks, but closer to home we might also learn how to carry space inside ourselves in the effortless way we carry our skins. Space represents sanity, not a life purified, dull, or "spaced out" but one that might accommodate intelligently any idea or situation.

From the clayey soil of northern Wyoming is mined bentonite,   43 which is used as a filler in candy, gum, and lipstick. We Americans are great on fillers, as if what we have, what we are, is not enough. We have a cultural tendency toward denial, but, being affluent, we strangle ourselves with what we can buy. We have only to look at the houses we build to see how we build *against* space, the way we drink against pain and loneliness. We fill up space as if it were a pie shell, with things whose opacity further obstructs our ability to see what is already there.

H. D. F. KITTO

The Polis

H(enry) D(avy) F(indley) Kitto (1897–1982) was born in Gloucestershire, England, and received his B.A. in classics from Cambridge University. He continued his study while serving as a lecturer in ancient Greek at the University of Glasgow from 1920 to 1944, interrupting his scholarly life long enough to travel extensively in Greece and record his observations of the modern culture and land in *In the Mountains of Greece* (1933). In 1944 he became Professor at the University of Bristol, where he remained for the rest of his career. Kitto's reputation as a leading Greek scholar was established with works such as *Greek Tragedy* (1939) and *Form and Meaning in Drama* (1956), in which he concentrated on recovering the cultural context surrounding works of the classical period. By far his most influential book, however, has been *The Greeks* (1951), which offers the student unfamiliar with classical culture an in-depth portrait of the history and character of Greek civilization. This book, admired as much for the wit and vigor of its prose as for its excellent scholarship, has been reprinted over thirty times and translated into six languages. "The Polis" is excerpted from *The Greeks*.

"Polis" is the Greek word which we translate "city-state." It is a bad   1
translation, because the normal polis was not much like a city, and was very much more than a state. But translation, like politics, is the art of the possible; since we have not got the thing which the Greeks called "the polis," we do not possess an equivalent word. From now on, we will avoid the misleading term "city-state," and use the Greek word instead. In this chapter we will first inquire how this political system arose, then we will try to reconstitute the word "polis" and recover its real meaning by watching it in action. It may be a long task, but all the time we shall be improving our acquaintance with the Greeks. Without a clear conception what the polis was, and what it meant to the Greeks, it is quite impossible to understand properly Greek history, the Greek mind, or the Greek achievement.

First then, what was the polis? In the *Iliad* we discern a political   2
structure that seems not unfamiliar—a structure that can be called an advanced or a degenerate form of tribalism, according to taste. There are kings, like Achilles, who rule their people, and there is the great king, Agamemnon, King of Men, who is something like a feudal overlord. He is under obligation, whether of right or of custom, to consult the other kings or chieftains in matters of common interest. They form a regular council, and in its debates the sceptre, symbol of authority, is held by the speaker for the time being. This is recognizably European, not Oriental; Agamemnon is no despot, ruling with the unquestioned authority of a god. There are also signs of a shadowy Assembly of the People, to be consulted on important occasions: though Homer, a courtly poet, and in any case not a constitutional historian, says little about it.

Such, in outline, is the tradition about pre-conquest Greece. When   3
the curtain goes up again after the Dark Age we see a very different

picture. No longer is there a "wide-ruling Agamemnon" lording it in
Mycenae. In Crete, where Idomeneus had been ruling as sole king, we
find over fifty quite independent poleis, fifty small "states" in the place
of one. It is a small matter that the kings have disappeared; the important thing is that the kingdoms have gone too. What is true of Crete is
true of Greece in general, or at least of those parts which play any
considerable part in Greek history—Ionia, the islands, the Peloponnesus
except Arcadia, Central Greece except the western parts, and South
Italy and Sicily when they became Greek. All these were divided into
an enormous number of quite independent and autonomous political
units.

It is important to realize their size. The modern reader picks up a   4
translation of Plato's *Republic* or Aristotle's *Politics;* he finds Plato or-
daining that his ideal city shall have 5,000 citizens, and Aristotle that
each citizen should be able to know all the others by sight; and he
smiles, perhaps, at such philosophic fantasies. But Plato and Aristotle
are not fantasts. Plato is imagining a polis on the normal Hellenic scale;
indeed he implies that many existing Greek poleis are too small—for
many had less than 5,000 citizens. Aristotle says, in his amusing way—
Aristotle sometimes sounds very like a don[1]—that a polis of ten citizens
would be impossible, because it could not be self-sufficient, and that a
polis of a hundred thousand would be absurd, because it could not
govern itself properly. And we are not to think of these "citizens" as a
"master-class" owning and dominating thousands of slaves. The ordinary Greek in these early centuries was a farmer, and if he owned a
slave he was doing pretty well. Aristotle speaks of a hundred thousand
citizens; if we allow each to have a wife and four children, and then
add a liberal number of slaves and resident aliens, we shall arrive at
something like a million—the population of Birmingham; and to Aristotle an independent "state" as populous as Birmingham is a lecture-
room joke. Or we may turn from the philosophers to a practical man,
Hippodamas, who laid out the Piraeus in the most up-to-date American
style; he said that the ideal number of citizens was ten thousand, which
would imply a total population of about 100,000.

In fact, only three poleis had more than 20,000 citizens—Syracuse   5
and Acragas (Girgenti) in Sicily, and Athens. At the outbreak of the
Peloponnesian War the population of Attica was probably about
350,000, half Athenian (men, women and children), about a tenth
resident aliens, and the rest slaves. Sparta, or Lacedaemon, had a much
smaller citizen-body, though it was larger in area. The Spartans had
conquered and annexed Messenia, and possessed 3,200 square miles of

---

1. A tutor or fellow of one of the colleges at Oxford or Cambridge. That is, Aristotle
sounds professorial.

territory. By Greek standards this was an enormous area: it would take a good walker two days to cross it. The important commercial city of Corinth had a territory of 330 square miles—about the size of Huntingdonshire. The island of Ceos, which is about as big as Bute, was divided into four poleis. It had therefore four armies, four governments, possibly four different calendars, and, it may be, four different currencies and systems of measures—though this is less likely. Mycenae was in historical times a shrunken relic of Agamemnon's capital, but still independent. She sent an army to help the Greek cause against Persia at the battle of Plataea; the army consisted of eighty men. Even by Greek standards this was small, but we do not hear that any jokes were made about an army sharing a cab.

To think on this scale is difficult for us, who regard a state of ten 6 million as small, and are accustomed to states which, like the U.S.A. and the U.S.S.R., are so big that they have to be referred to by their initials; but when the adjustable reader has become accustomed to the scale, he will not commit the vulgar error of confusing size with significance. The modern writer is sometimes heard to speak with splendid scorn of "those petty Greek states, with their interminable quarrels." Quite so; Plataea, Sicyon, Aegina and the rest are petty, compared with modern states. The Earth itself is petty, compared with Jupiter—but then, the atmosphere of Jupiter is mainly ammonia, and that makes a difference. We do not like breathing ammonia—and the Greeks would not much have liked breathing the atmosphere of the vast modern State. They knew of one such, the Persian Empire—and thought it very suitable, for barbarians. Difference of scale, when it is great enough, amounts to difference of kind.

But before we deal with the nature of the polis, the reader might 7 like to know how it happened that the relatively spacious pattern of pre-Dorian Greece became such a mosaic of small fragments. The Classical scholar too would like to know; there are no records, so that all we can do is to suggest plausible reasons. There are historical, geographical and economic reasons; and when these have been duly set forth, we may conclude perhaps that the most important reason of all is simply that this is the way in which the Greeks preferred to live.

The coming of the Dorians was not an attack made by one organized 8 nation upon another. The invaded indeed had their organization, loose though it was; some of the invaders—the main body that conquered Lacedaemon—must have been a coherent force; but others must have been small groups of raiders, profiting from the general turmoil and seizing good land where they could find it. A sign of this is that we find members of the same clan in different states. Pindar, for example, was a citizen of Thebes and a member of the ancient family of the Aegidae. But there were Aegidae too in Aegina and Sparta, quite independent poleis, and Pindar addresses them as kinsmen. This particular clan therefore was split up in the invasions. In a country like Greece this would be very natural.

In a period so unsettled the inhabitants of any valley or island might at a moment's notice be compelled to fight for their fields. Therefore a local strong-point was necessary, normally a defensible hill-top somewhere in the plain. This, the "acropolis" ("high-town"), would be fortified, and here would be the residence of the king. It would also be the natural place of assembly, and the religious centre. 9

This is the beginning of the town. What we have to do is to give reasons why the town grew, and why such a small pocket of people remained an independent political unit. The former task is simple. To begin with, natural economic growth made a central market necessary. We saw that the economic system implied by Hesiod and Homer was "close household economy"; the estate, large or small, produced nearly everything that it needed, and what it could not produce it did without. As things became more stable a rather more specialized economy became possible: more goods were produced for sale. Hence the growth of a market. 10

At this point we may invoke the very sociable habits of the Greeks, ancient or modern. The English farmer likes to build his house on his land, and to come into town when he has to. What little leisure he has he likes to spend on the very satisfying occupation of looking over a gate. The Greek prefers to live in the town or village, to walk out to his work, and to spend his rather ampler leisure talking in the town or village square. Therefore the market becomes a market-town, naturally beneath the Acropolis. This became the centre of the communal life of the people—and we shall see presently how important that was. 11

But why did not such towns form larger units? This is the important question. 12

There is an economic point. The physical barriers which Greece has so abundantly made the transport of goods difficult, except by sea, and the sea was not yet used with any confidence. Moreover, the variety of which we spoke earlier enabled quite a small area to be reasonably self-sufficient for a people who made such small material demands on life as the Greek. Both of these facts tend in the same direction; there was in Greece no great economic interdependence, no reciprocal pull between the different parts of the country, strong enough to counteract the desire of the Greek to live in small communities. 13

There is a geographical point. It is sometimes asserted that this system of independent poleis was imposed on Greece by the physical character of the country. The theory is attractive, especially to those who like to have one majestic explanation of any phenomenon, but it does not seem to be true. It is of course obvious that the physical subdivision of the country helped; the system could not have existed, for example, in Egypt, a country which depends entirely on the proper 14 management of the Nile flood, and therefore must have a central government. But there are countries cut up quite as much as Greece—Scotland, for instance—which have never developed the polis-system; and conversely there were in Greece many neighbouring poleis, such as Corinth and Sicyon, which remained independent of each other although between them there was no physical barrier that would seriously incommode a modern cyclist. Moreover, it was precisely the most mountainous parts of Greece that never developed poleis, or not until later days—Arcadia and Aetolia, for example, which had something like a canton-system. The polis flourished in those parts where communications were relatively easy. So that we are still looking for our explanation.

Economics and geography helped, but the real explanation is the 15 character of the Greeks—which those determinists may explain who have the necessary faith in their omniscience. As it will take some time to deal with this, we may first clear out of the way an important historical point. How did it come about that so preposterous a system was able to last for more than twenty minutes?

The ironies of history are many and bitter, but at least this must be 16 put to the credit of the gods, that they arranged for the Greeks to have the Eastern Mediterranean almost to themselves long enough to work out what was almost a laboratory-experiment to test how far, and in what conditions, human nature is capable of creating and sustaining a civilization. In Asia, the Hittite Empire had collapsed, the Lydian kingdom was not aggressive, and the Persian power, which eventually overthrew Lydia, was still embryonic in the mountainous recesses of the continent; Egypt was in decay; Macedon, destined to make nonsense of the polis-system, was and long remained in a state of ineffective semi-barbarism; Rome had not yet been heard of, nor any other power in Italy. There were indeed the Phoenicians, and their western colony, Carthage, but these were traders first and last. Therefore this lively and intelligent Greek people was for some centuries allowed to live under the apparently absurd system which suited and developed its genius instead of becoming absorbed in the dull mass of a large empire, which would have smothered its spiritual growth, and made it what it afterwards became, a race of brilliant individuals and opportunists. Obviously some day somebody would create a strong centralized power in the Eastern Mediterranean—a successor to the ancient sea-power of King Minos. Would it be Greek, Oriental, or something else? This question must be the theme of a later chapter, but no history of Greece can be intelligible until one has understood what the polis meant to the Greek; and when we have understood that, we shall also understand why the Greeks developed it, and so obstinately tried to maintain it. Let us then examine the word in action.

It meant at first that which was later called the Acropolis, the 17 stronghold of the whole community and the centre of its public life. The town which nearly always grew up around this was designated by another word, "asty." But "polis" very soon meant either the citadel or the whole people which, as it were, "used" this citadel. So we read in Thucydides, "Epidamnus is a polis on the right as you sail into the Ionian gulf." This is not like saying "Bristol is a city on the right as you sail up the Bristol Channel," for Bristol is not an independent state which might be at war with Gloucester, but only an urban area with a purely local administration. Thucydides' words imply that there is a town—though possibly a very small one—called Epidamnus, which is the political centre of the Epidamnians, who live in the territory of which the town is the centre—not the "capital"—and are Epidamnians whether they live in the town or in one of the villages in this territory.

Sometimes the territory and the town have different names. Thus, Attica is the territory occupied by the Athenian people; it comprised Athens—the "polis" in the narrower sense—the Piraeus, and many villages; but the people collectively were Athenians, not Attics, and a citizen was an Athenian in whatever part of Attica he might live. 18

In this sense "polis" is our "state." In Sophocles' *Antigone* Creon comes forward to make his first proclamation as king. He begins, "Gentlemen, as for the polis, the gods have brought it safely through the storm, on even keel." It is the familiar image of the Ship of State, and we think we know where we are. But later in the play he says what we should naturally translate, "Public proclamation has been made . . ." He says in fact, "It has been proclaimed to the polis . . ."—not to the "state," but to the "people." Later in the play he quarrels violently with his son: "What?" he cries, "is anyone but me to rule in this land?" Haemon answers, "It is no polis that is ruled by one man only." The answer brings out another important part of the whole conception of a polis, namely that it is a community, and that its affairs are the affairs of all. The actual business of governing might be entrusted to a monarch, acting in the name of all according to traditional usages, or to the heads of certain noble families, or to a council of citizens owning so much property, or to all the citizens. All these, and many modifications of them, were natural forms of "polity"; all were sharply distinguished by the Greek from Oriental monarchy, in which the monarch is irresponsible, not holding his powers in trust by the grace of god, but being himself a god. If there was irresponsible government there was no polis. Haemon is accusing his father of talking like a "tyrannos"[2] and thereby destroying the polis—but not "the State." 19

To continue our exposition of the word. The chorus in Aristophanes' 20

---

2. I prefer to use the Greek form of this (apparently) Oriental word. It is the Greek equivalent of "dictator," but it does not necessarily have the colour of our word "tyrant." [author's note]

Acharnians, admiring the conduct of the hero, turns to the audience with an appeal which I render literally, "Dost thou see, O whole polis?" The last words are sometimes translated "thou thronging city," which sounds better, but obscures an essential point, namely that the size of the polis made it possible for a member to appeal to all his fellow-citizens in person, and this he naturally did if he thought that another member of the polis had injured him. It was the common assumption of the Greeks that the polis took its origin in the desire for Justice. Individuals are lawless, but the polis will see to it that wrongs are redressed. But not by an elaborate machinery of state-justice, for such a machine could not be operated except by individuals, who may be as unjust as the original wrongdoer. The injured party will be sure of obtaining justice only if he can declare his wrongs to the whole polis. The word therefore now means "people" in actual distinction from "state."

Iocasta, the tragic Queen in the *Oedipus,* will show us a little more 21
of the range of the word. It becomes a question if Oedipus her husband is not after all the accursed man who had killed the previous king Laius. "No, no," cries Iocasta, "it cannot be! The slave said it was 'brigands' who had attacked them, not 'a brigand.' He cannot go back on his word now. The polis heard him, not I alone." Here the word is used without any "political" association at all; it is, as it were, off duty, and signifies "the whole people." This is a shade of meaning which is not always so prominent, but is never entirely absent.

Then Demosthenes the orator talks of a man who, literally, "avoids 22
the city"—a translation which might lead the unwary to suppose that he lived in something corresponding to the Lake District, or Purley. But the phrase "avoids the polis" tells us nothing about his domicile; it means that he took no part in public life—and was therefore something of an oddity. The affairs of the community did not interest him.

We have now learned enough about the word polis to realize that 23
there is no possible English rendering of such a common phrase as, "It is everyone's duty to help the polis." We cannot say "help the state," for that arouses no enthusiasm; it is "the state" that takes half our incomes from us. Not "the community," for with us "the community" is too big and too various to be grasped except theoretically. One's village, one's trade union, one's class, are entities that mean something to us at once, but "work for the community," though an admirable sentiment, is to most of us vague and flabby. In the years before the war, what did most parts of Great Britain know about the depressed areas? How much do bankers, miners and farmworkers understand each other? But the "polis" every Greek knew; there it was, complete, before his eyes. He could see the fields which gave it its sustenance—or did not, if the crops failed; he could see how agriculture, trade and industry dove-tailed into one another; he knew the frontiers, where

they were strong and where weak; if any malcontents were planning
a *coup*, it was difficult for them to conceal the fact. The entire life of the
polis, and the relation between its parts, were much easier to grasp,
because of the small scale of things. Therefore to say "It is everyone's
duty to help the polis" was not to express a fine sentiment but to speak
the plainest and most urgent common sense.[3] Public affairs had an
immediacy and a concreteness which they cannot possibly have for us.

One specific example will help. The Athenian democracy taxed the   24
rich with as much disinterested enthusiasm as the British, but this could
be done in a much more gracious way, simply because the State was
so small and intimate. Among us, the payer of super-tax (presumably)
pays much as the income-tax payer does: he writes his cheque and
thinks, "There! *That's* gone down the drain!" In Athens, the man whose
wealth exceeded a certain sum had, in a yearly rota, to perform certain
"liturgies"—literally, "folk-works." He had to keep a warship in commission for one year (with the privilege of commanding it, if he chose),
or finance the production of plays at the Festival, or equip a religious
procession. It was a heavy burden, and no doubt unwelcome, but at
least some fun could be got out of it and some pride taken in it. There
was satisfaction and honour to be gained from producing a trilogy wor-
thily before one's fellow-citizens. So, in countless other ways, the size
of the polis made vivid and immediate, things which to us are only
abstractions or wearisome duties. Naturally this cut both ways. For
example, an incompetent or unlucky commander was the object not of
a diffused and harmless popular indignation, but of direct accusation;
he might be tried for his life before an Assembly, many of whose past
members he had led to death.

Pericles' Funeral Speech, recorded or recreated by Thucydides, will   25
illustrate this immediacy, and will also take our conception of the polis
a little further. Each year, Thucydides tell us, if citizens had died in
war—and they had, more often than not—a funeral oration was delivered by "a man chosen by the polis." Today, that would be someone
nominated by the Prime Minister, or the British Academy, or the B.B.C.
In Athens it meant that someone was chosen by the Assembly who had
often spoken to that Assembly; and on this occasion Pericles spoke from
a specially high platform, that his voice might reach as many as possible.
Let us consider two phrases that Pericles used in that speech.

He is comparing the Athenian polis with the Spartan, and makes   26
the point that the Spartans admit foreign visitors only grudgingly, and
from time to time expel all strangers, "while we make our polis common to all." "Polis" here is not the political unit; there is no question
of naturalizing foreigners—which the Greeks did rarely, simply because

3. It did not, of course, follow that the Greek obeyed common sense any oftener than
we do. [author's note]

the polis was so intimate a union. Pericles means here: "We throw open to all our common cultural life," as is shown by the words that follow, difficult though they are to translate: "nor do we deny them any instruction or spectacle"—words that are almost meaningless until we realize that the drama, tragic and comic, the performance of choral hymns, public recitals of Homer, games, were all necessary and normal parts of "political" life. This is the sort of thing Pericles has in mind when he speaks of "instruction and spectacle," and of "making the polis open to all."

But we must go further than this. A perusal of the speech will show that in praising the Athenian polis Pericles is praising more than a state, a nation, or a people: he is praising a way of life; he means no less when, a little later, he calls Athens the "school of Hellas."—And what of that? Do not we praise "the English way of life"? The difference is this; we expect our State to be quite indifferent to "the English way of life"—indeed, the idea that the State should actively try to promote it would fill most of us with alarm. The Greeks thought of the polis as an active, formative thing, training the minds and characters of the citizens; we think of it as a piece of machinery for the production of safety and convenience. The training in virtue, which the medieval state left to the Church, and the polis made its own concern, the modern state leaves to God knows what.

"Polis," then, originally "citadel," may mean as much as "the whole communal life of the people, political, cultural, moral"—even "economic," for how else are we to understand another phrase in this same speech, "the produce of the whole world comes to us, because of the magnitude of our polis"? This must mean "our national wealth."

Religion too was bound up with the polis—though not every form of religion. The Olympian gods were indeed worshipped by Greeks everywhere, but each polis had, if not its own gods, at least its own particular cults of these gods. Thus, Athena of the Brazen House was worshipped at Sparta, but to the Spartans Athena was never what she was to the Athenians, "Athena Polias," Athena guardian of the City. So Hera, in Athens, was a goddess worshipped particularly by women, as the goddess of hearth and home, but in Argos "Argive Hera" was the supreme deity of the people. We have in these gods tribal deities, like Jehovah, who exist as it were on two levels at once, as gods of the individual polis, and gods of the whole Greek race. But beyond these Olympians, each polis had its minor local deities, "heroes" and nymphs, each worshipped with his immemorial rite, and scarcely imagined to exist outside the particular locality where the rite was performed. So that in spite of the panhellenic Olympian system, and in spite of the philosophic spirit which made merely tribal gods impossible for the Greek, there is a sense in which it is true to say that the polis is an independent religious, as well as political, unit. The tragic poets at least could make use of the old belief that the gods desert a city which is about to be captured. The gods are the unseen partners in the city's welfare.

How intimately religious and "political" thinking were connected we can best see from the *Oresteia* of Aeschylus. This trilogy is built around the idea of Justice. It moves from chaos to order, from conflict to reconciliation; and it moves on two planes at once, the human and the divine. In the *Agamemnon* we see one of the moral Laws of the universe, that punishment must follow crime, fulfilled in the crudest possible way; one crime evokes another crime to avenge it, in apparently endless succession—but always with the sanction of Zeus. In the *Choephori* this series of crimes reaches its climax when Orestes avenges his father by killing his mother. He does this with repugnance, but he is commanded to do it by Apollo, the son and the mouthpiece of Zeus—Why? Because in murdering Agamemnon the King and her husband, Clytemnestra has committed a crime which, unpunished, would shatter the very fabric of society. It is the concern of the Olympian gods to defend Order; they are particularly the gods of the Polis. But Orestes' matricide outrages the deepest human instincts; he is therefore implacably pursued by other deities, the Furies. The Furies have no interest in social order, but they cannot permit this outrage on the sacredness of the blood-tie, which it is their office to protect. In the *Eumenides* there is a terrific conflict between the ancient Furies and the younger Olympians over the unhappy Orestes. The solution is that Athena comes with a new dispensation from Zeus. A jury of Athenian citizens is empanelled to try Orestes on the Acropolis where he has fled for protection—this being the first meeting of the Council of the Areopagus. The votes on either side are equal; therefore, as an act of mercy, Orestes is acquitted. The Furies, cheated of their legitimate prey, threaten Attica with destruction, but Athena persuades them to make their home in Athens, with their ancient office not abrogated (as at first they think) but enhanced, since henceforth they will punish violence within the polis, not only within the family.

So, to Aeschylus, the mature polis becomes the means by which the Law is satisfied without producing chaos, since public justice supersedes private vengeance; and the claims of authority are reconciled with the instincts of humanity. The trilogy ends with an impressive piece of pageantry. The awful Furies exchange their black robes for red ones, no longer Furies, but "Kindly Ones" (Eumenides); no longer enemies of Zeus, but his willing and honoured agents, defenders of his now perfected social order against intestine violence. Before the eyes of the Athenian citizens assembled in the theatre just under the Acropolis— and indeed guided by citizen-marshals—they pass out of the theatre to their new home on the other side of the Acropolis. Some of the most acute of man's moral and social problems have been solved, and the means of the reconciliation is the Polis.

A few minutes later, on that early spring day of 458 B.C., the citizens 32 too would leave the theatre, and by the same exits as the Eumenides. In what mood? Surely no audience has had such an experience since. At the time, the Athenian polis was confidently riding the crest of the wave. In this trilogy there was exaltation, for they had seen their polis emerge as the pattern of Justice, of Order, of what the Greeks called Cosmos; the polis, they saw, was—or could be—the very crown and summit of things. They had seen their goddess herself acting as President of the first judicial tribunal—a steadying and sobering thought. But there was more than this. The rising democracy had recently curtailed the powers of the ancient Court of the Areopagus, and the reforming statesman had been assassinated by his political enemies. What of the Eumenides, the awful inhabitants of the land, the transformed Furies, whose function it was to avenge the shedding of a kinsman's blood? There was warning here, as well as exaltation, in the thought that the polis had its divine as well as its human members. There was Athena, one of those Olympians who had presided over the formation of ordered society, and there were the more primitive deities who had been persuaded by Athena to accept this pattern of civilized life, and were swift to punish any who, by violence from within, threatened its stability.

To such an extent was the religious thought of Aeschylus inter- 33 twined with the idea of the polis; and not of Aeschylus alone, but of many other Greek thinkers too—notably of Socrates, Plato, and Aristotle. Aristotle made a remark which we most inadequately translate "Man is a political animal." What Aristotle really said is "Man is a creature who lives in a polis"; and what he goes on to demonstrate, in his *Politics*, is that the polis is the only framework within which man can fully realize his spiritual, moral and intellectual capacities.

Such are some of the implications of this word: we shall meet 34 more later, for I have deliberately said little about its purely "political" side—to emphasize the fact that it is so much more than a form of political organization. The polis was a living community, based on kinship, real or assumed—a kind of extended family, turning as much as possible of life into family life, and of course having its family quarrels, which were the more bitter because they were family quarrels.

This it is that explains not only the polis but also much of what the 35 Greek made and thought, that he was essentially social. In the winning of his livelihood he was essentially individualist: in the filling of his life he was essentially "communist." Religion, art, games, the discussion of things—all these were needs of life that could be fully satisfied only through the polis—not, as with us, through voluntary associations of like-minded people, or through *entrepreneurs* appealing to individuals. (This partly explains the difference between Greek drama and the modern cinema.) Moreover, he wanted to play his own part in running the affairs of the community. When we realize how many of the necessary, interesting and exciting activities of life the Greek enjoyed through the polis, all of them in the open air, within sight of the same acropolis, with the same ring of mountains or of sea visibly enclosing the life of every member of the state—then it becomes possible to understand Greek history, to understand that in spite of the promptings of common sense the Greek could not bring himself to sacrifice the polis, with its vivid and comprehensive life, to a wider but less interesting unity. We may perhaps record an Imaginary Conversation between an Ancient Greek and a member of the Athenaeum. The member regrets the lack of political sense shown by the Greeks. The Greek replies, "How many clubs are there in London?" The member, at a guess, says about five hundred. The Greek then says, "Now, if all these combined, what splendid premises they could build. They could have a club-house as big as Hyde Park." "But," says the member, "that would no longer be a club." "Precisely," says the Greek, "and a polis as big as yours is no longer a polis."

After all, modern Europe, in spite of its common culture, common   36 interests, and ease of communication, finds it difficult to accept the idea of limiting national sovereignty, though this would increase the security of life without notably adding to its dullness; the Greek had possibly more to gain by watering down the polis—but how much more to lose. It was not common sense that made Achilles great, but certain other qualities.

PLATO

Crito

Plato (c. 427–347 B.C.) was probably born in Athens and is regarded as the father of rationalist philosophy. His works such as the *Republic* and the *Laws* suggest that Plato had the makings of a great statesman, but he retreated from public life in 399 B.C., disillusioned by the political system of Athens and claiming that the only hope for Greek cities was for "philosophers [to] become kings or kings philosophers." When Plato returned to Athens after traveling for several years, he founded the Academy, establishing an educational community that made Athens the center of educational life in Greece. There he taught for forty years, educating several famous thinkers and statesmen, most notably the philosopher Aristotle. Scholars are hard pressed to distinguish between Plato's thought and that of his mentor, Socrates, largely because Plato's writings are dialogues that feature Socrates as a character. The dialogue, which resembles what we might call today a cross-examination, pits Socrates against an antagonist who is inexorably led to concede the point Socrates wishes to make. The question of whether Plato is faithfully recording the debate or putting words in the mouths of his "characters" cannot be answered. His works include *Gorgias, Symposium, Timaeus,* and the following dialogue, *Crito.*

Socrates.[1]   Why have you come at this hour, Crito? it must be quite   1
early?

Crito.   Yes, certainly.

Soc.   What is the exact time?

Cr.   The dawn is breaking.

Soc.   I wonder that the keeper of the prison would let you in.   5

Cr.   He knows me, because I often come, Socrates; moreover, I have done him a kindness.

Soc.   And are you only just arrived?

Cr.   No, I came some time ago.

Soc.   Then why did you sit and say nothing, instead of at once awakening me?

Cr.   I should not have liked myself, Socrates, to be in such great   10
trouble and unrest as you are—indeed I should not: I have been watching with amazement your peaceful slumbers; and for that reason I did not awake you, because I wished to minimize the pain. I have always thought you to be of a happy disposition; but never did I see anything like the easy, tranquil manner in which you bear this calamity.

Soc.   Why, Crito, when a man has reached my age he ought not to be repining at the approach of death.

Cr.   And yet other old men find themselves in similar misfortunes, and age does not prevent them from repining.

Soc.   That is true. But you have not told me why you come at this early hour.

Cr.   I come to bring you a message which is sad and painful; not, as I believe, to yourself, but to all of us who are your friends, and saddest of all to me.

Soc.   What? Has the ship come from Delos, on the arrival of which   15
I am to die?

---

1. Socrates (469–399 B.C.), a Greek teacher and philosopher, is known to posterity through the writings of Plato. Accused of corrupting the youth of Athens by his questioning manner of teaching, he was brought to trial and sentenced to death; subsequently, he was given poison hemlock to drink. Crito, a friend and follower of Socrates, here tries to persuade him to escape from prison, but Socrates refuses to break the laws of Athens.

Cr.　No, the ship has not actually arrived, but she will probably be here to-day, as persons who have come from Sunium tell me that they left her there; and therefore tomorrow, Socrates, will be the last day of your life.

Soc.　Very well, Crito; if such is the will of God, I am willing; but my belief is that there will be a delay of a day.

Cr.　Why do you think so?

Soc.　I will tell you. I am to die on the day after the arrival of the ship.

Cr.　Yes; that is what the authorities say.　　　　　　　　　　　20

Soc.　But I do not think that the ship will be here until tomorrow; this I infer from a vision which I had last night, or rather only just now, when you fortunately allowed me to sleep.

Cr.　And what was the nature of the vision?

Soc.　There appeared to me the likeness of a woman, fair and comely, clothed in bright raiment, who called to me and said: O Socrates,

　　　The third day hence to fertile Phthia shalt thou go.

Cr.　What a singular dream, Socrates!

Soc.　There can be no doubt about the meaning, Crito, I think.　　25

Cr.　Yes; the meaning is only too clear. But, oh! my beloved Socrates, let me entreat you once more to take my advice and escape. For if you die I shall not only lose a friend who can never be replaced, but there is another evil: people who do not know you and me will believe that I might have saved you if I had been willing to give money, but that I did not care. Now, can there be a worse disgrace than this—that I should be thought to value money more than the life of a friend? For the many will not be persuaded that I wanted you to escape, and that you refused.

Soc.　But why, my dear Crito, should we care about the opinion of the many? Good men, and they are the only persons who are worth considering, will think of these things truly as they occurred.

Cr.　But you see, Socrates, that the opinion of the many must be regarded, for what is now happening shows that they can do the greatest evil to any one who has lost their good opinion.

Soc.　I only wish it were so, Crito; and that the many could do the greatest evil; for then they would also be able to do the greatest good—and what a fine thing this would be! But in reality they can do neither; for they cannot make a man either wise or foolish; and whatever they do is the result of chance.

Cr.　Well, I will not dispute with you; but please to tell me, Socra-　30
tes, whether you are not acting out of regard to me and your other friends: are you not afraid that if you escape from prison we may get into trouble with the informers for having stolen you away, and lose

either the whole or a great part of our property; or that even a worse evil may happen to us? Now, if you fear on our account, be at ease; for in order to save you, we ought surely to run this, or even a greater risk; be persuaded, then, and do as I say.

Soc. Yes, Crito, that is one fear which you mention, but by no means the only one.

Cr. Fear not—there are persons who are willing to get you out of prison at no great cost; and as for the informers, they are far from being exorbitant in their demands—a little money will satisfy them. My means, which are certainly ample, are at your service, and if you have a scruple about spending all mine, here are strangers who will give you the use of theirs; and one of them, Simmias the Theban, has brought a large sum of money for this very purpose; and Cebes and many others are prepared to spend their money in helping you to escape. I say, therefore, do not hesitate on our account, and do not say, as you did in the court, that you will have a difficulty in knowing what to do with yourself anywhere else. For men will love you in other places to which you may go, and not in Athens only; there are friends of mine in Thessaly, if you like to go to them, who will value and protect you, and no Thessalian will give you any trouble. Nor can I think that you are at all justified, Socrates, in betraying your own life when you might be saved; in acting thus you are playing into the hands of your enemies, who are hurrying on your destruction. And further I should say that you are deserting your own children; for you might bring them up and educate them; instead of which you go away and leave them, and they will have to take their chance; and if they do not meet with the usual fate of orphans, there will be small thanks to you. No man should bring children into the world who is unwilling to persevere to the end of their nurture and education. But you appear to be choosing the easier part, not the better and manlier, which would have been more becoming in one who professes to care for virtue in all his actions, like yourself. And, indeed, I am ashamed not only of you, but of us who are your friends, when I reflect that the whole business will be attributed entirely to our want of courage. The trial need never have come on, or might have been managed differently; and this last act, or crowning folly, will seem to have occurred through our negligence and cowardice, who might have saved you, if we had been good for anything; and you might have saved yourself, for there was no difficulty at all. See now, Socrates, how sad and discreditable are the consequences, both to us and you. Make up your mind, then, or rather have your mind already made up, for the time of deliberation is over, and there is only one thing to be done, which must be done this very night, and if we delay at all will be no longer practicable or possible; I beseech you therefore, Socrates, be persuaded by me, and do as I say.

Soc. Dear Crito, your zeal is invaluable, if a right one; but if wrong, the greater the zeal the greater the danger; and therefore we ought to consider whether I shall or shall not do as you say. For I am and always have been one of those natures who must be guided by reason, whatever the reason may be which upon reflection appears to me to be the best; and now that this chance has befallen me, I cannot repudiate my own words: the principles which I have hitherto honoured and revered I still honour, and unless we can at once find other and better principles, I am certain not to agree with you; no, not even if the power of the multitude could inflict many more imprisonments, confiscations, deaths, frightening us like children with hobgoblin terrors. What will be the fairest way of considering the question? Shall I return to our old argument about the opinions of men?—we were saying that some of them are to be regarded, and others, not. Now, were we right in maintaining this before I was condemned? And has the argument which was once good now proved to be talk for the sake of talking—mere childish nonsense? That is what I want to consider with your help, Crito:—whether, under my present circumstances, the argument appears to be in any way different or not; and is to be allowed by me or disallowed. That argument, which, as I believe, is maintained by many persons of authority, was to the effect, as I was saying, that the opinions of some men are to be regarded, and of other men not to be regarded. Now you, Crito, are not going to die tomorrow—at least, there is no human probability of this—and therefore you are disinterested and not liable to be deceived by the circumstances in which you are placed. Tell me, then, whether I am right in saying that some opinions, and the opinions of some men only, are to be valued, and that other opinions, and the opinions of other men, are not to be valued. I ask you whether I was right in maintaining this?

Cr.   Certainly.

Soc.   The good are to be regarded, and not the bad?   35

Cr.   Yes.

Soc.   And the opinions of the wise are good, and the opinions of the unwise are evil?

Cr.   Certainly.

Soc.   And what was said about another matter? Is the pupil who devotes himself to the practice of gymnastic supposed to attend to the praise and blame and opinion of every man, or of one man only—his physician or trainer, whoever he may be?

Cr.   Of one man only.   40

Soc.   And he ought to fear the censure and welcome the praise of that one only, and not of the many?

Cr.   Clearly so.

Soc.   And he ought to act and train, and eat and drink in the way which seems good to his single master who has understanding, rather than according to the opinion of all other men put together?

Cr.   True.

Soc.   And if he disobeys and disregards the opinion and approval   45
of the one, and regards the opinion of the many who have no understanding, will he not suffer evil?

Cr.   Certainly he will.

Soc.   And what will the evil be, whither tending and what affecting, in the disobedient person?

Cr.   Clearly, affecting the body; that is what is destroyed by the
evil.

Soc.   Very good; and is not this true, Crito, of other things which
we need not separately enumerate? In questions of just and unjust, fair
and foul, good and evil, which are the subjects of our present consulta-
tion, ought we to follow the opinion of the many and to fear them; or
the opinion of the one man who has understanding? ought we not to
fear and reverence him more than all the rest of the world: and if we
desert him shall we not destroy and injure that principle in us which
may be assumed to be improved by justice and deteriorated by injustice;
—there is such a principle?

Cr.   Certainly there is, Socrates.   50

Soc.   Take a parallel instance:—if, acting under the advice of those
who have no understanding, we destroy that which is improved by
health and is deteriorated by disease, would life be worth having? And
that which has been destroyed is—the body?

Cr.   Yes.

Soc.   Could we live, having an evil and corrupted body?

Cr.   Certainly not.

Soc.   And will life be worth having, if that higher part of man be   55
destroyed, which is improved by justice and depraved by injustice? Do
we suppose that principle, whatever it may be in man, which has to
do with justice and injustice, to be inferior to the body?

Cr.   Certainly not.

Soc.   More honourable than the body?

Cr.   Far more.

Soc.   Then, my friend, we must not regard what the many say of
us: but what he, the one man who has understanding of just and unjust,
will say, and what the truth will say. And therefore you begin in error
when you advise that we should regard the opinion of the many about
just and unjust, good and evil, honourable and dishonourable.—
"Well," some one will say, "But the many can kill us."

Cr.   Yes, Socrates; that will clearly be the answer.   60

Soc.   And it is true: but still I find with surprise that the old argument is unshaken as ever. And I should like to know whether I may
say the same of another proposition—that not life, but a good life, is
to be chiefly valued?

Cr.   Yes, that also remains unshaken.

Soc. And a good life is equivalent to a just and honourable one—that holds also?

Cr. Yes, it does.

Soc. From these premises I proceed to argue the question whether 65
I ought or ought not to try to escape without the consent of the Athenians: and if I am clearly right in escaping, then I will make the attempt; but if not, I will abstain. The other considerations which you mention, of money and loss of character and the duty of educating one's children, are, I fear, only the doctrines of the multitude, who would be as ready to restore people to life, if they were able, as they are to put them to death—and with as little reason. But now, since the argument has thus far prevailed, the only question which remains to be considered is, whether we shall do rightly either in escaping or in suffering others to aid in our escape and paying them in money and thanks, or whether in reality we shall not do rightly; and if the latter, then death or any other calamity which may ensue on my remaining here must not be allowed to enter into the calculation.

Cr. I think that you are right, Socrates; how then shall we proceed?

Soc. Let us consider the matter together, and do you either refute me if you can, and I will be convinced; or else cease, my dear friend, from repeating to me that I ought to escape against the wishes of the Athenians; for I highly value your attempts to persuade me to do so, but I may not be persuaded against my own better judgment. And now please to consider my first position, and try how you can best answer me.

Cr. I will.

Soc. Are we to say that we are never intentionally to do wrong, or that in one way we ought and in another way we ought not to do wrong, or is doing wrong always evil and dishonourable, as I was just now saying, and as has been already acknowledged by us? Are all our former admissions which were made within a few days to be thrown away? And have we, at our age, been earnestly discoursing with one another all our life long only to discover that we are no better than children? Or, in spite of the opinion of the many, and in spite of consequences whether better or worse, shall we insist on the truth of what was then said, that injustice is always an evil and dishonour to him who acts unjustly? Shall we say so or not?

Cr. Yes. 70

Soc. Then we must do no wrong?

Cr. Certainly not.

Soc. Nor when injured injure in return, as the many imagine; for we must injure no one at all?

Cr. Clearly not.

Soc. Again, Crito, may we do evil? 75

Cr.   Surely not, Socrates.

Soc.   And what of doing evil in return for evil, which is the morality of the many—is that just or not?

Cr.   Not just.

Soc.   For doing evil to another is the same as injuring him?

Cr.   Very true.   80

Soc.   Then we ought not to retaliate or render evil for evil to any one, whatever evil we may have suffered from him. But I would have you consider, Crito, whether you really mean what you are saying. For this opinion has never been held, and never will be held, by any considerable number of persons; and those who are agreed and those who are not agreed upon this point have no common ground, and can only despise one another when they see how widely they differ. Tell me, then, whether you agree with and assent to my first principle, that neither injury nor retaliation nor warding off evil is ever right. And shall that be the premise of our argument? Or do you decline and dissent from this? For so I have ever thought, and continue to think; but, if you are of another opinion, let me hear what you have to say. If, however, you remain of the same mind as formerly, I will proceed to the next step.

Cr.   You may proceed, for I have not changed my mind.

Soc.   Then I will go on to the next point, which may be put in the form of a question:—Ought a man to do what he admits to be right, or ought he to betray the right?

Cr.   He ought to do what he thinks right.

Soc.   But if this is true, what is the application? In leaving the   85
prison against the will of the Athenians, do I wrong any? or rather do I not wrong those whom I ought least to wrong? Do I not desert the principles which were acknowledged by us to be just—what do you say?

Cr.   I cannot tell, Socrates; for I do not know.

Soc.   Then consider the matter in this way:—Imagine that I am about to play truant (you may call the proceeding by any name which you like), and the laws and the government come and interrogate me: "Tell us, Socrates," they say; "what are you about? are you not going by an act of yours to overturn us—the laws, and the whole state, as far as in you lies? Do you imagine that a state can subsist and not be overthrown, in which the decisions of law have no power, but are set aside and trampled upon by individuals?" What will be our answer, Crito, to these and the like words? Any one, and especially a rhetorician, will have a good deal to say on behalf of the law which requires a sentence to be carried out. He will argue that this law should not be set aside; and shall we reply, "Yes; but the state has injured us and given an unjust sentence." Suppose I say that?

Cr.   Very good, Socrates.

Soc. "And was that our agreement with you?" the laws would answer; "or were you to abide by the sentence of the state?" And if I were to express my astonishment at their words, the laws would probably add: "Answer, Socrates, instead of opening your eyes—you are in the habit of asking and answering questions. Tell us,—What complaint have you to make against us which justifies you in attempting to destroy us and the state? In the first place did we not bring you into existence? Your father married your mother by our aid and begat you. Say whether you have any objection to urge against those of us who regulate marriage?" None, I should reply. "Or against those of us who after birth regulate the nurture and education of children, in which you also were trained? Were not the laws, which have the charge of education, right in commanding your father to train you in music and gymnastic?" Right, I should reply. "Well, then, since you were brought into the world and nurtured and educated by us, can you deny in the first place that you are our child and slave, as your fathers were before you? And if this is true, you are not on equal terms with us; nor can you think that you have a right to do to us what we are doing to you. Would you have any right to strike or revile or do any other evil to your father or your master, if you had one, because you have been struck or reviled by him, or received some other evil at his hands?—you would not say this? And because we think right to destroy you, do you think that you have any right to destroy us in return, and your country as far as in you lies? Will you, O professor of true virtue, pretend that you are justified in this? Has a philosopher like you failed to discover that our country is more to be valued and higher and holier far than mother or father or any ancestor, and more to be regarded in the eyes of the gods and of men of understanding? also to be soothed, and gently and reverently entreated when angry, even more than a father, and either to be persuaded, or if not persuaded, to be obeyed? And when we are punished by her, whether with imprisonment or stripes, the punishment is to be endured in silence; and if she lead us to wounds or death in battle, thither we follow as is right; neither may any one yield or retreat or leave his rank, but whether in battle or in a court of law, or in any other place, he must do what his city and his country order him; or he must change their view of what is just: and if he may do no violence to his father or mother, much less may he do violence to his country." What answer shall we make to this, Crito? Do the laws speak truly, or do they not?

Cr. I think that they do.

Soc. Then the laws will say: "Consider, Socrates, if we are speaking truly that in your present attempt you are going to do us an injury. For, having brought you into the world, and nurtured and educated you, and given you and every other citizen a share in every good which we had to give, we further proclaim to any Athenian by the liberty

90

which we allow him, that if he does not like us when he has become of age and has seen the ways of the city, and made our acquaintance, he may go where he pleases and take his goods with him. None of our laws will forbid him or interfere with him. Any one who does not like us and the city, and who wants to emigrate to a colony or to any other city, may go where he likes, retaining his property. But he who has experience of the manner in which we order justice and administer the State, and still remains, has entered into an implied contract that he will do as we command him. And he who disobeys us is, as we maintain, thrice wrong; first, because in disobeying us he is disobeying his parents; secondly, because we are the authors of his education; thirdly, because he has made an agreement with us that he will duly obey our commands; and he neither obeys them nor convinces us that our commands are unjust; and we do not rudely impose them, but give him the alternative of obeying or convincing us;—that is what we offer, and he does neither.

"These are the sort of accusations to which, as we were saying, you, Socrates, will be exposed if you accomplish your intentions; you, above all other Athenians." Suppose now I ask, why I rather than anybody else? they will justly retort upon me that I above all other men have acknowledged the agreement. "There is clear proof," they will say, "Socrates, that we and the city were not displeasing to you. Of all Athenians you have been the most constant resident in the city, which, as you never leave, you may be supposed to love. For you never went out of the city either to see the games, except once when you went to the Isthmus, or to any other place unless when you were on military service; nor did you travel as other men do. Nor had you any curiosity to know other States or their laws: your affections did not go beyond us and our State; we were your special favourites, and you acquiesced in our government of you; and here in this city you begat your children, which is a proof of your satisfaction. Moreover, you might in the course of the trial, if you had liked, have fixed the penalty at banishment; the State which refuses to let you go now would have let you go then. But you pretended that you preferred death to exile, and that you were not unwilling to die. And now you have forgotten these fine sentiments, and pay no respect to us, the laws, of whom you are the destroyer; and are doing what only a miserable slave would do, running away and turning your back upon the compacts and agreements which you made as a citizen. And, first of all, answer this very question: Are we right in saying that you agreed to be governed according to us in deed, and not in word only? Is that true or not?" How shall we answer, Crito? Must we not assent?

Cr. We cannot help it, Socrates.

Soc. Then will they not say: "You, Socrates, are breaking the covenants and agreements which you made with us at your leisure, not in any haste or under any compulsion or deception, but after you have had seventy years to think of them, during which time you were at liberty to leave the city, if we were not to your mind, or if our covenants appeared to you to be unfair. You had your choice, and might have gone either to Lacedaemon or Crete, both which States are often praised by you for their good government, or to some other Hellenic or foreign State. Whereas you, above all other Athenians, seemed to be so fond of the State, or, in other words, of us, her laws (and who would care about a State which has no laws?), that you never stirred out of her; the halt, the blind, the maimed were not more stationary in her than you were. And now you run away and forsake your agreements. Not so, Socrates, if you will take our advice; do not make yourself ridiculous by escaping out of the city.

"For just consider, if you transgress and err in this sort of way, what 95 good will you do either to yourself or to your friends? That your friends will be driven into exile and deprived of citizenship, or will lose their property, is tolerably certain; and you yourself, if you fly to one of the neighbouring cities, as, for example, Thebes or Megara, both of which are well governed, will come to them as an enemy, Socrates, and their government will be against you, and all patriotic citizens will cast an evil eye upon you as a subverter of the laws, and you will confirm in the minds of the judges the justice of their own condemnation of you. For he who is a corrupter of the laws is more than likely to be a corrupter of the young and foolish portion of mankind. Will you then flee from well-ordered cities and virtuous men? and is existence worth having on these terms? Or will you go to them without shame, and talk to them, Socrates? And what will you say to them? What you say here about virtue and justice and institutions and laws being the best things among men? Would that be decent of you? Surely not. But if you go away from well-governed states to Crito's friends in Thessaly, where there is great disorder and license, they will be charmed to hear the tale of your escape from prison, set off with ludicrous particulars of the manner in which you were wrapped in a goatskin or some other disguise, and metamorphosed as the manner is of runaways; but will there be no one to remind you that in your old age you were not ashamed to violate the most sacred laws for a miserable desire of a little more life? Perhaps not, if you keep them in a good temper; but if they are out of temper you will hear many degrading things; you will live, but how?—as the flatterer of all men, and the servant of all men; and doing what?—eating and drinking in Thessaly, having gone abroad in order that you may get a dinner. And where will be your fine sentiments about justice and virtue? Say that you wish to live for the sake of your children—you want to bring them up and educate them—will you take them into Thessaly and deprive them of Athenian citizenship? Is this the benefit which you will confer upon them? Or are you under the impression that they will be better cared for and educated here if you are still alive, although absent from them; for your friends will take care of them? Do you fancy that if you are an inhabitant of Thessaly they will take care of them, and if you are an inhabitant of the other world that they will not take care of them? Nay; but if they who call themselves friends are good for anything, they will—to be sure they will.

"Listen, then, Socrates, to us who have brought you up. Think not of life and children first, and of justice afterward, but of justice first, that you may be justified before the princes of the world below. For neither will you nor any that belong to you be happier or holier or juster in this life, or happier in another, if you do as Crito bids. Now you depart in innocence, a sufferer and not a doer of evil; a victim, not of the laws but of men. But if you go forth, returning evil for evil, and injury for injury, breaking the covenants and agreements which you have made with us, and wronging those whom you ought least of all to wrong, that is to say, yourself, your friends, your country, and us, we shall be angry with you while you live, and our brethren, the laws in the world below, will receive you as an enemy; for they will know that you have done your best to destroy us. Listen, then, to us and not to Crito."

This, dear Crito, is the voice which I seem to hear murmuring in my ears, like the sound of the flute in the ears of the mystic; that voice, I say, is humming in my ears, and prevents me from hearing any other. And I know that anything more which you may say will be vain. Yet speak, if you have anything to say.

Cr.   I have nothing to say, Socrates.

Soc.   Leave me then, Crito, to fulfill the will of God, and to follow whither he leads.

TONI CADE BAMBARA

The Hammer Man

Toni Cade Bambara (1939–   ) grew up in Harlem and the Bedford-Stuyvesant district of New York City. She began writing as a child, most notably influenced by the women of Harlem who surrounded her; Bambara claims they taught her that "the laws of hospitality, kinship obligation, and caring neighborliness remain eternal, 'cause first and foremost there's us: community.'" Bambara values writing, then, because she sees it as a "legitimate way, an important way, to participate in the empowerment of the community that names [her]."

Primarily educated at Queen's College and City College, New York,
Bambara studied theater, mime, dance, film, and linguistics at eight
other institutions in Europe and America. Prodigiously talented and
politically committed, she has been a welfare investigator, a community organizer, a college professor, and a director of plays and films.
At the same time, she has published two books of short stories, *Gorilla,
My Love* (1972) and *The Sea Birds Are Still Alive* (1977), two novels,
The Salt Eaters (1980) and *If Blessing Comes* (1987), and numerous
screenplays. In 1991 Bambara collaborated on a book about the films
of Spike Lee, *Five for Five*. "The Hammer Man" was first published in
Negro Digest in 1966.

I was glad to hear that Manny had fallen off the roof. I had put out   1
the tale that I was down with yellow fever, but nobody paid me no
mind, least of all Dirty Red who stomped right in to announce that
Manny had fallen off the roof and that I could come out of hiding now.
My mother dropped what she was doing, which was the laundry, and
got the whole story out of Red. "Bad enough you gots to hang around
with boys," she said. "But fight with them too. And you would pick
the craziest one at that."

Manny was supposed to be crazy. That was his story. To say you   2
were bad put some people off. But to say you were crazy, well, you
were officially not to be messed with. So that was his story. On the
other hand, after I called him what I called him and said a few choice
things about his mother, his face did go through some piercing changes.
And I did kind of wonder if maybe he sure was nuts. I didn't wait to
find out. I got in the wind. And then he waited for me on my stoop all
day and all night, not hardly speaking to the people going in and out.
And he was there all day Saturday, with his sister bringing him peanut-
butter sandwiches and cream sodas. He must've gone to the bathroom
right there cause every time I looked out the kitchen window, there he
was. And Sunday, too. I got to thinking the boy was mad.

"You got no sense of humor, that's your trouble," I told him. He   3
looked up, but he didn't say nothing. All at once I was real sorry about
the whole thing. I should've settled for hitting off the little girls in the
school yard, or waiting for Frankie to come in so we could raise some
kind of hell. This way I had to play sick when my mother was around
cause my father had already taken away my BB gun and hid it.

I don't know how they got Manny on the roof finally. Maybe the   4
Wakefield kids, the ones who keep the pigeons, called him up. Manny
was a sucker for sick animals and things like that. Or maybe Frankie
got some nasty girls to go up on the roof with him and got Manny to
join him. I don't know. Anyway, the catwalk had lost all its cement
and the roof always did kind of slant downward. So Manny fell off the
roof. I got over my yellow fever right quick, needless to say, and ven-

tured outside. But by this time I had already told Miss Rose that Crazy Manny was after me. And Miss Rose, being who she was, quite naturally went over to Manny's house and said a few harsh words to his mother, who, being who she was, chased Miss Rose out into the street and they commenced to get with it, snatching bottles out of the garbage cans and breaking them on the johnny pumps and stuff like that.

Dirty Red didn't have to tell us about this. Everybody could see and hear all. I never figured the garbage cans for an arsenal, but Miss Rose came up with sticks and table legs and things, and Manny's mother had her share of scissor blades and bicycle chains. They got to rolling in the streets and all you could see was pink drawers and fat legs. It was something else. Miss Rose is nutty but Manny's mother's crazier than Manny. They were at it a couple of times during my sick spell. Everyone would congregate on the window sills or the fire escape, commenting that it was still much too cold for this kind of nonsense. But they watched anyway. And then Manny fell off the roof. And that was that. Miss Rose went back to her dream books and Manny's mother went back to her tumbled-down kitchen of dirty clothes and bundles and bundles of rags and children.

My father got in on it too, cause he happened to ask Manny one night why he was sitting on the stoop like that every night. Manny told him right off that he was going to kill me first chance he got. Quite naturally this made my father a little warm, me being his only daughter and planning to become a doctor and take care of him in his old age. So he had a few words with Manny first, and then he got hold of the older brother, Bernard, who was more his size. Bernard didn't see how any of it was his business or my father's business, so my father got mad and jammed Bernard's head into the mailbox. Then my father started getting messages from Bernard's uncle about where to meet him for a showdown and all. My father didn't say a word to my mother all this time; just sat around mumbling and picking up the phone and putting it down, or grabbing my stickball bat and putting it back. He carried on like this for days till I thought I would scream if the yellow fever didn't have me so weak. And then Manny fell off the roof, and my father went back to his beer-drinking buddies.

I was in the school yard, pitching pennies with the little boys from the elementary school, when my friend Violet hits my brand-new Spaudeen over the wall. She came running back to tell me that Manny was coming down the block. I peeked beyond the fence and there he was all right. He had his head all wound up like a mummy and his arm in a sling and his leg in a cast. It looked phony to me, especially that walking cane. I figured Dirty Red had told me a tale just to get me out there so Manny could stomp me, and Manny was playing it up with costume and all till he could get me.

"What happened to him?" Violet's sister whispered. But I was too busy trying to figure out how this act was supposed to work. Then Manny passed real close to the fence and gave me a look.

"You had enough, Hammer Head," I yelled. "Just bring your crummy self in this yard and I'll pick up where I left off." Violet was knocked out and the other kids went into a huddle. I didn't have to say anything else. And when they all pressed me later, I just said, "You know that hammer he always carries in his fatigues?" And they'd all nod waiting for the rest of a long story. "Well, I took it away from him." And I walked off nonchalantly. 9

Manny stayed indoors for a long time. I almost forgot about him. New kids moved into the block and I got all caught up with that. And then Miss Rose finally hit the numbers and started ordering a whole lot of stuff through the mail and we would sit on the curb and watch these weird-looking packages being carried in, trying to figure out what simple-minded thing she had thrown her money away on when she might just as well wait for the warm weather and throw a block party for all her godchildren. 10

After a while a center opened up and my mother said she'd increase my allowance if I went and joined because I'd have to get out of my pants and stay in skirts, on account of that's the way things were at the center. So I joined and got to thinking about everything else but old Hammer Head. It was a rough place to get along in, the center, but my mother said that I needed to be be'd with and she needed to not be with me, so I went. And that time I sneaked into the office, that's when I really got turned on. I looked into one of those not-quite-white folders and saw that I was from a deviant family in a deviant neighborhood. I showed my mother the word in the dictionary, but she didn't pay me no mind. It was my favorite word after that. I ran it in the ground till one day my father got the strap just to show how deviant he could get. So I gave up trying to improve my vocabulary. And I almost gave up my dungarees. 11

Then one night I'm walking past the Douglas Street park cause I got thrown out of the center for playing pool when I should've been sewing, even though I had already decided that this was going to be my last fling with boy things, and starting tomorrow I was going to fix my hair right and wear skirts all the time just so my mother would stop talking about her gray hairs, and Miss Rose would stop calling me by my brother's name by mistake. So I'm walking past the park and there's ole Manny on the basketball court, perfecting his lay-ups and talking with himself. Being me, I quite naturally walk right up and ask what the hell he's doing playing in the dark, and he looks up and all around like the dark had crept up on him when he wasn't looking. So I knew right away that he'd been out there for a long time with his eyes just going along with the program. 12

"There was two seconds to go and we were one point behind," he   13
said, shaking his head and staring at his sneakers like they was somebody. "And I was in the clear. I'd left the men in the backcourt and
there I was, smiling, you dig, cause it was in the bag. They passed the
ball and I slid the ball up nice and easy cause there was nothing to
worry about. And . . ." He shook his head. "I muffed the goddamn
shot. Ball bounced off the rim . . ." He stared at his hands. "The game
of the season. Last game." And then he ignored me altogether, though
he wasn't talking to me in the first place. He went back to the lay-ups,
always from the same spot with his arms crooked in the same way,
over and over. I must've gotten hypnotized cause I probably stood there
for at least an hour watching like a fool till I couldn't even see the
damn ball, much less the basket. But I stood there anyway for no reason
I know of. He never missed. But he cursed himself away. It was torture.
And then a squad car pulled up and a short cop with hair like one of
the Marx Brothers came out hitching up his pants. He looked real hard
at me and then at Manny.

"What are you two doing?"   14

"He's doing a lay-up. I'm watching," I said with my smart self.   15

Then the cop just stood there and finally turned to the other one   16
who was just getting out of the car.

"Who unlocked the gate?" the big one said.   17

"It's always unlocked," I said. Then we three just stood there like   18
a bunch of penguins watching Manny go at it.

"This on the level?" the big guy asked, tilting his hat back with the   19
thumb the way big guys do in hot weather. "Hey you," he said, walking
over to Manny. "I'm talking to you." He finally grabbed the ball to get
Manny's attention. But that didn't work. Manny just stood there with
his arms out waiting for the pass so he could save the game. He wasn't
paying no mind to the cop. So, quite naturally, when the cop slapped
him upside his head it was a surprise. And when the cop starting counting three to go, Manny had already recovered from the slap and was
just ticking off the seconds before the buzzer sounded and all was lost.

"Gimme the ball, man." Manny's face was all tightened up and   20
ready to pop.

"Did you hear what I said, black boy?"   21

Now, when somebody says that word like that, I gets warm. And   22
crazy or no crazy, Manny was my brother at that moment and the cop
was the enemy.

"You better give him back his ball," I said. "Manny don't take no   23
mess from no cops. He ain't bothering nobody. He's gonna be Mister
Basketball when he grows up. Just trying to get a little practice in before
the softball season starts."

"Look here, sister, we'll run you in too," Harpo said.   24

"I damn sure can't be your sister seeing how I'm a black girl. Boy,   25
I sure will be glad when you run me in so I can tell everybody about
that. You must think you're in the South, Mister."

The big guy screwed his mouth up and let out one of them hard-day   26
sighs. "The park's closed, little girl, so why don't you and your boyfriend go on home."

That really got me. The "little girl" was bad enough but that "boy-   27
friend" was too much. But I kept cool, mostly because Manny looked
so pitiful waiting there with his hands in a time-out and there being
no one to stop the clock. But I kept my cool mostly cause of that
hammer in Manny's pocket and no telling how frantic things can get
what with a big-mouth like me, a couple of wise cops, and a crazy boy
too.

"The gates are open," I said real quiet-like, "and this here's a free   28
country. So why don't you give him back his ball?"

The big cop did another one of those sighs, his specialty I guess,   29
and then he bounced the ball to Manny who went right into his gliding
thing clear up to the backboard, damn near like he was some kind of
very beautiful bird. And then he swooshed that ball in, even if there
was no net, and you couldn't really hear the swoosh. Something happened to the bones in my chest. It was something.

"Crazy kids anyhow," the one with the wig said and turned to go.   30
But the big guy watched Manny for a while and I guess something
must've snapped in his head, cause all of a sudden he was hot for taking
Manny to jail or court or somewhere and starting yelling at him and
everything, which is a bad thing to do to Manny, I can tell you. And
I'm standing there thinking that none of my teachers, from kindergarten
right on up, none of them knew what they were talking about. I'll be
damned if I ever knew one of them rosy-cheeked cops that smiled and
helped you get to school without neither you or your little raggedy dog
getting hit by a truck that had a smile on its face, too. Not that I ever
believed it. I knew Dick and Jane was full of crap from the get-go,
especially them cops. Like this dude, for example, pulling on Manny's
clothes like that when obviously he had just done about the most beautiful thing a man can do and not be a fag. No cop could swoosh without
a net.

"Look out, man," was all Manny said, but it was the way he pushed   31
the cop that started the real yelling and threats. And I thought to myself,
Oh God here I am trying to change my ways, and not talk back in
school, and do like my mother wants, but just have this last fling, and
now this—getting shot in the stomach and bleeding to death in Douglas
Street park and poor Manny getting pistol-whipped by those bastards
and whatnot. I could see it all, practically crying too. And it just wasn't
no kind of thing to happen to a small child like me with my confirmation picture in the paper next to my weeping parents and schoolmates.

I could feel the blood sticking to my shirt and my eyeballs slipping away, and then that confirmation picture again; and my mother and her gray hair; and Miss Rose heading for the precinct with a shotgun; and my father getting old and feeble with no one to doctor him up and all.

And I wished Manny had fallen off the damn roof and died right   32
then and there and saved me all this aggravation of being killed with him by these cops who surely didn't come out of no fifth-grade reader. But it didn't happen. They just took the ball and Manny followed them real quiet-like right out of the park into the dark, then into the squad car with his head drooping and his arms in a crook. And I went on home cause what the hell am I going to do on a basketball court, and it getting to be nearly midnight?

I didn't see Manny no more after he got into that squad car. But   33
they didn't kill him after all cause Miss Rose heard he was in some kind of big house for people who lose their marbles. And then it was spring finally, and me and Violet was in this very boss fashion show at the center. And Miss Rose bought me my first corsage—yellow roses to match my shoes.

ROBERT FROST

Mending Wall

Robert Frost (1874–1963), son of a San Francisco newspaperman and a schoolteacher, published his first poem in 1894 and continued to publish actively until 1962. After attending classes at Dartmouth and Harvard, but graduating from neither, he farmed and taught school in New Hampshire before turning full-time to poetry. His numerous honors and awards include four Pulitzer Prizes for Poetry (1924, 1931, 1937, and 1943), the American Academy of Poets Award (1953), and induction into the American Poet's Corner at the Cathedral of St. John the Divine in 1986. Having lived most of his adult life in New England, Frost was heavily influenced by the region's characteristic speech and landscape, but it might be a mistake to think of him as having been entirely at home there: The speakers in his poems often seem to view both their Yankee neighbors and the natural landscape with an outsider's eye. "Mending Wall" was first published in *North of Boston* (1914).

Something there is that doesn't love a wall,
That sends the frozen-ground-swell under it,
And spills the upper boulders in the sun;
And makes gaps even two can pass abreast.
The work of hunters is another thing: 5
I have come after them and made repair
Where they have left not one stone on a stone,
But they would have the rabbit out of hiding,
To please the yelping dogs. The gaps I mean,
No one has seen them made or heard them made, 10
But at spring mending-time we find them there.
I let my neighbor know beyond the hill;
And on a day we meet to walk the line
And set the wall between us once again.
We keep the wall between us as we go. 15
To each the boulders that have fallen to each.
And some are loaves and some so nearly balls
We have to use a spell to make them balance:
'Stay where you are until our backs are turned!'
We wear our fingers rough with handling them. 20
Oh, just another kind of outdoor game,
One on a side. It comes to little more:
There where it is we do not need the wall:
He is all pine and I am apple orchard.
My apple trees will never get across 25
And eat the cones under his pines. I tell him.
He only says, 'Good fences make good neighbors.'
Spring is the mischief in me, and I wonder
If I could put a notion in his head:
'Why do they make good neighbors? Isn't it 30
Where there are cows? But here there are no cows.
Before I built a wall I'd ask to know
What I was walling in or walling out,
And to whom I was like to give offense.
Something there is that doesn't love a wall. 35
That wants it down. I could say 'Elves' to him,
But it's not elves exactly, and I'd rather
He said it for himself. I see him there
Bringing a stone grasped firmly by the top
In each hand, like an old-stone savage armed. 40
He moves in darkness as it seems to me.
Not of woods only and the shade of trees.
He will not go behind his father's saying.
And he likes having thought of it so well
He says again, 'Good fences make good neighbors.' 45

INSIDERS AND OUTSIDERS

We find ourselves dislodged and excluded.

Insiders and Outsiders: Preview

229

Overview and Ideas for Writing

"To an ordinary human being," George Orwell once wrote, "love means nothing if it does not mean loving some individuals more than others." One way or another, all the selections in this unit have to do with the problems created by our inability to spread love, admiration, or even respect, evenly in society. Every circle that defines a cozy "us" leaves the rest of the world defined as "them."

As the essays in the unit demonstrate, our social inclusions and exclusions are often rather complicated. Terry Galloway, for instance, writes about the gradual onset of deafness, which left her neither part of the able-bodied population nor, really, one of the disabled. Roger Wilkins recalls his schooldays, when he was held at arm's length by both his white schoolmates and the boys in his African-American church. Perri Klass finds that she is included in the medical profession partly because she learns a language that excludes her patients and even dehumanizes them.

The doubleness of inclusion and exclusion shows strongly in George Orwell's essay about imperialism and Adrienne Rich's about her Jewish-Christian-Southern heritage. It is strong in "Letter from Birmingham Jail," in which Martin Luther King, Jr. writes to an audience separated from him by race but connected to him by a religious tradition. And E. M. Forster, "having been a Gentile at my first preparatory school and a Jew at my second," shows that his double identity has given him something to say about anti-Semitism. The speaker in Gwendolyn Brooks's "The Chicago Defender Sends a Man to Little Rock" could be seen as a man befuddled into silence by the difficulty of distinguishing "them" from "us."

The writers in the unit reveal the ironies and the humor in our struggles to win a place in what C. S. Lewis calls "the Inner Ring." But we can hardly read them without feeling the ache of exclusion, perhaps most simply expressed in the disappointment of the snubbed girl in Liliana Heker's "The Stolen Party."

If Lewis is right when he says that the desire to be an insider is "one of the great permanent mainsprings of human action," then simply by virtue of being human, you should have some important personal experience to communicate on the subject of being an outsider, or an insider, or both at the same time. Writing about this experience thoughtfully could deepen your understanding—and your reader's understanding—of a social force that can control us from the day we enter preschool until the day we die.

The section also opens up some opportunities for research. You might want to examine the social forces that have created, and continue to create, prejudices against entire groups of people. How can we account for attitudes toward African-Americans, Jews, and women that were widespread a generation or two ago but that now are almost universally condemned? You might look for answers not only in the writings of historians and sociologists, but in primary sources as well: examine for yourself the books, newspapers, and magazines people used to read; see what you can learn from autobiographical writing or fiction. You might also examine the ways that groups of "outsiders" are treated in the media today. Is our society freer of irrational biases than it was fifty years ago, or is the level of prejudice about the same, with some change of targets or code words?

E. M. FORSTER

Jew-Consciousness

E. M. Forster (1879–1970) was one of the great novelists of his time and one of its finest essayists. Although he stopped publishing novels after 1924, the rise of fascism led him to produce some of his best nonfiction in the 1930s, including several essays collected in *Two Cheers for Democracy* (1951). Always sympathetic to the individual, however idiosyncratic, Forster raised in opposition to the fascist aristocracy of power the idea of "an aristocracy of the sensitive, the considerate, and the plucky." His ideal aristocrats, he said, "are sensitive for others as well as for themselves, they are considerate without being fussy, their pluck is not swankiness but the power to endure, and they can take a joke." In "Jew-Consciousness," originally published in *New Statesman and Nation* on January 7, 1939, Forster gives a humanist response to the tide of anti-Semitism that was sweeping not only Germany but England and, as he put it, "assailing the human mind at its source."

How would you describe the relationship Forster strikes with the reader in the opening paragraph? Formal or informal? Personal or distant? Does he treat the reader like an insider or an outsider?

Long, long ago, while Queen Victoria[1] reigned, I attended two preparatory schools. At the first of these, it was held to be a disgrace to have a sister. Any little boy who possessed one was liable to get teased. The word would go round: "Oh, you men, have you seen the Picktoes' sister?" The men would then reel about with sideway motions, uttering cries of "sucks" and pretending to faint with horror, while the Picktoes, who had hitherto held their own socially in spite of their name, found themselves banished into the wilderness, where they mourned, Major with Minor, in common shame. Naturally anyone who had a sister hid her as far as possible, and forbade her to sit with him at a Prizegiving or to speak to him except in passing and in a very formal manner. Public opinion was not bitter on the point, but it was quite definite. Sisters were disgraceful. I got through all right myself, because my conscience was clear, and though charges were brought against me from time to time they always fell through.

Why wouldn't Forster simply say, "I got through all right myself because I didn't have a sister."?

It was a very different story at my second school. Here, sisters were negligible, but it was

---

1. Queen of England from 1837 to 1901. Forster was at preparatory school during the last years of her reign.

a disgrace to have a mother. Crabbe's mother, Gob's mother, eeugh! No words were too strong, no sounds too shrill. And since mothers at that time of life are commoner than sisters, and also less biddable, the atmosphere of this school was less pleasant, and the sense of guilt stronger. Nearly every little boy had a mother in a cupboard, and dreadful revelations occurred. A boy would fall ill and a mother would swoop and drive him away in a cab. A parcel would arrive with "From Mummy for her darling" branded upon it. Many tried to divert suspicion by being aggressive and fastening female parents upon the weak. One or two, who were good at games and had a large popularity-surplus, took up a really heroic line, acknowledged their mother brazenly, and would even be seen walking with her across the playing-field, like King Carol with Madame Lupescu.[2] We admired such boys and envied them, but durst not imitate them. The margin of safety was too narrow. The convention was established that a mother spelt disgrace, and no individual triumph could reverse this.

> Can you remember similar prejudices from your schooldays?

> Forster's style is never flat. By what techniques does he keep his prose lively?

Those preparatory schools prepared me for life better than I realised, for having passed through two imbecile societies, a sister-conscious and a mother-conscious, I am now invited to enter a third. I am asked to consider whether the people I meet and talk about are or are not Jews, and to form an opinion on them until this fundamental point has been settled. What revolting tosh! Neither science nor religion nor common sense has one word to say in its favour. All the same, Jew-consciousness is in the air, and it remains to be seen how far it will succeed in poisoning it. I don't think we shall ever reintroduce ghettos into England; I wouldn't say for certain, since no one knows what wickedness may not develop in his country or in himself if circumstances change. I don't think we shall go savage. But I do think we shall go silly. Many people have gone so already. Today, the average man suspects the people he dislikes of being Jews, and is surprised when the people he likes are Jews. Having been a Gentile at my first preparatory school and a Jew at my second, I know what I am talking about. I know how the poison works, and I know that if the average man is anyone in particular he is a preparatory school boy.

> Forster uses words like "imbecile" and "silly" in this essay. C. S. Lewis favors grander phrases like "the lure of the caucus" and "the quest for the Inner Ring." Why is their language so far apart?

3

---

2. Carol II (1893–1953), King of Romania, and his mistress, with whom he lived after being forced to renounce his right of succession to the throne in 1925.

Is Forster serious about the "average man" being essentially like a schoolboy? What exactly does he mean? Is he right?

Have you seen instances in contemporary America of similar sniggering?

Why put "grand" before Nordic?

Do you believe that any of Forster's techniques would defeat prejudices you have seen in your own society? As you read other selections in this unit, consider whether they make Forster's techniques look less promising or more.

On the surface, things do not look too bad. Labour and Liberalism behave with their expected decency and denounce persecution, and respectability generally follows suit. But beneath the surface things are not so good and anyone who keeps his ears open in railway carriages or pubs or country lanes can hear a very different story. A nasty side of our nation's character has been scratched up—the sniggering side. People who would not ill-treat Jews themselves, or even be rude to them, enjoy tittering over their misfortunes; they giggle when pogroms are instituted by someone else and synagogues defiled vicariously. "Serve them right really, Jews." This makes unpleasant reading, but anyone who cares to move out of his own enlightened little corner will discover that it is true. The grand Nordic argument, "He's a bloody capitalist so he must be a Jew, and as he's a Jew he must be a Red," has already taken root in our fillingstations and farms. Men employ it more frequently than women, and young men more frequently than old ones. The best way of confuting it is to say sneeringly, "That's propaganda." When "That's propaganda" has been repeated several times, the sniggering stops, for no goose likes to think that he has been got at. There is another reply which is more intellectual but which requires more courage. It is to say, "Are you sure you're not a Jew yourself? Do you know who your eight great-grandparents were? Can you swear that all the eight are Aryan?"

Cool reasonableness would be best of all, of course, but it does not work in the world of today any better than in my preparatory schools. The only effective check to silliness is silliness of a cleverer type.

Jew-mania was the one evil which no one foretold at the close of   4
the last war. All sorts of troubles were discerned and discernible—nationalism, class-warfare, the split between the haves and the havenots, the general lowering of cultural values. But no prophet, so far as I know, had foreseen this anti-Jew horror, whereas today no one can see the end of it. There had been warnings, of course, but they seemed no more ominous than a poem by Hilaire Belloc.[3] Back in India, in

3. English writer (1870–1953) of essays and children's verse.

1921, a Colonel lent me the Protocols of the Elders of Zion,[4] and it was such an obvious fake that I did not worry. I had forgotten my preparatory schools, and did not see that they were about to come into their own. To me, anti-Semitism is now the most shocking of all things. It is destroying much more than the Jews; it is assailing the human mind at its source, and inviting it to create false categories before exercising judgment. I am sure we shall win through. But it will take a long time. Perhaps a hundred years must pass before men can think back to the mentality of 1918, or can say with the Prophet Malachi,"Have we not all one father? Hath not one God created us?"[5] For the moment, all that we can do is to dig in our heels, and prevent silliness from sliding into insanity.

A strong statement. What would you list as the most shocking of all things, and why?

Why would Forster use the Malachi quotation here? How does it affect you as a reader?

TERRY GALLOWAY

I'm Listening as Hard as I Can

Terry Galloway (1950–   ) is a deaf playwright, poet, and performer who grew up in Germany and Texas. She holds a degree in American Studies from the University of Texas at Austin and had, she reports, a "two years combative relationship with Columbia University." In the early eighties, she began presenting one-woman shows, one of which she opens by noting, "I'm a Texan and am proud of it. Unfortunately, I share with most Texans a fatal flaw. I presume an intimacy—and most often where there is none." The combination of tough humor and assumed intimacy in the monologues make Galloway, as one reviewer said, "a hoot and a provocateur from the get-go." Galloway's shows have been produced throughout the United States and in England, Canada, and Mexico. She has also created alternative theater groups in Austin, Texas, and Tallahassee, Florida. To date she has published a play, a performance text, a book of poetry, several individual poems, and many comic and dramatic monologues. She also co-wrote an award-winning children's show for PBS. Her more personal life, she reports, "is the subject of gossipy speculation." The following essay was first published in *Texas Monthly* in April 1981.

At the age of twelve I won the swimming award at the Lions Camp for Crippled Children. When my name echoed over the PA system the

4. A fake document purporting to give the proceedings of a conference of Jews in the late nineteenth century, at which they proposed to overthrow Christianity and control the world.
5. Mal. 2:10.

girl in the wheelchair next to me grabbed the box speaker of my hearing aid and shouted, "You won!" My ear quaking, I took the cue. I stood up straight—the only physically unencumbered child in a sea of braces and canes—affixed a pained but brave grin to my face, then limped all the way to the stage.

Later, after the spotlight had dimmed, I was overcome with re- 2 morse, but not because I'd played the crippled heroine. The truth was that I was ashamed of my handicap. I wanted to have something more visibly wrong with me. I wanted to be in the same league as the girl who'd lost her right leg in a car accident; her artificial leg attracted a bevy of awestruck campers. I, on the other hand, wore an unwieldy box hearing aid buckled to my body like a dog halter. It attracted no one. Deafness wasn't, in my eyes, a blue-ribbon handicap. Mixed in with my envy, though, was an overwhelming sense of guilt; at camp I was free to splash in the swimming pool, while most of the other children were stranded at the shallow end, where lifeguards floated them in lazy circles. But seventeen years of living in the "normal" world has diminished my guilt considerably, and I've learned that every handicap has its own particular hell.

I'm something of an anomaly in the deaf world. Unlike most deaf 3 people, who were either born deaf or went deaf in infancy, I lost my hearing in chunks over a period of twelve years. Fortunately I learned to speak before my loss grew too profound, and that ability freed me from the most severe problem facing the deaf—the terrible difficulty of making themselves understood. My opinion of deafness was just as biased as that of a person who can hear. I had never met a deaf child in my life, and I didn't know how to sign. I imagined deaf people to be like creatures from beyond: animallike because their language was so physical, threatening because they were unable to express themselves with sophistication—that is, through speech. I *could* make myself understood, and because I had a talent for lipreading it was easy for me to pass in the wider world. And for most of my life that is exactly what I did—like a black woman playing white, I passed for something other than what I was. But in doing so I was avoiding some very painful facts. And for many years I was inhibited not only by my deafness but my own idea of what it meant to be deaf.

My problems all started when my mother, seven months pregnant 4 with me, developed a serious kidney infection. Her doctors pumped her full of antibiotics. Two months later I was born, with nothing to suggest that I was anything more or less than a normal child. For years nobody knew that the antibiotics had played havoc with my fetal nervous system. I grew up bright, happy, and energetic.

But by the time I was ten I knew, if nobody else did, that something 5 somewhere had gone wrong. The people around me had gradually developed fuzzy profiles, and their speech had taken on a blurred and foreign character. But I was such a secure and happy child that it didn't enter my mind to question my new perspective or mention the changes to anyone else. Finally, my behavior became noticeably erratic—I would make nonsensical replies to ordinary questions or simply fail to reply at all. My teachers, deciding that I was neither a particularly creative child nor an especially troublesome one, looked for a physical cause. They found two: I wasn't quite as blind as a bat, but I was almost as deaf as a doornail.

My parents took me to Wilford Hall Air Force Hospital in San Antonio, where I was examined from ear to ear. My tonsils were removed and studied, ice water was injected into my inner ear, and I underwent a series of inexplicable and at times painful exploratory tests. I would forever after associate deafness with kind attention and unusual punishment. Finally a verdict was delivered: "Congenital interference has resulted in a neural disorder for which there is no known medical or surgical treatment." My hearing loss was severe and would grow progressively worse.

I was fitted with my first hearing aid and sent back home to resume my childhood. I never did. I had just turned twelve, and my body was undergoing enormous changes. I had baby fat, baby breasts, hairy legs, and thick pink cat-eye glasses. My hearing aid was about the size of a small transistor radio and rode in a white linen pouch that hit exactly at breast level. It was not a welcome addition to my pubescent woe.

As a vain child trapped in a monster's body, I was frantic for a way to survive the next few years. Glimpsing my reflection in mirrors became such agony that I acquired a habit of brushing my teeth and hair with my eyes closed. Everything I did was geared to making my body more inhabitable, but I only succeeded in making it less so. I kept my glasses in my pocket and developed an unbecoming squint; I devised a smile that hid two broken front teeth, but it looked disturbingly like the grin of a piranha; I kept my arms folded over my would-be breasts. But the hearing aid was a different story. There was no way to disguise it. I could tuck it under my blouse, but then all I could hear was the static of cotton. Besides, whenever I took a step the box bounced around like a third breast. So I resigned myself: a monster I was, a monster I would be.

I became more withdrawn, more suspicious of other people's intentions. I imagined that I was being deliberately excluded from schoolyard talk because the other children didn't make much of an effort to involve me—they simply didn't have the time or patience to repeat snatches of gossip ten times and slowly. Conversation always reached the point of ridiculousness before I could understand something as simple as "The movie starts at five." (The groovy shark's alive? The moving stars that thrive?) I didn't make it to many movies. I cultivated a lofty sense of superiority, and I was often brutal with people who offered the "wrong" kind of help at the "wrong" time. Right after my thirteenth birthday some well-meaning neighbors took me to a revivalist faith healing. I already had doubts about exuberant religions, and the knee-deep hysteria of the preacher simply confirmed them. He bounded to my side and put his hands on my head. "O Lord," he cried, "heal this poor little lamb!"

I leaped up as if transported and shouted, "I can walk!"   10

For the first few years my parents were as bewildered as I was.   11
Nothing had prepared them for a handicapped child on the brink of adolescence. They sensed a whole other world of problems, but in those early stages I still seemed so normal that they just couldn't see me in a school for the deaf. They felt that although such schools were there to help, they also served to isolate. I have always been grateful for their decision. Because of it, I had to contend with public schools, and in doing so I developed two methods of survival: I learned to read not just lips but the whole person, and I learned the habit of clear speech by taking every speech and drama course I could.

That is not to say my adolescent years were easy going—they were   12
misery. The lack of sound cast a pall on everything. Life seemed less fun than it had been before. I didn't associate that lack of fun with the lack of sound. I didn't begin to make the connection between the failings of my body and the failings of the world until I was well out of college. I simply did not admit to myself that deafness caused certain problems—or even that I was deaf.

From the time I was twelve until I was twenty-four, the loss of my   13
hearing was erratic. I would lose a decibel or two of sound and then my hearing would stabilize. A week or a year later there would be another slip and then I'd have to adjust all over again. I never knew when I would hit bottom. I remember going to bed one night still being able to make out the reassuring purr of the refrigerator and the late-night conversation of my parents, then waking the next morning to nothing—even my own voice was gone. These fits and starts continued until my hearing finally dropped to the last rung of amplifiable sound. I was a college student at the time, and whenever anyone asked about my hearing aid, I admitted to being only slightly hard of hearing.

My professors were frequently alarmed by my almost maniacal in-   14
tensity in class. I was petrified that I'd have to ask for special privileges just to achieve marginal understanding. My pride was in flames. I became increasingly bitter and isolated. I was terrified of being marked a deaf woman, a label that made me sound dumb and cowlike, enveloped in a protective silence that denied me my complexity. I did everything I could to hide my handicap. I wore my hair long and never wore earrings, thus keeping attention away from my ears and their riders. I monopolized conversations so that I wouldn't slip up and reveal what I was or wasn't hearing; I took on a disdainful air at large parties, hoping that no one would ask me something I couldn't instantly reply

to. I lied about the extent of my deafness so I could avoid the stigma of being thought "different" in a pathetic way.

It was not surprising that in my senior year I suffered a nervous collapse and spent three days in the hospital crying like a baby. When I stopped crying I knew it was time to face a few things—I had to start asking for help when I needed it because I couldn't handle my deafness alone, and I had to quit being ashamed of my handicap so I could begin to live with its consequences and discover what (if any) were its rewards.

When I began telling people that I was *really* deaf I did so with grim determination. Some were afraid to talk to me at any length, fearing perhaps that they were talking into a void; others assumed that I was somehow an unsullied innocent and always inquired in carefully enunciated sentences: "Doooooooo youuuuuuuu driiinnk liquor?" But most people were surprisingly sympathetic—they wanted to know the best way to be understood, they took great pains to talk directly to my face, and they didn't insult me by using only words of one syllable.

It was, in part, that gentle acceptance that made me more curious about my own deafness. Always before it had been an affliction to wrestle with as one would with angels, but when I finally accepted it as an inevitable part of my life, I relaxed enough to do some exploring. I would take off my hearing aid and go through a day, a night, an hour or two—as long as I could take it—in absolute silence. I felt as if I were indulging in a secret vice because I was perceiving the world in a new way—stripped of sound.

Of course I had always known that sound is vibration, but I didn't know, until I stopped straining to hear, how truly sound is a refinement of feeling. Conversations at parties might elude me, but I seldom fail to pick up on moods. I enjoy watching people talk. When I am too far away to read lips I try reading postures and imagining conversations. Sometimes, to everyone's horror, I respond to things better left unsaid when I'm trying to find out what's going on around me. I want to see, touch, taste, and smell everything within reach; I especially have to curb a tendency to judge things by their smell—not just potato salad but people as well—a habit that seems to some people entirely too barbaric for comfort. I am not claiming that my other senses stepped up their work to compensate for the loss, but the absence of one does allow me to concentrate on the others. Deafness has left me acutely aware of both the duplicity that language is capable of and the many expressions the body cannot hide.

Over the last twenty years I've worked exclusively in speaking theatre. I've performed both male and female roles in a variety of Shakespearean productions; co-wrote and starred in a PBS children's show; toured my performance art pieces, nationally and internationally; helped found, then wrote and performed for two major musical/satirical cabarets; and still I make my living performing and conducting work-shops in performance. Some people think it's odd that, as deaf as I am, I've spent so much of my life working in the theater, but I find it to be a natural consequence of my particular circumstance. The loss of sound has enhanced my fascination with language and the way meaning is conveyed. I love to perform. Exactly the same processes occur onstage as off—except that onstage, once I've memorized the script, I know what everybody is saying as they say it. I am delighted to be so immedi-ately in the know. It has provided a direct way to keep in touch with the rest of the world despite the imposed isolation.

Silence is not empty; it is simply more sobering than sound. At times I prefer the sobriety. I can still "hear" with a hearing aid—that is, I can discern noise, but I can't tell you where it's coming from or if it is laughter or a faulty drain. When there are many people talking together I hear a strange music, a distant rumbling in my consciousness. But when I take off my hearing aid at night and lie in bed surrounded by my fate, I wonder, "What is this—a foul subtraction or a blessing in disguise?" For despite my fears there is a kind of peace in the si-lence—albeit an uneasy one. There is, after all, less to distract me from my thoughts. [20]

But I know what I've lost. The process of becoming deaf has at times been frightening, akin perhaps to dying, and early in life it took away my happy confidence in the image of a world where things always work right. When I first came back from the Lions Camp that summer I cursed heaven and earth for doing such terrible wrong to me and to my friends. My grandmother tried to comfort me by promising, "Honey, God's got something special planned for you." [21]

But I thought, "Yes. He plans to make me deaf." [22]

ROGER WILKINS

Confessions of a Blue-Chip Black

Roger Wilkins (1932–   ) was born in Kansas City and grew up there, in Harlem, and in Grand Rapids, Michigan. He received his undergraduate and legal education at the University of Michigan. After serving briefly as a welfare worker in Cleveland and as a private attor-ney in New York, Wilkins went to Washington, D.C., to serve in vari-ous administrative posts. He was assistant attorney general from 1966 to 1969, a post he left to serve as director of the Ford Foundation's domestic programs. This position gave him "daily association with blackness," since he helped develop projects intended to aid the urban black underclass. But, as Wilkins realized with increasing discomfort, the Ford Foundation itself was part of a white power structure safely

isolated from the reality of urban poverty. In 1972 he resigned and
began writing articles and editorials for *The New York Times*. Currently
he is a professor of history at George Mason University and a regular
columnist for *Mother Jones*. "Confessions of a Blue-Chip Black," which
first appeared in *Harper's* in April 1982, is from Wilkins's autobiography, *A Man's Life* (1982).

Early in the spring of 1932—six months after Earl's brother, Roy,   1
left Kansas City to go to New York to join the national staff of the
National Association for the Advancement of Colored People, and eight
months before Franklin Roosevelt was elected president for the first
time—Earl and Helen Wilkins had the first and only child to be born
of their union. I was born in a little segregated hospital in Kansas City
called Phillis Wheatley.[1] The first time my mother saw me, she cried.
My head was too long and my color, she thought, was blue.

My parents never talked about slavery or my ancestors. Images of   2
Africa were images of backwardness and savagery. Once, when I was
a little boy, I said to my mother after a friend of my parents left the
house: "Mr. Bledsoe is black, isn't he, mama."

"Oh," she exclaimed. "Never say anybody is black. That's a terrible   3
thing to say."

Next time Mr. Bledsoe came to the house, I commented, "Mama,   4
Mr. Bledsoe is navy blue."

When I was two years old and my father was in the tuberculosis   5
sanitarium, he wrote me a letter, which I obviously couldn't read, but
which tells a lot about how he planned to raise his Negro son.

Friday, March 22, 1934

Dear Roger—

   Let me congratulate you upon having reached your second birthday.
Your infancy is now past and it is now that you should begin to turn your
thoughts upon those achievements which are expected of a brilliant young
gentleman well on his way to manhood.

   During the next year, you should learn the alphabet; you should learn
certain French and English idioms which are a part of every cultivated
person's vocabulary: you should gain complete control of those natural
functions which, uncontrolled, are a source of worry and embarrassment
to even the best of grandmothers: you should learn how to handle table
silver so that you will be able to eat gracefully and conventionally: and you
should learn the fundamental rules of social living—politeness, courtesy,
consideration for others, and the rest.

   This should not be difficult for you. You have the best and most patient
of mothers in your sterling grandmother and your excellent mother. Great
things are expected of you. Never, never forget that.

Love,
Your Father

---

1. Phillis Wheatley (1753?–1784) was a black American poet.

We lived in a neat little stucco house on a hill in a small Negro   6
section called Roundtop. I had no sense of being poor or of any anxiety
about money. At our house, not only was there food and furniture and
all the rest, there was even a baby grand piano that my mother would
play sometimes. And there was a cleaning lady, Mrs. Turner, who came
every week.

When it was time for me to go to school, the board of education   7
provided us with a big yellow bus, which carried us past four or five
perfectly fine schools down to the middle of the large Negro community,
to a very old school called Crispus Attucks.[2] I have no memories of
those bus rides except for my resentment of the selfishness of the whites
who wouldn't let us share those newer-looking schools near to home.

My father came home when I was four and died when I was almost   8
nine. He exuded authority. He thought the women hadn't been sufficiently firm with me, so he instituted a spanking program with that
same hard hairbrush that my grandmother had used so much to try to
insure that I didn't have "nigger-looking" hair.

After my father's death, the family moved to New York. Our apart-   9
ment was in that legendary uptown area called Sugar Hill, where blacks
who had it made were said to live the sweet life. I lived with my mother,
my grandmother, and my mother's younger sister, Zelma. My Uncle
Roy and his wife, Minnie, a New York social worker, lived on the same
floor. My Aunt Marvel and her husband, Cecil, lived one floor down.

As life in New York settled into a routine, my life came to be domi-   10
nated by four women: my mother, her sisters, and her mother. Nobody
else had any children, so everybody concentrated on me.

Sometime early in 1943 my mother's work with the YMCA took   11
her to Grand Rapids, Michigan, where she made a speech and met a
forty-four-year-old bachelor doctor who looked like a white man. He
had light skin, green eyes, and "good hair"—that is, hair that was as
straight and as flat as white people's hair. He looked so like a white
person that he could have passed for white. There was much talk about
people who had passed. They were generally deemed to be bad people,
for they were not simply selfish, but also cruel to those whom they left
behind. On the other hand, people who could pass, but did not, were
respected.

My mother remarried in October 1943, and soon I was once more   12
on a train with my grandmother, heading toward Grand Rapids and
my new home. This train also took me, at the age of twelve, beyond
the last point in my life when I would feel totally at peace with my
blackness.

---

2. Crispus Attucks (1723?–1770) was an American mulatto who led the mob in the
Boston Massacre and was killed by British troops.

My new home was in the north end of Grand Rapids, a completely   13
white neighborhood. This would be the place I would henceforth think
of as home. And it would be the place where I would become more
Midwestern than Harlemite, more American than black, and more complex than was comfortable or necessary for the middle-class conformity
that my mother had in mind for me.

Grand Rapids was pretty single-family houses and green spaces.   14
The houses looked like those in *Look* magazine or in *Life.* You could
believe, and I did, that there was happiness inside. To me, back then,
the people seemed to belong to the houses as the houses belonged to
the land, and all of it had to do with being white. They moved and
walked and talked as if the place, the country, and the houses were
theirs, and I envied them.

I spent the first few weeks exploring Grand Rapids on a new bike   15
my stepfather had bought for me. The people I passed would look back
at me with intense and sometimes puzzled looks on their faces as I
pedaled by. Nobody waved or even smiled. They just stopped what they
were doing to stand and look. As soon as I saw them looking, I would
look forward and keep on riding.

One day I rode for miles, down and up and down again. I was past   16
Grand Rapids' squatty little downtown, and farther south until I began
to see some Negro people. There were black men and women and some
girls, but it was the boys I was looking for. Then I saw a group: four
of them. They were about my age, and they were dark. Though their
clothes were not as sharp as the boys' in the Harlem Valley, they were
old, and I took the look of poverty and the deep darkness of their faces
to mean that they were like the hard boys of Harlem.

One of them spotted me riding toward them and pointed. "Hey,   17
lookit that bigole skinny bike," he said. Then they all looked at my
bike and at me. I couldn't see expressions on their faces; only the
blackness and the coarseness of their clothes. Before any of the rest of
them had a chance to say anything, I stood up on the pedals and
wheeled the bike in a U-turn and headed back on up toward the north
end of town. It took miles for the terror to finally subside.

Farther on toward home, there was a large athletic field. As I neared   18
the field, I could see some large boys in shorts moving determinedly
around a football. When I got to the top of the hill that overlooked the
field, I stopped and stood, one foot on the ground and one leg hanging
over the crossbar, staring down at them. All the boys were white and
big and old—sixteen to eighteen. I had never seen a football workout
before, and I was fascinated. I completely forgot everything about color,
theirs or mine.

Then one of them saw me. He pointed and said, "Look, there's the   19
little coon watchin us."

I wanted to be invisible. I was horrified. My heart pounded, and   20 my arms and legs shook, but I managed to get back on my bike and ride home.

The first white friend I made was named Jerry Schild. On the second day of our acquaintance, he took me to his house, above a store run by his parents. I met his three younger siblings, including a very little one toddling around in bare feet and a soiled diaper.

While Jerry changed the baby, I looked around the place. It was cheap, all chintz and linoleum. The two soft pieces of furniture, a couch and an overstuffed chair, had gaping holes and were hemorrhaging their fillings. And there were an awful lot of empty brown beer bottles sitting around, both in the kitchen and out on the back porch. While the place was not dirty, it made me very sad. Jerry and his family were poor in a way I had never seen people be poor before, in Kansas City or even in Harlem.

Jerry's father wasn't there that day and Jerry didn't mention him. But later in the week, when I went to call for Jerry, I saw him. I yelled for Jerry from downstairs in the back and his father came to the railing of the porch on the second floor. He was a skinny man in overalls with the bib hanging down crookedly because it was fastened only on the shoulder. His face was narrow and wrinkled and his eyes were set deep in dark hollows. He had a beer bottle in his hand and he looked down at me. "Jerry ain't here," he said. He turned away and went back inside.

One day our front doorbell rang and I could hear my mother's troubled exclamation. "Jerry! What's wrong?" Jerry was crying so hard he could hardly talk. "My father says I can't play with you anymore because you're not good enough for us."

Creston High School, which served all the children from the north end of Grand Rapids, was all white and middle-class. Nobody talked to me that first day, but I was noticed. When I left school at the end of the day I found my bike leaning up against the fence where I had left it, with a huge glob of slimy spit on my shaggy saddle cover. People passed by on their way home and looked at me and spit. I felt a hollowness behind my eyes, but I didn't cry. I just got on the bike, stood up on the pedals, and rode it home without sitting down. And it went that way for about the first two weeks. After the third day, I got rid of the saddle cover because the plain leather was a lot easier to clean.

But the glacier began to thaw. One day in class, the freckle-faced kid with the crewcut sitting next to me was asking everybody for a pencil. And then he looked at me and said, "Maybe you can lend me one." Those were the best words I had heard since I first met Jerry. This kid had included me in the human race in front of everybody. His name was Jack Waltz.

And after a while when the spitters had subsided and I could ride home sitting down, I began to notice that little kids my size were playing pickup games in the end zones of the football field. It looked interesting, but I didn't know anybody and didn't know how they would respond to me. So I just rode on by for a couple of weeks, slowing down each day, trying to screw up my courage to go in.

But then one day, I saw Jack Waltz there. I stood around the edges   28
of the group watching. It seemed that they played forever without even noticing me, but finally someone had to go home and the sides were unbalanced. Somebody said, "Let's ask him."

As we lined up for our first huddle, I heard somebody on the other   29
side say, "I hope he doesn't have a knife." One of the guys on my side asked me, "Can you run the ball?" I said yes, so they gave me the ball and I ran three quarters of the length of the field for a touchdown. And I made other touchdowns and other long runs before the game was over. When I thought about it later that night, I became certain that part of my success was due to the imaginary knife that was running interference for me. But no matter. By the end of the game, I had a group of friends. Boys named Andy and Don and Bill and Gene and Rich. We left the field together and some of them waved and yelled, "See ya tomorra, Rog."

And Don De Young, a pleasant round-faced boy, even lived quite   30
near me. So, after parting from everybody else, he and I went on together down to the corner of Coit and Knapp. As we parted, he suggested that we meet to go to school together the next day. I had longed for that but I hadn't suggested it for fear of a rebuff for overstepping the limits of my race. I had already learned one of the great tenets of Negro survival in America: to live the reactive life. It was like the old Negro comedian who once said, "When the man asks how the weather is, I know nuff to look keerful at his face 'fore even I look out the window." So, I waited for him to suggest it, and my patience was rewarded. I was overjoyed and grateful.

I didn't spend all my time in the north end. Soon after I moved to   31
Grand Rapids, Pop introduced me to some patients he had with a son my age. The boy's name was Lloyd Brown, and his father was a bellman downtown at the Pantlind Hotel. Lloyd and I often rode bikes and played basketball in his backyard. After a while, my mother asked me why I never had Lloyd come out to visit me. It was a question I dreaded, but she pressed on. "After all," she said, "you've had a lot of meals at his house and it's rude not to invite him back." I knew she was right and I also hated the whole idea of it.

With my friends in the north, race was never mentioned. Ever. I   32
carried my race around with me like an open basket of rotten eggs. I knew I could drop one at any moment and it would explode with a stench over everything. This was in the days when the movies either had no blacks at all or featured rank stereotypes like Stepin Fetchit,[3]

3. A lazy black character in the film *Hearts in Dixie* (1929).

and the popular magazines like *Life*, *Look*, the *Saturday Evening Post*, and *Collier's* carried no stories about Negroes, had no ads depicting Negroes, and generally gave the impression that we did not exist in this society. I knew that my white friends, being well brought up, were just too polite to mention this disability that I had. And I was grateful to them, but terrified, just the same, that maybe someday one of them would have the bad taste to notice what I was.

It seemed to me that my tenuous purchase in this larger white   33
world depended on the maintenance between me and my friends in the north end of our unspoken bargain to ignore my difference, my shame, and their embarrassment. If none of us had to deal with it, I thought, we could all handle it. My white friends behaved as if they perceived the bargain exactly as I did. It was a delicate equation, and I was terrified that Lloyd's presence in the North End would rip apart the balance.

I am so ashamed of that shame now that I cringe when I write it.   34
But I understand that boy now as he could not understand himself then. I was an American boy, though I did not fully comprehend that either. I was fully shaped and formed by America, where white people had all the power in sight, and they owned everything in sight except our house. Their beauty was the real beauty; there wasn't any other beauty. A real human being had straight hair, a white face, and thin lips. Other people, who looked different, were lesser beings.

No wonder, then, that most black men desired the forbidden fruit   35
of white loins. No wonder, too, that we thought that the most beautiful and worthy Negro people were those who looked most white. We blacks used to have a saying, "If you're white, you're all right. If you're brown, stick around. If you're black, stand back." I was brown.

It was not that we in my family were direct victims of racism. On   36
the contrary, my stepfather clearly had a higher income than the parents of most students in my high school. Unlike those of most of my contemporaries, black and white, my parents had college degrees. Within Grand Rapids' tiny Negro community, they were among the elite. The others were the lawyer, the dentist, the undertaker, and the other doctor.

But that is what made race such exquisite agony. I did have a sense   37
that it was unfair for poor Negroes to be relegated to bad jobs—if they had jobs at all—and to bad or miserable housing, but I didn't feel any great sense of identity with them. After all, the poor blacks in New York had also been the hard ones: the ones who tried to take my money, to beat me up, and to keep me perpetually intimidated. Besides, I had heard it intimated around my house that their behavior, sexual or otherwise, left a good deal to be desired.

So I thought that maybe they just weren't ready for this society,   38
but that I was. And it was dreadfully unfair for white people to just

look at my face and lips and hair and decide that I was inferior. By being a model student and leader, I thought I was demonstrating how well Negroes could perform if only the handicaps were removed and they were given a chance. But deep down I guess I was also trying to demonstrate that I was not like those other people; that I was different. My message was quite clear: I was *not nigger*. But the world didn't seem quite ready to make such fine distinctions, and it was precisely that fact—though at the time I could scarcely even have admitted it to myself—that was the nub of the race issue for me.

I would sometimes lie on my back and stare up at passing clouds and wonder why God had played a dirty trick by making me a Negro. It all seemed so random. So unfair to me. To *me*! But in school I was gaining more friends, and the teachers respected me. It got so that I could go for days not thinking very much about being Negro, until something made the problem unavoidable. [39]

One day in history class, for instance, the teacher asked each of us to stand and tell in turn where our families had originated. Many of the kids in the class were Dutch with names like Vander Jagt, De Young, and Ripstra. My pal Andy was Scots-Irish. When it came my turn, I stood up and burned with shame and when I would speak, I lied. And then I was even more ashamed because I exposed a deeper shame. "Some of my family was English," I said—Wilkins is an English name—"and the rest of it came from . . . Egypt." Egypt! [40]

One Saturday evening after one of our sandlot games, I went over to Lloyd's. Hearing my stories, Lloyd said mildly that he'd like to come up and play some Saturday. I kept on talking, but all the time my mind was repeating: "Lloyd wants to play. He wants to come up to the North End on Saturday. Next Saturday. Next Saturday." I was trapped. [41]

So, after the final story about the final lunge, when I couldn't put it off any longer, I said, "Sure. Why not?" But, later in the evening, after I had had some time to think, I got Lloyd alone. "Say, look," I said. "Those teams are kinda close, ya know. I mean, we don't switch around. From team to team. Or new guys, ya know?" [42]

Lloyd nodded, but he was getting a funny look on his face . . . part unbelieving and part hurt. So I quickly interjected before he could say anything, "Naw, man. Naw. Not like you shouldn't come and play. Just that we gotta have some good reason for you to play on our team, you dig?" [43]

"Yeah," Lloyd said, his face still puzzled, but no longer hurt. [44]

"Hey, I know," I said. "I got it. We'll say you're my cousin. If you're my cousin, see, then you gotta play. Nobody can say you can't be on my team, because you're family, right?" [45]

"Oh, right. Okay," Lloyd said, his face brightening. "Sure, we'll say we're cousins. Solid." [46]

I felt relieved as well. I could have a Negro cousin. It wasn't voluntary. It wouldn't be as if I had gone out and made a Negro friend deliberately. A person couldn't help who his cousins were.

There began to be a cultural difference between me and other blacks my age too. Black street language had evolved since my Harlem days, and I had not kept pace. Customs, attitudes, and the other common social currencies of everyday black life had evolved away from me. I didn't know how to talk, to banter, to move my body. If I was tentative and responsive in the North End, where I lived, I was tense, stiff, and awkward when I was with my black contemporaries. One day I was standing outside the church trying, probably at my mother's urging, to make contact. Conversational sallies flew around me while I stood there stiff and mute, unable to participate. Because the language was so foreign to me, I understood little of what was being said, but I did know that the word used for a white was *paddy*. Then a boy named Nickerson, the one whom my mother particularly wanted me to be friends with, inclined his head slightly toward me and said, to whoops of laughter, "technicolor paddy." My feet felt rooted in stone, and my head was aflame. I never forgot that phrase.

I have rarely felt so alone as I did that day riding home from church. Already partly excluded by my white friends, I was now almost completely alienated from my own people as well. But I felt less uncomfortable and less vulnerable in the white part of town. It was familiar enough to enable me to ward off most unpleasantness.

And then there was the problem of girls. They were everywhere, the girls. They all had budding bosoms, they all smelled pink, they all brushed against the boys in the hall, they were all white, and, in 1947–49, they were all inaccessible.

There were some things you knew without ever knowing how you knew them. You knew that Mississippi was evil and dangerous, that New York was east, and the Pacific ocean was west. And in the same way you knew that white women were the most desirable and dangerous objects in the world. Blacks were lynched in Mississippi and such places sometimes just for looking with the wrong expression at white women. Blacks of a very young age knew that white women of any quality went with the power and style that went with the governance of America—though, God knows, we had so much self-hate that when a white woman went with a Negro man, we promptly decided she was trash, and we also figured that if she would go with him she would go with any Negro.

Nevertheless, as my groin throbbed at fifteen and sixteen and seventeen, *they* were often the only ones there. One of them would be in the hallway opening her locker next to mine. Her blue sweater sleeve would be pushed up to just below the elbow, and as she would reach high on a shelf to stash away a book, I would see the tender dark hair against the white skin of her forearm. And I would ache and want to touch that arm and follow that body hair to its source.

Some of my friends, of course, did touch some of those girls. My   53
friends and I would talk about athletics and school and their loves. But they wouldn't say a word about the dances and the hayrides they went to.

I perceived they liked me and accepted me as long as I moved aside   54
when life's currents took them to where I wasn't supposed to be. I fit into their ways when they talked about girls, even their personal girls. And, indeed, I fit into the girls' lives when they were talking about boys, most particularly their own personal boys. Because I was a boy, I had insight. But I was also Negro, and therefore a neuter. So a girl who was alive and sensuous night after night in my fantasies would come to me earnestly in the day and talk about Rich or Gene or Andy. She would ask what he thought about her, whether he liked to dance, whether, if she invited him to her house for a party, he would come. She would tell me her fears and her yearnings, never dreaming for an instant that I had yearnings too and that she was their object.

There may be few more powerful obsessions than a teenage boy's   55
fixation on a love object. In my case it came down to a thin brunette named Marge McDowell. She was half a grade behind me, and she lived in a small house on a hill. I found excuses to drive by it all the time. I knew her schedule at school, so I could manage to be in most of the hallways she had to use going from class to class. We knew each other, and she had once confided a strong but fleeting yearning for my friend Rich Kippen. I thought about her constantly.

Finally, late one afternoon after school, I came upon her alone in   56
a hallway. "Marge," I blurted, "can I ask you something?"

She stopped and smiled and said, "Sure, Roger, what?"   57

"Well I was wondering," I said. "I mean. Well, would you go to   58
the hayride next week with me."

Her jaw dropped and her eyes got huge. Then she uttered a small   59
shriek and turned, hugging her books to her bosom the way girls do, and fled. I writhed with mortification in my bed that night and for many nights after.

In my senior year, I was elected president of the Creston High   60
School student council. It was a breakthrough of sorts.

ADRIENNE RICH

Split at the Root: An Essay on Jewish Identity

Adrienne Rich (1929–   ) knows what it means to be an outsider. She grew up in an "assimilated" Jewish family in Baltimore; became a writer at Radcliffe, where she studied male poets taught by an all-male faculty; lived the life of a faculty wife and mother; and eventually became a leader among America's politically active lesbians. As a civil rights activist and a teacher in New York City's SEEK program for disadvantaged young people, Rich has devoted much of her career to improving the lives of other "outsiders." She has also been an activist in the women's movement and, since 1986, a professor of English and feminist studies at Stanford University. Rich has published several books of poetry since her college years, including *A Change of World* (1951), *The Diamond Cutters* (1955), *Diving into the Wreck* (1973), and *Time's Power: Poems 1985–1988* (1992). "Split at the Root" was originally published in *Nice Jewish Girls: A Lesbian Anthology* (ed. Evelyn Tort Beck, 1984) and is collected in Rich's *Blood, Bread, and Poetry: Selected Prose, 1979–1985* (1986).

For about fifteen minutes I have been sitting chin in hand in front 1
of the typewriter, staring out at the snow. Trying to be honest with myself, trying to figure out why writing this seems to be so dangerous an act, filled with fear and shame, and why it seems so necessary. It comes to me that in order to write this I have to be willing to do two things: I have to claim my father, for I have my Jewishness from him and not from my gentile mother; and I have to break his silence, his taboos; in order to claim him I have in a sense to expose him.

And there is, of course, the third thing: I have to face the sources 2
and the flickering presence of my own ambivalence as a Jew; the daily, mundane anti-Semitisms of my entire life.

These are stories I have never tried to tell before. Why now? Why, 3
I asked myself sometime last year, does this question of Jewish identity float so impalpably, so ungraspably around me, a cloud I can't quite see the outlines of, which feels to me to be without definition?

And yet I've been on the track of this longer than I think. 4

In a long poem written in 1960, when I was thirty-one years old, 5
I described myself as "Split at the root, neither Gentile nor Jew, / Yankee nor Rebel."[1] I was still trying to have it both ways: to be neither/nor,

---

1. Adrienne Rich, "Readings of History," in *Snapshots of a Daughter-in-Law* (New York: W. W. Norton, 1967), pp. 36–40. [author's note]

trying to live (with my Jewish husband and three children more Jewish in ancestry than I) in the predominantly gentile Yankee academic world of Cambridge, Massachusetts.

But this begins, for me, in Baltimore, where I was born in my   6
father's workplace, a hospital in the Black ghetto, whose lobby contained an immense white marble statue of Christ.

My father was then a young teacher and researcher in the depart-   7
ment of pathology at the Johns Hopkins Medical School, one of the very few Jews to attend or teach at that institution. He was from Birmingham, Alabama; his father, Samuel, was Ashkenazic,[2] an immigrant from Austria-Hungary and his mother, Hattie Rice, a Sephardic Jew from Vicksburg, Mississippi. My grandfather had had a shoe store in Birmingham, which did well enough to allow him to retire comfortably and to leave my grandmother income on his death. The only souvenirs of my grandfather, Samuel Rich, were his ivory flute, which lay on our living-room mantel and was not to be played with; his thin gold pocket watch, which my father wore; and his Hebrew prayer book, which I discovered among my father's books in the course of reading my way through his library. In this prayer book there was a newspaper clipping about my grandparents' wedding, which took place in a synagogue.

My father, Arnold, was sent in adolescence to a military school   8
in the North Carolina mountains, a place for training white southern Christian gentlemen. I suspect that there were few, if any, other Jewish boys at Colonel Bingham's, or at "Mr. Jefferson's university" in Charlottesville, where he studied as an undergraduate. With whatever conscious forethought, Samuel and Hattie sent their son into the dominant southern WASP culture to become an "exception," to enter the professional class. Never, in describing these experiences, did he speak of having suffered—from loneliness, cultural alienation, or outsiderhood. Never did I hear him use the word *anti-Semitism*.

It was only in college, when I read a poem by Karl Shapiro begin-   9
ning "To hate the Negro and avoid the Jew / is the curriculum," that it flashed on me that there was an untold side to my father's story of his student years. He looked recognizably Jewish, was short and slender in build with dark wiry hair and deep-set eyes, high forehead and curved nose.

My mother is a gentile. In Jewish law I cannot count myself a Jew.   10
If it is true that "we think back through our mothers if we are women" (Virginia Woolf)—and I myself have affirmed this—then even according to lesbian theory, I cannot (or need not?) count myself a Jew.

2. Ashkenazic: descended from the Yiddish-speaking Jews of northern Europe, as opposed to Sephardic, descended from the Jews of Spain, Portugal, and Africa.

The white southern Protestant woman, the gentile, has always been 11
there for me to peel back into. That's a whole piece of history in itself,
for my gentile grandmother and my mother were also frustrated artists
and intellectuals, a lost writer and a lost composer between them. Readers and annotators of books, note takers, my mother a good pianist still,
in her eighties. But there was also the obsession with ancestry, with
"background," the southern talk of family, not as people you would
necessarily know and depend on, but as heritage, the guarantee of
"good breeding." There was the inveterate romantic heterosexual fantasy, the mother telling the daughter how to attract men (my mother
often used the word "fascinate"); the assumption that relations between the sexes could only be romantic, that it was in the woman's
interest to cultivate "mystery," conceal her actual feelings. Survival
tactics of a kind, I think today, knowing what I know about the white
woman's sexual role in the southern racist scenario. Heterosexuality as
protection, but also drawing white women deeper into collusion with
white men.

It would be easy to push away and deny the gentile in me—that 12
white southern woman, that social christian. At different times in my
life I have wanted to push away one or the other burden of inheritance,
to say merely *I am a woman; I am a lesbian.* If I call myself a Jewish
lesbian, do I thereby try to shed some of my southern gentile white
woman's culpability? If I call myself only through my mother, is it
because I pass more easily through a world where being a lesbian often
seems like outsiderhood enough?

According to Nazi logic, my two Jewish grandparents would have 13
made me a *Mischling, first-degree*—nonexempt from the Final Solution.

The social world in which I grew up was christian virtually without 14
needing to say so—christian imagery, music, language, symbols, assumptions everywhere. It was also a genteel, white, middle-class world
in which "common" was a term of deep opprobrium. "Common"
white people might speak of "niggers"; *we* were taught never to use
that word—*we* said "Negroes" (even as we accepted segregation, the
eating taboo, the assumption that Black people were simply of a separate species). Our language was more polite, distinguishing us from the
"red-necks" or the lynch-mob mentality. But so charged with negative
meaning was even the word "Negro" that as children we were taught
never to use it in front of Black people. We were taught that any mention of skin color in the presence of colored people was treacherous,
forbidden ground. In a parallel way, the word "Jew" was not used by
polite gentiles. I sometimes heard my best friend's father, a Presbyterian
minister, allude to "the Hebrew people" or "people of the Jewish faith."
The world of acceptable folk was white, gentile (christian, really), and
had "ideals" (which colored people, white "common" people, were

not supposed to have). "Ideals" and "manners" included not hurting someone's feelings by calling her or him a Negro or a Jew—naming the hated identity. This is the mental framework of the 1930s and 1940s in which I was raised.

(Writing this, I feel dimly like the betrayer: of my father, who did   15
not speak the word; of my mother, who must have trained me in the messages; of my caste and class; of my whiteness itself.)

Two memories: I am in a play reading at school of *The Merchant of*   16
Venice. Whatever Jewish law says, I am quite sure I was *seen* as Jewish (with a reassuringly gentile mother) in that double vision that bigotry allows. I am the only Jewish girl in the class, and I am playing Portia.[3] As always, I read my part aloud for my father the night before, and he tells me to convey, with my voice, more scorn and contempt with the word "Jew": "Therefore, Jew . . ." I have to say the word out, and say it loudly. I was encouraged to pretend to be a non-Jewish child acting a non-Jewish character who has to speak the word "Jew" emphatically. Such a child would not have had trouble with the part. But *I* must have had trouble with the part, if only because the word itself was really taboo. I can see that there was a kind of terrible, bitter bravado about my father's way of handling this. And who would not dissociate from Shylock in order to identify with Portia? As a Jewish child who was also a female, I loved Portia—and, like every other Shakespearean heroine, she proved a treacherous role model.

A year or so later I am in another play, *The School for Scandal*, in   17
which a notorious spendthrift is described as having "many excellent friends . . . among the Jews." In neither case was anything explained, either to me or to the class at large, about this scorn for Jews and the disgust surrounding Jews and money. Money, when Jews wanted it, had it, or lent it to others, seemed to take on a peculiar nastiness; Jews and money had some peculiar and unspeakable relation.

At this same school—in which we had Episcopalian hymns and   18
prayers, and read aloud through the Bible morning after morning—I gained the impression that Jews were in the Bible and mentioned in English literature, that they had been persecuted centuries ago by the wicked Inquisition, but that they seemed not to exist in everyday life. These were the 1940s, and we were told a great deal about the Battle of Britain, the noble French Resistance fighters, the brave, starving Dutch—but I did not learn of the resistance of the Warsaw ghetto until I left home.

I was sent to the Episcopal church, baptized and confirmed, and   19
attended it for about five years, though without belief. That religion seemed to have little to do with belief or commitment; it was liturgy

---

3. Portia, disguised as a lawyer, defends the life of Antonio against a claim filed by the Jewish moneylender Shylock.

that mattered, not spiritual passion. Neither of my parents ever entered that church, and my father would not enter *any* church for any reason—wedding or funeral. Nor did I enter a synagogue until I left Baltimore. When I came home from church, for a while, my father insisted on reading aloud to me from Thomas Paine's *The Age of Reason*—a diatribe against institutional religion. Thus, he explained, I would have a balanced view of these things, a choice. He—they—did not give me the choice to be a Jew. My mother explained to me when I was filling out forms for college that if any question was asked about "religion," I should put down "Episcopalian" rather than "none"—to seem to have no religion was, she implied, dangerous.

But it was white social christianity, rather than any particular christian sect, that the world was founded on. The very word *Christian* was used as a synonym for virtuous, just, peace-loving, generous, etc., etc.[4] The norm was christian: "religion: none" was indeed not acceptable. Anti-Semitism was so intrinsic as not to have a name. I don't recall exactly being taught that the Jews killed Jesus—"Christ killer" seems too strong a term for the bland Episcopal vocabulary—but certainly we got the impression that the Jews had been caught out in a terrible mistake, failing to recognize the true Messiah, and were thereby less advanced in moral and spiritual sensibility. The Jews had actually allowed *moneylenders in the Temple* (again, the unexplained obsession with Jews and money). They were of the past, archaic, primitive, as older (and darker) cultures are supposed to be primitive; christianity was lightness, fairness, peace on earth, and combined the feminine appeal of "The meek shall inherit the earth" with the masculine stride of "Onward, Christian Soldiers."

Sometime in 1946, while still in high school, I read in the newspaper that a theater in Baltimore was showing films of the Allied liberation of the Nazi concentration camps. Alone, I went downtown after school one afternoon and watched the stark, blurry, but unmistakable newsreels. When I try to go back and touch the pulse of that girl of sixteen, growing up in many ways so precocious and so ignorant, I am overwhelmed by a memory of despair, a sense of inevitability more enveloping than any I had ever known. Anne Frank's diary and many other personal narratives of the Holocaust were still unknown or unwritten. But it came to me that every one of those piles of corpses, mountains of shoes and clothing had contained, simply, individuals, who had believed, as I now believed of myself, that they were intended to live out a life of some kind of meaning, that the world possessed some kind of

---

4. In a similar way the phrase "That's white of you" implied that you were behaving with the superior decency and morality expected of white but not of Black people. [author's note]

sense and order; yet *this* had happened to them. And I, who believed my life was intended to be so interesting and meaningful, was connected to those dead by something—not just mortality but a taboo name, a hated identity. Or was I—did I really have to be? Writing this now, I feel belated rage that I was so impoverished by the family and social worlds I lived in, that I had to try to figure out by myself what this did indeed mean for me. That I had never been taught about resistance, only about passing. That I had no language for anti-Semitism itself.

When I went home and told my parents where I had been, they   22
were not pleased. I felt accused of being morbidly curious, not healthy, sniffing around death for the thrill of it. And since, at sixteen, I was often not sure of the sources of my feelings or of my motives for doing what I did, I probably accused myself as well. One thing was clear: there was nobody in my world with whom I could discuss those films. Probably at the same time, I was reading accounts of the camps in magazines and newspapers; what I remember were the films and having questions that I could not even phrase, such as *Are those men and women "them" or "us"?*

To be able to ask even the child's astonished question *Why do they*   23
hate us so? means knowing how to say "we." The guilt of not knowing, the guilt of perhaps having betrayed my parents or even those victims, those survivors, through mere curiosity—these also froze in me for years the impulse to find out more about the Holocaust.

1947: I left Baltimore to go to college in Cambridge, Massachusetts,   24
left (I thought) the backward, enervating South for the intellectual, vital North. New England also had for me some vibration of higher moral rectitude, of moral passion even, with its seventeenth-century Puritan self-scrutiny, its nineteenth-century literary "flowering," its abolitionist righteousness, Colonel Shaw and his Black Civil War regiment depicted in granite on Boston Common.[5] At the same time, I found myself, at Radcliffe, among Jewish women. I used to sit for hours over coffee with what I thought of as the "real" Jewish students, who told me about middle-class Jewish culture in America. I described my background— for the first time to strangers—and they took me on, some with amusement at my illiteracy, some arguing that I could never marry into a strict Jewish family, some convinced I didn't "look Jewish," others that I did. I learned the names of holidays and foods, which surnames are Jewish and which are "changed names"; about girls who had had their noses "fixed," their hair straightened. For these young Jewish women, students in the late 1940s, it was acceptable, perhaps even necessary, to strive to look as gentile as possible; but they stuck proudly to being

---

5. Colonel Robert Gould Shaw (1837–1863), a white officer, led the first regiment of African-American troops mustered into the Union Army.

Jewish, expected to marry a Jew, have children, keep the holidays, carry on the culture.

I felt I was testing a forbidden current, that there was danger in   25
these revelations. I bought a reproduction of a Chagall portrait of a rabbi in striped prayer shawl and hung it on the wall of my room. I was admittedly young and trying to educate myself, but I was also doing something that *is* dangerous: I was flirting with identity.

One day that year I was in a small shop where I had bought a   26
dress with a too-long skirt. The shop employed a seamstress who did alterations, and she came in to pin up the skirt on me. I am sure that she was a recent immigrant, a survivor. I remember a short, dark woman wearing heavy glasses, with an accent so foreign I could not understand her words. Something about her presence was very power-ful and disturbing to me. After marking and pinning up the skirt, she sat back on her knees, looked up at me, and asked in a hurried whisper: "You Jewish?" Eighteen years of training in assimilation sprang into the reflex by which I shook my head, rejecting her, and muttered, "No."

What was I actually saying "no" to? She was poor, older, struggling   27
with a foreign tongue, anxious; she had escaped the death that had been intended for her, but I had no imagination of her possible courage and foresight, her resistance—I did not see in her a heroine who had perhaps saved many lives, including her own. I saw the frightened immigrant, the seamstress hemming the skirts of college girls, the wan-dering Jew. But I was an American college girl having her skirt hemmed. And I was frightened myself, I think, because she had recog-nized me ("It takes one to know one," my friend Edie at Radcliffe had said) even if I refused to recognize myself or her, even if her recognition was sharpened by loneliness or the need to feel safe with me.

But why should she have felt safe with me? I myself was living   28
with a false sense of safety.

There are betrayals in my life that I have known at the very moment   29
were betrayals: this was one of them. There are other betrayals commit-ted so repeatedly, so mundanely, that they leave no memory trace be-hind, only a growing residue of misery, of dull, accreted self-hatred. Often these take the form not of words but of silence. Silence before the joke at which everyone is laughing: the anti-woman joke, the racist joke, the anti-Semitic joke. Silence and then amnesia. Blocking it out when the oppressor's language starts coming from the lips of one we admire, whose courage and eloquence have touched us: *She didn't really mean that; he didn't really say that.* But the accretions build up out of sight, like scale inside a kettle.

1948: I come home from my freshman year at college, flaming with   30
new insights, new information. I am the daughter who has gone out

into the world, to the pinnacle of intellectual prestige, Harvard, fulfilling
my father's hopes for me, but also exposed to dangerous influences. I
have already been reproved for attending a rally for Henry Wallace and
the Progressive party.[6] I challenge my father: "Why haven't you told
me that I am Jewish? Why do you never talk about being a Jew?" He
answers measuredly, "You know that I have never denied that I am a
Jew. But it's not important to me. I am a scientist, a deist. I have no
use for organized religion. I choose to live in a world of many kinds of
people. There are Jews I admire and others whom I despise. I am a
person, not simply a Jew." The words are as I remember them, not
perhaps exactly as spoken. But that was the message. And it contained
enough truth—as all denial drugs itself on partial truth—so that it remained for the time being unanswerable, leaving me high and dry, split
at the root, gasping for clarity, for air.

At that time Arnold Rich was living in suspension, waiting to be   31
appointed to the professorship of pathology at Johns Hopkins. The ap-
pointment was delayed for years, no Jew ever having held a professional chair in that medical school. And he wanted it badly. It must
have been a very bitter time for him, since he had believed so greatly
in the redeeming power of excellence, of being the most brilliant, inspired man for the job. With enough excellence, you could presumably
make it stop mattering that you were Jewish; you could become the
only Jew in the gentile world, a Jew so "civilized," so far from "common," so attractively combining southern gentility with European cultural values that no one would ever confuse you with the raw, "pushy"
Jews of New York, the "loud, hysterical" refugees from eastern Europe,
the "overdressed" Jews of the urban South.

We—my sister, mother, and I—were constantly urged to speak   32
quietly in public, to dress without ostentation, to repress all vividness
or spontaneity, to assimilate with a world which might see us as too
flamboyant. I suppose that my mother, pure gentile though she was,
could be seen as acting "common" or "Jewish" if she laughed too
loudly or spoke aggressively. My father's mother, who lived with us
half the year, was a model of circumspect behavior, dressed in dark
blue or lavender, retiring in company, ladylike to an extreme, wearing
no jewelry except a good gold chain, a narrow brooch, or a string of
pearls. A few times, within the family, I saw her anger flare, felt the
passion she was repressing. But when Arnold took us out to a restaurant
or on a trip, the Rich women were always tuned down to some WASP
level my father believed, surely, would protect us all—maybe also make
us unrecognizable to the "real Jews" who wanted to seize us, drag us
back to the *shtetl,* the ghetto, in its many manifestations.

6. Henry Wallace, a former vice president, ran for president on the Progressive party
ticket in 1948.

For, yes, that *was* a message—that some Jews would be after you,   33
once they "knew," to rejoin them, to re-enter a world that was messy,
noisy, unpredictable, maybe poor—"even though," as my mother once
wrote me, criticizing my largely Jewish choice of friends in college,
"some of them will be the most brilliant, fascinating people you'll ever
meet." I wonder if that isn't one message of assimilation—of America—
that the unlucky or the unachieving want to pull you backward, that
to identify with them is to court downward mobility, lose the precious
chance of passing, of token existence. There was always within this
sense of Jewish identity a strong class discrimination. Jews might be
"fascinating" as individuals but came with huge unruly families who
"poured chicken soup over everyone's head" (in the phrase of a white
southern male poet). Anti-Semitism could thus be justified by the bad
behavior of certain Jews; and if you did not effectively deny family and
community, there would always be a remote cousin claiming kinship
with you who was the "wrong kind" of Jew.

I have always believed his attitude toward other Jews depended on who   34
they were. . . . It was my impression that Jews of this background looked
down on Eastern European Jews, including Polish Jews and Russian Jews,
who generally were not as well educated. This from a letter written to me
recently by a gentile who had worked in my father's department, whom
I had asked about anti-Semitism there and in particular regarding my
father. This informant also wrote me that it was hard to perceive anti-
Semitism in Baltimore because the racism made so much more intense
an impression: *I would almost have to think that blacks went to a different*
heaven than the whites, because the bodies were kept in a separate morgue,
and some white persons did not even want blood transfusions from black
donors. My father's mind was predictably racist and misogynist; yet as
a medical student he noted in his journal that southern male chivalry
stopped at the point of any white man in a streetcar giving his seat to
an old, weary Black woman standing in the aisle. Was this a Jewish
insight—an outsider's insight, even though the outsider was striving to
be on the inside?

Because what isn't named is often more permeating than what is,   35
I believe that my father's Jewishness profoundly shaped my own identity and our family existence. They were shaped both by external anti-
Semitism and my father's self-hatred, and by his Jewish pride. What
Arnold did, I think, was call his Jewish pride something else: achievement, aspiration, genius, idealism. Whatever was unacceptable got left
back under the rubric of Jewishness or the "wrong kind" of Jews—
uneducated, aggressive, loud. The message I got was that we were really
superior: nobody else's father had collected so many books, had traveled so far, knew so many languages. Baltimore was a musical city, but
for the most part, in the families of my school friends, culture was
for women. My father was an amateur musician, read poetry, adored

encyclopedic knowledge. He prowled and pounced over my school papers, insisting I use "grown-up" sources; he criticized my poems for faulty technique and gave me books on rhyme and meter and form. His investment in my intellect and talent was egotistical, tyrannical, opinionated, and terribly wearing. He taught me, nevertheless, to believe in hard work, to mistrust easy inspiration, to write and rewrite; to feel that I *was* a person of the book, even though a woman; to take ideas seriously. He made me feel, at a very young age, the power of language and that I could share in it.

The Riches were proud, but we also had to be very careful. Our behavior had to be more impeccable than other people's. Strangers were not to be trusted, nor even friends; family issues must never go beyond the family; the world was full of potential slanderers, betrayers, *people who could not understand.* Even within the family, I realize that I never in my whole life knew what my father was really feeling. Yet he spoke —monologued—with driving intensity. You could grow up in such a house mesmerized by the local electricity, the crucial meanings assumed by the merest things. This used to seem to me a sign that we were all living on some high emotional plane. It was a difficult force field for a favored daughter to disengage from. 36

Easy to call that intensity Jewish; and I have no doubt that passion is one of the qualities required for survival over generations of persecution. But what happens when passion is rent from its original base, when the white gentile world is softly saying "Be more like us and you can be almost one of us"? What happens when survival seems to mean closing off one emotional artery after another? His forebears in Europe had been forbidden to travel or expelled from one country after another, had special taxes levied on them if they left the city walls, had been forced to wear special clothes and badges, restricted to the poorest neighborhoods. He had wanted to be a "free spirit," to travel widely, among "all kinds of people." Yet in his prime of life he lived in an increasingly withdrawn world, in his house up on a hill in a neighborhood where Jews were not supposed to be able to buy property, depending almost exclusively on interactions with his wife and daughters to provide emotional connectedness. In his home, he created a private defense system so elaborate that even as he was dying, my mother felt unable to talk freely with his colleagues or others who might have helped her. Of course, she acquiesced in this. 37

The loneliness of the "only," the token, often doesn't feel like loneliness but like a kind of dead echo chamber. Certain things that ought to don't resonate. Somewhere Beverly Smith writes of women of color "inspiring the behavior" in each other. When there's nobody to "inspire the behavior," act out of the culture, there is an atrophy, a dwindling, which is partly invisible. 38

I was married in 1953, in the Hillel House at Harvard, under a   39
portrait of Albert Einstein. My parents refused to come. I was marrying
a Jew of the "wrong kind" from an Orthodox eastern European background. Brooklyn-born, he had gone to Harvard, changed his name,
was both indissolubly connected to his childhood world and terribly
ambivalent about it. My father saw this marriage as my having fallen
prey to the Jewish family, eastern European division.

Like many women I knew in the fifties living under a then-   40
unquestioned heterosexual imperative, I married in part because I knew
no better way to disconnect from my first family. I married a "real
Jew" who was himself almost equally divided between a troubled yet
ingrained Jewish identity, and the pull toward Yankee approval, assimilation. But at least he was not adrift as a single token in a gentile world.
We lived in a world where there was much intermarriage and where a
certain "Jewish flavor" was accepted within the dominant gentile culture. People talked glibly of "Jewish self-hatred," but anti-Semitism
was rarely identified. It was as if you could have it both ways—identity
and assimilation—without having to think about it very much.

I was moved and gratefully amazed by the affection and kindliness   41
my husband's parents showed me, the half *shiksa*. I longed to embrace
that family, that new and mysterious Jewish world. It was never a
question of conversion—my husband had long since ceased being observant—but of a burning desire to do well, please these new parents,
heal the split consciousness in which I had been raised, and, of course,
to belong. In the big, sunny apartment on Eastern Parkway, the table
would be spread on Saturday afternoons with a white or an embroi-
dered cloth and plates of coffeecake, spongecake, mohncake, cookies
for a family gathering where everyone ate and drank—coffee, milk,
cake—and later the talk still eddied among the women around the table
or in the kitchen, while the men ended up in the living room watching
the ball game. I had never known this kind of family, in which mock
insults were cheerfully exchanged, secrets whispered in corners among
two or three, children and grandchildren boasted about, and the new
daughter-in-law openly inspected. I was profoundly attracted by all
this, including the punctilious observance of *kashrut*, the symbolism
lurking behind daily kitchen tasks. I saw it all as quintessentially and
authentically Jewish, and I objectified both the people and the culture.
My unexamined anti-Semitism allowed me to do this. But also, I had
not yet recognized that as a woman I stood in a particular and unexamined relationship to the Jewish family and to Jewish culture.

There were several years during which I did not see, and barely   42
communicated with, my parents. At the same time, my father's personality haunted my life. Such had been the force of his will in our household that for a long time I felt I would have to pay in some terrible

way for having disobeyed him. When finally we were reconciled, and my husband and I and our children began to have some minimal formal contact with my parents, the obsessional power of Arnold's voice or handwriting had given way to a dull sense of useless anger and pain. I wanted him to cherish and approve of me, not as he had when I was a child, but as the woman I was, who had her own mind and had made her own choices. This, I finally realized, was not to be; Arnold demanded absolute loyalty, absolute submission to his will. In my separation from him, in my realization at what price that once-intoxicating approval had been bought, I was learning in concrete ways a great deal about patriarchy, in particular how the "special" woman, the favored daughter, is controlled and rewarded.

Arnold Rich died in 1968 after a long, deteriorating illness; his   43
mind had gone, and he had been losing his sight for years. It was a year of intensifying political awareness for me; the Martin Luther King and Robert Kennedy assassinations, the Columbia strike.[7] But it was not that these events, and the meetings and demonstrations that surrounded them, pre-empted the time of mourning for my father; I had been mourning a long time for an early, primary, and intense relationship, by no means always benign, but in which I had been ceaselessly made to feel that what I did with my life, the choices I made, the attitudes I held, were of the utmost consequence.

Sometime in my thirties, on visits to Brooklyn, I sat on Eastern   44
Parkway, a baby stroller at my feet—one of many rows of young Jewish women on benches with children in that neighborhood. I used to see the Lubavitcher Hasidim—then beginning to move into the Crown Heights neighborhood—walking out on *Shabbes,* the women in their *shaytls*[8] a little behind the men. My father-in-law pointed them out as rather exotic—too old-country, perhaps, too unassimilated even for his devout yet Americanized sense of Jewish identity. It took many years for me to understand—partly because I understood so little about class in America—how in my own family, and in the very different family of my in-laws, there were degrees and hierarchies of assimilation which looked askance upon each other—and also geographic lines of difference, as between southern Jews and New York Jews, whose manners and customs varied along class as well as regional lines.

I had three sons before I was thirty, and during those years I often   45
felt that to be a Jewish woman, a Jewish mother, was to be perceived

7. In the spring of 1968, student protestors closed Columbia University to block the school's plan to build a gymnasium in Morningside Park, a popular recreational area for residents of Harlem.
8. Wigs traditionally worn by Orthodox Jewish women after their marriage.

in the Jewish family as an entirely physical being, a producer and nour-
isher of children. The experience of motherhood was eventually to radi-
calize me. But before that, I was encountering the institution of motherhood most directly in a Jewish cultural version; and I felt rebellious,
moody, defensive, unable to sort out what was Jewish from what was
simply motherhood or female destiny. (I lived in Cambridge, not Brooklyn; but there, too, restless, educated women sat on benches with baby
strollers, half-stunned, not by Jewish cultural expectations, but by the
middle-class American social expectations of the 1950s.)

My children were taken irregularly to Seders, to bar mizvahs, and to   46
special services in their grandfather's temple. Their father lit Hanukkah
candles while I stood by, having rememorized each year the English
meaning of the Hebrew blessing. We all celebrated a secular, liberal
Christmas. I read aloud from books about Esther and the Maccabees
and Moses, and also from books about Norse trolls and Chinese grandmothers and Celtic dragon slayers. Their father told stories of his boyhood in Brooklyn, his grandmother in the Bronx who had to be visited
by subway every week, of misdeeds in Hebrew school, of being a bright
Jewish kid at Boys' High. In the permissive liberalism of academic Cambridge, you could raise your children to be as vaguely or distinctly
Jewish as you would, but Christian myth and calendar organized the
year. My sons grew up knowing far more about the existence and
concrete meaning of Jewish culture than I had. But I don't recall sitting
down with them and telling them that millions of people like themselves, many of them children, had been rounded up and murdered in
Europe in their parents' lifetime. Nor was I able to tell them that they
came in part out of the rich, thousand-year-old Ashkenazic culture of
eastern Europe, which the Holocaust destroyed; or that they came from
a people whose traditions, religious and secular, included a hatred
of oppression and an imperative to pursue justice and care for the
stranger—an anti-racist, a socialist, and even sometimes a feminist vision. I could not tell them these things because these things were still
too indistinct in my own mind.

The emergence of the Civil Rights movement in the sixties I remem-   47
ber as lifting me out of a sense of personal frustration and hopelessness.
Reading James Baldwin's early essays in the fifties had stirred me with
a sense that apparently "given" situations like racism could be analyzed
and described and that this could lead to action, to change. Racism had
been so utter and implicit a fact of my childhood and adolescence, had
felt so central among the silences, negations, cruelties, fears, supersti-
tions of my early life, that somewhere among my feelings must have
been the hope that if Black people could become free of the immense
political and social burdens they were forced to bear, I, too, could become free of all the ghosts and shadows of my childhood, named and

unnamed. When "the movement" began, it felt extremely personal to me. And it was often Jews who spoke up for the justice of the cause, Jewish students and civil rights lawyers who travelled South; it was two young Jews who were found murdered with a young Black man in Mississippi: Schwerner, Goodman, Chaney.

Moving to New York in the mid-sixties meant being plunged almost   48
immediately into the debate over community control of public schools, in which Black and Jewish teachers and parents were often on opposite sides of extremely militant barricades. It was easy as a white liberal to deplore and condemn the racism of middle-class Jewish parents or angry Jewish schoolteachers, many of them older women; to displace our own racism onto them; or to feel it as too painful to think about. The struggle for Black civil rights had such clarity about it for me: I knew that segregation was wrong, that unequal opportunity was wrong; I knew that segregation in particular was more than a set of social and legal rules—it meant that even "decent" white people lived in a network of lies and arrogance and moral collusion. In the world of Jewish assimilationist and liberal politics which I knew best, however, things were far less clear to me, and anti-Semitism went almost unmentioned. It was even possible to view concern about anti-Semitism as a reactionary agenda, a monomania of *Commentary* magazine or, later, the Jewish Defense League. Most of the political work I was doing in the late 1960s was on racial issues, in particular as a teacher in the City University during the struggle for open admissions. The white colleagues I thought of as allies were, I think, mostly Jewish. Yet it was easy to see other New York Jews, who had climbed out of poverty and exploitation through the public-school system and the free city colleges, as now trying to block Black and Puerto Rican students trying to do likewise. I didn't understand then that I was living between two strains of Jewish social identity: the Jew as radical visionary and activist who understands oppression firsthand, and the Jew as part of America's devouring plan in which the persecuted, called to assimilation, learn that the price is to engage in persecution.

And, indeed, there *was* intense racism among Jews as well as white   49
gentiles in the City University, part of the bitter history of Jews and Blacks which James Baldwin had described much earlier, in his 1948 essay "The Harlem Ghetto";[9] part of the divide-and-conquer script still being rehearsed by those of us who have the least to gain from it.

By the time I left my marriage, after seventeen years and three   50
children, I had become identified with the Women's Liberation move-

9. James Baldwin, "The Harlem Ghetto," in *Notes of a Native Son* (Boston: Beacon, 1955). [author's note]

ment. It was an astonishing time to be a woman of my age. In the 1950s, seeking a way to grasp the pain I seemed to be feeling most of the time, to set it in some larger context, I had read all kinds of things; but it was James Baldwin and Simone de Beauvoir who had described the world—though differently—in terms that made the most sense to me. By the end of the sixties there were two political movements—one already meeting severe repression, one just emerging—which addressed those descriptions of the world.

And there was, of course, a third movement, or a movement- 51
within-a-movement: the early lesbian manifestoes, the new visibility and activism of lesbians everywhere. I had known very early on that the women's movement was not going to be a simple walk across an open field; that it would pull on every fiber of my existence; that it would mean going back and searching the shadows of my conscious-ness. Reading *The Second Sex* in the 1950s isolation of an academic housewife had felt less dangerous than reading "The Myth of Vaginal Orgasm" or "Woman-identified Woman" in a world where I was in constant debate and discussion with women over every aspect of our lives that we could as yet name. De Beauvoir had placed "The Lesbian" on the margins, and there was little in her book to suggest the power of woman bonding. But the passion of debating ideas with women was an erotic passion for me, and the risking of self with women that was necessary in order to win some truth out of the lies of the past was also erotic. The suppressed lesbian I had been carrying in me since adolescence began to stretch her limbs, and her first full-fledged act was to fall in love with a Jewish woman.

Some time during the early months of that relationship, I dreamed 52
that I was arguing feminist politics with my lover. *Of course,* I said to her in this dream, *if you're going to bring up the Holocaust against me, there's nothing I can do.* If, as I believe, I was both myself and her in this dream, it spoke of the split in my consciousness. I had been, more or less, a Jewish heterosexual woman. But what did it mean to be a Jewish lesbian? What did it mean to feel myself, as I did, both anti-Semite and Jew? And, as a feminist, how was I charting for myself the oppressions within oppression?

The earliest feminist papers on Jewish identity that I read were 53
critiques of the patriarchal and misogynist elements in Judaism, or of the caricaturing of Jewish women in literature by Jewish men. I remem-ber hearing Judith Plaskow give a paper called "Can a Woman Be a Jew?" (Her conclusion was "Yes, but . . .") I was soon after in corre-spondence with a former student who had emigrated to Israel, was a passionate feminist, and wrote to me at length of the legal and social constraints on women there, the stirrings of contemporary Israeli femi-nism, and the contradictions she felt in her daily life. With the new politics, activism, literature of a tumultuous feminist movement around

me, a movement which claimed universality though it had not yet
acknowledged its own racial, class, and ethnic perspectives or its fears of
the differences among women, I pushed aside for one last time thinking
further about myself as a Jewish woman. I saw Judaism simply as
another strand of patriarchy. If asked to choose, I might have said (as
my father had said in other language): *I am a woman, not a Jew.* (But,
I always added mentally, if Jews had to wear yellow stars again, I too,
would wear one—as if I would have the choice to wear it or not.)

Sometimes I feel I have seen too long from too many disconnected   54
angles: white, Jewish, anti-Semite, racist, anti-racist, once-married, lesbian, middle-class, feminist, exmatriate southerner, *split at the root*—that
I will never bring them whole. I would have liked, in this essay, to
bring together the meanings of anti-Semitism and racism as I have
experienced them and as I believe they intersect in the world beyond
my life. But I'm not able to do this yet. I feel the tension as I think,
make notes: *If you really look at the one reality, the other will waver and
disperse.* Trying in one week to read Angela Davis and Lucy Davidowicz;[10] trying to hold throughout to a feminist, a lesbian, perspective—
what does this mean? Nothing has trained me for this. And sometimes
I feel inadequate to make any statement as a Jew; I feel the history of
denial within me like an injury, a scar. For assimilation has affected *my*
perceptions; those early lapses in meaning, those blanks, are with me
still. My ignorance can be dangerous to me and to others.

Yet we can't wait for the undamaged to make our connections for   55
us; we can't wait to speak until we are perfectly clear and righteous.
There is no purity and, in our lifetimes, no end to this process.

This essay, then, has no conclusions: it is another beginning for   56
me. Not just a way of saying, in 1982 Right Wing America, *I, too, will
wear the yellow star.* It's a moving into accountability, enlarging the
range of accountability. I know that in the rest of my life, the next half
century or so, every aspect of my identity will have to be engaged. The
middle-class white girl taught to trade obedience for privilege. The Jewish lesbian raised to be a heterosexual gentile. The woman who first
heard oppression named and analyzed in the Black Civil Rights struggle.
The woman with three sons, the feminist who hates male violence. The
woman limping with a cane, the woman who has stopped bleeding are
also accountable. The poet who knows that beautiful language can lie,
that the oppressor's language sometimes sounds beautiful. The woman
trying, as part of her resistance, to clean up her act.

10. Angela Y. Davis, *Women, Race and Class* (New York: Random House, 1981); Lucy S.
Davidowicz, *The War against the Jews 1933–1945* (1975) (New York: Bantam, 1979).
[author's note]

PERRI KLASS

Learning the Language

Perri Klass (1958–   ) graduated from Harvard Medical School in 1986. During her years as a medical student, she not only published a novel (*Recombinations*, 1985) and gave birth to a son but also contributed essays to *Mademoiselle, Discover, Massachusetts Medicine*, and *The New York Times*. These essays gave a fresh and sometimes discomforting picture of medical school education; several were later collected in *A Not Entirely Benign Procedure: Four Years as a Medical Student* (1987). In 1990 she published a second novel, *Other Women's Children*, and in 1992 continued the story of her medical training with *Baby Doctor*, an account of her years as a pediatric resident. Now a practicing pediatrician, Klass is also a regular contributor of articles and stories to several magazines. Klass says that writing about medical school while going through it changed the nature of the experience: "I have found that in order to write about my training so that people outside the medical profession can understand what I am talking about I have had to preserve a certain level of naiveté for myself." In "Learning the Language," first published in the "Hers" column of *The New York Times* in 1984, Klass's naiveté allows her to see some hidden functions of medical jargon.

"Mrs. Tolstoy is your basic LOL in NAD, admitted for a soft rule-out MI," the intern announces. I scribble that on my patient list. In other words, Mrs. Tolstoy is a Little Old Lady in No Apparent Distress who is in the hospital to make sure she hasn't had a heart attack (rule out a Myocardial Infarction). And we think it's unlikely that she has had a heart attack (a *soft* rule-out).   1

If I learned nothing else during my first three months of working in the hospital as a medical student, I learned endless jargon and abbreviations. I started out in a state of primeval innocence, in which I didn't even know that "s̄ CP, SOB, N/V" meant "without chest pain, shortness of breath, or nausea and vomiting." By the end I took the abbreviations so much for granted that I would complain to my mother the English professor, "And can you believe I had to put down *three* NG tubes last night?"   2

"You'll have to tell me what an NG tube is if you want me to sympathize properly," my mother said. NG, nasogastric—isn't it obvious?   3

I picked up not only the specific expressions but also the patterns of speech and the grammatical conventions; for example, you never say that a patient's blood pressure fell or that his cardiac enzymes rose. Instead, the patient is always the subject of the verb: "He dropped his   4

pressure." "He bumped his enzymes." This sort of construction probably reflects the profound irritation of the intern when the nurses come
in the middle of the night to say that Mr. Dickinson has disturbingly
low blood pressure. "Oh, he's gonna hurt me bad tonight," the intern
might say, inevitably angry at Mr. Dickinson for dropping his pressure
and creating a problem.

When chemotherapy fails to cure Mrs. Bacon's cancer, what we   5
say is, "Mrs. Bacon failed chemotherapy."

"Well, we've already had one hit today, and we're up next, but at   6
least we've got mostly stable players on our team." This means that our
team (group of doctors and medical students) has already gotten one
new admission today, and it is our turn again, so we'll get whoever is
admitted next in emergency, but at least most of the patients we already
have are fairly stable, that is, unlikely to drop their pressures or in any
other way get suddenly sicker and hurt us bad. Baseball metaphor is
pervasive. A no-hitter is a night without any new admissions. A player
is always a patient—a nitrate player is a patient on nitrates, a unit
player is a patient in the intensive care unit, and so on, until you reach
the terminal player.

It is interesting to consider what it means to be winning, or doing   7
well, in this perennial baseball game. When the intern hangs up the
phone and announces, "I got a hit," that is not cause for congratula-
tions. The team is not scoring points; rather, it is getting hit, being
bombarded with new patients. The object of the game from the point of
view of the doctors, considering the players for whom they are already
responsible, is to get as few new hits as possible.

This special language contributes to a sense of closeness and profes-   8
sional spirit among people who are under a great deal of stress. As a
medical student, I found it exciting to discover that I'd finally cracked
the code, that I could understand what doctors said and wrote, and
could use the same formulations myself. Some people seem to become
enamored of the jargon for its own sake, perhaps because they are so
deeply thrilled with the idea of medicine, with the idea of themselves
as doctors.

I knew a medical student who was referred to by the interns on   9
the team as Mr. Eponym because he was so infatuated with eponymous
terminology, the more obscure the better. He never said "capillary pulsations" if he could say "Quincke's pulses." He would lovingly tell over
the multinamed syndromes—Wolff-Parkinson-White, Lown-Ganong-
Levine, Schönlein-Henoch—until the temptation to suggest Schleswig-
Holstein or Stevenson-Kefauver or Baskin-Robbins became irresistible
to his less reverent colleagues.

And there is the jargon that you don't ever want to hear yourself   10

using. You know that your training is changing you, but there are
certain changes you think would be going a little too far.

The resident was describing a man with devastating terminal pan- 11
creatic cancer. "Basically he's CTD," the resident concluded. I reminded
myself that I had resolved not to be shy about asking when I didn't
understand things. "CTD?" I asked timidly.

The resident smirked at me. "Circling The Drain."   12

The images are vivid and terrible. "What happened to Mrs. Mel-   13
ville?"

"Oh, she boxed last night." To box is to die, of course.   14

Then there are the more pompous locutions that can make the   15
beginning medical student nervous about the effects of medical training.
A friend of mine was told by his resident, "A pregnant woman with
sickle-cell represents a failure of genetic counseling."

Mr. Eponym, who tried hard to talk like the doctors, once explained 16
to me, "An infant is basically a brainstem preparation." The term
"brainstem preparation," as used in neurological research, refers to an
animal whose higher brain functions have been destroyed so that only
the most primitive reflexes remain, like the sucking reflex, the startle
reflex, and the rooting reflex.

And yet at other times the harshness dissipates into a strangely 17
elusive euphemism. "As you know, this is a not entirely benign procedure," some doctor will say, and that will be understood to imply
agony, risk of complications, and maybe even a significant mortality
rate.

The more extreme forms aside, one most important function of   18
medical jargon is to help doctors maintain some distance from their
patients. By reformulating a patient's pain and problems into a language
that the patient doesn't even speak, I suppose we are in some sense
taking those pains and problems under our jurisdiction and also reducing their emotional impact. This linguistic separation between doctors
and patients allows conversations to go on at the bedside that are unin-
telligible to the patient. "Naturally, we're worried about adeno-CA,"
the intern can say to the medical student, and lung cancer need never
be mentioned.

I learned a new language this past summer. At times it thrills me 19
to hear myself using it. It enables me to understand my colleagues, to
communicate effectively in the hospital. Yet I am uncomfortably aware
that I will never again notice the peculiarities and even atrocities of
medical language as keenly as I did this summer. There may be specific
expressions I manage to avoid, but even as I remark them, promising
myself I will never use them, I find that this language is becoming my
professional speech. It no longer sounds strange in my ears—or coming

from my mouth. And I am afraid that as with any new language, to use it properly you must absorb not only the vocabulary but also the structure, the logic, the attitudes. At first you may notice these new and alien assumptions every time you put together a sentence, but with time and increased fluency you stop being aware of them at all. And as you lose that awareness, for better or for worse, you move closer and closer to being a doctor instead of just talking like one.

GEORGE ORWELL

Shooting an Elephant

George Orwell (1903–1950), originally named Eric Arthur Blair, was born in Bengal, India. His father was a minor British colonial officer and his mother the daughter of a French merchant. When his family moved to England in 1911, Orwell spent six unpleasant years in a snobbish preparatory school before winning a scholarship to Eton, a still more exclusive school where his relative poverty made him feel like an outsider. On the advice of one of his tutors, he elected not to enter Cambridge University, but instead to join the Indian Imperial Police in Burma, a job he held until 1927, when guilt at being "part of that evil despotism" drove him out. To experience life unprotected by the privileges of the British middle class, he then lived among the poor in Paris and London, working as a dishwasher and day laborer. In 1933 he published an account of this life in *Down and Out in Paris and London* under the pseudonym by which he has been known ever since. While Orwell is perhaps best known for his novels *Animal Farm* (1945) and *1984* (1949), he is considered one of the finest essayists of this century; among his collections of nonfiction are *Dickens, Dali and Others* (1946) and *Shooting an Elephant* (1950). "Shooting an Elephant" was first published in *New Writing*, Autumn 1936.

In Moulmein, in Lower Burma, I was hated by large numbers of 1 people—the only time in my life that I have been important enough for this to happen to me. I was sub-divisional police officer of the town, and in an aimless, petty kind of way anti-European feeling was very bitter. No one had the guts to raise a riot, but if a European woman went through the bazaars alone somebody would probably spit betel juice over her dress. As a police officer I was an obvious target and was baited whenever it seemed safe to do so. When a nimble Burman tripped me up on the football field and the referee (another Burman) looked the other way, the crowd yelled with hideous laughter. This happened more than once. In the end the sneering yellow faces of young men that met me everywhere, the insults hooted after me when I was at a safe distance, got badly on my nerves. The young Buddhist priests were the worst of all. There were several thousands of them in the town and none of them seemed to have anything to do except stand on street corners and jeer at Europeans.

All this was perplexing and upsetting. For at that time I had already made up my mind that imperialism was an evil thing and the sooner I chucked up my job and got out of it the better. Theoretically—and secretly, of course—I was all for the Burmese and all against their oppressors, the British. As for the job I was doing, I hated it more bitterly than I can perhaps make clear. In a job like that you see the dirty work of Empire at close quarters. The wretched prisoners huddling in the stinking cages of the lockups, the grey, cowed faces of the long-term convicts, the scarred buttocks of the men who had been flogged with bamboos—all these oppressed me with an intolerable sense of guilt. But I could get nothing into perspective. I was young and ill-educated and I had to think out my problems in the utter silence that is imposed on every Englishman in the East. I did not even know that the British Empire is dying, still less did I know that it is a great deal better than the younger empires that are going to supplant it. All I knew was that I was stuck between my hatred of the empire I served and my rage against the evil-spirited little beasts who tried to make my job impossible. With one part of my mind I thought of the British Raj as an unbreakable tyranny, as something clamped down, in *saecula saeculorum*,[1] upon the will of prostrate peoples; with another part I thought that the greatest joy in the world would be to drive a bayonet into a Buddhist priest's guts. Feelings like these are the normal by-products of imperialism; ask any Anglo-Indian official, if you can catch him off duty.

One day something happened which in a roundabout way was enlightening. It was a tiny incident in itself, but it gave me a better glimpse than I had had before of the real nature of imperialism—the real motives for which despotic governments act. Early one morning the sub-inspector at a police station the other end of the town rang me up on the 'phone and said that an elephant was ravaging the bazaar. Would I please come and do something about it? I did not know what I could do, but I wanted to see what was happening and I got on to a pony and started out. I took my rifle, an old .44 Winchester and much too small to kill an elephant, but I thought the noise might be useful *in terrorem*. Various Burmans stopped me on the way and told me about the elephant's doings. It was not, of course, a wild elephant, but a tame one which had gone "must." It had been chained up, as tame elephants

---

1. "For ages of ages" (Latin); until the end of time.

always are when their attack of "must" is due, but on the previous
night it had broken its chain and escaped. Its mahout, the only person
who could manage it when it was in that state, had set out in pursuit,
but had taken the wrong direction and was now twelve hours' journey
away, and in the morning the elephant had suddenly reappeared in the
town. The Burmese population had no weapons and were quite helpless
against it. It had already destroyed somebody's bamboo hut, killed a
cow and raided some fruit-stalls and devoured the stock; also it had
met the municipal rubbish van and, when the driver jumped out and
took to his heels, had turned the van over and inflicted violences
upon it.

The Burmese sub-inspector and some Indian constables were wait-   4
ing for me in the quarter where the elephant had been seen. It was a
very poor quarter, a labyrinth of squalid bamboo huts, thatched with
palm-leaf, winding all over a steep hillside. I remember that it was a
cloudy, stuffy morning at the beginning of the rains. We began questioning the people as to where the elephant had gone and, as usual,
failed to get any definite information. That is invariably the case in the
East; a story always sounds clear enough at a distance, but the nearer
you get to the scene of events the vaguer it becomes. Some of the people
said that the elephant had gone in one direction, some said that he had
gone in another, some professed not even to have heard of any elephant. I had almost made up my mind that the whole story was a pack
of lies, when we heard yells a little distance away. There was a loud,
scandalized cry of "Go away, child! Go away this instant!" and an old
woman with a switch in her hand came round the corner of a hut,
violently shooing away a crowd of naked children. Some more women
followed, clicking their tongues and exclaiming; evidently there was
something that the children ought not to have seen. I rounded the hut
and saw a man's dead body sprawling in the mud. He was an Indian,
a black Dravidian coolie, almost naked, and he could not have been
dead many minutes. The people said that the elephant had come suddenly upon him round the corner of the hut, caught him with its trunk,
put its foot on his back and ground him into the earth. This was the
rainy season and the ground was soft, and his face had scored a trench
a foot deep and a couple of yards long. He was lying on his belly with
arms crucified and head sharply twisted to one side. His face was coated
with mud, the eyes wide open, the teeth bared and grinning with an
expression of unendurable agony. (Never tell me, by the way, that the
dead look peaceful. Most of the corpses I have seen look devilish.) The
friction of the great beast's foot had stripped the skin from his back as
neatly as one skins a rabbit. As soon as I saw the dead man I sent an
orderly to a friend's house nearby to borrow an elephant rifle. I had
already sent back the pony, not wanting it to go mad with fright and
throw me if it smelt the elephant.

The orderly came back in a few minutes with a rifle and five cartridges, and meanwhile some Burmans had arrived and told us that the elephant was in the paddy fields below, only a few hundred yards away. As I started forward practically the whole population of the quarter flocked out of the houses and followed me. They had seen the rifle and were all shouting excitedly that I was going to shoot the elephant. They had not shown much interest in the elephant when he was merely ravaging their homes, but it was different now that he was going to be shot. It was a bit of fun to them, as it would be to an English crowd; besides they wanted the meat. It made me vaguely uneasy. I had no intention of shooting the elephant—I had merely sent for the rifle to defend myself if necessary—and it is always unnerving to have a crowd following you. I marched down the hill, looking and feeling a fool, with the rifle over my shoulder and an ever-growing army of people jostling at my heels. At the bottom, when you got away from the huts, there was a metalled road and beyond that a miry waste of paddy fields a thousand yards across, not yet ploughed but soggy from the first rains and dotted with coarse grass. The elephant was standing eight yards from the road, his left side towards us. He took not the slightest notice of the crowd's approach. He was tearing up bunches of grass, beating them against his knees to clean them and stuffing them into his mouth.

I had halted on the road. As soon as I saw the elephant I knew with perfect certainty that I ought not to shoot him. It is a serious matter to shoot a working elephant—it is comparable to destroying a huge and costly piece of machinery—and obviously one ought not to do it if it can possibly be avoided. And at that distance, peacefully eating, the elephant looked no more dangerous than a cow. I thought then and I think now that his attack of "must" was already passing off; in which case he would merely wander harmlessly about until the mahout came back and caught him. Moreover, I did not in the least want to shoot him. I decided that I would watch him for a little while to make sure that he did not turn savage again, and then go home.

But at that moment I glanced round at the crowd that had followed me. It was an immense crowd, two thousand at the least and growing every minute. It blocked the road for a long distance on either side. I looked at the sea of yellow faces above the garish clothes—faces all happy and excited over this bit of fun, all certain that the elephant was going to be shot. They were watching me as they would watch a conjurer about to perform a trick. They did not like me, but with the magical rifle in my hands I was momentarily worth watching. And suddenly I realized that I should have to shoot the elephant after all. The people expected it of me and I had got to do it; I could feel their two thousand wills pressing me forward, irresistibly. And it was at this moment, as I stood there with the rifle in my hands, that I first grasped the hollowness, the futility of the white man's dominion in the East.

Here was I, the white man with his gun, standing in front of the unarmed native crowd—seemingly the leading actor of the piece; but in
reality I was only an absurd puppet pushed to and fro by the will of
those yellow faces behind. I perceived in this moment that when the
white man turns tyrant it is his own freedom that he destroys. He
becomes a sort of hollow, posing dummy, the conventionalized figure
of a sahib. For it is the condition of his rule that he shall spend his life
in trying to impress the "natives," and so in every crisis he has got to
do what the "natives" expect of him. He wears a mask, and his face
grows to fit it. I had got to shoot the elephant. I had committed myself
to doing it when I sent for the rifle. A sahib has got to act like a sahib;
he has got to appear resolute, to know his own mind and do definite
things. To come all that way, rifle in hand, with two thousand people
marching at my heels, and then to trail feebly away, having done nothing—no, that was impossible. The crowd would laugh at me. And my
whole life, every white man's life in the East, was one long struggle
not to be laughed at.

But I did not want to shoot the elephant. I watched him beating   8
his bunch of grass against his knees, with that preoccupied grandmoth-
erly air that elephants have. It seemed to me that it would be murder
to shoot him. At that age I was not squeamish about killing animals,
but I had never shot an elephant and never wanted to. (Somehow it
always seems worse to kill a *large* animal.) Besides, there was the beast's
owner to be considered. Alive, the elephant was worth at least a hundred pounds; dead, he would only be worth the value of his tusks,
five pounds, possibly. But I had got to act quickly. I turned to some
experienced-looking Burmans who had been there when we arrived,
and asked them how the elephant had been behaving. They all said the
same thing; he took no notice of you if you left him alone, but he might
charge if you went too close to him.

It was perfectly clear to me what I ought to do. I ought to walk up   9
to within, say, twenty-five yards of the elephant and test his behavior.
If he charged, I could shoot; if he took no notice of me, it would be
safe to leave him until the mahout came back. But also I knew that I
was going to do no such thing. I was a poor shot with a rifle and the
ground was soft mud into which one would sink at every step. If the
elephant charged and I missed him, I should have about as much
chance as a toad under a steamroller. But even then I was not thinking
particularly of my own skin, only of the watchful yellow faces behind.
For at that moment, with the crowd watching me, I was not afraid in
the ordinary sense, as I would have been if I had been alone. A white
man mustn't be frightened in front of "natives"; and so, in general, he
isn't frightened. The sole thought in my mind was that if anything went
wrong those two thousand Burmans would see me pursued, caught,
trampled on and reduced to a grinning corpse like that Indian up the

hill. And if that happened it was quite probable that some of them would laugh. That would never do. There was only one alternative. I shoved the cartridges into the magazine and lay down on the road to get a better aim.

The crowd grew very still, and a deep, low, happy sigh, as of people who see the theatre curtain go up at last, breathed from innumerable throats. They were going to have their bit of fun after all. The rifle was a beautiful German thing with cross-hair sights. I did not then know that in shooting an elephant one would shoot to cut an imaginary bar running from ear-hole to ear-hole. I ought, therefore, as the elephant was sideways on, to have aimed straight at his ear-hole; actually I aimed several inches in front of this, thinking the brain would be further forward. 10

When I pulled the trigger I did not hear the bang or feel the kick— one never does when a shot goes home—but I heard the devilish roar of glee that went up from the crowd. In that instant, in too short a time, one would have thought, even for the bullet to get there, a mysterious, terrible change had come over the elephant. He neither stirred nor fell, but every line of his body had altered. He looked suddenly stricken, shrunken, immensely old, as though the frightful impact of the bullet had paralysed him without knocking him down. At last, after what seemed a long time—it might have been five seconds, I dare say—he sagged flabbily to his knees. His mouth slobbered. An enormous senility seemed to have settled upon him. One could have imagined him thousands of years old. I fired again into the same spot. At the second shot he did not collapse but climbed with desperate slowness to his feet and stood weakly upright, with legs sagging and head drooping. I fired a third time. That was the shot that did for him. You could see the agony of it jolt his whole body and knock the last remnant of strength from his legs. But in falling he seemed for a moment to rise, for as his hind legs collapsed beneath him he seemed to tower upward like a huge rock toppling, his trunk reaching skywards like a tree. He trumpeted, for the first and only time. And then down he came, his belly towards me, with a crash that seemed to shake the ground even where I lay. 11

I got up. The Burmans were already racing past me across the mud. It was obvious that the elephant would never rise again, but he was not dead. He was breathing very rhythmically with long rattling gasps, his great mound of a side painfully rising and falling. His mouth was wide open—I could see far down into caverns of pale pink throat. I waited a long time for him to die, but his breathing did not weaken. Finally I fired my two remaining shots into the spot where I thought his heart must be. The thick blood welled out of him like red velvet, but still he did not die. His body did not even jerk when the shots hit him, the tortured breathing continued without a pause. He was dying, 12 very slowly and in great agony, but in some world remote from me where not even a bullet could damage him further. I felt that I had got to put an end to that dreadful noise. It seemed dreadful to see the great beast lying there, powerless to move and yet powerless to die, and not even to be able to finish him. I sent back for my small rifle and poured shot after shot into his heart and down his throat. They seemed to make no impression. The tortured gasps continued as steadily as the ticking of a clock.

In the end I could not stand it any longer and went away. I heard   13
later that it took him half an hour to die. Burmans were bringing dahs and baskets even before I left, and I was told they had stripped his body almost to the bones by the afternoon.

Afterwards, of course, there were endless discussions about the   14
shooting of the elephant. The owner was furious, but he was only an Indian and could do nothing. Besides, legally I had done the right thing, for a mad elephant has to be killed, like a mad dog, if its owner fails to control it. Among the Europeans opinion was divided. The older men said I was right, the younger men said it was a damn shame to shoot an elephant for killing a coolie, because an elephant was worth more than any damn Coringhee coolie. And afterwards I was very glad that the coolie had been killed; it put me legally in the right and it gave me a sufficient pretext for shooting the elephant. I often wondered whether any of the others grasped that I had done it solely to avoid looking a fool.

C. S. LEWIS

The Inner Ring

C. S. Lewis (1898–1963), professor of medieval and Renaissance English at Cambridge University, was also a novelist, a writer of children's books, and a popular speaker on moral and religious issues. In the early 1940s, he delivered a series of radio talks on the BBC that were later collected in *Mere Christianity* (1952), a book still very popular among Christians of all denominations. In 1942 he published his best-known book, *The Screwtape Letters*, in which he impersonated a veteran devil in hell who writes letters encouraging the efforts of a novice devil hard at work on earth. Lewis's witty, intelligent defenses of traditional morality and religion led him to challenge many of the secular orthodoxies of the twentieth century. "The Inner Ring" was the Memorial Lecture at King's College, University of London, in 1944. In it you will find a challenge to Sigmund Freud's assumption that sex is the strongest of all human drives.

May I read you a few lines from Tolstoi's *War and Peace*?　　　1

When Boris entered the room, Prince Andrey was listening to an old general, wearing his decorations, who was reporting something to Prince Andrey, with an expression of soldierly servility on his purple face. "Alright. Please wait!" he said to the general, speaking in Russian with the French accent which he used when he spoke with contempt. The moment he noticed Boris he stopped listening to the general who trotted imploringly after him and begged to be heard, while Prince Andrey turned to Boris with a cheerful smile and a nod of the head. Boris now clearly understood—what he had already guessed—that side by side with the system of discipline and subordination which were laid down in the Army Regulations, there existed a different and a more real system—the system which compelled a tightly laced general with a purple face to wait respectfully for his turn while a mere captain like Prince Andrey chatted with a mere second lieutenant like Boris. Boris decided at once that he would be guided not by the official system but by this other unwritten system.[1]

When you invite a middle-aged moralist to address you, I suppose 　2
I must conclude, however unlikely the conclusion seems, that you have a taste for middle-aged moralising. I shall do my best to gratify it. I shall in fact give you advice about the world in which you are going to live. I do not mean by this that I am going to attempt to talk on what are called current affairs. You probably know quite as much about them as I do. I am not going to tell you—except in a form so general that you will hardly recognise it—what part you ought to play in post-war reconstruction. It is not, in fact, very likely that any of you will be able, in the next ten years, to make any direct contribution to the peace or prosperity of Europe. You will be busy finding jobs, getting married, acquiring facts. I am going to do something more old-fashioned than you perhaps expected. I am going to give advice. I am going to issue warnings. Advice and warnings about things which are so perennial that no one calls them "current affairs."

And of course everyone knows what a middle-aged moralist of my 　3
type warns his juniors against. He warns them against the World, the Flesh, and the Devil. But one of this trio will be enough to deal with today. The Devil, I shall leave strictly alone. The association between him and me in the public mind has already gone quite as deep as I wish: in some quarters it has already reached the level of confusion, if not of identification. I begin to realise the truth of the old proverb that he who sups with that formidable host needs a long spoon. As for the Flesh, you must be very abnormal young people if you do not know quite as much about it as I do. But on the World I think I have something to say.

1. Part III, chapter 9. [author's note]

In the passage I have just read from Tolstoi, the young second   4
lieutenant Boris Dubretskoi discovers that there exist in the army two
different systems or hierarchies. The one is printed in some little red
book and anyone can easily read it up. It also remains constant. A
general is always superior to a colonel and a colonel to a captain. The
other is not printed anywhere. Nor is it even a formally organised secret
society with officers and rules which you would be told after you had
been admitted. You are never formally and explicitly admitted by anyone. You discover gradually, in almost indefinable ways, that it exists
and that you are outside it; and then later, perhaps, that you are inside
it. There are what correspond to passwords, but they too are spontaneous and informal. A particular slang, the use of particular nicknames, an
allusive manner of conversation, are the marks. But it is not constant. It
is not easy, even at a given moment, to say who is inside and who is
outside. Some people are obviously in and some are obviously out, but
there are always several on the border-line. And if you come back to
the same Divisional Headquarters, or Brigade Headquarters, or the same
regiment or even the same company, after six weeks' absence, you may
find this second hierarchy quite altered. There are no formal admissions
or expulsions. People think they are in it after they have in fact been
pushed out of it, or before they have been allowed in: this provides
great amusement for those who are really inside. It has no fixed name.
The only certain rule is that the insiders and outsiders call it by different
names. From inside it may be designated, in simple cases, by mere
enumeration: it may be called "You and Tony and me." When it is
very secure and comparatively stable in membership it calls itself "we."
When it has to be suddenly expanded to meet a particular emergency
it calls itself "All the sensible people at this place." From outside, if you
have despaired of getting into it, you call it "That gang" or "They" or
"So-and-so and his set" or "the Caucus" or "the Inner Ring." If you
are a candidate for admission you probably don't call it anything. To
discuss it with the other outsiders would make you feel outside yourself.
And to mention it in talking to the man who is inside, and who may
help you if this present conversation goes well, would be madness.

Badly as I may have described it, I hope you will all have recognised   5
the thing I am describing. Not, of course, that you have been in the
Russian Army or perhaps in any army. But you have met the phenomenon of an Inner Ring. You discovered one in your house at school
before the end of the first term. And when you had climbed up to
somewhere near it by the end of your second year, perhaps you discovered that within the Ring there was a Ring yet more inner, which in
its turn was the fringe of the great school Ring to which the house
Rings were only satellites. It is even possible that the School Ring was
almost in touch with a Masters' Ring. You were beginning, in fact, to
pierce through the skins of the onion. And here, too, at your uni-

versity—shall I be wrong in assuming that at this very moment, invisible to me, there are several rings—independent systems or concentric rings—present in this room? And I can assure you that in whatever hospital, inn of court, diocese, school, business, or college you arrive after going down, you will find the Rings—what Tolstoi calls the second or unwritten systems.

All this is rather obvious. I wonder whether you will say the same of my next step, which is this. I believe that in all men's lives at certain periods, and in many men's lives at all periods between infancy and extreme old age, one of the most dominant elements is the desire to be inside the local Ring and the terror of being left outside. This desire, in one of its forms, has indeed had ample justice done to it in literature. I mean, in the form of snobbery. Victorian fiction is full of characters who are hag-ridden by the desire to get inside that particular Ring which is, or was, called Society. But it must be clearly understood that "Society," in that sense of the word, is merely one of a hundred Rings and snobbery therefore only one form of the longing to be inside. People who believe themselves to be free, and indeed are free, from snobbery, and who read satires on snobbery with tranquil superiority, may be devoured by the desire in another form. It may be the very intensity of their desire to enter some quite different Ring which renders them immune from the allurements of high life. An invitation from a duchess would be very cold comfort to a man smarting under the sense of exclusion from some artistic or communist côterie. Poor man—it is not large, lighted rooms, or champagne, or even scandals about peers and Cabinet Ministers that he wants: it is the sacred little attic or studio, the heads bent together, the fog of tobacco smoke, and the delicious knowledge that we—we four or five all huddled beside this stove—are the people who *know*. Often the desire conceals itself so well that we hardly recognise the pleasures of fruition. Men tell not only their wives but themselves that it is a hardship to stay late at the office or the school on some bit of important extra work which they have been let in for because they and So-and-so and the two others are the only people left in the place who really know how things are run. But it is not quite true. It is a terrible bore, of course, when old Fatty Smithson draws you aside and whispers "Look here, we've got to get you in on this examination somehow" or "Charles and I saw at once that you've got to be on this committee." A terrible bore . . . ah, but how much more terrible if you were left out! It is tiring and unhealthy to lose your Saturday afternoons: but to have them free because you don't matter, that is much worse.

Freud would say, no doubt, that the whole thing is a subterfuge of the sexual impulse. I wonder whether the shoe is not sometimes on the other foot, I wonder whether, in ages of promiscuity, many a virginity has not been lost less in obedience to Venus than in obedience to the lure of the caucus. For of course, when promiscuity is the fashion, the chaste are outsiders. They are ignorant of something that other people know. They are uninitiated. And as for lighter matters, the number who first smoked or first got drunk for a similar reason is probably very large.

I must now make a distinction. I am not going to say that the existence of Inner Rings is an evil. It is certainly unavoidable. There must be confidential discussions: and it is not only not a bad thing, it is (in itself) a good thing, that personal friendship should grow up between those who work together. And it is perhaps impossible that the official hierarchy of any organisation should quite coincide with its actual workings. If the wisest and most energetic people invariably held the highest posts, it might coincide; since they often do not, there must be people in high positions who are really deadweights and people in lower positions who are more important than their rank and seniority would lead you to suppose. In that way the second, unwritten system is bound to grow up. It is necessary; and perhaps it is not a necessary evil. But the desire which draws us into Inner Rings is another matter. A thing may be morally neutral and yet the desire for that thing may be dangerous. As Byron has said:

> *Sweet is a legacy, and passing sweet*
> *The unexpected death of some old lady.*

The painless death of a pious relative at an advanced age is not an evil. But an earnest desire for her death on the part of her heirs is not reckoned a proper feeling, and the law frowns on even the gentlest attempt to expedite her departure. Let Inner Rings be an unavoidable and even an innocent feature of life, though certainly not a beautiful one: but what of our longing to enter them, our anguish when we are excluded, and the kind of pleasure we feel when we get in?

I have no right to make assumptions about the degree to which any of you may already be compromised. I must not assume that you have ever first neglected, and finally shaken off, friends whom you really loved and who might have lasted you a lifetime, in order to court the friendship of those who appeared to you more important, more esoteric. I must not ask whether you have ever derived actual pleasure from the loneliness and humiliation of the outsiders after you yourself were in: whether you have talked to fellow members of the Ring in the presence of outsiders simply in order that the outsiders might envy; whether the means whereby, in your days of probation, you propitiated the Inner Ring, were always wholly admirable. I will ask only one question—and it is, of course, a rhetorical question which expects no answer. In the whole of your life as you now remember it, has the desire to be on the right side of that invisible line ever prompted you to any act or word on which, in the cold small hours of a wakeful

night, you can look back with satisfaction? If so, your case is more
fortunate than most.

But I said I was going to give advice, and advice should deal with   10
the future, not the past. I have hinted at the past only to awake you to
what I believe to be the real nature of human life. I don't believe that
the economic motive and the erotic motive account for everything that
goes on in what we moralists call the World. Even if you add Ambition
I think the picture is still incomplete. The lust for the esoteric, the
longing to be inside, take many forms which are not easily recognisable
as Ambition. We hope, no doubt, for tangible profits from every Inner
Ring we penetrate: power, money, liberty to break rules, avoidance of
routine duties, evasion of discipline. But all these would not satisfy us
if we did not get in addition the delicious sense of secret intimacy. It is
no doubt a great convenience to know that we need fear no official
reprimands from our official senior because he is old Percy, a fellow-
member of our Ring. But we don't value the intimacy only for the sake
of convenience; quite equally we value the convenience as a proof of
the intimacy.

My main purpose in this address is simply to convince you that this   11
desire is one of the great permanent mainsprings of human action. It is
one of the factors which go to make up the world as we know it—this
whole pell-mell of struggle, competition, confusion, graft, disappointment, and advertisement, and if it is one of the permanent mainsprings
then you may be quite sure of this. Unless you take measures to prevent
it, this desire is going to be one of the chief motives of your life, from
the first day on which you enter your profession until the day when
you are too old to care. That will be the natural thing—the life that
will come to you of its own accord. Any other kind of life, if you lead
it, will be the result of conscious and continuous effort. If you do nothing about it, if you drift with the stream, you will in fact be an "inner
ringer." I don't say you'll be a successful one; that's as may be. But
whether by pining and moping outside Rings that you can never enter,
or by passing triumphantly further and further in—one way or the
other you will be that kind of man.

I have already made it fairly clear that I think it better for you not   12
to be that kind of man. But you may have an open mind on the question. I will therefore suggest two reasons for thinking as I do.

It would be polite and charitable, and in view of your age reason-   13
able too, to suppose that none of you is yet a scoundrel. On the other
hand, by the mere law of averages (I am saying nothing against free
will) it is almost certain that at least two or three of you before you die
will have become something very like scoundrels. There must be in this
room the makings of at least that number of unscrupulous, treacherous,
ruthless egotists. The choice is still before you: and I hope you will not
take my hard words about your possible future characters as a token

of disrespect to your present characters. And the prophecy I make is
this. To nine out of ten of you the choice which could lead to scoun-
drelism will come, when it does come, in no very dramatic colours.
Obviously bad men, obviously threatening or bribing, will almost certainly not appear. Over a drink or a cup of coffee, disguised as a triviality
and sandwiched between two jokes, from the lips of a man, or woman,
whom you have recently been getting to know rather better and whom
you hope to know better still—just at the moment when you are most
anxious not to appear crude, or naïf, or a prig—the hint will come. It
will be the hint of something which is not quite in accordance with the
technical rules of fair play: something which the public, the ignorant,
romantic public, would never understand: something which even the
outsiders in your own profession are apt to make a fuss about: but
something, says your new friend, which "we"—and at the word "we"
you try not to blush for mere pleasure—something "we always do."
And you will be drawn in, if you are drawn in, not by desire for gain
or ease, but simply because at that moment, when the cup was so near
your lips, you cannot bear to be thrust back again into the cold outer
world. It would be so terrible to see the other man's face—that genial,
confidential, delightfully sophisticated face—turn suddenly cold and
contemptuous, to know that you had been tried for the Inner Ring and
rejected. And then, if you are drawn in, next week it will be something
a little further from the rules, and next year something further still, but
all in the jolliest, friendliest spirit. It may end in a crash, a scandal, and
penal servitude: it may end in millions, a peerage and giving the prizes
at your old school. But you will be a scoundrel.

That is my first reason. Of all the passions the passion for the Inner   14
Ring is most skilful in making a man who is not yet a very bad man
do very bad things.

My second reason is this. The torture allotted to the Danaids in the   15
classical underworld, that of attempting to fill sieves with water, is the
symbol not of one vice but of all vices. It is the very mark of a perverse
desire that it seeks what is not to be had. The desire to be inside the
invisible line illustrates this rule. As long as you are governed by that
desire you will never get what you want. You are trying to peel an
onion: if you succeed there will be nothing left. Until you conquer the
fear of being an outsider, an outsider you will remain.

This is surely very clear when you come to think of it. If you want   16
to be made free of a certain circle for some wholesome reason—if, say,
you want to join a musical society because you really like music—then
there is a possibility of satisfaction. You may find yourself playing in a
quartet and you may enjoy it. But if all you want is to be in the know,
your pleasure will be short-lived. The circle cannot have from within
the charm it had from outside. By the very act of admitting you it has
lost its magic. Once the first novelty is worn off the members of this

circle will be no more interesting than your old friends. Why should they be? You were not looking for virtue or kindness or loyalty or humour or learning or wit or any of the things that can be really enjoyed. You merely wanted to be "in." And that is a pleasure that cannot last. As soon as your new associates have been staled to you by custom, you will be looking for another Ring. The rainbow's end will still be ahead of you. The old Ring will now be only the drab background for your endeavour to enter the new one.

And you will always find them hard to enter, for a reason you very   17
well know. You yourself, once you are in, want to make it hard for the next entrant, just as those who are already in made it hard for you. Naturally. In any wholesome group of people which holds together for a good purpose, the exclusions are in a sense accidental. Three or four people who are together for the sake of some piece of work exclude others because there is work only for so many or because the others can't in fact do it. Your little musical group limits its numbers because the rooms they meet in are only so big. But your genuine Inner Ring exists for exclusion. There'd be no fun if there were no outsiders. The invisible line would have no meaning unless most people were on the wrong side of it. Exclusion is no accident: it is the essence.

The quest of the Inner Ring will break your hearts unless you break   18
it. But if you break it, a surprising result will follow. If in your working hours you make the work your end, you will presently find yourself all unawares inside the only circle in your profession that really matters. You will be one of the sound craftsmen, and other sound craftsmen will know it. This group of craftsmen will by no means coincide with the Inner Ring or the Important People or the People in the Know. It will not shape that professional policy or work up that professional influence which fights for the profession as a whole against the public: nor will it lead to those periodic scandals and crises which the Inner Ring produces. But it will do those things which that profession exists to do and will in the long run be responsible for all the respect which that profession in fact enjoys and which the speeches and advertisements cannot maintain. And if in your spare time you consort simply with the people you like, you will again find that you have come unawares to a real inside: that you are indeed snug and safe at the centre of something which, seen from without, would look exactly like an Inner Ring. But the difference is that its secrecy is accidental, and its exclusiveness a by-product, and no one was led thither by the lure of the esoteric: for it is only four or five people who like one another meeting to do things that they like. This is friendship. Aristotle placed it among the virtues. It causes perhaps half of all the happiness in the world, and no Inner Ring can ever have it.

We are told in Scripture that those who ask get. That is true, in   19
senses I can't now explore. But in another sense there is much truth in

the schoolboy's principle "them as asks shan't have." To a young person, just entering on adult life, the world seems full of "insides," full of delightful intimacies and confidentialities, and he desires to enter them. But if he follows that desire he will reach no "inside" that is worth reaching. The true road lies in quite another direction. It is like the house in *Alice Through the Looking Glass.*[2]

MARTIN LUTHER KING, JR.

Letter from Birmingham Jail

Martin Luther King, Jr. (1929–1968), was the dominant leader of the American civil rights movement from 1955 until his assassination. A gifted student and the son and grandson of eloquent Baptist ministers, he received his B.A. from Morehouse College when he was nineteen years old. At Crozer Theological Seminary, where he studied until 1951, he became acquainted with the ideas of Mohandas Gandhi, the great Indian advocate of nonviolent protest. After taking his Ph.D. from Boston University in 1955, he became pastor of a church in Montgomery, Alabama, where he led the famous bus boycott that initiated more than a decade of civil rights protests. Soon King organized the Southern Christian Leadership Conference, a network of civil rights leaders extending throughout the South. Arrested in 1963 during desegregation demonstrations in Birmingham, Alabama, King wrote his "Letter from Birmingham Jail" in response to a public letter from a group of eight clergymen who opposed the demonstrations. His letter received national attention when it was republished in *The Christian Century* and *The Atlantic Monthly*. The following version is from King's *Why We Can't Wait* (1964).

April 16, 1963[1]

My Dear Fellow Clergymen:

While confined here in the Birmingham city jail, I came across your recent statement calling my present activities "unwise and untimely."   1

---

2. Lewis Carroll's Alice imagines that the mirror over her mantel is actually a window through which she sees another room in another house.

---

1. This response to a published statement by eight fellow clergymen from Alabama (Bishop C. C. J. Carpenter, Bishop Joseph A. Durick, Rabbi Hilton L. Grafman, Bishop Paul Hardin, Bishop Holan B. Harmon, the Reverend George M. Murray, the Reverend Edward V. Ramage and the Reverend Earl Stallings) was composed under somewhat constricting circumstances. Begun on the margins of the newspaper in which the state-

Seldom do I pause to answer criticism of my work and ideas. If I sought to answer all the criticisms that cross my desk, my secretaries would have little time for anything other than such correspondence in the course of the day, and I would have no time for constructive work. But since I feel that you are men of genuine good will and that your criticisms are sincerely set forth, I want to try to answer your statement in what I hope will be patient and reasonable terms.

I think I should indicate why I am here in Birmingham, since you 2 have been influenced by the view which argues against "outsiders coming in." I have the honor of serving as president of the Southern Christian Leadership Conference, an organization operating in every southern state, with headquarters in Atlanta, Georgia. We have some eighty-five affiliated organizations across the South, and one of them is the Alabama Christian Movement for Human Rights. Frequently we share staff, educational, and financial resources with our affiliates. Several months ago the affiliate here in Birmingham asked us to be on call to engage in a nonviolent direct-action program if such were deemed necessary. We readily consented, and when the hour came we lived up to our promise. So I, along with several members of my staff, am here because I was invited here. I am here because I have organizational ties here.

But more basically, I am in Birmingham because injustice is here. 3 Just as the prophets of the eighth century B.C. left their villages and carried their "thus saith the Lord" far beyond the boundaries of their home towns, and just as the Apostle Paul left his village of Tarsus and carried the gospel of Jesus Christ to the far corners of the Greco-Roman world, so am I compelled to carry the gospel of freedom beyond my own home town. Like Paul, I must constantly respond to the Macedonian call for aid.

Moreover, I am cognizant of the interrelatedness of all communities 4 and states. I cannot sit idly by in Atlanta and not be concerned about what happens in Birmingham. Injustice anywhere is a threat to justice everywhere. We are caught in an inescapable network of mutuality, tied in a single garment of destiny. Whatever affects one directly, affects all indirectly. Never again can we afford to live with the narrow, provincial "outside agitator" idea. Anyone who lives inside the United States can never be considered an outsider anywhere within its bounds.

You deplore the demonstrations taking place in Birmingham. But 5 your statement, I am sorry to say, fails to express a similar concern for the conditions that brought about the demonstrations. I am sure that

---

ment appeared while I was in jail, the letter was continued on scraps of writing paper supplied by a friendly Negro trusty, and concluded on a pad my attorneys were eventually permitted to leave me. Although the text remains in substance unaltered, I have indulged in the author's prerogative of polishing it for publication. [author's note]

none of you would want to rest content with the superficial kind of social analysis that deals merely with effects and does not grapple with underlying causes. It is unfortunate that demonstrations are taking place in Birmingham, but it is even more unfortunate that the city's white power structure left the Negro community with no alternative.

In any nonviolent campaign there are four basic steps: collection 6 of the facts to determine whether injustices exist; negotiation; self-purification; and direct action. We have gone through all these steps in Birmingham. There can be no gainsaying the fact that racial injustice engulfs this community. Birmingham is probably the most thoroughly segregated city in the United States. Its ugly record of brutality is widely known. Negroes have experienced grossly unjust treatment in the courts. There have been more unsolved bombings of Negro homes and churches in Birmingham than in any other city in the nation. These are the hard, brutal facts of the case. On the basis of these conditions, Negro leaders sought to negotiate with the city fathers. But the latter consistently refused to engage in good-faith negotiation.

Then, last September, came the opportunity to talk with leaders of 7 Birmingham's economic community. In the course of the negotiations, certain promises were made by the merchants—for example, to remove the stores' humiliating racial signs. On the basis of these promises, the Reverend Fred Shuttlesworth and the leaders of the Alabama Christian Movement for Human Rights agreed to a moratorium on all demonstrations. As the weeks and months went by, we realized that we were the victims of a broken promise. A few signs, briefly removed, returned; the others remained.

As in so many past experiences, our hopes had been blasted, and 8 the shadow of deep disappointment settled upon us. We had no alternative except to prepare for direct action, whereby we would present our very bodies as a means of laying our case before the conscience of the local and the national community. Mindful of the difficulties involved, we decided to undertake a process of self-purification. We began a series of workshops on nonviolence, and we repeatedly asked ourselves: "Are you able to accept blows without retaliating?" "Are you able to endure the ordeal of jail?" We decided to schedule our direct-action program for the Easter season, realizing that except for Christmas, this is the main shopping period of the year. Knowing that a strong economic-withdrawal program would be the by-product of direct action, we felt that this would be the best time to bring pressure to bear on the merchants for the needed change.

Then it occurred to us that Birmingham's mayoral election was 9 coming up in March, and we speedily decided to postpone action until after election day. When we discovered that the Commissioner of Public Safety, Eugene "Bull" Connor, had piled up enough votes to be in the runoff, we decided again to postpone action until the day after the run-off so that the demonstrations could not be used to cloud the issues. Like many others, we waited to see Mr. Connor defeated, and to this end we endured postponement after postponement. Having aided in this community need, we felt that our direct-action program could be delayed no longer.

You may well ask: "Why direct action? Why sit-ins, marches, and so forth? Isn't negotiation a better path?" You are quite right in calling for negotiation. Indeed, this is the very purpose of direct action. Nonviolent direct action seeks to create such a crisis and foster such a tension that a community which has constantly refused to negotiate is forced to confront the issue. It seeks so to dramatize the issue that it can no longer be ignored. My citing the creation of tension as part of the work of the nonviolent-resister may sound rather shocking. But I must confess that I am not afraid of the word "tension." I have earnestly opposed violent tension, but there is a type of constructive, nonviolent tension which is necessary for growth. Just as Socrates felt that it was necessary to create a tension in the mind so that individuals could rise from the bondage of myths and half-truths to the unfettered realm of creative analysis and objective appraisal, so must we see the need for nonviolent gadflies to create the kind of tension in society that will help men rise from the dark depths of prejudice and racism to the majestic heights of understanding and brotherhood.

The purpose of our direct-action program is to create a situation so crisis-packed that it will inevitably open the door to negotiation. I therefore concur with you in your call for negotiation. Too long has our beloved Southland been bogged down in a tragic effort to live in monologue rather than dialogue.

One of the basic points in your statement is that the action that I and my associates have taken in Birmingham is untimely. Some have asked: "Why didn't you give the new city administration time to act?" The only answer that I can give to this query is that the new Birmingham administration must be prodded about as much as the outgoing one, before it will act. We are sadly mistaken if we feel that the election of Albert Boutwell as mayor will bring the millennium to Birmingham. While Mr. Boutwell is a much more gentle person than Mr. Connor, they are both segregationists, dedicated to maintenance of the status quo. I have hope that Mr. Boutwell will be reasonable enough to see the futility of massive resistance to desegregation. But he will not see this without pressure from devotees of civil rights. My friends, I must say to you that we have not made a single gain in civil rights without determined legal and nonviolent pressure. Lamentably, it is an historical fact that privileged groups seldom give up their privileges voluntarily. Individuals may see the moral light and voluntarily give up their unjust posture; but, as Reinhold Niebuhr has reminded us, groups tend to be more immoral than individuals.

We know through painful experience that freedom is never volun- 13
tarily given by the oppressor; it must be demanded by the oppressed.
Frankly, I have yet to engage in a direct-action campaign that was "well
timed" in the view of those who have not suffered unduly from the
disease of segregation. For years now I have heard the word "Wait!"
It rings in the ear of every Negro with piercing familiarity. This "Wait"
has almost always meant "Never." We must come to see, with one
of our distinguished jurists, that "justice too long delayed is justice
denied."

We have waited for more than 340 years for our constitutional and 14
God-given rights. The nations of Asia and Africa are moving with jetlike
speed toward gaining political independence, but we still creep at horse-
and-buggy pace toward gaining a cup of coffee at a lunch counter.
Perhaps it is easy for those who have never felt the stinging darts of
segregation to say, "Wait." But when you have seen vicious mobs lynch
your mothers and fathers at will and drown your sisters and brothers
at whim; when you have seen hate-filled policemen curse, kick, and
even kill your black brothers and sisters; when you see the vast majority
of your twenty million Negro brothers smothering in an airtight cage
of poverty in the midst of an affluent society; when you suddenly find
your tongue twisted and your speech stammering as you seek to explain
to your six-year-old daughter why she can't go to the public amusement
park that has just been advertised on television, and see tears welling
up in her eyes when she is told that Funtown is closed to colored
children, and see ominous clouds of inferiority beginning to form in
her little mental sky, and see her beginning to distort her personality
by developing an unconscious bitterness toward white people; when
you have to concoct an answer for a five-year-old son who is asking:
"Daddy, why do white people treat colored people so mean?"; when
you take a cross-country drive and find it necessary to sleep night after
night in the uncomfortable corners of your automobile because no motel will accept you; when you are humiliated day in and day out by
nagging signs reading "white" and "colored"; when your first name
becomes "nigger," your middle name becomes "boy" (however old you
are) and your last name becomes "John," and your wife and mother are
never given the respected title "Mrs."; when you are harried by day
and haunted by night by the fact that you are a Negro, living constantly
at tiptoe stance, never quite knowing what to expect next, and are
plagued with inner fears and outer resentments; when you are forever
fighting a degenerating sense of "nobodiness"—then you will understand why we find it difficult to wait. There comes a time when the
cup of endurance runs over, and men are no longer willing to be
plunged into the abyss of despair. I hope, sirs, you can understand our
legitimate and unavoidable impatience.

You express a great deal of anxiety over our willingness to break 15 laws. This is certainly a legitimate concern. Since we so diligently urge people to obey the Supreme Court's decision of 1954 outlawing segregation in the public schools, at first glance it may seem rather paradoxical for us consciously to break laws. One may well ask: "How can you advocate breaking some laws and obeying others?" The answer lies in the fact that there are two types of laws: just and unjust. I would be the first to advocate obeying just laws. One has not only a legal but a moral responsibility to obey just laws. Conversely, one has a moral responsibility to disobey unjust laws. I would agree with St. Augustine that "an unjust law is no law at all."

Now, what is the difference between the two? How does one determine whether a law is just or unjust? A just law is a man-made code that squares with the moral law or the law of God. An unjust law is a code that is out of harmony with the moral law. To put it in the terms of St. Thomas Aquinas: An unjust law is a human law that is not rooted in eternal law and natural law. Any law that uplifts human personality is just. Any law that degrades human personality is unjust. All segregation statutes are unjust because segregation distorts the soul and damages the personality. It gives the segregator a false sense of superiority and the segregated a false sense of inferiority. Segregation, to use the terminology of the Jewish philosopher Martin Buber, substitutes an "I–it" relationship for an "I–thou" relationship and ends up relegating persons to the status of things. Hence segregation is not only politically, economically, and sociologically unsound, it is morally wrong and sinful. Paul Tillich has said that sin is separation. Is not segregation an existential expression of man's tragic separation, his awful estrangement, his terrible sinfulness? Thus it is that I can urge men to obey the 1954 decision of the Supreme Court, for it is morally right; and I can urge them to disobey segregation ordinances, for they are morally wrong. 16

Let us consider a more concrete example of just and unjust laws. An unjust law is a code that a numerical or power majority group compels a minority group to obey but does not make binding on itself. This is *difference* made legal. By the same token, a just law is a code that a majority compels a minority to follow and that it is willing to follow itself. This is *sameness* made legal. 17

Let me give another explanation. A law is unjust if it is inflicted on a minority that, as a result of being denied the right to vote, had no part in enacting or devising the law. Who can say that the legislature of Alabama which set up that state's segregation laws was democratically elected? Throughout Alabama all sorts of devious methods are used to prevent Negroes from becoming registered voters, and there are some counties in which, even though Negroes constitute a majority of the population, not a single Negro is registered. Can any law enacted under such circumstances be considered democratically structured? 18

Sometimes a law is just on its face and unjust in its application. For   19
instance, I have been arrested on a charge of parading without a permit.
Now, there is nothing wrong in having an ordinance which requires a
permit for a parade. But such an ordinance becomes unjust when it is
used to maintain segregation and to deny citizens the First-Amendment
privilege of peaceful assembly and protest.

I hope you are able to see the distinction I am trying to point out.   20
In no sense do I advocate evading or defying the law, as would the
rabid segregationist. That would lead to anarchy. One who breaks an
unjust law must do so openly, lovingly, and with a willingness to accept
the penalty. I submit that an individual who breaks a law that conscience tells him is unjust, and who willingly accepts the penalty of
imprisonment in order to arouse the conscience of the community over
its injustice, is in reality expressing the highest respect for law.

Of course, there is nothing new about this kind of civil disobedi-   21
ence. It was evidenced sublimely in the refusal of Shadrach, Meshach,
and Abednego to obey the laws of Nebuchadnezzar,[2] on the ground
that a higher moral law was at stake. It was practiced superbly by
the early Christians, who were willing to face hungry lions and the
excruciating pain of chopping blocks rather than submit to certain unjust laws of the Roman Empire. To a degree, academic freedom is a
reality today because Socrates practiced civil disobedience. In our own
nation, the Boston Tea Party represented a massive act of civil disobedience.

We should never forget that everything Adolf Hitler did in Germany   22
was "legal" and everything the Hungarian freedom fighters did in Hun-
gary was "illegal." It was "illegal" to aid and comfort a Jew in Hitler's
Germany. Even so, I am sure that, had I lived in Germany at the time,
I would have aided and comforted my Jewish brothers. If today I lived
in a Communist country where certain principles dear to the Christian
faith are suppressed, I would openly advocate disobeying that country's
antireligious laws.

I must make two honest confessions to you, my Christian and Jew-   23
ish brothers. First, I must confess that over the past few years I have
been gravely disappointed with the white moderate. I have almost
reached the regrettable conclusion that the Negro's great stumbling
block in his stride toward freedom is not the White Citizen's Counciler
or the Ku Klux Klanner, but the white moderate, who is more devoted
to "order" than to justice; who prefers a negative peace which is the
absence of tension to a positive peace which is the presence of justice;
who constantly says: "I agree with you in the goal you seek, but I
cannot agree with your methods of direct action"; who paternalistically
believes he can set the timetable for another man's freedom; who lives

2. King refers to the biblical story recorded in Dan. 3.

by a mythical concept of time and who constantly advises the Negro to wait for a "more convenient season." Shallow understanding from people of good will is more frustrating than absolute misunderstanding from people of ill will. Lukewarm acceptance is much more bewildering than outright rejection.

I had hoped that the white moderate would understand that law 24 and order exist for the purpose of establishing justice and that when they fail in this purpose they become the dangerously structured dams that block the flow of social progress. I had hoped that the white moderate would understand that the present tension in the South is a necessary phase of the transition from an obnoxious negative peace, in which the Negro passively accepted his unjust plight, to a substantive and positive peace, in which all men will respect the dignity and worth of human personality. Actually, we who engage in nonviolent direct action are not the creators of tension. We merely bring to the surface the hidden tension that is already alive. We bring it out in the open, where it can be seen and dealt with. Like a boil that can never be cured so long as it is covered up but must be opened with all its ugliness to the natural medicines of air and light, injustice must be exposed, with all the tension its exposure creates, to the light of human conscience and the air of national opinion before it can be cured.

In your statement you assert that our actions, even though peaceful, 25 must be condemned because they precipitate violence. But is this a logical assertion? Isn't this like condemning a robbed man because his possession of money precipitated the evil act of robbery? Isn't this like condemning Socrates because his unswerving commitment to truth and his philosophical inquiries precipitated the act by the misguided populace in which they made him drink hemlock? Isn't this like condemning Jesus because his unique God-consciousness and never-ceasing devotion to God's will precipitated the evil act of crucifixion? We must come to see that, as the federal courts have consistently affirmed, it is wrong to urge an individual to cease his efforts to gain his basic constitutional rights because the quest may precipitate violence. Society must protect the robbed and punish the robber.

I had also hoped that the white moderate would reject the myth 26 concerning time in relation to the struggle for freedom. I have just received a letter from a white brother in Texas. He writes: "All Christians know that the colored people will receive equal rights eventually, but it is possible that you are in too great a religious hurry. It has taken Christianity almost two thousand years to accomplish what it has. The teachings of Christ take time to come to earth." Such an attitude stems from a tragic misconception of time, from the strangely irrational notion that there is something in the very flow of time that will inevitably cure all ills. Actually, time itself is neutral; it can be used either destructively or constructively. More and more I feel that the people of ill will have used time much more effectively than have the people of good will. We will have to repent in this generation not merely for the hateful words and actions of the bad people but for the appalling silence of the good people. Human progress never rolls in on wheels of inevitability; it comes through the tireless efforts of men willing to be co-workers with God, and without this hard work, time itself becomes an ally of the forces of social stagnation. We must use time creatively, in the knowledge that the time is always ripe to do right. Now is the time to make real the promise of democracy and transform our pending national elegy into a creative psalm of brotherhood. Now is the time to lift our national policy from the quicksand of racial injustice to the solid rock of human dignity.

You speak of our activity in Birmingham as extreme. At first I was 27 rather disappointed that fellow clergymen would see my nonviolent efforts as those of an extremist. I began thinking about the fact that I stand in the middle of two opposing forces in the Negro community. One is a force of complacency, made up in part of Negroes who, as a result of long years of oppression, are so drained of self-respect and a sense of "somebodiness" that they have adjusted to segregation; and in part of a few middle-class Negroes who, because of a degree of academic and economic security and because in some ways they profit by segregation, have become insensitive to the problems of the masses. The other force is one of bitterness and hatred, and it comes perilously close to advocating violence. It is expressed in the various black nationalist groups that are springing up across the nation, the largest and best-known being Elijah Muhammad's Muslim movement. Nourished by the Negro's frustration over the continued existence of racial discrimination, this movement is made up of people who have lost faith in America, who have absolutely repudiated Christianity, and who have concluded that the white man is an incorrigible "devil."

I have tried to stand between these two forces, saying that we need 28 emulate neither the "do-nothingism" of the complacent nor the hatred and despair of the black nationalist. For there is the more excellent way of love and nonviolent protest. I am grateful to God that, through the influence of the Negro church, the way of nonviolence became an integral part of our struggle.

If this philosophy had not emerged, by now many streets of the 29 South would, I am convinced, be flowing with blood. And I am further convinced that if our white brothers dismiss as "rabble-rousers" and "outside agitators" those of us who employ nonviolent direct action, and if they refuse to support our nonviolent efforts, millions of Negroes will, out of frustration and despair, seek solace and security in black-nationalist ideologies—a development that would inevitably lead to a frightening racial nightmare.

Oppressed people cannot remain oppressed forever. The yearning 30 for freedom eventually manifests itself, and that is what has happened to the American Negro. Something within has reminded him of his birthright of freedom, and something without has reminded him that it can be gained. Consciously or unconsciously, he has been caught up by the *Zeitgeist*,[3] and with his black brothers of Africa and his brown and yellow brothers of Asia, South America and the Caribbean, the United States Negro is moving with a sense of great urgency toward the promised land of racial justice. If one recognizes this vital urge that has engulfed the Negro community, one should readily understand why public demonstrations are taking place. The Negro has many pent-up resentments and latent frustrations, and he must release them. So let him march; let him make prayer pilgrimages to the city hall; let him go on freedom rides—and try to understand why he must do so. If his repressed emotions are not released in nonviolent ways, they will seek expression through violence; this is not a threat but a fact of history. So I have not said to my people: "Get rid of your discontent." Rather, I have tried to say that this normal and healthy discontent can be channeled into the creative outlet of nonviolent direct action. And now this approach is being termed extremist.

But though I was initially disappointed at being categorized as an extremist, as I continued to think about the matter I gradually gained a measure of satisfaction from the label. Was not Jesus an extremist for love: "Love your enemies, bless them that curse you, do good to them that hate you, and pray for them which despitefully use you, and persecute you." Was not Amos an extremist for justice: "Let justice roll down like waters and righteousness like an ever-flowing stream." Was not Paul an extremist for the Christian gospel: "I bear in my body the marks of the Lord Jesus." Was not Martin Luther an extremist: "Here I stand; I cannot do otherwise, so help me God." And John Bunyan: "I will stay in jail to the end of my days before I make a butchery of my conscience." And Abraham Lincoln: "This nation cannot survive half slave and half free." And Thomas Jefferson: "We hold these truths to be self-evident, that all men are created equal . . ." So the question is not whether we will be extremists, but what kind of extremists we will be. Will we be extremists for hate or for love? Will we be extremists for the preservation of injustice or for the extension of justice? In that dramatic scene on Calvary's hill three men were crucified. We must never forget that all three were crucified for the same crime—the crime of extremism. Two were extremists for immorality, and thus fell below their environment. The other, Jesus Christ, was an extremist for love, truth, and goodness, and thereby rose above his environment. Perhaps the South, the nation, and the world are in dire need of creative extremists.

3. The spirit of the age. (German)

I had hoped that the white moderate would see this need. Perhaps   32
I was too optimistic; perhaps I expected too much. I suppose I should
have realized that few members of the oppressor race can understand
the deep groans and passionate yearnings of the oppressed race, and
still fewer have the vision to see that injustice must be rooted out by
strong, persistent, and determined action. I am thankful, however, that
some of our white brothers in the South have grasped the meaning of
this social revolution and committed themselves to it. They are still all
too few in quantity, but they are big in quality. Some—such as Ralph
McGill, Lillian Smith, Harry Golden, James McBride Dabbs, Ann Bra-
den, and Sarah Patton Boyle—have written about our struggle in eloquent and prophetic terms. Others have marched with us down nameless streets of the South. They have languished in filthy, roach-infested
jails, suffering the abuse and brutality of policemen who view them as
"dirty nigger-lovers." Unlike so many of their moderate brothers and
sisters, they have recognized the urgency of the moment and sensed
the need for powerful "action" antidotes to combat the disease of segregation.

Let me take note of my other major disappointment. I have been   33
so greatly disappointed with the white church and its leadership. Of
course, there are some notable exceptions. I am not unmindful of the
fact that each of you has taken some significant stands on this issue. I
commend you, Reverend Stallings, for your Christian stand on this past
Sunday, in welcoming Negroes to your worship service on a nonsegre-
gated basis. I commend the Catholic leaders of this state for integrating
Spring Hill College several years ago.

But despite these notable exceptions, I must honestly reiterate that   34
I have been disappointed with the church. I do not say this as one of
those negative critics who can always find something wrong with the
church. I say this as a minister of the gospel, who loves the church;
who was nurtured in its bosom; who has been sustained by its spiritual
blessings and who will remain true to it as long as the cord of life shall
lengthen.

When I was suddenly catapulted into the leadership of the bus   35
protest in Montgomery, Alabama, a few years ago, I felt we would be
supported by the white church. I felt that the white ministers, priests,
and rabbis of the South would be among our strongest allies. Instead,
some have been outright opponents, refusing to understand the freedom movement and misrepresenting its leaders; all too many others
have been more cautious than courageous and have remained silent
behind the anesthetizing security of stained-glass windows.

In spite of my shattered dreams, I came to Birmingham with the   36
hope that the white religious leadership of this community would see
the justice of our cause and, with deep moral concern, would serve as
the channel through which our just grievances could reach the power

structure. I had hoped that each of you would understand. But again I have been disappointed.

I have heard numerous southern religious leaders admonish their worshipers to comply with a desegregation decision because it is the law, but I have longed to hear white ministers declare: "Follow this decree because integration is morally right and because the Negro is your brother." In the midst of blatant injustices inflicted upon the Negro, I have watched white churchmen stand on the sideline and mouth pious irrelevancies and sanctimonious trivialities. In the midst of a mighty struggle to rid our nation of racial and economic injustice, I have heard many ministers say: "Those are social issues, with which the gospel has no real concern." And I have watched many churches commit themselves to a completely otherworldly religion which makes a strange, un-Biblical distinction between body and soul, between the sacred and the secular. 37

I have traveled the length and breadth of Alabama, Mississippi, and all the other southern states. On sweltering summer days and crisp autumn mornings I have looked at the South's beautiful churches with their lofty spires pointing heavenward. I have beheld the impressive outlines of her massive religious-education buildings. Over and over I have found myself asking: "What kind of people worship here? Who is their God? Where were their voices when the lips of Governor Barnett[4] dripped with words of interposition and nullification? Where were they when Governor Wallace[5] gave a clarion call for defiance and hatred? Where were their voices of support when bruised and weary Negro men and women decided to rise from the dark dungeons of complacency to the bright hills of creative protest?" 38

Yes, these questions are still in my mind. In deep disappointment I have wept over the laxity of the church. But be assured that my tears have been tears of love. There can be no deep disappointment where there is not deep love. Yes, I love the church. How could I do otherwise? I am in the rather unique position of being the son, the grandson and the great-grandson of preachers. Yes, I see the church as the body of Christ. But, oh! How we have blemished and scarred that body through social neglect and through fear of being nonconformists. 39

There was a time when the church was very powerful—in the time when the early Christians rejoiced at being deemed worthy to suffer for what they believed. In those days the church was not merely a thermometer that recorded the ideas and principles of popular opinion; it was a thermostat that transformed the mores of society. Whenever 40

4. Ross Barnett, governor of Mississippi, in 1962 ordered resistance to the registration of a black student, James Meredith, at the University of Mississippi.
5. George Wallace, governor of Alabama, stood in a doorway of the University of Alabama in a symbolic effort to block the registration of two black students in 1963.

the early Christians entered a town, the people in power became disturbed and immediately sought to convict the Christians for being "disturbers of the peace" and "outside agitators." But the Christians pressed on, in the conviction that they were "a colony of heaven," called to obey God rather than man. Small in number, they were big in commitment. They were too God-intoxicated to be "astronomically intimidated." By their effort and example they brought an end to such ancient evils as infanticide and gladiatorial contests.

Things are different now. So often the contemporary church is a 41 weak, ineffectual voice with an uncertain sound. So often it is an arch-defender of the status quo. Far from being disturbed by the presence of the church, the power structure of the average community is consoled by the church's silent—and often even vocal—sanction of things as they are.

But the judgment of God is upon the church as never before. If 42 today's church does not recapture the sacrificial spirit of the early church, it will lose its authenticity, forfeit the loyalty of millions, and be dismissed as an irrelevant social club with no meaning for the twentieth century. Every day I meet young people whose disappointment with the church has turned into outright disgust.

Perhaps I have once again been too optimistic. Is organized religion 43 too inextricably bound to the status quo to save our nation and the world? Perhaps I must turn my faith to the inner spiritual church, the church within the church, as the true *ekklesia*[6] and the hope of the world. But again I am thankful to God that some noble souls from the ranks of organized religion have broken loose from the paralyzing chains of conformity and joined us as active partners in the struggle for freedom. They have left their secure congregations and walked the streets of Albany, Georgia, with us. They have gone down the highways of the South on tortuous rides for freedom. Yes, they have gone to jail with us. Some have been dismissed from their churches, have lost the support of their bishops and fellow ministers. But they have acted in the faith that right defeated is stronger than evil triumphant. Their witness has been the spiritual salt that has preserved the true meaning of the gospel in these troubled times. They have carved a tunnel of hope through the dark mountain of disappointment.

I hope the church as a whole will meet the challenge of this decisive 44 hour. But even if the church does not come to the aid of justice, I have no despair about the future. I have no fear about the outcome of our struggle in Birmingham, even if our motives are at present misunderstood. We will reach the goal of freedom in Birmingham and all over the nation, because the goal of America is freedom. Abused and scorned though we may be, our destiny is tied up with America's destiny. Before

6. Literally, "assembly of the people." (Greek)

the pilgrims landed at Plymouth, we were here. Before the pen of Jefferson etched the majestic words of the Declaration of Independence across the pages of history, we were here. For more than two centuries our forebears labored in this country without wages; they made cotton king; they built the homes of their masters while suffering gross injustice and shameful humiliation—and yet out of a bottomless vitality they continued to thrive and develop. If the inexpressible cruelties of slavery could not stop us, the opposition we now face will surely fail. We will win our freedom because the sacred heritage of our nation and the eternal will of God are embodied in our echoing demands.

Before closing I feel impelled to mention one other point in your   45
statement that has troubled me profoundly. You warmly commended the Birmingham police force for keeping "order" and "preventing violence." I doubt that you would have so warmly commended the police force if you had seen its dogs sinking their teeth into unarmed, nonviolent Negroes. I doubt that you would so quickly commend the policemen if you were to observe their ugly and inhumane treatment of Negroes here in the city jail; if you were to watch them push and curse old Negro women and young Negro girls; if you were to see them slap and kick old Negro men and young boys; if you were to observe them, as they did on two occasions, refuse to give us food because we wanted to sing our grace together. I cannot join you in your praise of the Birmingham police department.

It is true that the police have exercised a degree of discipline in   46
handling the demonstrators. In this sense they have conducted themselves rather "nonviolently" in public. But for what purpose? To preserve the evil system of segregation. Over the past few years I have consistently preached that nonviolence demands that the means we use must be as pure as the ends we seek. I have tried to make clear that it is wrong to use immoral means to attain moral ends. But now I must affirm that it is just as wrong, or perhaps even more so, to use moral means to preserve immoral ends. Perhaps Mr. Connor and his policemen have been rather nonviolent in public, as was Chief Pritchett in Albany, Georgia, but they have used the moral means of nonviolence to maintain the immoral end of racial injustice. As T. S. Eliot has said: "The last temptation is the greatest treason: To do the right deed for the wrong reason."

I wish you had commended the Negro sit-inners and demonstrators   47
of Birmingham for their sublime courage, their willingness to suffer, and their amazing discipline in the midst of great provocation. One day the South will recognize its real heroes. They will be the James Merediths, with the noble sense of purpose that enables them to face jeering and hostile mobs, and with the agonizing loneliness that characterizes the life of the pioneer. They will be old, oppressed, battered Negro women, symbolized in a seventy-two-year-old woman in Montgomery,

Alabama, who rose up with a sense of dignity and with her people
decided not to ride segregated buses, and who responded with ungram-
matical profundity to one who inquired about her weariness: "My feets
is tired, but my soul is at rest." They will be the young high school and
college students, the young ministers of the gospel and a host of their
elders, courageously and nonviolently sitting in at lunch counters and
willingly going to jail for conscience' sake. One day the South will
know that when these disinherited children of God sat down at lunch
counters, they were in reality standing up for what is best in the American dream and for the most sacred values in our Judaeo-Christian heritage, thereby bringing our nation back to those great wells of democracy
which were dug deep by the founding fathers in their formulation of
the Constitution and the Declaration of Independence.

   Never before have I written so long a letter. I'm afraid it is much   48
too long to take your precious time. I can assure you that it would have
been much shorter if I had been writing from a comfortable desk, but
what else can one do when he is alone in a narrow jail cell, other than
write long letters, think long thoughts, and pray long prayers?

   If I have said anything in this letter that overstates the truth and   49
indicates an unreasonable impatience, I beg you to forgive me. If I have
said anything that understates the truth and indicates my having a
patience that allows me to settle for anything less than brotherhood, I
beg God to forgive me.

   I hope this letter finds you strong in the faith. I also hope that   50
circumstances will soon make it possible for me to meet each of you,
not as an integrationist or a civil-rights leader but as a fellow clergyman
and a Christian brother. Let us all hope that the dark clouds of racial
prejudice will soon pass away and the deep fog of misunderstanding
will be lifted from our fear-drenched communities, and in some not too
distant tomorrow the radiant stars of love and brotherhood will shine
over our great nation with all their scintillating beauty.

                           Yours for the cause of Peace and Brotherhood,
                                             MARTIN LUTHER KING, JR.

LILIANA HEKER

The Stolen Party

Liliana Heker (1943–   ), born in Buenos Aires, began writing as a
teenager. Her first book of short stories, *Los que vieron la zarza* (*Those
Who Beheld the Burning Bush*), was published in 1966, and she has

been writing ever since. Most of Heker's career has been devoted to serving as editor in chief for *El ornitorrinco* (*The Platypus*), a literary magazine that survived years of chaos in Argentina's civil life. In addition to short stories, Heker writes novels; her second, *Zona de clivaje* (*Zone of Cleavage*, 1987), won the Buenos Aires Municipal Prize. In her journalism and fiction, Heker encourages loyalty to Argentina, believing that writers should stay in the country and work to improve it rather than writing about its problems in exile. "The Stolen Party" was translated into English by Alberto Manguel for his *Other Fires: Short Fiction by Latin American Women* (1986).

As soon as she arrived she went straight to the kitchen to see if the   1
monkey was there. It was: what a relief! She wouldn't have liked to admit that her mother had been right. *Monkeys at a birthday?* her mother had sneered. *Get away with you, believing any nonsense you're told!* She was cross, but not because of the monkey, the girl thought; it's just because of the party.

"I don't like you going," she told her. "It's a rich people's party."   2

"Rich people go to Heaven too," said the girl, who studied religion   3
at school.

"Get away with Heaven," said the mother. "The problem with you,   4
young lady, is that you like to fart higher than your ass."

The girl didn't approve of the way her mother spoke. She was   5
barely nine, and one of the best in her class.

"I'm going because I've been invited," she said. "And I've been   6
invited because Luciana is my friend. So there."

"Ah yes, your friend," her mother grumbled. She paused. "Listen,   7
Rosaura," she said at last. "That one's not your friend. You know what you are to them? The maid's daughter, that's what."

Rosaura blinked hard: she wasn't going to cry. Then she yelled: 8
"Shut up! You know nothing about being friends!"

Every afternoon she used to go to Luciana's house and they would   9
both finish their homework while Rosaura's mother did the cleaning. They had their tea in the kitchen and they told each other secrets. Rosaura loved everything in the big house, and she also loved the people who lived there.

"I'm going because it will be the most lovely party in the whole   10
world, Luciana told me it would. There will be a magician, and he will bring a monkey and everything."

The mother swung around to take a good look at her child, and   11
pompously put her hands on her hips.

"Monkeys at a birthday?" she said. "Get away with you, believing   12
any nonsense you're told!"

Rosaura was deeply offended. She thought it unfair of her mother   13 to accuse other people of being liars simply because they were rich. Rosaura too wanted to be rich, of course. If one day she managed to live in a beautiful palace, would her mother stop loving her? She felt very sad. She wanted to go to that party more than anything else in the world.

"I'll die if I don't go," she whispered, almost without moving her lips.   14

And she wasn't sure whether she had been heard, but on the morning of the party she discovered that her mother had starched her Christmas dress. And in the afternoon, after washing her hair, her mother rinsed it in apple vinegar so that it would be all nice and shiny. Before going out, Rosaura admired herself in the mirror, with her white dress and glossy hair, and thought she looked terribly pretty.   15

Señora Ines also seemed to notice. As soon as she saw her, she said: 16

"How lovely you look today, Rosaura."   17

Rosaura gave her starched skirt a slight toss with her hands and walked into the party with a firm step. She said hello to Luciana and asked about the monkey. Luciana put on a secretive look and whispered into Rosaura's ear: "He's in the kitchen. But don't tell anyone, because it's a surprise."   18

Rosaura wanted to make sure. Carefully she entered the kitchen and there she saw it: deep in thought, inside its cage. It looked so funny that the girl stood there for a while, watching it, and later, every so often, she would slip out of the party unseen and go and admire it. Rosaura was the only one allowed into the kitchen. Señora Ines had said: "You yes, but not the others, they're much too boisterous, they might break something." Rosaura had never broken anything. She even managed the jug of orange juice, carrying it from the kitchen into the dining-room. She held it carefully and didn't spill a single drop. And Señora Ines had said: "Are you sure you can manage a jug as big as that?" Of course she could manage. She wasn't a butterfingers, like the others. Like that blonde girl with the bow in her hair. As soon as she saw Rosaura, the girl with the bow had said: 19

"And you? Who are you?"   20

"I'm a friend of Luciana," said Rosaura.   21

"No," said the girl with the bow, "you are not a friend of Luciana because I'm her cousin and I know all her friends. And I don't know you."   22

"So what," said Rosaura. "I come here every afternoon with my mother and we do our homework together."   23

"You and your mother do your homework together?" asked the girl, laughing.   24

"I and Luciana do our homework together," said Rosaura, very   25
seriously.

The girl with the bow shrugged her shoulders.   26

"That's not being friends," she said. "Do you go to school to-   27
gether?"

"No."   28

"So where do you know her from?" said the girl, getting impatient.   29

Rosaura remembered her mother's words perfectly. She took a deep   30
breath.

"I'm the daughter of the employee," she said.   31

Her mother had said very clearly: "If someone asks, you say you're   32
the daughter of the employee; that's all." She also told her to add:
"And proud of it." But Rosaura thought that never in her life would
she dare to say something of the sort.

"What employee?" said the girl with the bow. "Employee in a   33
shop?"

"No," said Rosaura angrily. "My mother doesn't sell anything in   34
any shop, so there."

"So how come she's an employee?" said the girl with the bow.   35

Just then Señora Ines arrived saying *shh shh,* and asked Rosaura if   36
she wouldn't mind helping serve out the hot-dogs, as she knew the
house so much better than the others.

"See?" said Rosaura to the girl with the bow, and when no one   37
was looking she kicked her in the shin.

Apart from the girl with the bow, all the others were delightful.   38
The one she liked best was Luciana, with her golden birthday crown;
and then the boys. Rosaura won the sack race, and nobody managed
to catch her when they played tag. When they split into two teams to
play charades, all the boys wanted her for their side. Rosaura felt she
had never been so happy in all her life.

But the best was still to come. The best came after Luciana blew   39
out the candles. First the cake. Señora Ines had asked her to help pass
the cake around, and Rosaura had enjoyed the task immensely, because
everyone called out to her, shouting "Me, me!" Rosaura remembered
a story in which there was a queen who had the power of life or death
over her subjects. She had always loved that, having the power of
life or death. To Luciana and the boys she gave the largest pieces,
and to the girl with the bow she gave a slice so thin one could see
through it.

After the cake came the magician, tall and bony, with a fine red   40
cape. A true magician: he could untie handkerchiefs by blowing on
them and make a chain with links that had no openings. He could
guess what cards were pulled out from a pack, and the monkey was
his assistant. He called the monkey "partner." "Let's see here, partner,"

he would say, "Turn over a card." And, "Don't run away, partner: time
to work now."

The final trick was wonderful. One of the children had to hold   41
the monkey in his arms and the magician said he would make him
disappear.

"What, the boy?" they all shouted.   42

"No, the monkey!" shouted back the magician.   43

Rosaura thought that this was truly the most amusing party in the   44
whole world.

The magician asked a small fat boy to come and help, but the small   45
fat boy got frightened almost at once and dropped the monkey on the
floor. The magician picked him up carefully, whispered something in
his ear, and the monkey nodded almost as if he understood.

"You mustn't be so unmanly, my friend," the magician said to the   46
fat boy.

"What's unmanly?" said the fat boy.   47

The magician turned around as if to look for spies.   48

"A sissy," said the magician. "Go sit down."   49

Then he stared at all the faces, one by one. Rosaura felt her heart   50
tremble.

"You, with the Spanish eyes," said the magician. And everyone   51
saw that he was pointing at her.

She wasn't afraid. Neither holding the monkey, nor when the magi-   52
cian made him vanish; not even when, at the end, the magician flung
his red cape over Rosaura's head and uttered a few magic words . . . and
the monkey reappeared, chattering happily, in her arms. The children
clapped furiously. And before Rosaura returned to her seat, the magician said:

"Thank you very much, my little countess."   53

She was so pleased with the compliment that a while later, when   54
her mother came to fetch her, that was the first thing she told her.

"I helped the magician and he said to me, 'Thank you very much,   55
my little countess.'"

It was strange because up to then Rosaura had thought that she   56
was angry with her mother. All along Rosaura had imagined that she
would say to her: "See that the monkey wasn't a lie?" But instead
she was so thrilled that she told her mother all about the wonderful
magician.

Her mother tapped her on the head and said: "So now we're a   57
countess!"

But one could see that she was beaming.   58

And now they both stood in the entrance, because a moment ago   59
Señora Ines, smiling, had said: "Please wait here a second."

Her mother suddenly seemed worried.   60

"What is it?" she asked Rosaura.   61

"What is what?" said Rosaura. "It's nothing; she just wants to get   62
the presents for those who are leaving, see?"

She pointed at the fat boy and at a girl with pigtails who were   63
also waiting there, next to their mothers. And she explained about the
presents. She knew, because she had been watching those who left
before her. When one of the girls was about to leave, Señora Ines would
give her a bracelet. When a boy left, Señora Ines gave him a yo-yo.
Rosaura preferred the yo-yo because it sparkled, but she didn't mention
that to her mother. Her mother might have said: "So why don't you
ask for one, you blockhead?" That's what her mother was like. Rosaura
didn't feel like explaining that she'd be horribly ashamed to be the odd
one out. Instead she said:

"I was the best-behaved at the party."   64

And she said no more because Señora Ines came out into the hall   65
with two bags, one pink and one blue.

First she went up to the fat boy, gave him a yo-yo out of the blue   66
bag, and the fat boy left with his mother. Then she went up to the girl
and gave her a bracelet out of the pink bag, and the girl with the pigtails
left as well.

Finally she came up to Rosaura and her mother. She had a big   67
smile on her face and Rosaura liked that. Señora Ines looked down at
her, then looked up at her mother, and then said something that made
Rosaura proud:

"What a marvellous daughter you have, Herminia."   68

For an instant, Rosaura thought that she'd give her two presents: 69
the bracelet and the yo-yo. Señora Ines bent down as if about to look
for something. Rosaura also leaned forward, stretching out her arm.
But she never completed the movement.

Señora Ines didn't look in the pink bag. Nor did she look in the   70
blue bag. Instead she rummaged in her purse. In her hand appeared
two bills.

"You really and truly earned this," she said handing them over.   71
"Thank you for all your help, my pet."

Rosaura felt her arms stiffen, stick close to her body, and then she   72
noticed her mother's hand on her shoulder. Instinctively she pressed
herself against her mother's body. That was all. Except her eyes. Rosaura's eyes had a cold, clear look that fixed itself on Señora Ines's face.

Señora Ines, motionless, stood there with her hand outstretched.   73
As if she didn't dare draw it back. As if the slightest change might
shatter an infinitely delicate balance.

Translated by Alberto Manguel

GWENDOLYN BROOKS

The Chicago Defender Sends a Man
to Little Rock
Fall, 1957

Gwendolyn Brooks (1917–   ) has lived on Chicago's South Side
since she was one month old. Growing up in a family that loved books
and music, she spent her time reading: "I couldn't skate, I was never
a good rope-jumper, and I can remember thinking I must be a very
inferior kind of child since I couldn't play jacks." What she *could* do
was write: she published her first poem when she was thirteen and as
a high school and college student contributed regularly to *The Chicago
Defender*, the city's African-American newspaper. Failing to land a regular job with the *Defender*, she worked briefly as a maid and then as
a secretary. After attending poetry workshops from 1941 to 1943,
she began to publish frequently in important magazines. In 1945 she
published her first book of poems and in 1950 won the Pulitzer Prize
for her second, *Annie Allen*. By the mid-1960s, her reputation for social
realism and beautiful language well established, she taught in various
colleges and universities. Later, influenced by Imamu Amiri Baraka
and Ron Milner, she embraced a more radical view of the African-
American poet, allying herself with a Chicago street gang and publishing her works exclusively with a small, low-profit black press. Always
ready to experiment and change, Brooks continues to search for a way
of writing that is simultaneously political and, as she says, "Gwendo-
lyninan." The following poem is from her 1960 collection, *The Bean
Eaters*.

In Little Rock the people bear
Babes and comb and part their hair
And watch the want ads, put repair
To roof and latch. While wheat toast burns
A woman waters multiferns.   5

Time upholds and overturns
The many, tight, and small concerns.

In Little Rock the people sing
Sunday hymns like anything,
Through Sunday pomp and polishing.   10

And after testament and tunes,
Some soften Sunday afternoons
With lemon tea and Lorna Doones.

I forecast
And I believe   15
Come Christmas Little Rock will cleave
To Christmas tree and trifle, weave,
From laugh and tinsel, texture fast.

In Little Rock is baseball; Barcarolle.
That hotness in July . . . the uniformed figures raw and implacable   20
And not intellectual,
Batting the hotness or clawing the suffering dust.
The Open Air Concert, on the special twilight green. . . .
When Beethoven is brutal or whispers to lady-like air.
Blanket-sitters are solemn, as Johann troubles to lean   25
To tell them what to mean. . . .

There is love, too, in Little Rock. Soft women softly
Opening themselves in kindness.
Or, pitying one's blindness,
Awaiting one's pleasure   30
In azure
Glory with anguished rose at the root. . . .
To wash away old semi-discomfitures.
They re-teach purple and unsullen blue.
The wispy soils go and certain   35
Half-havings have they clarified to sures.

In Little Rock they know
Not answering the telephone is a way of rejecting life,
That it is our business to be bothered, is our business
To cherish bores or boredom, be polite   40
To lies and love and many-faceted fuzziness.

I scratch my head, massage the hate-I-had.
I blink across my prim and pencilled pad.
The saga I was sent for is not down.
Because there is a puzzle in this town.   45
The biggest News I do not dare
Telegraph to the Editor's chair:
''They are like people everywhere.''

The angry Editor would reply
In hundred harryings of Why.   50

And true, they are hurling spittle, rock,
Garbage and fruit in Little Rock.
And I saw coiling storm a-writhe
On bright madonnas. And a scythe
Of men harassing brownish girls.   55
(The bows and barrettes in the curls
And braids declined away from joy.)

I saw a bleeding brownish boy. . . .

The lariat lynch-wish I deplored.

The loveliest lynchee was our Lord.   60

NATURE AND CIVILIZATION

We find ourselves among the beasts.

Nature and Civilization: Preview

Overview and Ideas for Writing

Asking whether humans live in nature or in civilization is in some ways like asking whether they walk on their left feet or on their right. Since Darwin's time, we have known ourselves to be well-dressed apes, bundles of animal instincts barely covered by the veneer of civilization.

On the other hand, what we *know* is not always what we *feel,* and these days more and more of us feel that our "natural" environment is indoors, in rooms without weather or insects or decay. Close encounters with even little fragments of nature can feel uncomfortable, as we see in this unit's essays by Annie Dillard and Lewis Thomas. In a similar vein, Harry Crews aims to destroy the warm, fuzzy view of the natural world and our participation in it; Brigid Brophy, also wishing to stifle the sentimentality of nature lovers, claims that "there isn't and never was a natural man. We are a species that doesn't occur wild." Having a body ties us to nature; having a culture separates us from it.

This unit is filled with close observation of creatures, human and nonhuman. Diane Ackerman, Alice Walker, E. B. White, and Loren Eiseley—different as their styles and attitudes are—all ponder the thin line between nature and civilization. Drawing on close observations of animals, White gives us a simple, closely observed narrative of a visit to the zoo, while Ackerman and Eiseley want to understand how animals are like us and how we are like them; Walker goes one step further to consider how our various connections to animals—physical, emotional, spiritual—redefine the way we treat them as well as the way we treat each other. Like these writers, you have had some experiences that illustrate the relation of humans to nature: downtown, at the zoo, with pets, at the city's edge, in a small town or on a farm, in the wilderness. To write about such experiences in enough detail to allow your reader to understand them is a step toward turning sight into insight.

While Vicki Hearne begins where these writers do, she takes a decidedly different perspective in her essay, using her close ties to her dogs to come to terms with the issue of animal rights. If you are interested in extending your vision with some research, you might begin with Hearne and the *Harper's* forum she mentions in her essay or with Melissa Greene and other authors who have studied the history of zoos. In addition to your reading, interviews and surveys might turn up some useful information and point you in interesting directions. How, and how significantly, is nature treated in a popular magazine these days? Are the numbers of hunters, backpackers, and canoeists increasing or decreasing? Are vacationers seeking out encounters with animals or are they avoiding them? Greene raises similar questions along with vexing ones about the elimination of entire species and habitats. Research into these ecological problems and what can be done about them is obviously important.

E. B. WHITE

Twins

E(lywn) B(rooks) White (1899–1985), after failing as a newspaper reporter, became the principal writer of short comments for *The New Yorker*. Harold Ross, the magazine's founder and editor, insisted that these comments be unsigned and employ the editorial *we*, a practice that, White complained, could make the writer sound like "a composite personality." White, however, retained his singularity and his sanity: "Once in a while we think of ourself as 'we,' but not often." In 1938 White and his wife, Katharine Angell, moved to a farm in Maine, now famous as the setting of *Charlotte's Web* (1952), and White temporarily left *The New Yorker* to write monthly essays for *Harper's*, which are collected in *One Man's Meat* (1942). Other important collections include *The Second Tree from the Corner* (1954) and *Essays of E. B. White* (1977). "Twins," originally published as an unsigned comment in *The New Yorker* on June 12, 1948, shows White at the top of his form.

White builds this essay on contrasts, beginning with this first sentence and its images of the moose calf and the new pair of shoes. Make a list of all the contrasting images of nature and civilization in the essay. What is the effect of the intrusions from civilization on this natural scene?

What is the effect of "on legs that were just learning their business"? Why didn't White simply say "standing unsteadily"?

It is perfectly obvious that the two fawns born at the same time are twins. Why does White bother saying so?

On a warm, miserable morning last week we went up to the Bronx Zoo to see the moose calf and to break in a new pair of black shoes. We encountered better luck than we had bargained for. The cow moose and her young one were standing near the wall of the deer park below the monkey house, and in order to get a better view we strolled down to the lower end of the park, by the brook. The path there is not much travelled. As we approached the corner where the brook trickles under the wire fence, we noticed a red deer getting to her feet. Beside her, on legs that were just learning their business, was a spotted fawn, as small and perfect as a trinket seen through a reducing glass. They stood there, mother and child, under a gray beech whose trunk was engraved with dozens of hearts and initials. Stretched on the ground was another fawn, and we realized that the doe had just finished twinning. The second fawn was still wet, still unrisen. Here was a scene of rare sylvan splendor, in one of our five favorite boroughs, and we couldn't have asked for more. Even our new shoes seemed to be working out all right and weren't hurting much.

The doe was only a couple of feet from the wire, and we sat down ₂
on a rock at the edge of the footpath to see what sort of start young
fawns get in the deep fastnesses of Mittel Bronx. The mother, mildly
resentful of our presence and dazed from her labor, raised one forefoot
and stamped primly. Then she lowered her head,
picked up the afterbirth, and began dutifully to eat
it, allowing it to swing crazily from her mouth, as
though it were a bunch of withered beet greens.
From the monkey house came the loud, insane
hooting of some captious primate, filling the whole
woodland with a wild hooroar. As we watched,
the sun broke weakly through, brightened the rich
red of the fawns, and kindled their white spots.
Occasionally a sightseer would appear and wander
aimlessly by, but of all who passed none was aware that anything
extraordinary had occurred. "Looka the kangaroos!" a child cried. And
he and his mother stared sullenly at the deer and then walked on.

In a few moments the second twin gathered all his legs and all his ₃
ingenuity and arose, to stand for the first time sniffing the mysteries of
a park for captive deer. The doe, in recognition of his achievement, quit
her other work and began to dry him, running her tongue against the
grain and paying particular attention to the key
points. Meanwhile the first fawn tiptoed toward
the shallow brook, in little stops and goes, and
started across. He paused midstream to make a
slight contribution, as a child does in bathing.
Then, while his mother watched, he continued
across, gained the other side, selected a hiding
place, and lay down under a skunk-cabbage leaf
next to the fence, in perfect concealment, his legs
folded neatly under him. Without actually going
out of sight, he had managed to disappear completely in the shifting light and shade. From somewhere a long way off a twelve-o'clock whistle
sounded. We hung around awhile, but he never
budged. Before we left, we crossed the brook ourself, just outside the fence, knelt, reached through
the wire, and tested the truth of what we had once
heard: that you can scratch a new fawn between
the ears without starting him. You can indeed.

Most of White's comment is devoted to description of the fawns. In this paragraph, he digresses somewhat to include details about other animals and people. Was that a smart move on White's behalf? Why or why not?

Here White directly compares the fawn to a child. Is he saying anything in particular with the comparison? See how White's comment relates to Alice Walker's more direct use of a comparison between humans and animals.

Many of the essayists in this unit focus on a similar point of contact between humans and the natural world. You will find interesting comparisons with "Twins" in the essays by Ackerman, Dillard, and Crews. If you read these essays, note the various conclusions each writer draws.

DIANE ACKERMAN

The Moon by Whale Light

Diane Ackerman (1948–   ) received her M.F.A., M.A., and Ph.D.
from Cornell University. She taught English at the University of Pittsburgh and then was the director of the writers' program at Washington
University in St. Louis (1984–1986). Since then she has been a staff
writer for *The New Yorker* and has served as a visiting writer at several
universities. Ackerman's many interests include skin diving, horseback
riding, and flying airplanes. She has written several books of poetry
and several collections of nonfiction, including *A Natural History of the
Senses* (1990) and *The Moon by Whale Light* (1991), from which the
following selection is excerpted. These latest collections have established Ackerman as a science and nature writer of the stature of Stephen Jay Gould, John McPhee, and Annie Dillard. Most recently,
Ackerman published a book about love among humans (and occasionally their love of animals), *A Natural History of Love* (1994).

. . . We cut the motor about two hundred yards from the whales.   1
Juan[1] and I slipped over the side of the boat and began to swim toward
them, approaching as quietly as possible, so that they wouldn't construe
any of our movements as aggressive. In a few minutes, we were only
yards from the mother's head. Looking down, I saw the three-month-
old baby beside her underwater, its callosities bright in the murky green
water. Slowly, Juan and I swam all the way around them, getting closer
and closer. The long wound on Fang's[2] flank looked red and angry.
When her large tail lifted out of the water, its beauty stunned me for a
moment, and then I yanked Juan's hand, to draw his attention, and
we pulled back. At fifty feet long, weighing about fifty tons, all she
would have needed to do was hit us with a flipper to crush us, or swat
us with her tail to kill us instantly. But she was moving her tail gently,
slowly, without malice. It would be as if a human being, walking across
a meadow, had come upon a strange new animal. Our instinct wouldn't
be to kill it but to get closer and have a look, perhaps touch it. Right
whales are grazers, which have balleen plates, not teeth. We did not
look like lunch. She swung her head around so that her mouth was
within two feet of me, then turned her head on edge to reveal a large
white patch and, under that, an eye shaped much like a human eye. I

1. Juan: a student from the University of Buenos Aires spending the summer in Patagonia
conducting research on whales.
2. Fang: the mother whale who had been so frequently observed she had earned herself
a name.

looked directly into her eye, and she looked directly back at me, as we hung in the water, studying each other.

I wish you well, I thought, applying all the weight of my concentra- 2 tion, in case it was possible for her to sense my mood. I did not imagine she could decipher the words, but many animals can sense fear in humans. Perhaps they can also sense other emotions.

Her dark, plumlike eye fixed me and we stared deeply at one an- 3 other for some time. The curve of her mouth gave her a Mona Lisa smile, but that was just a felicity of her anatomy. The only emotion I sensed was her curiosity. That shone through her watchfulness, her repeated turning toward us, her extreme passivity, her caution with flippers and tail. Apparently, she was doing what we were—swimming close to a strange, fascinating life-form, taking care not to frighten or hurt it. Perhaps, seeing us slip over the side of the Zodiac,[3] she thought it had given birth and we were its young. In that case, she might have been thinking how little we resembled our parent. Or perhaps she understood only too well that we were intelligent beasts who lived in the strange, dangerous world of the land, where whales can get stranded, lose their bearings and equilibrium, and die. Perhaps she knew somehow that we live in that desert beyond the waves from which whales rarely return, a kingdom we rule, where we thrive. A whale's glimpse of us is almost as rare as our glimpse of a whale. They have never seen us mating, they have rarely if at all seen us feeding, they have never seen us give birth, suckle our young, die of old age. They have never observed our society, our normal habits. They would not know how to tell our sex, since we hide our reproductive organs. Perhaps they know that human males tend to have more facial hair than females, just as we know that male right whales tend to have more callosities on their faces than females. But they would still find it hard to distinguish between a clothed, short-haired, clean-shaven man and a clothed, short-haired woman.

When Fang had first seen us in the Zodiac, we were wearing large 4 smoked plastic eyes. Now we had small eyes shaped like hers—but two on the front of the head, like a flounder or a seal, not an eye on either side, like a fish or a whale. In the water, our eyes were encased in a glass jar, our mouths stretched around a rubber tube, and our feet were flippers. Instead of diving like marine mammals, we floated on the surface. To Fang, I must have looked spastic and octopuslike, with my thin limbs dangling. Human beings possess such immense powers that few animals cause us to feel truly humble. A whale does, swimming beside you, as big as a reclining building, its eye carefully observing you. It could easily devastate you with a twitch, and yet it doesn't. Still, although it lives in a gliding, quiet, investigate-it-first realm, it is not as

3. Zodiac: the small boat Ackerman used during her whaling explorations.

benign as a Zen monk.[4] Aggression plays a big role in its life, especially during courtship. Whales have weapons that are equal in their effects to our pointing a gun at somebody, squeezing a finger, and blowing him away. When they strike each other with their flukes in battles, they hit flat, but they sometimes slash the water with the edge. That fluke edge could break a person in two instantly. But such an attack has never happened in the times people have been known to swim with whales. On rare occasions, unprovoked whales have struck boats with their flukes, perhaps by accident, on at least one occasion killing a man. And there are three reported instances of a whale breaching onto a boat, again resulting in deaths. But they don't attack swimmers. In many of our science-fiction stories, aliens appear on earth and terrible fights ensue, with everyone shooting weapons that burn, sting, or blow others up. To us, what is alien is treacherous and evil. Whales do not visualize aliens in that way. So although it was frightening to float beside an animal as immense and powerful as a whale, I knew that if I showed her where I was and what I was and that I meant her no harm, she would return the courtesy.

Suddenly, Juan pulled me back a few feet and, turning, I saw the   5
calf swimming around to our side, though staying close to its mother. Big as an elephant, it still looked like a baby. Only a few months old, it was a frisky pup and rampantly curious. It swam right up, turned one eye at us, took a good look, then wheeled its head around to look at us with the other eye. When it turned, it swung its mouth right up to my chest, and I reached out to touch it, but Juan pulled my hand back. I looked at him and nodded. A touch could have startled the baby, which might not have known its own strength yet. In a reflex, its flipper or tail could have swatted us. It might not have known that if humans are held underwater—by a playful flipper, say—they can drown. Its flippers hung in the water by its sides, and its small callosities looked like a crop of fieldstones. When it rolled, it revealed a patch of white on its belly and an anal slit. Swimming forward, it fanned its tail, and the water suddenly felt chillier as it stirred up cold from the bottom. The mother was swimming forward to keep up with it, and we followed, hanging quietly in the water, trying to breathe slowly and kick our flippers as little as possible. Curving back around, Fang turned on her side so that she could see us, and waited as we swam up close again. Below me, her flipper hovered large as a freight elevator. Tilting it very gently in place, she appeared to be sculling; her tail, too, was barely moving. Each time she and the baby blew, a fine mist sprayed into the air, accompanied by a *whumping* sound, as of a pedal organ.

---

4. Zen monk: A member of a secluded community of men leading a stoic lifestyle dedicated to the principles of Zen Buddhism, a sect of Buddhism that stresses the practice of meditation as the means of enlightenment.

Both mother and calf made no sudden moves around us, no acts of aggression.

We did not have their insulation of blubber to warm us in such   6
frigid waters and, growing cold at last after an hour of traveling slowly along the bay with them, we began to swim back toward the beach. To save energy, we rolled onto our backs and kicked with our fins. When we were a few hundred yards away from her, Fang put her head up in a spy hop. Then she dove, rolled, lifted a flipper high into the air like a black rubber sail, and waved it back and forth. The calf did the same. Juan and I laughed. They were not waving at us, only rolling and playing now that we were out of the way. But it was so human a gesture that we automatically waved our arms overhead in reply. Then we turned back onto our faces again. Spears of sunlight cut through the thick green water and disappeared into the depths, a bottom soon revealed itself as tawny brown about thirty feet below us, and then the sand grew visible, along with occasional shells, and then the riot of shells near shore, and finally the pebbles of the shallows. Taking off our fins, we stepped from one liquid realm to another, from the whale road, as the Anglo-Saxons called the ocean, back onto the land of humans.

LOREN EISELEY

The Brown Wasps

Loren Eiseley (1907–1977) was one of those highly imaginative think-ers who cannot be neatly pigeonholed. He was a sociologist, anthro-pologist, historian of science, archeologist, and poet. Fascinated by evolution, he wrote such books as *Darwin's Century: Evolution and the Men Who Discovered It* (1958), *The Mind as Nature* (1962), and *Darwin and the Mysterious Mr. X: New Light on the Evolutionists* (1979). Eiseley spent a lifetime thinking about the long journey that began with the first living cell and has led to the diversity of life on earth. In his essays and poems, the present moment sometimes seems like a thin pane of glass through which he looks backward at an immense past; the evolutionary prehistory is always there, connecting the human jaw with the snake's jaw, the human hand with the bat's wing, human emotions with the emotions of our animal cousins. "The Brown Wasps" was originally published in *Gentry*, a small literary magazine, in 1957.

There is a corner in the waiting room of one of the great Eastern   1
stations where women never sit. It is always in the shadow and over-

hung by rows of lockers. It is, however, always frequented—not so much by genuine travelers as by the dying. It is here that a certain element of the abandoned poor seeks a refuge out of the weather, clinging for a few hours longer to the city that has fathered them. In a precisely similar manner I have seen, on a sunny day in midwinter, a few old brown wasps creep slowly over an abandoned wasp nest in a thicket. Numbed and forgetful and frost-blackened, the hum of the spring hive still resounded faintly in their sodden tissues. Then the temperature would fall and they would drop away into the white oblivion of the snow. Here in the station it is in no way different save that the city is busy in its snows. But the old ones cling to their seats as though these were symbolic and could not be given up. Now and then they sleep, their gray old heads resting with painful awkwardness on the backs of the benches.

Also they are not at rest. For an hour they may sleep in the gasping 2 exhaustion of the ill-nourished and aged who have to walk in the night. Then a policeman comes by on his round and nudges them upright.

"You can't sleep here," he growls. 3

A strange ritual then begins. An old man is difficult to waken. After 4 a muttered conversation the policeman presses a coin into his hand and passes fiercely along the benches prodding and gesturing toward the door. In his wake, like birds rising and settling behind the passage of a farmer through a cornfield, the men totter up, move a few paces and subside once more upon the benches.

One man, after a slight, apologetic lurch, does not move at all. 5 Tubercularly thin, he sleeps on steadily. The policeman does not look back. To him, too, this has become a ritual. He will not have to notice it again officially for another hour.

Once in a while one of the sleepers will not awake. Like the brown 6 wasps, he will have had his wish to die in the great droning center of the hive rather than in some lonely room. It is not so bad here with the shuffle of footsteps and the knowledge that there are others who share the bad luck of the world. There are also the whistles and the sounds of everyone, everyone in the world, starting on journeys. Amidst so many journeys somebody is bound to come out all right. Somebody.

Maybe it was on a like thought that the brown wasps fell away 7 from the old paper nest in the thicket. You hold till the last, even if it is only to a public seat in a railroad station. You want your place in the hive more than you want a room or a place where the aged can be eased gently out of the way. It is the place that matters, the place at the heart of things. It is life that you want, that bruises your gray old head with the hard chairs; a man has a right to his place.

But sometimes the place is lost in the years behind us. Or sometimes 8 it is a thing of air, a kind of vaporous distortion above a heap of rubble. We cling to a time and place because without them man is lost, not

only man but life. This is why the voices, real or unreal, which speak
from the floating trumpets at spiritualist seances are so unnerving. They
are voices out of nowhere whose only reality lies in their ability to stir
the memory of a living person with some fragment of the past. Before
the medium's cabinet both the dead and the living revolve endlessly
about an episode, a place, an event that has already been engulfed by
time.

This feeling runs deep in life; it brings stray cats running over end-   9
less miles, and birds homing from the ends of the earth. It is as though
all living creatures, and particularly the more intelligent, can survive
only by fixing or transforming a bit of time into space or by securing a
bit of space with its objects immortalized and made permanent in time.
For example, I once saw, on a flower pot in my own living room, the
efforts of a field mouse to build a remembered field. I have lived to see
this episode repeated in a thousand guises, and since I have spent a
large portion of my life in the shade of a nonexistent tree, I think I am
entitled to speak for the field mouse.

One day as I cut across the field which at that time extended on   10
one side of our suburban shopping center, I found a giant slug feeding
from a runnel of pink ice cream in an abandoned Dixie cup. I could
see his eyes telescope and protrude in a kind of dim, uncertain ecstasy
as his dark body bunched and elongated in the curve of the cup. Then,
as I stood there at the edge of the concrete, contemplating the slug, I
began to realize it was like standing on a shore where a different type
of life creeps up and fumbles tentatively among the rocks and sea wrack.
It knows its place and will only creep so far until something changes.
Little by little as I stood there I began to see more of this shore that
surrounds the place of man. I looked with sudden care and attention
at things I had been running over thoughtlessly for years. I even waded
out a short way into the grass and the wild-rose thickets to see more. A
huge black-belted bee went droning by and there were some indistinct
scurryings in the underbrush.

Then I came to a sign which informed me that this field was to be   11
the site of a new Wanamaker suburban store. Thousands of obscure
lives were about to perish, the spores of puffballs would go smoking
off to new fields, and the bodies of little white-footed mice would be
crunched under the inexorable wheels of the bulldozers. Life disappears
or modifies its appearances so fast that everything takes on an aspect
of illusion—a momentary fizzing and boiling with smoke rings, like
pouring dissident chemicals into a retort. Here man was advancing, but
in a few years his plaster and bricks would be disappearing once more
into the insatiable maw of the clover. Being of an archaeological cast
of mind, I thought of this fact with an obscure sense of satisfaction and
waded back through the rose thickets to the concrete parking lot. As I
did so, a mouse scurried ahead of me, frightened of my steps if not of

that ominous Wanamaker sign. I saw him vanish in the general direction of my apartment house, his little body quivering with fear in the great open sun on the blazing concrete. Blinded and confused, he was running straight away from his field. In another week scores would follow him.

I forgot the episode then and went home to the quiet of my living room. It was not until a week later, letting myself into the apartment, that I realized I had a visitor. I am fond of plants and had several ferns standing on the floor in pots to avoid the noon glare by the south window. 12

As I snapped on the light and glanced carelessly around the room, I saw a little heap of earth on the carpet and a scrabble of pebbles that had been kicked merrily over the edge of one of the flower pots. To my astonishment I discovered a full-fledged burrow delving downward among the fern roots. I waited silently. The creature who had made the burrow did not appear. I remembered the wild field then, and the flight of the mice. No house mouse, no *Mus domesticus,* had kicked up this little heap of earth or sought refuge under a fern root in a flower pot. I thought of the desperate little creature I had seen fleeing from the wild-rose thicket. Through intricacies of pipes and attics, he, or one of his fellows, had climbed to this high green solitary room. I could visualize what had occurred. He had an image in his head, a world of seed pods and quiet, of green sheltering leaves in the dim light among the weed stems. It was the only world he knew and it was gone. 13

Somehow in his flight he had found his way to this room with drawn shades where no one would come till nightfall. And here he had smelled green leaves and run quickly up the flower pot to dabble his paws in common earth. He had even struggled half the afternoon to carry his burrow deeper and had failed. I examined the hole, but no whiskered twitching face appeared. He was gone. I gathered up the earth and refilled the burrow. I did not expect to find traces of him again. 14

Yet for three nights thereafter I came home to the darkened room and my ferns to find the dirt kicked gaily about the rug and the burrow reopened, though I was never able to catch the field mouse within it. I dropped a little food about the mouth of the burrow, but it was never touched. I looked under beds or sat reading with one ear cocked for rustlings in the ferns. It was all in vain; I never saw him. Probably he ended in a trap in some other tenant's room. 15

But before he disappeared I had come to look hopefully for his evening burrow. About my ferns there had begun to linger the insubstantial vapor of an autumn field, the distilled essence, as it were, of a mouse brain in exile from its home. It was a small dream, like our dreams, carried a long and weary journey along pipes and through spider webs, past holes over which loomed the shadows of waiting cats, 16 and finally, desperately, into this room where he had played in the shuttered daylight for an hour among the green ferns on the floor. Every day these invisible dreams pass us on the street, or rise from beneath our feet, or look out upon us from beneath a bush.

Some years ago the old elevated railway in Philadelphia was torn   17
down and replaced by a subway system. This ancient El with its barnlike stations containing nut-vending machines and scattered food scraps had, for generations, been the favorite feeding ground of flocks of pigeons, generally one flock to a station along the route of the El. Hundreds of pigeons were dependent upon the system. They flapped in and out of its stanchions and steel work or gathered in watchful little audiences about the feet of anyone who rattled the peanut-vending machines. They even watched people who jingled change in their hands, and prospected for food under the feet of the crowds who gathered between trains. Probably very few among the waiting people who tossed a crumb to an eager pigeon realized that this El was like a food-bearing river, and that the life which haunted its banks was dependent upon the running of the trains with their human freight.

I saw the river stop.   18

The time came when the underground tubes were ready; the traffic   19
was transferred to a realm unreachable by pigeons. It was like a great river subsiding suddenly into desert sands. For a day, for two days, pigeons continued to circle over the El or stand close to the red vending machines. They were patient birds, and surely this great river which had flowed through the lives of unnumbered generations was merely suffering from some momentary drought.

They listened for the familiar vibrations that had always heralded   20
an approaching train; they flapped hopefully about the head of an occasional workman walking along the steel runways. They passed from one empty station to another, all the while growing hungrier. Finally they flew away.

I thought I had seen the last of them about the El, but there was a   21
revival and it provided a curious instance of the memory of living things for a way of life or a locality that has long been cherished. Some weeks after the El was abandoned workmen began to tear it down. I went to work every morning by one particular station, and the time came when the demolition crews reached this spot. Acetylene torches showered passersby with sparks, pneumatic drills hammered at the base of the structure, and a blind man who, like the pigeons, had clung with his cup to a stairway leading to the change booth, was forced to give up his place.

It was then, strangely, momentarily, one morning that I witnessed   22
the return of a little band of the familiar pigeons. I even recognized one or two members of the flock that had lived around this particular station before they were dispersed into the streets. They flew bravely in and

out among the sparks and the hammers and the shouting workmen. They had returned—and they had returned because the hubbub of the wreckers had convinced them that the river was about to flow once more. For several hours they flapped in and out through the empty windows, nodding their heads and watching the fall of girders with attentive little eyes. By the following morning the station was reduced to some burned-off stanchions in the street. My bird friends had gone. It was plain, however, that they retained a memory for an insubstantial structure now compounded of air and time. Even the blind man clung to it. Someone had provided him with a chair, and he sat at the same corner staring sightlessly at an invisible stairway where, so far as he was concerned, the crowds were still ascending to the trains.

I have said my life has been passed in the shade of a nonexistent 23 tree, so that such sights do not offend me. Prematurely I am one of the brown wasps and I often sit with them in the great droning hive of the station, dreaming sometimes of a certain tree. It was planted sixty years ago by a boy with a bucket and a toy spade in a little Nebraska town. That boy was myself. It was a cottonwood sapling and the boy remembered it because of some words spoken by his father and because everyone died or moved away who was supposed to wait and grow old under its shade. The boy was passed from hand to hand, but the tree for some intangible reason had taken root in his mind. It was under its branches that he sheltered; it was from this tree that his memories, which are my memories, led away into the world.

After sixty years the mood of the brown wasps grows heavier upon 24 one. During a long inward struggle I thought it would do me good to go and look upon that actual tree. I found a rational excuse in which to clothe this madness. I purchased a ticket and at the end of two thousand miles I walked another mile to an address that was still the same. The house had not been altered.

I came close to the white picket fence and reluctantly, with great 25 effort, looked down the long vista of the yard. There was nothing there to see. For sixty years that cottonwood had been growing in my mind. Season by season its seeds had been floating farther on the hot prairie winds. We had planted it lovingly there, my father and I, because he had a great hunger for soil and live things growing, and because none of these things had long been ours to protect. We had planted the little sapling and watered it faithfully, and I remembered that I had run out with my small bucket to drench its roots the day we moved away. And all the years since it had been growing in my mind, a huge tree that somehow stood for my father and the love I bore him. I took a grasp on the picket fence and forced myself to look again.

A boy with the hard bird eye of youth pedaled a tricycle slowly up 26 beside me.

"What'cha lookin' at?" he asked curiously. 27

"A tree," I said.   28

"What for?" he said.   29

"It isn't there," I said, to myself mostly, and began to walk away   30
at a pace just slow enough not to seem to be running.

"What isn't there?" the boy asked. I didn't answer. It was obvious   31
I was attached by a thread to a thing that had never been there, or
certainly not for long. Something that had to be held in the air, or
sustained in the mind, because it was part of my orientation in the
universe and I could not survive without it. There was more than an
animal's attachment to a place. There was something else, the attachment of the spirit to a grouping of events in time; it was part of our
morality.

So I had come home at last, driven by a memory in the brain as   32
surely as the field mouse who had delved long ago into my flower pot
or the pigeons flying forever amidst the rattle of nut-vending machines.
These, the burrow under the greenery in my living room and the red-
bellied bowls of peanuts now hovering in midair in the minds of pigeons, were all part of an elusive world that existed nowhere and yet
everywhere. I looked once at the real world about me while the persistent boy pedaled at my heels.

It was without meaning, though my feet took a remembered path.   33
In sixty years the house and street had rotted out of my mind. But the
tree, the tree that no longer was, that had perished in its first season,
bloomed on in my individual mind, unblemished as my father's words.
"We'll plant a tree here, son, and we're not going to move any more.
And when you're an old, old man you can sit under it and think how
we planted it here, you and me, together."

I began to outpace the boy on the tricycle.   34

"Do you live here, Mister?" he shouted after me suspiciously. I   35
took a firm grasp on airy nothing—to be precise, on the bole of a great
tree. "I do," I said. I spoke for myself, one field mouse, and several
pigeons. We were all out of touch but somehow permanent. It was the
world that had changed.

ALICE WALKER

Am I Blue?

Alice Walker (1944–   ) was born in Eatonton, Georgia, the youngest of eight children. Her father, who she says was "wonderful at
math" but "a terrible farmer," earned only about three hundred dollars a year as a sharecropper. The example of her mother, a determined
woman who helped in the fields and worked as a maid, helped make
Walker a "womanist," a term she invented to mean "a black feminist

or woman of color." Both her parents were storytellers: Walker's career began when she was eight and started to write their stories down. After graduating at the top of her high school class, Walker attended Spelman College in Atlanta, then graduated from Sarah Lawrence College in Bronxville, New York, in 1965. Best known for her third novel, *The Color Purple* (1982), which won the American Book Award and the Pulitzer Prize, Walker is also an accomplished essayist and poet. Her essays are collected in *In Search of Our Mothers' Gardens: Womanist Prose* (1983) and *Living by the Word* (1988), in which "Am I Blue?" was first published. Recently, Walker has devoted her attention to the subject of female genital mutilation, which is practiced in some parts of Africa and the Middle East; her novel *Possessing the Secret of Joy* (1992) and recent documentary film, *Warrior Marks* (1993), both address this issue.

"Ain't these tears in these eyes tellin' you?"[1]

For about three years my companion and I rented a small house in the country that stood on the edge of a large meadow that appeared to run from the end of our deck straight into the mountains. The mountains, however, were quite far away, and between us and them there was, in fact, a town. It was one of the many pleasant aspects of the house that you never really were aware of this.

It was a house of many windows, low, wide, nearly floor to ceiling in the living room, which faced the meadow, and it was from one of these that I first saw our closest neighbor, a large white horse, cropping grass, flipping its mane, and ambling about—not over the entire meadow, which stretched well out of sight of the house, but over the five or so fenced-in acres that were next to the twenty-odd that we had rented. I soon learned that the horse, whose name was Blue, belonged to a man who lived in another town, but was boarded by our neighbors next door. Occasionally, one of the children, usually a stocky teen-ager, but sometimes a much younger girl or boy, could be seen riding Blue. They would appear in the meadow, climb up on his back, ride furiously for ten or fifteen minutes, then get off, slap Blue on the flanks, and not be seen again for a month or more.

There were many apple trees in our yard, and one by the fence that Blue could almost reach. We were soon in the habit of feeding him apples, which he relished, especially because by the middle of summer the meadow grasses—so green and succulent since January—had dried out from lack of rain, and Blue stumbled about munching the dried stalks half-heartedly. Sometimes he would stand very still just by the apple tree, and when one of us came out he would whinny, snort loudly, or stamp the ground. This meant, of course: I want an apple.

It was quite wonderful to pick a few apples, or collect those that

1. From "Am I Blue?", a song popularized by the great jazz singer Billie Holiday.

had fallen to the ground overnight, and patiently hold them, one by one, up to his large, toothy mouth. I remained as thrilled as a child by his flexible dark lips, huge, cubelike teeth that crunched the apples, core and all, with such finality, and his high broad-breasted *enormity;* beside which, I felt small indeed. When I was a child, I used to ride horses, and was especially friendly with one named Nan until the day I was riding and my brother deliberately spooked her and I was thrown, head first, against the trunk of a tree. When I came to, I was in bed and my mother was bending worriedly over me; we silently agreed that perhaps horseback riding was not the safest sport for me. Since then I have walked, and prefer walking to horseback riding—but I had forgotten the depth of feeling one could see in horses' eyes.

I was therefore unprepared for the expression in Blue's. Blue was 5 lonely. Blue was horribly lonely and bored. I was not shocked that this should be the case; five acres to tramp by yourself, endlessly, even in the most beautiful of meadows—and his was—cannot provide many interesting events, and once rainy season turned to dry that was about it. No, I was shocked that I had forgotten that human animals and nonhuman animals can communicate quite well; if we are brought up around animals as children we take this for granted. By the time we are adults we no longer remember. However, the animals have not changed. They are in fact *completed* creations (at least they seem to be, so much more than we) who are not likely *to* change; it is their nature to express themselves. What else are they going to express? And they do. And, generally speaking, they are ignored.

After giving Blue the apples, I would wander back to the house, 6 aware that he was observing me. Were more apples not forthcoming then? Was that to be his sole entertainment for the day? My partner's small son had decided he wanted to learn how to piece a quilt; we worked in silence on our respective squares as I thought . . .

Well, about slavery: about white children, who were raised by black 7 people, who knew their first all-accepting love from black women, and then, when they were twelve or so, were told they must "forget" the deep levels of communication between themselves and "mammy" that they knew. Later they would be able to relate quite calmly, "My old mammy was sold to another good family." "My old mammy was ————." Fill in the blank. Many more years later a white woman would say: "I can't understand these Negroes, these blacks. What do they want? They're so different from us."

And about the Indians, considered to be "like animals" by the 8 "settlers" (a very benign euphemism for what they actually were), who did not understand their description as a compliment.

And about the thousands of American men who marry Japanese, Ko- 9 rean, Filipina, and other non-English-speaking women and of how happy they report they are, *"blissfully,"* until their brides learn to speak

English, at which point the marriages tend to fall apart. What then did the men see, when they looked into the eyes of the women they married, before they could speak English? Apparently only their own reflections.

I thought of society's impatience with the young. "Why are they playing the music so loud?" Perhaps the children have listened to much of the music of oppressed people their parents danced to before they were born, with its passionate but soft cries for acceptance and love, and they have wondered why their parents failed to hear.

I do not know how long Blue had inhabited his five beautiful, boring acres before we moved into our house; a year after we had arrived—and had also traveled to other valleys, other cities, other worlds—he was still there.

But then, in our second year at the house, something happened in Blue's life. One morning, looking out the window at the fog that lay like a ribbon over the meadow, I saw another horse, a brown one, at the other end of Blue's field. Blue appeared to be afraid of it, and for several days made no attempt to go near. We went away for a week. When we returned, Blue had decided to make friends and the two horses ambled or galloped along together, and Blue did not come nearly as often to the fence underneath the apple tree.

When he did, bringing his new friend with him, there was a different look in his eyes. A look of independence, of self-possession, of inalienable *horse*ness. His friend eventually became pregnant. For months and months there was, it seemed to me, a mutual feeling between me and the horses of justice, of peace. I fed apples to them both. The look in Blue's eyes was one of unabashed, "this is *it*ness."

It did not, however, last forever. One day, after a visit to the city, I went out to give Blue some apples. He stood waiting, or so I thought, though not beneath the tree. When I shook the tree and jumped back from the shower of apples, he made no move. I carried some over to him. He managed to half-crunch one. The rest he let fall to the ground. I dreaded looking into his eyes—because I had of course noticed that Brown, his partner, had gone—but I did look. If I had been born into slavery, and my partner had been sold or killed, my eyes would have looked like that. The children next door explained that Blue's partner had been "put with him" (the same expression that old people used, I had noticed, when speaking of an ancestor during slavery who had been impregnated by her owner) so that they could mate and she conceive. Since that was accomplished, she had been taken back by her owner, who lived somewhere else.

Will she be back? I asked.

They didn't know.

Blue was like a crazed person. Blue *was*, to me, a crazed person. He galloped furiously, as if he were being ridden, around and around his five beautiful acres. He whinnied until he couldn't. He tore at the ground with his hooves. He butted himself against his single shade tree. He looked always and always toward the road down which his partner had gone. And then, occasionally, when he came up for apples, or I took apples to him, he looked at me. It was a look so piercing, so full of grief, a look so *human*, I almost laughed (I felt too sad to cry) to think there are people who do not know that animals suffer. People like me who have forgotten, and daily forget, all that animals try to tell us. "Everything you do to us will happen to you; we are your teachers, as you are ours. We are one lesson" is essentially it, I think. There are those who never once have even considered animals' rights: those who have been taught that animals actually want to be used and abused by us, as small children "love" to be frightened, or women "love" to be mutilated and raped. . . . They are the great-grandchildren of those who honestly thought, because someone taught them this: "Women can't think," and "niggers can't faint." But most disturbing of all, in Blue's large brown eyes was a new look, more painful than the look of despair: the look of disgust with human beings, with life, the look of hatred. And it was odd what the look of hatred did. It gave him, for the first time, the look of a beast. And what that meant was that he had put up a barrier within to protect himself from further violence; all the apples in the world wouldn't change that fact.

And so Blue remained, a beautiful part of our landscape, very   18
peaceful to look at from the window, white against the grass. Once a friend came to visit and said, looking out on the soothing view: "And it *would* have to be a *white* horse; the very image of freedom." And I thought, yes, the animals are forced to become for us merely "images" of what they once so beautifully expressed. And we are used to drinking milk from containers showing "contented" cows, whose real lives we want to hear nothing about, eating eggs and drumsticks from "happy" hens, and munching hamburgers advertised by bulls of integrity who seem to command their fate.

As we talked of freedom and justice one day for all, we sat down   19
to steaks. I am eating misery, I thought, as I took the first bite. And spit it out.

MELISSA GREENE

No Rms, Jungle Vu

Melissa Greene (1952–   ) is a freelance writer in Atlanta, Georgia. After graduating from Oberlin College in 1975, she joined VISTA as a volunteer in McIntosh County, Georgia. The knowledge she gained through personal contacts there resulted in her first book, *Praying for Sheetrock* (1991), a portrait of a community belatedly struggling with the issue of civil rights. Greene says that her motive in writing is often to preserve the memory of things that might otherwise vanish unnoticed. When she read a profile of zoologist Jon Coe in her local newspaper, she was impressed that he, too, was a preservationist, working to save or re-create fragments of natural habitats. She was also eager to meet the man who said that he could design a zoo that would make the zoo-goer's hair stand on end. "No Rms, Jungle Vu" appeared in a slightly longer form in *The Atlantic Monthly* in December 1987.

"The Egyptians have been civilized for four thousand years . . . my own ancestors probably a lot less," Jon Charles Coe says. "We evolved over millions of years in the wild, where survival depended on our awareness of the landscape, the weather, and the animals. We haven't been domesticated long enough to have lost those senses. In my opinion, it is the business of the zoo to slice right through that sophisticated veneer, to recall us to our origins. I judge the effectiveness of a zoo exhibit in the pulse rate of the zoo-goer. We can design a zoo that will make the hair stand up on the back of your neck." 1

A revolution is under way in zoo design, which was estimated to be a $20 million business last year. Jon Coe and Grant Jones are the vanguard. Coe, forty-six, is a stocky man with a long, curly beard. He is an associate professor of landscape architecture at the University of Pennsylvania and a senior partner in the zoo-design firm of Coe Lee Robinson Roesch, in Philadelphia. Grant Jones, a senior partner in the architectural firm Jones & Jones, in Seattle, is at forty-eight a trendsetter in the design of riverfront areas, botanical gardens, and historical parks, as well as zoos. Coe and Jones were classmates at the Harvard School of Design, and Coe worked for Jones & Jones until 1981. 2

Ten years ago in Seattle they created the Woodland Park gorilla exhibit in collaboration with Dennis Paulson, a biologist, and with David Hancocks, an architect and the director of the Woodland Park Zoo. The exhibit is still praised by experts as the best ever done. It has become an international standard for the replication of wilderness in a zoo exhibit and for the art of including and engaging the zoo-goer. Dian Fossey, the field scientist who lived for fifteen years near the wild mountain gorillas of Rwanda before her murder there, in December of 1985, flew to Seattle as a consultant to the designers of Woodland Park. When the exhibit was completed, Johnpaul Jones, Grant Jones's partner (the two are not related), sent photographs to her. She wrote back that she had shown the photos to her colleagues at the field station and they had believed them to be photos of wild gorillas in Rwanda. "Your 3 firm, under the guidance of [Mr.] Hancocks, has made a tremendously important advancement toward the captivity conditions of gorillas," Fossey wrote. "Had such existed in the past, there would undoubtedly be more gorillas living in captivity."

"Woodland Park has remained a model for the zoo world," says   4
Terry Maple, the new director of Zoo Atlanta, a professor of comparative psychology (a field that examines the common origins of animal and human behavior) at the Georgia Institute of Technology, and the author of numerous texts and articles on primate behavior. "Woodland Park changed the way we looked at the zoo environment. Before Woodland Park, if the gorillas weren't in cages, they were on beautiful mown lawns, surrounded by moats. In good zoos they had playground equipment. In Woodland Park the staff had to teach the public not to complain that the gorilla exhibit looked unkempt."

"As far as gorilla habitats go," Maple says, "Cincinnati's is pretty   5
good; San Diego's is pretty good; Columbus's has a huge cage, so aesthetically it loses a great deal, but socially it's terrific; San Francisco's is a more technical solution, naturalistic but surrounded by walls. Woodland Park's is the best in the world."

In Woodland Park the zoo-goer must step off the broad paved cen-   6
tral boulevard onto a narrow path engulfed by vegetation to get to the gorillas. Coe planted a big-leaf magnolia horizontally, into the bank of a man-made hill, so that it would grow over the path. ("People forget that a landscape architect not only can do this," he said on a recent tour of the exhibit, indicating a pretty circle of peonies, "but can also do *this*"—he pointed to a shaggy, weed-covered little hill. "I *designed* that hill.")

The path leads to a wooden lean-to with a glass wall on one side   7
that looks into a rich, weedy, humid clearing. Half a dozen heavy-set, agile gorillas part the tall grasses, stroll leaning on their knuckles, and sit nonchalantly among clumps of comfrey, gnawing celery stalks. The blue-black sheen of their faces and fur on a field of green is electrifying. The social organization of the gorillas is expressed by their interaction around a couple of boulders in the foreground of the exhibit. All the gorillas enjoy climbing on the boulders, but the young ones yield to their elders and the adult females yield to the adult males, two silverback gorillas. The silverbacks drum their chests with their fists rapidly and perfunctorily while briefly rising on two feet—not at all like Tarzan. The fists make a rapid thudding noise, which seems to mean, "Here I come." Each silverback climbs to his rostrum, folds his arms, and glares at the other. As in nature, their relationship is by turns civil but not friendly, and contentious but not bullying.

The zoo-goers in the lean-to, observing all this, feel fortunate that   8
the troop of gorillas chooses to stay in view, when it apparently has acres and acres in which to romp. Moss-covered boulders overlap other

boulders in the distance, a stream fringed with ferns wanders among them, birds roost in the forty-foot-high treetops, and caves and nests beyond the bend in the stream are available to the gorillas as a place of retreat. "Flight distance" is the zoological term for the distance an animal needs to retreat from an approaching creature in order to feel safe—the size of the cushion of empty space it wishes to maintain around itself. (Several years ago Jon Coe accepted an assignment to design a nursing home, a conventional job that was unusual for him. He designed the home with flight distance. Sitting rooms and visiting areas were spacious near the front door but grew smaller as one progressed down the hall toward the residents' rooms. A resident overwhelmed by too much bustle in the outer areas could retreat down the hall to quieter and quieter environments.)

In fact the gorillas in Woodland Park do not have so much space to explore. The exhibit is 13,570 square feet (about a third of an acre), which is generous but not limitless. The arrangement of overlapping boulders and trees in the distance is meant to trick the eye. There are no fences or walls against which to calculate depth, and the visitor's peripheral vision is deliberately limited by the dimensions of the lean-to. Wider vision might allow a visitor to calculate his position within Woodland Park, or might give him an inappropriate glimpse—as happens in almost every other zoo in the world—of a snowshoe rabbit or an Amazon porcupine or a North American zoo-goer, over the heads of the West African gorillas. Coe measured and calculated the sight lines to ensure that the view was an uncorrupted one into the heart of the rain forest.

The boulders themselves contain a trick. Coe designed them to contain heating coils, so that in the miserable, misty Seattle winter they give off a warm aura, like an electric blanket. The boulders serve two purposes: they help the tropical gorillas put up with the Seattle winter, and they attract the gorillas to within several feet of the lean-to and the zoo-goers. It is no coincidence that much of the drama of the gorillas' everyday life is enacted three feet away from the lean-to. The patch of land in front of the lean-to is shady and cool in summer. The gorillas freely choose where to spend their day, but the odds have been weighted heavily in favor of their spending it in front of the lean-to.

"Their old exhibit was a six-hundred-square-foot tile bathroom," says Grant Jones, a tall, handsome, blue-eyed man. "The gorillas displayed a lot of very neurotic behavior. They were aggressive, sad, angry, lethargic. They had no flight distance. The people were behind the glass day and night, the people pounded on the glass, the gorillas were stressed out, totally, all the time. Their only way to deal with it was to sleep or to show intense anger. They'd pick up their own feces and smear it across the glass. They were not interacting with one another.

"My assumption was that when they left their cage to enter their

new outdoor park, that behavior would persist. On the first day, although they were frightened when they came into the new park, they
were tranquil. They'd never felt the wind; they'd never seen a bird fly
over; they'd never seen water flowing except for the drain in the bottom
of their cubicle. Instantly they became quiet and curious. The male was
afraid to enter into the environment and stood at the door for hours.
His mate came and took him by the hand and led him. They only went
about halfway. They stopped at a small stream. They sat and picked up
some leaves and dipped them in the water and took a bite of the leaves.
They leaned back and saw clouds moving over. It was spellbinding. I
assumed they would never recover from the trauma of how they'd been
kept. It turned out to be a matter of two or three days."

"Picture the typical zoo exhibit," Jon Coe says. "You stroll along a   13
sidewalk under evenly spaced spreading maples, beside colorful bedding plants. On your right is a polar-bear exhibit. There is a well-pruned
hedge of boxwood with a graphic panel in it. The panel describes interesting features of the species, including the fact that polar bears often
are seen swimming far out to sea. In the exhibit a bear is splashing in
a bathtub. Very little is required of the viewers and very little is gained
by them. The visitor is bored for two reasons: first because the setting
is too obvious, and second because of a feeling of security despite the
close presence of a wild animal.

"When planning this exhibit, we learned that in the wild, gorillas   14
like to forage at the edge of a forest, in clearings created by tribal people
who fell the trees, burn off the undergrowth, farm for a couple of years,
then move on. After they move on, the forest moves back in and the
gorillas forage there. We set about to re-create that scene. We got lots
of charred stumps, and we took a huge dead tree from a power-line
clearing a few miles from here. The story is plant succession, and how
the gorillas exploit the early plants growing back over the abandoned
farmland."

Coe relies on stagecraft and drama to break down the zoo-goer's   15
sense of security. When walking through a client zoo for the first time,
long before he has prepared a master plan, he offers a few suggestions:
Get rid of the tire swings in the chimp exhibit. Get rid of the signs
saying NIMBA THE ELEPHANT and JOJO THE CHEETAH. Stop the publicized
feeding of the animals, the baby elephant's birthday party, and any
other element contributing to either an anthropomorphized view ("Do
the elephants call each *other* Nimba and Bomba?") or a view of wild
beasts as tame pets.

"How can we improve our ability to get and hold the attention of   16
the zoo-goer?" he asks. "We must create a situation that transcends
the range of stimulation people are used to and enhances the visitor's
perception of the animal. A zoo animal that *appears* to be unrestrained

and dangerous should receive our full attention, possibly accompanied by an adrenal rush, until its potential for doing us harm is determined."

For ten years Coe and others have been experimenting with the [17] relative positions of zoo-goers and zoo animals. Coe now designs exhibits in which the animal terrain surrounds and is actually higher than the zoo paths, so that zoo-goers must look up to see the animals. The barriers between animals and people are camouflaged so effectively that zoo-goers may be uncertain whether an animal has access to them or not. In JungleWorld, the Bronx Zoo's recently opened $9.5 million indoor tropical forest nearly an acre in size, conceived by William Conway, the director of the zoo, a python lives inside a tree trunk that apparently has fallen across the zoo-goers' walkway. "We made the interior of the log brighter and tilted the glass away from the outside light to avoid all reflections," says Charles Beier, an associate curator. "It's an old jeweler's trick. When people glance overhead, there appears to be no barrier between them and the snake." The screams of horror provoked by the python are quite a different matter from the casual conversations that people engage in while strolling past rows of terrariums with snakes inside.

"We are trying to get people to be prepared to look for animals in [18] the forest, not have everything brightly lighted and on a platform in front of them," says John Gwynne, the deputy director for design of the New York Zoological Society, which operates the Bronx Zoo. "We have lots of dead trees and dead grass in here. It's actually very hard to train a gardener not to cut off the dead branches. We're trying to create a wilderness, not a garden—something that can catch people by surprise."

.   .   .

The profession of zoo design is a relatively new one. In the past, [19] when a zoo director said that a new lion house was required, the city council solicited bids and hired a popular local architect—the one who did the suburban hospital and the new high school—and paid him to fly around the country and get acquainted with lion houses. He visited four or five and learned design tips from each: how wide to space the bars, for example, and how thick to pour the cement. Then he flew home and drew a lion house.

"As recently as fifteen years ago there was no Jones & Jones or Jon [20] Coe," says William Conway, of the Bronx Zoo. "There were very few architects around then who had any concept of what animals were all about or who would go—as Jon Coe has gone—to Africa to see and sketch and try to understand, so that he knew what the biologist was talking about. The problem of the zoologist in the zoo was that, in the past, he was very often dealing with an architect who wanted to make a monument."

"The downfall of most zoos has been that they've hired architects," says Ace Torre, a designer in New Orleans, who holds degrees in architecture and landscape architecture. "Some of the more unfortunate zoos hired six different architects. Each one made his own statement. As a result, the zoo is a patchwork of architectural tributes." 21

In 1975 the City of Seattle asked Grant Jones, whose firm had restored the splendid Victorian copper-roofed pergolas and the elegant walkways and the granite statuary of the city's Pioneer Square Historic District, to design the Woodland Park Zoo gorilla house. The City of Seattle—specifically, David Hancocks, the zoo director—had made a novel choice. Jones was an anomaly in the world of architecture in that he prided himself on having never designed anything taller than three stories. Most of his buildings were made of wood, and they tended to be situated in national parks. Instead of making a grand tour of gorilla houses, Jones consulted field scientists and gorilla experts who had seen how gorillas lived in the wild. 22

"When they asked me to design a gorilla exhibit," Jones says, "I naturally rephrased the problem in my own mind as designing a landscape with gorillas in it. In what sort of landscape would I want to behold gorillas? I would want to include mystery and discovery. I'd like to see the gorillas from a distance first, and then up close. I'd like to be able to intrude on them and see what's going on without their knowing I'm there. I'd want to give them flight distance, a place to back off and feel secure. And I would want an experience that would take me back to a primordial depth myself. How did I spend my day some millions of years ago, living in proximity to this animal?" 23

"We asked Dian Fossey to visit Seattle," David Hancocks says, "and she became the most crucial member of the design team. We had so many people telling us we were being very foolish. A zoo director on the East Coast called to say he'd put a potted palm in a cage where a gorilla had lived for fifteen years. The gorilla pulled it out by the roots, ate it, and got sick." 24

"Driving in from the airport, we asked Fossey what the rain forest looked like," Jon Coe says. "She kept turning this way and that way in her seat, saying, 'It looks like that! It looks just like that!' Of course, Seattle is in a belt of temperate rain forest. Fossey was in an alpine tropical rain forest. The plants are not identical, but they are very similar. We realized that we could stand back and let the native plants take over the exhibit and the overall effect would be very much the same. 25

"And there were trees, forty-foot-tall trees, in the area slated for the gorillas. What to do about the trees? No zoo in the world had let gorillas have unlimited access to trees. We thought of the gorilla as a terrestrial animal. The wisdom at the time said that the trees had to 26 come down. We brought George Schaller, probably the world's preeminent field scientist, to Seattle, and asked him about the trees. His response was, 'I don't know if they're going to fall out of them or not, but somebody has to do this.' "

"They didn't fall out of the trees," Jones says, "but Kiki [one of 27 the silverbacks] escaped. We'd brought in some rock-climbers to try to get out of the exhibit when it was finished, and we'd made a few modifications based on their suggestions. Jon figured out an elaborate jumping matrix: if a gorilla can jump this far on the horizontal, how far can he go on a downward slope, et cetera. The problem is, you can't program in motivation. At some point the motivation may be so great that you'll find yourself saying, 'Whoops, the tiger can jump thirteen feet, not twelve. Guess we should have made it wider.'

"We had planted some hawthorn trees about four to five inches in 28 diameter, ten feet high, and had hoped they were large enough that the gorillas would accept them. They accepted everything else, but these trees were standing too much alone, too conspicuous. Kiki pulled all the branches off of one, then ripped it out of the ground. It stood by itself; the roots were like a tripod. He played with that thing for a number of days.

"The keepers were aware of how we must never let them have a 29 big long stick because they might put it across the moat, walk across it, and get out. They saw that tree but it was clearly not long enough to bridge the moat. We all discussed it, and decided it wasn't a problem. During that same period Kiki began disappearing for three hours at a time, and we didn't know where he was. It's a large environment, and he could have been off behind some shrubbery. One of the keepers told us later that he'd seen Kiki sitting on the edge of the big dry moat at the back of the habitat. One day Kiki climbed down into the moat.

"I imagine he took his tree with him to the far corner, leaned it up 30 against the wall, and considered it. At some point he must have made a firm decision. He got a toehold on the roots, pressed his body to the wall, lifted himself up in one lunge, and hung from the top of the moat. Then he pulled himself up and landed in the rhododendrons. He was out, he was in the park."

"He was sitting in the bushes and some visitors saw him," Coe 31 says. "They raced to the director's office and reported it to Hancocks." His response was calm, according to Coe. Anxious visitors often reported that there were gorillas loose in the trees. "The gorilla's not out," said Hancocks. "The exhibit, you see, is called landscape immersion. It's intended to give you the *impression* that the gorillas are free."

The visitors thanked Hancocks and left. He overheard one remark 32 to the other, "Still, it just doesn't seem right having him sit there on the sidewalk like that."

"Sidewalk?" Hancocks said.   33

"We called the police," says Hancocks, "not to control the gorilla   34
but to stop people from coming into the zoo. Jim Foster, the vet, fed
fruit to Kiki and calmed him down while we tried to figure out what
to do. We put a ladder across the moat and Jim climbed on it to show
Kiki how to cross. Kiki actually tried it, but the ladder wobbled and
fell, and he retreated. It was getting dark. We finally had to tranquilize
him and carry him back."

"It's been seven years since," Jones says, "and Kiki never has tried   35
again, although he clearly knows how to do it. He doesn't want to
leave. In fact I am frequently called in by zoos that are having problems
with escape. They always want to know, Should we make the moats
wider? The bars closer together? Should we chain the animal? Yet
escape is almost never a design problem. It is a question of motivation.
It is a social problem."

"One of the roles a silverback has in life," Coe says, "is to patrol   36
his territory. Kiki wasn't escaping *from* something. He was exploring
outward from the center of his territory to define its edges."

"If Kiki had escaped from a conventional ape house, the city would   37
have panicked," Hancocks says. "But in the year or two the exhibit
had been open, Seattle had lost the hairy-monster-of-the-ape-house
image, and saw gorillas as quiet and gentle."

Shortly after, one of the local papers carried a cartoon of Kiki roller-   38
skating arm-in-arm with two buxom beauties through the adjacent
Greenlake Park, and another had a cartoon of him pole-vaulting over
the moat.

.   .   .

The current revolution in zoo design—the landscape revolution—is   39
driven by three kinds of change that have occurred during this century.
First are great leaps in animal ecology, veterinary medicine, landscape
design, and exhibit technology, making possible unprecedented realism
in zoo exhibits. Second, and perhaps most important, is the progressive
disappearance of wilderness—the very subject of zoos—from the earth.
Third is knowledge derived from market research and from environmental psychology, making possible a sophisticated focus on the zoo-
goer.

Zoo-related sciences like animal ecology and veterinary medicine   40
for exotic animals barely existed fifty years ago and tremendous advances have been made in the last fifteen years. Zoo veterinarians now
inoculate animals against diseases they once died of. Until recently,
keeping the animals alive required most of a zoo's resources. A cage
modeled after a scientific laboratory or an operating room—tile-lined
and antiseptic, with a drain in the floor—was the best guarantee of
continued physical health. In the late 1960s and early 1970s zoo veteri-

narians and comparative psychologists began to realize that stress was as great a danger as disease to the captive wild animals. Directors thus sought less stressful forms of confinement than the frequently-hosed-down sterile cell.

Field scientists also published findings about the complex social 41 relations among wild animals. Zoos began to understand that captive animals who refused to mate often were reacting to the improper social configurations in which they were confined. Gorillas, for example, live in large groups in the wild. Zoos had put them in pairs, and then only at breeding time—"believing them monogamous, as we'd like to think we are," Coe says. Interaction between the male and the female gorilla was stilted, hostile, abnormal. Successful breeding among captive gorillas didn't begin until they were housed in large family groups. Golden lion tamarins, in contrast, refused to mate when they were caged in groups. Only very recently did researchers affiliated with the National Zoo discover that these beautiful little monkeys *are* monogamous.

Science first affected the design of zoos in 1735, when Linnaeus 42 published his *Systema Naturae* and people fell in love with classification. The resultant primate house, carnivore house, and reptile house allowed the public to grasp the contemporary scientific understanding of the animal world. "At the turn of the century a zoo was a place where you went to learn what kinds of animals there were," Conway says. "The fact that they were in little cages didn't matter. You could see this was an Arabian oryx, a scimitar-horned oryx, a beisa oryx, and so on. It wasn't at that time so important to have an idea of what they do, or the way they live, or how they evolved." The taxonomic approach informed the design of science museums, aquariums, botanical gardens, and arboretums.

Today zoo directors and designers can draw on whole libraries of 43 information about animal behavior and habitat. Exhibit designers can create entire forests of epoxy and fiber-glass trees, reinforced concrete boulders, waterfalls, and artificial vines, with mist provided by cloud machines. A zoo director can oversee the creation of astoundingly realistic habitats for the animals.

But zoo directors and designers cannot simply create magnificent 44 animal habitats and call them a zoo. That would be something else—a wildlife preserve, a national park. A zoo director has to think about bathrooms: zoos are for people, not animals. A zoo director has to think about bond issues and the fact that the city council, which also finances garbage collection, trims a little more from his budget each year. He has to be aware that the zoo is competing with a vast entertainment industry for the leisure hours and dollars of the public.

"If you're not smiling at Disney World, you're fired the next day," 45 says Robert Yokel, the director of the Miami Metrozoo. He is a laid-back, blue-jeaned, suntanned man with wild, scant hair. "Happy,

happy, happy, that's the whole concept. They are the premier operators. They taught the rest of the industry how a park should be run: keep it clean, make it convenient, make the ability to spend dollars very easy. They do everything top drawer. They drew over thirteen million people last year. It's an escape. It's a fantasy." Obviously, the director of the Miami zoo, more than most, has to worry about Disney World. He is surrounded, as well, by Monkey Jungle, the Miami Seaquarium, Busch Gardens, Parrot Jungle, Orchid Jungle, Flamingo Gardens, Lion Country Safari, and the beach. If Florida legalizes gambling, he may never see anyone again. But Yokel is not alone in the zoo world in appreciating what commercial entertainment parks offer the public.

The public today has more leisure time and disposable income than   46
ever before, more children than at any time since the 1950s, and more sophistication about animals—thanks to television, movies, and libraries—than at any time in history. Although a Greek in the age of Homer might not have been able to identify an anteater or a koala, many two-year-olds today can. However, there are other claims on people's time. Although, according to statistics, zoo-going is an entrenched habit with Americans, it is no longer likely that a station wagon packed with kids and heading down the highway on Sunday afternoon will turn in at the zoo. The family has been to Disney World, to Six Flags; they've been to theme parks where the hot-dog vendors wear period costumes and the concession stands look like log cabins; they've visited amusement parks where the whole environment, from the colorful banners to the trash cans, all sparkling clean and brightly painted, shrieks of fun. The local zoo, with its broad tree-lined avenues, pacing leopards, and sleeping bears, seems oddly antiquated and sobering by comparison. So zoo directors must ask, Are our visitors having a good time? Will they come back soon? Would they rather be at Disney World? What will really excite them?

Zoos used to be simpler. Once upon a time—in pharaonic Egypt,   47
in Imperial Rome, in the Austro-Hungarian Empire, in the traveling menageries and bear shows of Western Europe and Russia in the 1800s, even in the United States at the turn of the century—it was sufficient for the zoo to pluck an animal from the teeming wild populations in Asia and Africa and display it, as an exotic specimen, to an amazed populace. (And if the animal sickened in captivity, there was nothing to do but wait for it to die and send for another one. Not only had veterinary medicine not evolved adequately but there was no pressure by concerned wildlife groups for zoos to maintain and reproduce their own stock. The animals were out there.)

Already occupied with the welfare of their animals and the amuse-   48
ment of their zoo-goers, zoo directors today must be responsible to the larger reality that the wilderness is disappearing and the animals with it. Today the cement-block enclosure or quarter-acre plot allotted by a

zoo may be the last protected ground on earth for an animal whose habitat is disappearing under farmland, villages, or cities. The word *ark* is used with increasing frequency by zoo professionals. In this country, zoos house members of half a dozen species already extinct in the wild, and of hundreds more on the verge of extinction. Zoo-goers are confronted by skull logos denoting vanishing animals. The new designers like Coe and Jones, and directors like Conway, Maple, Graham, Dolan, George Rabb, at Chicago Brookfield, and Michael Robinson, at the National Zoo, belong as no designers or directors ever before belonged to the international community of zoologists and conservationists who have as their goal the preservation of the wild.

"This is a desperate time," William Conway says. The New York Zoological Society, under his leadership, also operates one of the largest and oldest wildlife-conservation organizations in the world, Wildlife Conservation International, which sponsors sixty-two programs in thirty-two countries. Conway is a slender, distinguished, avuncular gentleman with a pencil-line moustache. For him it seems quite a personal matter, a subject of intense private distress, that the earth is losing its wildlife and he doesn't know how many species are going, or what they are, or where they are, or how to save them.

"We are certainly at the rate of losing a species a day now, probably more," he says. "Who knows how many species there are on earth? Suppose, for the sake of argument, there are ten million species of animals out there. If we have one million in the year 2087 we will be doing very well. The human population is increasing at the rate of a hundred and fifty a minute. The tropical moist forest is decreasing at the rate of fifty acres a minute. And there is not a hope in the world of slowing this destruction and this population increase for quite some time. Most of the animals we hold dear, the big, charismatic megavertebrates, almost all of them will be endangered within the next twenty years. The people who are going to do that have already been born.

"And the destruction is being effected by some poor guy and his wife and their five children who are hacking out a few acres of ground to try to eat. That's where most of the fifty acres a minute are going: forty-eight that way and two to the bulldozers. In Rwanda there is a mountain-gorilla preserve that supports two hundred and forty gorillas. It recently was calculated that the park could sustain two thousand human families, people with no other place to live, no land. Now, how can you justify saving the land for two hundred and forty gorillas when you could have two thousand human families? That's one side of the story. Here's the other: if you were to do that, to put those two thousand families in there, the mountain gorilla would disappear completely, and that would take care of Rwanda's population-expansion needs for slightly less than three months. It's a very discouraging picture."

Michael Robinson, the director of the National Zoo, is a rotund and   52
rosy-cheeked Englishman. "I have spent twenty years in the tropics,
and it is difficult to talk about them in a detached, scientific manner,"
he says. "They are the richest ecosystem on earth. They have been here
for millions of years. Perhaps eighty percent of all the animals in the
world live there and have evolved relationships of breathtaking complexity. The northern hardwood forests have perhaps forty species of
trees per hectare. The rain forest has closer to a hundred and fifty to
two hundred species per hectare. Once the rain forest is cut down, it
takes about a hundred years for the trees to grow back. We estimate that
it would take at least six hundred years before the forest has returned to
its original state, with all the plants and animals there."

"The American Association of Zoological Parks and Aquariums   53
Species Survival Plan has only thirty-seven endangered species," Conway says. "We should have at least a thousand. How are we going to
do it? My God, there are only one thousand seven hundred and eighty-
five spaces for big cats in the United States. One thousand seven hundred and eighty-five. How many races of tigers are out there? Five or
six. Several races of lions. Several races of leopards, to say nothing of
snow leopards, jaguars, fishing cats, cheetahs, and so on. And you have
to maintain a minimum population of two to three hundred animals
each to have a population that is genetically and demographically
sound. What in bloody hell are we going to do?"

Zoos in America are doing two things to try to save the wild ani-   54
mals. The front-line strategy is conservation biology and captive propa-
gation, employing all the recent discoveries in human fertility, such as
in vitro fertilization, embryo transplantation, and surrogate motherhood. Zoos around the world have hooked into a computerized data-
base called ISIS, so that if a rare Indian rhino goes into heat in Los
Angeles—or, for that matter, in the wilds of India—a healthy male
rhino to donate sperm can be located.

The second-line strategy is to attempt to save the wilderness itself   55
through educating the public. Zoo directors and designers point out that
there are 115 million American zoo-goers each year, and that if even
10 percent of them were to join conservation organizations, to boycott
goods produced from the bones, horns, organs, and hides of endangered
species, to vote to assist poor nations that are attempting to preserve
their forests (perhaps by allowing debt payments to be eased in proportion to the numbers of wild acres preserved), their strength would be
felt. The point of the landscape-immersion exhibits is to give the public
a taste of what is out there, what is being lost.

It is dawning on zoo professionals that they are, in part, responsible   56
for the American public's unfamiliarity with ecology and lack of awareness that half a dozen species a week are being driven into extinction,

and that the precious tropical rain forest may vanish within our lifetime. "By itself, the sight of caged animals does not engender respect for animals," the environmental psychologist Robert Sommer wrote in 1972 in a pioneering essay titled "What Did We Learn at the Zoo?" "Despite excellent intentions, even the best zoos may be creating animal stereotypes that are not only incorrect but that actually work against the interests of wildlife preservation." Terry Maple says, "Zoos used to teach that animals are weird and they live alone."

In the past the only zoo people who paid much attention to zoo-goers were the volunteers assigned to drum up new members. The question they usually asked about zoo-goers was, Can we attract ten thousand of them in August? rather than, How have we influenced their attitudes about wildlife? With the decline of the wild and the dedication of zoos to educating the public, zoo professionals have grown curious about zoo-goers. What do they think? What are they saying as they nudge each other and point? Why do they shoot gum balls at the hippos? What exactly *are* they learning at the zoo? In search of answers to such questions, behavioral scientists are strolling through zoos around the country. They clock the number of seconds zoo-goers look at an exhibit. They count how many zoo-goers read the educational placards. They record the casual utterances of passers-by. And they note the age and gender of the zoo-goers who carve their initials on the railings. (They excite the envy of their co-equals in the science-museum world. "Researchers [at zoos] can linger for inordinate amounts of time at exhibits under the guise of waiting for an animal to do something," Beverly Serrell wrote in *Museum News* in 1980. "Standing next to a skeleton doesn't afford such a convenient cover.")

A fairly sharply focused portrait of the average North American zoo-goer has emerged. For example, data collected by the Smithsonian Institution at the National Zoo in 1979 revealed that zoo-goers arrive at the gates in any one of eighty-four "visitor constellations." One of the most common constellations is one parent accompanied by one or more children. On weekdays mothers predominate. On weekends fathers are sighted. In another study Professor Edward G. Ludwig, of State University College at Fredonia, New York, observed that the adult unaccompanied by children seemed to have "an aura of embarrassment." A survey published in 1976 found that zoo-goers tend to have more education and larger annual incomes than the population at large, and a 1979 survey found that zoo-goers are ignorant of basic ecological principles much more than are backpackers, birdwatchers, and members of wildlife organizations.

In a group of four zoo-goers, it's likely that only one or two will read an informational sign. Nearly all conversation will be confined to the friends and family members with whom the zoo-goer arrives. The most common form of conversation at the zoo is a declarative sentence following "Watch!" or "Look!" The second most common form is a question. Robert Yokel, in Miami, believes that the two questions asked most frequently by zoo-goers are "Where is the bathroom?" and "Where is the snack bar?" Zoo-goers typically look at exhibits for about ninety seconds. Some never stop walking. Ludwig found that most people will stop for animals that beg, animals that are feeding, baby animals, animals that make sounds, or animals that are mimicking human behavior. People express irritation or annoyance with animals that sleep, eliminate, or regurgitate.

Zoo visitors do not like to lose their way within a zoo, and they get disgruntled when they find themselves backtracking. "We do not enjoy walking in circles and we invariably do," said one of the 300 respondents to the Smithsonian study. "Then we get irritated with ourselves."

Jim Peterson, a senior partner in the natural-history exhibit design firm of Bios, in Seattle, has identified the "first-fish syndrome." Within twenty feet of the entrance to an aquarium, visitors need to see a fish or they become unhappy. They will rush past the finest backlighted high-tech hands-on exhibitry to find that first fish. Similarly, Peterson has noted that visitors in zoos can tolerate only fifty feet between animals. Any greater distance inspires them to plow through foliage and create their own viewing blind.

Most "noncompliant behavior," such as unauthorized feeding of animals or attempting to climb over barriers, comes from juveniles and teens in mixed-gender groupings and children accompanied by both parents. A 1984 study by Valerie D. Thompson suggested that two parents tend to be involved with each other, freeing the children to perform antisocial acts; and that among teenagers there is "a close tie between noncompliant behavior and attempting to impress a member of the opposite sex."

Ted Finlay, a graduate student working with Terry Maple at Zoo Atlanta, wrote a master's thesis titled "The Influence of Zoo Environments on Perceptions of Animals," one of the first studies to focus on zoo design. Finlay majored in psychology and animal behavior with a minor in architecture, with the intention of becoming a zoo psychologist. For the research for his dissertation he prepared a slide show of animals in three environments: free, caged, and in various types of naturalistic zoo exhibits. Two hundred and sixty-seven volunteers viewed the slides and rated their feelings about the animals. The free animals were characterized as "free," "wild," and "active." Caged animals were seen as "restricted," "tame," and "passive." Animals in naturalistic settings were rated like the free animals if no barrier was visible. If the barrier *was* visible, they were rated like caged animals—that is to say, less favorably.

The zoo-goer who emerges from the research literature—benighted and happy-go-lucky, chomping his hot dog, holding his nose in the elephant house and scratching under his arms in the monkey house to make his children laugh—is a walking anachronism. He is the creation of an outmoded institution—the conventional zoo—in which the primate house, carnivore house, and reptile house, all lined with tile, glow with an unreal greenish light as if the halls were subterranean, and in which giraffes, zebras, and llamas stand politely, and as if on tiptoe, on the neatly mown lawns of the moated exhibits.

Once it was education enough for the public to file past the captive 65 gorilla in its cage and simply absorb the details of its peculiar or frightening countenance. "One ape in a cage, shaking its steel bars," Terry Maple says, "was a freak show, a horror show, King Kong! You'd go there to be scared, to scream, to squeeze your girlfriend." Despite gilded, or dingy, surroundings, a tusked creature in eighteenth-century Versailles, or downtown Pittsburgh, had the aura of a savage, strange, flowered wilderness.

"Pee-you!" is the primal, universal response of schoolchildren 66 herded into an elephant house. Adults more discreetly crinkle their noses, turn their heads, and laugh. The unspoken impressions are that elephants are filthy, tread in their own feces, attract flies, require hosing down, eat mush, and no wonder they are housed in cinder-block garages. These are not the sort of impressions that might inspire a zoo-goer to resist—much less protest—the marketing of souvenirs made of ivory.

Moated exhibits display animals in garden-like settings, with bed- 67 ding plants along cement walkways. A koala seated alone in the branch of a single artificial tree above a bright-green lawn looks as if he'd be at home in a Southern California back yard, next to the patio. The visitors looking at such exhibits appreciate the animals in them more and pronounce them "beautiful" or "interesting," but the subliminal message here is that animals are like gentle pets and thrive nicely in captivity. The visitors are hard pressed to explain what the big deal is about the rain forest or why zoologists talk about it, their voices cracking, the way twelfth-century Crusaders must have discussed the Holy Land.

. . .

One evening, just at dusk, Coe hurried alone through the Woodland 68 Park Zoo. He'd worked late on some sketches, and the zoo had closed. He would have to let himself out. The lions in the Serengeti Plains exhibit galloped back and forth through their yellow grass, whipping their tails. They ran and ran and pulled up short at the brink of their hidden moat, panting, their nostrils flaring. Coe just happened to be passing by. One of the dun-colored male lions approached and crouched at the very edge of the moat, and growled. Jon Coe froze.

Now, Coe had designed the exhibit. He knew that he was looking   69
up at the lion because he'd elevated its territory to instill fear and respect
in the zoo-goer. He knew that he seemed to be walking beside the wild,
dark African plains because he'd considered issues like sight lines and
cross-viewing. He knew that a concealed moat lay between him and
the lion, and that the width of the moat was the standard width used
by zoos all over the world. But he also knew that you can't program
in motivation. The lion looked at him and crouched; he could hear it
snorting. Then it growled again—king of the darkness on the grassy
plain. The hair stood up on the back of Coe's neck.

ANNIE DILLARD

The Fixed

Annie Dillard (1945–   ) wrote her master's thesis on Henry David
Thoreau's *Walden* in 1968. Like Thoreau, she combines a philosophical
interest in nature with unusual abilities as a close observer and recorder of the world around her. The combination is so striking that it
brought Dillard from obscurity to national prominence at one stroke
with the publication of her Pulitzer Prize–winning *Pilgrim at Tinker
Creek* (1974), from which "The Fixed" is excerpted. Since then she
has published a steady stream of poetry and prose, including *Holy the
Firm* (1978), *Tickets for a Prayer Wheel* (1982), *Teaching a Stone to Talk*
(1982), *An American Childhood* (1987), and *The Writing Life* (1989).
Her first novel, *The Living,* was published in 1992. *Pilgrim at Tinker
Creek* is a guidebook to the author's neighborhood: its most common
gesture is a pointing finger and a plea for us to look at what we
commonly overlook. If we follow her instructions, we discover once
again that our neighborhood is the earth and that our relationship
with our neighbors is troubling.

I have just learned to see praying mantis egg cases. Suddenly I see   1
them everywhere; a tan oval of light catches my eye, or I notice a blob
of thickness in a patch of slender weeds. As I write I can see the one I
tied to the mock orange hedge outside my study window. It is over an
inch long and shaped like a bell, or like the northern hemisphere of an
egg cut through its equator. The full length of one of its long sides is
affixed to a twig; the side that catches the light is perfectly flat. It has
a dead straw, deadweed color, and a curious brittle texture, hard as
varnish, but pitted minutely, like frozen foam. I carried it home this
afternoon, holding it carefully by the twig, along with several others—

they were light as air. I dropped one without missing it until I got home and made a count.

Within the week I've seen thirty or so of these egg cases in a rose-grown field on Tinker Mountain, and another thirty in weeds along Carvin's Creek. One was on a twig of tiny dogwood on the mud lawn of a newly built house. I think the mail-order houses sell them to gardeners at a dollar apiece. It beats spraying, because each case contains between one hundred twenty-five to three hundred fifty eggs. If the eggs survive ants, woodpeckers, and mice—and most do—then you get the fun of seeing the new mantises hatch, and the smug feeling of knowing, all summer long, that they're out there in your garden devouring gruesome numbers of fellow insects all nice and organically. When a mantis has crunched up the last shred of its victim, it cleans its smooth green face like a cat.

In late summer I often see a winged adult stalking the insects that swarm about my porch light. Its body is a clear, warm green; its naked, triangular head can revolve uncannily, so that I often see one twist its head to gaze at me as it were over its shoulder. When it strikes, it jerks so suddenly and with such a fearful clatter of raised wings, that even a hardened entomologist like J. Henri Fabre[1] confessed to being startled witless every time.

Adult mantises eat more or less everything that breathes and is small enough to capture. They eat honeybees and butterflies, including monarch butterflies. People have actually seen them seize and devour garter snakes, mice, and even *hummingbirds*. Newly hatched mantises, on the other hand, eat small creatures like aphids and each other. When I was in elementary school, one of the teachers brought in a mantis egg case in a Mason jar. I watched the newly hatched mantises emerge and shed their skins; they were spidery and translucent, all over joints. They trailed from the egg case to the base of the Mason jar in a living bridge that looked like Arabic calligraphy, some baffling text from the Koran inscribed down the air by a fine hand. Over a period of several hours, during which time the teacher never summoned the nerve or the sense to release them, they ate each other until only two were left. Tiny legs were still kicking from the mouths of both. The two survivors grappled and sawed in the Mason jar; finally both died of injuries. I felt as though I myself should swallow the corpses, shutting my eyes and washing them down like jagged pills, so all that life wouldn't be lost.

When mantises hatch in the wild, however, they straggle about prettily, dodging ants, till all are lost in the grass. So it was in hopes of seeing an eventual hatch that I pocketed my jackknife this afternoon before I set out to walk. Now that I can see the egg cases, I'm embarrassed to realize how many I must have missed all along. I walked east

1. Noted French observer of the behavior of insects (1823–1915).

through the Adams' woods to the cornfield, cutting three undamaged egg cases I found at the edge of the field. It was a clear, picturesque day, a February day without clouds, without emotion or spirit, like a beautiful woman with an empty face. In my fingers I carried the thorny stems from which the egg cases hung like roses; I switched the bouquet from hand to hand, warming the free hand in a pocket. Passing the house again, deciding not to fetch gloves, I walked north to the hill by the place where the steers come to drink from Tinker Creek. There in the weeds on the hill I found another eight egg cases. I was stunned—I cross this hill several times a week, and I always look for egg cases here, because it was here that I had once seen a mantis laying her eggs.

It was several years ago that I witnessed this extraordinary proce- 6 dure, but I remember, and confess, an inescapable feeling that I was watching something not real and present, but a horrible nature movie, a "secrets-of-nature" short, beautifully photographed in full color, that I had to sit through unable to look anywhere else but at the dimly lighted EXIT signs along the walls, and that behind the scenes some amateur moviemaker was congratulating himself on having stumbled across this little wonder, or even on having contrived so natural a set- ting, as though the whole scene had been shot very carefully in a terrar- ium in someone's greenhouse.

I was ambling across this hill that day when I noticed a speck of 7 pure white. The hill is eroded; the slope is a rutted wreck of red clay broken by grassy hillocks and low wild roses whose roots clasp a pit- tance of topsoil. I leaned to examine the white thing and saw a mass of bubbles like spittle. Then I saw something dark like an engorged leech rummaging over the spittle, and then I saw the praying mantis.

She was upside-down, clinging to a horizontal stem of wild rose 8 by her feet which pointed to heaven. Her head was deep in dried grass. Her abdomen was swollen like a smashed finger; it tapered to a fleshy tip out of which bubbled a wet, whipped froth. I couldn't believe my eyes. I lay on the hill this way and that, my knees in thorns and my cheeks in clay, trying to see as well as I could. I poked near the female's head with a grass; she was clearly undisturbed, so I settled my nose an inch from that pulsing abdomen. It puffed like a concertina, it throbbed like a bellows; it roved, pumping, over the glistening, clabbered surface of the egg case testing and patting, thrusting and smoothing. It seemed to act so independently that I forgot the panting brown stick at the other end. The bubble creature seemed to have two eyes, a frantic little brain, and two busy, soft hands. It looked like a hideous, harried mother slicking up a fat daughter for a beauty pageant, touching her up, slob- bering over her, patting and hemming and brushing and stroking.

The male was nowhere in sight. The female had probably eaten 9 him. Fabre says that, at least in captivity, the female will mate with and devour up to seven males, whether she has laid her egg cases or not. The mating rites of mantises are well known: a chemical produced in the head of the male insect says, in effect, "No, don't go near her, you fool, she'll eat you alive." At the same time a chemical in his abdomen says, "Yes, by all means, now and forever yes."

While the male is making up what passes for his mind, the female tips the balance in her favor by eating his head. He mounts her. Fabre describes the mating, which sometimes lasts six hours, as follows: "The male, absorbed in the performance of his vital functions, holds the female in a tight embrace. But the wretch has no head; he has no neck; he has hardly a body. The other, with her muzzle turned over her shoulder continues very placidly to gnaw what remains of the gentle swain. And, all the time, that masculine stump, holding on firmly, goes on with the business! . . . I have seen it done with my own eyes and have not yet recovered from my astonishment."

I watched the egg-laying for over an hour. When I returned the next day, the mantis was gone. The white foam had hardened and browned to a dirty suds; then, and on subsequent days, I had trouble pinpointing the case, which was only an inch or so off the ground. I checked on it every week all winter long. In the spring the ants discovered it; every week I saw dozens of ants scrambling over the sides, unable to chew a way in. Later in the spring I climbed the hill every day, hoping to catch the hatch. The leaves of the trees had long since unfolded, the butterflies were out, and the robins' first broods were fledged; still the egg case hung silent and full on the stem. I read that I should wait for June, but still I visited the case every day. One morning at the beginning of June everything was gone. I couldn't find the lower thorn in the clump of three to which the egg case was fixed. I couldn't find the clump of three. Tracks ridged the clay, and I saw the lopped stems: somehow my neighbor had contrived to run a tractor-mower over that steep clay hill on which there grew nothing to mow but a few stubby thorns.

So. Today from this same hill I cut another three undamaged cases and carried them home with the others by their twigs. I also collected a suspiciously light cynthia moth cocoon. My fingers were stiff and red with cold, and my nose ran. I had forgotten the Law of the Wild, which is, "Carry Kleenex." At home I tied the twigs with their egg cases to various sunny bushes and trees in the yard. They're easy to find because I used white string; at any rate, I'm unlikely to mow my own trees. I hope the woodpeckers that come to the feeder don't find them, but I don't see how they'd get a purchase on them if they did.

Night is rising in the valley; the creek has been extinguished for an hour, and now only the naked tips of trees fire tapers into the sky like trails of sparks. The scene that was in the back of my brain all afternoon, obscurely, is beginning to rise from night's lagoon. It really has nothing to do with praying mantises. But this afternoon I threw tiny string lashings and hitches with frozen hands, gingerly, fearing to touch the egg cases even for a minute because I remembered the Polyphemus moth.[2]

I have no intention of inflicting all my childhood memories on   14
anyone. Far less do I want to excoriate my old teachers who, in their bungling, unforgettable way, exposed me to the natural world, a world covered in chitin, where implacable realities hold sway. The Polyphemus moth never made it to the past; it crawls in that crowded, pellucid pool at the lip of the great waterfall. It is as present as this blue desk and brazen lamp, as this blackened window before me in which I can no longer see even the white string that binds the egg case to the hedge, but only my own pale, astonished face.

Once, when I was ten or eleven years old, my friend Judy brought   15
in a Polyphemus moth cocoon. It was January; there were doily snowflakes taped to the schoolroom panes. The teacher kept the cocoon in her desk all morning and brought it out when we were getting restless before recess. In a book we found what the adult moth would look like; it would be beautiful. With a wingspread of up to six inches, the Polyphemus is one of the few huge American silk moths, much larger than, say, a giant or tiger swallowtail butterfly. The moth's enormous wings are velveted in a rich, warm brown, and edged in bands of blue and pink delicate as a watercolor wash. A startling "eyespot," immense, and deep blue melding to an almost translucent yellow, luxuriates in the center of each hind wing. The effect is one of a masculine splendor foreign to the butterflies, a fragility unfurled to strength. The Polyphemus moth in the picture looked like a mighty wraith, a beating essence of the hardwood forest, alien-skinned and brown, with spread, blind eyes. This was the giant moth packed in the faded cocoon. We closed the book and turned to the cocoon. It was an oak leaf sewn into a plump oval bundle; Judy had found it loose in a pile of frozen leaves.

We passed the cocoon around; it was heavy. As we held it in our   16
hands, the creature within warmed and squirmed. We were delighted, and wrapped it tighter in our fists. The pupa began to jerk violently, in heart-stopping knocks. Who's there? I can still feel those thumps, urgent through a muffling of spun silk and leaf, urgent through the swaddling of many years, against the curve of my palm. We kept passing it around. When it came to me again it was hot as a bun; it jumped half out of my hand. The teacher intervened. She put it, still heaving and banging, in the ubiquitous Mason jar.

2. Polyphemus, in classical mythology, was a one-eyed giant (a Cyclops) whom the hero Odysseus blinded (*Odyssey*, Book 9). A Polyphemus moth has a large eyespot on each hind wing.

It was coming. There was no stopping it now, January or not. One   17
end of the cocoon dampened and gradually frayed in a furious battle.
The whole cocoon twisted and slapped around in the bottom of the jar.
The teacher fades, the classmates fade, I fade: I don't remember anything but that thing's struggle to be a moth or die trying. It emerged at
last, a sodden crumple. It was a male; his long antennae were thickly
plumed, as wide as his fat abdomen. His body was very thick, over an
inch long, and deeply furred. A gray, furlike plush covered his head; a
long, tan furlike hair hung from his wide thorax over his brown-furred,
segmented abdomen. His multijointed legs, pale and powerful, were
shaggy as a bear's. He stood still, but he breathed.

He couldn't spread his wings. There was no room. The chemical   18
that coated his wings like varnish, stiffening them permanently, dried,
and hardened his wings as they were. He was a monster in a Mason
jar. Those huge wings stuck on his back in a torture of random pleats
and folds, wrinkled as a dirty tissue, rigid as leather. They made a single
nightmare clump still wracked with useless, frantic convulsions.

The next thing I remember, it was recess. The school was in   19
Shadyside, a busy residential part of Pittsburgh. Everyone was playing
dodgeball in the fenced playground or racing around the concrete
schoolyard by the swings. Next to the playground a long delivery drive
sloped downhill to the sidewalk and street. Someone—it must have
been the teacher—had let the moth out. I was standing in the driveway,
alone, stock-still, but shivering. Someone had given the Polyphemus
moth his freedom, and he was walking away.

He heaved himself down the asphalt driveway by infinite degrees,   20
unwavering. His hideous crumpled wings lay glued and rucked on his
back, perfectly still now, like a collapsed tent. The bell rang twice; I
had to go. The moth was receding down the driveway, dragging on. I
went; I ran inside. The Polyphemus moth is still crawling down the
driveway, crawling down the driveway hunched, crawling down the
driveway on six furred feet, forever.

LEWIS THOMAS

Ponds

Lewis Thomas (1913–1993) was a physician by vocation and a naturalist by avocation. He became a writer almost by accident: In 1970
he was asked to deliver the keynote address at a medical symposium
on inflammation. "This kind of conference," he later observed, "tends
to be rather heavy going and my talk was designed to lighten the

proceedings at the outset by presenting a rather skewed view of inflammation." The address was such a success that Thomas was soon
asked to become a regular columnist for the *New England Journal of
Medicine.* The terms were simple: no pay for Thomas but an absolutely
free hand to write what he wished. "Ponds" was published in the
Journal in 1978. Like many of Thomas's essays, it presents a "rather
skewed" view of contemporary America's relationship with nature. It
is precisely the skewing that gave Thomas a wide audience and led to
the reprinting of his essays as a series of popular books: *The Lives of a
Cell* (1974), *The Medusa and the Snail* (1979), *Late Night Thoughts on
Listening to Mahler's Ninth Symphony* (1983), *Et Cetera, et Cetera* (1990),
and *The Fragile Species* (1992). In 1983 he published *The Youngest Science,* a mixture of memoir and history that reminds us how closely
his own career paralleled the development of truly modern medicine.
Thomas was president emeritus at the Memorial Sloan-Kettering Cancer Center in New York City until his death in 1993.

Large areas of Manhattan are afloat. I remember when the new   1
Bellevue Hospital was being built, fifteen years ago; the first stage was
the most spectacular and satisfying, an enormous square lake. It was
there for the two years, named Lake Bellevue, while the disconsolate
Budget Bureau went looking for cash to build the next stage. It was
fenced about and visible only from the upper windows of the old hospital, but pretty to look at, cool and blue in midsummer, frozen gleaming
as Vermont in January. The fence, like all city fences, was always broken, and we could have gone down to the lake and used it, but it was
known to be an upwelling of the East River. At Bellevue there were
printed rules about the East River: if anyone fell in, it was an emergency
for the Infectious-Disease Service, and the first measures, after resuscitation, were massive doses of whatever antibiotics the hospital pharmacy
could provide.

But if you cleaned the East River you could have ponds all over   2
town, up and down the East Side of Manhattan anyway. If you lifted
out the Empire State Building and the high structures nearby, you
would have, instantly, an inland sea. A few holes bored in the right
places would let water into the subways, and you'd have lovely underground canals all across to the Hudson, uptown to the Harlem River,
downtown to the Battery, a Venice underground, without pigeons.

It wouldn't work, though, unless you could find a way to keep out   3
the fish. New Yorkers cannot put up with live fish out in the open. I
cannot explain this, but it is so.

There is a new pond, much smaller than Lake Bellevue, on First   4
Avenue between Seventieth and Seventy-first, on the east side of the
street. It emerged sometime last year, soon after a row of old flats had
been torn down and the hole dug for a new apartment building. By
now it is about average size for Manhattan, a city block long and about

forty feet across, maybe eight feet deep at the center, more or less kid-
ney-shaped, rather like an outsized suburban swimming pool except
for the things floating, and now the goldfish.

With the goldfish, it is almost detestable. There are, clearly visible   5
from the sidewalk, hundreds of them. The neighborhood people do not
walk by and stare into it through the broken fence, as would be normal
for any other Manhattan pond. They tend to cross the street, looking
away.

Now there are complaints against the pond, really against the gold-   6
fish. How could people do such a thing? Bad enough for pet dogs and
cats to be abandoned, but who could be so unfeeling as to abandon
goldfish? They must have come down late at night, carrying their bowls,
and simply dumped them in. How could they?

The ASPCA[1] was called, and came one afternoon with a rowboat.   7
Nets were used, and fish taken away in new custodial bowls, some to
Central Park, others to ASPCA headquarters, to the fish pound. But the
goldfish have multiplied, or maybe those people with their bowls keep
coming down late at night for their furtive, unfeeling dumping. Anyway, there are too many fish for the ASPCA, for which this seems to
be a new kind of problem. An official stated for the press that the
owners of the property would be asked to drain the pond by pumping,
and then the ASPCA would come back with nets to catch them all.

You'd think they were rats or roaches, the way people began to   8
talk. Get those goldfish out of that pond, I don't care how you do it.
Dynamite, if necessary. But get rid of them. Winter is coming, someone
said, and it is deep enough so that they'll be swimming around underneath the ice. Get them out.

It is this knowledge of the East River, deep in the minds of all   9
Manhattan residents, more than the goldfish themselves, I think. Goldfish in a glass bowl are harmless to the human mind, maybe even
helpful to minds casting about for something, anything, to think about.
But goldfish let loose, propagating themselves, worst of all *surviving* in
what has to be a sessile eddy of the East River, somehow threaten us
all. We do not like to think that life is possible under some conditions,
especially the conditions of a Manhattan pond. There are four abandoned tires, any number of broken beer bottles, fourteen shoes and a
single sneaker, and a visible layer, all over the surface, of that grayish-
green film that settles on all New York surfaces. The mud at the banks
of the pond is not proper country mud but reconstituted Manhattan
landfill, ancient garbage, fossilized coffee grounds and grapefruit rind,
the defecation of a city. For goldfish to be swimming in such water,
streaking back and forth mysteriously in small schools, feeding, obviously feeding, looking as healthy and well-off as goldfish in the costliest

1. American Society for the Prevention of Cruelty to Animals.

kind of window-box aquarium, means something is wrong with our standards. It is, in some deep sense beyond words, insulting.

I thought I noticed a peculiar sort of fin on the under-surface of two of the fish. Perhaps, it occurs to me now in a rush of exultation, in such a pond as this, with all its chemical possibilities, there are contained some mutagens, and soon there will be schools of mutant goldfish. Give them just a little more time, I thought. And then, with the most typically Manhattan thought I've ever thought, I thought: The ASPCA will come again, next month, with their rowboat and their nets. The proprietor will begin pumping out the pond. The nets will flail, the rowboat will settle, and then the ASPCA officials will give a sudden shout of great dismay. And with a certain amount of splashing and grayish-greenish spray, at all the edges of the pond, up all the banks of ancient New York landfill mud, crawling on their new little feet, out onto the sidewalks, up and down and across the street, into doorways and up the fire escapes, some of them with little suckers on their little feet, up the sides of buildings and into open windows, looking for something, will come the goldfish.

It won't last, of course. Nothing like this ever does. The mayor will come and condemn it in person. The Health Department will come and recommend the purchase of cats from out of town because of the constitutional boredom of city cats. The NIH will send up teams of professionals from Washington with a new kind of antifish spray, which will be recalled four days later because of toxicity to cats.

After a few weeks it will be finished anyway, like a lot of New York events. The goldfish will dive deep and vanish, the pond will fill up with sneakers, workmen will come and pour concrete over everything, and by next year the new building will be up and occupied by people all unaware of their special environmental impact. But what a time it was.

HARRY CREWS

Pages from the Life of a Georgia Innocent

Harry Crews (1935–   ) grew up in Bacon County, Georgia, part of a poor family living in one of the most impoverished regions of the rural South. He now teaches English at the University of Florida at Gainesville and is the author of many novels, including *The Knockout Artist* (1988), and *Body* (1990), both of which depict confrontations between the urban and the rural. *Scar Lover*, published in 1992, is his most recent novel. "Pages from the Life of a Georgia Innocent" appeared in Crews's monthly column in *Esquire* in July 1976. That Crews chose to call this column "Grits" (a slang term for rough-edged Southerners) tells a great deal about where he is, quite literally, coming from. Crews is known for mixing pain, humor, and deliberate roughness of style. One critic has said that reading his work is like undergoing major surgery while under the influence of laughing gas. You can read more about Crews's difficult early years in Bacon County in his autobiography, *A Childhood: A Biography of a Place* (1978).

Not very long ago I went with my twelve-year-old boy to a Disney   1
movie, one of those things that show a farm family, poor but God knows honest, out there on the land building character through hunger and hard work. The hunger and hard work seemed to be a hell of a lot of fun. The deprivation was finally so rewarding you could hardly stand it. The farm was full of warm, fuzzy, furry, damp-nosed creatures: bawling calves and braying mules and dogs that were treated like people. There was a little pain here and there but just so much as would teach important lessons to all of us. It sometimes even brought a tear to the eye, but not a real tear because the tear only served to prove that a family out in the middle of nowhere scratching in the earth for survival didn't have it so bad after all. Somebody was forever petting and stroking the plump little animals, crooning to them, as they were raised for strange, unstated reasons, but surely not to be castrated and slaughtered and skinned and eaten. They were, after all, friends.

If somebody got sick, he'd just pop into an old, rattling but trust-   2
worthy pickup truck and go off to town, where a kindly doctor would receive him immediately into his office and effect an instant cure by looking down his throat and asking him to say Ah. No mention was made of payment.

As my boy and I came out of the movie, blinking in the sunlight,   3
it occurred to me that Disney and others—the folks who bring you *The Waltons,* say, or *The Little House on the Prairie*—had managed to sell this strange vision of poverty and country life not only to suburbanites, while the suburbanites stuffed themselves with malt balls and popcorn, but also to people in little towns throughout the South who had proof in their daily lives to the contrary.

All fantasy. Now there is nothing wrong with fantasy. I love it,   4
even live off it at times. But driving home, the reality behind the fantasy began to go bad on me. It seemed immoral and dangerous to show so many smiles without an occasional glimpse of the skull underneath.

As we were going down the driveway, my boy, Byron, said: "That   5
was a great movie, huh, Dad?"

"Yeah," I said. "Great."   6

"I wish I could've lived in a place like that," he said.   7

"No, you don't," I said. "You just think you do."   8

My grandmother in Bacon County, Georgia, raised biddies: tiny   9
cheeping bits of fluff that city folk allow their children to squeeze to
death at Easter. But city children are not the only ones who love biddies; hawks love them, too. Hawks like to swoop into the yard and
carry off one impaled on their curved talons. Perhaps my grandmother,
in her secret heart, knew that hawks even then were approaching the
time when they would be on the endangered-species list. Whether she
did or not, I'm sure she often felt she and her kind were already on the
list. It would not do.

I'll never forget the first time I saw her get rid of a hawk. Chickens,   10
as everybody knows, are cannibals. Let a biddy get a spot of blood on
it from a scrape or a raw place and the other biddies will simply eat it
alive. My grandmother penned up all the biddies except the puniest
one, already half pecked to death by the other cute little bits of fluff,
and she set it out in the open yard by itself. First, though, she put arsenic
on its head. I—about five years old and sucking on a sugar-tit—saw the
hawk come in low over the fence, its red tail fanned, talons stretched,
and nail the poisoned biddy where it squatted in the dust. The biddy
never made a sound as it was carried away. My gentle grandmother
watched it all with satisfaction before she let her other biddies out of
the pen.

Another moment from my childhood that comes instantly to mind   11
was about a chicken, too; a rooster. He was boss cock of the whole
farm, a magnificent bird nearly two feet tall. At the base of a chicken's
throat is its craw, a kind of pouch into which the bird swallows food,
as well as such things as grit, bits of rock and shell. For reasons I don't
understand they sometimes become craw-bound. The stuff in the craw
does not move; it remains in the craw and swells and will ultimately
cause death. That's what would have happened to the rooster if the
uncle who practically raised me hadn't said one day: "Son, we got to
fix him."

He tied the rooster's feet so we wouldn't be spurred and took out   12
his castrating knife, honed to a razor's edge, and sterilized it over a little
fire. He soaked a piece of fine fishing line and a needle in alcohol. I
held the rooster on its back, a wing in each hand. With the knife my
uncle split open the craw, cleaned it out, then sewed it up with the
fishing line. The rooster screamed and screamed. But it lived to be cock
of the walk again.

Country people never did anything worse to their stock than they   13
sometimes were forced to do to themselves. We had a man who farmed
with us, a man from up north somewhere who had drifted down into

Georgia with no money and a mouth full of bad teeth. Felix was his name and he was good with a plow and an ax, a hard worker. Most of the time you hardly knew he was on the place, he was so quiet and well-mannered. Except when his teeth began to bother him. And they bothered him more than a little. He lived in a shedlike little room off the side of the house. The room didn't have much in it: a ladder-back chair, a kerosene lamp, a piece of broken glass hanging on the wall over a pan of water where he shaved as often as once a week, a slat-board bed, and in one corner a chamber pot—which we called a slop jar—for use in the middle of the night when nature called. I slept in a room on the other side of the wall from him. I don't remember how old I was the night of his terrible toothache, but I do remember I was still young enough to wear a red cotton gown with five little pearl buttons down the front my grandmother had made for me.

When I heard him kick the slop jar, I knew it was his teeth. I just [14] didn't know how bad it was. When the ladder-back chair splintered, I knew it was a bad hurt, even for Felix. A few times that night I managed to slip off to sleep only to be jarred awake when he would run blindly into the thin wall separating us. He groaned and cursed, not loudly but steadily, sometimes for as long as half an hour. Ordinarily, my mother would have fixed a hot poultice for his jaw or at least tried to do *something*, but he was a proud man and when he was really dying from his teeth, he preferred to suffer, if not in silence, at least by himself. The whole house was kept awake most of the night by his thrashing and groaning, by the wash pan being knocked off the shelf, by his broken shaving mirror being broken again, and by his blind charges into the wall.

See, our kindly country dentist would not have gotten out of his [15] warm bed for anything less than money. And Felix didn't have any money. Besides, the dentist was in town ten miles away and we didn't have a rattling, trustworthy old truck. The only way we had to travel was two mules. And so there was nothing for Felix to do but what he was doing and it built practically no character at all. Looking back on it now, I can see that it wasn't even human. The sounds coming through the wall sure as hell weren't human anyway. On a Georgia dirt farm, pain reduced everything—man and beast alike—to the lowest common denominator. And it was pretty low and pretty common. Not something you'd want to watch while you ate malt balls and popcorn.

I was huddled under the quilts shaking with dread—my nerves [16] were shot by the age of four and so they have remained—when I heard Felix kick open the door to his room and thump down the wooden steps in his heavy brogan work shoes, which he'd not taken off all night. I couldn't imagine where he was going but I knew I wanted to watch whatever was about to happen. The only thing worse than my nerves is my curiosity, which has always been untempered by pity or compassion, a serious character failing in most societies but a sanity-saving virtue in Georgia when I was a child.

It was February and I went out the front door barefoot onto the 17 frozen ground. I met Felix coming around the corner of the house. In the dim light I could see the craziness in his eyes, the same craziness you see in the eyes of a trapped fox when it has not quite been able to chew through its own leg. Felix headed straight for the well, with me behind him, shaking in my thin cotton gown. He took the bucket from the nail on the rack built over the open well and sent it shooting down hard as he could to break the inch of ice that was over the water. As he was drawing the bucket up on the pulley, he seemed to see me for the first time.

"What the hell, boy! What the hell!" His voice was as mad as his 18 eyes and he either would not or could not say anything else. He held the bucket and took a mouthful of the freezing water. He held it a long time, spat it out, and filled his mouth again.

He turned the bucket loose and let it fall again into the well instead 19 of hanging it back on the nail where it belonged. With his cheeks swelling with water he took something out of the back pocket of his overalls. As soon as I saw what he had I knew beyond all belief and good sense what he meant to do, and suddenly I was no longer cold but stood on the frozen ground in a hot passion waiting to see him do it, to see if he *could* do it.

He had a piece of croker sack about the size of a half-dollar in his 20 left hand and a pair of wire pliers in his right. He spat the water out and reached way back in his rotten mouth and put the piece of sack over the tooth. He braced his feet against the well and stuck the pliers in over the sackcloth. He took the pliers in both hands and immediately a forked vein leapt in his forehead. The vein in his neck popped big as a pencil. He pulled and twisted and pulled and never made a sound.

It took him a long time and finally as he fought with the pliers and 21 with himself his braced feet slipped so that he was flat on his back when the blood broke from his mouth, followed by the pliers holding a tooth with roots half an inch long. He got slowly to his feet, sweat running off his face, and held the bloody tooth up between us.

He looked at the tooth and said in his old, recognizable voice: *"Hurt* 22 *now, you sumbitch!"*

BRIGID BROPHY

The Menace of Nature

Brigid Brophy (1929–   ), after completing an undergraduate degree
in classics at Oxford University, found work as a secretary first for a
London camera firm and later for a distributor of pornographic books.
By 1954, however, she had established herself as a prize-winning novelist. Since then she has produced several novels, scores of essays, a
psychoanalytic study of civilization (*Black Ship to Hell,* 1962), a book
on Mozart, and another on the "decadent" artist Aubrey Beardsley.
Perhaps the most characteristic of her titles, however, is *Fifty Works of
English Literature We Could Do Without* (1968). Brophy is an iconoclast
by nature: She challenges every complacent assumption she finds.
"The Menace of Nature" (first published in London's *New Statesman*
in 1965) attacks several beliefs most of us accept without a second
thought: that the city is stressful and the country relaxing, that a rural
landscape is more beautiful than a block of buildings, that when we
get "back to the land" we are making contact with something basic
to human nature. Not only does Brophy challenge beliefs some of
us cherish, but she addresses us with more familiarity than we are
accustomed to: She seems to pluck at our sleeves rather than address
us from behind a lectern.

So? Are you just back? Or are you, perhaps, staying on there for   1
the extra week? By "there" I mean, of course, one of the few spots left
where the machine has not yet gained the upper hand; some place as
yet unstrangled by motorways and unfouled by concrete mixers; a place
where the human spirit can still—but for how much longer?—steep
itself in natural beauty and recuperate after the nervous tension, the
sheer stress, of modern living.

Well (I assume you're *enough* recuperated to stand this informa-   2
tion?): I think you've been piously subscribing to a heresy. It's a heresy
I incline offhand to trace, with an almost personally piqued sense of
vendetta, to the old heresiarch himself, the sometimes great, often ba-
thetic but never cogently thoughtful poet, William Wordsworth. Since
the day he let the seeds of heresy fall (on, no doubt, the Braes of the
Yarrow or the Banks of Nith), the thing has spread and enlarged itself
into one of the great parroted, meaningless (but slightly paranoid) un-
truths of our age.

I am not trying to abolish the countryside. (I *state* this because it is   3
true; I emphasise it because I don't want the lynch mob outside my
window.) I'm not such a pig as to want the country built on or littered
up with bottles and plastic bags merely because it doesn't appeal to *me*.
As it happens, my own taste for countryside, though small, is existent.

I've found the country very pleasant to be driven through in a tolerably fast car by someone whose driving I trust and whose company I like. But I admit that landscape as such bores me—to the extent that I have noticed myself in picture galleries automatically pausing to look at "Landscape with Ruins" or "Bandits in a Landscape" but walking straight past the pure landscapes at a speed which is obviously trying to simulate the effect of being driven past in a car.

I'm not, however, out to dissuade *you* from spending your holiday 4 as a sort of legalised bandit in the landscape. Neither am I anti-holiday. Holidays have been sniped at lately as things everyone feels an obligation to enjoy but no one really does. Yet I suspect there would be fewer dissatisfied holiday-makers if social pressure didn't try to limit our choice to "Landscape" or "Landscape with Seascape." You can be made to feel quite guiltily antisocial in the summer months if you are, like me, constitutionally unable either to relax or to take a suntan. Indeed, relaxation is becoming this decade's social *sine qua non*, like Bridge in the 'thirties. They'll scarcely let you have a baby these days if you can't satisfy them beforehand you're adept at relaxing. But on the in some ways more private question of having a holiday, constitutional urbanites are still free, if only they can resist being shamed onto the beaches, to opt out of a rest and settle for the change which even the proverb allows to be as good as it. By simply exchanging their own for a foreign city, they are released from the routine of earning their daily bread and washing up after it, but don't suffer the disorientation, the uncorseted discomfort, which overtakes an urbanite cast up on a beach with no timetable to live by except the tides.

Still, it isn't in the holidays but during the rest of the year that the 5 great rural heresy does its damage. How many, for example, of the middle-class parents who bring up their children in London do so with unease or even apology, with a feeling that they are selfishly depriving the children of some "natural heritage" and sullying their childhood with urban impurities? Some parents even let this guilt drive them out to the suburbs or further, where they believe they cancel the egocentricity of their own need or desire for the town by undergoing the martyrdom of commuting. This parental masochism may secure the child a rural heritage (though parents should enquire, before moving, whether their child has the rural temperament and *wants* the rural heritage) but it deprives him of the cultural one; he gains the tennis club but is condemned to the tennis club light-opera society's amateur production of *No, No, Nanette* because the trains don't run late enough to bring him home after Sadler's Wells.[1]

The notion that "nature" and "nature study" are somehow "nice" 6 for children, regardless of the children's own temperament, is a senti-

---

1. Theater in London, primarily used by visiting theatrical companies.

mental piety—and often a hypocritical one, like the piety which thinks Sunday School nice for *them* though we don't go to church ourselves. (In fact, it is we middle-aged who may need fresh air and exercise; the young are cat-like enough to remain lithe without.) Historically, it is not inept to trace the supposed affinity between children and "nature" to Wordsworth's time. It was about that time that there settled on England, like a drizzle, the belief that sex is *not* "nice" for children. Children's sexual curiosity was diverted to "the birds and the bees" and gooseberry bushes; and birds, bees and bushes—in other words, "nature"—have remained "suitable" for children ever since.

If the romantic belief in children's innocence is now exploded, its   7 numinous energy has only gone to strengthen the even more absurd romantic belief in the innocence of landscape's, as opposed to man-created, beauty. But I reject utterly the imputation that a brook is purer than Bach or a breeze more innocent than *As You Like It*. I warn you I shall be suspicious of this aesthetic faculty of yours that renders you so susceptible to the beauty of Snowdon if it leaves you unable to see anything in All Souls', Langham Place; and I shall be downright sceptical of it if (I am making allowance for your sensibility to run exclusively in that landscape groove which mine leaves out) you doat on the Constable country but feel it vaguely impure to take a 74 to the V.&A. to see a Constable.[2]

You'll protest you feel no such impurity. Yet didn't you read the   8 first paragraph of this article without taking so much as a raised eye-brow's worth of exception? Didn't you let the assumption pass that the city is corrupt? Weren't you prepared to accept from me, as you have from a hundred august authorities—sociologists, physicians, psychologists—that *idée reçue*[3] about the nervous tension and stress of modern urban life? But what in heaven's name is this stressful modern urban life being compared with? Life in a medieval hamlet? Will no one take into account the symptoms into which the stress of *that* erupted—the epidemics of dancing madness and flagellation frenzy? Or life in a neolithic cave—whose stress one can only imagine and flinch at?

The truth is that the city is a device for *reducing* stress—by giving   9 humans a freer choice of escapes from the pressure (along with the weather) of their environment. The device doesn't always work perfectly: traffic jams *are* annoying; the motor car does maim and must be prevented from doing so: but the ambulance which arrives so mercifully

---

2. The references in the last sentence in the paragraph are *Snowdon*, highest mountain in Wales, in a district noted for scenic beauty; *All Souls', Langham Place*, church in London built from 1822 to 1825 by John Nash; *Constable country*, rural areas in southern Great Britain painted by the famous landscape painter John Constable (1776–1837); *a 74*, a bus; *the V.&A.*, the Victoria & Albert Museum in London, where a number of Constables are hung.
3. An idea generally accepted by everyone.

quick is also powered by a motor. The city is one of the great indispensable devices of civilisation (itself only a device for centralising beauty
and transmitting it as a heritage). It is one of the cardinal simple brilliant
inventions, like currency. Like currency, it is a medium of exchange
and thereby of choice—whereas the country is a place where one is
under the thumb of chance, constrained to love one's neighbour not
out of philanthropy but because there's no other company.

What's more, in the eighteenth century the city was suddenly up-   10
graded from a device of civilisation to a manifestation of it. The city
became an art form. (The form had been discovered, but not very consciously remarked, earlier. It was discovered, like many art forms, by
accident—often, as at Venice and Bruges, an accident of water.) We
are in dire danger now of clogging up our cities as devices and at the
same time despoiling them as works of art; and one of the biggest
villains in this process is our rural heresy.

Most western European beings have to live in cities, and all but   11
the tiny portion of them who are temperamental rustics would do so
contentedly, without wasting energy in guilt, and with an appreciative
eye for the architecturescapes round them, had they not been told that
liking the country is purer and more spiritual. Our cities run to squalor
and our machines run amok because our citizens' minds are not on the
job of mastering the machines and using them to make the cities efficient and beautiful. Their eyes are blind to the Chirico-esque[4] hand-
someness of the M1, because their hearts are set on a rustic Never-Never
Land. Rustic sentimentality makes us build our suburban villas to mimic
cottages, and then pebble-dash their outside walls in pious memory of
the holiday we spent sitting agonised on the shingle. The lovely terraced
façades of London are being undermined, as by subsidence, by our
yearning, our sickly nostalgia, for a communal country childhood that
never existed. We neglect our towns for a fantasy of going "back" to
the land, back to our "natural" state. But there isn't and never was a
natural man. We are a species that doesn't occur wild. No pattern in
his genes instructs man on what pattern to build his nest. Instead, if
he's fortunate, the Muses whisper to him the ground-plan of an architectural folly. Even in his cave, he frescoed the walls. All that is infallibly
natural to our species is to make things that are artificial. We are *homo
artifex, homo faber, homo Fabergé.*[5] Yet we are so ignorant of our own

---

4. The allusion is to Giorgio de Chirico, an early-twentieth-century Italian painter whose
mysterious, symbolic work influenced surrealist painters. The M1 is a major northbound
highway out of London.
5. Very freely translatable either as "man the craftsman, man the builder, man the perfumed" or as "man the tool-user, man the engineer, man the jeweler." Fabergé is the
name of both an international manufacturer of fragrances and a brilliant Russian goldsmith, known especially for his Imperial Easter eggs.

human nature that our cities are falling into disrepair and all we worry about is their encroachment on "nature."

For, as I said at the start, the rural fantasy is paranoid. A glance at history shews that it is human life which is frail, and civilisation which flickers in constant danger of being blown out. But the rural fantasy insists that every plant is a delicate plant. The true paranoid situation is on the other foot. I wouldn't wish to do (and if we live at sensibly high densities there's no need to do) either, but were I forced either to pull down a Nash terrace or to build over a meadow, I'd choose the latter. If you don't like what you've put up on the meadow, you can take it away again and the meadow will re-seed itself in a year or two; but human semen is lucky if it engenders an architectural genius a century. The whole Wordsworthian fallacy consists in gravely underestimating the toughness of plants. In fact, no sooner does civilisation admit a crack—no sooner does a temple of Apollo lapse into disuse—than a weed forces its wiry stem through the crack and urges the blocks of stone further apart. During the last war, the bomber engines were hardly out of earshot before the loosestrife[6] leapt up on the bombed site. Whether we demolish our cities in a third world war or just let them tumble into decay, the seeds of the vegetable kingdom are no doubt waiting to seize on the rubble or sprout through the cracks. *Aux armes, citoyens.*[7] To your trowels and mortar. Man the concrete mixers. The deep mindless silence of the countryside is massing in the Green Belt, ready to move in.

VICKI HEARNE

What's Wrong with Animal Rights

Vicki Hearne (1946–   ), known equally for her creative writing and animal training, is a professor of English at Yale and consultant for the Yale Institution for Social and Policy Studies. Born in Austin, Texas, Hearne received her B.A. from the University of California at Riverside, where she served as a lecturer in the early eighties. Her books of poetry include *Nervous Horses* (1980) and *The Parts of Light: Poems* (1994), and she has also written a novel, *The White German Shepherd* (1988). Hearne is also a weekly columnist on animal issues for the *Los Angeles Times* and has published several works of nonfiction

6. A wild flowering plant.
7. "To arms, citizens"—a call to battle (the third line of the French national anthem, *La Marseillaise,* written at the time of the French Revolution, 1792).

about animals, including *Adam's Task: Calling Animals by Name* (1988), *Bandit: Dossier of a Dangerous Dog* (1991), and *Animal Happiness* (1993). In *Adam's Task,* a well-received but controversial book, Hearne spells out her philosophy of domesticated animals and their relationship to humans; this book lays the foundation for her essay "What's Wrong with Animal Rights," first published in *Harper's* (September 1991) and then collected in *The Best American Essays, 1992.*

Not all happy animals are alike. A Doberman going over a hurdle   1
after a small wooden dumbbell is sleek, all arcs of harmonious power. A basset hound cheerfully performing the same exercise exhibits harmonies of a more lugubrious nature. There are chimpanzees who love precision the way musicians or fanatical housekeepers or accomplished hypochondriacs do; others for whom happiness is a matter of invention and variation—chimp vaudevillians. There is a rhinoceros whose happiness, as near as I can make out, is in needing to be trained every morning, all over again, or else he "forgets" his circus routine, and in this you find a clue to the slow, deep, quiet chuckle of his happiness and to the glory of the beast. Happiness for Secretariat[1] is in his ebullient bound, that joyful length of stride. For the draft horse or the weight-pull dog, happiness is of a different shape, more awesome and less obviously intelligent. When the pulling horse is at its most intense, the animal goes into himself, allocating all of the educated power that organizes his desire to dwell in fierce and delicate intimacy with that power, leans into the harness, and MAKES THAT SUCKER MOVE.

If we are speaking of human beings and use the phrase "animal   2
happiness," we tend to mean something like "creature comforts." The emblems of this are the golden retriever rolling in the grass, the horse with his nose deep in the oats, the kitty by the fire. Creature comforts are important to animals—"Grub first, then ethics" is a motto that would describe many a wise Labrador retriever, and I have a pit bull named Annie whose continual quest for the perfect pillow inspires her to awesome feats. But there is something more to animals, a capacity for satisfactions that come from work in the fullest sense—what is known in philosophy and in this country's Declaration of Independence as "happiness." This is a sense of personal achievement, like the satisfaction felt by a good wood-carver or a dancer or a poet or an accomplished dressage horse. It is a happiness that, like the artist's, must come from something within the animal, something trainers call "talent." Hence, it cannot be imposed on the animal. But it is also something that does not come *ex nihilo.*[2] If it had not been a fairly ordinary thing,

---

1. Secretariat: U.S. racehorse who won the Kentucky Derby in 1973.
2. ex nihilo: Latin phrase meaning "from" or "out of nothing."

in one part of the world, to teach young children to play the pianoforte, it is doubtful that Mozart's music would exist.

Happiness is often misunderstood as a synonym for pleasure or as an antonym for suffering. But Aristotle associated happiness with ethics—codes of behavior that urge us toward the sensation of getting it right, a kind of work that yields the "click" of satisfaction upon solving a problem or surmounting an obstacle. In his *Ethics*, Aristotle wrote, "If happiness is activity in accordance with excellence, it is reasonable that it should be in accordance with the highest excellence." Thomas Jefferson identified the capacity for happiness as one of the three fundamental rights on which all others are based: "life, liberty, and the pursuit of happiness."

I bring up this idea of happiness as a form of work because I am an animal trainer, and work is the foundation of the happiness a trainer and an animal discover together. I bring up these words also because they cannot be found in the lexicon of the animal-rights movement. This absence accounts for the uneasiness toward the movement of most people, who sense that rights advocates have a point but take it too far when they liberate snails or charge that goldfish at the county fair are suffering. But the problem with the animal-rights advocates is not that they take it too far; it's that they've got it all wrong.

Animal rights are built upon a misconceived premise that rights were created to prevent us from unnecessary suffering. You can't find an animal-rights book, video, pamphlet, or rock concert in which someone doesn't mention the Great Sentence, written by Jeremy Bentham in 1789. Arguing in favor of such rights, Bentham wrote: "The question is not, Can they *reason*? nor, can they *talk*? but, can they suffer?"

The logic of the animal-rights movement places suffering at the iconographic center of a skewed value system. The thinking of its proponents—given eerie expression in a virtually sadopornographic sculpture of a tortured monkey that won a prize for its compassionate vision—has collapsed into a perverse conundrum. Today the loudest voices calling for—demanding—the destruction of animals are the humane organizations. This is an inevitable consequence of the apotheosis of the drive to relieve suffering: death is the ultimate release. To compensate for their contradictions, the humane movement has demonized, in this century and the last, those who made animal happiness their business: veterinarians, trainers, and the like. We think of Louis Pasteur as the man whose work saved you and me and your dog and cat from rabies, but antivivisectionists of the time claimed that rabies increased in areas where there were Pasteur[3] Institutes.

3. Pasteur (1822–1895): French chemist and microbiologist whose experiments with rabbits allowed him to develop a vaccine that protected humans from rabies and bankrolled further research at his Institute.

An anti-rabies public relations campaign mounted in England in ⁷ the 1880s by the Royal Society for the Prevention of Cruelty to Animals and other organizations led to orders being issued to club any dog found not wearing a muzzle. England still has her cruel and unnecessary law that requires an animal to spend six months in quarantine before being allowed loose in the country. Most of the recent propaganda about pit bulls—the crazy claim that they "take hold with their front teeth while they chew away with their rear teeth" (which would imply, incorrectly, that they have double jaws)—can be traced to literature published by the Humane Society of the United States during the fall of 1987 and earlier. If your neighbors want your dog or horse impounded and destroyed because he is a nuisance—say the dog barks, or the horse attracts flies—it will be the local Humane Society to whom your neighbors turn for action.

In a way, everyone has the opportunity to know that the history ⁸ of the humane movement is largely a history of miseries, arrests, prosecutions, and death. The Humane Society is the pound, the place with the decompression chamber or the lethal injections. You occasionally find worried letters about this in Ann Landers's column.

Animal-rights publications are illustrated largely with photographs ⁹ of two kinds of animals—"Helpless Fluff" and "Agonized Fluff," the two conditions in which some people seem to prefer their animals, because any other version of an animal is too complicated for propaganda. In the introduction to his book *Animal Liberation,* Peter Singer says somewhat smugly that he and his wife have no animals and, in fact, don't much care for them. This is offered as evidence of his objectivity and ethical probity. But it strikes me as an odd, perhaps obscene underpinning for an ethical project that encourages university and high school students to cherish their ignorance of, say, great bird dogs as proof of their devotion to animals.

I would like to leave these philosophers behind, for they are inept ¹⁰ connoisseurs of suffering who might revere my Airedale for his capacity to scream when subjected to a blowtorch but not for his wit and courage, not for his natural good manners that are a gentle rebuke to ours. I want to celebrate the moment not long ago when, at his first dog show, my Airedale, Drummer, learned that there can be a public place where his work is respected. I want to celebrate his meticulousness, his happiness upon realizing at the dog show that no one would swoop down upon him and swamp him with the goo-goo excesses known as the "teddy-bear complex" but that people actually got out of his way, gave him room to work. I want to say, "There can be a six-and-a-half-month-old puppy who can care about accuracy, who can be fastidious, and whose fastidiousness will be a foundation for courage later." I want to say, "Leave my puppy alone!"

I want to leave the philosophers behind, but I cannot, in part be-   11
cause the philosophical problems that plague academicians of the animal-rights movement are illuminating. They wonder, do animals have
rights or do they have interests? Or, if these rightists lead particularly
unexamined lives, they dismiss that question as obvious (yes, of course
animals have rights, prima facie[4]) and proceed to enumerate them,
James Madison style. This leads to the issuance of bills of rights—the
right to an environment, the right not to be used in medical experiments—and other forms of trivialization.

The calculus of suffering can be turned against the philosophers of   12
festering flesh, even in the case of food animals, or exotic animals who
perform in movies and circuses. It is true that it hurts to be slaughtered
by man, but it doesn't hurt nearly as much as some of the cunningly
cruel arrangements meted out by "Mother Nature." In Africa, 75 percent of the lions cubbed do not survive to the age of two. For those
who make it to two, the average age at death is ten years. Asali, the
movie and TV lioness, was still working at age twenty-one. There are
fates worse than death, but twenty-one years of a close working relationship with Hubert Wells, Asali's trainer, is not one of them. Dorset
sheep and polled Herefords would not exist at all were they not in a
symbiotic relationship with human beings.

A human being living in the "wild"—somewhere, say, without the   13
benefits of medicine and advanced social organization—would probably have a life expectancy of from thirty to thirty-five years. A human
being living in "captivity"—in, say, a middle-class neighborhood of
what the Centers for Disease Control call a Metropolitan Statistical
Area—has a life expectancy of seventy or more years. For orangutans
in the wild in Borneo and Malaysia, the life expectancy is thirty-five
years; in captivity, fifty years. The wild is not a suffering-free zone or
all that frolicsome a location.

The questions asked by animal-rights activists are flawed, because   14
they are built on the concept that the origin of rights is in the avoidance
of suffering rather than in the pursuit of happiness. The question that
needs to be asked—and that will put us in closer proximity to the
truth—is not, do they have rights? or, what are those rights? but rather,
what is a right?

Rights originate in committed relationships and can be found, both   15
intact and violated, wherever one finds such relationships—in social
compacts, within families, between animals, and between people and
nonhuman animals. This is as true when the nonhuman animals in
question are lions or parakeets as when they are dogs. It is my Airedale
whose excellencies have my attention at the moment, so it is with
reference to him that I will consider the question, what is a right?

4. prima facie: Latin phrase meaning "at first sight" or "before close inspection."

When I imagine situations in which it naturally arises that A de- [16] fends or honors or respects B's rights, I imagine situations in which the relationship between A and B can be indicated with a possessive pronoun. I might say, "Leave her alone, she's my daughter" or "That's what she wants, and she is my daughter. I think I am bound to honor her wants." Similarly, "Leave her alone, she's my mother." I am more tender of the happiness of my mother, my father, my child, than I am of other people's family members; more tender of my friends' happinesses than your friends' happinesses, unless you and I have a mutual friend.

Possession of a being by another has come into more and more [17] disrepute, so that the common understanding of one person possessing another is slavery. But the important detail about the kind of possessive pronoun that I have in mind is reciprocity: if I have a friend, she has a friend. If I have a daughter, she has a mother. The possessive does not bind one of us while freeing the other; it cannot do that. Moreover, should the mother reject the daughter, the word that applies is "disown." The form of disowning that most often appears in the news is domestic violence. Parents abuse children; husbands batter wives.

Some cases of reciprocal possessives have built-in limitations, such [18] as "my patient/my doctor" or "my student/my teacher" or "my agent/ my client." Other possessive relations are extremely limited but still remarkably binding: "my neighbor" and "my country" and "my president."

The responsibilities and the ties signaled by reciprocal possession [19] typically are hard to dissolve. It can be as difficult to give up an enemy as to give up a friend, and often the one becomes the other, as though the logic of the possessive pronoun outlasts the forms it chanced to take at a given moment, as though we were stuck with one another. In these bindings, nearly inextricable, are found the origin of our rights. They imply a possessiveness but also recognize an acknowledgment by each side of the other's existence.

The idea of democracy is dependent on the citizens' having knowl- [20] edge of the government; that is, realizing that the government exists and knowing how to claim rights against it. I know this much because I get mail from the government and see its "representatives" running about in uniforms. Whether I actually have any rights in relationship to the government is less clear, but the idea that I do is symbolized by the right to vote. I obey the government, and, in theory, it obeys me, by counting my ballot, reading the *Miranda*[5] warning to me, agreeing to be bound by the Constitution. My friend obeys me as I obey her; the

---

5. Miranda warning: "You have the right to remain silent," etc. The formulaic warning police officers deliver to suspects to inform them of their right to avoid self-incrimination.

government "obeys" me to some extent, and, to a different extent, I obey it.

What kind of thing can my Airedale, Drummer, have knowledge 21
of? He can know that I exist and through that knowledge can claim his happinesses, with varying degrees of success, both with me and against me. Drummer can also know about larger human or dog communities than the one that consists only of him and me. There is my household—the other dogs, the cats, my husband. I have had enough dogs on campuses to know that he can learn that Yale exists as a neighborhood or village. My older dog, Annie, not only knows that Yale exists but can tell Yalies from townies, as I learned while teaching there during labor troubles.

Dogs can have elaborate conceptions of human social structures, 22
and even of something like their rights and responsibilities within them, but these conceptions are never elaborate enough to construct a rights relationship between a dog and the state, or a dog and the Humane Society. Both of these are concepts that depend on writing and memoranda, officers in uniform, plaques and seals of authority. All of these are literary constructs, and all of them are beyond a dog's ken, which is why the mail carrier who doesn't also happen to be a dog's friend is forever an intruder—this is why dogs bark at mailmen.

It is clear enough that natural rights relations can arise between 23
people and animals. Drummer, for example, can insist, "Hey, let's go outside and do something!" if I have been at my computer several days on end. He can both refuse to accept various of my suggestions and tell me when he fears for his life—such as the time when the huge, white flapping flag appeared out of nowhere, as it seemed to him, on the town green one evening when we were working. I can (and do) say to him either, "Oh, you don't have to worry about that" or, "Uh oh, you're right, Drum, that guy looks dangerous." Just as the government and I—two different species of organism—have developed improvised ways of communicating, such as the vote, so Drummer and I have worked out a number of ways to make our expressions known. Largely through obedience, I have taught him a fair amount about how to get responses from me. Obedience is reciprocal; you cannot get responses from a dog to whom you do not respond accurately. I have enfranchised him in a relationship to me by educating him, creating the conditions by which he can achieve a certain happiness specific to a dog, maybe even specific to an Airedale, inasmuch as this same relationship has allowed me to plumb the happiness of being a trainer and writing this article.

Instructions in this happiness are given terms that are alien to a 24
culture in which liver treats, fluffy windup toys, and miniature sweaters are confused with respect and work. Jack Knox, a sheepdog trainer

originally from Scotland, will shake his crook at a novice handler who makes a promiscuous move to praise a dog, and will call out in his Scottish accent, "Eh! Eh! Get back, get BACK! Ye'll no be abusin' the dogs like that in my clinic." America is a nation of abused animals, Knox says, because we are always swooping at them with praise, "no gi'ing them their freedom." I am reminded of Rainer Maria Rilke's account in which the Prodigal Son leaves—has to leave—because everyone loves him, even the dogs love him, and he has no path to the delicate and fierce truth of himself. Unconditional praise and love, in Rilke's story, disenfranchise us, distract us from what truly excites our interest.

In the minds of some trainers and handlers, praise is dishonesty. 25 Paradoxically, it is a kind of contempt for animals that masquerades as a reverence for helplessness and suffering. The idea of freedom means that you do not, at least not while Jack Knox is nearby, helpfully guide your dog through the motions of, say, herding over and over—what one trainer calls "explainy-wainy." This is rote learning. It works tolerably well on some handlers, because people have vast unconscious minds and can store complex preprogrammed behaviors. Dogs, on the other hand, have almost no unconscious minds, so they can learn only by thinking. Many children are like this until educated out of it.

If I tell my Airedale to sit and stay on the town green, and someone 26 comes up and burbles, "What a pretty thing you are," he may break his stay to go for a caress. I pull him back and correct him for breaking. Now he holds his stay because I have blocked his way to movement but not because I have punished him. (A correction blocks one path as it opens another for desire to work; punishment blocks desire and opens nothing.) He holds his stay now, and—because the stay opens this possibility of work, new to a heedless young dog—he watches. If the person goes on talking, and isn't going to gush with praise, I may heel Drummer out of his stay and give him an "Okay" to make friends. Sometimes something about the person makes Drummer feel that reserve is in order. He responds to an insincere approach by sitting still, going down into himself, and thinking, "This person has no business pawing me. I'll sit very still, and he will go away." If the person doesn't take the hint from Drummer, I'll give the pup a little backup by saying, "Please don't pet him, he's working," even though he was not under any command.

The pup reads this, and there is a flicker of a working trust now 27 stirring in the dog. Is the pup grateful? When the stranger leaves, does he lick my hand, full of submissive blandishments? This one doesn't. This one says nothing at all, and I say nothing much to him. This is a working trust we are developing, not a mutual congratulation society. My backup is praise enough for him; the use he makes of my support is praise enough for me.

Listening to a dog is often praise enough. Suppose it is just after   28
dark and we are outside. Suddenly there is a shout from the house.
The pup and I both look toward the shout and then toward each other:
"What do you think?" I don't so much as cock my head, because
Drummer is growing up, and I want to know what he thinks. He takes
a few steps toward the house, and I follow. He listens again and compre-
hends that it's just Holly, who at fourteen is much given to alarming
cries and shouts. He shrugs at me and goes about his business. I say
nothing. To praise him for this performance would make about as much
sense as praising a human being for the same thing. Thus:

A. What's that?
B. I don't know. [Listens] Oh, it's just Holly.
A. What a gooooooood human being!
B. Huh?

This is one small moment in a series of like moments that will   29
culminate in an Airedale who on a Friday will have the discrimination
and confidence required to take down a man who is attacking me with
a knife and on Saturday clown and play with the children at the annual
Orange Empire Dog Club Christmas party.

People who claim to speak for animal rights are increasingly de-   30
voted to the idea that the very keeping of a dog or a horse or a gerbil
or a lion is in and of itself an offense. The more loudly they speak, the
less likely they are to be in a rights relation to any given animal, because
they are spending so much time in airplanes or transmitting fax an-
nouncements of the latest Sylvester Stallone anti-fur rally. In a 1988
Harper's forum, for example, Ingrid Newkirk, the national director of
People for the Ethical Treatment of Animals, urged that domestic pets be
spayed and neutered and ultimately phased out. She prefers, it appears,
wolves—and wolves someplace else—to Airedales and, by a logic
whose interior structure is both emotionally and intellectually forever
closed to Drummer, claims thereby to be speaking for "animal rights."

She is wrong. I am the only one who can own up to my Airedale's   31
inalienable rights. Whether or not I do it perfectly at any given moment
is no more refutation of this point than whether I am perfectly my
husband's mate at any given moment refutes the fact of marriage. Only
people who know Drummer, and whom he can know, are capable of
this relationship. PETA[6] and the Humane Society and the ASPCA and
the Congress and NOW—as institutions—do have the power to affect
my ability to grant rights to Drummer but are otherwise incapable of
creating conditions or laws or rights that would increase his happiness.

---

6. PETA: People for the Ethical Treatment of Animals; ASPCA: American Society for the
Prevention of Cruelty to Animals; NOW: National Organization for Women.

Only Drummer's owner has the power to obey him—to obey who he is and what he is capable of—deeply enough to grant him his rights and open up the possibility of happiness.

JOSEPH BRUCHAC III

Turtle Meat

Joseph Bruchac III (1942–   ), a descendant of Abnaki Indians and Slovakian immigrants to the United States, has lived most of his life in upper New York state. Born in Saratoga Springs, he took his bachelor's degree at Cornell University, served three years as a high school teacher in Ghana, West Africa, and returned to his native state to do graduate work at Syracuse University, SUNY-Albany, and Union Graduate School (Ph.D., 1975). A prolific writer and translator of West African and Iroquois literature, he has contributed poems to over four hundred periodicals and published several collections, including *Entering Onondaga* (1978), *Translator's Son* (1981), and *Remembering the Dawn* (1983). He is also the author of several novels and collections of short stories, including *The Dreams of Jesse Brown* (1977), *Fox Song* (1993), and *The Earth Under Sky Bear's Feet* (1995), and a collector of Native American tales and legends, found in such works as *The Native American Sweat Lodge: History and Legends* (1993) and *The First Strawberries: A Cherokee Story* (1993). Recently Bruchac has devoted himself to promoting the works of fellow Native Americans, West Africans, and American prison inmates. Not a cloistered scholar, Bruchac says he likes "to work outside, in the earthmother's soil, with my hands." Bruchac's religion is animism—belief in an indwelling soul in both animate beings and inanimate objects. "Turtle Meat" appeared in *Earth Power Coming: Short Fiction in Native American Literature* (1983).

"Old Man, come in. I need you!"   1

The old woman's cracked voice carried out to the woodshed near   2
the overgrown field. Once it had been planted with corn and beans, the whole two acres. But now mustard rolled heads in the wind and wild carrot bobbed among nettles and the blue flowers of thistles. *A goat would like to eat those thistles,* Homer LaWare thought. *Too bad I'm too old to keep a goat.* He put down the ax handle he had been carving, cast one quick look at the old bamboo fishing pole hanging over the door and then stood up.

"Coming over," he called out. With slow careful steps he crossed   3
the fifty yards between his shed and the single-story house with the picture window and the gold-painted steps. He swung open the screen

door and stepped over the dishes full of dog food. *Always in front of the door,* he thought.

"Where?" he called from the front room. 4

"Back here, I'm in the bathroom. I can't get up." 5

He walked as quickly as he could through the cluttered kitchen. 6
The breakfast dishes were still on the table. He pushed open the bathroom door. Mollie was sitting on the toilet.

"Amalia Wind, what's wrong?" he said. 7

"My legs seem to of locked, Homer. Please just help me to get up. 8
I've been hearing the dogs yapping for me outside the door and the
poor dears couldn't even get to me. Just help me up."

He slipped his hand under her elbow and lifted her gently. He could 9
see that the pressure of his fingers on the white wrinkled flesh of her
arm was going to leave marks. She'd always been like that. She always
bruised easy. But it hadn't stopped her from coming for him . . . and
getting him, all those years ago. It hadn't stopped her from throwing
Jake Wind out of her house and bringing Homer LaWare to her farm
to be the hired man.

Her legs were unsteady for a few seconds but then she seemed to 10
be all right. He removed his arms from her.

"Just don't know how it happened, Homer. I ain't so old as that, 11
am I, Old Man?"

"No, Amalia. That must of was just a cramp. Nothing more than 12
that."

They were still standing in the bathroom. Her long grey dress had 13
fallen down to cover her legs but her underpants were still around her
ankles. He felt awkward. Even after all these years, he felt awkward.

"Old Man, you just get out and do what you were doing. A woman 14
has to have her privacy. Get now."

"You sure?" 15

"Sure? My Lord! If I wasn't sure you think I'd have any truck with 16
men like you?" She poked him in the ribs. "You know what you should
do, Old Man? You should go down to the pond and do that fishing
you said you were going to."

He didn't want to leave her alone, but he didn't want to tell her 17
that. And there was something in him that urged him towards that
pond, the pond where the yellow perch had been biting for the last few
days according to Jack Crandall. Jack had told him that when he
brought his ax by to have Homer fit a new handle.

"I still got Jack's ax to fix, Amalia." 18

"And when did it ever take you more than a minute to fit a handle 19
into anything, *Old Man*?" There was a wicked gleam in her eye. For a
few seconds she looked forty years younger in the old man's eyes.

He shook his head. 20

"Miss Wind, I swear those ladies were right when they said you 21 was going to hell." She made a playful threatening motion with her hand and he backed out the door. "But I'm going."

It took him another hour to finish carving the handle to the right   22
size. It slid into the head like a hand going into a velvet glove. His hands shook when he started the steel wedge that would hold it tight, but it took only three strokes with the maul to put the wedge in. He looked at his hands, remembering the things they'd done. Holding the reins of the last horse they'd had on the farm—twenty years ago. Or was it thirty? Lifting the sheets back from Mollie's white body that first night. Swinging in tight fists at the face of Jake Wind the night he came back, drunk and with a loaded .45 in his hand. He'd gone down hard and Homer had emptied the shells out of the gun and broken its barrel with his maul on his anvil. Though Jake had babbled of the law that night, neither the law nor Jake ever came back to the Wind farm. It had been Amalia's all along. Her father'd owned it and Jake had married her for it. She'd never put the property in any man's name, never would. That was what she always said.

"I'm not asking, Amalia," that was what Homer had said to her   23
after the first night they'd spent in the brass bed, just before he'd dressed and gone back to sleep the night away in his cot in the shed. He always slept there. All the years. "I'm not asking for any property, Amalia. It's the Indian in me that don't want to own no land."

That was Homer's favorite saying. Whenever there was something   24
about him that seemed maybe different from what others expected he would say simply, "It's the Indian in me." Sometimes he thought of it not just as a part of him but as another man, a man with a name he didn't know but would recognize if he heard it.

His father had said that same phrase often. His father had come   25
down from Quebec and spoke French and, sometimes, to his first wife who had died when Homer was six, another language that Homer never heard again after her death. His father had been a quiet man who made baskets from the ash trees that grew on their farm. "But he never carried them into town," Homer said with pride. "He just stayed on the farm and let people come to him if they wanted to buy them."

The farm had gone to a younger brother who sold out and moved   26
West. There had been two other children. None of them got a thing, except Homer who got his father's best horse. In those years Homer was working for Seneca Smith at his mill. Woods work, two-man saws and sledding the logs out in the snow. He had done it until his thirtieth year when Amalia had asked him to come and work her farm. Though people had talked, he had done it. When anyone asked why he let himself be run by a woman that way he said, in the same quiet voice his father had used, "It's the Indian in me."

The pond was looking glass smooth. Homer stood beside the boat.   27
Jack Crandall had given him the key to it. He looked in the water. He

saw his face, the skin lined and brown as an old map. Wattles of flesh hung below his chin like the comb of a rooster.

"Shit, you're a good-looking man, Homer LaWare," he said to his   28
reflection. "Easy to see what a woman sees in you." He thought again of Mollie sitting in the rocker and looking out the picture window. As he left he heard her old voice calling the names of the small dogs she loved so much. *Those dogs were the only ones ever give back her love,* he thought, *not that no-good daughter. Last time she come was Christmas in '68 to give her that pissy green shawl and try to run me off again.*

Homer stepped into the boat. Ripples wiped his face from the sur-   29
face of the pond. He put his pole and the can of worms in front of him and slipped the oars into the oarlocks, one at a time, breathing hard as he did so. He pulled the anchor rope into the boat and looked out across the water. A brown stick projected above the water in the middle of the pond. *Least it looks like a stick, but if it moves it . . .* The stick moved . . . slid across the surface of the water for a few feet and then disappeared. He watched with narrowed eyes until it reappeared a hundred feet further out. It was a turtle, a snapping turtle. Probably a big one.

"I see you out there, Turtle," Homer said. "Maybe you and me are   30
going to see more of each other."

He felt in his pocket for the familiar feel of his bone-handled knife.   31
He pushed the red handkerchief that held it deep in his pocket more firmly into place. Then he began to row. He stopped in the middle of the pond and began to fish. Within a few minutes he began to pull in the fish, yellow-stomached perch with bulging dark eyes. Most of them were a foot long. He stopped when he had a dozen and began to clean them, leaving the baited line in the water. He pulled out the bone-handled knife and opened it. The blade was thin as the handle of a spoon from thirty years of sharpening. It was like a razor. Homer always carried a sharp knife. He made a careful slit from the ventral opening of the fish up to its gills and spilled out the guts into the water, leaning over the side of the boat as he did so. He talked as he cleaned the fish.

"Old Knife, you cut good," he said. He had cleaned nearly every   32
fish, hardly wasting a moment. Almost as fast as when he was a boy. *Some things didn't go from you so . . .*

The jerking of his pole brought him back from his thoughts. It was   33
being dragged overboard. He dropped the knife on the seat and grabbed the pole as it went over. He pulled up on it and it bent almost double. *No fish pulls like that.* It was the turtle. He began reeling the line in, slow and steady so it wouldn't break. Soon he saw it, wagging its head back and forth, coming up from the green depths of the pond where it had been gorging on the perch guts and grabbed his worm.

"Come up and talk, Turtle," Homer said.   34

The turtle opened its mouth as if to say something and the hook   35 slipped out, the pole jerking back in Homer's hands. Its jaws were too tough for the hook to stick in. But the turtle stayed there, just under the water. It was big, thirty pounds at least. It was looking for more food. Homer put another worm on the hook with trembling hands and dropped it in front of the turtle's mouth.

"Turtle, take this one too."   36

He could see the wrinkled skin under its throat as it turned its head.   37
A leech of some kind was on the back of its head, another hanging onto its right leg. It was an old turtle. Its skin was rough, its shell green with algae. It grabbed the hook with a sideways turn of its head. As Homer pulled up to snag the hook it reached forward with its paws and grabbed the line like a man grabbing a rope. Its front claws were as long as the teeth of a bear.

Homer pulled. The turtle kept the hook in its mouth and rose to   38
the surface. It was strong and the old man wondered if he could hold it up. Did he want turtle meat that much? But he didn't cut the line. The mouth was big enough to take off a finger, but he kept pulling in line. It was next to the boat and the hook was only holding because of the pressure on the line. A little slack and it would be gone. Homer slipped the pole under his leg and grabbed with his other hand for the anchor rope, began to fasten a noose in it as the turtle shook its head, moving the twelve-foot boat as it struggled. He could smell it now. The heavy musk of the turtle was everywhere. It wasn't a good smell or a bad smell. It was only the smell of the turtle.

Now the noose was done. He hung it over the side. It was time for   39
the hard part now, the part that was easy for him when his arms were young and his chest wasn't caved in like a broken box. He reached down fast and grabbed the tail, pulling it so that the turtle came half out of the water. The boat almost tipped but Homer kept his balance. The turtle swung its head, mouth open and wide enough to swallow a softball. It hissed like a snake, ready to grab at anything within reach. With his other hand, gasping as he did it, feeling the turtle's rough tail tear the skin of his palm as it slipped from his other hand, Homer swung the noose around the turtle's head. Its own weight pulled the slip knot tight. The turtle's jaws clamped tight with a snap on Homer's sleeve.

"Turtle, I believe I got you and you got me," Homer said. He slipped   40
a turn of rope around his left foot with his free arm. He kept pulling back as hard as he could to free his sleeve but the turtle had it. "I understand you, Turtle," he said, "you don't like to let go." He breathed hard, closed his eyes for a moment. Then he took the knife in his left hand. He leaned over and slid it across the turtle's neck. Dark fluid blossomed out into the water. A hissing noise came from between the clenched jaws, but the turtle held onto the old man's sleeve. For a long time the blood came out but the turtle still held on. Finally Homer took

the knife and cut the end of his sleeve off, leaving it in the turtle's mouth.

He sat up straight for the first time since he had hooked the turtle 41 and looked around. It was dark. He could hardly see the shore. He had been fighting the turtle for longer than he thought.

By the time he had reached the shore and docked the boat the 42 sounds of the turtle banging itself against the side of the boat had stopped. He couldn't tell if blood was still flowing from its cut throat because night had turned all of the water that same color. He couldn't find the fish in the bottom of the boat. It didn't matter. The raccoons could have them. He had his knife and his pole and the turtle. He dragged it back up to the old Ford truck. It was too heavy to carry.

There were cars parked in the driveway when he pulled in. He had 43 to park near the small mounds beside his shed that were marked with wooden plaques and neatly lettered names. He could hear voices as he walked through the darkness.

"Old fool's finally come back," he heard a voice saying. The voice 44 was rough as a rusted hinge. It was the voice of Amalia's daughter.

He pushed through the door. "Where's Amalia?" he said. Someone 45 screamed. The room was full of faces and they were all looking at him.

"Old bastard looks like he scalped someone," a pock-faced man 46 with grey crew-cut hair muttered.

Homer looked at himself. His arms and hands were covered with 47 blood of the turtle. His tattered right sleeve barely reached his elbow. His trousers were muddy. His fly was half-way open. "Where's Amalia?" he demanded again.

"What the hell have you been up to, you old fart?" said the raspy 48 voice of the daughter. He turned to stare into her loose-featured face. She was sitting in Amalia's rocker.

"I been fishin'." 49

The daughter stood up and walked toward him. She looked like 50 her father. Jake Wind was written all over her face, carved into her bones.

"You want to know where Moms is, huh? Wanta know where 51 your old sweetheart's gone to? Well, I'll tell you. She's been sent off to a home that'll take care of her, even if she is cracked. Come in and find her sittin' talking to dogs been dead for years. Dishes full of dog food for ghosts. Maybe you better eat some of it because your meal ticket's been cancelled, you old bastard. This man is a doctor and he's decided my dear mother was mentally incompetent. The ambulance took her outta here half an hour ago."

She kept talking, saying things she had longed to say for years. 52 Homer LaWare wasn't listening. His eyes took in the details of the room he had walked through every day for the last forty years, the furniture he had mended when it was broken, the picture window he had installed, the steps he had painted, the neatly stacked dishes he had eaten his food from three times each day for almost half a century. The daughter was still talking, talking as if this were a scene she had rehearsed for many years. But he wasn't listening. Her voice was getting louder. She was screaming. Homer hardly heard her. He closed his eyes, remembering how the turtle held onto his sleeve even after its throat was cut and its life was leaking out into the pond.

The screaming stopped. He opened his eyes and saw that the man 53 with the grey crew-cut hair was holding the daughter's arms. She was holding a plate in her hands. Maybe she had been about to hit him with it. It didn't matter. He looked at her. He looked at the other people in the room. They seemed to be waiting for him to say something.

"I got a turtle to clean out," he said, knowing what it was in him 54 that spoke. Then he turned and walked into the darkness.

RANDALL JARRELL

Field and Forest

Randall Jarrell (1914–1965), literary critic, poet, and translator, grew up in the South and in California and graduated from Vanderbilt University. He began teaching as an instructor at Kenyon College in the late 1930s and was a professor of English at several universities during his life, including the University of North Carolina, Princeton, and the University of Cincinnati. Author of several books of criticism, numerous translations, and even a few children's books, Jarrell was well respected for his poetry. His collections include *Selected Poems* (1955) and *The Woman at the Washington Zoo* (1960), which won a National Book Award. Jarrell's poetry often includes images of nature, but he generally uses these images to study the complexity, and the sadness or tragedy, he found in human nature. Jarrell was killed in an automobile accident in 1965. "Field and Forest" is from his last book of poetry, *The Lost World*, which was published that same year.

> *When you look down from the airplane you see lines,*   1
> *Roads, ruts, braided into a net or web—*
> *Where people go, what people do: the ways of life.*
>
> *Heaven says to the farmer: 'What's your field?'*   2
> *And he answers: 'Farming,' with a field,*
> *Or: 'Dairy-farming,' with a herd of cows.*
> *They seem a boys' toy cows, seen from this high.*
>
> *Seen from this high,*   3
> *The fields have a terrible monotony.*

But between the lighter patches there are dark ones. 4
A farmer is separated from a farmer
By what farmers have in common: forests,
Those dark things—what the fields were to begin with.
At night a fox comes out of the forest, eats his chickens.
At night the deer come out of the forest, eat his crops.

If he could he'd make farm out of all the forest, 5
But it isn't worth it: some of it's marsh, some rocks,
There are things there you couldn't get rid of
With a bulldozer, even—not with dynamite.
Besides, he likes it. He had a cave there, as a boy;
He hunts there now. It's a waste of land,
But it would be a waste of time, a waste of money,
To make it into anything but what it is.

At night, from the airplane, all you see is lights, 6
A few lights, the lights of houses, headlights,
And darkness. Somewhere below, beside a light,
The farmer, naked, takes out his false teeth:
He doesn't eat now. Takes off his spectacles:
He doesn't see now. Shuts his eyes:
If he were able to he'd shut his ears,
And as it is, he doesn't hear with them.
Plainly, he's taken out his tongue: he doesn't talk.
His arms and legs: at least, he doesn't move them.

They are knotted together, curled up, like a child's. 7
And after he has taken off the thoughts
It has taken him his life to learn,
He takes off, last of all, the world.

When you take off everything what's left? A wish, 8
A blind wish; and yet the wish isn't blind,
What the wish wants to see, it sees.

There in the middle of the forest is the cave 9
And there, curled up inside it, is the fox.
He stands looking at it.
Around him the fields are sleeping: the fields dream.
At night there are no more farmers, no more farms.
At night the fields dream, the fields are the forest.
The boy stands looking at the fox
As if, if he looked long enough—

                          he looks at it. 10
Or is it the fox that's looking at the boy?
The trees can't tell the two of them apart.

PROGRESS
AND ITS PRICE

We find ourselves in our work and works.

Progress and Its Price: Preview

Overview and Ideas for Writing

In the days before houseflies were controlled by chemicals or sealed out of air-conditioned houses, the fly bottle was a common household implement. In its simplest form it amounted to a bottle standing upright with a paper funnel in its mouth. In the bottom of the bottle was a spoonful of honey ("You catch more flies with honey than vinegar," we still say). Flies attracted by the scent would enter the funnel at the large end, pass through a tiny hole at the small end, and eat their fill. Then they would attempt to fly away, but would find themselves blocked by glass or paper in every direction. Without a scent to guide them, they would be unable to find their way through the small end of the funnel to freedom.

Three of the writers in this unit—Adam Smith, Thomas Edison, and Aldous Huxley—remind us that our escape from the bad old days of fly bottles and heavy physical labor has given Americans at the end of the twentieth century advantages that the kings of earlier periods would envy. Other writers in the unit, however, might say that the fly bottle is a good metaphor for an economic and technological trap that we may have fallen into. Henry David Thoreau, writing after Smith discovered the principles of the factory system and before Edison invented the lightbulb and the phonograph, foresaw a world in which individual lives would be increasingly narrow, repetitious, and unfulfilling. "Progress" might give the promised sweets of more leisure and more goods, but also bottle us up in a set of planned environments (tract houses, shopping malls, office buildings) that seem to merge into what Alice Bloom describes as one great "international accommodation" that "resembles a large airport lounge."

Most of the essays in the unit focus on one area of life and consider the changes, good or bad, that technology has brought to it. Thus Adam Smith, Henry David Thoreau, and Jomo Kenyatta all deal with the way we produce goods, including the houses we live in. Thomas Edison and Juliet B. Schor concentrate on the way we do our housekeeping. Carol Bly deals with physical labor and Alice Bloom with leisure. The broadest surveys of how technology has changed our lives are presented by Aldous Huxley (an enthusiast of progress in this essay, though readers of *Brave New World* know he has seen the dark side) and Daniel Boorstin (a doubter here, though he usually writes as an enthusiast).

The story in the unit, Nathaniel Hawthorne's "The Birthmark," is a classic tale of humanity's attempt to improve on the imperfect material nature supplies. The poem, Mark Halliday's "Population," gives a picture of contemporary life, streamlined in ways Hawthorne could hardly have foreseen.

Whether you are inclined to be enthusiastic or skeptical about material progress, your own experience can provide you with some valuable insights for writing. You could, for example, carefully observe a day, hour, or even a few minutes of your own life and then consider the role that recent technology has played. How much were you affected by products that did not exist a hundred years ago? Fifty? Twenty-five? In what ways were you a beneficiary of progress and in what ways a victim? You might also write interestingly about your experience with a state of technology higher or lower than that most of us are accustomed to.

If you want to do some research, the history of technology provides an inexhaustible supply of topics. You might, for example, trace the evolution of one of the inventions that shape our lives, show how it came into general use, and evaluate its impact. Daniel Boorstin's essay will give you some ideas with which to work. You could analyze the process by which something is done or made: Adam Smith, Henry David Thoreau, Jomo Kenyatta, Juliet B. Schor, and Carol Bly give you a varied set of patterns for such analysis and a variety of ways to think about the connection between how people work and who they are.

CAROL BLY

Getting Tired

Carol Bly (1930–   ) was born in Duluth, Minnesota, and graduated from Wellesley College in 1951. Between 1958 and 1971, with
her husband, poet Robert Bly, she managed a literary magazine series, *Fifties, Sixties,* and finally *Seventies.* In the 1970s she began writing essays—what she called "letters"—for *Preview* and *Minnesota
Monthly,* published by Minnesota Public Radio. These essays focus on
rural life in Minnesota, depicting the dullness as well as the romance,
and they often encourage rural people to put aside societal expectations in order to cultivate their internal lives and learn to live passionately. Her short stories, published in *The New Yorker, Ploughshares,* and
American Review and collected in *Backbone* (1985), echo this interest.
"Getting Tired" comes from Bly's collection of essays, *Letters from the
Country* (1981).

Readers sometimes find
Bly's first sentence disorienting. Why? Is this disorientation a good or bad thing?

How does Bly manage to
make the machine sound
like a living thing?

The men have left a gigantic 6600 combine   1
a few yards from our grove, at the edge of the
stubble. For days it was working around the
farm; we heard it on the east, later on the west,
and finally we could see it grinding back and
forth over the windrows on the south. But now
it has been simply squatting at the field's edge,
huge, tremendously still, very professional,
slightly dangerous.

We all have the correct feelings about this   2
new combine: this isn't the good old farming
where man and soil are dusted together all day;
this isn't farming a poor man can afford, either,
and therefore it further threatens his hold on the American "family
farm" operation. We have been sneering at this machine for days, as
its transistor radio, amplified well over the engine roar, has been grinding up our silence, spreading a kind of shrill ghetto evening all over the
farm.

But now it is parked, and after a while I walk over to it and climb   3
up its neat little John-Deere-green ladder on the left. Entering the big
cab up there is like coming up into a large ship's bridge on visitors'
day—heady stuff to see the inside workings of a huge operation like
the Queen Elizabeth II. On the other hand I feel left out, being only a
dumbfounded passenger. The combine cab has huge windows flaring
wider at the top; they lean forward over the ground, and the driver sits
so high behind the glass in its rubber moldings it is like a movie-set
spaceship. He has obviously come to dominate the field, whether he
farms it or not.

The value of the 66 is that it can do anything, and to change it   4
from a combine into a cornpicker takes one man about half an hour,
whereas most machine conversions on farms take several men a half
day. It frees its owner from a lot of monkeying.

Monkeying, in city life, is what little boys do   5
to clocks so they never run again. In farming it has
two quite different meanings. The first is small side
projects. You monkey with poultry, unless you're
a major egg handler. Or you monkey with ducks
or geese. If you have a very small milk herd, and
finally decide that prices plus state regulations
don't make your few Holsteins worthwhile, you
"quit monkeying with them." There is a hidden
dignity in this word: it precludes mention of
money. It lets the wife of a very marginal farmer
have a conversation with a woman who may be
helping her husband run fifteen hundred acres.

> How is what Bly calls "monkeying" related to what Adam Smith calls "sauntering" in his 7th paragraph and what Thoreau calls working "deliberately" in his 7th paragraph? What role does monkeying play in your work or your studying? What limits your monkeying?

"How you coming with those geese?" "Oh, we've been real disgusted.
We're thinking of quitting monkeying with them." It saves her having
to say, "We lost our shirts on those darn geese."

The other meaning of monkeying is wrestling with and maintaining   6
machinery, such as changing heads from combining to cornpicking.
Farmers who cornpick the old way, in which the corn isn't shelled
automatically during picking in the field but must be elevated to the
top of a pile by belt and then shelled, put up with some monkeying.

Still, cornpicking and plowing is a marvelous time of the year on   7
farms; one of the best autumns I've had recently had a few days of
fieldwork in it. We were outside all day, from six in the morning to
eight at night—coming in only for noon dinner. We ate our lunches
on a messy truck flatbed. (For city people who don't know it: *lunch*
isn't a noon meal; it is what you eat out of a black lunch pail at 9 A.M.
and 3 P.M. If you offer a farmer a cup of coffee at 3:30 P.M. he or she is
likely to say, "No thanks, I've already had lunch.") There were four of
us hired to help—a couple to plow, Celia (a skilled
farmhand who worked steady for our boss), and
me. Lunch was always two sandwiches of white
commercial bread with luncheon meat, and one
very generous piece of cake-mix cake carefully
wrapped in Saran Wrap. (I never found anyone
around here self-conscious about using Saran
Wrap when the Dow Chemical Company was also
making napalm.)

> Daniel Boorstin talks about the way technology can "attenuate" experience. In what ways is Bly's experience here more attenuated than that of a farmhand from the nineteenth century? How would it be further attenuated by the Deere 6600?

It was very pleasant on the flatbed, squinting   8
out over the yellow picked cornstalks—each time
we stopped for lunch, a larger part of the field had

been plowed black. We fell into the easy psychic habit of farmworkers: admiration of the boss. "Ja, I see he's buying one of those big 4010s," someone would say. We always perked up at inside information like that. Or "Ja," as the woman hired steady told us, "he's going to plow the home fields first this time, instead of the other way round." We temporary help were impressed by that, too. Then, with real flair, she brushed a crumb of luncheon meat off her jeans, the way you would make sure to flick a gnat off spotless tennis whites. It is the true feminine touch to brush a crumb off pants that are encrusted with Minnesota Profile A heavy loam, many swipes of SAE 40 oil, and grain dust.

All those days, we never tired of exchanging information on how *he* was making out, what *he* was buying, whom *he* was going to let drive the new tractor, and so on. There is always something to talk about with the other hands, because farming is genuinely absorbing. It has the best quality of work: nothing else seems real. And everyone doing it, even the cheapest helpers like me, can see the layout of the whole—from spring work, to cultivating, to small grain harvest, to corn-picking, to fall plowing.

Can you think of work you do, or have done, where it is impossible to see "the layout of the whole"?

The second day I was promoted from elevating corncobs at the corn pile to actual plowing. Hour after hour I sat up there on the old Alice, as she was called (an Allis-Chalmers WC that looked rusted from the Flood). You have to sit twisted part way around, checking that the plowshares are scouring clean, turning over and dropping the dead crop and soil, not clogging. For the first two hours I was very political. I thought about what would be good for American farming—stronger marketing organizations, or maybe a law like the Norwegian Odal law, preventing the breaking up of small farms or selling them to business interests. Then the sun got high, and each time I reached the headlands area at the field's end I dumped off something else, now my cap, next my jacket, finally my sweater.

Since the headlands are the last to be plowed, they serve as a field road until the very end. There are usually things parked there—a pickup or a corn trailer—and things dumped—my warmer clothing, our afternoon lunch pails, a broken furrow wheel someone picked up.

Is this "dropping" of political thought a good or a bad thing? Does technological progress make us more or less political?

By noon I'd dropped all political interest, and was thinking only: how unlike this all is to Keats's picture of autumn, a "season of mists and mellow fruitfulness." This gigantic expanse of horizon, with everywhere the easy growl of tractors, was simply teeming with extrovert energy. It wouldn't calm down for another week, when whoever was lowest on the totem pole

9

10

11

12

would be sent out to check a field for dropped parts or to drive away the last machines left around.

The worst hours for all common labor are the hours after noon   13
dinner. Nothing is inspiring then. That is when people wonder how they ever got stuck in the line of work they've chosen for life. Or they wonder where the cool Indian smoke of secrets and messages began to vanish from their marriage. Instead of plugging along like a cheerful beast working for me, the Allis now smelled particularly gassy. To stay awake I froze my eyes onto an indented circle in the hood around the gas cap. Someone had apparently knocked the screw cap fitting down into the hood, so there was a moat around it. In this moat some overflow gas leapt in tiny waves. Sometimes the gas cap was a castle, this was the moat; sometimes it was a nuclear-fission plant, this was the horrible hot-water waste. Sometimes it was just the gas cap on the old Alice with the spilt gas bouncing on the hot metal.

> Would Bly be better off if technology removed this after-dinner depression with drugs or air-conditioning or piped-in music?

Row after row. I was stupefied. But then around 2:30 the shadows   14
appeared again, and the light, which had been dazing and white, grew fragile. The whole prairie began to gather itself for the cool evening. All of a sudden it was wonderful to be plowing again, and when I came to the field end, the filthy jackets and the busted furrow wheel were just benign mistakes: that is, if it chose to, the jacket could be a church robe, and the old wheel could be something with some pride to it, like a helm. And I felt the same about myself: instead of being someone with a half interest in literature and a half interest in farming doing a half-decent job plowing, I could have been someone desperately needed in Washington or Zurich. I drank my three o'clock coffee joyously, and traded the other plowman a Super-Valu cake-mix lemon cake slice for a Holsum baloney sandwich because it had garlic in it.

By seven at night we had been plowing with headlights for an   15
hour. I tried to make up games to keep going, on my second wind, on my third wind, but labor is labor after the whole day of it; the mind refuses to think of ancestors. It refuses to pretend the stalks marching up to the right wheel in the spooky light are men-at-arms, or to imagine a new generation coming along. It doesn't care. Now the Republicans could have announced a local meeting in which they would propose a new farm program whereby every farmer owning less than five hundred acres must take half price for his crop, and every farmer owning more than a thousand acres shall receive triple price for his crop, and I was so tired I wouldn't have shown up to protest.

> Bly clearly has opinions on such political matters. Is the purpose of this essay to argue for those opinions?

A million hours later we sit around in a daze at the dining-room   16
table, and nobody says anything. In low, courteous mutters we ask for

the macaroni hotdish down this way, please.
Then we get up in ones and twos and go home.
Now the farm help are all so tired we *are* a little
like the various things left out on the headlands—some tools, a jacket, someone's thermos
top—used up for that day. Thoughts won't even
stick to us any more.

> What image does the con-
> cluding sentence of para-
> graph 16 bring to your
> mind?

Such tiredness must be part of farmers' wanting huge machinery 17
like the Deere 6600. That tiredness that feels so good to the occasional
laborer and the athlete is disturbing to a man destined to it eight months
of every year. But there is a more hidden psychology in the issue of
enclosed combines versus open tractors. It is this: one gets too many
impressions on the open tractor. A thousand impressions enter as you
work up and down the rows: nature's beauty or nature's stubbornness,
politics, exhaustion, but mainly the feeling that all this repetition—last
year's cornpicking, this year's cornpicking, next year's cornpicking—is
taking up your lifetime. The mere repetition reveals your eventual
death.

When you sit inside a modern combine, on the other hand, you 18
are so isolated from field, sky, all the real world,
that the brain is dulled. You are not sensitized
to your own mortality. You aren't sensitive to
anything at all.

> Do you agree with the obser-
> vations that end Bly's essay?
> Could the observations
> about the 6600 be applied
> equally to television, com-
> puters, VCRs?

This must be a common choice of our me- 19
chanical era: to hide from life inside our machinery. If we can hide from life in there, some
idiotic part of the psyche reasons, we can hide
from death in there as well.

JOMO KENYATTA

Gikuyu Industries

Jomo Kenyatta (1894?–1978) was born in a small Kikuyu[1] agricul-
tural village in Kenya, then part of British East Africa. When he was
ten years old, he developed a serious infection and was taken for
surgery to a Christian mission, where he met his first Europeans. Fascinated, he ran away from home and became a pupil at the mission.
Later he moved to Nairobi and held various government posts, becom-

1. *Kikuyu* and *Gikuyu* are alternate spellings for the name of Kenyatta's tribe. *Kikuyu* is
more commonly used.

ing active in organizations that promoted the rights of Kikuyu natives suffering under the domination of white settlers. In 1929 he moved to London to lobby for the rights of his people. There he met and studied with Bronislaw Malinowski, the renowned anthropologist, and completed an academic thesis that he revised for popular publication as *Facing Mount Kenya* (1938). As the following excerpt shows, this book describes Kikuyu customs that were beginning to decline in the face of European influences. After World War II, Kenyatta established himself as one of Africa's leading politicians. Jailed from 1952 to 1961 for alleged terrorist connections, Kenyatta was released in time to negotiate the terms of Kenya's independence and to become its first president in 1964. Kenyatta's speeches have been collected in two volumes, *Harambee!* (1964) and *Suffering Without Bitterness* (1968).

IRONWORK

For centuries the Gikuyu people have developed the technique of procuring iron ore from the sand, and so the use of iron tools has been well established in the Gikuyu country from time immemorial. In Gikuyu legends and stories we are told how, in the beginning of things, the animals were divided into two sections for domestication purposes. The divider, Mogai, gave one section of the animals to men and the other to women. At this time people did not possess any iron tools; they used wooden knives and spears. The women took to slaughtering their animals for food and other purposes; they did this with wooden knives, and it took a long time to kill and skin one animal. The legends go on to tell us that owing to the pain inflicted on the animals through this slow process of killing and skinning with blunt wooden knives, the animals could not stand it much longer. One night, when the women were sleeping, the animals gathered together and decided to run away from these cruel human beings. All the animals possessed by the women ran away and scattered in the forests and plains; at the same time they selected their own chiefs and leaders and defended themselves from being captured by the human beings. The lion and leopard were chosen as the defenders of jungles; the elephant, buffalo, and rhinoceros as the defenders of the forests; the hippopotamus as the defender of rivers and lakes, and so on. From this time the animals which were possessed by the women became wild animals, and the men's animals, which at that time were not used for killing, remained domesticated.

Women tried hard to get their animals back from the forests and jungles, but they did not succeed; they pleaded with the Mogai to help them get their animals back, but Mogai would not listen to their petition, for he said that the women had treated their animals cruelly and therefore he had given them freedom to roam freely in the forests, plains, and jungles. When the men saw the crisis which had befallen the women they held a conference and decided to send a delegation to the Mogai and ask him what they should do with their animals, which were increasing by leaps and bounds. The delegates took with them a fine lamb which was fawn-coloured all over its body. They told Mogai that they wanted to sacrifice the lamb to him, but they did not like to kill and skin it with the blunt wooden knives for fear of losing their herds as had happened to the women. To their request the Mogai replied: "You are wise men, for you have remembered to seek my advice. I can see that you know that I have given you these animals and I have power to take them away from you. For your faith in me I will give you good advice about how to get better tools, not only for sacrifices, but also for your general use. I will make you the masters of your animals with new tools, but I command you to share these with your unfortunate womenfolk."

At this juncture Mogai directed the men to a site in a river-bed and said to them: "Take sand from this site. Dry it in the sun; then make a fire and put the sand therein, and through this process you will get iron. I will give you wisdom to make better tools and you will not have to use blunt wooden tools any more." From this time the Gikuyu, following the advice of Mogai, entered into the phase of metal or iron culture.

Apart from these legends and stories which have been handed down from generation to generation, we have no other records to show exactly when and how this evolution took place.

The fact that the Gikuyu have been well acquainted with the technique and the development of ironwork can be proved by the number of iron implements and ornaments of purely Gikuyu origin which are to be found in all branches of activities in the Gikuyu community. The chief iron articles in the Gikuyu society are the following: spears, swords, digging- and clearing-knives of different sizes, ear- and finger-rings, arrow heads, bracelets of various shapes and sizes, axes and fine chains, hammers and tongs, tweezers, etc.

With these preliminary remarks we will proceed to describe how the work of procuring iron is done. The iron is obtained from ore. The method adopted by the Gikuyu for this purpose of collecting iron ore is that of washing sand which is secured from certain districts and in a particular river. The sand is carefully washed in a river by experienced men; the black substances that contain ore are put together and are handed over to the women and children, who help to spread the ore in the sun to dry. It is worth noting that the whole family of a smith takes part in the work, and the work is divided among the group. When a man is busy in the river washing the sand, his wife or wives and children are busy spreading the iron ore in the sun to dry. This method of working may seem primitive in the eyes of the machine-man of the Western world, but nevertheless the system fulfilled the needs of the community. In the olden days there was only one great demand for iron—namely, during the time of initiation, when the young warriors needed new equipment for war or protection. The chief demand in this direction was for spears and swords. This did not necessarily mean that a new supply of iron was to follow, for there was always a bit of iron in every homestead left over from worn-out tools or those which had broken and could not be mended. These bits of iron were collected and put away to be used in the future for supplying a spear or a sword to the son of the homestead. For this reason the iron production, as mentioned above, was not everyday work. Some smiths had never participated in the work of iron production; they lived on repairs and renewing or joining up together the old bits of iron to produce a new tool or weapon.

After the sand containing iron ore is dried it is carried to the smithy. 7 There it is put in a fire made of a special mixture of charcoals. Some of these are made from a particular tree and others from a special banana plant. The two kinds of charcoals are mixed. The banana charcoal is said to have particular value in smelting iron. Its substances help to put the pure iron together and to separate it from impure matters.

Before the process of smelting is actually started, a short ritual is 8 performed by the smith and his assistants. The ritual consists of sprinkling a little Gikuyu beer over the furnace, accompanied by a few ceremonial words directed to Mogai and the ancestral spirits. In the absence of beer a little water fulfils the ritual duty. After the ceremony of invoking the spirits of ancestors and appealing to Mogai for guidance and protection in the enterprise, the work of smelting iron is proceeded with. Two bellows are employed simultaneously to keep the fire burning. They are worked by assistants, who learn the profession by means of watching the smith doing the work. In other words, they learn by example. The bellows are put in motion, the charcoals are carefully laid, and then the sand is slowly sprinkled over the burning fire by the trained hands of the smith. The heat is kept at a regulated temperature by adding the required amount of charcoals in the furnace. At the same time the blowing of the bellows is kept in check. Sometimes the heat is intensified, and at other times it is slowed down. In this way the temperature is kept at the required degree, which reduces the ore to metallic iron, which is technically called "blooms" (*gekama*).

The smith, with his assistants, continues to work from morning till 9 the evening, especially when they have plenty of sand containing ore to melt. In the evening the melted iron is left in the furnace to cool. Early the next morning the smith, followed by his assistants, takes a small quantity of beer made of sugar-cane or honey. On his arrival at the smithy he performs a short ceremony of greeting the ancestral spirits who have guarded the work during the night. The ceremony consists of sprinkling the beer over and round the furnace and again over the working tools. The communion between the smith and the ancestor spirits in this respect is considered to be of great importance, for the spirits of ancestors are said to be very closely connected with ironwork, and especially male spirits. It is believed that unless these are appeased they can render the ironwork unsuccessful by causing the tools or weapons which are made of the iron to break, and thus reduce the popularity of the smith. This belief is founded on the ground that the male ancestors have had their bitter experiences as warriors and some of them had met their deaths in battle-fields in which the iron weapons were used. And even those who had not met their deaths in this way have suffered pain in one way or another, by being wounded either in battle or in the general activities of a warrior's life.

When the ritual of communing with the ancestral spirits is com- 10 pleted, the iron "blooms," which have run together into small lumps, are taken out from the furnace. These are joined into a big heap by a mass of slag which has flowed during the melting. After the big pile of slag is taken out, the "blooms" are knocked out and collected together. The next step that follows is to heat the "blooms" and hammer a few of them together, according to the quantity required, to make a spear or sword or other iron articles. The irons thus beaten in heaps are known as *mondwa,* and they are sold according to sizes.

If a man wants a spear he will not buy a ready-made spear but the 11 *mondwa,* and then pay the smith for making the spear. Sometimes the same smith fulfils both tasks of selling the *mondwa* and of making the spear. But there are others who do not make iron, and their duty is merely to make articles with material supplied by their customers.

The smith clan holds an important position in the community; 12 members of that clan are respected and feared. In the first place they command respect because of their skill in ironwork, without which the community would have difficulty in obtaining the necessary imple- ments for various activities, for iron implements play an important part in the economic, religious, social, and political life of the Gikuyu. In the second place the smiths are feared for the fact that strong curses rest with the smith clan. If a smith should curse a man or family there is no form of purification that could cleanse the cursed individual or the group. The curse consists of cutting a piece of red-hot iron on an anvil and at the same time uttering spells, e.g. *Ng'ania wa Ng'ania arutwika ta kiriha geeke. Mahori maake marohehenjeka, ngoro yake erot- weka ta kiriha geeke.* This means: "May So and-so (proper name given) be cut like this iron. Let his lungs be smashed to smithereens. Let his heart be cut off like this iron."

HUT-BUILDING

It is a common ambition of every Gikuyu young man to own a hut 13 or huts, which means implicitly to have a wife or wives. The establish- ment of a homestead gives a man special status in the community; he is referred to as *muthuri* (an elder), and is considered capable of holding a responsible position in tribal affairs. Thus, it is the desire of every Gikuyu man to work hard and accumulate property which will enable him to build a homestead of his own. There is a proverb in Gikuyu which says: *"Wega uumaga na mocie,"* that is, the quality of a man is judged by his homestead. With these few remarks we will proceed to describe how a hut is built.

Gikuyu huts are of the round type, with wooden walls and grass 14 thatched roofs. The actual building of a hut takes only one day; and as soon as it is completed, a new fire is drilled from sacred fire-sticks, *"githegethi na Geka kia Igongona."* But in case of rebuilding, the fire from the old hut is preserved to be transferred to the new hut. The fire is ritually lit in the new hut, and after a short ceremony of communing with the ancestral spirits the owner moves into the new homestead. Sometimes two or more huts are built simultaneously, as in the case of a man having more than one wife or a large family which could not be housed in one hut. But general custom requires that even a man with one wife should have two huts, one for his wife's private use and one for himself for general use. The woman's hut is called *nyomba*. Here it is taboo for a mere stranger to enter, because *nyomba* is considered as the traditional sacred abode of the family and the proper place to hold communion with their ancestral spirits. All aspects of religious and magical ceremonies and sacrifices which concern the family are centered around the *nyomba*. It is for fear of defilement and ill-luck that strangers are not allowed to cross this sacred threshold. The man's hut is called *thingira;* in this, friends and casual visitors are entertained.

Nowadays the system of having two huts for a man with only one 15 wife is dying out, owing to the heavy burden of hut taxes imposed on the people by the British Government. The result has been congestion, whole families being crowded in one hut, for many such families can hardly maintain their livelihood and at the same time afford to find money for hut taxation.

We have mentioned that a hut is built and occupied in the same 16 day; this statement may puzzle those who are not acquainted with the Gikuyu method of building. To avoid this, let us at once explain how the work that expedites the putting up of a hut is organised. Most important of all is the Gikuyu collective method of working. A few days before the erection of a hut or huts the building materials are collected. In doing this the division of labour according to sex plays an important role. The work of cutting wood necessary for building falls on men; women take the responsibility of providing thatching grass and other materials.

When a family is engaged in the work of building a hut or huts 17 the help of neighbours and friends is necessary in order to expedite the work. A man goes round asking his friends to help him, and at the same time telling them what kind of building materials he would like them to supply him with. In the same manner the wife visits her women friends, requesting them to help in various ways. Those who cannot take part in collecting building materials are asked to help in providing food and drink for the builders' feast, which is called *"iruga ria mwako."* On the day appointed many of these friends will turn up, bringing with them the required materials for building. The man and his wife or wives receive their helpers joyfully and bid them to sit down and rest. After all have arrived a feast is provided, consisting of a variety of food and drink. During the feasting this group of men and women entertain themselves with traditional songs relating to team-work. Before they part, a day is appointed when the actual building of a hut or huts will take place.

It is obvious that without this system of team-work it would take 18 a man a long time to complete the work, especially in a community where the system of paid labour is traditionally unknown. In its place, mutual help guided by the rules of give and take plays a significant part. In every branch of work reciprocity is the fundamental principle governing the relationship between a man and his neighbours, and also between various groups or clans and the tribe. If a man, after having been asked to give his service, absents himself without a good reason, especially when his neighbour has urgent work, such as building a hut or a cattle kraal, which has to be completed in one day (for it is feared that should a hut or a kraal be left unfinished and unoccupied, evil spirits might dwell therein and, therefore, cause constant misfortune to the future occupants and their herd), the result will be that the defaulter will find himself socially boycotted for his individualistic attitude. When a man has thus been ostracised, *"kohingwo,"* he will have to pay a fine of one sheep or a he-goat to his neighbours for his bad behaviour. When the fine is paid, the animal is slaughtered for a feast, and then, after a short ceremony of reunion, the man's status as a good and helpful neighbour is re-acknowledged.

After the building materials have been collected, the head of the 19 family selects a plot where he wishes to establish his new homestead. In selecting the plot care is taken to see that the land is not associated with any ancestral curse or taboo. The plot must also be one that has been lawfully acquired. The homestead must not be built on or near a graveyard, or on a place where a fierce battle has taken place, resulting in loss of lives. Such places are considered as the resting homes for the departed spirits, and to disturb them would mean to invoke their anger.

When these preliminary arrangements have been made, the man 20 prepares sugar-cane or honey beer for the foundation ceremony. Early in the morning, on the day of building a hut or huts, a small quantity of the beer is taken to the selected plot and, in communion with the ancestral spirits, it is sprinkled on the ground where the new home is

to be built. Sometimes milk or uncooked gruel, *"gethambio,"* is preferred for this ceremony, according to the custom of the clan to which
the individual belongs. After the ancestral spirits have been summoned
to join in the work of building, the friends who have gathered to help
their neighbour start to clear and to level the ground. Then the foundation is marked according to the size of the hut which a man wants. To
make a good circle a kind of string compass is employed. A stick is put
in the centre of the circle and a string tied to it, then a man holds one
end of the string and, after measuring the required paces, he holds the
string tight and then goes round, marking the ground until the circle
lines meet. This is called *"gokurura kiea."* When this is done the builders
start digging holes in the ground for the outer wall. The holes are about
one foot deep and about six inches in diameter. After this the inner
circle is marked, which divides the hut into several apartments. Immediately the wall is erected and the roof put on. This completes the men's
work in building, leaving the thatching to the womenfolk.

While the women are engaged in thatching, the men retire to a   21
feast which has been awaiting them. During the feasting the men sing
songs relating to the art of building; those who are clever and hard
workers are highly praised in these songs; at the same time contemptuous phrases are uttered for laziness. In some of the phrases men call on
the women in teasing tones, saying: "Look on those lazy-bones who
are working like chameleons, the sun is going down, do you want us
to make torches for you? Do hurry up and join us in feasting, and let
us utter blessings for the homestead before the sun is completely gone
down." To this the women answer in chorus, saying: "You men, you
lack the most important art in building, namely, thatching. A wall and
an empty roof cannot protect you from heavy rain, nor from burning
sun. It is our careful thatching that makes a hut worth living in. We
are not chameleons, but we do thatch our huts like *'nyoni ya nyagathanga'* (this is the name of a small bird in Gikuyu which is well known
by its sweet songs and the neatness of its nest)." In many of the Gikuyu
cradle stories and legends *nyoni ya nyagathanga* and its work is highly
praised. This acts as an encouragement to both boys and girls to become
industrious in their future activities in life. It is characteristic of the
Gikuyu people to sing inspiring songs while performing a task, for it is
said: "to work in a happy mood is to make the task easier, and to
relieve the heart from fatigue." (*"Koruta wera na ngoro theru ni kohothia
wera na konyihia minoga."*)

When the women have finally finished thatching they join the men   22
in feasting. Before the party comes to a close the owner of the homestead brings the remainder of the beer or the milk which has been
sprinkled on the foundation; he hands it to a ceremonial elder, who
after pouring the liquid into a ritual horn, calls upon those present to
stand up. Then the ceremonial elder, with his hands raised holding the

horn, turns towards Kere-Nyaga (Mount Kenya). In this position he chants a prayer, calling for a blessing for the homestead and its future prosperity. The following is the form of the prayer used for such an occasion:

"Wee Githuri oikaraga Kere-Nyaga; kerathimo geaku nikeo getomaga mecie ethegee. Namo marakara maku, nemo mahukagia mecie. Togogothaitha twetura-neire ohamwe na ngoma cia aciari aito. Togokoria ate orinderere mocie oyo na otome wethegee. Reke atumia ona mahio mathathare. Thaaai, thathayai Ngai, thaaaai."

The following is the translation of the above prayer: "You, the Great 23 Elder, who dwells on the Kere-Nyaga, your blessing allows homesteads to spread. Your anger destroys homesteads. We beseech You, and in this we are in harmony with the spirits of our ancestors: we ask You to guard this homestead and let it spread. Let the women, herd, and flock be prolific. (Chorus) Peace, praise, or beseech ye, Ngai (God), peace be with us."

After this the homestead is declared open. The next thing is to 24 light the fire which we have mentioned in our earlier description. Two children, male and female, are selected for this ritual; they are looked upon as a symbol of peace and prosperity for the homestead. The ceremonial elder hands the fire to the children and instructs them how to light it; at the same time he gives them the ritual words to be used in this connection. The children enter the hut, with the elder following behind them, to see that the ritual is correctly carried out. Behind this small procession the owner of the homestead and his wife follow carrying firewood to kindle the fire, for it is considered as a bad omen for such a fire to go out. After the fire has been properly lit, things are moved in without any further ceremony.

Let us glance inside a woman's hut. It may be some six paces from 25 the entrance to the fire-place in the centre. The roof is supported at the outside by the wall, in the inside by a series of poles equidistant from the centre. The poles fulfil a twofold purpose; besides supporting the roof, they are the mainstays of partitions which divide the hut into apartments. These apartments depend upon the needs of the occupant—her bedroom is essential, and no less so is the store-room next door to it. Should a daughter live with her mother, her room will be next to the store-room, and should the woman keep one or two animals (sheep or goats) for fattening, they will have their compartment farther round the wall, just inside the door, on the right as you enter. These rooms will occupy the whole of the right inside of the hut, leaving free only the space between the fire-place and the inner circle of poles. Each apartment communicates immediately with this space.

To the left of a person entering the hut is a long partition, extend- 26 ing almost from the door to the woman's bedroom. Between this and the outer wall the animals sleep at night. The scheme is thus simple; first the fire-place, then the circle in which people may sit, then the outer apartments. The accompanying diagram will make this clear. A woman's hut is considered as the cradle of the family tradition; it has many taboos which, for the harmony and the prosperity of the family, must be strictly observed. Among other things, fire must be lit in the hut every evening, and there must be someone to sleep in it every night. The wife is debarred by custom from having sexual intercourse

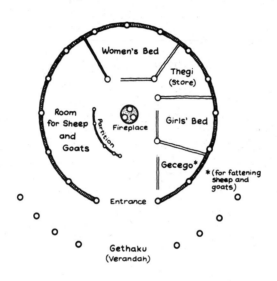

anywhere else but inside the hut. Sexual intercourse must not take place in the day-time, even with her husband, neither must it be performed whilst food is being cooked, or the food will have to be thrown away, for an act of this nature renders the food unclean and unfit for human consumption. Anyone eating such food will have *thahu* (defilement), and will have to be cleansed by a *mondo mogo* (witch-doctor), for it is feared that unless this is done, disaster will befall such a man.

The man's hut, unlike that of the woman, is very simple; it has only one partition, and sometimes none at all. When there is one, it is used to divide the bedstead from the fire-place. The rest of the hut is left open; this is to provide a large sitting-place for the family and their visitors. For the man's hut is used for general purposes, whereas the woman's hut is strictly used for her private purposes and family matters. 27

A well-built hut generally lasts for about ten or more years; occasionally the roof has to be re-thatched, especially in the interval between the heavy and the short rains. The wall has also to be repaired every now and again; holes between the wood are filled with cow or 28 sheep dung. This method serves two purposes; in the first place it keeps draughts out, and in the second it preserves the wood and prevents it being eaten by the ants. The wood preserved in this way becomes useful in the future building of new huts, especially when old ones are pulled down. Some building materials have been with a family for a considerable number of years, and they are looked upon as sacred relics.

ADAM SMITH

Division of Labour

Adam Smith (1723–1790) was born in the small Scottish fishing village of Kirkcaldy. At the age of four, according to his biographer John Rae, Smith was kidnapped by gypsies, but soon recaptured. Rae adds wryly that Smith would "have made a poor gypsy." A notoriously absent-minded professor at the University of Glasgow (he once fell into a pit while deep in conversation), he was fascinated by economics and the development of new manufacturing processes. He was a friend of James Watt, inventor of the steam engine, and an acute observer of the state of technology at the beginning of the Industrial Revolution. *The Wealth of Nations* (1776) is Smith's masterpiece. In it he argues that people's natural desire to trade leads logically to division of labor and that the "invisible hand" of a free marketplace adjusts production to meet the needs of society. In the following excerpt, Smith illustrates the benefits of division of labor by introducing the famous example of a pin factory.

The greatest improvement in the productive powers of labour, and 1 the greater part of the skill, dexterity, and judgment with which it is any where directed, or applied, seem to have been the effects of the division of labour.

The effects of the division of labour, in the general business of 2 society, will be more easily understood, by considering in what manner it operates in some particular manufactures. It is commonly supposed to be carried furthest in some very trifling ones; not perhaps that it really is carried further in them than in others of more importance: but in those trifling manufactures which are destined to supply the small wants of but a small number of people, the whole number of workmen must necessarily be small; and those employed in every different branch of the work can often be collected into the same workhouse, and placed at once under the view of the spectator. In those great manufactures, on the contrary, which are destined to supply the great wants of the great body of the people, every different branch of the work employs so great a number of workmen, that it is impossible to collect them all into the same workhouse. We can seldom see more, at one time, than those employed in one single branch. Though in such manufactures, therefore, the work may really be divided into a much greater number of parts, than in those of a more trifling nature, the division is not near so obvious, and has accordingly been much less observed.

To take an example, therefore, from a very trifling manufacture; but one in which the division of labour has been very often taken notice of, the trade of the pin-maker; a workman not educated to this business (which the division of labour has rendered a distinct trade), nor acquainted with the use of the machinery employed in it (to the invention of which the same division of labour has probably given occasion), could scarce, perhaps, with his utmost industry, make one pin in a day, and certainly could not make twenty. But in the way in which this business is now carried on, not only the whole work is a peculiar trade, but it is divided into a number of branches, of which the greater part are likewise peculiar trades. One man draws out the wire, another straights it, a third cuts it, a fourth points it, a fifth grinds it at the top for receiving the head; to make the head requires two or three distinct operations; to put it on, is a peculiar business, to whiten the pins is another; it is even a trade by itself to put them into the paper; and the important business of making a pin is, in this manner, divided into about eighteen distinct operations, which, in some manufactories, are all performed by distinct hands, though in others the same man will sometimes perform two or three of them. I have seen a small manufactory of this kind where ten men only were employed, and where some of them consequently performed two or three distinct operations. But though they were very poor, and therefore but indifferently accommodated with the necessary machinery, they could, when they exerted themselves, make among them about twelve pounds of pins in a day. There are in a pound upwards of four thousand pins of a middling size. Those ten persons, therefore, could make among them upwards of forty-eight thousand pins in a day. Each person, therefore, making a tenth part of forty-eight thousand pins, might be considered as making four thousand eight hundred pins in a day. But if they had all wrought separately and independently, and without any of them having been educated to this peculiar business, they certainly could not each of them have made twenty, perhaps not one pin in a day; that is, certainly, not the two hundred and fortieth, perhaps not the four thousand eight hundredth part of what they are at present capable of performing, in consequence of a proper division and combination of their different operations.

In every other art and manufacture, the effects of the division of labour are similar to what they are in this very trifling one; though, in many of them, the labour can neither be so much subdivided, nor reduced to so great a simplicity of operation. The division of labour, however, so far as it can be introduced, occasions, in every art, a proportionable increase of the productive powers of labour. The separation of different trades and employments from one another, seems to have taken place, in consequence of this advantage. This separation too is generally carried furthest in those countries which enjoy the highest degree of industry and improvement; what is the work of one man in a rude state of society, being generally that of several in an improved one. In every improved society, the farmer is generally nothing but a farmer; the manufacturer, nothing but a manufacturer. The labour too which is necessary to produce any one complete manufacture, is almost always divided among a great number of hands. How many different trades are employed in each branch of the linen and woollen manufactures, from the growers of the flax and the wool, to the bleachers and smoothers of the linen, or to the dyers and dressers of the cloth!

This great increase of the quantity of work, which, in consequence ⁵ of the division of labour, the same number of people are capable of performing, is owing to three different circumstances; first, to the increase of dexterity in every particular workman; secondly, to the saving of the time which is commonly lost in passing from one species of work to another; and lastly, to the invention of a great number of machines which facilitate and abridge labour, and enable one man to do the work of many.

First, the improvement of the dexterity of the workman necessarily ⁶ increases the quantity of the work he can perform; and the division of labour, by reducing every man's business to some one simple operation, and by making this operation the sole employment of his life, necessarily increases very much the dexterity of the workman. A common smith, who, though accustomed to handle the hammer, has never been used to make nails, if upon some particular occasion he is obliged to attempt it, will scarce, I am assured, be able to make above two or three hundred nails in a day, and those too very bad ones. A smith who has been accustomed to make nails, but whose sole or principal business has not been that of a nailer, can seldom with his utmost diligence make more than eight hundred or a thousand nails in a day. I have seen several boys under twenty years of age who had never exercised any other trade but that of making nails, and who, when they exerted themselves, could make, each of them, upwards of two thousand three hundred nails in a day. The making of a nail, however, is by no means one of the simplest operations. The same person blows the bellows, stirs or mends the fire as there is occasion, heats the iron, and forges every part of the nail: In forging the head too he is obliged to change his tools. The different operations into which the making of a pin, or of a metal button, is subdivided, are all of them much more simple, and the dexterity of the person, of whose life it has been the sole business to perform them, is usually much greater. The rapidity with which some of the operations of those manufactures are performed, exceeds what the human hand could, by those who had never seen them, be supposed capable of acquiring.

Secondly, the advantage which is gained by saving the time com- 7 monly lost in passing from one sort of work to another, is much greater than we should at first view be apt to imagine it. It is impossible to pass very quickly from one kind of work to another, that is carried on in a different place, and with quite different tools. A country weaver, who cultivates a small farm, must lose a good deal of time in passing from his loom to the field, and from the field to his loom. When the two trades can be carried on in the same workhouse, the loss of time is no doubt much less. It is even in this case, however, very considerable. A man commonly saunters a little in turning his hand from one sort of employment to another. When he first begins the new work he is seldom very keen and hearty; his mind, as they say, does not go to it, and for some time he rather trifles than applies to good purpose. The habit of sauntering and of indolent careless application, which is naturally, or rather necessarily acquired by every country workman who is obliged to change his work and his tools every half hour, and to apply his hand in twenty different ways almost every day of his life; renders him almost always slothful and lazy, and incapable of any vigorous application even on the most pressing occasions. Independent, therefore, of his deficiency in point of dexterity, this cause alone must always reduce considerably the quantity of work which he is capable of performing.

Thirdly, and lastly, every body must be sensible how much labour 8 is facilitated and abridged by the application of proper machinery. It is unnecessary to give any example. I shall only observe, therefore, that the invention of all those machines by which labour is so much facilitated and abridged, seems to have been originally owing to the division of labour. Men are much more likely to discover easier and readier methods of attaining any object, when the whole attention of their minds is directed towards that single object, than when it is dissipated among a great variety of things. But in consequence of the division of labour, the whole of every man's attention comes naturally to be directed towards some one very simple object. It is naturally to be expected, therefore, that some one or other of those who are employed in each particular branch of labour should soon find out easier and readier methods of performing their own particular work, wherever the nature of it admits of such improvement. A great part of the machines made use of in those manufactures in which labour is most subdivided, were originally the inventions of common workmen, who, being each of them employed in some very simple operation, naturally turned their thoughts towards finding out easier and readier methods of performing it. Whoever has been much accustomed to visit such manufactures, must frequently have been shewn very pretty machines, which were the inventions of such workmen, in order to facilitate and quicken their own particular part of the work. In the first fire-engines, a boy was constantly employed to open and shut alternately the communication between the boiler and the cylinder, according as the piston either ascended or descended. One of those boys, who loved to play with his companions, observed that, by tying a string from the handle of the valve which opened this communication to another part of the machine, the valve would open and shut without his assistance, and leave him at liberty to divert himself with his play-fellows. One of the greatest improvements that has been made upon this machine, since it was first invented, was in this manner the discovery of a boy who wanted to save his own labour.

All the improvements in machinery, however, have by no means 9 been the inventions of those who had occasion to use the machines. Many improvements have been made by the ingenuity of the makers of the machines, when to make them became the business of a peculiar trade; and some by that of those who are called philosophers or men of speculation, whose trade it is not to do any thing, but to observe every thing; and who, upon that account, are often capable of combining together the powers of the most distant and dissimilar objects. In the progress of society, philosophy or speculation becomes, like every other employment, the principal or sole trade and occupation of a particular class of citizens. Like every other employment too, it is subdivided into a great number of different branches, each of which affords occupation to a peculiar tribe or class of philosophers; and this subdivision of employment in philosophy, as well as in every other business, improves dexterity, and saves time. Each individual becomes more expert in his own peculiar branch, more work is done upon the whole, and the quantity of science is considerably increased by it.

It is the great multiplication of the productions of all the different 10 arts, in consequence of the division of labour, which occasions, in a well-governed society, that universal opulence which extends itself to the lowest ranks of the people. Every workman has a great quantity of his own work to dispose of beyond what he himself has occasion for; and every other workman being exactly in the same situation, he is enabled to exchange a great quantity of his own goods for a great quantity, or, what comes to the same thing, for the price of a great quantity of theirs. He supplies them abundantly with what they have occasion for, and they accommodate him as amply with what he has occasion for, and a general plenty diffuses itself through all the different ranks of the society.

Observe the accommodation of the most common artificer or day- 11

labourer in a civilized and thriving country, and you will perceive that
the number of people of whose industry a part, though but a small part,
has been employed in procuring him this accommodation, exceeds all
computation. The woollen coat, for example, which covers the day-
labourer, as coarse and rough as it may appear, is the produce of the
joint labour of a great multitude of workmen. The shepherd, the sorter
of the wool, the wool-comber or carder, the dyer, the scribbler, the
spinner, the weaver, the fuller, the dresser, with many others, must all
join their different arts in order to complete even this homely production. How many merchants and carriers, besides, must have been employed in transporting the materials from some of those workmen to
others who often live in a very distant part of the country! how much
commerce and navigation in particular, how many ship-builders, sail-
ors, sail-makers, rope-makers, must have been employed in order to
bring together the different drugs made use of by the dyer, which often
come from the remotest corners of the world! What a variety of labour
too is necessary in order to produce the tools of the meanest of those
workmen! To say nothing of such complicated machines as the ship of
the sailor, the mill of the fuller, or even the loom of the weaver, let us
consider only what a variety of labour is requisite in order to form that
very simple machine, the shears with which the shepherd clips the
wool. The miner, the builder of the furnace for smelting the ore, the
feller of the timber, the burner of the charcoal to be made use of in
the smelting-house, the brick-maker, the brick-layer, the workmen who
attend the furnace, the mill-wright, the forger, the smith, must all of
them join their different arts in order to produce them. Were we to
examine, in the same manner, all the different parts of his dress and
household furniture, the coarse linen shirt which he wears next his
skin, the shoes which cover his feet, the bed which he lies on, and all
the different parts which compose it, the kitchen-grate at which he
prepares his victuals, the coals which he makes use of for that purpose,
dug from the bowels of the earth, and brought to him perhaps by a
long sea and a long land carriage, all the other utensils of his kitchen,
all the furniture of his table, the knives and forks, the earthen or pewter
plates upon which he serves up and divides his victuals, the different
hands employed in preparing his bread and his beer, the glass window
which lets in the heat and the light, and keeps out the wind and the
rain, with all the knowledge and art requisite for preparing that beautiful and happy invention, without which these northern parts of the
world could scarce have afforded a very comfortable habitation, together with the tools of all the different workmen employed in producing those different conveniencies; if we examine, I say, all these things,
and consider what a variety of labour is employed about each of them,
we shall be sensible that without the assistance and co-operation of
many thousands, the very meanest person in a civilized country could

not be provided, even according to, what we very falsely imagine, the easy and simple manner in which he is commonly accommodated. Compared, indeed, with the more extravagant luxury of the great, his accommodation must no doubt appear extremely simple and easy; and yet it may be true, perhaps, that the accommodation of an European prince does not always so much exceed that of an industrious and frugal peasant, as the accommodation of the latter exceeds that of many an African king, the absolute master of the lives and liberties of ten thousand naked savages.

HENRY DAVID THOREAU

The Fitness in a Man's Building His Own House

Henry David Thoreau (1817–1862), after an education at Harvard College, returned to his native town of Concord, Massachusetts, where he worked sporadically as a schoolteacher and a surveyor. From July 4, 1845, to September 6, 1847, he lived in a cabin made with his own hands by the shore of Walden Pond, near Concord. There he wrote his first book, *A Week on the Concord and Merrimack Rivers* (published in 1849), and completed the first draft of *Walden, or Life in the Woods* (1854). Thoreau, more than any other writer in America, has become identified with a spirit of independence that resists all forms of centralization and specialization. American nationalism had no appeal for him: During his stay at Walden he was arrested for refusing to pay his poll tax to a government that tolerated slavery and fought an imperialistic war against Mexico. Similarly, he would not endorse an economic system that turned men into wage slaves, even if the system increased their supposed prosperity: "It is hard to have a southern overseer; it is worse to have a northern one; but worst of all when you are the slave-driver of yourself." The excerpt below is taken from *Walden*'s first chapter, "Economy," which responds to the theories of thinkers like Adam Smith.

Near the end of March, 1845, I borrowed an axe and went down   1
to the woods by Walden Pond, nearest to where I intended to build my house, and began to cut down some tall, arrowy white pines, still in their youth, for timber. It is difficult to begin without borrowing, but perhaps it is the most generous course thus to permit your fellow-men to have an interest in your enterprise. The owner of the axe, as he

released his hold on it, said that it was the apple of his eye; but I
returned it sharper than I received it. It was a pleasant hillside where I
worked, covered with pine woods, through which I looked out on the
pond, and a small open field in the woods where pines and hickories
were springing up. The ice in the pond was not yet dissolved, though
there were some open spaces, and it was all dark-colored and saturated
with water. There were some slight flurries of snow during the days
that I worked there; but for the most part when I came out on to the
railroad, on my way home, its yellow sand-heap stretched away gleaming in the hazy atmosphere, and the rails shone in the spring sun, and
I heard the lark and pewee and other birds already come to commence
another year with us. They were pleasant spring days, in which the
winter of man's discontent was thawing as well as the earth, and the
life that had lain torpid began to stretch itself. One day, when my axe
had come off and I had cut a green hickory for a wedge, driving it with
a stone, and had placed the whole to soak in a pond-hole in order to
swell the wood, I saw a striped snake run into the water, and he lay
on the bottom, apparently without inconvenience, as long as I stayed
there, or more than a quarter of an hour; perhaps because he had not
yet fairly come out of the torpid state. It appeared to me that for a like
reason men remain in their present low and primitive condition; but if
they should feel the influence of the spring of springs arousing them,
they would of necessity rise to a higher and more ethereal life. I had
previously seen the snakes in frosty mornings in my path with portions
of their bodies still numb and inflexible, waiting for the sun to thaw
them. On the 1st of April it rained and melted the ice, and in the early
part of the day, which was very foggy, I heard a stray goose groping
about over the pond and cackling as if lost, or like the spirit of the fog.

So I went on for some days cutting and hewing timber, and also   2
studs and rafters, all with my narrow axe, not having many communi-
cable or scholar-like thoughts, singing to myself,—

> *Men say they know many things;*
> *But lo! they have taken wings,—*
> *The arts and sciences,*
> *And a thousand appliances:*
> *The wind that blows*
> *Is all that anybody knows.*

I hewed the main timbers six inches square, most of the studs on two
sides only, and the rafters and floor timbers on one side, leaving the
rest of the bark on, so that they were just as straight and much stronger
than sawed ones. Each stick was carefully mortised or tenoned by its
stump, for I had borrowed other tools by this time. My days in the
woods were not very long ones; yet I usually carried my dinner of bread
and butter, and read the newspaper in which it was wrapped, at noon,

sitting amid the green pine boughs which I had cut off, and to my bread was imparted some of their fragrance, for my hands were covered with a thick coat of pitch. Before I had done I was more the friend than the foe of the pine tree, though I had cut down some of them, having become better acquainted with it. Sometimes a rambler in the wood was attracted by the sound of my axe, and we chatted pleasantly over the chips which I had made.

By the middle of April, for I made no haste in my work, but rather made the most of it, my house was framed and ready for the raising. I had already bought the shanty of James Collins, an Irishman who worked on the Fitchburg Railroad, for boards. James Collins' shanty was considered an uncommonly fine one. When I called to see it he was not at home. I walked about the outside, at first unobserved from within, the window was so deep and high. It was of small dimensions, with a peaked cottage roof, and not much else to be seen, the dirt being raised five feet all around as if it were a compost heap. The roof was the soundest part, though a good deal warped and made brittle by the sun. Doorsill there was none, but a perennial passage for the hens under the door-board. Mrs. C. came to the door and asked me to view it from the inside. The hens were driven in by my approach. It was dark, and had a dirt floor for the most part, dank, clammy, and aguish, only here a board and there a board which would not bear removal. She lighted a lamp to show me the inside of the roof and the walls, and also that the board floor extended under the bed, warning me not to step into the cellar, a sort of dust hole two feet deep. In her own words, they were "good boards overhead, good boards all around, and a good window,"—of two whole squares originally, only the cat had passed out that way lately. There was a stove, a bed, and a place to sit, an infant in the house where it was born, a silk parasol, gilt-framed looking-glass, and a patent new coffee-mill nailed to an oak sapling, all told. The bargain was soon concluded, for James had in the meanwhile returned. I to pay four dollars and twenty-five cents to-night, he to vacate at five to-morrow morning, selling to nobody else meanwhile: I to take possession at six. It were well, he said, to be there early, and anticipate certain indistinct but wholly unjust claims on the score of ground rent and fuel. This he assured me was the only encumbrance. At six I passed him and his family on the road. One large bundle held their all,—bed, coffee-mill, looking-glass, hens,—all but the cat; she took to the woods and became a wild cat, and, as I learned afterward, trod in a trap set for woodchucks, and so became a dead cat at last.

I took down this dwelling the same morning, drawing the nails, and removed it to the pond-side by small cartloads, spreading the boards on the grass there to bleach and warp back again in the sun. One early thrush gave me a note or two as I drove along the woodland path. I was informed treacherously by a young Patrick that neighbor Seeley, an Irishman, in the intervals of the carting, transferred the still tolerable, straight, and drivable nails, staples, and spikes to his pocket, and then stood when I came back to pass the time of day, and look freshly up, unconcerned, with spring thoughts, at the devastation; there being a dearth of work, as he said. He was there to represent spectatordom, and help make this seemingly insignificant event one with the removal of the gods of Troy.[1]

I dug my cellar in the side of a hill sloping to the south, where a   5
woodchuck had formerly dug his burrow, down through sumach and blackberry roots, and the lowest stain of vegetation, six feet square by seven deep, to a fine sand where potatoes would not freeze in any winter. The sides were left shelving, and not stoned; but the sun having never shone on them, the sand still keeps its place. It was but two hours' work. I took particular pleasure in this breaking of ground, for in almost all latitudes men dig into the earth for an equable temperature. Under the most splendid house in the city is still to be found the cellar where they store their roots as of old, and long after the superstructure has disappeared posterity remark its dent in the earth. The house is still but a sort of porch at the entrance of a burrow.

At length, in the beginning of May, with the help of some of my   6
acquaintances, rather to improve so good an occasion for neighborliness than from any necessity, I set up the frame of my house. No man was ever more honored in the character of his raisers than I. They are destined, I trust, to assist at the raising of loftier structures one day. I began to occupy my house on the 4th of July, as soon as it was boarded and roofed, for the boards were carefully feather-edged and lapped, so that it was perfectly impervious to rain, but before boarding I laid the foundation of a chimney at one end, bringing two cartloads of stones up the hill from the pond in my arms. I built the chimney after my hoeing in the fall, before a fire became necessary for warmth, doing my cooking in the meanwhile out of doors on the ground, early in the morning: which mode I still think is in some respects more convenient and agreeable than the usual one. When it stormed before my bread was baked, I fixed a few boards over the fire, and sat under them to watch my loaf, and passed some pleasant hours in that way. In those days, when my hands were much employed, I read but little, but the least scraps of paper which lay on the ground, my holder, or tablecloth, afforded me as much entertainment, in fact answered the same purpose as the *Iliad*.

It would be worth the while to build still more deliberately than I   7
did, considering, for instance, what foundation a door, a window, a

---

1. The Roman poet Virgil begins his epic, the *Aeneid*, with the hero's moving the household gods from the destroyed city of Troy.

cellar, a garret, have in the nature of man, and perchance never raising any superstructure until we found a better reason for it than our temporal necessities even. There is some of the same fitness in a man's building his own house that there is in a bird's building its own nest. Who knows but if men constructed their dwellings with their own hands, and provided food for themselves and families simply and honestly enough, the poetic faculty would be universally developed, as birds universally sing when they are so engaged? But alas! we do like cowbirds and cuckoos, which lay their eggs in nests which other birds have built, and cheer no traveller with their chattering and unmusical notes. Shall we forever resign the pleasure of construction to the carpenter? What does architecture amount to in the experience of the mass of men? I never in all my walks came across a man engaged in so simple and natural an occupation as building his house. We belong to the community. It is not the tailor alone who is the ninth part of a man;[2] it is as much the preacher, and the merchant, and the farmer. Where is this division of labor to end? and what object does it finally serve? No doubt another *may* also think for me; but it is not therefore desirable that he should do so to the exclusion of my thinking for myself.

True, there are architects so called in this country, and I have heard ⁸ of one at least possessed with the idea of making architectural ornaments have a core of truth, a necessity, and hence a beauty, as if it were a revelation to him. All very well perhaps from his point of view, but only a little better than the common dilettantism. A sentimental reformer in architecture, he began at the cornice, not at the foundation. It was only how to put a core of truth within the ornaments, that every sugarplum, in fact, might have an almond or caraway seed in it,—though I hold that almonds are most wholesome without the sugar,—and not how the inhabitant, the indweller, might build truly within and without, and let the ornaments take care of themselves. What reasonable man ever supposed that ornaments were something outward and in the skin merely,—that the tortoise got his spotted shell, or the shell-fish its mother-o'-pearl tints, by such a contract as the inhabitants of Broadway their Trinity Church? But a man has no more to do with the style of architecture of his house than a tortoise with that of its shell: nor need the soldier be so idle as to try to paint the precise *color* of his virtue on his standard. The enemy will find it out. He may turn pale when the trial comes. This man seemed to me to lean over the cornice, and timidly whisper his half truth to the rude occupants who really knew it better than he. What of architectural beauty I now see, I know has gradually grown from within outward,

---

2. "It takes nine tailors to make a man": a popular saying of the nineteenth century.

out of the necessities and character of the indweller, who is the only builder,—out of some unconscious truthfulness, and nobleness, without ever a thought for the appearance and whatever additional beauty of this kind is destined to be produced will be preceded by a like unconscious beauty of life. The most interesting dwellings in this country, as the painter knows, are the most unpretending, humble log huts and cottages of the poor commonly; it is the life of the inhabitants whose shells they are, and not any peculiarity in their surfaces merely, which makes them *picturesque;* and equally interesting will be the citizen's suburban box, when his life shall be as simple and as agreeable to the imagination, and there is as little straining after effect in the style of his dwelling. A great proportion of architectural ornaments are literally hollow, and a September gale would strip them off, like borrowed plumes, without injury to the substantials. They can do without *architecture* who have no olives nor wines in the cellar. What if an equal ado were made about the ornaments of style in literature, and the architects of our Bibles spent as much time about their cornices as the architects of our churches do? So are made the *belles-lettres* and the *beaux-arts* and their professors. Much it concerns a man, forsooth, how a few sticks are slanted over him or under him, and what colors are daubed upon his box. It would signify somewhat, if, in any earnest sense, *he* slanted them and daubed it; but the spirit having departed out of the tenant, it is of a piece with constructing his own coffin,—the architecture of the grave,—and "carpenter" is but another name for "coffin-maker." One man says, in his despair or indifference to life, take up a handful of the earth at your feet, and paint your house that color. Is he thinking of his last and narrow house? Toss up a copper for it as well. What an abundance of leisure he must have! Why do you take up a handful of dirt? Better paint your house your own complexion; let it turn pale or blush for you. An enterprise to improve the style of cottage architecture! When you have got my ornaments ready, I will wear them.

Before winter I built a chimney, and shingled the sides of my house, which were already impervious to rain, with imperfect and sappy shingles made of the first slice of the log, whose edges I was obliged to straighten with a plane. 9

I have thus a tight shingled and plastered house, ten feet wide by fifteen long, and eight-feet posts, with a garret and a closet, a large window on each side, two trap-doors, one door at the end, and a brick fireplace opposite. The exact cost of my house, paying the usual price for such materials as I used, but not counting the work, all of which was done by myself, was as follows; and I give the details because very few are able to tell exactly what their houses cost, and fewer still, if any, the separate cost of the various materials which compose them:— 10

Boards	$8 03½ , mostly shanty boards.	
Refuse shingles for roof and sides	4 00	
Laths	1 25	
Two second-hand windows with glass	2 43	
One thousand old brick	4 00	
Two casks of lime	2 40	That was high.
Hair	0 31	More than I needed.
Mantle-tree iron	0 15	
Nails	3 90	
Hinges and screws	0 14	
Latch	0 10	
Chalk	0 01	
Transportation	1 40	{ carried a good part on my back.
In all	$28 12½	

These are all the materials, excepting the timber, stones, and sand, which I claimed by squatter's right. I have also a small woodshed adjoining, made chiefly of the stuff which was left after building the house.

I intend to build me a house which will surpass any on the main street in Concord in grandeur and luxury, as soon as it pleases me as much and will cost me no more than my present one.

I thus found that the student who wishes for a shelter can obtain one for a lifetime at an expense not greater than the rent which he now pays annually. If I seem to boast more than is becoming, my excuse is that I brag for humanity rather than for myself; and my shortcomings and inconsistencies do not affect the truth of my statement. Notwithstanding much cant and hypocrisy,—chaff which I find it difficult to separate from my wheat, but for which I am as sorry as any man,—I will breathe freely and stretch myself in this respect, it is such a relief to both the moral and physical system; and I am resolved that I will not through humility become the devil's attorney. I will endeavor to speak a good word for the truth. At Cambridge College the mere rent of a student's room, which is only a little larger than my own, is thirty dollars each year, though the corporation had the advantage of building thirty-two side by side and under one roof, and the occupant suffers the inconvenience of many and noisy neighbors, and perhaps a residence in the fourth story. I cannot but think that if we had more true wisdom in these respects, not only less education would be needed, because, forsooth, more would already have been acquired, but the pecuniary expense of getting an education would in a great measure vanish. Those conveniences which the student requires at Cambridge or elsewhere cost him or somebody else ten times as great a sacrifice of life as they would with proper management on both sides. Those things for which the most money is demanded are never the things which the student most wants. Tuition, for instance, is an important item in the term bill, while for the far more valuable education which he gets by associating with the most cultivated of his contemporaries no charge is made. The mode of founding a college is, commonly, to get up a subscription of dollars and cents, and then, following blindly the principles of a division of labor to its extreme,—a principle which should never be followed but with circumspection,—to call in a contractor who makes this a subject of speculation, and he employs Irishmen or other operatives actually to lay the foundations, while the students that are to be are said to be fitting themselves for it; and for these oversights successive generations have to pay. I think that it would be *better than this*, for the students, or those who desire to be benefited by it, even to lay the foundation themselves. The student who secures his coveted leisure and retirement by systematically shirking any labor necessary to man obtains but an ignoble and unprofitable leisure, defrauding himself of the experience which alone can make leisure fruitful. "But," says one, "you do not mean that the students should go to work with their hands instead of their heads?" I do not mean that exactly, but I mean something which he might think a good deal like that; I mean that they should not *play* life, or *study* it merely, while the community supports them at this expensive game, but earnestly *live* it from beginning to end. How could youths better learn to live than by at once trying the experiment of living? Methinks this would exercise their minds as much as mathematics. If I wished a boy to know something about the arts and sciences, for instance, I would not pursue the common course, which is merely to send him into the neighborhood of some professor, where anything is professed and practised but the art of life;—to survey the world through a telescope or a microscope, and never with his natural eye; to study chemistry, and not learn how his bread is made, or mechanics, and not learn how it is earned; to discover new satellites to Neptune, and not detect the motes in his eyes, or to what vagabond he is a satellite himself; or to be devoured by the monsters that swarm all around him, while contemplating the monsters in a drop of vinegar. Which would have advanced the most at the end of a month,—the boy who had made his own jackknife from the ore which he had dug and smelted, reading as much as would be necessary for this—or the boy who had attended the lectures on metallurgy at the Institute in the meanwhile, and had received a Rodgers penknife from his father? Which would be most likely to cut his fingers? . . . To my astonishment I was informed on leaving college that I had studied navigation!—why, if I had taken one turn down the harbor I should have known more about it. Even the *poor* student studies and is taught only *political* economy, while that economy of living which is synonymous with philosophy is not even sincerely professed in our colleges. The consequence is, that while he is reading Adam Smith, Ricardo, and Say,[3] he runs his father in debt irretrievably.

As with our colleges, so with a hundred "modern improvements"; there is an illusion about them; there is not always a positive advance. The devil goes on exacting compound interest to the last for his early share and numerous succeeding investments in them. Our inventions are wont to be pretty toys, which distract our attention from serious things. They are but improved means to an unimproved end, an end which it was already but too easy to arrive at; as railroads lead to Boston or New York. We are in great haste to construct a magnetic telegraph from Maine to Texas; but Maine and Texas, it may be, have nothing important to communicate. Either is in such a predicament as the man who was earnest to be introduced to a distinguished deaf woman, but when he was presented, and one end of her ear trumpet was put into his hand, had nothing to say. As if the main object were to talk fast and not to talk sensibly. We are eager to tunnel under the Atlantic and bring the Old World some weeks nearer to the New; but perchance the first news that will leak through into the broad, flapping American ear will be that the Princess Adelaide has the whooping cough. After all, the man whose horse trots a mile a minute does not carry the most important messages; he is not an evangelist, nor does he come round eating locusts and wild honey.[4] I doubt if Flying Childers[5] ever carried a peck of corn to mill.

One says to me, "I wonder that you do not lay up money; you love to travel; you might take the cars and go to Fitchburg today and see the country." But I am wiser than that. I have learned that the swiftest traveller is he that goes afoot. I say to my friend, Suppose we try who will get there first. The distance is thirty miles; the fare ninety cents. That is almost a day's wages. I remember when wages were sixty cents a day for laborers on this very road. Well, I start now on foot, and get there before night; I have travelled at that rate by the week together. You will in the meanwhile have earned your fare, and arrive there sometime to-morrow, or possibly this evening, if you are lucky enough to get a job in season. Instead of going to Fitchburg, you will be working here the greater part of the day. And so, if the railroad reached round the world, I think that I should keep ahead of you; and as for seeing the country and getting experience of that kind, I should have to cut your acquaintance altogether.

Such is the universal law, which no man can ever outwit, and with regard to the railroad even we may say it is as broad as it is long. To make a railroad round the world available to all mankind is equivalent

3. Noted political economists.
4. As John the Baptist did.
5. An undefeated English racehorse of the eighteenth century.

to grading the whole surface of the planet. Men have an indistinct notion that if they keep up this activity of joint stocks and spades long enough all will at length ride somewhere, in next to no time, and for nothing; but though a crowd rushes to the depot, and the conductor shouts "All aboard!" when the smoke is blown away and the vapor condensed, it will be perceived that a few are riding, but the rest are run over,—and it will be called, and will be, "A melancholy accident." No doubt they can ride at last who shall have earned their fare, that is, if they survive so long, but they will probably have lost their elasticity and desire to travel by that time. This spending of the best part of one's life earning money in order to enjoy a questionable liberty during the least valuable part of it reminds me of the Englishman who went to India to make a fortune first, in order that he might return to England and live the life of a poet. He should have gone up garret at once. "What!" exclaim a million Irishmen starting up from all the shanties in the land, "is not this railroad which we have built a good thing?" Yes, I answer, *comparatively* good, that is, you might have done worse; but I wish, as you are brothers of mine, that you could have spent your time better than digging in this dirt.

THOMAS EDISON

The Woman of the Future

Thomas Alva Edison (1847–1931) was expelled from school in Port Huron, Michigan, at age seven because his teacher thought he was retarded. Educated by his mother, he developed an interest in chemistry and electricity and built a homemade telegraph. By the time he was sixteen he was a professional telegraph operator, spending most of his wages experimenting with ways to improve the device he operated. In 1868 he bought a copy of the research journals of the English scientist Michael Faraday and taught himself proper scientific methods. From this point forward, his life is the stuff of legend. He invented the electric lightbulb, the phonograph, the mimeograph, the fluoroscope, and the alkaline storage battery. He produced the first practical motion picture cameras and projectors, and though Alexander Graham Bell beat him to the telephone, Edison improved it by inventing the crucial carbon transmitter for its speaker. His laboratories at Menlo Park and West Orange, New Jersey, employed a large staff of technicians and scientists and became the prototype for today's industrial research parks. By the time he died, he owned the patents on more than a thousand inventions. In his later years, Edison began to be quoted as a sage, as in this interview with journalist Edward Marshall, published in *Good Housekeeping* in October 1912.

"The housewife of the future will be neither a slave to servants nor   1
herself a drudge. She will give less attention to the home, because the
home will need less; she will be rather a domestic engineer than a
domestic laborer, with the greatest of all handmaidens, electricity, at
her service. This and other mechanical forces will so revolutionize the
woman's world that a large portion of the aggregate of woman's energy
will be conserved for use in broader, more constructive fields."

As we talked, Thomas A. Edison, doubtless the greatest inventor of   2
all time, said some things which may offend the woman of now, but
he said others so appreciative and inspiring that they surely will wipe
offense away. He declared, without reserve, his concord with the suffrage workers; he explained that woman as she is, and speaking generally, is an undeveloped creature and—here is where the women's wrath
will rise at first—vastly man's inferior. But he went on to say that
anatomical investigation of the female brain[1] has shown it to be finer
and more capable of ultimate aesthetic development than man's, and
he explained that that development is undoubtedly, at last, well under
way.

"It may be a perfectly natural detail of the development of the race   3
that the modern woman not only does not wish to be, but will not be,
a servant," Mr. Edison declared. "This has had its really unfortunate
effect in that it has led, of late years, to general neglect of woman's
work, and has resulted in the refusal, or, at least the failure, of many
mothers to rightly teach their daughters. But good will ultimately come
of it, for the necessities arising out of womankind's unwillingness, have
turned the minds of the inventors toward creation of mechanical devices
to perform that work which woman used to do. The first requisite of
such machinery was a power which could be easily and economically
subdivided into small units. Such a power has been found in electricity,
which is now not only available in the cities, where it can be obtained
from the great electrical supply concerns, but is becoming constantly
more easily available in the rural districts, through the development of
the small dynamo and of the gasoline engine and the appreciation and
utilization of small water powers which are becoming general even on
our farms.

"Electricity will do practically all of the manual work about the   4
home. Just as it has largely supplanted the broom and dustpan, and
even the carpet sweeper, by being harnessed to the vacuum cleaner, it
will be applied to the hundreds of other littler drudgeries in the house
and in the yard. Attached to various simple but entirely effective mechanical contrivances now everywhere upon the market, and many
others soon to be there, it will eliminate the task of maintaining cleanliness in other ways as well as in cleaning up dirt. No labor is much

1. Apparently by means of phrenology, a "science" based on analysis of the skull's shape.

worse than sweeping. It has killed many women. Did you ever stop to think what a boon to women the vacuum cleaner really has been?

"Electricity will not only, as now, wash the clothes when turned   5 on in a laundry and plugged into any one of dozens of existent patent washers, but will dry them, gather them, and iron them without the use of the little manual labor even now required in ironing by electrically heated individual irons and by the application of electricity to the other parts of the process. Electricity already dries clothes, after washing, quickly and with great economy of fabric, in easily equipped and inexpensive drying rooms, electrically heated, free from the dust of coal fires and from the winds which tore grandmother's wash to tatters when it was hung upon the outdoor lines of the old days. These electric laundries have already been reduced to what approaches absolute perfection in the larger establishments, such as commercial laundries, hotels, and the more luxurious apartment buildings, but it will not be long before they will be made possible for the small home in the cities or on farms.

"By supplying light through bulbs containing neither wicks to trim   6 nor reservoirs to be filled with dust-accumulating oil, and involving no lamp chimneys to be cleaned of soot, electricity is constantly eliminating one large detail of the old-time household drudgery.

"As improved methods of production are developed, especially as   7 waterpower comes into use for its creation, the electric current is becoming cheaper, so that it is now available, even in the kitchen, as a substitute for coal or oil, or gas in cooking. A vast advantage which comes from it, lies in the fact that it does not heat up a kitchen and that, with nominal expenditure for additional current, ventilators can be arranged and operated which will keep the kitchen absolutely free of fumes. Many a woman's life in old days was shortened; many a woman's life in these days is being shortened, by her presence for long hours each day in an overheated atmosphere above a cook-stove. The application of electricity to domestic work will do away with this.

"A kitchen in which the cooking is electrically done and in which   8 a ventilation system electrically operated is installed, cannot become unduly heated even in the worst days of our terrific American summers. Electricity will cool the room as readily as it will cook the food. The kitchen of the future will be all electric, and the electric kitchen will be as comfortable as any room in the house.

"And the electric cooking of the future will, in many instances,   9 improve the food. It will permit the preparation of many dishes literally on the dining table, by means of the electric chafing dish, and more complete utensils, and so reduce the labor of food preparation that there will be no temptation to prepare it in large quantities and put parts of it aside for future use, a system which results frequently in sad deterioration of the food involved.

"And not only will it make cooking simple and economical, but it will make it better, for electric heat can be locally applied as no other heat can be. The electrically cooked roast will be the perfect roast. No part of it need be underdone, no part of it need be burned in the oven. The housewife's great problem of imperfectly adjusted draughts and dampers will be solved—indeed, it has been solved—in many kitchens, for electric cooking is already widely practiced.

"The housewife's work, in days to come, will amount to little more than superintendence, not of Norah, fresh from Ireland, or Gretchen, fresh from Germany, but of simplified electrical appliances; and that is why I said, to start with, that electricity will change the housewives of the future from drudges into engineers.

"Electricity has already cheapened very greatly; it is getting cheaper every day. It used to cost ten cents a kilowatt hour, but the price has been reduced to five cents, four cents, even three cents to large consumers of power. An element in the cost is the time at which the current is consumed. If it is not used at the times known as 'peak hours,' that is, at hours when it is most in demand for lighting and for power, it can be manufactured and served very cheaply.

"The problem of the storage of electricity must enter our calculations when we endeavor to make predictions of its future cost, and that is, perhaps, too complicated to go into here; but I do not hesitate to say that in the not far distant future electricity will be sold in New York City at 50 percent of its present cost. In cities where water power is available for its manufacture, the rate already is much lower than it is in New York City, and it will continue to decrease until electricity becomes the cheapest power which man has ever known.

"Even as things are now, all sort of minor mechanical appliances such as brushes to clear the hair from dust in barber shops, factories, and homes, vacuum cleaners and a hundred other things operated through air condensed by electricity are in daily and growing use—a use which must be economical or it would not exist. There are lawn mowers which are chargeable 'off the line,' and indeed if I were to attempt to make a catalog of all the minor uses to which electricity is already put, the list would fill a good part of an issue of *Good Housekeeping*. Here is a distinct advance, for everything performing labor without requiring power from human muscles must be regarded as real progress.

"To diminish the necessity for utilizing man himself, or woman herself, as the motor-furnishing force for this life's mechanical tasks, is to increase the potentiality of humanity's brain power. When all our mental energy can be devoted to the highest tasks of which it may be capable, then shall we have made the greatest forward step in this world's history. To so conserve our energy as to trend toward this eventuality is the tendency of the age.

"It is there that electricity will play its greatest part in the develop-

ment of womankind. It will not only permit women to more generally
exercise their mental force, but will compel this exercise, and thus insure a brain development in them such as has been prevented in the
past.

"It will develop woman to that point where she can think straight.   17
Direct thought is not at present an attribute of femininity. In this woman
is now centuries, ages, even epochs behind man. That it is true is not
her fault, but her misfortune, and the misfortune of the race. Man must
accept responsibility for it, for it has been through his superior physical
strength that he has held his dominance over woman and delayed her
growth. For ages woman was man's chattel, and in such condition
progress for her was impossible; now she is emerging into real sex
independence, and the resulting outlook is a dazzling one. This must
be credited very largely to progression in mechanics; more especially to
progression in electrical mechanics.

"Under these new influences woman's brain will change and   18
achieve new capabilities, both of effort and accomplishment. Woman
will grow more involved cross fibers and that will mean a new race of
mankind.

"Man is at present little, if any, more than half what he might   19
be. The child may be considered the mean between his father and his
mother—between the undeveloped female and the developed male.
The male has had his full of mental exercise since society first organized;
it has been denied the female. To growth, exercise is an essential. An
arm which never has been used will show weak muscles. A blacksmith's
arm is mighty because it lifts great weights, strikes heavy blows. Development of brain is not so very different from muscular development.
The idle brain will atrophy, as will the idle arm.

"The brain of woman in the past has been, to an extent, an idle   20
brain. She has been occupied with petty tasks which, while holding her
attention closely, have not given her brain exercise; such thinking as
she has had time for, she has very largely found unnecessary because
the stronger sex has done it for her. Through exercise men's brains have
developed from the low standard of the aborigine to the high standard
of the modern man, and if, in the new era which is dawning, woman's
mental power increases with as great rapidity as that with which man's
has grown, the children of the future—the children of the exercised,
developed man, and of the exercised, developed woman—will be of
mental power incredible to us today.

"The evolution of the brain of the male human has been the most   21
wonderful of all the various phenomena of nature. When, in the new
era of emancipation from the thraldom of the everyday mechanical
task, the brain of woman undergoes a similar development, then, and
only then, will the race begin to reach its ultimate. Yes, the mental

power of the child born in the future will be marvelous, for to it women will make a contribution as great as that of man.

"There never was any need for woman's retardation. Man's selfishness, his lust for ownership, must be held responsible for it. He was not willing to make woman equal partner in his various activities, and so he held her back from an ability to fill an equal partnership. [22]

"Less of this is evident in the development of the Jewish than in that of any other race. The almost supernatural business instinct of the Jew may be, I think, attributed to the fact that the various persecutions of the race have forced it to develop all its strength—its strength of women as well as that of men. Women have, from the beginning, taken part in Jewish councils; Jewish women have shared, always, in the pursuits of Jewish men; especially have they been permitted to play their part in business management. The result is that the Jewish child receives commercial acumen not only from the father's but from the mother's side. This may be taken as an evidence of what may come in future when womankind in general is equally developed with men along all lines. [23]

"This development of woman through the evolution of mechanics will, by means of those mechanics, probably be the quickest which the world has ever seen. The refinements of life in the future will be carried to a point not dreamed of now. I think the time has just arrived when the menial phases of existence may be said to be upon the verge of disappearing. This undoubtedly accounts for the great difficulty we experience now in hiring men, and more especially in hiring women, to do menial labor. The servant girl performs her tasks unwillingly in these days, and when she sees an opportunity, deserts them for the factory, where, through mechanical appliances, her potentiality as a human being finds new effectiveness. [24]

"The drudgery of life will, by and by, entirely disappear. In days to come, through a small outlay of money, both men and women will be gratified by an infinite variety of delightful sights, sounds, and experiences that today are unknown and unimagined. [25]

"An illustration of what may eventually be accomplished has arisen recently in my own experience. I have been once more working on the phonograph, endeavoring to bring it to perfection, and, within a few months, have succeeded in so doing. Here at my laboratory we now know not only that we can make records of and reproduce the finest music which humanity has yet created, but through our work we have discovered imperfections in the music of the past which, now that they have been found out, will be corrected. In a short time it will be possible to produce within the humblest home the best music of the world, and to produce it there as perfectly as it was in its first form. The reproduction will be presented so that any individual listening to it will hear the [26] music to far better advantage than could any individual listening to the original production, unless his seat, while listening, were located in a scientifically determined spot in the auditorium wherein the music was produced. At concerts, now, the listener on one side of the hall hears too much brass. On the other side wood instruments or the strings are dominant.

"In playing for the phonographic records of the future, the orches-   27
tras will be so carefully distributed that each instrument will have its uttermost value in relation to the one spot where the phonograph is located and recording. Therefore, the person hearing music reproduced for them by this new instrument will have advantages which hitherto have been among the possibilities for but a small group at each concert. In the phonographic concert of the future, all will be balanced. I am informed that balance is secured in New York's Metropolitan Opera House only in a few seats near the center aisles, back, close to the doors. In front, on either side, and above, the music must, of necessity, be more or less unbalanced, and the cleverest acoustics cannot counteract this.

"In order to learn what was true and what was false about our   28
records, I made a minute microscopical examination of tremendous numbers of them, and eventually reduced music to a minutely meas-ured science. I was enabled to reproduce singers' notes exactly as they had been sung. This gave us all the beauties of the original rendition, but, alas! it gave us all the flaws as well. The latter was appalling, both in number and magnitude. I shall not give a list of the world-famous singers who worked with us, but I shall reveal the surprising fact that the greatest of them dramatically are correspondingly poor vocally. When the tiny dots which register the sound upon a phonographic cylinder can be subjected to a microscopical examination and exact measurement, the slightest falsity is at once scientifically and mathemat-ically discernible.

"The influence of this advance will be to startlingly improve the   29
singing of the world, because it will make possible the discovery of imperfections which in the past have been glossed by emotions. These faults, thus revealed, will undoubtedly be found subject to correction, and thus singing will improve. All this will enormously simplify the labors of anxious mothers and of teachers who strive to impart musical training to the young. I have been studying music with as much inten-sity, of late, as I ever gave to any task, and I find few instruments, and practically no human voices without glaring imperfections. I have had a great number of teachers in my laboratory, and have found them all at sea. They have had no standards, no measurements. Music has been, like other things, unorganized. Its standardization, its measurement, its organization, were the first steps in our experimenting.

"I have in five months tried nine thousand five hundred tunes or   30 songs in an earnest endeavor to find what it all means, to learn why certain music dies, why other music lives. Once, in a brief period, I studied one thousand seven hundred waltzes, as reproduced day by day without pause on pianos, and at another time seven hundred more. It was only in this way that a real investigation of the facts of music became possible. The study necessitated elaborate investigations of each musical instrument. I knew the mechanics of them, but did not know the musical aesthetics. My investigations have been accurate, for they have been founded upon measurement; actual physical measurement of sound vibrations, as recorded on the phonographic cylinder. Helmholtz in his studies was thrown off badly by the imperfect instruments which he used in experimenting. I have been able to avoid all that. I can make a record, reproduce it, and then examine with a microscope the vibrations of which it is made up, and this makes their measurement quite possible and proves out the quality of tone by actually hearing it. The method was not known to Helmholtz,[2] and he therefore drew many wrong conclusions.

"It will be with music as it has been with electricity. When we first began in electricity we had no measurements; we had to guess at everything. It was only when we reduced currents down to units of measurements such as volts and amperes that measurement was possible, and until measurement was possible, no true knowledge of electricity was possible. Music has, likewise, floundered about, misunderstood, unsystematized. It has been a complicated matter in which the personal equation has played the largest part and in which accuracy—which means Truth—has played a very small part.

"I have gone into this matter of the new phonograph (which has not hitherto been announced) because it indicates advance along those special lines you ask me to consider. It will save the woman of the future one more of those tasks which have absorbed her in the past, and will perform it for her better than she could perform it for herself. It will open to her and her children, at small cost, a vast mass of music which has hitherto been denied them at any price whatever of money or of effort, and will leave no real excuse for such expenditure of mothers' time as has been given to producing for, and teaching to, the children of the past crude music on pianos or what not.

"Science has, by this advance, removed one more of the great time eaters which have so oppressed all women. With the home-picture machine, now well developed, taking moving pictures into the family circle, it will be possible to furnish, quickly and concretely, such knowledge of the wonders of the nature which surrounds us as was impossible for our forefathers to obtain through any means of study. The revela-

2. Hermann Ludvig Ferdinand von Helmholtz (1821–1894), a great German physiologist and physicist.

tions are illimitable. We could start at eight each morning, and watch films till eight each night for a period of a thousand years, and see new things each moment, without more than slightly touching on the surface of the facts which are available. The moving picture is developing the circumstance that we live in an environment of which we know practically nothing, and of which we even surmise little.

"All these things will do more for the development of women than   34 they will for the development of men, and they are but a few of many influences which now are working toward that end. They occur to me because they are involved in those things which most engage my thought. They will help develop those cells in a woman's mind which have not in the past had opportunity or encouragement to grow. Give them opportunity and encouragement, and they will grow with great rapidity. They are very smart—these little cells! I have not much muscle, because I never have had reason to develop muscle. If I had had to do hard manual labor in the past, my little cells would have built muscle for me.

"The exercise of women's brains will build for them new fibers,   35 new involutions, and new folds. If women had had the same struggle for existence which has confronted men, they would have been physically as strong, as capable of mind. But in the past they were protected, or, if not protected, forced to drudgery. These days are the days of woman's start upon the race—her first fair start.

"More and more she must be pushed, and more and more she will   36 advance herself. It is lack of those brain folds which has made her so illogical. Now, as they begin to come to her she will gain in logic. When she has to meet, in future, the same crises which men in the past have had to meet, the conservation of her time, which modern science has made possible, will have armed her for the encounter. This will make Earth a splendid planet to live upon.

"The development of women will solve many problems which we   37 now deem quite insoluble. When women progress side by side with men, matrimony will become the perfect partnership. This perfect partnership will produce a childhood made up of individuals who would now be thought not only mental, but physical and moral prodigies. There will be no drawbacks to life. We shall stop the cry for more births and raise instead a cry for better births. We shall wake up presently to the dire fact that this world is getting settled at a rate which presently will occupy its total space. The less of that space which is occupied by the unfit and the imperfect, certainly the better for the race. The development of women which has now begun and is progressing with such startling speed, will do more to solve this problem than any other thing could do. What we want now is quality, not quantity. The woman of the future—the domestic engineer, not the domestic drudge—the wife, not the dependent; not alone the mother, but the teacher and developer, will help to bring this quality about."

JULIET B. SCHOR

Housewives' Hours

Juliet B. Schor (1955–   ), who took her B.A. from Wesleyan University in Connecticut in 1975 and her Ph.D. in economics from the University of Massachusetts in 1982, has had the sort of solid academic career that rarely produces best-sellers. After teaching briefly at Williams College and Columbia University, she settled in at Harvard, published three books, and was promoted to associate professor in 1989. Three years later she published *The Overworked American: The Unexpected Decline of Leisure.* The book received so much critical and media attention that Schor found herself suddenly in the limelight, frequently interviewed and asked to make public appearances. The cause of this stir was her portrait of American workers lured by the desire for a higher and higher material standard of living into a work-and-spend lifestyle that leaves them unhappy and unfulfilled. "Many of us," she says in her preface, "need to relax, unwind, and, yes, to work less." The following excerpt, which surveys the effect of technology on housewives, combines Schor's interest in economics with her increasing interest in women's studies. Schor's footnotes citing *Scientific American, Ladies' Home Journal, Ms.* magazine, and several academic books and articles have been omitted.

The twentieth century radically transformed America. We went from the horse and buggy to the Concorde, from farm to city and then to suburb, from silent movies to VCRs. Throughout all these changes, one thing stayed constant: the amount of work done by the American housewife. In the 1910s, she was doing about fifty-two hours a week. Fifty or sixty years later, the figure wasn't much different. 1

This conclusion comes from a set of studies recording the daily 2 activities of full-time housewives. The first was carried out in 1912–14 by a Ph.D. candidate at Columbia University named John Leeds. Leeds surveyed a group of sixty middle-class families, with employed husbands, full-time homemakers, and an average of 2.75 children. After watching the routine of the housewives in his group, Leeds found that they spent an average of fifty-six hours each week at their work. This number is actually slightly higher than most subsequent findings, but the difference appears not to be meaningful and is attributable to some peculiarities of Leeds's families.

Over the next few decades, many more housewives were surveyed 3 under the auspices of the U.S. Bureau of Home Economics. Another Ph.D. candidate, Joann Vanek from the University of Michigan, compiled the results of these surveys, all of which followed a common set of guidelines. Vanek found that in 1926–27, and again in 1929,

Figure 4.1 The Constancy of Housewives' Weekly Hours

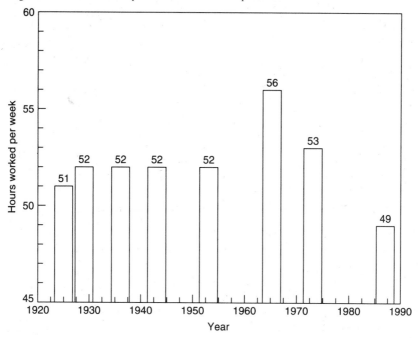

SOURCE: Estimates from 1926–27 through 1965–66 are from Joann Vanek, "Time Spent in Housework," *Scientific American*, 231 (5 November 1974): 116–20. 1973 and 1987 are author's calculations.
All data are for full-time housewives.

housewives were putting in about fifty-two hours. The strange thing is that in 1936, 1943, and 1953, years of additional studies, the findings were unchanged. The housewife was still logging in fifty-two hours. In the 1960s and 1970s, more surveys were undertaken. A large one in Syracuse, New York, in 1967 and 1968 found that housewives averaged fifty-six hours per week. And according to my own estimates, from 1973, a married, middle-class housewife with three children did an average of fifty-three hours of domestic work each week (see figure 4.1).

The odd thing about the constancy of hours is that it coincided with a technological revolution in the household. When the early studies were done, American homes had little sophisticated equipment. Many were not yet wired for gas and electricity. They did not have automatic washers and dryers or refrigerators. Some homes even lacked indoor plumbing, so that every drop of water that entered the house had to be carried in by hand and then carried out again.

By 1950, the amount of capital equipment in the home had risen dramatically. Major technological systems, such as indoor plumbing, electricity, and gas, had been installed virtually everywhere. At the same time, many labor-saving appliances also came into vogue—automatic washing machines and dryers, electric irons, vacuum cleaners, refrigerators and freezers, garbage disposals. By the 1990s, we had added dishwashers, microwaves, and trash compacters. Each of these innovations had the potential to save countless hours of labor. Yet none of them did. In terms of reducing time spent on domestic work, all this expensive labor-saving technology was an abject failure.

Researchers have documented this failure. After conducting a large, twelve-country study, in which conditions ranged from the most modern to rather primitive (lack of indoor plumbing, appliances, and so forth), the authors tentatively suggested the opposite: technical sophistication may *increase* the amount of time given over to household work. Studies of U.S. women also found that those with more durable equipment in their homes work no fewer hours than those with less. Only one major appliance has been shown to save significant amounts of time (the microwave oven). Some actually increase housework (freezers and washing machines).

Of course, technology was not without its effects. Some activities became less time consuming and others more. Between the 1920s and the 1960s, food preparation fell almost ten hours a week, but was offset by a rise in shopping, managerial tasks, and child care. Certain innovations were labor saving on their own, but led to new tasks. The refrigerator eliminated the need for daily shopping and storing ice at home, but helped drive the door-to-door vendor out of business, thereby contributing to the rise of the supermarket, with its self-service and greater travel time.

Laundry provides the best example of how technology failed to reduce labor time. During the period from 1925 to 1965, automatic washers and dryers were introduced. The new machines did cut the time needed to wash and dry a load of clothes. Yet laundry time rose. The reason was that housewives were doing more loads—in part, because investment in household-level capital undermined commercial establishments. Laundry that had previously been sent out began to stay home. At the same time, standards of cleanliness went up.

The escalation of standards for laundering has been a long process, stretching back to colonial times. In those days, washing would be done once a month at most and, in many families, much less—perhaps four times per year. Nearly everyone wore dirty clothes nearly all the time. Slowly the frequency of washing rose. When the electric washer was introduced (1925), many Americans enjoyed a clean set of clothes (or at least a fresh shirt or blouse) every Saturday night. By the 1950s and 1960s, we washed after one wearing.

Standards have crept up for nearly everything housewives do—laundry, cooking, care of children, shopping, care of the sick, cleaning.

Estimates from a mid-1970s survey show that the housewife spent an
average of 10.3 hours a week getting the floors "spic and span," cleaning toilets, dusting, and waxing. In recent decades, homes have received
"deep cleaning," with concerted attacks on "germs" and an "eat-off-
the-floor" standard. Americans have taken seriously the dictum that
"cleanliness is next to godliness." One 1920s housewife realized:

> Because we housewives of today have the tools to reach it, we dig every
> day after dust that grandmother left to a spring cataclysm. If few of us have
> nine children for a weekly bath, we have two or three for a daily immer-
> sion. If our consciences don't prick over vacant pie shelves or empty cookie
> jars, they do over meals in which a vitamin may be omitted or a calorie
> lacking.

But we were not always like this. Contemporary standards of housecleaning are a modern invention, like the vacuum cleaners and furniture polishes that make them possible. Europeans (and Americans)
joined the cleanliness bandwagon quite recently. It was not until the
late eighteenth century that people in England even began to wash
themselves systematically. And it was only the rich who did so. Body
odors and excretions offended no one. For example, menstrual blood
just dripped onto the floor. In terms of personal hygiene, a crust of dirt
was thought to foster a good complexion underneath. Noses would be
blown onto clothing; feces were often left lying around the house, even
among the genteel classes.

In other parts of the world, higher standards of hygiene prevailed.   11
Medieval and early modern European travelers to Asia, for example,
were considered to be extremely uncouth. In matters of housekeeping,
filth and neglect were the order of the day. Anything more was considered "a waste of time." These habits were transported to America with
the first European settlers, whose bodies and homes reproduced Euro-
pean-style filth. The culture of cleanliness was at least a century away.

It was delayed because it was expensive. The labor of colonial   12
women was far too valuable to be spent creating spic-and-span. For
most colonists, survival entailed the labor of both adults (and their
children and perhaps someone else's children as well). Women were
busy making yarn, cloth, candles, and soap. They were butchering animals, baking bread, churning butter, and brewing beer. They tended
gardens and animals, concocted medicines, and cared for the sick. They
sewed and mended garments, and typically had time to clean their
houses only once a year. According to historian Mary Beth Norton, "it
seems clear either that cleanliness was not highly valued or that farm
wives, fully occupied with other tasks, simply had no time to worry
about sweeping floors, airing bedding, or putting things away." Undoubtedly, some colonial women did take great pains with their homes,
but sanitation could be infeasible. Rural dwellings were rudimentary,

with dirt floors and few pieces of furniture or other possessions. Open-hearth fires spewed out soot. Hauling and heating water was arduous and expensive; it was used sparingly for luxuries such as washing dishes.

The less well-off segments of U.S. society, who were by no means 13 a minority, faced similar living conditions throughout the nineteenth century. Slaves, and then sharecroppers, lived in primitive cabins, which were "extremely difficult to keep clean and tidy." In urban tenements, housekeeping was hard even to recognize:

> There was no furniture to speak of, few clothes to wash, little food to prepare. . . . Washing and cleaning were difficult since all water had to be carried up the stairs. People tracked in dirt from the muddy streets; plaster crumbled; chimneys clogged and stoves smoked. . . . Cleaning was only a small part of complicated and arduous family economies. The major effort went into acquiring necessities—food, fuel and water.

As the nation grew richer, it got cleaner. Prosperity freed many married women from the burdens of earning money and producing necessities and gave them time to devote to housekeeping. As they did, higher standards emerged. The shift began among the middle classes and eventually filtered down to the less well-to-do. By the last quarter of the nineteenth century, America was well into its longstanding affair with the immaculate. Victorian-era homes were subjected to strenuous cleaning exercises, which were further complicated by the clutter and bric-a-brac that was the fashion of the day. In households with servants, requirements would be even more exacting. By the turn of the century, the once-yearly cleaning had given way to a daily routine. Each and every morning, women would be sweeping, dusting, cleaning, washing, and straightening up. And those were just the daily tasks. Bigger jobs (washing clothes, ironing clothes, baking, canning, washing walls, and so on) were done on a weekly, monthly, and seasonal basis. The rituals had become endless.

The trend to more and better was not confined to housecleaning 14 and laundry but included activities such as cooking and baking. To some extent, what occurred was a shift from the production of the food itself (gardening, raising animals, making butter or beer) to more elaborate preparation. In earlier days, "the simplest and least exerting forms of cooking had to be utilized most frequently; hence the ubiquity and centrality of those classic 'one-pot' dishes, soup and stew." Now women learned the art and craft of cooking, as soup and stew gave way to fried chicken and angel food cake. Nutrition and esthetics became preoccupations. All these changes in the standards of housekeeping helped keep the housewife's hours long even as progress made it possible to save her labor. But the area where the upgrading was most dramatic was in the care of children.

Being a mother—and increasingly, being a father as well—is a 15
highly labor-intensive and demanding job. It is an article of faith that
infants and small children need constant attention, supervision, and
love. As they grow older, they also require education and moral training. All these needs translate into countless hours. One might have
thought that mothering was always like this. Newborn babies in the
fifteenth century were just as helpless as those in the twentieth. But
three hundred years ago, parents acted very differently. Children were
hardly "raised" in today's sense of the term. Historians of the family
and "private life" have discovered that we cannot project contemporary
child-rearing practices backward in time. Like housecleaning, laundering, cooking, and many other domestic labors, the standards and
norms of mothering have been dramatically upgraded.

Part of the transformation has been psychological. In the past (be- 16
fore about the sixteenth century in England and later in other parts
of Europe), parent-child relationships appear to have been much less
emotional. What is seen today as a deep biological bond between parent
and child, particularly mother and child, is very much a social construction. For the most part, children were not "cared for" by their parents.
The rich had little to do with their offspring until they were grown.
Infants were given to wet-nurses, despite widespread evidence of neglect and markedly lower chances of survival. Older children were sent
off to school. Those in less economically fortunate families fared no
better. They would be sent as servants or into apprenticeships, often in
the homes of strangers. In all social classes, infants and children were
routinely left unattended for long periods of time. To make them less
of a nuisance, babies were wrapped in swaddling clothes, their limbs
completely immobilized, for the first months of their lives. Another
custom was the violent rocking of infants "which puts the babe into a
dazed condition, in order that he may not trouble those that have the
care of him." However harmful these practices may have been for children, they were convenient for their elders.

Among the poor and laboring classes, economic stress made proper 17
care virtually impossible. In the worst cases, there was not sufficient
income to feed children, and infanticide and abandonment were not
unusual. When families did keep (and feed) their offspring, they could
rarely spare even the ill-paid labor of women. Time for mothering was
an unaffordable luxury. Women had to work for pay, and the children
were frequently left alone:

> The children are then in many cases left without any person in charge of
> them, a sufficient quantity [of opium] being given by the parents to keep
> them in a state of stupor until they return home. . . . When under the
> influence of this mixture, the children lie in a perfectly torpid state for
> hours together. "The young 'uns all lay about on the floor," said one
> woman to me who was in the habit of dosing her children with it, "like

dead 'uns, and there's no bother with 'em. When they cry we gives 'em a little of it—p'raps half a spoonful, and that quiets 'em."

The relative lack of parental love and attention can partly be explained by the high probability that children might not survive. The ephemerality of life until at least the mid-eighteenth century is revealed by the practice of giving two children the same name, in the expectation that only one would live. Under these circumstances, the absence of deep emotional ties to children is understandable. But the picture is actually more complicated. Parental indifference was not merely a result of infant mortality. It was also a cause. Historians now realize that one reason many children died is that their parents did not, or could not, take sufficient pains to keep them alive. Neglect and abuse were dangerous, in both rich and poor families.

More caring attitudes began to emerge in the eighteenth century, [18] in both Europe and the United States. Eventually some of the more odious child-rearing practices started to fade away, such as swaddling; and by the end of the century, wetnursing was in decline. Parental affection became more common, and the individuality of the child was recognized. Middle-class families, often religious reformers, began to devote considerable attention to the education of their children. The biggest changes came in the nineteenth century. The idealization of mother love, vigilant attention to the needs of children, and recognition of the unique potential of each individual came to dominate child-rearing ideology. These beliefs may appear natural; but, as a leading historian of the family has noted, "motherhood as we know it today is a surprisingly new institution."

By the last quarter of the nineteenth century, what historians have [19] called "conscious motherhood" and a bona-fide mothers' movement emerged. As the "century of the child" opened, mothers were providing their children with all manner of new services. They breast-fed. They began to toilet-train, schedule, and educate. They learned to worry about germs, nutrition, and the quality of the air. They practiced "scientific nursing" on sick children. The long legacy of child neglect gave way, particularly in America, to the most labor-intensive mothering process in human history.

Children benefited from all this attention. "But the burden that it [20] placed upon the new American housewife was immense. Children had to be kept in bed for weeks at a time; bedpans had to be provided and warmed . . . utensils had to be boiled, alcohol baths administered, hands scrupulously washed, mouths carefully masked." And all these practical duties were embedded in a new cultural icon: the selfless mother. She was a romantic ideal, but eventually became a reality. Mothers actually did become altruistic—and unsparing with their time.

In all these ways, then, was the American household and the labor [21] of its mistress transformed. The old tasks of animal husbandry, sewing, and candlemaking disappeared, and women took on new ones. They made their family's beds and breast-fed their own babies. The motto was more and better. Looking back on this history, some observers have noted the operation of a Parkinson's Law of housework, in which "work expands to fill the time available for its completion." And there is a certain amount of truth in this characterization: the housewife's work *did* expand to fill her customary schedule. As the market economy produced low-cost versions of what women had made at home, they transferred their labor to other tasks. Housewifery remained a full-time job irrespective of the appliances or the technological systems at the housewife's disposal. The 1950s and 1960s were particularly labor-intensive. Middle-class women were trapped in a stultifying domesticity, following "Hints from Heloise" on how to prepare homemade dog food or turn Clorox bottles into birdfeeders.

DANIEL J. BOORSTIN

Technology and Democracy

Daniel J. Boorstin (1914–   ), a summa cum laude graduate of Harvard and a Rhodes scholar with two degrees from Oxford University, is a lawyer by training. He has, however, become one of America's best-known historians, largely because of his interest in topics that historians with more formal training have tended to ignore, including the effects of mass media on the lives of ordinary citizens. Among his many books, perhaps the best known are *The Decline of Radicalism: Reflections of America Today* (1969), *The Americans: The Democratic Experience* (Pulitzer Prize, 1974), and *The Republic of Technology* (1978). In all these works, there is an optimism about the effects of technology and prosperity that some critics have labeled as "boosterism" and even "vulgarity." When Boorstin talks about the drawbacks of technological progress, as he did in this 1972 lecture delivered at the University of Michigan and later collected in *Democracy and Its Discontents* (1974), he deserves special attention because he is examining the limitations of his own pet thesis.

One of the most interesting and characteristic features of democracy   1
is, of course, the difficulty of defining it. And this difficulty has been compounded in the United States, where we have been giving new meanings to almost everything. It is, therefore, especially easy for anyone to say that democracy in America has failed.

"Democracy," according to political scientists, usually describes a   2
form of government by the people, either directly or through their
elected representatives. But I prefer to describe a democratic society as
one which is governed by a spirit of equality and dominated by the
desire to equalize, to give everything to everybody. In the United States
the characteristic wealth and skills and know-how and optimism of our
country have dominated this quest.

My first and overshadowing proposition is that our problems arise   3
not so much from our failures as from our successes. Of course no
success is complete; only death is final. But we have probably come
closer to attaining our professed objectives than any other society of
comparable size and extent, and it is from this that our peculiarly American problems arise.

The use of technology to democratize our daily life has given a   4
quite new shape to our hopes. In this final chapter I will explore some of
the consequences of democracy, not for government but for experience.
What are the consequences for everybody every day of this effort to
democratize life in America? And especially the consequences of our
fantastic success in industry and technology and in invention?

There have been at least four of these consequences. I begin with   5
what I call *attenuation,* which means the thinning out or the flattening
of experience. We might call this the democratizing of experience. It
might otherwise be described as the decline of poignancy. One of the
consequences of our success in technology, of our wealth, of our energy
and our imagination, has been the removal of distinctions, not just
between people but between everything and everything else, between
every place and every other place, between every time and every other
time. For example, television removes the distinction between being
here and being there. And the same kind of process, of thinning out,
of removing distinctions, has appeared in one area after another of our
lives.

For instance, in the seasons. One of the great unheralded achieve-   6
ments of American civilization was the rise of transportation and refrigeration, the development of techniques of canning and preserving
meat, vegetables, and fruits in such a way that it became possible to
enjoy strawberries in winter, to enjoy fresh meat at seasons when the
meat was not slaughtered, to thin out the difference between the diet
of winter and the diet of summer. There are many unsung heroic stories
in this effort.

One of them, for example, was the saga of Gustavus Swift in Chi-   7
cago. In order to make fresh meat available at a relatively low price to
people all over the country, it was necessary to be able to transport it
from the West, where the cattle were raised, to the Eastern markets and
the cities where population was concentrated. Gustavus Swift found the

railroad companies unwilling to manufacture refrigerator cars. They were afraid that, if refrigeration was developed, the cattle would be butchered in the West and then transported in a more concentrated form than when the cattle had to be carried live. The obvious consequence, they believed, would be to reduce the amount of freight. So they refused to develop the refrigerator car. Gustavus Swift went ahead and developed it, only to find that he had more cars than he had use for. The price of fresh meat went down in the Eastern cities, and Gustavus Swift had refrigerator cars on his hands. He then sent agents to the South and to other parts of the country, and tried to encourage people to raise produce which had to be carried in refrigerator cars. One of the consequences of this was the development of certain strains of fruit and vegetables, especially of fruit, which would travel well. And Georgia became famous for the peaches which were grown partly as a result of Swift's efforts to encourage people to raise something that he could carry in his refrigerator cars.

There were other elements in this story which we may easily for- 8 get—for example, how central heating and air conditioning have affected our attitude toward the seasons, toward one time of year or another. Nowadays visitors from abroad note that wherever they are in our country, it is not unusual to find that in winter it is often too warm indoors, and in summer, often too cool.

But the development of central heating during the latter part of the 9 nineteenth century had other, less obvious consequences. For example, as people built high-rise apartments in the cities they found it impossible to have a fireplace in every room. You could not construct a high building with hundreds of apartments and have enough room for all the chimneys. So central heating was developed and this became a characteristic of city life. As central heating was developed it was necessary to have a place to put the machinery, and the machinery went in the cellar. But formerly people, even in the cities, had used their cellars to store fruit and vegetables over the winter. When the basement was heated by a furnace, of course it was no longer possible to store potatoes or other vegetables or fruit there. This increased the market for fresh fruits and vegetables that were brought in from truck farms just outside the cities or by refrigerator cars from greater distances. And this was another way of accelerating the tendency toward equalizing the seasons and equalizing the diet of people all over the country.

Also important in attenuating experience was the development of 10 what I would call homogenized space, especially the development of vertical space as a place to live in. There is a great deal less difference between living on the thirty-fifth floor and living on the fortieth floor of an apartment building than there is between living in a house in the middle of a block and living on the corner. The view is pretty much the same as you go up in the air. Vertical space is much more homogenized, and as we live in vertical space more and more, we live in places where "where we are" makes much less difference than it used to.

An important element in this which has been a product of American technology is, of course, glass. We forget that the innovations in the production of glass resulting in large sheets which you could look through was an achievement largely of American technology in the nineteenth century. Of course, one by-product was the development of the technology of bottling, which is related to some of the levelings-out of the seasons which I mentioned before in relation to food. But we forget that when we admire those old leaded-glass windows which we see in medieval or early modern buildings, what we are admiring is the inability of people to produce plate glass. 11

When a large plate of glass became technologically possible, this affected daily life in the United States. It affected merchandising, for example, because the "show window" became possible in which you could, with a relatively unobstructed view, display garments and other large objects in a way to make them appealing to people who passed by. But glass was also important in producing one of the main characteristics of modern American architecture—an architecture in which there is relatively less difference between the indoors and the outdoors than elsewhere. And that is one of the great functions of glass in modern architecture. 12

Along with the attenuation of places and time comes the attenuation of occasions and events. One of the more neglected aspects of modern technology is what I have called the rise of "repeatable experience." It used to be thought that one of the characteristics of life, one of the things that distinguished being alive from being dead, was the uniqueness of the individual moment. Something happened which could never happen again. If you missed it then, you were out of luck. But the growth of popular photography, which we can trace from about 1888 when Kodak #1 went on the market, began to allow everybody to make his own experience repeatable. If you had not seen this baby when he was so cute, you could still see him that way right now if you were so unlucky as to be in the living room with the parents who wanted to show you. Kodak #1 was a great achievement and was the beginning of our taking for granted that there was such a thing as a repeatable experience. 13

The phonograph, of course, beginning about 1877, created new opportunities to repeat audible experience. If you want to hear the voice of Franklin Delano Roosevelt now, you can hear him on a record. At the opening of the Woodrow Wilson Center for International Scholars at the Smithsonian Institution in 1971, part of the dedicating ceremony was the playing of a record with the voice of Woodrow Wilson. It was 14 not a very warm voice, but it was identifiable and distinctive. The growth of the phonograph, then, has accustomed us to the fact that experience is not a onetime thing.

When we watch the Winter Olympics in our living room and see   15 the ski jumper in the seventy-meter jump who makes a mistake or who performs very well, we can see the same performance just a minute later with all the failures and successes pointed out. Is instant replay the last stage in the technology of repeatable experience?

In the attenuating of events there is another element which I call   16 the "pseudo-event." As more and more of the events which have public notice are planned in advance, as the accounts of them are made available before they happen, then it becomes the responsibility of the event to live up to its reputation. In this way the spontaneity of experience, the unpredictableness of experience, dissolves and disappears. The difference between the present and the future becomes less and less.

Another aspect of this is what I have called the "neutralization of   17 risks," a result of the rise of insurance. For insurance, too, is a way of reducing the difference between the future and the present. You reduce risks by assuring yourself that if your house burns down, at least you will have the money so you can rebuild it. In this sense, insurance, and especially casualty insurance, provides a way of thinning out the difference between present and future, removing the suspense and the risk of experience.

What have been the everyday consequences of the democratizing   18 of property for our experience of property? In his classic defense of property in his essay *On Civil Government* (1690), John Locke argued that because property is the product of the mixing of a person's labor with an object, no government has the right to take it without his consent. This simplistic conception of property has dominated a great deal of political and economic thinking. It was prominent in the thinking of the authors of the Declaration of Independence and of the Founding Fathers of the Constitution. It was based on a simpler society where there was something poignant and characteristic about the experience of ownership. Owning meant the right to exclude people. You had the pleasure of possession.

But what has happened to property in our society? Of course, the   19 most important new form of property in modern American life is corporate property: shares of stock in a corporation. And the diffusion of the ownership of shares is one of the most prominent features of American life. There are companies like AT&T, for example, which have as many as a million stockholders. What does it mean to be a stockholder? You are a lucky person. You own property and you have some shares. So what? One doesn't need to be rich or even middle-class in this country to own shares of stock. But very few of my friends who own shares of stock know precisely what it means or what their legal powers are as stockholders. They are solicited to send in their proxies—by somebody who has a special interest in getting them to vote for something or other. They feel very little pleasure of control; they don't have the sense of wreaking themselves on any object. Yet this—a share of stock—is the characteristic and most important form of property in modern times. This property, too, is attenuated.

Other developments in American life concerning property have had   20 a similar effect. For example, installment and credit buying. This phenomenon first grew in connection with the wide marketing of the sewing machine and then in relation to the cash register, but its efflorescence has come with the automobile. When it became necessary to sell millions of automobiles—and necessary in order to keep the machinery of our society going to sell them to people who could not afford to lay out the full cost of an automobile—it was necessary to find ways of financing their purchases. Installment and credit buying was developed. One of the results was that people became increasingly puzzled over whether they did or did not (and if so in what sense) own their automobile. Of course, it is not uncommon for people to divest themselves of their physical control of an object like an automobile or a color television set before they have really acquired full ownership—and then to enter on another ambiguous venture of part ownership.

Another aspect of this is the rise of franchising: the development   21 of what I would call the "semi-independent businessman." In the United States today, between 35 percent and 50 percent of all retail merchandising is done through franchised outlets. Well, of course, we all know what a franchised outlet is; a typical example would be a McDonald's hamburger stand or any other outlet in which the person who is in control of the shop has been authorized to use a nationally advertised name like Midas Mufflers or Colonel Sanders' Kentucky Fried Chicken. He is then instructed in the conduct of his business. He must meet certain standards in order to be allowed to continue to advertise as a Holiday Inn or Howard Johnson or whatever. And he is in business "for himself." Now, what does that mean? If you go into a franchised outlet and you find the hamburger unsatisfactory, what can you do? Whom would you complain to? The man who runs the shop has received his instructions and his materials from the people who have franchised him. It is not his fault. And, of course, it's not the fault of the people at the center who franchised him, because the shop is probably badly run by the franchisee.

This phenomenon grew out of the needs of the automobile because   22 in order to sell Fords or any other makes, it was necessary to have an outlet which would take continuous responsibility for stocking parts. Then the purchaser could replace that part at the outlet where he had purchased the car. After automobile franchising came the franchising of filling stations. People wanted some assurance about the quality of the fuel they put in their cars; they were given this by the identification of what they purchased with some nationally advertised brand in which they had confidence.

Now, perhaps the most important example of attenuation, of the 23 decline of poignancy in our experience in relation to property, is so obvious and so universal that it has hardly been discussed. That is packaging. Until relatively recently if you went into a store to buy coffee, you would have to bring a container to the grocery store, and the grocer would ladle out the coffee to you.

Packaging began to develop in this country after the Civil War. In 24 a sense it was a by-product of the Civil War because the necessities of the war (especially the need to package flour) produced certain innovations which were important. And later there were decisive, although what seem to us rather trivial, innovations. For example, the invention of the folding box was important. Until there was a way to make boxes which could be transported and stored compactly, it was impossible or impractical to use them for industrial purposes. The folding box and certain improvements in the paper bag, such as the paper bag that had a square bottom so that it could stand up, and on the side of which you could print an advertisement—these were American inventions.

If we will risk seeming pompous or pedantic, we can say that the 25 most important consequences of packaging have been epistemological. They have had to do with the nature of knowledge and they have especially had the effect of confusing us about what knowledge is, and what's real, about what's form and what's substance. When you think about a Winston cigarette, you don't think about the tobacco inside the cigarette. You think about the package. And in one area after another of American life, the form and the content become confused, and the form becomes that which dominates our consciousness. One area perhaps in which this has ceased to be true, happily or otherwise, is the area which I have always thought of as an aspect of packaging—namely, clothing. In the United States we have developed ready-made clothing, too, in such a way as to obscure the differences of social class and even of sex.

All around us we see attenuation—as our technology has suc- 26 ceeded, as we have tried to make everything available to everybody. The very techniques we use in preparing our food, in transporting our food, in controlling the climate and temperature of the rooms we live in, the shapes of the buildings in which we do business and reside, the ways we look at past experience—in all these ways our experience becomes attenuated. As we democratize experience, the poignancy of the moment, of the season, of the control of the object, of the spontaneous event, declines.

Now to a second consequence of the success of our technology for 27
our daily experience. This is what I would call the *decline of congregation*.
Or it might be called a new segregation. This is the consequence of
increasingly organized and centralized sources of anything and everything. Example: Rebecca at the well.[1] When I wrote an article for the
issue of *Life* magazine which was intended to celebrate the twenty-fifth
anniversary of the introduction of television in this country, I entitled
the article at first "Rebecca at the TV Set." But my friends at *Life* said,
"Rebecca who?" Deferring to their greater, wider knowledge of American life and of the literariness of the American people, instead we called
it simply "The New Segregation."

When Rebecca lived in her village and needed to get water for the 28
household, she went to the well. At the well she met the other women
of the village; she heard the gossip; she met her fiancé there, as a matter
of fact. And then what happened? With the progress of democracy and
technology, running water was introduced; and Rebecca stayed in the
kitchenette of her eighth-floor apartment. She turned the faucet on and
got the water out of the faucet; she didn't have to go to the well any
more. She had only the telephone to help her collect gossip and she
would have to find other ways to meet her fiancé. This is a parable of
the problem of centralizing sources of everything.

The growth of centralized plumbing was itself, of course, a neces- 29
sary by-product of the development of the skyscraper and the concentration of population in high buildings. You had to have effective sanitary facilities. But we forget other features of this development. Even
those of us who have never made much use of the old "privy" know
that the privy characteristically had more than one hole in it. Why was
this? The plural facility was not peculiar simply to the privy; it was also
found in the sanitary arrangements of many older buildings, including
some of the grandest remaining medieval structures. The development
of centralized plumbing led to privatizing; "privy" was the wrong word
for the old facility. The privatizing of the bodily functions made them
less sociable. People engaged in them in private.

The most dramatic example today of the privatizing of experience 30
by centralizing a facility is, of course, television. We could start with
the newspaper, for that matter. The town crier communicated the news
to people in their presence. If you wanted to hear it you had to be
there, or talk to somebody else who was there when he brought the
news. But as the newspaper developed, with inexpensive printing, the
messages were brought to you and you could look at them privately as
you sat by yourself at breakfast. Television is perhaps one of the most
extreme examples of the decline of congregation. Until the development

1. The wife of Isaac and mother of Jacob and Esau, Gen. 24.

of television, if you wanted to see a play you had to go out to a theater; if you wanted to hear a concert you had to go to a concert hall. These performances were relatively rare. They were special events. But with the coming of television, everybody acquired his private theater. Rebecca had her theater in her kitchen. She no longer needed to go out for entertainment.

The centralized source, the centralizing of the source, then, led to the isolating of the consumer. Of course, much was gained by this. But one of the prices paid was the decline of congregation—congregation being the drawing together of people where they could enjoy and react to and respond to the reactions and feelings of their fellows. [31]

There is a third consequence of our technological success in democratic America, which I would call the new determinism, or *the rising sense of momentum*. Technology has had a deep and pervasive effect on our attitude toward history, and especially on the citizen's attitude toward his control over the future. In the seventeenth century the Puritans spoke about Providence; that was their characteristic way of describing the kind of control that God exercised over futurity. In the nineteenth century, when people became more scientifically minded, they still retained some notion of divine foresight in the form of the concept of destiny or mission or purpose. But in our time in this country we have developed a different kind of approach toward futurity; and this is what I would call the sense of momentum. [32]

Momentum in physics is the product of a body's mass and its linear velocity. Increasing scale and speed of operation increase the momentum. One of the characteristics of our technology and especially of our most spectacular successes has been to increase this sense of momentum. I will mention three obvious examples. It happens that each of these developments came, too, as a result of overwhelming international pressure. When such pressures added to the forces at work inside the nation, in each case they produced a phenomenon of great mass and velocity which became very difficult to stop. [33]

The first example is, of course, atomic research. The large-scale concerted efforts in this country to build an atomic bomb began and were accelerated at the time of World War II because of rumors that the Nazis were about to succeed in nuclear fission. When this information became available, national resources were massed and organized in an unprecedented fashion; futurity was scheduled and groups were set to work in all parts of the continent exploring different possible ways of finding the right form of uranium or of some other element. And the search for the first atomic chain reaction, which was accomplished at my University of Chicago, went on. [34]

One of the more touching human aspects of this story is the account, now well chronicled by several historians, of the frantic efforts of the atomic scientists, the people who had been most instrumental in [35] getting this process started (Albert Einstein, Leo Szilard, and James Franck, among others), when they saw that the atomic bomb was about to become possible, to persuade the President of the United States either not to use the bomb or to use it only in a demonstration in the uninhabited mid-Pacific. Such a use, they urged, would so impress the enemy with the horrors of the bomb that he would surrender, eliminating the need for us to use the bomb against a live target. They pursued this purpose—trying to put the brakes on military use of the bomb—with a desperation that even exceeded the energy they had shown in developing the bomb. But, of course, they had no success.

They could develop the bomb, but they couldn't stop it. Why? There were many reasons, including President Truman's reasonable belief that use of the bomb could in the long run save the hundreds of thousands of Japanese and American lives that would have been lost in an invasion, and also would shorten the war. But surely one reason was that there had already been too much investment in the bomb. Billions of dollars had gone into the making of it. People were organized all over the country in various ways. It was impossible to stop. ³⁶

Another example of this kind of momentum is the phenomenon of space exploration. I happen to be an enthusiast for space exploration, so by describing this momentum I do not mean to suggest that I think the space enterprise itself has not been a good thing. Nevertheless, as a historian I am increasingly impressed by the pervasive phenomenon of momentum in our time. Billions of dollars have been spent in developing the machinery for going off to the moon or going then to Mars or elsewhere. The mass of the operation has been enormous. The velocity of it is enormous, and it becomes virtually impossible to stop. The recent problem with the SST is a good example. For when any enterprise in our society has reached a certain scale, the consequences in unemployment and in dislocation of the economy are such that it becomes every year more difficult to cease doing what we are already doing. ³⁷

A third example, more in the area of institutions, is foreign aid: the international pressures to give foreign aid to one country or another. We have an enormous mass of wealth being invested, a great velocity with lots of people going off all over the world and performing this operation of giving aid, and it becomes almost impossible to stop it. The other countries resent the decline of aid and consider it a hostile act, even though they might not have felt that way if we hadn't started the aid in the first place. Foreign aid is, I think, the most characteristic innovation in foreign policy in this century. ³⁸

Each of these three enterprises illustrates the attitude of the American citizen in the later twentieth century toward his control over experience. Increasingly, the citizen comes to feel that events are moving, and moving so fast with such velocity and in such mass that he has very little ³⁹

control. The sense of momentum itself becomes possible only because of our success in achieving these large purposes which no other democratic society, no other society before us, had even imagined.

Now, what does this bring us to? Before I come to my fourth and   40
concluding point on the ways in which the successes of democracy have affected our experience, I would like briefly to recall some of the remedies that have been suggested for the ills of democracy and the problems of democracy in the past. Al Smith once said, "All the ills of democracy can be cured by more democracy." I must confess, though I admire Al Smith for some of his enterprises, the Empire State Building for example, I think he was on the wrong track here. In fact, I would take an almost contrary position. Even at the risk of seeming flip, I might sum up the democratic paradoxes that I have been describing: "Getting there is *all* the fun."

Is there a law of democratic impoverishment? Is it possible that   41
while *democratizing* enriches experience, *democracy* dilutes experience?

Example: photography. Before the invention of photography, it was   42
a remarkable experience to see an exact likeness of the Sphinx or of Notre Dame or of some exotic animal or to see a portrait of an ancestor. Then, as photography was publicized in the 1880's and thoroughly popularized in this century, it opened up a fantastic new range of experience for everybody. Suddenly people were able to see things they had never been able to see before. And then what happened? Everyone had a camera, or two or three cameras; and everywhere he went he took pictures and when he came home he had to find a victim, somebody to show the pictures to. And this became more and more difficult.

While photography was being introduced, it was life-enriching and   43
vista-opening; but once it was achieved, once everybody had a camera, the people were looking in their cameras instead of looking at the sight they had gone to see. It had an attenuating effect. A picture came to mean less and less, simply because people saw pictures everywhere. And the experience of being there also somehow meant less because the main thing people saw everywhere was the inside of their viewfinders, and their concern over their lens cap and finding the proper exposure made it hard for them to notice what was going on around them at the moment.

Another example is, of course, the phonograph. Has the phono   44
graph—in its universal late-twentieth-century uses—necessarily made people more appreciative of music? In the 1920's when I was raised in Tulsa, Oklahoma, I had never heard an opera, nor had I really heard any classical music properly performed by an orchestra. But in our living room we had a wind-up Victrola, and I heard Galli-Curci singing arias from *Rigoletto*, and I heard Caruso, and I heard some symphonies,

and it was fantastic. And then hi-fi came and everybody had a phono-graph, a hi-fi machine or a little transistor radio which you could carry with you and hear music any time.

Today when I walk into the elevator in an office building, it is not impossible that I will hear Beethoven or Verdi. Sitting in the airplane I hear Mozart coming out of the public-address system. Wherever we go we hear music whether we want to hear it or not, whether we are in the mood for it or not. It becomes an everywhere, all-the-time thing. The experience is attenuated.

And one of the most serious consequences of all this, finally, is the attenuation of community itself. What holds people together? What has held people together in the past? For the most part it has been their sense of humanity, their pleasure in the presence of one another, their feeling for another person's expression, the sound of a voice, the look on his or her face. But the kind of community I describe increasingly becomes attenuated. People are trying to enjoy the community all by themselves.

We are led to certain desperate quests in American life. These, the by-products of our success, are clues to the vitality and energy of our country, to the quest for novelty to keep life interesting and vistas open, to the quest for community and the quest for autonomy. Can we inoculate ourselves against these perils of our technological success? Samuel Butler once said, "If I die prematurely, at any rate I shall be saved from being bored by my own success." Our problem, too, is partly that.

And now a fourth characteristic of the relation of technology to democracy in our time: *the belief in solutions*. One of the most dangerous popular fallacies—nourished by American history and by some of our most eloquent and voluble patriots—is the notion that democracy is attainable. There is a subtle difference between American democratic society and many earlier societies in the extent to which their ideals could be attained. The objectives of other societies have for the most part been definable and attainable. Aristocracy and monarchy do present attainable ideals. Even totalitarianism presents objectives which can be attained in the sense in which the objectives of democracy never can be.

This nation has been a place of renewal, of new beginnings for nations and for man. Vagueness has been a national resource: the vagueness of the continent, the mystery of our resources, the vagueness of our social classes, the misty miasma of our hopes.

Our society has been most distinctively a way of reaching for rather than of finding. American democracy, properly speaking, has been a process and not a product, a quest and not a discovery. But a great danger which has been nourished by our success in technology has been the belief in solutions. For technological problems there *are* solutions. It is possible to set yourself the task of developing an economic and workable internal-combustion engine, a prefabricated house, or a way of reaching the moon. Technological problems are capable of solutions.

We are inclined, then, using the technological problem as our prototype, to believe that somehow democracy itself is a solution, a dissolving of the human condition. But we should have learned, and even the history of technology—especially the history of technology in our democratic society—should have taught us otherwise. 51

In human history in the long run there are no solutions, only problems. This is what I have suggested in my description of "self-liquidating" ideals. And the examples are all around us—in our effort to create a pluralistic society by assimilating and Americanizing people, in our effort to give everybody an uncrowded wilderness vacation, in our effort to find an exciting new model each year. 52

Every seeming solution is a new problem. When you democratize the speedy automobile and give everybody an automobile, the result is a traffic jam; and this is the sense in which the "solution" of technological problems presents us with obstacles to the fulfillment of what is human in our society. When we think about American democratic society, then, we must learn not to think about a condition, but about a process; not about democracy, but about the quest for democracy, which we might call "democratizing." 53

The most distinctive feature of our system is not a system, but a quest, not a neat arrangement of men and institutions, but a flux. What other society has ever committed itself to so tantalizing, so fulfilling, so frustrating a community enterprise? 54

To prepare ourselves for this view of American democracy there are two sides to our personal need. One is on the side of prudence and wisdom; the other on the side of poetry and imagination. 55

On the side of prudence, there is a need for a sense of history. Only by realizing the boundaries that we have been given can we discover how to reach beyond them. Only so can we have the wisdom not to mistake passing fads for great movements, not to mistake the fanaticisms of a few for the deep beliefs of the many, not to mistake fashion for revolution. This wisdom is necessary if we are to secure sensibly the benefits of a free society for those who have for whatever reason been deprived of its benefits. We were not born yesterday, nor was the nation. And between the day before yesterday and yesterday, crucial events have happened. We can discover these and come to terms with them only through history. As Pascal said, "It is only by knowing our condition that we can transcend it." Our technology brings us the omnipresent present. It dulls our sense of history, and if we are not careful it can destroy it. 56

We in the U.S.A. are always living in an age of transition. Yet we 57

have tended to believe that our present is always the climax of history,
even though American history shows that the climax is always in the
future. By keeping suspense alive, we can prepare ourselves for the
shocks of change.

And finally, on the side of poetry and imagination, how do we   58
keep alive the spirit of adventure, what I would call the exploring spirit?
This should be the easiest because it is the most traditional of our
achievements and efforts. We must remember that we live in a new
world. We must keep alive the exploring spirit. We must not sacrifice
the infinite promise of the unknown, of man's unfulfilled possibilities
in the universe's untouched mysteries, for the cozy satisfactions of predictable, statistical benefits. Space exploration is a symbol.

Recently I had the pleasure of talking with Thor Heyerdahl, the *Kon*   59
Tiki man, whose latest venture was the Ra expedition, in which he
explored the possibilities of men having come from Egypt or elsewhere
in the Mediterranean to this continent long ago in boats made of reeds.
He and his crew, to test their hypothesis, actually crossed the Atlantic
in a reed boat. And as I talked to Thor Heyerdahl about the Ra expedition, I said that it must have been a terrible feeling of risk when you
suddenly left the sight of land and got out into the open sea. It seemed
to me that the fear and perils of the open sea would be the greatest.
Thor Heyerdahl said not at all: the great dangers, the dangers of shoals
and rocks, existed along the shore. The wonderful sense of relief, he
observed, came when he went out on the ocean where there was openness all around, although also high waves and strong currents. The
promise of American democracy, I suggest, depends on our ability to
stay at sea, to work together in community while we all reach to the
open horizon.

ALDOUS HUXLEY

Hyperion to a Satyr[1]

Aldous Huxley (1894–1963) was planning a career as a physician
when, at the age of sixteen, he contracted an eye disease that left
him temporarily blind and changed his plans. His scientific interests,
however, shaped his literary career; Huxley was a prolific novelist,
essayist, and poet. His early works, including the novels *Chrome Yellow*
(1921) and *Antic Hay* (1923), are full of skeptical social comment, as
is his most famous novel, *Brave New World* (1932). In general, his later

1. In Shakespeare's *Hamlet*, the prince compares his dead father to his stepfather: "So
excellent a king, that was, to this, / Hyperion to a Satyr."

novels and essays replace skepticism with mysticism. *The Perennial Philosophy* (1945) explores Oriental religion, and *The Doors of Perception* (1954) and *Heaven and Hell* (1956) report on Huxley's experiences with hallucinogenic drugs. "Hyperion to a Satyr" (from *Tomorrow and Tomorrow and Tomorrow*, 1956) shows that even in Huxley's mystical years, his interest in science and technology was strong. In this essay, in fact, he argues that technicians may be doing more than mystics to bring about the ideal of human benevolence.

A few months before the outbreak of the Second World War I took   1
a walk with Thomas Mann on a beach some fifteen or twenty miles southwest of Los Angeles. Between the breakers and the highway stretched a broad belt of sand, smooth, gently sloping and (blissful surprise!) void of all life but that of the pelicans and godwits. Gone was the congestion of Santa Monica and Venice. Hardly a house was to be seen; there were no children, no promenading loincloths and brassières, not a single sun-bather was practicing his strange obsessive cult. Miraculously, we were alone. Talking of Shakespeare and the musical glasses, the great man and I strolled ahead. The ladies followed. It was they, more observant than their all too literary spouses, who first remarked the truly astounding phenomenon. "Wait," they called, "wait!" And when they had come up with us, they silently pointed. At our feet, and as far as the eye could reach in all directions, the sand was covered with small whitish objects, like dead caterpillars. Recognition dawned. The dead caterpillars were made of rubber and had once been contraceptives of the kind so eloquently characterized by Mantegazza as *"una tela di ragno contro l'infezione, una corazza contro il piacere."*[2]

> *Continuous as the stars that shine*
> *And twinkle in the milky way,*
> *They stretched in never-ending line*
> *Along the margin of a bay:*
> *Ten thousand saw I at a glance . . .*[3]

Ten thousand? But we were in California, not the Lake District. The scale was American, the figures astronomical. Ten million saw I at a glance. Ten million emblems and mementoes of Modern Love.

> *O bitter barren woman! what's the name,*
> *The name, the name, the new name thou hast won?*

2. "A cobweb against infection, a breastplate against pleasure": Paolo Mantegazza (1831–1910) was an Italian physiologist and anthropologist known for his popular works on medicine.
3. The lines are from William Wordsworth's "I Wandered Lonely as a Cloud." They describe daffodils.

And the old name, the name of the bitter fertile woman—what was that? These are questions that can only be asked and talked about, never answered in any but the most broadly misleading way. Generalizing about Woman is like indicting a Nation—an amusing pastime, but very unlikely to be productive either of truth or utility.

Meanwhile, there was another, a simpler and more concrete question: How on earth had these objects got here, and why in such orgiastic profusion? Still speculating, we resumed our walk. A moment later our noses gave us the unpleasant answer. Offshore from this noble beach was the outfall through which Los Angeles discharged, raw and untreated, the contents of its sewers. The emblems of modern love and the other things had come in with the spring tide. Hence that miraculous solitude. We turned and made all speed towards the parked car.

Since that memorable walk was taken, fifteen years have passed. Inland from the beach, three or four large cities have leapt into existence. The bean fields and Japanese truck gardens of those ancient days are now covered with houses, drugstores, supermarkets, drive-in theaters, junior colleges, jet-plane factories, laundromats, six-lane highways. But instead of being, as one would expect, even more thickly constellated with Malthusian flotsam and unspeakable jetsam, the sands are now clean, the quarantine has been lifted. Children dig, well-basted sun-bathers slowly brown, there is splashing and shouting in the surf. A happy consummation—but one has seen this sort of thing before. The novelty lies, not in the pleasantly commonplace end—people enjoying themselves—but in the fantastically ingenious means whereby that end has been brought about.

Forty feet above the beach, in a seventy-five-acre oasis scooped out of the sand dunes, stands one of the marvels of modern technology, the Hyperion Activated Sludge Plant. But before we start to discuss the merits of activated sludge, let us take a little time to consider sludge in its unactivated state, as plain, old-fashioned dirt.

Dirt, with all its concomitant odors and insects, was once accepted as an unalterable element in the divinely established Order of Things. In his youth, before he went into power politics as Innocent III, Lotario de' Conti found time to write a book on the *Wretchedness of Man's Condition*. "How filthy the father," he mused, "how low the mother, how repulsive the sister!" And no wonder! For "dead, human beings give birth to flies and worms; alive, they generate worms and lice." Moreover, "consider the plants, consider the trees. They bring forth flowers and leaves and fruits. But what do *you* bring forth? Nits, lice, vermin. Trees and plants exude oil, wine, balm—and *you*, spittle, snot, urine, ordure. *They* diffuse the sweetness of all fragrance—*you*, the most abominable stink." In the Age of Faith, Homo sapiens was also Homo pediculosus, also Homo immundus—a little lower than the angels, but dirty by definition, lousy, not *per accidens*,[4] but in his very essence. And as for man's helpmate—*si nec extremis digitis flegma vel stercus tangere patimur, quomodo ipsum stercoris saccum amplecti desideramus?* "We who shrink from touching, even with the tips of our fingers, a gob of phlegm or a lump of dung, how is it that we crave for the embraces of this mere bag of night-soil?" But men's eyes are not, as Odo of Cluny wished they were, "like those of the lynxes of Boeotia"; they cannot see through the smooth and milky surfaces into the palpitating sewage within. That is why

> *There swims no goose so grey but soon or late*
> *Some honest gander takes her for his mate.*

That is why (to translate the notion into the language of medieval orthodoxy), every muck-bag ends by getting herself embraced—with the result that yet another stinker-with-a-soul finds himself embarked on a sea of misery, bound for a port which, since few indeed can hope for salvation, is practically certain to be Hell. The embryo of this future reprobate is composed of "foulest seed," combined with "blood made putrid by the heat of lust." And as though to make it quite clear what He thinks of the whole proceeding, God has decreed that "the mother shall conceive in stink and nastiness."

That there might be a remedy for stink and nastiness—namely soap and water—was a notion almost unthinkable in the thirteenth century. In the first place, there was hardly any soap. The substance was known to Pliny, as an import from Gaul and Germany. But more than a thousand years later, when Lotario de' Conti wrote his book, the burgesses of Marseilles were only just beginning to consider the possibility of manufacturing the stuff in bulk. In England no soap was made commercially until halfway through the fourteenth century. Moreover, even if soap had been abundant, its use for mitigating the "stink and nastiness," then inseparable from love, would have seemed, to every right-thinking theologian, an entirely illegitimate, because merely physical, solution to a problem in ontology and morals—an escape, by means of the most vulgarly materialistic trick, from a situation which God Himself had intended, from all eternity, to be as squalid as it was sinful. A conception without stink and nastiness would have the appearance—what a blasphemy!—of being Immaculate. And finally there was the virtue of modesty. Modesty, in that age of codes and pigeonholes, had its Queensberry Rules—no washing below the belt. Sinful in itself, such an offense against modesty in the present was fraught with all kinds of perils for modesty in the future. Havelock Ellis observed, when he was practicing obstetrics in the London slums, that modesty was due, in large measure, to a fear of being disgusting. When his patients realized

6

---

4. "By accident." (Latin)

that "I found nothing disgusting in whatever was proper and necessary to be done under the circumstances, it almost invariably happened that every sign of modesty at once disappeared." Abolish "stink and nastiness," and you abolish one of the most important sources of feminine modesty, along with one of the most richly rewarding themes of pulpit eloquence.

A contemporary poet has urged his readers not to make love to those who wash too much. There is, of course, no accounting for tastes; but there *is* an accounting for philosophical opinions. Among many other things, the greatly gifted Mr. Auden is a belated representative of the school which held that sex, being metaphysically tainted, ought also to be physically unclean.

Dirt, then, seemed natural and proper, and dirt in fact was everywhere. But, strangely enough, this all-pervading squalor never generated its own psychological antidote—the complete indifference of habit. Everybody stank, everybody was verminous; and yet, in each successive generation, there were many who never got used to these familiar facts. What has changed in the course of history is not the disgusted reaction to filth, but the moral to be drawn from that reaction. "Filth," say the men of the twentieth century, "is disgusting. Therefore let us quickly do something to get rid of filth." For many of our ancestors, filth was as abhorrent as it seems to almost all of us. But how different was the moral they chose to draw! "Filth is disgusting," they said. "Therefore the human beings who produce the filth are disgusting, and the world they inhabit is a vale, not merely of tears, but of excrement. This state of things has been divinely ordained, and all we can do is cheerfully to bear our vermin, loathe our nauseating carcasses and hope (without much reason, since we shall probably be damned) for an early translation to a better place. Meanwhile it is an observable fact that villeins are filthier even than lords. It follows, therefore, that they should be treated as badly as they smell." This loathing for the poor on account of the squalor in which they were condemned to live outlasted the Middle Ages and has persisted to the present day. The politics of Shakespeare's aristocratic heroes and heroines are the politics of disgust. "Footboys" and other members of the lower orders are contemptible because they are lousy—not in the metaphorical sense in which that word is now used, but literally; for the louse, in Sir Hugh Evans' words, "is a familiar beast to man, and signifies love." And the lousy were also the smelly. Their clothes were old and unclean, their bodies sweaty, their mouths horrible with decay. It made no difference that, in the words of a great Victorian reformer, "by no prudence on their part can the poor avoid the dreadful evil of their surroundings." They were disgusting and that, for the aristocratic politician, was enough. To canvass the common people's suffrages was merely to "beg their stinking breath." Candidates for elective office were men who "stand upon the breath of garlic eaters.'' When the citizens of Rome voted against him, Coriolanus told them that they were creatures,[5]

> *whose breath I hate*
> *As reek o' th' rotten fens, whose loves I prize*
> *As the dead carcasses of unburied men*
> *That do corrupt my air.*

And, addressing these same citizens, "You are they," says Menenius,

> *You are they*
> *That made the air unwholesome when you cast*
> *Your stinking greasy caps in hooting at*
> *Coriolanus' exile.*

Again, when Caesar was offered the crown, "the rabblement shouted and clapped their chopped hands, and threw up their sweaty night-caps, and uttered such a deal of stinking breath, because Caesar had refused the crown, that it had almost choked Caesar; for he swounded and fell down at it; and for mine own part," adds Casca, "I durst not laugh for fear of opening my lips and receiving the bad air." The same "mechanic slaves, with greasy aprons" haunted Cleopatra's imagination in her last hours.

> *In their thick breaths,*
> *Rank of gross diet, shall we be enclouded,*
> *And forced to drink their vapours.*

In the course of evolution man is supposed to have sacrificed the greater part of his olfactory center to his cortex, his sense of smell to his intelligence. Nevertheless, it remains a fact that in politics, no less than in love and social relations, smell judgments continue to play a major role. In the passages cited above, as in all the analogous passages penned or uttered since the days of Shakespeare, there is the implication of an argument, which can be formulated in some such terms as these. "Physical stink is a symbol, almost a symptom, of intellectual and moral inferiority. All the members of a certain group stink physically. Therefore, they are intellectually and morally vile, inferior and, as such, unfit to be treated as equals."

Tolstoy, who was sufficiently clear-sighted to recognize the undesirable political consequences of cleanliness in high places and dirt among the poor, was also sufficiently courageous to advocate, as a remedy, a general retreat from the bath. Bathing, he saw, was a badge of class distinction, a prime cause of aristocratic exclusiveness. For those who, in Mr. Auden's words, "wash too much," find it exceedingly distasteful to

---

5. The three indented quotations that follow are from Shakespeare's plays *Coriolanus, Julius Caesar,* and *Antony and Cleopatra.*

associate with those who wash too little. In a society where, let us say, only one in five can afford the luxury of being clean and sweet-smelling, Christian brotherhood will be all but impossible. Therefore, Tolstoy argued, the bathers should join the unwashed majority. Only where there is equality in dirt can there be a genuine and unforced fraternity.

Mahatma Gandhi, who was a good deal more realistic than his 13
Russian mentor, chose a different solution to the problem of differential cleanliness. Instead of urging the bathers to stop washing, he worked indefatigably to help the non-bathers to keep clean. Brotherhood was to be achieved, not by universalizing dirt, vermin and bad smells, but by building privies and scrubbing floors.

Spengler, Sorokin, Toynbee—all the philosophical historians and 14
sociologists of our time have insisted that a stable civilization cannot be built except on the foundations of religion. But if man cannot live by bread alone, neither can he live exclusively on metaphysics and worship. The gulf between theory and practice, between the ideal and the real, cannot be bridged by religion alone. In Christendom, for example, the doctrines of God's fatherhood and the brotherhood of man have never been self-implementing. Monotheism has proved to be powerless against the divisive forces first of feudalism and then of nationalistic idolatry. And within these mutually antagonistic groups, the injunction to love one's neighbor as oneself has proved to be as ineffective, century after century, as the commandment to worship one God.

A century ago the prophets who formulated the theories of the 15
Manchester School were convinced that commerce, industrialization and improved communications were destined to be the means whereby the age-old doctrines of monotheism and human brotherhood would at last be implemented. Alas, they were mistaken. Instead of abolishing national rivalries, industrialization greatly intensified them. With the march of technological progress, wars became bloodier and incomparably more ruinous. Instead of uniting nation with nation, improved communications merely extended the range of collective hatreds and military operations. That human beings will, in the near future, voluntarily give up their nationalistic idolatry, seems, in these middle years of the twentieth century, exceedingly unlikely. Nor can one see, from this present vantage point, any technological development capable, by the mere fact of being in existence, of serving as an instrument for realizing those religious ideals, which hitherto mankind has only talked about. Our best consolation lies in Mr. Micawber's hope that, sooner or later, "Something will Turn Up."[6]

In regard to brotherly love within the mutually antagonistic groups, 16
something *has* turned up. That something is the development, in many different fields, of techniques for keeping clean at a cost so low that practically everybody can afford the luxury of not being disgusting.

6. Micawber is a luckless optimist in Charles Dickens's *David Copperfield*.

For creatures which, like most of the carnivores, make their home 17
in a den or burrow, there is a biological advantage in elementary cleanliness. To relieve nature in one's bed is apt, in the long run, to be
unwholesome. Unlike the carnivores, the primates are under no evolutionary compulsion to practice the discipline of the sphincters. For these
free-roaming nomads of the woods, one tree is as good as another and
every moment is equally propitious. It is easy to house-train a cat or a
dog, all but impossible to teach the same desirable habits to a monkey.
By blood we are a good deal closer to poor Jocko than to Puss or Tray.
Man's instincts were developed in the forest; but ever since the dawn
of civilization, his life has been lived in the more elaborate equivalent
of a rabbit warren. His notions of sanitation were not, like those of
the cat, inborn, but had to be painfully acquired. In a sense the older
theologians were quite right in regarding dirt as natural to man—an
essential element in the divinely appointed order of his existence.

But in spite of its unnaturalness, the art of living together without 18
turning the city into a dunghill has been repeatedly discovered. Mo-
henjo-daro, at the beginning of the third millennium B.C., had a water-
borne sewage system; so, several centuries before the siege of Troy, did
Cnossos; so did many of the cities of ancient Egypt, albeit only for the
rich. The poor were left to demonstrate their intrinsic inferiority by
stinking, in their slums, to high heaven. A thousand years later Rome
drained her swamps and conveyed her filth to the contaminated Tiber
by means of the Cloaca Maxima. But these solutions to the problem of
what we may politely call "unactivated sludge" were exceptional. The
Hindus preferred to condemn a tithe of their population to untouchability and the daily chore of carrying slops. In China the thrifty house-
holder tanked the family sludge and sold it, when mature, to the highest
bidder. There was a smell, but it paid, and the fields recovered some of
the phosphorus and nitrogen of which the harvesters had robbed them.
In medieval Europe every alley was a public lavatory, every window a
sink and garbage chute. Droves of pigs were dedicated to St. Anthony
and, with bells round their necks, roamed the streets, battening on the
muck. (When operating at night, burglars and assassins often wore
bells. Their victims heard the reassuring tinkle, turned over in their beds
and went to sleep again—it was only the blessed pigs.) And meanwhile
there were cesspools (like the black hole into which that patriotic Franciscan, Brother Salimbene,[7] deliberately dropped his relic of St. Dominic), there was portable plumbing, there were members of the lower
orders, whose duty it was to pick up the unactivated sludge and deposit

---

7. Huxley slightly misremembers a story of monastic rivalry in the *Chronicle* of the thir-
teenth-century monk. He assumes that it was the Franciscan Salimbene who visited a
Dominican monastery, begged for a relic of St. Dominic, "put it to the vilest uses, and
cast it at last into the cesspool. Then he cried aloud, saying, 'Alas! help me, brothers, for
I seek the relic of your saint which I have lost among the filth.'" The outline of the story
is accurate, but Huxley has confused the characters.

it outside the city limits. But always the sludge accumulated faster than it could be removed. The filth was chronic and, in the slummier quarters, appalling. It remained appalling until well into the nineteenth century. As late as the early years of Queen Victoria's reign sanitation in the East End of London consisted in dumping everything into the stagnant pools that still stood between the jerry-built houses. From the peak of their superior (but still very imperfect) cleanliness the middle and upper classes looked down with unmitigated horror at the Great Unwashed. "The Poor" were written and spoken about as though they were creatures of an entirely different species. And no wonder! Nineteenth-century England was loud with Non-Conformist and Tractarian piety; but in a society most of whose members stank and were unclean the practice of brotherly love was out of the question.

The first modern sewage systems, like those of Egypt before them, were reserved for the rich and had the effect of widening still further the gulf between rulers and ruled. But endemic typhus and several dangerous outbreaks of Asiatic cholera lent weight to the warnings and denunciations of the sanitary reformers. In self-defense the rich had to do something about the filth in which their less fortunate neighbors were condemned to live. Sewage systems were extended to cover entire metropolitan areas. The result was merely to transfer the sludge problem from one place to another. "The Thames," reported a Select Committee of 1836, "receives the excrementitious matter from nearly a million and a half of human beings; the washing of their foul linen; the filth and refuse of many hundred manufactories; the offal and decomposing vegetable substances from the markets; the foul and gory liquid from the slaughter-houses; and the purulent abominations from hospitals and dissecting rooms, too disgusting to detail. Thus that most noble river, which has been given us by Providence for our health, recreation and beneficial use, is converted into the Common sewer of London, and the sickening mixture it contains is daily pumped up into the water for the inhabitants of the most civilized capital of Europe."

In England the heroes of the long campaign for sanitation were a strangely assorted band. There was a bishop, Blomfield of London; there was the radical Edwin Chadwick, a disciple of Jeremy Bentham; there was a physician, Dr. Southwood Smith; there was a low-church man of letters, Charles Kingsley; and there was the seventh Earl of Shaftesbury, an aristocrat who had troubled to acquaint himself with the facts of working-class life. Against them were marshaled the confederate forces of superstition, vested interest, and brute inertia. It was a hard fight; but the cholera was a staunch ally, and by the end of the century the worst of the mess had been cleared up, even in the slums. Writing in 1896, Lecky[8] called it "the greatest achievement of our age." In the historian's estimation, the sanitary reformers had done more for general

8. British intellectual and social historian.

happiness and the alleviation of human misery than all the more spectacular figures of the long reign put together. Their labors, moreover,
were destined to bear momentous fruit. When Lecky wrote, upper-class
noses could still find plenty of occasions for passing olfactory judgments
on the majority. But not nearly so many as in the past. The stage was
already set for the drama which is being played today—the drama
whose theme is the transformation of the English caste system into an
equalitarian society. Without Chadwick and his sewers, there might
have been violent revolution, never that leveling by democratic process,
that gradual abolition of untouchability, which are in fact taking place.

    Hyperion—what joy the place would have brought to those passion-   21
ately prosaic lovers of humanity, Chadwick and Bentham! And the
association of the hallowed name with sewage, of sludge with the great
god of light and beauty—what romantic furies it would have evoked
in Keats and Blake! And Lotario de' Conti—how thunderously, in the
name of religion, he would have denounced this presumptuous demonstration that Homo immundus can effectively modify the abjection of
his predestined condition! And Dean Swift,[9] above all—how deeply the
spectacle would have disturbed him! For, if Celia could relieve nature
without turning her lover's bowels, if Yahoos, footmen and even ladies
of quality did not *have* to stink, then, obviously, his occupation was
gone and his neurosis would be compelled to express itself in some
other, some less satisfactory, because less excruciating, way.

    An underground river rushes into Hyperion. Its purity of 99.7 per   22
cent exceeds that of Ivory Soap. But two hundred million gallons are
a lot of water; and the three thousandth part of that daily quota represents a formidable quantity of muck. But happily the ratio between
muck and muckrakers remains constant. As the faecal tonnage rises, so
does the population of aerobic and anaerobic bacteria. Busier than bees
and infinitely more numerous, they work unceasingly on our behalf.
First to attack the problem are the aerobes. The chemical revolution
begins in a series of huge shallow pools, whose surface is perpetually
foamy with the suds of Surf, Tide, Dreft and all the other monosyllables
that have come to take the place of soap. For the sanitary engineers,
these new detergents are a major problem. Soap turns very easily into
something else; but the monosyllables remain intractably themselves,
frothing so violently that it has become necessary to spray the surface
of the aerobes' pools with overhead sprinklers. Only in this way can
the suds be prevented from rising like the foam on a mug of beer and
being blown about the countryside. And this is not the only price that
must be paid for easier dishwashing. The detergents are greedy for oxygen. Mechanically and chemically, they prevent the aerobes from get-

9. Jonathan Swift (1667–1745), whose works frequently refer to the unsanitary side of
life.

ting all the air they require. Enormous compressors must be kept working night and day to supply the needs of the suffocating bacteria. A cubic foot of compressed air to every cubic foot of sludgy liquid. What will happen when Zoom, Bang, and Whiz come to replace the relatively mild monosyllables of today, nobody, in the sanitation business, cares to speculate.

When, with the assistance of the compressors, the aerobes have done all they are capable of doing, the sludge, now thickly concentrated, is pumped into the Digestion System. To the superficial glance, the Digestion System looks remarkably like eighteen very large Etruscan mausoleums. In fact it consists of a battery of cylindrical tanks, each more than a hundred feet in diameter and sunk fifty feet into the ground. Within these huge cylinders steam pipes maintain a cherishing heat of ninety-five degrees—the temperature at which the anaerobes are able to do their work with maximum efficiency. From something hideous and pestilential the sludge is gradually transformed by these most faithful of allies into sweetness and light—light in the form of methane, which fuels nine supercharged Diesel engines, each of seventeen hundred horsepower, and sweetness in the form of an odorless solid which, when dried, pelleted, and sacked, sells to farmers at ten dollars a ton. The exhaust of the Diesels raises the steam which heats the Digestion System, and their power is geared either to electric generators or centrifugal blowers. The electricity works the pumps and the machinery of the fertilizer plant, the blowers supply the aerobes with oxygen. Nothing is wasted. Even the emblems of modern love contribute their quota of hydrocarbons to the finished products, gaseous and solid. And meanwhile another torrent, this time about 99.95 per cent pure, rushes down through the submarine outfall and mingles, a mile offshore, with the Pacific. The problem of keeping a great city clean without polluting a river or fouling the beaches, and without robbing the soil of its fertility, has been triumphantly solved.

But untouchability depends on other things besides the bad sanitation of slums. We live not merely in our houses, but even more continuously in our garments. And we live not exclusively in health, but very often in sickness. Where sickness rages unchecked and where people cannot afford to buy new clothes or keep their old ones clean, the occasions for being disgusting are innumerable.

Thersites, in *Troilus and Cressida*, lists a few of the commoner ailments of Shakespeare's time: "the rotten diseases of the south, the guts-griping, ruptures, catarrhs, loads o' gravel i' the back, lethargies, cold palsies, raw eyes, dirt-rotten livers, wheezing lungs, bladders full of imposthume, sciaticas, lime-kilns i' the palm, incurable bone-ache, and the rivelled fee-simple of the tetter." And there were scores of others even more repulsive. Crawling, flying, hopping, the insect carriers of infection swarmed uncontrollably. Malaria was endemic, typhus

never absent, bubonic plague a regular visitor, dysentery, without benefit of plumbing, a commonplace. And meanwhile, in an environment
that was uniformly septic, everything that *could* suppurate *did* suppurate. The Cook, in Chaucer's "Prologue," had a "mormal," or gangre-
nous sore, on his shin. The Summoner's face was covered with the
"whelkes" and "knobbes" of a skin disease that would not yield to any
known remedy. Every cancer was inoperable, and gnawed its way,
through a hideous chaos of cellular proliferation and breakdown, to its
foregone conclusion. The unmitigated horror surrounding illness explains the admiration felt, throughout the Middle Ages and early modern times, for those heroes and heroines of charity who voluntarily
undertook the care of the sick. It explains, too, certain actions of the
saints—actions which, in the context of modern life, seem utterly in-
comprehensible. In their filth and wretchedness, the sick were unspeak-
ably repulsive. This dreadful fact was a challenge to which those who
took their Christianity seriously responded by such exploits as the em-
bracing of lepers, the kissing of sores, the swallowing of pus. The modern response to this challenge is soap and water, with complete asepsis
as the ultimate ideal. The great gulf of disgust which used to separate
the sick and the chronically ailing from their healthier fellows, has been,
not indeed completely abolished, but narrowed everywhere and, in
many places, effectively bridged. Thanks to hygiene, many who, because of their afflictions, used to be beyond the pale of love or even
pity, have been re-admitted into the human fellowship. An ancient
religious ideal has been implemented, at least in part, by the development of merely material techniques for dealing with problems previously soluble (and then how very inadequately, so far as the sick themselves were concerned!) only by saints.

"The essential act of thought is symbolization." Our minds trans- 26
form experiences into signs. If these signs adequately represent the experiences to which they refer, and if we are careful to manipulate them
according to the rules of a many-valued logic, we can deepen our understanding of experience and thereby achieve some control of the
world and our own destiny. But these conditions are rarely fulfilled. In
all too many of the affairs of life we combine ill-chosen signs in all
kinds of irrational ways, and are thus led to unrealistic conclusions and
inappropriate acts.

There is nothing in experience which cannot be transformed by the 27
mind into a symbol—nothing which cannot be made to signify something else. We have seen, for example, that bad smells may be made to
stand for social inferiority, dirt for a low IQ, vermin for immorality,
sickness for a status beneath the human. No less important than these
purely physiological symbols are the signs derived, not from the body
itself, but from its coverings. A man's clothes are his most immediately
perceptible attribute. Stinking rags or clean linen, liveries, uniforms,
canonicals, the latest fashions—these are the symbols in terms of which

men and women have thought about the relations of class with class, of person with person. In the *Institutions of Athens,* written by an anonymous author of the fifth century B.C., we read that it was illegal in Athens to assault a slave even when he refused to make way for you in the street. "The reason why this is the local custom shall be explained. If it were legal for the slave to be struck by the free citizen, your Athenian citizen himself would always be getting assaulted through being mistaken for a slave. Members of the free proletariat of Athens are no better dressed than slaves or aliens and no more respectable in appearance." But Athens—a democratic city state with a majority of "poor whites"—was exceptional. In almost every other society the wearing of cheap and dirty clothes has been regarded (such is the power of symbols) as the equivalent of a moral lapse—a lapse for which the wearers deserved to be ostracized by all decent people. In *Les Précieuses Ridicules*[10] the high-flown heroines take two footmen, dressed up in their masters' clothes, for marquises. The comedy comes to its climax when the pretenders are stripped of their symbolic finery and the girls discover the ghastly truth. *Et eripitur persona, manet res*[11]—or, to be more precise, *manet altera persona.* The mask is torn off and there remains—what? Another mask—the footman's.

In eighteenth-century England the producers of woolens were able 28 to secure legislation prohibiting the import of cotton prints from the Orient and imposing an excise duty, not repealed until 1832, on the domestic product. But in spite of this systematic discouragement, the new industry prospered—inevitably; for it met a need, it supplied a vast and growing demand. Wool could not be cleaned, cotton was washable. For the first time in the history of Western Europe it began to be possible for all but the poorest women to look clean. The revolution then begun is still in progress. Garments of cotton and the new synthetic fibers have largely abolished the ragged and greasy symbols of earlier class distinctions. And meanwhile, for such fabrics as cannot be washed, the chemical industry has invented a host of new detergents and solvents. In the past, grease spots were a problem for which there was no solution. Proletarian garments were darkly shiny with accumulated fats and oils, and even the merchant's broadcloth, even the velvets and satins of lords and ladies displayed the ineradicable traces of last year's candle droppings, of yesterday's gravy. Dry cleaning is a modern art, a little younger than railway travel, a little older than the first Atlantic cable.

In recent years, and above all in America, the revolution in clothing 29 has entered a new phase. As well as cleanliness, elegance is being placed within the reach of practically everyone. Cheap clothes are massproduced from patterns created by the most expensive designers. Unfashionableness was once a stigma hardly less damning, as a symbol of

10. *The Affected Young Women,* a play by Molière.
11. "And snatch away the mask, the thing remains." (Latin)

inferiority, than dirt. Fifty years ago a girl who wore cheap clothes proclaimed herself, by their obvious dowdiness, to be a person whom it was all but out of the question, if one were well off, to marry. Misalliance is still deplored; but, thanks to Sears and Ohrbach, it seems appreciably less dreadful than it did to our fathers.

Sewage systems and dry cleaning, hygiene and washable fabrics, DDT and penicillin—the catalogue represents a series of technological victories over two great enemies: dirt and that system of untouchability, that unbrotherly contempt, to which, in the past, dirt has given rise.

It is, alas, hardly necessary to add that these victories are in no sense definitive or secure. All we can say is that, in certain highly industrialized countries, technological advances have led to the disappearance of some of the immemorial symbols of class distinction. But this does not guarantee us against the creation of new symbols no less compulsive in their anti-democratic tendencies than the old. A man may be clean; but if, in a dictatorial state, he lacks a party card, he figuratively stinks and must be treated as an inferior at the best and, at the worst, an untouchable.

In the nominally Christian past two irreconcilable sets of symbols bedeviled the Western mind—the symbols, inside the churches, of God's fatherhood and the brotherhood of man; and the symbols, outside, of class distinction, mammon worship and dynastic, provincial or national idolatry. In the totalitarian future—and if we go on fighting wars, the future of the West is bound to be totalitarian—the time-hallowed symbols of monotheism and brotherhood will doubtless be preserved. God will be One and men will all be His children, but in a strictly Pickwickian sense. Actually there will be slaves and masters, and the slaves will be taught to worship a parochial Trinity of Nation, Party, and Political Boss. Samuel Butler's Musical Banks[12] will be even more musical than they are today, and the currency in which they deal will have even less social and psychological purchasing power than the homilies of the Age of Faith.

Symbols are necessary—for we could not think without them. But they are also fatal—for the thinking they make possible is just as often unrealistic as it is to the point. In this consists the essentially tragic nature of the human situation. There is no way out, except for those who have learned how to go beyond all symbols to a direct experience of the basic fact of the divine immanence. *Tat tvam asi*—thou art That. When this is perceived, the rest will be added. In the meantime we must be content with such real but limited goods as Hyperion, and such essentially precarious and mutable sources of good as are provided by the more realistic of our religious symbols.

---

12. In Butler's *Erewhon* (1872), English institutions are ironically reflected in an imaginary land. Equivalent to the English churches are the Erewhonian Musical Banks, the money in which "had no direct commercial value in the outside world."

ALICE BLOOM

On a Greek Holiday

Alice Bloom (1935–   ) took both her B.A. and her M.A. in English at Washington University in St. Louis. She teaches at the University of Maine in Farmington and lives at the end of a snowplow route in a house so isolated that the sound of an automobile will bring both dogs and people to the window. After living much of her adult life in Midwestern suburbs, she has recently learned how to fish for smelt and make maple syrup. Bloom has published essays in several journals, including *The Hudson Review*, where a version of "On a Greek Holiday" appeared in August 1983. The following excerpt picks up after she has set the scene, an isolated strip of bare sand to which tourists are ferried so that they can take off as many of their clothes as they dare and lie exposed to a burning sun that the local Greeks avoid. Most of the women are bare-breasted. The men "lie on their beach mats, clothed in their tiny suits," reading the latest best-sellers or "adjusting the knobs on multiwave radios."

. . . Two women are walking toward us, at noon, across the nearly   1
deserted rocks. Most of the other swimmers and sunbathers are up in the cafe, eating lunch under the fig trees, the grapevine. These two women are not together, they walk several feet apart, and they do not look at each other. One is tall and blond, dressed in a flowered bikini and clogs, a tourist, English or American or Scandinavian or German. The other woman, a Greek, is carrying a basket, walking quickly, and gives the impression of being on a neighborhood errand. She is probably from one of the small old farms—sheep, olive trees, hens, gardens, goats—that border this stretch of sea and climb a little way into the pine and cypress woods.

Both are smoking and both walk upright. Beyond that, there is so   2
little similarity they could belong to different planets, eras, species, sexes. The tourist looks young, the Greek looks old; actually, she looks as old as a village well and the blonde looks like a drawn-out infant, but there could be as little as five or ten years difference between them.

The Greek woman is short and heavy, waistless, and is wearing a   3
black dress, a black scarf pulled low around her eyes, a black sweater, thick black stockings, black shoes. She is stupendously there, black but for the walnut of her face, in the white sun, against the white space. She looks, at once, as if she could do everything she's ever done, anything needed, and also at once, she gives off an emanation of humor, powers, secrets, determinations, acts. She is moving straight ahead, like a moving church, a black peaked roof, a hot black hat, a dark tent, like a doom, a government, a force for good and evil, an ultimatum, a determined animal. She probably can't read, or write; she may never

in her life have left this island; but she is beautiful, she could crush you, love you, mend you, deliver you of child or calf or lamb or illusion, bleed a pig, spear a fish, wring a supper's neck, till a field, coax an egg into life. Her sex is like a votive lamp flickering in a black, airless room. As she comes closer, she begins to crochet—that's what's in her basket, balls of cotton string and thick white lace coming off the hook and her brown fingers.

The blond tourist, struggling along the hot pebbles in her clogs, is coming back to her beach mat and friends. She looks as though she couldn't dress a doll without having a fit of sulks and throwing it down in a tantrum. It may not be the case, of course. She is on holiday, on this Greek island, which fact means both money and time. She is no doubt capable, well meaning, and by the standards and expectations of most of the world's people, well educated and very rich and very comfortable. She can undoubtedly read and write, most blond people can, and has, wherever she comes from, a vote, a voice, a degree of some kind, a job, a career perhaps, money certainly, opinions, friends, health, talents, habits, central heating, living relatives, personalized checks, a return ticket, a summer wardrobe, the usual bits and clamor we all, tourists, have. But presence, she has not. Nor authority, nor immediacy, nor joy for the eye, nor a look of adding to the world, not of strength nor humor nor excitement. Nearly naked, pretty, without discernible blemish, blond, tall, tan, firm, the product of red meat and whole milk, vitamins, orange juice, women's suffrage, freedom of religion, child labor laws, compulsory education, the anxious, dancing, lifelong attendance of uncounted numbers of furrow-browed adults, parents, teachers, pediatricians, orthodontists, counselors, hairdressers, diet and health and career and exercise and fashion consultants, still, she is not much to look at. She looks wonderful, but your eye, your heart, all in you that wants to look out on the substance of the people of the day, doesn't care, isn't interested long, is, in fact, diminished a little.

She could be anything—a professor of Romance languages at a major university, a clerk in a Jermyn Street shop, a flight attendant, a Stockholm lawyer, but nothing shows of that life or luck or work or history, not world, not pain or freedom or sufficiency. What you think of, what her person walking toward you in the fierce noon light forces you to think of, after the momentary, automatic envy of her perfections, is that she looks as though she's never had enough—goods or rights or attention or half-decent days. Whether she is or not, she looks unutterably dissatisfied and peevish. And yet, in order to be here on this blue-white beach on this July day, unless you are chasing your own stray goat across the rocks, requires a position of luxury, mobility, and privilege common to us but beyond any imagining of the Greek woman who walks here too with a basket of string and her hot, rusty clothes

thought little or nothing of the matter before,—Aylmer discovered that this was the case with himself.

Had she been less beautiful,—if Envy's self could have found aught 8
else to sneer at,—he might have felt his affection heightened by the prettiness of this mimic hand, now vaguely portrayed, now lost, now stealing forth again and glimmering to and fro with every pulse of emotion that throbbed within her heart; but, seeing her otherwise so perfect, he found this one defect grow more and more intolerable with every moment of their united lives. It was the fatal flaw of humanity which Nature, in one shape or another, stamps ineffaceably on all her productions, either to imply that they are temporary and finite, or that their perfection must be wrought by toil and pain. The crimson hand expressed the ineludible gripe in which mortality clutches the highest and purest of earthly mould, degrading them into kindred with the lowest, and even with the very brutes, like whom their visible frames return to dust. In this manner, selecting it as the symbol of his wife's liability to sin, sorrow, decay, and death, Aylmer's sombre imagination was not long in rendering the birthmark a frightful object, causing him more trouble and horror than ever Georgiana's beauty, whether of soul or sense, had given him delight.

At all the seasons which should have been their happiest he invari- 9
ably, and without intending it, nay, in spite of a purpose to the contrary, reverted to this one disastrous topic. Trifling as it at first appeared, it so connected itself with innumerable trains of thought and modes of feeling that it became the central point of all. With the morning twilight Aylmer opened his eyes upon his wife's face and recognized the symbol of imperfection; and when they sat together at the evening hearth his eyes wandered stealthily to her cheek, and beheld, flickering with the blaze of the wood fire, the spectral hand that wrote mortality where he would fain have worshipped. Georgiana soon learned to shudder at his gaze. It needed but a glance with the peculiar expression that his face often wore to change the roses of her cheek into a deathlike paleness, amid which the crimson hand was brought strongly out, like a bas-relief of ruby on the whitest marble.

Late one night, when the lights were growing dim so as hardly to 10
betray the stain on the poor wife's cheek, she herself, for the first time, voluntarily took up the subject.

"Do you remember, my dear Aylmer," said she, with a feeble at- 11
tempt at a smile, "have you any recollection, of a dream last night about this odious hand?"

"None! none whatever!" replied Aylmer, starting; but then he 12
added, in a dry, cold tone, affected for the sake of concealing the real depth of his emotion, "I might well dream of it; for, before I fell asleep, it had taken a pretty firm hold of my fancy."

"And you did dream of it?" continued Georgiana, hastily; for she 13 dreaded lest a gush of tears should interrupt what she had to say. "A terrible dream! I wonder that you can forget it. Is it possible to forget this one expression?—'It is in her heart now; we must have it out!' Reflect, my husband; for by all means I would have you recall that dream."

The mind is in a sad state when Sleep, the all-involving, cannot   14 confine her spectres within the dim region of her sway, but suffers them to break forth, affrighting this actual life with secrets that perchance belong to a deeper one. Aylmer now remembered his dream. He had fancied himself with his servant Aminadab, attempting an operation for the removal of the birthmark; but the deeper went the knife, the deeper sank the hand, until at length its tiny grasp appeared to have caught hold of Georgiana's heart; whence, however, her husband was inexorably resolved to cut or wrench it away.

When the dream had shaped itself perfectly in his memory Aylmer   15 sat in his wife's presence with a guilty feeling. Truth often finds its way to the mind close muffled in robes of sleep, and then speaks with uncompromising directness of matters in regard to which we practise an unconscious self-deception during our waking moments. Until now he had not been aware of the tyrannizing influence acquired by one idea over his mind, and of the lengths which he might find in his heart to go for the sake of giving himself peace.

"Aylmer," resumed Georgiana, solemnly, "I know not what may   16 be the cost to both of us to rid me of this fatal birthmark. Perhaps its removal may cause cureless deformity; or it may be the stain goes as deep as life itself. Again: do we know that there is a possibility, on any terms, of unclasping the firm gripe of this little hand which was laid upon me before I came into the world?"

"Dearest Georgiana, I have spent much thought upon the subject,"   17 hastily interrupted Aylmer. "I am convinced of the perfect practicability of its removal."

"If there be the remotest possibility of it," continued Georgiana,   18 "let the attempt be made, at whatever risk. Danger is nothing to me; for life, while this hateful mark makes me the object of your horror and disgust,—life is a burden which I would fling down with joy. Either remove this dreadful hand, or take my wretched life! You have deep science. All the world bears witness of it. You have achieved great wonders. Cannot you remove this little, little mark, which I cover with the tips of two small fingers? Is this beyond your power, for the sake of your own peace, and to save your poor wife from madness?"

"Noblest, dearest, tenderest wife," cried Aylmer, rapturously,   19 "doubt not my power. I have already given this matter the deepest thought—thought which might almost have enlightened me to create a being less perfect than yourself. Georgiana, you have led me deeper than ever into the heart of science. I feel myself fully competent to render this dear cheek as faultless as its fellow; and then, most beloved, what will be my triumph when I shall have corrected what Nature left imperfect in her fairest work! Even Pygmalion, when his sculptured woman assumed life, felt not greater ecstasy than mine will be."

"It is resolved, then," said Georgiana, faintly smiling. "And, 20 Aylmer, spare me not, though you should find the birthmark take refuge in my heart at last."

Her husband tenderly kissed her cheek—her right cheek—not that 21 which bore the impress of the crimson hand.

The next day Aylmer apprised his wife of a plan that he had formed 22 whereby he might have opportunity for the intense thought and constant watchfulness which the proposed operation would require; while Georgiana, likewise, would enjoy the perfect repose essential to its success. They were to seclude themselves in the extensive apartments occupied by Aylmer as a laboratory, and where, during his toilsome youth, he had made discoveries in the elemental powers of Nature that had roused the admiration of all the learned societies in Europe. Seated calmly in this laboratory, the pale philosopher had investigated the secrets of the highest cloud region and of the profoundest mines; he had satisfied himself of the causes that kindled and kept alive the fires of the volcano; and had explained the mystery of the fountains, and how it is that they gush forth, some so bright and pure, and others with such rich medicinal virtues, from the dark bosom of the earth. Here, too, at an earlier period, he had studied the wonders of the human frame, and attempted to fathom the very process by which Nature assimilates all her precious influences from earth and air, and from the spiritual world, to create and foster man, her masterpiece. The latter pursuit, however, Aylmer had long laid aside in unwilling recognition of the truth—against which all seekers sooner or later stumble—that our great creative Mother, while she amuses us with apparently working in the broadest sunshine, is yet severely careful to keep her own secrets, and, in spite of her pretended openness, shows us nothing but results. She permits us, indeed, to mar, but seldom to mend, and, like a jealous patentee, on no account to make. Now, however, Aylmer resumed these half-forgotten investigations; not, of course, with such hopes or wishes as first suggested them; but because they involved much physiological truth and lay in the path of his proposed scheme for the treatment of Georgiana.

As he led her over the threshold of the laboratory, Georgiana was 23 cold and tremulous. Aylmer looked cheerfully into her face, with intent to reassure her, but was so startled with the intense glow of the birthmark upon the whiteness of her cheek that he could not restrain a strong convulsive shudder. His wife fainted.

"Aminadab! Aminadab!" shouted Aylmer, stamping violently on 24 the floor.

Forthwith there issued from an inner apartment a man of low stat-   25
ure, but bulky frame, with shaggy hair hanging about his visage, which
was grimed with the vapors of the furnace. This personage had been
Aylmer's underworker during his whole scientific career, and was ad-
mirably fitted for that office by his great mechanical readiness, and the
skill with which, while incapable of comprehending a single principle,
he executed all the details of his master's experiments. With his vast
strength, his shaggy hair, his smoky aspect, and the indescribable earthi-
ness that incrusted him, he seemed to represent man's physical nature;
while Aylmer's slender figure, and pale, intellectual face, were no less
apt a type of the spiritual element.

"Throw open the door of the boudoir, Aminadab," said Aylmer,   26
"and burn a pastil."

"Yes, master," answered Aminadab, looking intently at the lifeless   27
form of Georgiana; and then he muttered to himself, "If she were my
wife, I'd never part with that birthmark."

When Georgiana recovered consciousness she found herself breath-   28
ing an atmosphere of penetrating fragrance, the gentle potency of which
had recalled her from her deathlike faintness. The scene around her
looked like enchantment. Aylmer had converted those smoky, dingy,
sombre rooms, where he had spent his brightest years in recondite
pursuits, into a series of beautiful apartments not unfit to be the secluded abode of a lovely woman. The walls were hung with gorgeous
curtains, which imparted the combination of grandeur and grace that
no other species of adornment can achieve; and, as they fell from the
ceiling to the floor, their rich and ponderous folds, concealing all angles
and straight lines, appeared to shut in the scene from infinite space. For
aught Georgiana knew, it might be a pavilion among the clouds. And
Aylmer, excluding the sunshine, which would have interfered with his
chemical processes, had supplied its place with perfumed lamps, emitting flames of various hue, but all uniting in a soft, impurpled radiance.
He now knelt by his wife's side, watching her earnestly, but without
alarm; for he was confident in his science, and felt that he could draw
a magic circle round her within which no evil might intrude.

"Where am I? Ah, I remember," said Georgiana, faintly; and she   29
placed her hand over her cheek to hide the terrible mark from her
husband's eyes.

"Fear not, dearest!" exclaimed he. "Do not shrink from me! Believe   30
me, Georgiana, I even rejoice in this single imperfection, since it will
be such a rapture to remove it."

"O, spare me!" sadly replied his wife. "Pray do not look at it again.   31
I never can forget that convulsive shudder."

In order to soothe Georgiana, and, as it were, to release her mind   32
from the burden of actual things, Aylmer now put in practice some of
the light and playful secrets which science had taught him among its

profounder lore. Airy figures, absolutely bodiless ideas, and forms of unsubstantial beauty came and danced before her, imprinting their momentary footsteps on beams of light. Though she had some indistinct idea of the method of these optical phenomena, still the illusion was almost perfect enough to warrant the belief that her husband possessed sway over the spiritual world. Then again, when she felt a wish to look forth from her seclusion, immediately, as if her thoughts were answered, the procession of external existence flitted across a screen. The scenery and the figures of actual life were perfectly represented, but with that bewitching yet indescribable difference which always makes a picture, an image, or a shadow so much more attractive than the original. When wearied of this, Aylmer bade her cast her eyes upon a vessel containing a quantity of earth. She did so, with little interest at first; but was soon startled to perceive the germ of a plant shooting upward from the soil. Then came the slender stalk; the leaves gradually unfolded themselves; and amid them was a perfect and lovely flower.

"It is magical!" cried Georgiana. "I dare not touch it."   33

"Nay, pluck it," answered Aylmer,—"pluck it, and inhale its brief   34 perfume while you may. The flower will wither in a few moments and leave nothing save its brown seed vessels; but thence may be perpetuated a race as ephemeral as itself."

But Georgiana had no sooner touched the flower than the whole   35 plant suffered a blight, its leaves turning coal-black as if by the agency of fire.

"There was too powerful a stimulus," said Aylmer, thoughtfully.   36

To make up for this abortive experiment, he proposed to take her   37 portrait by a scientific process of his own invention. It was to be effected by rays of light striking upon a polished plate of metal. Georgiana assented; but, on looking at the result, was affrighted to find the features of the portrait blurred and indefinable; while the minute figure of a hand appeared where the cheek should have been. Aylmer snatched the metallic plate and threw it into a jar of corrosive acid.

Soon, however, he forgot these mortifying failures. In the intervals   38 of study and chemical experiment he came to her flushed and exhausted, but seemed invigorated by her presence, and spoke in glowing language of the resources of his art. He gave a history of the long dynasty of the alchemists, who spent so many ages in quest of the universal solvent by which the golden principle might be elicited from all things vile and base. Aylmer appeared to believe that, by the plainest scientific logic, it was altogether within the limits of possibility to discover this long-sought medium; "but," he added, "a philosopher who should go deep enough to acquire the power would attain too lofty a wisdom to stoop to the exercise of it." Not less singular were his opinions in regard to the elixir vitae. He more than intimated that it was at his option to concoct a liquid that should prolong life for years, perhaps interminably; but that it would produce a discord in Nature which all the world, and chiefly the quaffer of the immortal nostrum, would find cause to curse.

"Aylmer, are you in earnest?" asked Georgiana, looking at him with amazement and fear. "It is terrible to possess such power, or even to dream of possessing it." 39

"O, do not tremble, my love," said her husband. "I would not wrong either you or myself by working such inharmonious effects upon our lives; but I would have you consider how trifling, in comparison, is the skill requisite to remove this little hand." 40

At the mention of the birthmark, Georgiana, as usual, shrank as if a red-hot iron had touched her cheek. 41

Again Aylmer applied himself to his labors. She could hear his voice in the distant furnace room giving directions to Aminadab, whose harsh, uncouth, misshapen tones were audible in response, more like the grunt or growl of a brute than human speech. After hours of absence, Aylmer reappeared and proposed that she should now examine his cabinet of chemical products and natural treasures of the earth. Among the former he showed her a small vial, in which, he remarked, was contained a gentle yet most powerful fragrance, capable of impregnating all the breezes that blow across a kingdom. They were of inestimable value, the contents of that little vial; and, as he said so, he threw some of the perfume into the air and filled the room with piercing and invigorating delight. 42

"And what is this?" asked Georgiana, pointing to a small crystal globe containing a gold-colored liquid. "It is so beautiful to the eye that I could imagine it the elixir of life." 43

"In one sense it is," replied Aylmer; "or rather, the elixir of immortality. It is the most precious poison that ever was concocted in this world. By its aid I could apportion the lifetime of any mortal at whom you might point your finger. The strength of the dose would determine whether he were to linger out years, or drop dead in the midst of a breath. No king on his guarded throne could keep his life if I, in my private station, should deem that the welfare of millions justified me in depriving him of it." 44

"Why do you keep such a terrific drug?" inquired Georgiana in horror. 45

"Do not mistrust me, dearest," said her husband, smiling; "its virtuous potency is yet greater than its harmful one. But see! here is a powerful cosmetic. With a few drops of this in a vase of water, freckles may be washed away as easily as the hands are cleansed. A stronger infusion would take the blood out of the cheek, and leave the rosiest beauty a pale ghost." 46

"Is it with this lotion that you intend to bathe my cheek?" asked Georgiana, anxiously. 47

"O, no," hastily replied her husband; "this is merely superficial. 48
Your case demands a remedy that shall go deeper."

In his interviews with Georgiana, Aylmer generally made minute 49
inquiries as to her sensations, and whether the confinement of the
rooms and the temperature of the atmosphere agreed with her. These
questions had such a particular drift that Georgiana began to conjecture
that she was already subjected to certain physical influences, either
breathed in with the fragrant air or taken with her food. She fancied
likewise, but it might be altogether fancy, that there was a stirring up
of her system—a strange, indefinite sensation creeping through her
veins, and tingling, half painfully, half pleasurably, at her heart. Still,
whenever she dared to look into the mirror, there she beheld herself
pale as a white rose and with the crimson birthmark stamped upon her
cheek. Not even Aylmer now hated it so much as she.

To dispel the tedium of the hours which her husband found it 50
necessary to devote to the processes of combination and analysis, Georgiana turned over the volumes of his scientific library. In many dark
old tomes she met with chapters full of romance and poetry. They were
the works of the philosophers of the middle ages, such as Albertus
Magnus, Cornelius Agrippa, Paracelsus, and the famous friar who created the prophetic Brazen Head. All these antique naturalists stood in
advance of their centuries, yet were imbued with some of their credu-
lity, and therefore were believed, and perhaps imagined themselves to
have acquired from the investigation of Nature a power above Nature,
and from physics a sway over the spiritual world. Hardly less curious
and imaginative were the early volumes of the Transactions of the Royal
Society, in which the members, knowing little of the limits of natural
possibility, were continually recording wonders or proposing methods
whereby wonders might be wrought.

But to Georgiana, the most engrossing volume was a large folio 51
from her husband's own hand, in which he had recorded every experiment of his scientific career, its original aim, the methods adopted for
its development, and its final success or failure, with the circumstances
to which either event was attributable. The book, in truth, was both
the history and emblem of his ardent, ambitious, imaginative, yet practical and laborious life. He handled physical details as if there were nothing beyond them; yet spiritualized them all and redeemed himself from
materialism by his strong and eager aspiration towards the infinite. In
his grasp the veriest clod of earth assumed a soul. Georgiana, as she
read, reverenced Aylmer and loved him more profoundly than ever,
but with a less entire dependence on his judgment than heretofore.
Much as he had accomplished, she could not but observe that his most
splendid successes were almost invariably failures, if compared with the
ideal at which he aimed. His brightest diamonds were the merest pebbles, and felt to be so by himself, in comparison with the inestimable

gems which lay hidden beyond his reach. The volume, rich with achievements that had won renown for its author, was yet as melancholy a record as ever mortal hand had penned. It was the sad confession and continual exemplification of the shortcomings of the composite man, the spirit burdened with clay and working in matter, and of the despair that assails the higher nature at finding itself so miserably thwarted by the earthly part. Perhaps every man of genius, in whatever sphere, might recognize the image of his own experience in Aylmer's journal.

So deeply did these reflections affect Georgiana that she laid her   52
face upon the open volume and burst into tears. In this situation she was found by her husband.

"It is dangerous to read in a sorcerer's books," said he with a smile,   53
though his countenance was uneasy and displeased. "Georgiana, there are pages in that volume which I can scarcely glance over and keep my senses. Take heed lest it prove detrimental to you."

"It has made me worship you more than ever," said she.   54

"Ah, wait for this one success," rejoined he, "then worship me if   55
you will. I shall deem myself hardly unworthy of it. But come, I have sought you for the luxury of your voice. Sing to me, dearest."

So she poured out the liquid music of her voice to quench the thirst   56
of his spirit. He then took his leave with a boyish exuberance of gayety, assuring her that her seclusion would endure but a little longer, and that the result was already certain. Scarcely had he departed when Georgiana felt irresistibly impelled to follow him. She had forgotten to inform Aylmer of a symptom which for two or three hours past had begun to excite her attention. It was a sensation in the fatal birthmark, not painful, but which induced a restlessness throughout her system. Hastening after her husband, she intruded for the first time into the laboratory.

The first thing that struck her eye was the furnace, that hot and   57
feverish worker, with the intense glow of its fire, which by the quantities of soot clustered above it seemed to have been burning for ages. There was a distilling apparatus in full operation. Around the room were retorts, tubes, cylinders, crucibles, and other apparatus of chemical research. An electrical machine stood ready for immediate use. The atmosphere felt oppressively close, and was tainted with gaseous odors which had been tormented forth by the processes of science. The severe and homely simplicity of the apartment, with its naked walls and brick pavement, looked strange, accustomed as Georgiana had become to the fantastic elegance of her boudoir. But what chiefly, indeed almost solely, drew her attention, was the aspect of Aylmer himself.

He was pale as death, anxious and absorbed, and hung over the   58
furnace as if it depended upon his utmost watchfulness whether the liquid which it was distilling should be the draught of immortal happi-

ness or misery. How different from the sanguine and joyous mien that he had assumed for Georgiana's encouragement!

"Carefully now, Aminadab; carefully, thou human machine; carefully, thou man of clay," muttered Aylmer, more to himself than his assistant. "Now, if there be a thought too much or too little, it is all over." 59

"Ho! ho!" mumbled Aminadab. "Look, master! look!" 60

Aylmer raised his eyes hastily, and at first reddened, then grew paler than ever, on beholding Georgiana. He rushed towards her and seized her arm with a gripe that left the print of his fingers upon it. 61

"Why do you come hither? Have you no trust in your husband?" cried he, impetuously. "Would you throw the blight of that fatal birthmark over my labors? It is not well done. Go, prying woman! go!" 62

"Nay, Aylmer," said Georgiana with the firmness of which she possessed no stinted endowment, "it is not you that have a right to complain. You mistrust your wife; you have concealed the anxiety with which you watch the development of this experiment. Think not so unworthily of me, my husband. Tell me all the risk we run, and fear not that I shall shrink; for my share in it is far less than your own." 63

"No, no, Georgiana!" said Aylmer, impatiently; "it must not be." 64

"I submit," replied she, calmly. "And, Aylmer, I shall quaff whatever draught you bring me; but it will be on the same principle that would induce me to take a dose of poison if offered by your hand." 65

"My noble wife," said Aylmer, deeply moved, "I knew not the height and depth of your nature until now. Nothing shall be concealed. Know, then, that this crimson hand, superficial as it seems, has clutched its grasp into your being with a strength of which I had no previous conception. I have already administered agents powerful enough to do aught except to change your entire physical system. Only one thing remains to be tried. If that fail us we are ruined." 66

"Why did you hesitate to tell me this?" asked she. 67

"Because, Georgiana," said Aylmer, in a low voice, "there is danger." 68

"Danger? There is but one danger—that this horrible stigma shall be left upon my cheek!" cried Georgiana. "Remove it, remove it, whatever be the cost, or we shall both go mad!" 69

"Heaven knows your words are too true," said Aylmer, sadly. "And now, dearest, return to your boudoir. In a little while all will be tested." 70

He conducted her back and took leave of her with a solemn tenderness which spoke far more than his words how much was now at stake. After his departure Georgiana became rapt in musings. She considered the character of Aylmer and did it completer justice than at any previous moment. Her heart exulted, while it trembled, at his honorable love—so pure and lofty that it would accept nothing less than perfection nor miserably make itself contented with an earthlier nature than he had 71 dreamed of. She felt how much more precious was such a sentiment than that meaner kind which would have borne with the imperfection for her sake, and have been guilty of treason to holy love by degrading its perfect idea to the level of the actual; and with her whole spirit she prayed that, for a single moment, she might satisfy his highest and deepest conception. Longer than one moment she well knew it could not be; for his spirit was ever on the march, ever ascending, and each instant required something that was beyond the scope of the instant before.

The sound of her husband's footsteps aroused her. He bore a crystal 72 goblet containing a liquor colorless as water, but bright enough to be the draught of immortality. Aylmer was pale; but it seemed rather the consequence of a highly-wrought state of mind and tension of spirit than of fear or doubt.

"The concoction of the draught has been perfect," said he, in an- 73 swer to Georgiana's look. "Unless all my science have deceived me, it cannot fail."

"Save on your account, my dearest Aylmer," observed his wife, "I 74 might wish to put off this birthmark of mortality by relinquishing mortality itself in preference to any other mode. Life is but a sad possession to those who have attained precisely the degree of moral advancement at which I stand. Were I weaker and blinder, it might be happiness. Were I stronger, it might be endured hopefully. But, being what I find myself, methinks I am of all mortals the most fit to die."

"You are fit for heaven without tasting death!" replied her husband. 75 "But why do we speak of dying? The draught cannot fail. Behold its effect upon this plant."

On the window seat there stood a geranium diseased with yellow 76 blotches which had overspread all its leaves. Aylmer poured a small quantity of the liquid upon the soil in which it grew. In a little time, when the roots of the plant had taken up the moisture, the unsightly blotches began to be extinguished in a living verdure.

"There needed no proof," said Georgiana, quietly. "Give me the 77 goblet. I joyfully stake all upon your word."

"Drink, then, thou lofty creature!" exclaimed Aylmer, with fervid 78 admiration. "There is no taint of imperfection on thy spirit. Thy sensible frame, too, shall soon be all perfect."

She quaffed the liquid and returned the goblet to his hand. 79

"It is grateful," said she, with a placid smile. "Methinks it is like 80 water from a heavenly fountain; for it contains I know not what of unobtrusive fragrance and deliciousness. It allays a feverish thirst that had parched me for many days. Now, dearest, let me sleep. My earthly senses are closing over my spirit like the leaves around the heart of a rose at sunset."

She spoke the last words with a gentle reluctance, as if it required 81 almost more energy than she could command to pronounce the faint and lingering syllables. Scarcely had they loitered through her lips ere she was lost in slumber. Aylmer sat by her side, watching her aspect with the emotions proper to a man the whole value of whose existence was involved in the process now to be tested. Mingled with this mood, however, was the philosophic investigation characteristic of the man of science. Not the minutest symptom escaped him. A heightened flush of the cheek, a slight irregularity of breath, a quiver of the eyelid, a hardly perceptible tremor through the frame,—such were the details which, as the moments passed, he wrote down in his folio volume. Intense thought had set its stamp upon every previous page of that volume; but the thoughts of years were all concentrated upon the last.

While thus employed, he failed not to gaze often at the fatal hand, 82 and not without a shudder. Yet once, by a strange and unaccountable impulse, he pressed it with his lips. His spirit recoiled, however, in the very act; and Georgiana, out of the midst of her deep sleep, moved uneasily and murmured as if in remonstrance. Again Aylmer resumed his watch. Nor was it without avail. The crimson hand, which at first had been strongly visible upon the marble paleness of Georgiana's check, now grew more faintly outlined. She remained not less pale than ever; but the birthmark, with every breath that came and went lost somewhat of its former distinctness. Its presence had been awful; its departure was more awful still. Watch the stain of the rainbow fading out of the sky, and you will know how that mysterious symbol passed away.

"By Heaven! it is well nigh gone!" said Aylmer to himself, in almost 83 irrepressible ecstasy. "I can scarcely trace it now. Success! success! And now it is like the faintest rose color. The lightest flush of blood across her cheek would overcome it. But she is so pale!"

He drew aside the window curtain and suffered the light of natural 84 day to fall into the room and rest upon her cheek. At the same time he heard a gross, hoarse chuckle, which he had long known as his servant Aminadab's expression of delight.

"Ah, clod! ah, earthly mass!" cried Aylmer, laughing in a sort of 85 frenzy, "you have served me well! Matter and spirit—earth and heaven—have both done their part in this! Laugh, thing of the senses! You have earned the right to laugh."

These exclamations broke Georgiana's sleep. She slowly unclosed 86 her eyes and gazed into the mirror which her husband had arranged for that purpose. A faint smile flitted over her lips when she recognized how barely perceptible was now that crimson hand which had once blazed forth with such disastrous brilliancy as to scare away all their happiness. But then her eyes sought Aylmer's face with a trouble and anxiety that he could by no means account for.

"My poor Aylmer!" murmured she. 87

"Poor? Nay, richest, happiest, most favored!" exclaimed he. "My 88 peerless bride, it is successful! You are perfect!"

"My poor Aylmer," she repeated, with a more than human tender- 89 ness, "you have aimed loftily; you have done nobly. Do not repent that, with so high and pure a feeling, you have rejected the best the earth could offer. Aylmer, dearest Aylmer, I am dying!"

Alas! it was too true! The fatal hand had grappled with the mystery 90 of life, and was the bond by which an angelic spirit kept itself in union with a mortal frame. As the last crimson tint of the birthmark—that sole token of human imperfection—faded from her cheek, the parting breath of the now perfect woman passed into the atmosphere, and her soul, lingering a moment near her husband, took its heavenward flight. Then a hoarse, chuckling laugh was heard again! Thus ever does the gross fatality of earth exult in its invariable triumph over the immortal essence which, in this dim sphere of half development, demands the completeness of a higher state. Yet, had Aylmer reached a profounder wisdom, he need not thus have flung away the happiness which would have woven his mortal life of the selfsame texture with the celestial. The momentary circumstance was too strong for him; he failed to look beyond the shadowy scope of time, and, living once for all in eternity, to find the perfect future in the present.

MARK HALLIDAY

Population

Mark Halliday (1949–   ) was born in Michigan and grew up in North Carolina and Connecticut. He took his B.A. from Brown University in 1971 and his M.A. in creative writing from Brown in 1976. In the interim between degrees, he was an actor and scriptwriter for the Rhode Island Feminist Theater. In 1983 he completed his Ph.D. at Brandeis with a dissertation on Thomas Hardy's poetry. He then taught for six years at the University of Pennsylvania and for four at the Wilmington Friends School in Delaware. Halliday began writing poetry as an undergraduate, "with more enthusiasm than serious effort," he reports. In 1978, helped by the poet Frank Bidart and other teachers, he developed the colloquial, speech-oriented style that has characterized most of his work since then. His poems often strive to reveal and explore feelings that are embarrassing and ostensibly unpoetic, particularly the struggle for attention and admiration that, in his view, "arises naturally from fear of death." Halliday's first book of poems was *Little Star* (1987); it was followed by *Tasker Street* (1992). His critical book on a major American poet, *Stevens and the Interpersonal*, appeared in 1991. "Population" is from *Tasker Street.*

Isn't it nice that everyone has a grocery list 1
except the very poor you hear about occasionally
we all have a grocery list on the refrigerator door;
at any given time there are thirty million lists in America
that say BREAD. *Isn't it nice*
not to be alone in this. Sometimes
you visit someone's house for the first time
and you spot the list taped up on a kitchen cabinet
and you think Yes, we're all in this together.
TOILET PAPER. *No getting around it.*
Nice to think of us all
unwrapping the new rolls at once,
forty thousand of us at any given moment.

Orgasm, of course, being the most vivid example: imagine 2
an electrified map wired to every American bed:
those little lights popping
on both sides of the Great Divide,
popping to beat the band. But
we never beat the band: within an hour or day
we're horny again, or hungry, or burdened with waste.
But isn't it nice not to be alone in
any of it; nice to be not noticeably responsible,
acquitted eternally in the rituals of the tribe:
it's only human! It's only human and that's not much.

So, aren't you glad we have such advanced farm machinery, 3
futuristic fertilizers, half a billion chickens
almost ready to die. Here come the loaves of bread for us
thup thup thup thup for all of us thup thup thup
except maybe the very poor
thup thup
and man all the cattle we can fatten up man,
there's no stopping our steaks. And that's why
we can make babies galore, baby:

let's get on with it. Climb aboard. 4
Let's be affirmative here, let's be pro-life for God's sake
how can life be wrong?
People need *people and the happiest people are*
surrounded with friendly flesh.
If you have ten kids they'll be so sweet—
ten really sweet kids! Have twelve!

What if there were 48 pro baseball teams,
you could see a damn lot more games!

And in this fashion we get away   5
from tragedy. Because tragedy comes when someone
gets too special. Whereas,

if forty thousand kitchen counters   6
on any given Sunday night
have notes on them that say
I CAN'T TAKE IT ANY MORE
I'M GONE, DON'T TRY TO FIND ME
you can feel how your *note is*
no big thing in America,
so, no horrible *heartbreak,*
it's more like a TV episode,
you've seen this whole plot lots of times
and everybody gets by—
you feel better already—
everybody gets by
and it's nice. It's a people thing.
You've got to admit it's nice.

MEDIA

We find ourselves in a hall of mirrors.

Media: Preview

As those images come to me I realize that, for nearly 20 years, I have been thinking that TV affected me more than it really did. For though what I saw on TV was important, I always saw it with people who had senses both of history and their own dignity; people who made certain that any televised message was subjected to interference. . . .

But the only movie I remember seeing for certain, some fifty-four years later, is *The Last Train From Madrid.* After we took the bus home to Ardmore Street, I burned my collection of war cards and put away my toy soldiers forever.

Irene shifted the control and invaded the privacy of several breakfast tables. She overheard demonstrations of indigestion, carnal love, abysmal vanity, faith, and despair. Irene's life was nearly as simple and sheltered as it appeared to be, and the forthright and sometimes brutal language that came from the loudspeaker that morning astonished and troubled her.

and the size of it,
the size of the great rear wall measures
the breadth of the dreams we have had here.

Overview and Ideas for Writing

It used to seem self-evident that art is a human copy of a reality which is not created by humans. In *Hamlet,* for instance, the prince reminds some actors that their purpose is to "hold, as 'twere, the mirror up to nature." Clearly he thinks of nature (human nature, primarily) as a solid reality that lies outside the play and is unaffected by it. The actors imitate real human beings. Hamlet apparently didn't foresee our world, where real human beings imitate actors.

But perhaps it was easier to separate art from reality in Shakespeare's day than it is in ours. Then, after all, the average person's exposure to "the media" was limited. A few hours per week in church, an occasional evening at a theater, and (for the few who could read) some hours spent with books would have been a high rate of exposure to experiences "scripted" by others. Today our exposure to "scripted" experience is so extensive that for many of us it permeates reality. Every minute of a television program or commercial is scripted, of course, and virtually every minute of a radio broadcast. The newspaper and magazine are filled almost entirely with "script" and "art," including the carefully posed or drawn figures in the advertisements. Only an occasional news photo seems to come directly from reality. When we go to the shopping mall, the building and the displays of merchandise inside it are artfully prepared by architects and designers, and the music in the background is programmed by Muzak or one of its competitors. The "reality" of our lives has become so entangled with "art" that if Hamlet were alive today—working in Hollywood or on Madison Avenue—he might instruct the actors that their purpose was, "as 'twere, to hold the mirror up to the mirror which is held up to nature." He might even add a few intervening mirrors. He might even question whether any of them needed to be pointed at nature.

The essays in this unit discuss the effect this intensive exposure to media has on our view of reality. Though several of them have their humorous moments, the writers generally seem worried. David Bradley and Wyatt Townley discuss the way that television has come to dominate both our homes and our public spaces. Randall Jarrell and Gloria Steinem remind us that the mass media, print and electronic, is controlled by people whose primary concern is not that we *understand* but that we *buy*. Neil Postman suggests that watching television news—an act many people treat as a civic duty—may be making us schizophrenic. Katha Pollitt worries about what her daughter is learning about women from books and television, and Barbara Ehrenreich tells us that Americans, who "used to be a great and restless people," are becoming "couch potatoes." Perhaps the most positive essay in the unit is Donald Hall's account of the movie that ended his boyish love affair with war and violence.

Not surprisingly, the unit's story and poem are more ambiguous than the typical Hollywood film. Each reader will have to decide for himself or herself whether John Cheever's story is about the effect of the media or about something else entirely. Each reader will need to decide whether John Updike's poem praises the movie house or ridicules it.

Your own experience with the media should allow you to discuss some of the questions these writers raise, and research might strengthen your discussion. Have the writers failed to see some of the media's virtues? Are children's books, movies, and television as sexist as Pollitt makes them out to be? Does network news bring us closer to the world or insulate us from it? Is there a movie that affected you and your classmates as strongly as Donald Hall was affected by *The Last Train From Madrid*?

KATHA POLLITT

The Smurfette Principle

Katha Pollitt (1949–   ) was born in Brooklyn and now lives and
works in Manhattan as a freelance writer. After receiving her B.A. in
philosophy from Radcliffe in 1972, she began to establish a name for
herself as a poet. Her 1982 collection, *Antarctic Traveller,* won the National Book Critics Circle Award in 1983. A committed political liberal,
she often writes essays and articles for such magazines as *The Atlantic
Monthly, Mother Jones, The New Yorker,* and *The Nation* (where she
serves as a contributing editor). "The Smurfette Principle" was published in *The New York Times Magazine* on April 7, 1991. In 1993 she
published *The Morning After: Sex, Fear and Femininity on Campus* and
in 1994 followed it with *Reasonable Creatures: Essays on Women and
Feminism.*

This Christmas, I finally caved in: I gave my 3-year-old daughter, 1
Sophie, her very own cassette of "The Little Mermaid." Now, she, too,
can sit transfixed by Ariel, the perky teen-ager
with the curvy tail who trades her voice for a
pair of shapely legs and a shot at marriage to a
prince. ("On land it's much preferred for ladies
not to say a word," sings the cynical sea witch,
"and she who holds her tongue will get her
man." Since she's the villain, we're not meant
to notice that events prove her correct.)

Are the media distorting reality for children, or are they
presenting a reality that people like Pollitt don't approve
of?

Usually when parents give a child some item they find repellent, 2
they plead helplessness before a juvenile filibuster. But "The Little Mermaid" was my idea. Ariel may look a lot like
Barbie, and her adventure may be limited to romance and over with the wedding bells, but unlike, say, Cinderella or Sleeping Beauty, she's
active, brave and determined, the heroine of her
own life. She even rescues the prince. And that
makes her a rare fish, indeed, in the world of
preschool culture.

Is Pollitt right about the passivity of Disney's pre-1989
heroines? Have heroines of
more recent Disney releases
been more passive than
Ariel or less?

Take a look at the kids' section of your local 3
video store. You'll find that features starring
boys, and usually aimed at them, account for 9
out of 10 offerings. Clicking the television dial
one recent week—admittedly not an encyclopedic study—I came across not a single network
cartoon or puppet show starring a female.
(Nickelodeon, the children's cable channel, has

If you tried Pollitt's tests today, would you find the
same dominance by boys in
the video store and on television?

one of each.) Except for the crudity of the animation and the general air of witlessness and hype, I might as well have been back in my own 1950's childhood, nibbling Frosted Flakes in front of Daffy Duck, Bugs Bunny, Porky Pig and the rest of the all-male Warner Brothers lineup.

Contemporary shows are either essentially all-male, like "Garfield," or are organized on what I call the Smurfette principle: a group of male buddies will be accented by a lone female, stereotypically defined. In the worst cartoons—the ones that blend seamlessly into the animated cereal commercials—the female is usually a little-sister type, a bunny in a pink dress and hair ribbons who tags along with the adventurous bears and badgers. But the Smurfette principle rules the more carefully made shows, too. Thus, Kanga, the only female in "Winnie-the-Pooh," is a mother. Piggy, of "Muppet Babies," is a pint-size version of Miss Piggy, the camp glamour queen of the Muppet movies. April, of the wildly popular "Teen-Age Mutant Ninja Turtles," functions as a girl Friday to a quartet of male superheroes. The message is clear. Boys are the norm, girls the variation; boys are central, girls peripheral; boys are individuals, girls types. Boys define the group, its story and its code of values. Girls exist only in relation to boys.

Well, commercial television—what did I expect? The surprise is that public television, for all its superior intelligence, charm and commitment to worthy values, shortchanges preschool girls, too. Mister Rogers lives in a neighborhood populated mostly by middle-aged men like himself. "Shining Time Station" features a cartoon in which the male characters are train engines and the female characters are passenger cars. And then there's "Sesame Street." True, the human characters are neatly divided between the genders (and among the races, too, which is another rarity). The film clips, moreover, are just about the only place on television in which you regularly see girls having fun together: practicing double Dutch, having a sleep-over. But the Muppets are the real stars of "Sesame Street," and the important ones—the ones with real personalities, who sing on the musical videos, whom kids identify with and cherish in dozens of licensed products—are *all* male. I know one little girl who was so outraged and heartbroken when she realized that even Big Bird—her last hope—was a boy that she hasn't watched the show since.

Margin notes:

Do you think this message is clear to children who watch these shows? Do you think that you received this message (consciously or unconsciously) from television and the movies when you were a child?

Randall Jarrell might have argued that the stronger message in children's programming is "Consume!" Would he be right?

Can any of these programs be defended against the charge that Pollitt is making? How?

Barbara Ehrenreich, though a notable feminist, describes another kind of danger in TV watching in her essay. Which danger is more serious?

Well, there's always the library. Some of the best children's books 6
ever written have been about girls—Madeline, Frances the badger. It's
even possible to find stories with funny, feminist messages, like "The
Paper-bag Princess." (She rescues the prince from a dragon, but he's so
ungrateful that she decides not to marry him, after all.) But books about
girls are a subset in a field that includes a much larger subset of books
about boys (12 of the14 storybooks singled out for praise in last year's
Christmas roundup in *Newsweek,* for instance)
and books in which the sex of the child is theoretically unimportant—in which case it usually
"happens to be" male. Dr. Seuss's books are less
about individual characters than about language
and imaginative freedom—but, somehow or
other, only boys get to go on beyond Zebra or
see marvels on Mulberry Street. Frog and Toad,
Lowly Worm, Lyle the Crocodile, all *could* have
been female. But they're not.

It might be worthwhile to
examine the books on the
most recent *Newsweek*
roundup (or other list of children's books). Are the
books dominated by male
characters?

Do kids pick up on the sexism in children's 7
culture? You bet. Preschoolers are like medieval
philosophers: the text—a book, a movie, a TV
show—is more authoritative than the evidence
of their own eyes. "Let's play weddings," says
my little niece. We grownups roll our eyes, but
face it: it's still the one scenario in which the
girl is the central figure. "Women are *nurses,*"
my friend Anna, a doctor, was informed by her
then 4-year-old, Molly. Even my Sophie is beginning to notice the back-seat role played by
girls in some of her favorite books. "Who's
that?" she asks every time we reread "The Cat
in the Hat." It's Sally, the timid little sister of the resourceful boy narrator. She wants Sally to matter, I think, and since Sally is really just a
name and a hair ribbon, we have to say her name again and again.

Pollitt answers her own
question confidently, but do
you agree with her answer?
How much actual influence
do the media have on the
way children view the
world? What issues besides
sexism might be at stake if
the media's influence is
strong?

The sexism in preschool culture deforms 8
both boys and girls. Little girls learn to split their
consciousness, filtering their dreams and ambi-
tions through boy characters while admiring the
clothes of the princess. The more privileged and
daring can dream of becoming exceptional
women in a man's world—Smurfettes. The others are being taught to accept the more usual
fate, which is to be a passenger car drawn
through life by a masculine train engine. Boys, who are rarely confronted with stories in which males play only minor roles, learn a simpler lesson: girls just don't matter much.

What lessons do you remember learning from the media
that you are *glad* to have
learned? See Donald Hall's
account of a movie that
changed his life.

How can it be that 25 years of feminist social changes have made   9
so little impression on preschool culture? Molly, now 6 and well aware
that women can be doctors, has one theory: children's entertainment
is mostly made by men. That's true, as it happens, and I'm sure it
explains a lot. It's also true that, as a society, we don't seem to care
much what goes on with kids, as long as they are reasonably quiet.
Marshmallow cereal, junky toys, endless hours in front of the tube—
a society that accepts all that is not going to get in a lather about a
little gender stereotyping. It's easier to focus on the bright side. I
had "Cinderella," Sophie has "The Little Mermaid"—that's progress,
isn't it?

David Bradley's essay in this
unit deals specifically with
the way parents can counteract objectional messages
from the media.

Can parents be so sure that
their children watch "very
little television"? See Wyatt
Townley's essay.

"We're working on it," Dulcy Singer, the exec-   10
utive producer of "Sesame Street," told me when
I raised the sensitive question of those all-male
Muppets. After all, the show has only been on the
air for a quarter of a century; these things take
time. The trouble is, our preschoolers don't have
time. My funny, clever, bold, adventurous daughter is forming her gender ideas right now. I do what
I can to counteract the messages she gets from her
entertainment, and so does her father—Sophie
watches very little television. But I can see we have
our work cut out for us. It sure would help if the
bunnies took off their hair ribbons, and if half of
the monsters were fuzzy, blue—and female.

RANDALL JARRELL

A Sad Heart at the Supermarket

Randall Jarrell (1914–1965) is primarily known as a poet and a critic
of poetry. His best-known early poems, collected in such books as
Little Friend, Little Friend (1945) and *Losses* (1948), were reactions to
the horrors of World War II. By the time he published his National
Book Award-winning *The Woman at the Washington Zoo* (1960), Jarrell
had become very concerned about the rise of a consumer culture in
America, a culture that seemed at odds with older and weightier aspects of human nature. He became interested in psychoanalysis,
dreams, myths, and folktales, all of which seemed to lead back to
something more significant than the world of television and household
appliances. Although Jarrell was in some ways a scholarly man—he
translated Chekhov from Russian and Goethe from German—his

words are plain, direct, and sharply opinionated. The passage below
is excerpted from an essay published in *Daedalus* in the spring of 1960.

Advertising men, businessmen speak continually of *media* or *the* 1
media or *the mass media*. One of their trade journals is named, simply,
Media. It is an impressive word: one imagines Mephistopheles offering
Faust[1] *media that no man has ever known;* one feels, while the word is
in one's ear, that abstract, overmastering powers, of a scale and intensity
unimagined yesterday, are being offered one by the technicians who
discovered and control them—offered, and at a price. The word has the
clear fatal ring of that new world whose space we occupy so luxuriously
and precariously; the world that produces mink stoles, rockabilly records, and tactical nuclear weapons by the million; the world that Attila,
Galileo, Hansel and Gretel never knew.

And yet, it's only the plural of *medium*. "Medium," says the diction- 2
ary, "that which lies in the middle; hence, middle condition or degree . . . A substance through which a force acts or an effect is transmitted . . . That through or by which anything is accomplished; as,
an advertising *medium . . . Biol.* A nutritive mixture or substance, as
broth, gelatin, agar, for cultivating bacteria, fungi, etc."

Let us name *our* trade journal *The Medium*. For all these media— 3
television, radio, movies, newspapers, magazines, and the rest—are a
single medium, in whose depths we are all being cultivated. This Medium is of middle condition or degree, mediocre; it lies in the middle
of everything, between a man and his neighbor, his wife, his child, his
self; it, more than anything else, is the substance through which the
forces of our society act upon us, and make us into what our society
needs.

And what does it need? For us to need. 4

Oh, it needs for us to do or be many things: workers, technicians, 5
executives, soldiers, housewives. But first of all, last of all, it needs for
us to be buyers; consumers; beings who want much and will want
more—who want consistently and insatiably. Find some spell to make
us turn away from the stoles, the records, and the weapons, and our
world will change into something to us unimaginable. Find some spell
to make us see that the product or service that yesterday was an unthinkable luxury today is an inexorable necessity, and our world will
go on. It is the Medium which casts this spell—which is this spell. As
we look at the television set, listen to the radio, read the magazines,
the frontier of necessity is always being pushed forward. The Medium

---

1. According to legend, Mephistopheles (the personification of the devil) offered the
learned Doctor Faust youth, knowledge, and magic—in exchange for his soul. In the
German dramatist Goethe's (1749–1832) *Faust*, Mephistopheles tells Faust, "I am giving
you things that no man has ever known."

shows us what our new needs are—how often, without it, we should not have known!—and it shows us how they can be satisfied by buying something. The act of buying something is at the root of our world; if anyone wishes to paint the genesis of things in our society, he will paint a picture of God holding out to Adam a check-book or credit card or Charge-A-Plate.

But how quickly our poor naked Adam is turned into a consumer,   6
is linked to others by the great chain of buying!

> *No outcast he, bewildered and depressed:*
> *Along his infant veins are interfused*
> *The gravitation and the filial bond*
> *Of nature that connect him with the world.*[2]

Children of three or four can ask for a brand of cereal, sing some soap's commercial; by the time that they are twelve or thirteen they are not children but teen-age consumers, interviewed, graphed, analyzed. They are well on their way to becoming that ideal figure of our culture, the knowledgeable consumer. Let me define him: the knowledgeable consumer is someone who, when he comes to Weimar,[3] knows how to buy a Weimaraner.

Daisy's voice sounded like money;[4] everything about the knowl-   7
edgeable consumer looks like or sounds like or feels like money, and informed money at that. To live is to consume, to understand life is to know what to consume: he has learned to understand this, so that his life is a series of choices—correct ones—among the products and services of the world. He is able to choose to consume something, of course, only because sometime, somewhere, he or someone else produced something—but just when or where or what no longer seems to us of as much interest. We may still go to Methodist or Baptist or Presbyterian churches on Sunday, but the Protestant ethic of frugal industry, of production for its own sake, is gone.

Production has come to seem to our society not much more than   8
a condition prior to consumption. "The challenge of today," an advertising agency writes, "is to make the consumer raise his level of demand." This challenge has been met: the Medium has found it easy to make its people feel the continually increasing lacks, the many specialized dissatisfactions (merging into one great dissatisfaction, temporarily assuaged by new purchases) that it needs for them to feel. When in some magazine we see the Medium at its most nearly perfect, we hardly know which half is entertaining and distracting us, which half making

2. Wordsworth, *The Prelude*, 2: 241–244.
3. Weimar is a German city rich with cultural and historical associations; a Weimaraner is a breed of dog.
4. Daisy Buchanan, in F. Scott Fitzgerald's *The Great Gatsby*.

us buy: some advertisement may be more ingeniously entertaining than the text beside it, but it is the text which has made us long for a product more passionately. When one finishes *Holiday* or *Harper's Bazaar* or *House and Garden* or *The New Yorker* or *High Fidelity* or *Road and Track* or—but make your own list—buying something, going somewhere seems a necessary completion to the act of reading the magazine.

Reader, isn't buying or fantasy-buying an important part of your 9 and my emotional life? (If you reply, *No,* I'll think of you with bitter envy as more than merely human; as deeply un-American.) It is a standard joke that when a woman is bored or sad she buys something, to cheer herself up; but in this respect we are all women together, and can hear complacently the reminder of how feminine this consumer-world of ours has become. One imagines as a characteristic dialogue of our time an interview in which someone is asking of a vague gracious figure, a kind of Mrs. America: "But while you waited for the interconti-nental ballistic missiles what did you *do*?" She answers: "I bought things."

She reminds one of the sentinel at Pompeii[5]—a space among ashes, 10 now, but at his post: she too did what she was supposed to do. Our society has delivered us—most of us—from the bonds of necessity, so that we no longer struggle to find food to keep from starving, cloth-ing and shelter to keep from freezing; yet if the ends for which we work and of which we dream are only clothes and restaurants and houses, possessions, consumption, how have we escaped?—we have exchanged man's old bondage for a new voluntary one. It is more than a figure of speech to say that the consumer is trained for his job of consuming as the factory-worker is trained for his job of producing; and the first can be a longer, more complicated training, since it is easier to teach a man to handle a tool, to read a dial, than it is to teach him to ask, always, for a name-brand aspirin—to want, someday, a stand-by generator.

What is that? You don't know? I used not to know, but the readers 11 of *House Beautiful* all know, so that now I know. It is the electrical generator that stands in the basement of the suburban houseowner, shining, silent, till at last one night the lights go out, the furnace stops, the freezer's food begins to—

Ah, but it's frozen for good, the lights are on forever; the owner 12 has switched on the stand-by generator.

But you don't see that he really needs the generator, you'd rather 13 have seen him buy a second car? He has two. A second bathroom? He has four. When the People of the Medium doubled everything, he dou-

5. The ancient Italian city of Pompeii was buried by an eruption of Mount Vesuvius in A.D. 79; the cinders and ashes remarkably preserved the city's ruins, including the remains of human beings who died on the spot.

bled everything; and now that he's gone twice round he will have to wait three years, or four, till both are obsolescent—but while he waits there are so many new needs that he can satisfy, so many things a man can buy. "Man wants but little here below/Nor wants that little long," said the poet;[6] what a lie! Man wants almost unlimited quantities of almost everything, and he wants it till the day he dies.

Sometimes in *Life* or *Look* we see a double-page photograph of   14 some family standing on the lawn among its possessions: station-wagon, swimming-pool, power-cruiser, sports-car, tape-recorder, television sets, radios, cameras, power lawn-mower, garden tractor, lathe, barbecue-set, sporting equipment, domestic appliances—all the gleaming, grotesquely imaginative paraphernalia of its existence. It was hard to get everything on two pages, soon it will need four. It is like a dream, a child's dream before Christmas; yet if the members of the family doubt that they are awake, they have only to reach out and pinch something. The family seems pale and small, a negligible appendage, beside its possessions; only a human being would need to ask: "Which owns which?" We are fond of saying that something is not just something but "a way of life"; this too is a way of life—our way, the way.

Emerson, in his spare stony New England, a few miles from Wal-   15 den, could write: "Things are in the saddle/And ride mankind."[7] He could say more now: that they are in the theater and studio, and entertain mankind; are in the pulpit and preach to mankind. The values of business, in a business society like our own, are reflected in every sphere: values which agree with them are reinforced, values which disagree are cancelled out or have lip service paid to them. In business what sells is good, and that's the end of it—that is what *good* means; if the world doesn't beat a path to your door, your mouse-trap wasn't better. The values of the Medium—which is both a popular business itself and the cause of popularity in other businesses—are business values: money, success, celebrity. If we are representative members of our society, the Medium's values are ours; and even if we are unrepresentative, non-conforming, our hands are—too often—subdued to the element they work in, and our unconscious expectations are all that we consciously reject. Darwin said that he always immediately wrote down evidence against a theory because otherwise, he'd noticed, he would forget it; in the same way, we keep forgetting the existence of those poor and unknown failures whom we might rebelliously love and admire.

If you're so smart why aren't you rich? is the ground-bass of our   16 society, a grumbling and quite unanswerable criticism, since the society's non-monetary values *are* directly convertible into money. Celeb-

6. British poet Oliver Goldsmith (1728–1774).
7. American poet and philosopher Ralph Waldo Emerson (1803–1882), a friend of Henry David Thoreau (see excerpt from Thoreau's *Walden*, page 405 in *The Dolphin Reader*).

rity turns into testimonials, lectures, directorships, presidencies, the capital gains of an autobiography *Told To* some professional ghost who
photographs the man's life as Bachrach[8] photographs his body. I read
in the newspapers a lyric and perhaps exaggerated instance of this direct
conversion of celebrity into money: his son accompanied Adlai Stevenson[9] on a trip to Russia, took snapshots of his father, and sold them (to
accompany his father's account of the trip) to *Look* for $20,000. When
Liberace said that his critics' unfavorable reviews hurt him so much
that he cried all the way to the bank, one had to admire the correctness
and penetration of his press-agent's wit—in another age, what might
not such a man have become!

GLORIA STEINEM

Sex, Lies, and Advertising

Gloria Steinem (1934–   ) grew up in relative poverty, living in a
trailer while her father traveled around Ohio looking for work. After
his death, she moved to a basement apartment in Toledo, where she
cared for her invalid mother and compiled a mediocre high school
record. High entrance-test scores allowed her to attend Smith College,
where she excelled academically. After traveling on a fellowship to
India, she returned to the United States determined to be a journalist.
The appearance of a 1962 article on the sexual revolution ("The Moral
Disarmament of Betty Coed") launched her career, and she was soon
writing feature stories for a number of magazines. Her feminism dates
from 1968, when she attended a meeting called to protest hearings
on New York's abortion laws: "Suddenly, I was no longer learning
intellectually what was wrong: I knew." In 1971 Steinem became
editor of *Ms.* magazine, a post she held until 1987, when financial
difficulties forced the sale of the magazine to a large Australian communications conglomerate. In addition to promoting the work of feminist writers while editing *Ms.*, Steinem has produced a significant body
of her own work, including *Outrageous Acts and Everyday Rebellions*
(1983), *Revolution from Within* (1992), and *Moving Beyond Words*
(1994).

About three years ago, as *glasnost* was beginning and *Ms.* seemed   1
to be ending, I was invited to a press lunch for a Soviet official. He
entertained us with anecdotes about new problems of democracy in his

8. Well-known American photography studio.
9. American statesman (1900–1965).

country. Local Communist leaders were being criticized in their media for the first time, he explained, and they were angry.

"So I'll have to ask my American friends," he finished pointedly, "how more *subtly* to control the press." In the silence that followed, I said, "Advertising."

The reporters laughed, but later, one of them took me aside: How *dare* I suggest that freedom of the press was limited? How dare I imply that his newsweekly could be influenced by ads?

I explained that I was thinking of advertising's media-wide influence on most of what we read. Even newsmagazines use "soft" cover stories to sell ads, confuse readers with "advertorials," and occasionally self-censor on subjects known to be a problem with big advertisers.

But, I also explained, I was thinking especially of women's magazines. There, it isn't just a little content that's devoted to attracting ads, it's almost all of it. That's why advertisers—not readers—have always been the problem for *Ms.* As the only women's magazine that didn't supply what the ad world euphemistically describes as "supportive editorial atmosphere" or "complementary copy" (for instance, articles that praise food/fashion/beauty subjects to "support" and "complement" food/fashion/beauty ads), *Ms.* could never attract enough advertising to break even.

"Oh, *women's* magazines," the journalist said with contempt. "Everybody knows they're catalogs—but who cares? They have nothing to do with journalism."

I can't tell you how many times I've had this argument in 25 years of working for many kinds of publications. Except as moneymaking machines—"cash cows" as they are so elegantly called in the trade—women's magazines are rarely taken seriously. Though changes being made by women have been called more far-reaching than the industrial revolution—and though many editors try hard to reflect some of them in the few pages left to them after all the ad-related subjects have been covered—the magazines serving the female half of this country are still far below the journalistic and ethical standards of news and general interest publications. Most depressing of all, this doesn't even rate an exposé.

If *Time* and *Newsweek* had to lavish praise on cars in general and credit General Motors in particular to get GM ads, there would be a scandal—maybe a criminal investigation. When women's magazines from *Seventeen* to *Lear's* praise beauty products in general and credit Revlon in particular to get ads, it's just business as usual.

I.

When *Ms.* began, we didn't consider *not* taking ads. The most important reason was keeping the price of a feminist magazine low enough for most women to afford. But the second and almost equal reason was providing a forum where women and advertisers could talk to each other and improve advertising itself. After all, it was (and still is) as potent a source of information in this country as news or TV and movie dramas.

We decided to proceed in two stages. First, we would convince makers of "people products" used by both men and women but advertised mostly to men—cars, credit cards, insurance, sound equipment, financial services, and the like—that their ads should be placed in a women's magazine. Since they were accustomed to the division between editorial and advertising in news and general interest magazines, this would allow our editorial content to be free and diverse. Second, we would add the best ads for whatever traditional "women's products" (clothes, shampoo, fragrance, food, and so on) that surveys showed *Ms.* readers used. But we would ask them to come in *without* the usual quid pro quo of "complementary copy."

We knew the second step might be harder. Food advertisers have always demanded that women's magazines publish recipes and articles on entertaining (preferably ones that name their products) in return for their ads; clothing advertisers expect to be surrounded by fashion spreads (especially ones that credit their designers); and shampoo, fragrance, and beauty products in general usually insist on positive editorial coverage of beauty subjects, plus photo credits besides. That's why women's magazines look the way they do. But if we could break this link between ads and editorial content, then we wanted good ads for "women's products," too.

By playing their part in this unprecedented mix of *all* the things our readers need and use, advertisers also would be rewarded: ads for products like cars and mutual funds would find a new growth market; the best ads for women's products would no longer be lost in oceans of ads for the same category; and both would have access to a laboratory of smart and caring readers whose response would help create effective ads for other media as well.

I thought then that our main problem would be the imagery in ads themselves. Carmakers were still draping blondes in evening gowns over the hoods like ornaments. Authority figures were almost always male, even in ads for products that only women used. Sadistic, he-man campaigns even won industry praise. (For instance, *Advertising Age* had hailed the infamous Silva Thin cigarette theme, "How to Get a Woman's Attention: Ignore Her," as "brilliant.") Even in medical journals, tranquilizer ads showed depressed housewives standing beside piles of dirty dishes and promised to get them back to work.

Obviously, *Ms.* would have to avoid such ads and seek out the best ones—but this didn't seem impossible. *The New Yorker* had been selecting ads for aesthetic reasons for years, a practice that only seemed to make advertisers more eager to be in its pages. *Ebony* and *Essence* were asking for ads with positive black images, and though their struggle was hard, they weren't being called unreasonable.

Clearly, what *Ms.* needed was a very special publisher and ad sales 15
staff. I could think of only one woman with experience on the business side of magazines—Patricia Carbine, who recently had become a vice president of *McCall's* as well as its editor in chief—and the reason I knew her name was a good omen. She had been managing editor at *Look* (really *the* editor, but its owner refused to put a female name at the top of his masthead) when I was writing a column there. After I did an early interview with Cesar Chavez, then just emerging as a leader of migrant labor, and the publisher turned it down because he was worried about ads from Sunkist, Pat was the one who intervened. As I learned later, she had told the publisher she would resign if the interview wasn't published. Mainly because *Look* couldn't afford to lose Pat, it *was* published (and the ads from Sunkist never arrived).

Though I barely knew this woman, she had done two things I 16
always remembered: put her job on the line in a way that editors often talk about but rarely do, and been so loyal to her colleagues that she never told me or anyone outside *Look* that she had done so.

Fortunately, Pat did agree to leave *McCall's* and take a huge cut in 17
salary to become publisher of *Ms.* She became responsible for training and inspiring generations of young women who joined the *Ms.* ad sales force, many of whom went on to become "firsts" at the top of publishing. When *Ms.* first started, however, there were so few women with experience selling space that Pat and I made the rounds of ad agencies ourselves. Later, the fact that *Ms.* was asking companies to do business in a different way meant our saleswomen had to make many times the usual number of calls—first to convince agencies and then client companies besides—and to present endless amounts of research. I was often asked to do a final ad presentation, or see some higher decision-maker, or speak to women employees so executives could see the interest of women they worked with. That's why I spent more time persuading advertisers than editing or writing for *Ms.* and why I ended up with an unsentimental education in the seamy underside of publishing that few writers see (and even fewer magazines can publish).

Let me take you with us through some experiences, just as they 18
happened:

■ Cheered on by early support from Volkswagen and one or two other 19
car companies, we scrape together time and money to put on a major reception in Detroit. We know U.S. carmakers firmly believe that women choose the upholstery, not the car, but we are armed with statistics and reader mail to prove the contrary: a car is an important purchase for women, one that symbolizes mobility and freedom.

But almost nobody comes. We are left with many pounds of shrimp 20 on the table, and quite a lot of egg on our face. We blame ourselves for not guessing that there would be a baseball pennant play-off on the same day, but executives go out of their way to explain they wouldn't have come anyway. Thus begins ten years of knocking on hostile doors, presenting endless documentation, and hiring a full-time saleswoman in Detroit; all necessary before *Ms.* gets any real results.

This long saga has a semihappy ending: foreign and, later, domestic 21 carmakers eventually provided *Ms.* with enough advertising to make cars one of our top sources of ad revenue. Slowly, Detroit began to take the women's market seriously enough to put car ads in other women's magazines, too, thus freeing a few pages from the hothouse of fashion-beauty-food ads.

But long after figures showed a third, even a half, of many car 22 models being bought by women, U.S. makers continued to be uncomfortable addressing women. Unlike foreign carmakers, Detroit never quite learned the secret of creating intelligent ads that exclude no one, and then placing them in women's magazines to overcome past exclusion. (*Ms.* readers were so grateful for a routine Honda ad featuring rack and pinion steering, for instance, that they sent fan mail.) Even now, Detroit continues to ask, "Should we make special ads for women?" Perhaps that's why some foreign cars still have a disproportionate share of the U.S. women's market.

■ In the *Ms.* Gazette, we do a brief report on a congressional hearing 23 into chemicals used in hair dyes that are absorbed through the skin and may be carcinogenic. Newspapers report this too, but Clairol, a Bristol-Myers subsidiary that makes dozens of products—a few of which have just begun to advertise in *Ms.*—is outraged. Not at newspapers or newsmagazines, just at us. It's bad enough that *Ms.* is the only women's magazine refusing to provide the usual "complementary" articles and beauty photos, but to criticize one of their categories—*that* is going too far.

We offer to publish a letter from Clairol telling its side of the story. 24 In an excess of solicitousness, we even put this letter in the Gazette, not in Letters to the Editors where it belongs. Nonetheless—and in spite of surveys that show *Ms.* readers are active women who use more of almost everything Clairol makes than do the readers of any other women's magazine—*Ms.* gets almost none of these ads for the rest of its natural life.

Meanwhile, Clairol changes its hair coloring formula, apparently in 25 response to the hearings we reported.

■ Our saleswomen set out early to attract ads for consumer electronics: 26 sound equipment, calculators, computers, VCRs, and the like. We know that our readers are determined to be included in the technological revolution. We know from reader surveys that *Ms.* readers are buying this stuff in numbers as high as those of magazines like *Playboy,* or "men 18 to 34," the prime targets of the consumer electronics industry. Moreover, unlike traditional women's products that our readers buy but don't need to read articles about, these are subjects they want covered in our pages. There actually *is* a supportive editorial atmosphere.

"But women don't understand technology," say executives at the end of ad presentations. "Maybe not," we respond, "but neither do men—and we all buy it." 27

"If women *do* buy it," say the decision-makers, "they're asking their husbands and boyfriends what to buy first." We produce letters from *Ms.* readers saying how turned off they are when salesmen say things like "Let me know when your husband can come in." 28

After several years of this, we get a few ads for compact sound systems. Some of them come from JVC, whose vice president, Harry Elias, is trying to convince his Japanese bosses that there is something called a women's market. At his invitation, I find myself speaking at huge trade shows in Chicago and Las Vegas, trying to persuade JVC dealers that showrooms don't have to be locker rooms where women are made to feel unwelcome. But as it turns out, the shows themselves are part of the problem. In Las Vegas, the only women around the technology displays are seminude models serving champagne. In Chicago, the big attraction is Marilyn Chambers, who followed Linda Lovelace of *Deep Throat* fame as Chuck Traynor's captive and/or employee. VCRs are being demonstrated with her porn videos. 29

In the end, we get ads for a car stereo now and then, but no VCRs; some IBM personal computers, but no Apple or Japanese ones. We notice that office magazines like *Working Woman* and *Savvy* don't benefit as much as they should from office equipment ads either. In the electronics world, women and technology seem mutually exclusive. It remains a decade behind even Detroit. 30

■ Because we get letters from little girls who love toy trains, and who ask our help in changing ads and box-top photos that feature little boys only, we try to get toy-train ads from Lionel. It turns out that Lionel executives *have* been concerned about little girls. They made a pink train, and were surprised when it didn't sell. 31

Lionel bows to consumer pressure with a photograph of a boy *and* a girl—but only on some of their boxes. They fear that, if trains are associated with girls, they will be devalued in the minds of boys. Needless to say, *Ms.* gets no train ads, and little girls remain a mostly unexplored market. By 1986, Lionel is put up for sale. 32

But for different reasons, we haven't had much luck with other kinds of toys either. In spite of many articles on child-rearing; an annual listing of nonsexist, multi-racial toys by Letty Cottin Pogrebin; Stories for Free Children, a regular feature also edited by Letty; and other prizewinning features for or about children, we get virtually no toy ads. Generations of *Ms.* saleswomen explain to toy manufacturers that a 33 larger proportion of *Ms.* readers have preschool children than do the readers of other women's magazines, but this industry can't believe feminists have or care about children.

- When *Ms.* begins, the staff decides not to accept ads for feminine 34
hygiene sprays or cigarettes: they are damaging and carry no appropriate health warnings. Though we don't think we should tell our readers what to do, we do think we should provide facts so they can decide for themselves. Since the antismoking lobby has been pressing for health warnings on cigarette adds, we decide to take them only as they comply.

Philip Morris is among the first to do so. One of its brands, Virginia 35
Slims, is also sponsoring women's tennis and the first national polls of women's opinions. On the other hand, the Virginia Slims theme, "You've come a long way, baby," has more than a "baby" problem. It makes smoking a symbol of progress for women.

We explain to Philip Morris that this slogan won't do well in our 36
pages, but they are convinced its success with some women means it will work with *all* women. Finally, we agree to publish an ad for a Virginia Slims calendar as a test. The letters from readers are critical— and smart. For instance: Would you show a black man picking cotton, the same man in a Cardin suit, and symbolize the antislavery and civil rights movements by smoking? Of course not. But instead of honoring the test results, the Philip Morris people seem angry to be proven wrong. They take away ads for *all* their many brands.

This costs *Ms.* about $250,000 the first year. After five years, we 37
can no longer keep track. Occasionally, a new set of executives listens to *Ms.* saleswomen, but because we won't take Virginia Slims, not one Philip Morris product returns to our pages for the next 16 years.

Gradually, we also realize our naiveté in thinking we *could* decide 38
against taking cigarette ads. They became a disproportionate support of magazines the moment they were banned on television, and few magazines could compete and survive without them; certainly not *Ms.*, which lacks so many other categories. By the time statistics in the 1980s showed that women's rate of lung cancer was approaching men's, the necessity of taking cigarette ads has become a kind of prison.

- General Mills, Pillsbury, Carnation, DelMonte, Dole, Kraft, Stouffer, 39
Hormel, Nabisco: you name the food giant, we try it. But no matter how desirable the *Ms.* readership, our lack of recipes is lethal.

We explain to them that placing food ads *only* next to recipes asso- 40
ciates food with work. For many women, it is a negative that works *against* the ads. Why not place food ads in diverse media without recipes (thus reaching more men, who are now a third of the shoppers in supermarkets anyway), and leave the recipes to specialty magazines like *Gourmet* (a third of whose readers are also men)?

These arguments elicit interest, but except for an occasional ad for 41 a convenience food, instant coffee, diet drinks, yogurt, or such extras as avocados and almonds, this mainstay of the publishing industry stays closed to us. Period.

■ Traditionally, wines and liquors didn't advertise to women: men were thought to make the brand decisions, even if women did the buying. But after endless presentations, we begin to make a dent in this category. Thanks to the unconventional Michel Roux of Carillon Importers (distributors of Grand Marnier, Absolut Vodka, and others), who assumes that food and drink have no gender, some ads are leaving their men's club.   42

Beermakers are still selling masculinity. It takes *Ms.* fully eight years to get its first beer ad (Michelob). In general, however, liquor ads are less stereotyped in their imagery—and far less controlling of the editorial content around them—than are women's products. But given the underrepresentation of other categories, these very facts tend to create a disproportionate number of alcohol ads in the pages of *Ms.* This in turn dismays readers worried about women and alcoholism.   43

■ We hear in 1980 that women in the Soviet Union have been producing feminist *samizdat* (underground, self-published books) and circulating them throughout the country. As punishment, four of the leaders have been exiled. Though we are operating on our usual shoestring, we solicit individual contributions to send Robin Morgan to interview these women in Vienna.   44

The result is an exclusive cover story that includes the first news of a populist peace movement against the Afghanistan occupation, a prediction of *glasnost* to come, and a grass-roots, intimate view of Soviet women's lives. From the popular press to women's studies courses, the response is great. The story wins a Front Page award.   45

Nonetheless, this journalistic coup undoes years of efforts to get an ad schedule from Revlon. Why? Because the Soviet women on our cover *are not wearing makeup*.   46

■ Four years of research and presentations go into convincing airlines that women now make travel choices and business trips. United, the first airline to advertise in *Ms.*, is so impressed with the response from our readers that one of its executives appears in a film for our ad presentations. As usual, good ads get great results.   47

But we have problems unrelated to such results. For instance: because American Airlines flight attendants include among their labor demands the stipulation that they could choose to have their last names preceded by "Ms." on their name tags—in a long-delayed revolt against the standard, "I am your pilot, Captain Rothgart, and this is your flight attendant, Cindy Sue"—American officials seem to hold the magazine responsible. We get no ads.   48

There is still a different problem at Eastern. A vice president cancels subscriptions for thousands of copies on Eastern flights. Why? Because   49 he is offended by ads for lesbian poetry journals in the *Ms.* Classified. A "family airline," as he explains to me coldly on the phone, has to "draw the line somewhere."

It's obvious that *Ms.* can't exclude lesbians and serve women. We've been trying to make that point ever since our first issue included an article by and about lesbians, and both Suzanne Levine, our managing editor, and I were lectured by such heavy hitters as Ed Kosner, then editor of *Newsweek* (and now of *New York Magazine*), who insisted that *Ms.* should "position" itself *against* lesbians. But our advertisers have paid to reach a guaranteed number of readers, and soliciting new subscriptions to compensate for Eastern would cost $150,000, plus rebating money in the meantime.

Like almost everything ad-related, this presents an elaborate organizing problem. After days of searching for sympathetic members of the Eastern board, Frank Thomas, president of the Ford Foundation, kindly offers to call Roswell Gilpatrick, a director of Eastern. I talk with Mr. Gilpatrick, who calls Frank Borman, then the president of Eastern. Frank Borman calls me to say that his airline is not in the business of censoring magazines: *Ms.* will be returned to Eastern flights.

■ Women's access to insurance and credit is vital, but with the exception of Equitable and a few other ad pioneers, such financial services address men. For almost a decade after the Equal Credit Opportunity Act passes in 1974, we try to convince American Express that women are a growth market—but nothing works.

Finally, a former professor of Russian named Jerry Welsh becomes head of marketing. He assumes that women should be cardholders, and persuades his colleagues to feature women in a campaign. Thanks to this 1980s series, the growth rate for female cardholders surpasses that for men.

For this article, I asked Jerry Welsh if he would explain why American Express waited so long. "Sure," he said, "they were afraid of having a 'pink' card."

■ Women of color read *Ms.* in disproportionate numbers. This is a source of pride to *Ms.* staffers, who are also more racially representative than the editors of other women's magazines. But this reality is obscured by ads filled with enough white women to make a reader snowblind.

Pat Carbine remembers mostly "astonishment" when she requested African American, Hispanic, Asian, and other diverse images. Marcia Ann Gillespie, a *Ms.* editor who was previously the editor in chief of *Essence*, witnesses ad bias a second time: having tried for *Essence* to get white advertisers to use black images (Revlon did so eventually, but L'Oréal, Lauder, Chanel, and other companies never did), she sees similar problems getting integrated ads for an integrated magazine. Indeed, the ad world often creates black and Hispanic ads only for black and

Hispanic media. In an exact parallel of the fear that marketing a product to women will endanger its appeal to men, the response is usually, "But your [white] readers won't identify."

In fact, those we are able to get—for instance, a Max Factor ad   57
made for *Essence* that Linda Wachner gives us after she becomes president—are praised by white readers, too. But there are pathetically few such images.

■ By the end of 1986, production and mailing costs have risen astro-   58
nomically, ad income is flat, and competition for ads is stiffer than ever. The 60/40 preponderance of edit over ads that we promised to readers becomes 50/50; children's stories, most poetry, and some fiction are casualties of less space; in order to get variety into limited pages, the length (and sometimes the depth) of articles suffers; and, though we do refuse most of the ads that would look like a parody in our pages, we get so worn down that some slip through. (See this issue's No Comment.) Still, readers perform miracles. Though we haven't been able to afford a subscription mailing in two years, they maintain our guaranteed circulation of 450,000.

Nonetheless, media reports on *Ms.* often insist that our unprofit-   59
ability must be due to reader disinterest. The myth that advertisers simply follow readers is very strong. Not one reporter notes that other comparable magazines our size (say, *Vanity Fair* or *The Atlantic*) have been losing more money in one year than *Ms.* has lost in 16 years. No matter how much never-to-be-recovered cash is poured into starting a magazine or keeping one going, appearances seem to be all that matter. (Which is why we haven't been able to explain our fragile state in public. Nothing causes ad-flight like the smell of nonsuccess.)

My healthy response is anger. My not-so-healthy response is con-   60
stant worry. Also an obsession with finding one more rescue. There is hardly a night when I don't wake up with sweaty palms and pounding heart, scared that we won't be able to pay the printer or the post office; scared most of all that closing our doors will hurt the women's movement.

Out of chutzpah and desperation, I arrange a lunch with Leonard   61
Lauder, president of Estée Lauder. With the exception of Clinique (the brainchild of Carol Phillips), none of Lauder's hundreds of products has been advertised in *Ms.* A year's schedule of ads for just three or four of them could save us. Indeed, as the scion of a family-owned company whose ad practices are followed by the beauty industry, he is one of the few men who could liberate many pages in all women's magazines just by changing his mind about "complementary copy."

Over a lunch that costs more than we can pay for some articles, I   62
explain the need for his leadership. I also lay out the record of *Ms.:* more literary and journalistic prizes won, more new issues introduced into the mainstream, new writers discovered, and impact on society

than any other magazine; more articles that became books, stories that became movies, ideas that became television series, and newly advertised products that became profitable; and, most important for him, a place for his ads to reach women who aren't reachable through any other women's magazine. Indeed, if there is one constant characteristic of the ever-changing *Ms.* readership, it is their impact as leaders. Whether it's waiting until later to have first babies, or pioneering PABA as sun protection in cosmetics, *whatever* they are doing today, a third to a half of American women will be doing three to five years from now. It's never failed.

But, he says, *Ms.* readers are not *our* women. They're not interested [63] in things like fragrance and blush-on. If they were, *Ms.* would write articles about them.

On the contrary, I explain, surveys show they are more likely to [64] buy such things than the readers of, say, *Cosmopolitan* or *Vogue*. They're good customers because they're out in the world enough to need several sets of everything: home, work, purse, travel, gym, and so on. They just don't need to read articles about these things. Would he ask a men's magazine to publish monthly columns on how to shave before he advertised Aramis products (his line for men)?

He concedes that beauty features are often concocted more for ad- [65] vertisers than readers. But *Ms.* isn't appropriate for his ads anyway, he explains. Why? Because Estée Lauder is selling "a kept-woman mentality."

I can't quite believe this. Sixty percent of the users of his products [66] are salaried, and generally resemble *Ms.* readers. Besides, his company has the appeal of having been started by a creative and hardworking woman, his mother, Estée Lauder.

That doesn't matter, he says. He knows his customers, and they [67] would *like* to be kept women. That's why he will never advertise in *Ms.*

In November 1987, by vote of the Ms. Foundation for Education [68] and Communication (*Ms.*'s owner and publisher, the media subsidiary of the Ms. Foundation for Women), *Ms.* was sold to a company whose officers, Australian feminists Sandra Yates and Anne Summers, raised the investment money in their country that *Ms.* couldn't find in its own. They also started *Sassy* for teenage women.

In their two-year tenure, circulation was raised to 550,000 by in- [69] vestment in circulation mailings, and, to the dismay of some readers, editorial features on clothes and new products made a more traditional bid for ads. Nonetheless, ad pages fell below previous levels. In addition, *Sassy*, whose fresh voice and sexual frankness were an unprecedented success with young readers, was targeted by two mothers from Indiana who began, as one of them put it, "calling every Christian organization I could think of." In response to this controversy, several crucial advertisers pulled out.

Such links between ads and editorial content were a problem in   70
Australia, too, but to a lesser degree. "Our readers pay two times more
for their magazines," Anne explained, "so advertisers have less power
to threaten a magazine's viability."

"I was shocked," said Sandra Yates with characteristic directness.   71
"In Australia, we think you have freedom of the press—but you don't."

Since Anne and Sandra had not met their budget's projections for   72
ad revenue, their investors forced a sale. In October 1989, *Ms.* and *Sassy*
were bought by Dale Lang, owner of *Working Mother, Working Woman,*
and one of the few independent publishing companies left among the
conglomerates. In response to a request from the original *Ms.* staff—as
well as to reader letters urging that *Ms.* continue, plus his own belief
that *Ms.* would benefit his other magazines by blazing a trail—he agreed
to try the ad-free, reader-supported *Ms.* you hold now and to give us
complete editorial control.

II.

Do you think, as I once did, that advertisers make decisions based   73
on solid research? Well, think again. "Broadly speaking," says Joseph
Smith of Oxtoby-Smith, Inc., a consumer research firm, "there is no
persuasive evidence that the editorial context of an ad matters."

Advertisers who demand such "complementary copy," even in the   74
absence of respectable studies, clearly are operating under a double
standard. The same food companies place ads in *People* with no recipes.
Cosmetics companies support *The New Yorker* with no regular beauty
columns. So where does this habit of controlling the content of
women's magazines come from?

Tradition. Ever since *Ladies Magazine* debuted in Boston in 1828,   75
editorial copy directed to women has been informed by something other
than its readers' wishes. There were no ads then, but in an age when
married women were legal minors with no right to their own money,
there was another revenue source to be kept in mind: husbands. "Husbands may rest assured," wrote editor Sarah Josepha Hale, "that nothing found in these pages shall cause her [his wife] to be less assiduous
in preparing for his reception or encourage her to 'usurp station' or
encroach upon prerogatives of men."

Hale went on to become the editor of *Godey's Lady's Book,* a maga-   76
zine featuring "fashion plates": engravings of dresses for readers to take
to their seamstresses or copy themselves. Hale added "how to" articles,
which set the tone for women's service magazines for years to come:
how to write politely, avoid sunburn, and—in no fewer than 1,200
words—how to maintain a goose quill pen. She advocated education
for women but avoided controversy. Just as most women's magazines
now avoid politics, poll their readers on issues like abortion but rarely

take a stand, and praise socially approved lifestyles, Hale saw to it that *Godey's* avoided the hot topics of its day: slavery, abolition, and women's suffrage.

What definitively turned women's magazines into catalogs, how- 77 ever, were two events: Ellen Butterick's invention of the clothing pattern in 1863 and the mass manufacture of patent medicines containing everything from colored water to cocaine. For the first time, readers could purchase what magazines encouraged them to want. As such magazines became more profitable, they also began to attract men as editors. (Most women's magazines continued to have men as top editors until the feminist 1970s.) Edward Bok, who became editor of *The Ladies' Home Journal* in 1889, discovered the power of advertisers when he rejected ads for patent medicines and found that other advertisers canceled in retribution. In the early 20th century, *Good Housekeeping* started its Institute to "test and approve" products. Its Seal of Approval became the grandfather of current "value added" programs that offer advertisers such bonuses as product sampling and department store promotions.

By the time suffragists finally won the vote in 1920, women's maga- 78 zines had become too entrenched as catalogs to help women learn how to use it. The main function was to create a desire for products, teach how to use products, and make products a crucial part of gaining social approval, pleasing a husband, and performing as a homemaker. Some related articles and short stories were included to persuade women to pay for these catalogs. But articles were neither consumerist nor rebellious. Even fiction was usually subject to formula: if a woman had any sexual life outside marriage, she was supposed to come to a bad end.

In 1965, Helen Gurley Brown began to change part of that formula 79 by bringing "the sexual revolution" to women's magazines—but in an ad-oriented way. Attracting multiple men required even more consumerism, as the Cosmo Girl made clear, than finding one husband.

In response to the workplace revolution of the 1970s, traditional 80 women's magazines—that is, "trade books" for women working at home—were joined by *Savvy, Working Woman,* and other trade books for women working in offices. But by keeping the fashion/beauty/entertaining articles necessary to get traditional ads and then adding career articles besides, they inadvertently produced the antifeminist stereotype of Super Woman. The male-imitative, dress-for-success woman carrying a briefcase became the media image of a woman worker, even though a blue-collar woman's salary was often higher than her glorified secretarial sister's, and though women at a real briefcase level are statistically rare. Needless to say, these dress-for-success women were also thin, white, and beautiful.

In recent years, advertisers' control over the editorial content of 81 women's magazines has become so institutionalized that it is written into "insertion orders" or dictated to ad salespeople as official policy. The following are recent typical orders to women's magazines:

■ Dow's Cleaning Products stipulates that ads for its Vivid and Spray 'n Wash products should be adjacent to "children or fashion editorial"; ads for Bathroom Cleaner should be next to "home furnishing/family" features; and so on for other brands. "If a magazine fails for 1/2 the brands or more," the Dow order warns, "it will be omitted from futher consideration."

■ Bristol-Myers, the parent of Clairol, Windex, Drano, Bufferin, and much more, stipulates that ads be placed next to "a full page of compati-ble editorial."

■ S.C. Johnson & Son, makers of Johnson Wax, lawn and laundry products, insect sprays, hair sprays, and so on, orders that its ads *'should not be opposite extremely controversial features or material antithetical to the nature/copy of the advertised product.''* (Italics theirs.)

■ Maidenform, manufacturer of bras and other apparel, leaves a blank for the particular product and states: "The creative concept of the ____ campaign, and the very nature of the product itself appeal to the positive emotions of the reader/consumer. Therefore, it is imperative that all editorial adjacencies reflect that same positive tone. The editorial must not be negative in content or lend itself contrary to the ____ product imagery/message (e.g., *editorial relating to illness, disillusionment, large size fashion, etc.*)." (Italics mine.)

■ The De Beers diamond company, a big seller of engagement rings, prohibits magazines from placing its ads with "adjacencies to hard news or anti/love-romance themed editorial."

■ Procter & Gamble, one of this country's most powerful and diversified advertisers, stands out in the memory of Anne Summers and Sandra Yates (no mean feat in this context): its products were not to be placed in *any* issue that included *any* material on gun control, abortion, the occult, cults, or the disparagement of religion. Caution was also de-manded in any issue covering sex or drugs, even for educational purposes.

Those are the most obvious chains around women's magazines. [82] There are also rules so clear they needn't be written down: for instance, an overall "look" compatible with beauty and fashion ads. Even "real" nonmodel women photographed for a woman's magazine are usually made up, dressed in credited clothes, and retouched out of all reality. When editors do include articles on less-than-cheerful subjects (for in-stance, domestic violence), they tend to keep them short and unillus-trated. The point is to be "upbeat." Just as women in the street are asked, "Why don't you smile, honey?" women's magazines acquire an institutional smile.

Within the text itself, praise for advertisers' products has become [83] so ritualized that fields like "beauty writing" have been invented. One of its frequent practitioners explained seriously that "It's a difficult art. How many new adjectives can you find? How much greater can you make a lipstick sound? The FDA restricts what companies can say on labels, but we create illusion. And ad agencies are on the phone all the time pushing you to get their product in. A lot of them keep the business based on how many editorial clippings they produce every month. The worst are products," like Lauder's as the writer confirmed, "with their own name involved. It's all ego."

Often, editorial becomes one giant ad. Last November, for instance, *Lear's* featured an elegant woman executive on the cover. On the contents page, we learned she was wearing Guerlain makeup and Samsara, a new fragrance by Guerlain. Inside were full-page ads for Samsara and Guerlain antiwrinkle cream. In the cover profile, we learned that this executive was responsible for launching Samsara and is Guerlain's director of public relations. When the *Columbia Journalism Review* did one of the few articles to include women's magazines in coverage of the influence of ads, editor Frances Lear was quoted as defending her magazine because "this kind of thing is done all the time." [84]

Often, advertisers also plunge odd-shaped ads into the text, no matter what the cost to the readers. At *Woman's Day,* a magazine originally founded by a supermarket chain, editor in chief Ellen Levine said, "The day the copy had to rag around a chicken leg was not a happy one." [85]

Advertisers are also adamant about where in a magazine their ads appear. When Revlon was not placed as the first beauty ad in one Hearst magazine, for instance, Revlon pulled its ads from *all* Hearst magazines. Ruth Whitney, editor in chief of *Glamour,* attributes some of these demands to "ad agencies wanting to prove to a client that they've squeezed the last drop of blood out of a magazine." She also is, she says, "sick and tired of hearing that women's magazines are controlled by cigarette ads." Relatively speaking, she's right. To be as censoring as are many advertisers for women's products, tobacco companies would have to demand articles in praise of smoking and expect glamorous photos of beautiful women smoking their brands. [86]

I don't mean to imply that the editors I quote here share my objections to ads: most assume that women's magazines have to be the way they are. But it's also true that only former editors can be completely honest. "Most of the pressure came in the form of direct product mentions," explains Sey Chassler, who was editor in chief of *Redbook* from the sixties to the eighties. "We got threats from the big guys, the Revlons, blackmail threats. They wouldn't run ads unless we credited them. [87]

"But it's not fair to single out the beauty advertisers because these pressures came from everybody. Advertisers want to know two things: What are you going to charge me? What *else* are you going to do for me? It's a holdup. For instance, management felt that fiction took up too much space. They couldn't put any advertising in that. For the last [88]

ten years, the number of fiction entries into the National Magazine
Awards had declined.

"And pressures are getting worse. More magazines are more bot-   89
tom-line oriented because they have been taken over by companies
with no interest in publishing.

"I also think advertisers do this to women's magazines especially,"   90
he concluded, "because of the general disrespect they have for women."

Even media experts who don't give a damn about women's maga-   91
zines are alarmed by the spread of this ad-edit linkage. In a climate *The
Wall Street Journal* describes as an unacknowledged Depression for media, women's products are increasingly able to take their low standards
wherever they go. For instance: newsweeklies publish uncritical stories
on fashion and fitness. *The New York Times Magazine* recently ran an
article on "firming creams," complete with mentions of advertisers.
Vanity Fair published a profile of one major advertiser, Ralph Lauren,
illustrated by the same photographer who does his ads, and turned the
lifestyle of another, Calvin Klein, into a cover story. Even the outrageous *Spy* has toned down since it began to go after fashion ads.

And just to make us really worry, films and books, the last media   92
that go directly to the public without having to attract ads first, are in
danger, too. Producers are beginning to depend on payments for dis-
playing products in movies, and books are now being commissioned
by companies like Federal Express.

But the truth is that women's products—like women's maga-   93
zines—have never been the subjects of much serious reporting anyway.
News and general interest publications, including the "style" or "living"
sections of newspapers, write about food and clothing as cooking and
fashion, and almost never evaluate such products by brand name.
Though chemical additives, pesticides, and animal fats are major health
risks in the United States, and clothes, shoddy or not, absorb more
consumer dollars than cars, this lack of information is serious. So is
ignoring the contents of beauty products that are absorbed into our
bodies through our skins, and that have profit margins so big they
would make a loan shark blush.

III.

What could women's magazines be like if they were as free as   94
books? as realistic as newspapers? as creative as films? as diverse as
women's lives? We don't know.

But we'll only find out if we take women's magazines seriously. If   95
readers were to act in a concerted way to change traditional practices
of *all* women's magazines and the marketing of *all* women's products,

we could do it. After all, they are operating on our consumer dollars; money that we now control. You and I could:

- write to editors and publishers (with copies to advertisers) that we're willing to pay *more* for magazines with editorial independence, but will *not* continue to pay for those that are just editorial extensions of ads;
- write to advertisers (with copies to editors and publishers) that we want fiction, political reporting, consumer reporting—whatever is, or is not, supported by their ads;
- put as much energy into breaking advertising's control over content as into changing the images in ads, or protesting ads for harmful products like cigarettes;
- support only those women's magazines and products that take *us* seriously as readers and consumers.

Those of us in the magazine world can also use the carrot-and-stick 96
technique. For instance: pointing out that, if magazines were a regulated medium like television, the demands of advertisers would be against FCC rules. Payola and extortion could be punished. As it is, there are probably illegalities. A magazine's postal rates are determined by the ratio of ad to edit pages, and the former costs more than the latter. So much for the stick.

The carrot means appealing to enlightened self-interest. For instance: there are many studies showing that the greatest factor in determining an ad's effectiveness is the credibility of its surroundings. The 97
"higher the rating of editorial believability," concluded a 1987 survey by the *Journal of Advertising Research*, "the higher the rating of the advertising." Thus, an impenetrable wall between edit and ads would also be in the best interest of advertisers.

Unfortunately, few agencies or clients hear such arguments. Editors 98
often maintain the false purity of refusing to talk to them at all. Instead, they see ad salespeople who know little about editorial, are trained in business as usual, and are usually paid by commission. Editors might also band together to take on controversy. That happened once when all the major women's magazines did articles in the same month on the Equal Rights Amendment. It could happen again.

It's almost three years away from life between the grindstones of 99
advertising pressures and readers' needs. I'm just beginning to realize how edges got smoothed down—in spite of all our resistance.

I remember feeling put upon when I changed "Porsche" to "car" 100
in a piece about Nazi imagery in German pornography by Andrea Dworkin—feeling sure Andrea would understand that Volkswagen, the distributor of Porsche and one of our few supportive advertisers, asked only to be far away from Nazi subjects. It's taken me all this time to realize that Andrea was the one with a right to feel put upon.

Even as I write this, I get a call from a writer for *Elle*, who is doing 101 a whole article on where women part their hair. Why, she wants to know, do I part mine in the middle?

It's all so familiar. A writer trying to make something of a nothing   102
assignment; an editor laboring to think of new ways to attract ads; readers assuming that other women must want this ridiculous stuff; more women suffering for lack of information, insight, creativity, and laughter that could be on these same pages.

I ask you: Can't we do better than this?   103

WYATT TOWNLEY

A Plea for Video-Free Zones

Wyatt Townley, educated at Purchase College of the State University of New York, has spent much of her life as a performer—running her own dance company, doing off-Broadway shows, and occasionally appearing in TV soap operas. As you will see in the following essay, she has forsaken the tube. She now concentrates primarily on her writing and has placed poems, nonfiction, and journalism in many publications, from *New Letters* to *Newsweek*. Her first book of poems, *Perfectly Normal* (which she says is "anything but") appeared in 1990. "A Plea for Video-Free Zones" is from *Newsweek*, January 31, 1994.

Turn it off, they say, if you don't like it. We tried that. Dismayed by   1
the banality of children's programming and the brutality of prime-time television, my husband and I canceled our cable service a few months ago—which in our part of the world means we get no reception at all.

But then we leave the house. We go to the health club and there's   2
Oprah chatting about incest on two wide screens above the treadmills. And in the club's day-care center, where we leave our 5-year-old, the television is blasting kidvid.

We take our little girl to the pediatrician's office and find a set tuned   3
to Special Report Television, which promotes health insurance and pharmaceuticals. When images of a violent drug bust flash on the screen (part of an anti-drug message), all the children become fascinated. We ask the nurse to turn the set off. "It can't be turned off," she says, smiling.

We go to a baseball game. What could be more outdoorsy? An   4
immense TV monitor the size of Grant's Tomb draws our attention throughout. It's useful for the occasional instant replay, but after every three outs it pounds us with loud, unzappable ads for blue jeans, soft

drinks, chewing gum, the local bank, the local supermarket—and the new lineup of television shows.

We go out to eat. A shouting television, like an offensive drunk, 5
drives us from the bars of upscale restaurants as well as family-style eateries. Even at the grocery store, TV sputters among the soda cans.

We take our car in for an oil change and carry a book along to read 6
while we wait. But there It perches, like Poe's raven, high in the corner of the waiting room, squawking about which price is right. No one in the room is paying attention to it, but no one can concentrate on anything else, either.

These days we find ourselves identifying with Winston in George 7
Orwell's "1984," who discovered that "The instrument [the telescreen, it was called] could be dimmed, but there was no way of shutting it off completely."

And so, when people ask us how it is to be without TV, we tell 8
them we don't know. Our child doesn't know either. Soon after we'd pulled the plug, we enrolled her in a day camp at a prestigious private school that offered water play, science demonstrations, field trips, art projects, stories—all kinds of imaginative programs for preschoolers. Tucked into the list was "films." They should have called it Television Camp. The set was on every day at nap time, as well as in the morning when it rained, on Fridays for a "treat" and when a teacher had trouble managing the kids.

It may be that, having disconnected our own television, we're extra 9
sensitive to all the TVs around us. Smokers who kick the habit, they say, are often irked by other people's smoke. On the other hand, sometimes there's an awful lot of smoke in the air. Maybe we need a television equivalent of the smoke alarm. Too much video in public places and a buzzer sounds.

Television saturates our lives so completely that it doesn't occur to 10
people to object to it. We all just assume that secondhand video is harmless. But that's what they used to say about secondhand smoke.

Educators bemoan the shortening attention span of TV-addicted 11
students and their inability to pursue a line of thought to its conclusion. The problem is not just with students. We're all TV-impaired. Whether the set is in our rec room, the departure lounge or the pediatrician's office, the result is the same: we can't concentrate. The big new federal study on literacy reports that barely half of adults can make sense of what they read—this in the era of the much vaunted Information Highway. Of course, television is not solely responsible for this appalling state of affairs, but it must share the blame. Our nation's romance with the tube and subsequent divorce from literature have compromised our ability to persevere in mental tasks, or even to *value* perseverance. Americans break for commercials.

As a marketing experiment, someone ought to open a restaurant 12 and advertise it as a "video-free environment." Or open a school and announce that television—yes, even "educational" programs—will not be used as a teaching aid. "All classes will be taught by an actual human being," the brochure would read.

If the idea flopped, we'd learn something valuable (if scary) about   13
ourselves. We'd learn that we love television so much that we'll stare at it every chance we get, no matter how inappropriate the context or vapid the content. From there it is but a short leap to imagine a brave new world of Orwellian intrusiveness, in which viewing is valued over doing, and "virtual reality" is preferred to the real thing.

But what if the idea took hold? What if video-free stores, lobbies,   14
day-care centers and waiting rooms turned out to have public appeal? What if all this time we'd been tolerating TV in public places because we didn't think we had a choice? We've heard so much from network apologists about free speech that we have forgotten other rights. What about noise pollution? What about thought pollution? What about the right to privacy—the right to daydream, read a book, write a poem without electronic interference?

Soon video-free zones, small pockets of resistance, would spring up   15
around the country. Before long, celebrities would spot the trend and make it "in" to turn off the tube. Sequential thinking might be reintroduced, first as a parlor game like Trivial Pursuit and ultimately as a normal human function.

But like all revolutions, this one must start with individuals, people   16
gutsy enough to stand up in a crowded room and say for all to hear, "Would anybody mind if I turned this thing off?"

NEIL POSTMAN

"*Now . . . This*"

Neil Postman is a professor of media ecology at New York University in New York City. He began his career as an educator in the 1960s and 1970s; his books on public education, written with Charles Weingartner, gave him a status comparable to that of John Holt as a spokesperson for radical education reform. One of Postman's best-known and most controversial works is *Teaching as a Subversive Activity* (1969). Ten years later, his writing took a sharp turn with the publication of *Teaching as a Conserving Activity*, which proposes that because of the media's bombardment of children and the fragmented education they receive through television, our schools must provide a learning environment that will counteract media-created disinformation. His most recent book on this subject is *Conscientious Objections: Stirring Up Trouble About Language, Technology, and Education* (1989). His interest in the effect of the media on adults as well as children is the focus of *Amusing Ourselves to Death* (1985), from which "Now . . . This" is excerpted, and of three more recent books, *How to Watch TV News* (1993), *Technopoly* (1994), and *The Disappearance of Childhood* (1994).

The American humorist H. Allen Smith once suggested that of all the worrisome words in the English language, the scariest is "uh oh," as when a physician looks at your X-rays, and with knitted brow says, "Uh oh." I should like to suggest that the words which are the title of this chapter are as ominous as any, all the more so because they are spoken without knitted brow—indeed, with a kind of idiot's delight. The phrase, if that's what it may be called, adds to our grammar a new part of speech, a conjunction that does not connect anything to anything but does the opposite: separates everything from everything. As such, it serves as a compact metaphor for the discontinuities in so much that passes for public discourse in present-day America. 1

"Now . . . this" is commonly used on radio and television newscasts to indicate that what one has just heard or seen has no relevance to what one is about to hear or see, or possibly to anything one is ever likely to hear or see. The phrase is a means of acknowledging the fact that the world as mapped by the speeded-up electronic media has no order or meaning and is not to be taken seriously. There is no murder so brutal, no earthquake so devastating, no political blunder so costly— for that matter, no ball score so tantalizing or weather report so threatening—that it cannot be erased from our minds by a newscaster saying, "Now . . . this." The newscaster means that you have thought long enough on the previous matter (approximately forty-five seconds), that you must not be morbidly preoccupied with it (let us say, for ninety seconds), and that you must now give your attention to another fragment of news or a commercial. 2

Television did not invent the "Now . . . this" world view. As I have tried to show, it is the offspring of the intercourse between telegraphy and photography. But it is through television that it has been nurtured and brought to a perverse maturity. For on television, nearly every half hour is a discrete event, separated in content, context, and emotional texture from what precedes and follows it. In part because television sells its time in seconds and minutes, in part because television must use images rather than words, in part because its audience can move freely to and from the television set, programs are structured so that almost each eight-minute segment may stand as a complete event in itself. Viewers are rarely required to carry over any thought or feeling from one parcel of time to another. 3

Of course, in television's presentation of the "news of the day," we   4
may see the "Now . . . this" mode of discourse in its boldest and
most embarrassing form. For there, we are presented not only with
fragmented news but news without context, without consequences,
without value, and therefore without essential seriousness; that is to
say, news as pure entertainment.

Consider, for example, how you would proceed if you were given   5
the opportunity to produce a television news show for any station concerned to attract the largest possible audience. You would, first, choose
a cast of players, each of whom has a face that is both "likable" and
"credible." Those who apply would, in fact, submit to you their eight-
by-ten glossies, from which you would eliminate those whose counte-
nances are not suitable for nightly display. This means that you will
exclude women who are not beautiful or who are over the age of fifty,
men who are bald, all people who are overweight or whose noses are
too long or whose eyes are too close together. You will try, in other
words, to assemble a cast of talking hair-do's. At the very least, you
will want those whose faces would not be unwelcome on a magazine
cover.

Christine Craft has just such a face, and so she applied for a co-   6
anchor position on KMBC-TV in Kansas City. According to a lawyer
who represented her in a sexism suit she later brought against the
station, the management of KMBC-TV "loved Christine's look." She
was accordingly hired in January 1981. She was fired in August 1981
because research indicated that her appearance "hampered viewer acceptance." What exactly does "hampered viewer acceptance" mean?
And what does it have to do with the news? Hampered viewer acceptance means the same thing for television news as it does for any television show: Viewers do not like looking at the performer. It also means
that viewers do not believe the performer, that she lacks credibility. In
the case of a theatrical performance, we have a sense of what that
implies: The actor does not persuade the audience that he or she is the
character being portrayed. But what does lack of credibility imply in
the case of a news show? What character is a co-anchor playing? And
how do we decide that the performance lacks verisimilitude? Does the
audience believe that the newscaster is lying, that what is reported did
not in fact happen, that something important is being concealed?

It is frightening to think that this may be so, that the perception of   7
the truth of a report rests heavily on the acceptability of the newscaster.
In the ancient world, there was a tradition of banishing or killing the
bearer of bad tidings. Does the television news show restore, in a curious form, this tradition? Do we banish those who tell us the news when
we do not care for the face of the teller? Does television countermand
the warnings we once received about the fallacy of the ad hominem
argument?

If the answer to any of these questions is even a qualified "Yes," then here is an issue worthy of the attention of epistemologists. Stated in its simplest form, it is that television provides a new (or, possibly, restores an old) definition of truth: The credibility of the teller is the ultimate test of the truth of a proposition. "Credibility" here does not refer to the past record of the teller for making statements that have survived the rigors of reality-testing. It refers only to the impression of sincerity, authenticity, vulnerability or attractiveness (choose one or more) conveyed by the actor/reporter. 8

This is a matter of considerable importance, for it goes beyond the question of how truth is perceived on television news shows. If on television, credibility replaces reality as the decisive test of truth-telling, political leaders need not trouble themselves very much with reality provided that their performances consistently generate a sense of verisimilitude. I suspect, for example, that the dishonor that now shrouds Richard Nixon results not from the fact that he lied but that on television he looked like a liar. Which, if true, should bring no comfort to anyone, not even veteran Nixon-haters. For the alternative possibilities are that one may look like a liar but be telling the truth; or even worse, look like a truth-teller but in fact be lying. 9

As a producer of a television news show, you would be well aware of these matters and would be careful to choose your cast on the basis of criteria used by David Merrick and other successful impresarios. Like them, you would then turn your attention to staging the show on principles that maximize entertainment value. You would, for example, select a musical theme for the show. All television news programs begin, end, and are somewhere in between punctuated with music. I have found very few Americans who regard this custom as peculiar, which fact I have taken as evidence for the dissolution of lines of demarcation between serious public discourse and entertainment. What has music to do with the news? Why is it there? It is there, I assume, for the same reason music is used in the theater and films—to create a mood and provide a leitmotif for the entertainment. If there were no music—as is the case when any television program is interrupted for a news flash— viewers would expect something truly alarming, possibly life-altering. But as long as the music is there as a frame for the program, the viewer is comforted to believe that there is nothing to be greatly alarmed about; that, in fact, the events that are reported have as much relation to reality as do scenes in a play. 10

This perception of a news show as a stylized dramatic performance whose content has been staged largely to entertain is reinforced by several other features, including the fact that the average length of any story is forty-five seconds. While brevity does not always suggest triviality, in this case it clearly does. It is simply not possible to convey a sense of seriousness about any event if its implications are exhausted 11 in less than one minute's time. In fact, it is quite obvious that TV news has no intention of suggesting that any story *has* any implications, for that would require viewers to continue to think about it when it is done and therefore obstruct their attending to the next story that waits panting in the wings. In any case, viewers are not provided with much opportunity to be distracted from the next story since in all likelihood it will consist of some film footage. Pictures have little difficulty in overwhelming words, and short-circuiting introspection. As a television producer, you would be certain to give both prominence and precedence to any event for which there is some sort of visual documentation. A suspected killer being brought into a police station, the angry face of a cheated consumer, a barrel going over Niagara Falls (with a person alleged to be in it), the President disembarking from a helicopter on the White House lawn—these are always fascinating or amusing, and easily satisfy the requirements of an entertaining show. It is, of course, not necessary that the visuals actually document the point of a story. Neither is it necessary to explain why such images are intruding themselves on public consciousness. Film footage justifies itself, as every television producer well knows.

It is also of considerable help in maintaining a high level of unreality that the newscasters do not pause to grimace or shiver when they speak their prefaces or epilogs to the film clips. Indeed, many newscasters do not appear to grasp the meaning of what they are saying, and some hold to a fixed and ingratiating enthusiasm as they report on earthquakes, mass killings and other disasters. Viewers would be quite disconcerted by any show of concern or terror on the part of newscasters. Viewers, after all, are partners with the newscasters in the "Now . . . this" culture, and they expect the newscaster to play out his or her role as a character who is marginally serious but who stays well clear of authentic understanding. The viewers, for their part, will not be caught contaminating their responses with a sense of reality, any more than an audience at a play would go scurrying to call home because a character on stage has said that a murderer is loose in the neighborhood. 12

The viewers also know that no matter how grave any fragment of news may appear (for example, on the day I write a Marine Corps general has declared that nuclear war between the United States and Russia is inevitable), it will shortly be followed by a series of commercials that will, in an instant, defuse the import of the news, in fact render it largely banal. This is a key element in the structure of a news program and all by itself refutes any claim that television news is designed as a serious form of public discourse. Imagine what you would think of me, and this book, if I were to pause here, tell you that I will return to my discussion in a moment, and then proceed to write a few words in behalf of United Airlines or the Chase Manhattan Bank. You would rightly think that I had no respect for you and, certainly, no 13 respect for the subject. And if I did this not once but several times in each chapter, you would think the whole enterprise unworthy of your attention. Why, then, do we not think a news show similarly unworthy? The reason, I believe, is that whereas we expect books and even other media (such as film) to maintain a consistency of tone and a continuity of content, we have no such expectation of television, and especially television news. We have become so accustomed to its discontinuities that we are no longer struck dumb, as any sane person would be, by a newscaster who having just reported that a nuclear war is inevitable goes on to say that he will be right back after this word from Burger King; who says, in other words, "Now . . . this." One can hardly overestimate the damage that such juxtapositions do to our sense of the world as a serious place. The damage is especially massive to youthful viewers who depend so much on television for their clues as to how to respond to the world. In watching television news, they, more than any other segment of the audience, are drawn into an epistemology based on the assumption that all reports of cruelty and death are greatly exaggerated and, in any case, not to be taken seriously or responded to sanely.

I should go so far as to say that embedded in the surrealistic frame 14 of a television news show is a theory of anticommunication, featuring a type of discourse that abandons logic, reason, sequence and rules of contradiction. In aesthetics, I believe the name given to this theory is Dadaism; in philosophy, nihilism; in psychiatry, schizophrenia. In the parlance of the theater, it is known as vaudeville.

For those who think I am here guilty of hyperbole, I offer the 15 following description of television news by Robert MacNeil, executive editor and co-anchor of the "MacNeil-Lehrer Newshour." The idea, he writes, "is to keep everything brief, not to strain the attention of anyone but instead to provide constant stimulation through variety, novelty, action, and movement. You are required . . . to pay attention to no concept, no character, and no problem for more than a few seconds at a time." He goes on to say that the assumptions controlling a news show are "that bite-sized is best, that complexity must be avoided, that nuances are dispensable, that qualifications impede the simple message, that visual stimulation is a substitute for thought, and that verbal precision is an anachronism."

Robert MacNeil has more reason than most to give testimony about 16 the television news show as vaudeville act. The "MacNeil-Lehrer Newshour" is an unusual and gracious attempt to bring to television some of the elements of typographic discourse. The program abjures visual stimulation, consists largely of extended explanations of events and in-depth interviews (which even there means only five to ten minutes), limits the number of stories covered, and emphasizes background and coherence. But television has exacted its price for MacNeil's rejection of a show business format. By television's standards, the audience is minuscule, the program is confined to public-television stations, and it is a good guess that the combined salary of MacNeil and Lehrer is one-fifth of Dan Rather's or Tom Brokaw's.

If you were a producer of a television news show for a commercial   17
station, you would not have the option of defying television's requirements. It would be demanded of you that you strive for the largest
possible audience, and, as a consequence and in spite of your best
intentions, you would arrive at a production very nearly resembling
MacNeil's description. Moreover, you would include some things Mac-
Neil does not mention. You would try to make celebrities of your newscasters. You would advertise the show, both in the press and on television itself. You would do "news briefs," to serve as an inducement to
viewers. You would have a weatherman as comic relief, and a sports-
caster whose language is a touch uncouth (as a way of his relating to
the beer-drinking common man). You would, in short, package the
whole event as any producer might who is in the entertainment
business.

The result of all this is that Americans are the best entertained and   18
quite likely the least well-informed people in the Western world. I say
this in the face of the popular conceit that television, as a window to
the world, has made Americans exceedingly well informed. Much depends here, of course, on what is meant by being informed. I will pass
over the now tiresome polls that tell us that, at any given moment, 70
percent of our citizens do not know who is the Secretary of State or
the Chief Justice of the Supreme Court. Let us consider, instead, the
case of Iran during the drama that was called the "Iranian Hostage
Crisis." I don't suppose there has been a story in years that received
more continuous attention from television. We may assume, then, that
Americans know most of what there is to know about this unhappy
event. And now, I put these questions to you: Would it be an exaggera-
tion to say that not one American in a hundred knows what language
the Iranians speak? Or what the word "Ayatollah" means or implies?
Or knows any details of the tenets of Iranian religious beliefs? Or the
main outlines of their political history? Or knows who the Shah was,
and where he came from?

Nonetheless, everyone had an opinion about this event, for in   19
America everyone is entitled to an opinion, and it is certainly useful to
have a few when a pollster shows up. But these are opinions of a quite
different order from eighteenth- or nineteenth-century opinions. It is
probably more accurate to call them emotions rather than opinions,
which would account for the fact that they change from week to week,
as the pollsters tell us. What is happening here is that television is
altering the meaning of "being informed" by creating a species of information that might properly be called *disinformation*. I am using this

word almost in the precise sense in which it is used by spies in the CIA or KGB. Disinformation does not mean false information. It means misleading information—misplaced, irrelevant, fragmented or superficial information—information that creates the illusion of knowing something but which in fact leads one away from knowing. In saying this, I do not mean to imply that television news deliberately aims to deprive Americans of a coherent, contextual understanding of their world. I mean to say that when news is packaged as entertainment, that is the inevitable result. And in saying that the television news show entertains but does not inform, I am saying something far more serious than that we are being deprived of authentic information. I am saying we are losing our sense of what it means to be well informed. Ignorance is always correctable. But what shall we do if we take ignorance to be knowledge?

Here is a startling example of how this process bedevils us. A *New York Times* article is headlined on February 15, 1983: 20

REAGAN MISSTATEMENTS GETTING LESS ATTENTION

The article begins in the following way:

President Reagan's aides used to become visibly alarmed at suggestions that he had given mangled and perhaps misleading accounts of his policies or of current events in general. That doesn't seem to happen much anymore.

Indeed, the President continues to make debatable assertions of fact but news accounts do not deal with them as extensively as they once did. In the view of White House officials, the declining news coverage mirrors a *decline in interest by the general public.* (my italics)

This report is not so much a news story as a story about the news, 21 and our recent history suggests that it is not about Ronald Reagan's charm. It is about how news is defined, and I believe the story would be quite astonishing to both civil libertarians and tyrants of an earlier time. Walter Lippmann, for example, wrote in 1920: "There can be no liberty for a community which lacks the means by which to detect lies." For all of his pessimism about the possibilities of restoring an eighteenth- and nineteenth-century level of public discourse, Lippmann assumed, as did Thomas Jefferson before him, that with a well-trained press functioning as a lie-detector, the public's interest in a President's mangling of the truth would be piqued, in both senses of that word. Given the means to detect lies, he believed, the public could not be indifferent to their consequences.

But this case refutes his assumption. The reporters who cover the 22 White House are ready and able to expose lies, and thus create the grounds for informed and indignant opinion. But apparently the public declines to take an interest. To press reports of White House dissembling, the public has replied with Queen Victoria's famous line: "We are not amused." However, here the words mean something the Queen did not have in mind. They mean that what is not amusing does not compel their attention. Perhaps if the President's lies could be demonstrated by pictures and accompanied by music the public would raise a curious eyebrow. If a movie, like *All the President's Men,* could be made from his misleading accounts of government policy, if there were a break-in of some sort or sinister characters laundering money, attention would quite likely be paid. We do well to remember that President Nixon did not begin to come undone until his lies were given a theatrical setting at the Watergate hearings. But we do not have anything like that here. Apparently, all President Reagan does is *say* things that are not entirely true. And there is nothing entertaining in that.

But there is a subtler point to be made here. Many of the President's   23
"misstatements" fall in the category of contradictions—mutually exclusive assertions that cannot possibly both, in the same context, be true. "In the same context" is the key phrase here, for it is context that defines contradiction. There is no problem in someone's remarking that he prefers oranges to apples, and also remarking that he prefers apples to oranges—not if one statement is made in the context of choosing a wallpaper design and the other in the context of selecting fruit for dessert. In such a case, we have statements that are opposites, but not contradictory. But if the statements are made in a single, continuous, and coherent context, then they are contradictions, and cannot both be true. Contradiction, in short, requires that statements and events be perceived as interrelated aspects of a continuous and coherent context. Disappear the context, or fragment it, and contradiction disappears. This point is nowhere made more clear to me than in conferences with my younger students about their writing. "Look here," I say. "In this paragraph you have said one thing. And in that you have said the opposite. Which is it to be?" They are polite, and wish to please, but they are as baffled by the question as I am by the response. "I know," they will say, "but that is *there* and this is *here*." The difference between us is that I assume "there" and "here," "now" and "then," one paragraph and the next to be connected, to be continuous, to be part of the same coherent world of thought. That is the way of typographic discourse, and typography is the universe I'm "coming from," as they say. But they are coming from a different universe of discourse altogether: the "Now . . . this" world of television. The fundamental assumption of that world is not coherence but discontinuity. And in a world of discontinuities, contradiction is useless as a test of truth or merit, because contradiction does not exist.

My point is that we are by now so thoroughly adjusted to the   24
"Now . . . this" world of news—a world of fragments, where events

stand alone, stripped of any connection to the past, or to the future, or to other events—that all assumptions of coherence have vanished. And so, perforce, has contradiction. In the context of *no context*, so to speak, it simply disappears. And in its absence, what possible interest could there be in a list of what the President says *now* and what he said *then*? It is merely a rehash of old news, and there is nothing interesting or entertaining in that. The only thing to be amused about is the bafflement of reporters at the public's indifference. There is an irony in the fact that the very group that has taken the world apart should, on trying to piece it together again, be surprised that no one notices much, or cares.

For all his perspicacity, George Orwell would have been stymied 25 by this situation; there is nothing "Orwellian" about it. The President does not have the press under his thumb. *The New York Times* and *The Washington Post* are not *Pravda*; the Associated Press is not Tass. And there is no Newspeak here. Lies have not been defined as truth nor truth as lies. All that has happened is that the public has adjusted to incoherence and been amused into indifference. Which is why Aldous Huxley would not in the least be surprised by the story. Indeed, he prophesied its coming. He believed that it is far more likely that the Western democracies will dance and dream themselves into oblivion than march into it, single file and manacled. Huxley grasped, as Orwell did not, that it is not necessary to conceal anything from a public insensible to contradiction and narcoticized by technological diversions. Although Huxley did not specify that television would be our main line to the drug, he would have no difficulty accepting Robert MacNeil's observation that "Television is the *soma* of Aldous Huxley's *Brave New World.*" Big Brother turns out to be Howdy Doody.

I do not mean that the trivialization of public information is all 26 accomplished *on* television. I mean that television is the paradigm for our conception of public information. As the printing press did in an earlier time, television has achieved the power to define the form in which news must come, and it has also defined how we shall respond to it. In presenting news to us packaged as vaudeville, television induces other media to do the same, so that the total information environment begins to mirror television.

For example, America's newest and highly successful national 27 newspaper, *USA Today*, is modeled precisely on the format of television. It is sold on the street in receptacles that look like television sets. Its stories are uncommonly short, its design leans heavily on pictures, charts and other graphics, some of them printed in various colors. Its weather maps are a visual delight; its sports section includes enough pointless statistics to distract a computer. As a consequence, *USA Today*, which began publication in September 1982, has become the third largest daily in the United States (as of July 1984, according to the Audit Bureau of Circulations), moving quickly to overtake the *Daily*

News and the *Wall Street Journal.* Journalists of a more traditional bent have criticized it for its superficiality and theatrics, but the paper's editors remain steadfast in their disregard of typographic standards. The paper's Editor-in-Chief, John Quinn, has said: "We are not up to undertaking projects of the dimensions needed to win prizes. They don't give awards for the best investigative paragraph." Here is an astonishing tribute to the resonance of television's epistemology: In the age of television, the paragraph is becoming the basic unit of news in print media. Moreover, Mr. Quinn need not fret too long about being deprived of awards. As other newspapers join in the transformation, the time cannot be far off when awards will be given for the best investigative sentence.

It needs also to be noted here that new and successful magazines   28
such as *People* and *Us* are not only examples of television-oriented print media but have had an extraordinary "ricochet" effect on television itself. Whereas television taught the mgazines that news is nothing but entertainment, the magazines have taught television that nothing but entertainment is news. Television programs, such as "Entertainment Tonight," turn information about entertainers and celebrities into "serious" cultural content, so that the circle begins to close: Both the form and content of news become entertainment.

Radio, of course, is the least likely medium to join in the descent   29
into a Huxleyan world of technological narcotics. It is, after all, particularly well suited to the transmission of rational, complex language. Nonetheless, and even if we disregard radio's captivation by the music industry, we appear to be left with the chilling fact that such language as radio allows us to hear is increasingly primitive, fragmented, and largely aimed at invoking visceral response; which is to say, it is the linguistic analogue to the ubiquitous rock music that is radio's principal source of income. As I write, the trend in call-in shows is for the "host" to insult callers whose language does not, in itself, go much beyond humanoid grunting. Such programs have little content, as this word used to be defined, and are merely of archeological interest in that they give us a sense of what a dialogue among Neanderthals might have been like. More to the point, the language of radio newscasts has become, under the influence of television, increasingly decontextualized and discontinuous, so that the possibility of anyone's knowing about the world, as against merely knowing *of* it, is effectively blocked. In New York City, radio station WINS entreats its listeners to "Give us twenty-two minutes and we'll give you the world." This is said without irony, and its audience, we may assume, does not regard the slogan as the conception of a disordered mind.

And so, we move rapidly into an information environment which   30
may rightly be called trivial pursuit. As the game of that name uses facts as a source of amusement, so do our sources of news. It has been

demonstrated many times that a culture can survive misinformation and false opinion. It has not yet been demonstrated whether a culture can survive if it takes the measure of the world in twenty-two minutes. Or if the value of its news is determined by the number of laughs it provides.

BARBARA EHRENREICH

Spudding Out

Barbara Ehrenreich (1941–   ) grew up in Butte, Montana, and received her Ph.D. from Rockefeller University. She was a staff member of the Health Policy Advisory Center and a professor of health sciences at SUNY College–Old Westbury before she began writing in the early 1970s. Her first books (which she wrote with her husband or with Deirdre English) focus on the politics of health, more specifically on male domination of women's health issues: *Complaints and Disorders: The Sexual Politics of Sickness* appeared in 1973 and *For Her Own Good: One Hundred Fifty Years of Experts' Advice to Women* in 1978. Since 1982 she has been a fellow of the Institute of Policy Studies in Washington, D.C., and a regular columnist for *Ms.* magazine and *Mother Jones.* She was cochairperson of the Democratic Socialists of America in 1983. Most of Ehrenreich's writing is nonfiction prose based on political and social issues. Ehrenreich also writes fiction. Her stories are collected in *Jump: And Other Stories* (1991); her first novel, *Kipper's Game,* appeared in 1993. In 1994 she returned to the subject of health care with *Hospital: An Oral History of Cook County Hospital.*

Someone has to speak for them, because they have, to a person, 1 lost the power to speak for themselves. I am referring to that great mass of Americans who were once known as the "salt of the earth," then as "the silent majority," more recently as "the viewing public," and now, alas, as "couch potatoes." What drives them—or rather, leaves them sapped and spineless on their reclining chairs? What are they seeking— beyond such obvious goals as a tastefully colorized version of *The Maltese Falcon*?

My husband was the first in the family to "spud out," as the expres- 2 sion now goes. Soon everyone wanted one of those zip-up "Couch Potato Bags," to keep warm in during David Letterman. The youngest, and most thoroughly immobilized, member of the family relies on a remote that controls his TV, stereo, and VCR, and can also shut down the neighbor's pacemaker at fifteen years.

But we never see the neighbors anymore, nor they us. This saddens 3
me, because Americans used to be a great and restless people, fond of
the outdoors in all of its manifestations, from Disney World to miniature
golf. Some experts say there are virtues in mass agoraphobia, that it
strengthens the family and reduces highway deaths. But I would point
out that there are still a few things that cannot be done in the den,
especially by someone zipped into a body bag. These include racquetball, voting, and meeting strange people in bars.

Most psychologists interpret the couch potato trend as a negative 4
reaction to the outside world. Indeed, the list of reasons to stay safely
tucked indoors lengthens yearly. First there was crime, then AIDS, then
side-stream smoke. To this list should be added "fear of the infrastruc-
ture," for we all know someone who rashly stepped outside only to be
buried in a pothole, hurled from a collapsing bridge, or struck by a
falling airplane.

But it is not just the outside world that has let us down. Let's face 5
it, despite a decade-long campaign by the "profamily" movement, the
family has been a disappointment. The reason lies in an odd circular
dynamic: we watch television to escape from our families because television shows us how dull our families really are.

Compare your own family to, for example, the Huxtables, the Kea- 6
tons, or the peppy young people on *Thirtysomething*. In those families,
even the three-year-olds are stand-up comics, and the most insipid
remark is hailed with heartening outbursts of canned laughter. When
television families aren't gathered around the kitchen table exchanging
wisecracks, they are experiencing brief but moving dilemmas, which
are handily solved by the youngest child or by some cute extraterrestrial
house-guest. Emerging from *Family Ties* or *My Two Dads*, we are forced
to acknowledge that our own families are made up of slow-witted,
emotionally crippled people who would be lucky to qualify for seats in
the studio audience of *Jeopardy!*

But gradually I have come to see that there is something besides 7
fear of the outside and disgust with our families that drives us to spud-
hood—some positive attraction, some deep cathexis to television itself.
For a long time it eluded me. When I watched television, mainly as a
way of getting to know my husband and children, I found that my
mind wandered to more interesting things, like whether to get up and
make ice cubes.

Only after many months of viewing did I begin to understand the 8
force that has transformed the American people into root vegetables. If
you watch TV for a very long time, day in, day out, you will begin to
notice something eerie and unnatural about the world portrayed
therein. I don't mean that it is two-dimensional or lacks a well-
developed critique of the capitalist consumer culture or something superficial like that. I mean something so deeply obvious that it's almost

scary: when you watch television, you will see people doing many things—chasing fast cars, drinking lite beer, shooting each other at close range, etc. But you will never see people *watching television*. Well, maybe for a second, before the phone rings or a brand-new, multi-racial adopted child walks into the house. But never *really watching*, hour after hour, the way *real* people do.

Way back in the beginning of the television era, this was not so strange, because real people actually did many of the things people do on TV, even if it was only bickering with their mothers-in-law about which toilet paper to buy. But modern people, i.e., couch potatoes, do nothing that is ever shown on television (because it is either dangerous or would involve getting up from the couch). And what they do do— watch television—is far too boring to be televised for more than a fraction of a second, not even by Andy Warhol, bless his boredom-proof little heart.   9

So why do we keep on watching? The answer, by now, should be perfectly obvious: we love television because television brings us a world in which television does not exist. In fact, deep in their hearts, this is what the spuds crave most: a rich, new, participatory life, in which family members look each other in the eye, in which people walk outside and banter with the neighbors, where there is adventure, possibility, danger, feeling, all in natural color, stereophonic sound, and three dimensions, without commercial interruptions, and starring . . . us.   10

"You mean some new kind of computerized interactive medium?" the children asked hopefully, pert as the progeny on a Tuesday night sitcom. But before I could expand on this concept—known to our an-cestors as "real life"—they were back at the box, which may be, after all, the only place left to find it.   11

DAVID BRADLEY

How TV Drew Our Family Together—
In Spite of Its Messages

David Bradley (1950–   ) grew up in Bedford County, Pennsylvania, a rural region he describes as "perilously close to the Mason-Dixon Line." Moving to Philadelphia in 1968 to attend the University of Pennsylvania, he managed to compile both a perfect academic tran-script and a novel (*South Street*, 1975) based on the life stories he heard at a local bar. In 1972, he moved to London to study the United

States from a British perspective, and he received an M.A. from King's College, London, in 1974. He returned to Philadelphia and worked as an editor and college teacher while he finished a ten-year struggle to complete *The Chaneyville Incident* (1981), an award-winning novel based on an incident Bradley learned about from his mother—the capture, killing, and burial of thirteen runaway slaves on a farm near Bradley's home. Currently a professor of English at Temple University in Philadelphia, Bradley is a frequent contributor to such magazines as *Esquire, Signature,* and *The New York Times Book Review.* The following essay is from *TV Guide,* July 11, 1987.

Thanksgiving evening, 1986, just before 8. Home for the holiday, I lie on the living-room carpet, full of pumpkin pie and pro football. My mother comes in and announces it's time for *The Cosby Show.* She says it with some trepidation; the last time she turned on *The Cosby Show,* I snorted angrily and left the room. But tonight, too stuffed to move, I only grunt as she turns on the set. I don't really mean to watch, but the announcer's voice, saying, "WJAC-TV, Johnstown, Channel 6, serving millions from atop the Alleghenies," draws my eye to the screen. As the image of Dr. Heathcliff Huxtable's Brooklyn brownstone blossoms, it occurs to me that, while the call sign, slogan, even the announcer have been the same for as long as I can remember, a picture so sharp and free of interference is something I could only dream of when I was young.

I was born in a fringe area, a place where television signals are weakened by distance. The town was Bedford, population 5000, situated in the Allegheny Mountains of Pennsylvania, 100 miles east of Pittsburgh along the Pennsylvania Turnpike—at Exit 11, to be precise. Bedford—like most of the region—could look back on a prosperous past but forward to only a marginal future. A local TV station was an impossibility, and the mountainous terrain cut down on what could be received from a distance—some people claimed to pick up Ch. 2 from Pittsburgh, but most could receive signals from only two stations: WJAC, an NBC affiliate (although in the '50s it sometimes strayed to ABC offerings, like *Lawrence Welk* and *Ted Mack's Original Amateur Hour*) and WFBG-TV, Ch. 10, Altoona, a CBS affiliate. On neither was reception perfect. Ch. 6 always had little dots all over the screen. Ch. 10 always had multiple images. Sometimes you could hear and not see clearly; sometimes you could see and not hear. Occasionally a channel would vanish for hours. Often a broadcast would hover just beyond the threshold of intelligibility.

In such an area one quickly learned some of the jargon of TV. Before I went to school I knew that my TV watching was subject to "interference" because I lived in a "fringe area" beyond "line of sight" of cities. I even knew that the dots on Ch. 6 were called "snow" and the multiple images on Ch. 10 were called "ghosts." Of course my understanding was childishly literal-minded. I thought "line of sight" meant I could see Johnstown and Altoona if I got up on the roof with the TV antenna (I nearly broke my neck trying), and that "snow" meant it was actually snowing between Bedford and Johnstown. And I believed "ghosts" were the spirits of dead people, trapped somehow in the glowing interior of our black-and-white Motorola. For years I feared those ghosts would escape once the set was turned off, and I would sit in the darkness, staring at the screen, refusing to turn my back until the white dot that lingered there had vanished.

The set in my mother's living room now is a 20-inch General Electric, with a heart of cool germanium, not hot vacuum tubes. It does not lend itself to ghostly fantasies. Still, as the action of *The Cosby Show* commences, I find that it can at least help me to conjure the spirits of my family, to bring them into the living room as they would come 30 years ago.   4

My grandmother occupies an overstuffed chair in the corner beyond the fireplace. She does not have a good view of the television, but she doesn't watch TV anyway—she just listens to it. One reason she doesn't watch is she is terrifically nearsighted but refuses to wear bifocals; her glasses are propped upon her forehead so she can see. But the real reason is that she is a devotee of radio.   5

My grandmother was born when TV was an inventor's dream. Her electronic revolution took place in 1921 or 1922, when she was invited to the home of a white neighbor to listen to one of the first commercial radio broadcasts from KDKA in Pittsburgh. It was years before she could afford a set, but by the time I was born radio was a part of her life. Every morning she would fire up her wood stove and her bulky, floor-model Zenith, and spend the day crocheting and listening to the scratchy AM broadcasts.   6

At dusk she would take up her cane and walk to our house to spend the night with the comfort of central heating and indoor plumbing—her home had neither. After dinner she would "listen to television," which meant sitting in the corner crocheting an infinite series of antimacassars and listening to the audio portions of the programs she enjoyed (most of which were carry-overs from radio—*The Jack Benny Show*, *The Lone Ranger*, Groucho Marx's *You Bet Your Life*). Once I asked her why she didn't look at the characters. "I know what they look like," she said.   7

One thing that drew her attention to the screen was a voice that seemed to belong to a black person. Eddie "Rochester" Anderson's gravelly tones would make her drop her glasses onto her nose and watch *Jack Benny* in earnest. A non-Caucasian accent from an unfamiliar source, such as a contestant on *You Bet Your Life*, would have her leaning forward and exclaiming, "Why . . . he's colored!" The only   8 broadcast she watched from the start was one where the audio gave no clue as to the race of the participants: *The Gillette Cavalcade of Sports*, aka the Friday Night Fights.

My grandmother was not a fight fan—she could name only two 9 boxers, Joe Louis and Sugar Ray Robinson (whose bouts she had heard on radio). But on Fridays at 10 she would pull her chair out to get a better view. As the announcer, Jimmy Powers, introduced each set of combatants, she would peer through the snow of Ch. 6, examining the boxers as if she had a bet down. If both were white, she would go back to her crocheting. If both were black, she would watch, interested but passive. But if a black was pitted against a white, she would perch on the edge of her seat, the frail lace of her handwork crumpled in her fists, and mutter, "Get him, get him!" every time the black threw a punch.

At the moment, my grandmother's ghost is relishing the sight of 10 the Huxtable family—a half-dozen black faces on the screen at one time. The other ghost in the living room, however, is oblivious to the number of black faces on the screen—or anything else. My father, stretched out in his recliner, is perfectly placed for TV viewing, but, as usual, he is asleep.

If my grandmother "listened to television," my father snored to it. 11 Settled in front of the television, he would go directly to sleep, dozing indiscriminately through laugh tracks, police sirens and war whoops. The only sound that roused him was the theme music of the *Eleven O'Clock News Roundup*. He would awaken to catch the national head-lines, nod off through the local news, wake for the weather and then announce it was bedtime. For years I found this behavior humorous, a bit perverse and totally inexplicable. But later I came to understand that putting my father to sleep was about all TV could do for him.

My father was denominational officer of the African Methodist 12 Episcopal Zion Church. Although an ordained minister, he was not assigned to a local parish but rather traveled extensively—about seven months a year, total—on denominational business. In the mid-'50s I began to travel with him. Our first trip was to New York, and when I felt the thrill of actually setting foot in the city I understood why television's black-and-white images, devoid of smell and color, could only put him to sleep. It was, I suppose, an early lesson in the difference between TV appearances and reality. But even had my father not been a traveler, TV would have been peripheral to his existence. I discovered that in Dinwiddie, Va., a wide place on U.S. Highway 1, south of Richmond, where the church held an annual "Institute"—a combination Bible school, summer camp and revival meeting.

My father started taking me to the South at an odd time: the sum- 13 mer of 1956. Some Southern whites were having violent reactions to civil-rights marches and Federal court rulings, and neither ministers nor children were immune to their wrath: the year before, the Rev. George Lee had been killed, and Emmett Till, a 14-year-old black boy from Chicago, who was visiting relatives in Mississippi, had been beaten to death, his body tied to a weight and dumped in the Tallahatchie River. Although I was too young to understand fully, I had seen enough on television to be more than a little afraid. But at the Institute we were cut off from all pictures, descriptions and accounts of the civil-rights struggle. The Institute building, a ramshackle three-story affair built on a former plantation, didn't even have a telephone. Television might have been a myth.

At first I was dismayed at missing *Captain Kangaroo* and *Mickey Mouse,* but soon I began to enjoy Dinwiddie's brand of entertainment: afternoon baseball games, evening firefly chases, the sweaty pomp and pageantry of the evening worship services. My father seemed to enjoy it too. In the afternoons he would sit beneath a shade tree, sipping iced tea and whipping all comers at Chinese checkers. In the evenings he would tell me a story before going to argue church politics on the porch with the other preachers. During the years we visited the Institute it gradually dawned on me that Dinwiddie was much like Bedford had been when my father was growing up, a place where entertainment was based on interaction between people, and I began to understand why he got annoyed at me for "sitting in front of the television," as he called it.   14

By then it was the mid-'60s, and a certain tension had grown between my father and me. Television did not cause it, but it became the focus of it. Whenever he saw me watching football and basketball he growled that I ought to watch things that had to do with brains, instead of brawn. He had no patience with the fantasy of *Star Trek.* We watched little together other than the *CBS Evening News,* and then Walter Cronkite's "And that's the way it is" tended to be drowned out by a frank exchange of views between my father and me, which ended when one of us—me, usually—left the room. The pattern persisted after I left home. It probably would have remained unchanged until he died if the television had not broken down.   15

I happened to be home visiting when the TV went dead. The repairman could only shake his head. The set was obsolete. Parts were unobtainable. The best solution was to buy a new TV. My father, then in his 70s, worried about retirement and medical bills, blanched at the price. So I went to town with my Mastercard and came back with an RCA XL-100. My father watched as I plugged it in and tuned it to the channel he wanted. As I started out of the room he touched my arm. "Watch a while," he said. "OK," I said, and sat down. He smiled, looked at the screen—and fell asleep.   16

From that moment our relationship changed. We did not suddenly   17 start agreeing, but, hours after one of us had made an angry exit, one of us would come back into the living room while the other was watching television, and watch, too. Sometimes my father would take his chair while I was disagreeing with the refs on *Monday Night Football*. Sometimes I would sit with him, suppressing groans, through *Little House on the Prairie*. I suppose you could call it reconciliation, but that would be a bit too grand. After all, Merlin Olsen was an ex-football player. And my father slept through every play.

My grandfather died in January of 1961, my father died in 1979. **18** Between those dates cable came to our house. In an electronic sense the cable moved Bedford out of the fringe area, melting the snow, exorcising the ghosts. All the shows of the three major networks are available now, along with religion on the CBN Cable Network, golden oldies on the USA Network, and un-American activities like 12-man football on ESPN. In a social sense, however, the cable has made it possible for Bedford to stay on the fringe; people who believed, 30 years ago, that cities were lousy with danger and sin can find confirmation aplenty on the local news out of Pittsburgh or D.C., and can touch up their family values with the *700 Club* and reruns of *Father Knows Best*. It's a temptation too to say that, in a cultural sense, the cable has brought new opportunities for enrichment, because you can turn on PBS and watch ballet from Lincoln Center and listen to longhair music from Wolf Trap. But those aren't new opportunities for at least one person: my mother.

I am a native of the fringe area. My mother was an exile there. She **19** was born in New Jersey in 1915, grew up there, married and lived with my father there when he was a local pastor. But, in 1948, when he became a denominational officer, they moved to Bedford. It must have been frustrating for my mother, a woman with artistic interests who was herself a pianist and a gifted soprano, after years of easy access to the culture of New York City, to be in a town where the local radio played Top 40 and country and went off the air at sundown. Although I was not born until 1950, I can recall the wistful tones in which she spoke of concerts she had attended and choirs in which she had sung. Fortunately, in the '50s, television networks had not yet learned that culture wouldn't sell and were airing programs like *Playhouse 90, Armstrong Circle Theater* and *The United States Steel Hour*.

My mother did not really watch television any more than my **20** grandmother or my father did. She would be in the room but would almost always be doing other things—knitting, ironing, reading. The one exception came on Sunday afternoons, when she would give undivided attention to the sampler of cultural events called *Omnibus*. I watched the show with her. And so, at 4 or 5, I was exposed to Aaron

Copland's "Billy the Kid" performed by the Ballet Theatre Company and Leonard Bernstein's explication of Beethoven's Fifth Symphony. I can't remember all the things we watched, but I can recall my mother's dismay when, in '56, *Omnibus* moved to ABC and was no longer broadcast in our area. But my mother did not stop watching television when *Omnibus* vanished from our airwaves. In fact, she made it a crusade to find shows of quality during the brief period between their debuts and cancellations, and was quick to recognize quality performers. She was a devotee of Richard Boone's dramatic anthology and of *East Side/West Side* with George C. Scott (both lasted only a season) and she started watching *The Garry Moore Show* when Carol Burnett joined the cast.

I watched those programs, too. Although most came on after my legislated bedtime, often, when my father was out of town, I would creep out into the living room, where my mother would be putting up her hair in front of the television. If my mother deemed the show "worth watching" she would pretend not to notice. When I was young what was "worth watching" tended to be what I had the least interest in seeing—I wanted *The Untouchables,* not *Alcoa Premiere.* But by the time I finished junior high school and was allowed to stay up until 11, my tastes were trained. In fact, it was I who insisted, in 1965, that my mother set aside her prejudice against shoot-'em-ups to watch a witty, often moving espionage thriller called *I Spy,* co-starring somebody named Bill Cosby. [21]

It occurs to me, now, as I watch that same Cosby registering dismay, suspicion, mollification, all at once (the bad news is another vehicle crashed into the Huxtable kids' car; the good news is the other vehicle was Stevie Wonder's limo and, in addition to paying for the damage, the singer has invited the family to a recording session), that he looks different than he did back in 1965. The explanation that comes to me is that back then fringe-area interference kept Cosby's expressive face a blur. But then I recall a moment when I saw Cosby's face clearly registering an even wider range of emotions. It was in one of the masterpiece episodes of *I Spy,* aired toward the end of the series, which Robert Culp directed and in which Cosby played the central role. He had been betrayed by a woman he loved, and there was nothing he needed to say; his face told everything. It was a powerful image then. My recollection of it now is powerful enough to challenge a line of thinking that began two decades ago. [22]

In the fall of 1968, I left the fringe area to attend college in Philadelphia. I couldn't afford a television, and I didn't have time to watch one anyway: I was studying or attending plays, poetry readings, concerts or—since it was the '60s—political seminars. One of those was a panel on "Black History." The discussion was fairly tame; the panelists agreed that the white power structure had tried to brainwash blacks into accepting second-class citizenship by promoting a version of history that [23] ignored any role blacks played in the development of America. The speakers disagreed only on the question of which medium had been the greatest brainwasher. One speaker nominated television, and suddenly I was reminded of *The Gray Ghost*.

The Gray Ghost was a syndicated dramatization of the life of John 24 Singleton Mosby, a Civil War cavalry officer who waged a guerrilla campaign that was both humorous and heroic—if you were a Confederate. At the time the show aired—1956 or 1957—I was too young to understand what the Civil War was about, so I cheered Mosby's escapes from his blue-coated enemies. But one day my father saw what I was doing and gave me a brief but unequivocal lesson in American history. The panelist's argument brought back the hot chagrin I had felt at my own ignorance and at, I realized, being deceived into thinking a "slave-holding rebel" was *my* hero.

In the weeks that followed, chagrin crystallized into a reasoned 25 hatred for the complex of finance, technology and show business that we call "television." For as I looked back to the shows I had watched in my childhood I realized that television had not only written blacks out of history, it had written them out of society. In the '50s you couldn't see a black on TV unless the role made it absolutely necessary. Amos, Andy and Rochester were holdovers from radio—they *had* to be black. But on shows TV originated, blacks appeared nowhere. Certainly they were not heroes or heroines, and they were not even domestics in continuing roles—John Forsythe's houseboy on *Bachelor Father* was Chinese. More important from the point of view of subliminal visual messages, they were not in the background. In television America you didn't see black folks walking down the street or sitting on a bus. The image would have delighted a segregationist. Even in the '60s, when television was supposedly "making blacks more visible," the only place you were sure to see them in casual roles was on offbeat shows set in Africa, like *Cowboy in Africa*, in which Chuck Connors taught the Kikuyu to rope steers (his sidekick was a Navajo, his employer an Englishman).

The truth, I realized, was that '60s television did not make all blacks 26 more visible—only some. TV news covered riots in Northern ghettos, but it made individual leaders visible only if they were Southern and nonviolent. It was Martin Luther King on the networks—Malcolm X was on talk shows aired by independent stations in the prime time of insomniacs and night watchmen. TV entertainment made black women more visible if they were middle class and prissy, like Diahann Carroll's Julia or Peggy on *Mannix*, both of whom were widows and apparently beyond sex—both seemed dedicated to the memories of dead husbands (both of whom died in uniform). Black men were more visible only as updated domestics, like Barney on *Mission: Impossible*, whose share of the Impossible Mission was usually to crawl through a sewer pipe with a screwdriver and drive the van; or Mark Sanger on *Ironside*, whose job was to cater to a crippled white man and drive the van. The answer to, "What does a black guy have to do to be on network TV and *not* drive a van?" was given by Cosby's Alexander Scott in *I Spy:* he has to be a Rhodes scholar (not just a college graduate and an athlete), speak six languages—and carry the bags of an Ivy-League dropout who gets almost all the girls.

I saw little in the '70s to stop my hating television. Black women   27 kept on losing their men while gaining about 60 pounds: Mabel King was divorced on *What's Happening,* Nell Carter was unmarried on *Gimme a Break,* Esther Rolle, Florida on *Good Times,* started out married but was widowed midway in the series. (Isabel Sanford, Louise on *The Jeffersons,* had a husband but might have wished she didn't.) Female characters who were not nor ever had been either domestics or over-weight were morally questionable good-time girls, like Willona (Ja'net DuBois) on *Good Times* . . . except for Helen Willis (Roxie Roker) on *The Jeffersons,* who was married to a white man. Black men had lots of problems, too. The good news was that Florida's husband, James, fi-nally got a job. The bad news was that it was in Mississippi. The worse news was that he died there (less violently, one hopes, than Emmett Till). George Jefferson was short, insecure and dominated by his wife, his mother and his (black) maid. Redd Foxx was a junkman. His son Lamont was still living at home. And all the shows that focused on black people were comedies—judging from television, blacks had no emotion too deep, commitment too strong or problem too complicated to be portrayed in 30 minutes and disposed of with a laugh.

To my eye, *The Cosby Show* changed none of that. Much was made   28 of the fact that each episode was vetted by a black Harvard psychiatrist to make sure only a positive image of blacks was presented, that nothing was said to make a child feel bad that his skin was black and his hair wasn't straight, but that, to my '60s-trained eye, was the same as smearing his face with bleaching cream and cutting his hair short so you couldn't tell it was kinky. Much was made of the show's high ratings among whites, but I saw that popularity—not only in America, but in places like South Africa—as evidence that it was letting whites see exactly the blacks they wanted doing exactly what they wanted for exactly as long as they wanted—middle-class, middle-of-the-road Negroes being funny as hell, for half an hour once a week.

The recollected image of Cosby's face from *I Spy* has not made me   29 change my mind about that. It has, however, made other images come bursting into my mind, as if some interference has been removed: my grandmother's parchment-colored fists gripping her doily as she watched a black man hit a white man, the look of satisfaction on her face as she talked of how, when they put *Amos 'n' Andy* on television they had to find "real colored men"; my father's eyes flashing indig-nantly as he insisted that what Walter Cronkite said was not "the way it was,'' his mouth twisted in sarcasm as he informed me that if the Gray Ghost had been victorious my great-grandfather, a freed slave, would have been carried back to ole Virginia; my mother's uncharacterizable expression as she footnoted a televised performance by Marian Anderson with the fact that once the Daughters of the American Revolution had refused to listen to Anderson sing, or her shoulders tensing as she watched Jackie Robinson come to bat in a televised baseball game. As those images come to me I realize that, for nearly 20 years, I have been thinking that TV affected me more than it really did. For though what I saw on TV was important, I always saw it with people who had senses both of history and their own dignity; people who made certain that any televised message was subjected to interference—to make sure that, when it came to the images that could harm me, I was protected in a fringe area.

And I realize too that, while I was lucky, I was not exceptionally so. 30 Though every black child does not have a militant for a grandmother, or a world traveler for a father, or a mother who can appreciate not only the arts but the artists, there are in each child's life black people who can offer, through explanation and example, antidotes to the poisonously . . . "negative" is too simple a word; perhaps "conventional" . . . images of blacks that television presents. There is danger in those images, of course, but those truly at risk are those who have no one to provide interference: black children whose parents do not insure that they live in a fringe area, white people who do not know the fringe is there.

Theme music rouses me. *Cosby Show* credits crawl across the screen. 31 I find I have an eerie urge to ask my mother what happened. She goes to the television, flips the dial to ESPN, where Texas is playing Texas A&M.

"Isn't there something you'd rather watch?" I ask as she resumes 32 her chair. I'm not being altruistic; I'm not interested in a game between two Southern schools.

"No," she says. "I'll just sit and put up my hair while you watch." 33

It occurs to me then that, in worrying about what television could 34 have done to me, I am forgetting what it has done for me; allowed me to keep my family. Despite the fact that we were separated by generation and politics and travel, despite the fact that I alone actually watched the thing, the television drew us, night after night, into the same room, like a fire on an ancient hearth. Like a lamp, it illuminated for me the expressions on the faces of my grandmother, my father, my mother. Like a camera, it helped me preserve their images. Now it has put them before me, clear and bright and free of interference.

And so, once again, my mother and I sit together. She puts up the 35 kinky hair *The Cosby Show* won't talk about. I doze just a bit, as we watch television together, never minding what is on the screen.

DONALD HALL

Purpose, Blame, and Fire

Donald Hall (1928–   ) was born in New Haven, Connecticut, and educated at Harvard and at Oxford University. Influenced by such undergraduate classmates as Robert Bly and Adrienne Rich, he turned his attention almost exclusively to poetry and in 1955 produced *Exiles and Marriages,* a book that won the American Academy of Poets' prestigious Lamont Award for that year. He became a professor of English at the University of Michigan in 1957 and continued to publish a steady stream of excellent poems. In 1975 he quit teaching, took up residence on a New Hampshire farm once owned by his grandparents, and devoted himself to writing full-time. Since then he has published several more volumes of award-winning poetry, as well as biographies, children's literature, textbooks, and essays. His essays are collected in *To Keep Moving: Essays 1959–1969* (1980) and in *Poetry and Ambition: Essays 1980–1988* (1988). In 1994 he published *Life Work,* half of which is a discussion of his life as a working writer and half the story of his dealing with terminal cancer. "Purpose, Blame, and Fire," written for the anthology *The Movie That Changed My Life,* was published in *Harper's* in May 1991.

My father was too young for the Great War, not fifteen when it [1] ended, and both of my grandfathers were too old. Their fathers fought in the Civil War—archaic blue figures, stiff-bearded in photographs—but in 1937, when I was eight, Gettysburg might have been Agincourt or Marathon.[1] As a second world war came closer, I understood that my father felt guilty about missing the Great War; but I understood that he wanted to miss the new one as well.

Everyone was nervous, the Depression hanging on and war ap- [2] proaching. I was an only child, alert to my parents' anxiety. My mother was thin and attentive. She had come to Connecticut from a remote farm in New Hampshire, and as I grew up I became aware that she felt lonely in the suburbs; she paid more attention to her child, in her displacement, than she would have done if she had stayed up north with her sisters.

Sometimes she took me on excursions to New Haven—Saturdays [3] during the school year, weekdays in summer. We walked up Ardmore Street to Whitney Avenue and waited for the bus that came every ten minutes to roll us four miles down Whitney and drop us at Church and Chapel outside Liggett's across from the New Haven Green. While I

---

1. Agincourt was a decisive victory of the English against the French in A.D. 1415; Marathon, a triumph of the Greeks against the Persians in 490 B.C.

tagged along, she shopped at Shartenberg's and Malley's. When we had
done shopping, we ate lunch at a place where I ordered franks and
beans—two grilled hot dogs and a tiny crock of pea beans dark with
molasses; dessert was Jell-O with real whipped cream or dry yellow
cake with white frosting. Lunch cost thirty-nine cents.

Then we went to the movies. At the theater we would see a first-run   4
film, a B-movie, one or two shorts, previews of coming attractions, and
a newsreel. In the year 1937 I am almost sure that I watched Spencer
Tracy in *Captains Courageous;* maybe Paul Muni in *The Life of Emile Zola,*
probably *Lost Horizon* and *A Star Is Born.* But the only movie I remember
seeing for certain, some fifty-four years later, is *The Last Train From
Madrid.* After we took the bus home to Ardmore Street, I burned my
collection of war cards and put away my toy soldiers forever.

In 1937 we boys wore long woolen stockings pulled up over the   5
bottoms of corduroy knickers as we walked to Spring Glen Grammar
School. There were no school buses. Children from my neighborhood
took several different routes to school—for variety or to avoid a bully—
but always passed the Glendower Drug Store, only two short blocks
from the school.

If we had change in our pockets, we spent it there. For a nickel,   6
we bought big candy bars or flat pieces of gum creased into five sticks
and pink as a dog's tongue. With the gum came cards that illustrated
our different obsessions: Of course there were baseball cards, and I seem
to recall cards for football as well; I remember G-man cards, each of
which illustrated a triumph of law and order such as J. Edgar Hoover's
agents flushing out Dillinger—shooting him in the lobby of a movie
theater—or Pretty Boy Floyd. Although G-man cards were violent, they
might have been the Society of Friends alongside another series that
we bought and collected. We called them war cards, and they thrived
in the bellicose air of 1937.

It was a time when the war in Spain[2] shrieked from the front pages   7
of newspapers, along with the Japanese invasion of China. In 1937
Stalin kept discovering to his astonishment that old colleagues had betrayed him; he shot seven of his best generals that year, doubtless a
great advantage when Hitler invaded. In 1937 Trotsky found his way to
Mexico,[3] the UAW[4] invented the sit-down strike, Neville Chamberlain[5]

2. The Spanish Civil War (1937–1939), which anticipated World War II and introduced
such horrors as the bombing of civilian targets. The war pitted fascist rebel General
Francisco Franco against Spanish Loyalists aided by liberals and leftists from around the
world.
3. Leon Trotsky (1879–1940), Russian revolutionary and political leader, was driven
into exile by dictator Joseph Stalin (1879–1953).
4. United Auto Workers.
5. British prime minister from May 1937 through May 1940.

asked Hitler for his cooperation in the interest of peace, the *Hindenburg* exploded and burned in New Jersey, and thousands of American progressives joined the Lincoln Brigade to fight fascism in Spain.

Even in the fourth grade we knew about Hitler, whose troops and planes fought alongside Franco against the Loyalists, who were aided by Stalin's troops and planes. Germany was again the enemy, less than twenty years after the Armistice of 1918. We were good, brave, loyal, outnumbered, and victorious against all odds; they were evil, cruel, cowardly, vicious, dumb, shrewd, and doomed. We knew who was right and who was wrong. (My father's mother's family had emigrated from Germany to New Haven in the 1880s, which was confusing.) In 1937 all of us—parents, teachers, children—understood that there would be another war and that America would join this war sooner than it had the Great War. Isolationists and pacifists campaigned against the war, but everyone knew that war was inevitable—whether it was or wasn't. A phenomenon like war cards makes it now seem as if we were being prepared, as if the adults were making sure that we grew up expecting to become soldiers, accepting the guns and the bombing and the death.

At least no one—so soon after the Great War—had the temerity to present war as a Cub Scout expedition. When we went to the movies, we saw a newsreel and sometimes even *The March of Time.* The late 1930s were endless parades in black and white, soldiers marching, weapons rolling past reviewing stands. I remember the bombing and strafing of refugees. I remember Hitler addressing rallies.

War cards used a lot of red ink. On the back of each card a short text described a notorious incident, and on the front an artist illustrated what had happened. I remember one card that showed a Japanese bomb hitting a crowded Chinese bus, maybe in Shanghai: Bodies being torn apart hurtled through the air, intestines stretched and tangled, headless bodies littering the ground. I don't believe these cards were particularly ideological; as I recollect, the cards claimed to be educational, illustrating the Horrors of War. Blood was the whole matter.

We cherished our war cards, chewing gum as we walked home to add a new one to our collections: Blood of war was the food on which we nurtured our boyish death-love. If you got a duplicate you could swap, maybe the exploded bus for a card that showed the shelling of a boat. We collected war cards as we collected ourselves for war.

Surely, at eight, my imagination was filled by war. I loved airplanes and read pulp stories about dogfights over the trenches. I loved the pilot heroes of the era—Wiley Post, Amelia Earhart, later Wrong-Way Corrigan. When I imagined myself going to war it was to join the Lafayette Escadrille,[6] fly Spads, and shoot down Fokker triplanes.

6. A unit of U.S. volunteers attached to the French air force in the early years of World War I.

Then I saw *The Last Train From Madrid.* Did it really change my life?   13
As I commit it to paper, the phrase sounds exaggerated, melodramatic. I
never registered as a C.O. (Nor did I serve in the military.) Although
I worked in Ann Arbor with the movement against the Vietnam War,
I was never a leader. Neither did I spell the country Amerika. It was
war horror that filled my chest, not political commitment: A horror is
not an idea, as a shudder is not a conviction. Certain horrors of war
retain the power to burst me into tears, especially the random slaughter
of civilians. And my first experience of such horrors, I now believe,
must have occurred on the day in 1937 when I saw *The Last Train From
Madrid.*

In September of 1990—as another war approached—I saw *The Last*   14
Train From Madrid again. Over the years I had thought of the film often
and assumed that it was antifascist, popular front. It is no such thing;
the film is astonishingly without political ideology. The plot is deriva-
tive, built of romantic clichés and stereotypes, and is impossible to take
seriously: a *Grand Hotel* on wheels. The writing is ghastly, from clumsy
exposition to flat dialogue. Its single import is the randomness of war
horror.

The film opens with the hurtling image of a locomotive and train.   15
A radio newscast tells us that tonight the last train will leave Madrid,
after which—we understand—the city will be overrun by the nameless
army that is besieging it. The army lacks not only name but idea, and
its only purpose is death. As characters speak of the train's terminus in
Valencia, Valencia becomes pure symbol: The destination is Arcadian
peace in a countryside antithetical to the city's panic, chaos, and violent
death. Naturally, everyone wants a seat on the train. The plot of the
movie turns on separate and intermingled stories of people seeking
passage on the train—their stratagems, their failures and successes. At
the end of the movie the train steams out of Madrid carrying some of
the people we've been introduced to and leaving others behind—not
only behind but dead.

A noble young officer (noble because he is handsome and stands   16
straight; noble because he is Anthony Quinn) listens at the film's beginning to impassioned pleas for passes, and in his dutiful nobility refuses
them. We dwell on an old lady, well played, who begs for a pass and
is refused. Most of our central figures are in couples, two by two like
the ark's animals: the romantic interest, which I doubtless ignored in
1937 and found myself ignoring last fall. Love between two men (Anthony Quinn and Gilbert Roland) who swore blood brotherhood as
soldiers in Africa years before is standard *Beau Geste*[7] stuff, but it does

---

7. A 1939 adventure film starring Gary Cooper as a member of the French Foreign
Legion.

provide the strongest human bond in the film—stronger for sure than the bonds each seeks to establish with Dorothy Lamour.

In one of the subplots a slaphappy American journalist (Lew Ayres) [17] picks up a girl (Olympe Bradna) who wants to get to Madrid to see her father before the firing squad kills him. (Naturally, they fall in love; later, this pair makes it onto the Valencia-bound train.) She sees her father, he is shot—and we never receive an inkling, not a *notion*, of what he did or stood for that led to his cold-blooded execution. The killing feels wholly arbitrary: No motive is supplied or suggested. In this film's eerie political emptiness, execution by firing squad is not a political act (and thus in some way purposeful) but routine, everyday—like sunrise and sunset.

One soldier on the firing squad (Robert Cummings) is tender- [18] hearted and will not fire his gun. For his sensitivity he will be sent to the front. He runs away—and runs into an unbelievable love. We see two people parting, a man and a woman whom we do not know. We understand that they have just made love, and that she is a prostitute. They seem fond of each other, happy, making plans for their next en- counter. As the man walks into the street, we suddenly spy his shape down the sight of a rifle—a sniper's rifle. The sniper shoots him dead. Although we may assume that the sniper waited for this particular man, the film provides not one detail to support this assumption. We know nothing of this man or his killer or any motive; we know nothing about the shooting except the brute fact. Like the earlier execution by firing squad, this street killing—idyll destroyed by bullet—presents itself as wholly arbitrary.

It is this young prostitute (Helen Mack) with whom Cummings falls [19] in love—and she with him—immediately. After Mack and Cummings drag her dead lover's body into her flat, they talk; Cummings wants the dead man's pass for the last train. Soon enough, they scheme a double escape. During their brief courtship, the couple construct of their lovers' talk the Arcadian Valencia to which the train will deliver them. Cummings eventually makes it to the train, but alone. Mack dies on the way—again arbitrarily.

By today's standards, of course, there are actually few deaths in [20] *The Last Train From Madrid*. Channel-surfing the television—happen- ing, say, upon a Chuck Norris movie—you will see more carnage before you can switch channels than you'll observe in eighty-five minutes of this old film. But the deaths I witnessed in 1937 stuck with me as those I see in movies today for the most part do not. One in particular: Near the film's end, before the train leaves the station, guards move through the cars rechecking passes. As they demand papers from everyone, our anxiety mounts because they are approaching a vulnerable protagonist. Suddenly, looking at one man's pass—a stranger to us—the guards ask him to step outside. He looks nervous; he tries to run—and they shoot him down. They kill him *on purpose,* aiming their guns, yet they kill him *for no reason* that we will ever understand.

Murderous paradox drives the film: Malignity exists everywhere,   21
yet most of the time it appears motiveless. To an eight-year-old in New Haven, the particular individuals shot and killed in the film suffered deaths as arbitrary as if they had been killed by bombs from the sky. An air raid takes place at the center of the film, a riot of civilian panic, people running and frightened. The sound track plays fear music, camera shots are jumpy and angular, and in one quick shot nervous pigeons scurry.

In Robert Frost's "Design" he writes about the malign coincidence   22
of an invisible spider haply arranged to kill a fly; the poet asks what could have caused this coming-together except for "design of darkness to appall." Then he qualifies the question in a further line: "If design govern in a thing so small." In *The Last Train From Madrid* we are surrounded by fear of imminent death, but, horribly, we lack design. As humans, we wish or perhaps even need to understand the cause or to place blame—on an enemy, on politicians who betrayed us, on the cupidity or moral squalor of a person or a class of people—because blame implies purpose, and purpose, meaning. *The Last Train From Madrid* suggests that design may not govern in a thing so small as human life and death.

Printed words at the very start of the film scroll its neutrality: This   23
movie will not uphold or defend either side of the war. When we read of battles in old histories we study the motives of each side, although the cause may mean little to us: We want to make sense. We may not keep with us the ideas behind a conflict—what we tend to remember are stories of heroism, cowardice, and suffering; "The river ran red with blood for seven days," we remember, not "Thus Centerville retained its access to the sea." Yet we make the effort to understand the history and politics, if only to satisfy ourselves that there appeared to be reasons for the blood: a design. By eschewing history and politics, *The Last Train From Madrid* leeches war of its particular temporal context, providing an eight-year-old with his first glimpse of war as eternal anonymous suffering. The film scrolls war's utter panic and sorrow. Oh, sorrow, sorrow, sorrow—the ripe life cut by hate without purpose, by anger lacking reason, by murder without blame.

How did my mother happen to take an eight-year-old to such a   24
movie? Microfilm of the *New Haven Register* explains. The newspaper printed paragraphs of studio puffery that wholly misrepresented the film: "With but two pictures to her credit, both of which were outstanding successes, Dorothy Lamour, the glamorous brunette, one of the season's most sensational 'finds,' moves into the ranks of the screen's

charming leading ladies. The event takes place in 'The Last Train from Madrid,' the romance laid in war-torn Spain." I find it breathtaking to read this notice of the film that horrified me. "In this story Miss Lamour appears as a beautiful patrician girl, who is the beloved of a young lieutenant in the government forces and his best friend." When I read Frank S. Nugent's *New York Times* review (6/19/37), I am almost as astonished. He notes the lack of politics in this "glib little fiction," but for Nugent also there was no horror. "True, it treats of the Spanish revolution, but merely as Hollywood has, in the past, regarded the melodramatic turmoils of Ruritania and Zenda."[8] He calls the film "a pre-tested melodrama which should suit the average palate," and in his conclusion makes a joke: "Its sympathies, neither Loyalist nor Rebel, are clearly on the side of the Ruritanians."

Frank S. Nugent was not eight years old. Was Nugent's cynicism   25 more appropriate than my horror? At eight, I ignored the silly romance at the film's center and registered only the panic of unmotivated murder. When I returned home after the Saturday matinee, I packed my lead toy soldiers with their flattish Great War helmets into a shoebox and tucked it deep in the long closet of my bedroom. I performed the ritual with so much solemnity that I might have played taps for background music. By this time I felt not panic but a sadness that would not relent, which may have derived from another melancholy that absorbed me that weekend. The film opened in New Haven on Saturday, July 10, 1937, while Amelia Earhart was missing over the Pacific. I remember playing outside the house, keeping the window open and a radio near the window; I remember a report that the Navy had spotted her plane on an atoll; I remember the correction of the report. In my mind's eye, Amelia Earhart circled continually, high in the air, the hum of the Lockheed's engine distant and plaintive, gas almost gone, the pilot in her leather helmet peering for land as she circled . . .

A day or two later, alone in the house, I carried my war cards down   26 to the coal furnace in the cellar. I was not allowed to open the furnace door, but I opened it anyway and threw the cards onto the red coals. At first they smoldered and turned brown, and I feared that they would not burn—would give me away when my father came home and stoked the furnace. Then one card burst into bright yellow flame, then another, then all together flared briefly in the shadow-and-red hellfire of the furnace on Ardmore Street.

8. Fictional kingdoms in *The Prisoner of Zenda*, a swashbuckling story made into movies in 1913, 1922, and 1937.

JOHN CHEEVER

The Enormous Radio

John Cheever (1912–1982) was expelled from high school in Quincy, Massachusetts, when he was seventeen for smoking and laziness, an event that ended his formal education but gave him material for his first story, "Expelled," which was published in *The New Republic* in 1930. He left home for Boston determined to be a writer and for a time supported himself by writing book synopses for a film studio and other odd jobs. Meanwhile, he began to place short stories in several magazines, most significantly *The New Yorker*, where he eventually published more than one hundred. Eventually, Cheever won a dozen major literary awards, including a Pulitzer Prize in 1980 for *The Stories of John Cheever*, and was awarded an honorary doctorate from Harvard University. "The Enormous Radio," first published in *The New Yorker* on May 17, 1947, is often cited as one of his finest works.

Jim and Irene Westcott were the kind of people who seem to strike   1
that satisfactory average of income, endeavor, and respectability that is reached by the statistical reports in college alumni bulletins. They were the parents of two young children, they had been married nine years, they lived on the twelfth floor of an apartment house near Sutton Place,[1] they went to the theatre on an average of 10.3 times a year, and they hoped someday to live in Westchester.[2] Irene Westcott was a pleasant, rather plain girl with soft brown hair and a wide, fine forehead upon which nothing at all had been written, and in the cold weather she wore a coat of fitch skins dyed to resemble mink. You could not say that Jim Westcott looked younger than he was, but you could at least say of him that he seemed to feel younger. He wore his graying hair cut very short, he dressed in the kind of clothes his class had worn at Andover,[3] and his manner was earnest, vehement, and intentionally naïve. The Westcotts differed from their friends, their classmates, and their neighbors only in an interest they shared in serious music. They went to a great many concerts—although they seldom mentioned this to anyone—and they spent a good deal of time listening to music on the radio.

Their radio was an old instrument, sensitive, unpredictable, and   2
beyond repair. Neither of them understood the mechanics of radio—or of any of the other appliances that surrounded them—and when the instrument faltered, Jim would strike the side of the cabinet with his

1. A "gentrified" neighborhood in New York City.
2. An upper-middle-class rustic suburb.
3. Home of Phillips Academy, a prestigious preparatory school.

hand. This sometimes helped. One Sunday afternoon, in the middle of a
Schubert quartet, the music faded away altogether. Jim struck the cabinet repeatedly, but there was no response; the Schubert was lost to
them forever. He promised to buy Irene a new radio, and on Monday
when he came home from work he told her that he had got one. He
refused to describe it, and said it would be a surprise for her when it
came.

The radio was delivered at the kitchen door the following after-   3
noon, and with the assistance of her maid and the handyman Irene
uncrated it and brought it into the living room. She was struck at once
with the physical ugliness of the large gumwood cabinet. Irene was
proud of her living room, she had chosen its furnishings and colors as
carefully as she chose her clothes, and now it seemed to her that the
new radio stood among her intimate possessions like an aggressive intruder. She was confounded by the number of dials and switches on
the instrument panel, and she studied them thoroughly before she put
the plug into a wall socket and turned the radio on. The dials flooded
with a malevolent green light, and in the distance she heard the music
of a piano quintet. The quintet was in the distance for only an instant;
it bore down upon her with a speed greater than light and filled the
apartment with the noise of music amplified so mightily that it knocked
a china ornament from a table to the floor. She rushed to the instrument
and reduced the volume. The violent forces that were snared in the
ugly gumwood cabinet made her uneasy. Her children came home from
school then, and she took them to the Park. It was not until later in
the afternoon that she was able to return to the radio.

The maid had given the children their suppers and was supervising   4
their baths when Irene turned on the radio, reduced the volume, and
sat down to listen to a Mozart quintet that she knew and enjoyed. The
music came through clearly. The new instrument had a much purer
tone, she thought, than the old one. She decided that tone was most
important and that she could conceal the cabinet behind a sofa. But as
soon as she had made her peace with the radio, the interference began.
A crackling sound like the noise of a burning powder fuse began to
accompany the singing of the strings. Beyond the music, there was a
rustling that reminded Irene unpleasantly of the sea, and as the quintet
progressed, these noises were joined by many others. She tried all the
dials and switches but nothing dimmed the interference, and she sat
down, disappointed and bewildered, and tried to trace the flight of the
melody. The elevator shaft in her building ran beside the living-room
wall, and it was the noise of the elevator that gave her a clue to the
character of the static. The rattling of the elevator cables and the opening and closing of the elevator doors were reproduced in her loudspeaker, and, realizing that the radio was sensitive to electrical currents
of all sorts, she began to discern through the Mozart the ringing of
telephone bells, the dialing of phones, and the lamentation of a vacuum

cleaner. By listening more carefully, she was able to distinguish door-bells, elevator bells, electric razors, and Waring mixers, whose sounds had been picked up from the apartments that surrounded hers and transmitted through her loudspeaker. The powerful and ugly instrument, with its mistaken sensitivity to discord, was more than she could hope to master, so she turned the thing off and went into the nursery to see her children.

When Jim Westcott came home that night, he went to the radio confidently and worked the controls. He had the same sort of experience Irene had had. A man was speaking on the station Jim had chosen, and his voice swung instantly from the distance into a force so powerful that it shook the apartment. Jim turned the volume control and reduced the voice. Then, a minute or two later, the interference began. The ringing of telephones and doorbells set in, joined by the rasp of the elevator doors and the whir of cooking appliances. The character of the noise had changed since Irene had tried the radio earlier; the last of the electric razors was being unplugged, the vacuum cleaners had all been returned to their closets, and the static reflected that change in pace that overtakes the city after the sun goes down. He fiddled with the knobs but couldn't get rid of the noises, so he turned the radio off and told Irene that in the morning he'd call the people who had sold it to him and give them hell.

The following afternoon, when Irene returned to the apartment from a luncheon date, the maid told her that a man had come and fixed the radio. Irene went into the living room before she took off her hat or her furs and tried the instrument. From the loudspeaker came a recording of the "Missouri Waltz." It reminded her of the thin, scratchy music from an old-fashioned phonograph that she sometimes heard across the lake where she spent her summers. She waited until the waltz had finished, expecting an explanation of the recording, but there was none. The music was followed by silence, and then the plaintive and scratchy record was repeated. She turned the dial and got a satisfactory burst of Caucasian music—the thump of bare feet in the dust and the rattle of coin jewelry—but in the background she could hear the ringing of bells and a confusion of voices. Her children came home from school then, and she turned off the radio and went to the nursery.

When Jim came home that night, he was tired, and he took a bath and changed his clothes. Then he joined Irene in the living room. He had just turned on the radio when the maid announced dinner, so he left it on, and he and Irene went to the table.

Jim was too tired to make even a pretense of sociability, and there was nothing about the dinner to hold Irene's interest, so her attention wandered from the food to the deposits of silver polish on the candlesticks and from there to the music in the other room. She listened for a few minutes to a Chopin prelude and then was surprised to hear a man's voice break in. "For Christ's sake, Kathy," he said, "do you always have to play the piano when I get home?" The music stopped abruptly. "It's the only chance I have," a woman said. "I'm at the office all day." "So am I," the man said. He added something obscene about an upright piano, and slammed a door. The passionate and melancholy music began again.

"Did you hear that?" Irene asked. 9

"What?" Jim was eating his dessert. 10

"The radio. A man said something while the music was still going on—something dirty." 11

"It's probably a play." 12

"I don't think it *is* a play," Irene said. 13

They left the table and took their coffee into the living room. Irene asked Jim to try another station. He turned the knob. "Have you seen my garters?" a man asked. "Button me up," a woman said. "Have you seen my garters?" the man said again. "Just button me up and I'll find your garters," the woman said. Jim shifted to another station. "I wish you wouldn't leave apple cores in the ashtrays," a man said. "I hate the smell." 14

"This is strange," Jim said. 15

"Isn't it?" Irene said. 16

Jim turned the knob again. " 'On the coast of Coromandel where the early pumpkins blow,' " a woman with a pronounced English accent said, " 'in the middle of the woods lived the Yonghy-Bonghy-Bò. Two old chairs, and half a candle, one old jug without a handle . . .' " 17

"My God!" Irene cried. "That's the Sweeneys' nurse." 18

" 'These were all his worldly goods,' " the British voice continued. 19

"Turn that thing off," Irene said. "Maybe they can hear *us*." Jim switched the radio off. "That was Miss Armstrong, the Sweeneys' nurse," Irene said. "She must be reading to the little girl. They live in 17-B. I've talked with Miss Armstrong in the Park. I know her voice very well. We must be getting other people's apartments." 20

"That's impossible," Jim said. 21

"Well, that was the Sweeneys' nurse," Irene said hotly. "I know her voice. I know it very well. I'm wondering if they can hear us." 22

Jim turned the switch. First from a distance and then nearer, nearer, as if borne on the wind, came the pure accents of the Sweeneys' nurse again: " '*Lady Jingly! Lady Jingly!*' " she said, " '*sitting where the pumpkins blow, will you come and be my wife?* said the Yonghy-Bonghy-Bò . . .' " 23

Jim went over to the radio and said "Hello" loudly into the speaker. 24

" '*I am tired of living singly,*' " the nurse went on, " '*on this coast so wild and shingly, I'm a-weary of my life; if you'll come and be my wife, quite serene would be my life . . .*' " 25

"I guess she can't hear us," Irene said. "Try something else." 26

Jim turned to another station, and the living room was filled with   27
the uproar of a cocktail party that had overshot its mark. Someone was
playing the piano and singing the "Whiffenpoof Song,"[4] and the voices
that surrounded the piano were vehement and happy. "Eat some more
sandwiches," a woman shrieked. There were screams of laughter and
a dish of some sort crashed to the floor.

"Those must be the Fullers, in 11-E," Irene said. "I knew they were   28
giving a party this afternoon. I saw her in the liquor store. Isn't this too
divine? Try something else. See if you can get those people in 18-C."

The Westcotts overheard that evening a monologue on salmon   29
fishing in Canada, a bridge game, running comments on home movies
of what had apparently been a fortnight at Sea Island, and a bitter
family quarrel about an overdraft at the bank. They turned off their
radio at midnight and went to bed, weak with laughter. Sometime in
the night, their son began to call for a glass of water and Irene got one
and took it to his room. It was very early. All the lights in the neighborhood were extinguished, and from the boy's window she could see the
empty street. She went into the living room and tried the radio. There
was some faint coughing, a moan, and then a man spoke. "Are you all
right, darling?" he asked. "Yes," a woman said wearily. "Yes, I'm all
right, I guess," and then she added with great feeling. "But, you know,
Charlie, I don't feel like myself any more. Sometimes there are about
fifteen or twenty minutes in the week when I feel like myself. I don't
like to go to another doctor, because the doctor's bills are so awful
already, but I just don't feel like myself, Charlie. I just never feel like
myself." They were not young, Irene thought. She guessed from the
timbre of their voices that they were middle-aged. The restrained melancholy of the dialogue and the draft from the bedroom window made
her shiver, and she went back to bed.

The following morning, Irene cooked breakfast for the family—the   30
maid didn't come up from her room in the basement until ten—braided
her daughter's hair, and waited at the door until her children and her
husband had been carried away in the elevator. Then she went into the
living room and tried the radio. "I don't want to go to school," a child
screamed. "I hate school. I won't go to school. I hate school." "You
will go to school," an enraged woman said. "We paid eight hundred
dollars to get you into that school and you'll go if it kills you." The
next number on the dial produced the worn record of the "Missouri
Waltz." Irene shifted the control and invaded the privacy of several
breakfast tables. She overheard demonstrations of indigestion, carnal
love, abysmal vanity, faith, and despair. Irene's life was nearly as simple
and sheltered as it appeared to be, and the forthright and sometimes
brutal language that came from the loudspeaker that morning aston-

4. The unofficial drinking song of Yale undergraduates.

ished and troubled her. She continued to listen until her maid came in. Then she turned off the radio quickly, since this insight, she realized, was a furtive one.

Irene had a luncheon date with a friend that day, and she left her 31 apartment at a little after twelve. There were a number of women in the elevator when it stopped at her floor. She stared at their handsome and impassive faces, their furs, and the cloth flowers in their hats. Which one of them had been to Sea Island? she wondered. Which one had overdrawn her bank account? The elevator stopped at the tenth floor and a woman with a pair of Skye terriers joined them. Her hair was rigged high on her head and she wore a mink cape. She was humming the "Missouri Waltz."

Irene had two Martinis at lunch, and she looked searchingly at her 32 friend and wondered what her secrets were. They had intended to go shopping after lunch, but Irene excused herself and went home. She told the maid that she was not to be disturbed; then she went into the living room, closed the doors, and switched on the radio. She heard, in the course of the afternoon, the halting conversation of a woman entertaining her aunt, the hysterical conclusion of a luncheon party, and a hostess briefing her maid about some cocktail guests. "Don't give the best Scotch to anyone who hasn't white hair," the hostess said. "See if you can get rid of that liver paste before you pass those hot things, and could you lend me five dollars? I want to tip the elevator man."

As the afternoon waned, the conversations increased in intensity. 33 From where Irene sat, she could see the open sky above the East River. There were hundreds of clouds in the sky, as though the south wind had broken the winter into pieces and were blowing it north, and on her radio she could hear the arrival of cocktail guests and the return of children and businessmen from their schools and offices. "I found a good-sized diamond on the bathroom floor this morning," a woman said. "It must have fallen out of that bracelet Mrs. Dunston was wearing last night." "We'll sell it," a man said. "Take it down to the jeweler on Madison Avenue and sell it. Mrs. Dunston won't know the difference, and we could use a couple of hundred bucks . . ." "'Oranges and lemons, say the bells of St. Clement's,'" the Sweeneys' nurse sang. "'Halfpence and farthings, say the bells of St. Martin's. When will you pay me? say the bells at old Bailey . . .'" "It's not a hat," a woman cried, and at her back roared a cocktail party. "It's not a hat, it's a love affair. That's what Walter Florell said. He said it's not a hat, it's a love affair," and then, in a lower voice, the same woman added, "Talk to somebody, for Christ's sake, honey, talk to somebody. If she catches you standing here not talking to anybody, she'll take us off her invitation list, and I love these parties."

The Westcotts were going out for dinner that night, and when Jim 34 came home, Irene was dressing. She seemed sad and vague, and he

brought her a drink. They were dining with friends in the neighborhood, and they walked to where they were going. The sky was broad
and filled with light. It was one of those splendid spring evenings that
excite memory and desire, and the air that touched their hands and
faces felt very soft. A Salvation Army band was on the corner playing
"Jesus Is Sweeter." Irene drew on her husband's arm and held him
there for a minute, to hear the music. "They're really such nice people,
aren't they?" she said. "They have such nice faces. Actually, they're so
much nicer than a lot of the people we know." She took a bill from
her purse and walked over and dropped it into the tambourine. There
was in her face, when she returned to her husband, a look of radiant
melancholy that he was not familiar with. And her conduct at the
dinner party that night seemed strange to him, too. She interrupted her
hostess rudely and stared at the people across the table from her with
an intensity for which she would have punished her children.

It was still mild when they walked home from the party, and Irene   35
looked up at the spring stars. " 'How far that little candle throws its
beams,' " she exclaimed. " 'So shines a good deed in a naughty world.' "
She waited that night until Jim had fallen asleep, and then went into
the living room and turned on the radio.

Jim came home at about six the next night. Emma, the maid, let   36
him in, and he had taken off his hat and was taking off his coat when
Irene ran into the hall. Her face was shining with tears and her hair
was disordered. "Go up to 16-C, Jim!" she screamed. "Don't take off
your coat. Go up to 16-C. Mr. Osborn's beating his wife. They've been
quarreling since four o'clock, and now he's hitting her. Go up there
and stop him."

From the radio in the living room, Jim heard screams, obscenities,   37
and thuds. "You know you don't have to listen to this sort of thing,"
he said. He strode into the living room and turned the switch. "It's
indecent," he said. "It's like looking in windows. You know you don't
have to listen to this sort of thing. You can turn it off."

"Oh, it's so horrible, it's so dreadful," Irene was sobbing. "I've been 38
listening all day, and it's so depressing."

"Well, if it's so depressing, why do you listen to it? I bought this   39
damned radio to give you some pleasure," he said. "I paid a great deal
of money for it. I thought it might make you happy. I wanted to make
you happy."

"Don't, don't, don't, don't quarrel with me," she moaned, and laid   40
her head on his shoulder. "All the others have been quarreling all day.
Everybody's been quarreling. They're all worried about money. Mrs.
Hutchinson's mother is dying of cancer in Florida and they don't have
enough money to send her to the Mayo Clinic. At least, Mr. Hutchinson
says they don't have enough money. And some woman in this building
is having an affair with the handyman—with that hideous handyman.

It's too disgusting. And Mrs. Melville has heart trouble and Mr. Hendricks is going to lose his job in April and Mrs. Hendricks is horrid about the whole thing and that girl who plays the 'Missouri Waltz' is a whore, a common whore, and the elevator man has tuberculosis and Mr. Osborn has been beating Mrs. Osborn." She wailed, she trembled with grief and checked the stream of tears down her face with the heel of her palm.

"Well, why do you have to listen?" Jim asked again. "Why do you 41 have to listen to this stuff if it makes you so miserable?"

"Oh, don't, don't, don't," she cried. "Life is too terrible, too sordid 42 and awful. But we've never been like that, have we, darling? Have we? I mean, we've always been good and decent and loving to one another, haven't we? And we have two children, two beautiful children. Our lives aren't sordid, are they, darling? Are they?" She flung her arms around his neck and drew his face down to hers. "We're happy, aren't we, darling? We are happy, aren't we?"

"Of course we're happy," he said tiredly. He began to surrender 43 his resentment. "Of course we're happy. I'll have that damned radio fixed or taken away tomorrow." He stroked her soft hair. "My poor girl," he said.

"You love me, don't you?" she asked. "And we're not hypercritical 44 or worried about money or dishonest, are we?"

"No, darling," he said. 45

A man came in the morning and fixed the radio. Irene turned it on 46 cautiously and was happy to hear a California-wine commercial and a recording of Beethoven's Ninth Symphony, including Schiller's "Ode to Joy." She kept the radio on all day and nothing untoward came from the speaker.

A Spanish suite was being played when Jim came home. "Is every- 47 thing all right?" he asked. His face was pale, she thought. They had some cocktails and went in to dinner to the "Anvil. Chorus" from Il Trovatore. This was followed by Debussy's "La Mer."

"I paid the bill for the radio today," Jim said. "It cost four hundred 48 dollars. I hope you'll get some enjoyment out of it."

"Oh, I'm sure I will," Irene said. 49

"Four hundred dollars is a good deal more than I can afford," he 50 went on. "I wanted to get something that you'd enjoy. It's the last extravagance we'll be able to indulge in this year. I see that you haven't paid your clothing bills yet. I saw them on your dressing table." He looked directly at her. "Why did you tell me you'd paid them? Why did you lie to me?"

"I just didn't want you to worry, Jim," she said. She drank some 51 water. "I'll be able to pay my bills out of this month's allowance. There were the slipcovers last month, and that party."

"You've got to learn to handle the money I give you a little more 52 intelligently, Irene," he said. "You've got to understand that we won't have as much money this year as we had last. I had a very sobering talk with Mitchell today. No one is buying anything. We're spending all our time promoting new issues, and you know how long that takes. I'm not getting any younger, you know. I'm thirty-seven. My hair will be gray next year. I haven't done as well as I'd hoped to do. And I don't suppose things will get any better."

"Yes, dear," she said.   53

"We've got to start cutting down," Jim said. "We've got to think   54
of the children. To be perfectly frank with you, I worry about money a great deal. I'm not at all sure of the future. No one is. If anything should happen to me, there's the insurance, but that wouldn't go very far today. I've worked awfully hard to give you and the children a comfortable life," he said bitterly. "I don't like to see all of my energies, all of my youth, wasted in fur coats and radios and slipcovers and—"

"Please, Jim," she said. "Please. They'll hear us."   55

"Who'll hear us? Emma can't hear us."   56

"The radio."   57

"Oh, I'm sick!" he shouted. "I'm sick to death of your apprehen-   58
siveness. The radio can't hear us. Nobody can hear us. And what if they can hear us? Who cares?"

Irene got up from the table and went into the living room. Jim   59
went to the door and shouted at her from there. "Why are you so Christly all of a sudden? What's turned you overnight into a convent girl? You stole your mother's jewelry before they probated her will. You never gave your sister a cent of that money that was intended for her—not even when she needed it. You made Grace Howland's life miserable, and where was all your piety and your virtue when you went to that abortionist? I'll never forget how cool you were. You packed your bag and went off to have that child murdered as if you were going to Nassau. If you'd had any reasons, if you'd had any good reasons—"

Irene stood for a minute before the hideous cabinet, disgraced and   60
sickened, but she held her hand on the switch before she extinguished the music and the voices, hoping that the instrument might speak to her kindly, that she might hear the Sweeneys' nurse. Jim continued to shout at her from the door. The voice on the radio was suave and noncommittal. "An early-morning railroad disaster in Tokyo," the loudspeaker said, "killed twenty-nine people. A fire in a Catholic hospital near Buffalo for the care of blind children was extinguished early this morning by nuns. The temperature is forty-seven. The humidity is eighty-nine."

JOHN UPDIKE

Movie House

John Updike (1932–   ) is now known primarily as a writer of novels, especially four that explore the life of an anxiety-ridden suburban-
ite, Harry ("Rabbit") Angstrom. Updike's talents, however, are not
limited to fiction. After graduating summa cum laude in 1954 from
Harvard, where he edited the *Harvard Lampoon*, he studied painting
for a year at Oxford University's Ruskin School of Art. While in England, he began writing light verse for *The New Yorker*. His interest in
writing poems, light or serious, has never waned, and along with his
novels (sixteen), collections of short stories (twenty-one), and books
of essays (ten), he has published fifteen books of poetry. "Movie
House" is from *Telephone Poles and Other Poems* (1963), a book that
has troubled some readers and reviewers because they couldn't be
certain of its tone: Is this a writer inviting us to examine our souls or
a writer inviting us to smile, or can he be both at once?

View it, by day, from the back,   1
from the parking lot in the rear,
for from this angle only
the beautiful brick blankness can be grasped.
Monumentality
wears one face in all ages.

No windows intrude real light   2
into this temple of shades,
and the size of it,
the size of the great rear wall measures
the breadth of the dreams we have had here.
It dwarfs the village bank,
outlooms the town hall, and even in its decline
makes the bright-ceilinged supermarkets seem mean.

Stark closet of stealthy rapture,   3
vast introspective camera
wherein our most daring self-projections
were given familiar names:
stand, stand by your macadam lake
and tell the aeons of our extinction
that we too could house our gods,
could secrete a pyramid
to sight the stars by.

UNDERSTANDING

We find ourselves in our findings.

Understanding: Preview

Overview and Ideas for Writing

In the opening pages of his novel *Hard Times*, Charles Dickens presents us with two neatly contrasted characters. Sitting in a classroom are a girl named Sissy Jupe and a boy named Bitzer. Sissy is a picture of health, robust and tanned from her life with a troupe of traveling entertainers who specialize in tricks of horsemanship. And yet, though she has been surrounded by horses all her life and undoubtedly knows how to groom, feed, and ride them, she is stumped when the superintendent of the school, Thomas Gradgrind, asks her to define a horse. "Girl number twenty possessed of no facts in reference to one of the commonest animals!" Gradgrind announces, and turns to Bitzer, a pale student who may never have touched a horse, but who has learned the definition very well: "Quadruped. Gramnivorous. Forty teeth, namely twenty-four grinders, four eye-teeth, and twelve incisive. Sheds coat in the spring; in marshy country, sheds hoofs, too. Hoofs hard, but requiring to be shod by iron. Age known by marks in the mouth."

"Now, girl number twenty," Gradgrind says, "you know what a horse is."

In Gradgrind's mind, and in the minds of many other people, understanding means no more than the accumulation of facts. You sometimes hear politicians complaining about the number of students who don't know who the sixteenth president of the United States was or what year Columbus discovered America. But, as William G. Perry points out, higher education requires more than memorization of facts.

> College raises other questions: by whose calendar is it proper to say that Columbus discovered America in 1492? How, when, and by whom was the year 1 established in this calendar? What of other calendars? In view of the evidence for Leif Ericson's previous visit (and the American Indians), what historical ethnocentrism is suggested by the use of the word "discover" in this sentence? As for Leif Ericson, in accord with what assumptions do you order the evidence?

In college, we learn (as Samuel Scudder did from the great scientist Louis Agassiz) that "facts are stupid things . . . until brought into connection with some general law." We learn, in short, that facts don't speak for themselves and that there are sharp and legitimate differences in the ways people choose to speak about facts. We learn, for reasons Carol Bly articulates, that Sissy Jupe's understanding may be preferable to Bitzer's. We may learn, like Malcolm X, that tremendous freedom comes through understanding the meaning of words, or we may learn, as Adrienne Rich claims, that such freedom is often squelched, as it has been for women when education is shaped and stifled by the presence and approval of men.

In one way or another, each selection in this unit is about a style of understanding that goes beyond Bitzer's. Patricia Hampl, for instance, shows that writing a memoir "creates" a life for us. Frank Conroy talks about the way some experiences, puzzling at the time, become meaningful in retrospect: "The light bulb may appear over your head . . . but it may be a while before it actually goes on." Taking us to a remote island in the Pacific, anthropologist William L. Rodman reveals the levels of meaning that may accumulate around a conversation between people from different cultures. Annie Dillard explores the complex relationship between attention and visual understanding, Li-Young Lee draws meaning from the relationship between things and ideas, and George Orwell examines the relationship between language and thought. Susan Glaspell's "Trifles" is a mystery story in which some clues invisible to the male investigators are visible and eloquent to the women.

Several of the writers reflect directly on personal experiences that revealed to them some of the complexity of what we mean by understanding. You may want to do the same, looking back on an event or set of events that changed a naive assumption or that showed you how differently people may respond to the same fact. If you want to go beyond your personal experience, bear in mind that a college campus is a laboratory that aims to produce understanding. You may want to investigate why it succeeds or fails at its business. You could locate an official statement of your college's educational goals and report on how these goals shape students' experience. You could use interviews and observation to compare the view faculty members take of education with the view students take. Or you could investigate the accuracy of some of the authors' controversial assertions: Perry's statement that "in a university setting good bull is . . . of more value than 'facts,'" for example, or Bly's statement that we train people to solve small problems and to avoid "the weight of vast considerations." To write on such topics is not easy, of course, because it requires us to examine our own understanding of understanding itself.

FRANK CONROY

Think About It

Frank Conroy (1936–   ) was born in New York and received his
B.A. from Haverford College. Conroy's reputation as a writer came
with the publication of his autobiographical *Stop-Time* (1967), which
is both a picture of a family unraveling and a re-creation of the pains
and joys of early adolescence. Nineteen years later he published a
collection of short prose pieces, *Midair* (1986); during the intervening
years, Conroy was teaching and, he claims, "out doing errands." In
addition, he has contributed essays and stories to several periodicals,
particularly *The New Yorker*, and he selected the stories for *The Iowa
Award: The Best Stories from Twenty Years* (1991). Conroy is a jazz
pianist as well as a writer, often performing with a group at the
Georgetown Fish House in Washington, D.C. His most recent work,
Body and Soul (1993), is a novel about a musical prodigy. After serving
for several years as the director of the literature program of the National Endowment for the Arts, Conroy has become the director of the
Writer's Workshop at the University of Iowa. "Think About It" was
published in *Harper's* in November 1988 and was collected in *Best
American Essays of 1989*.

<table>
<tr><td>

After this opening para-
graph, Conroy does not men-
tion the Puerto Rican men
again. Why do you think he
included this story about
them? What relation does
this paragraph have to what
follows?

</td><td>

When I was sixteen I worked selling hot dogs
at a stand in the Fourteenth Street subway sta-
tion in New York City, one level above the trains
and one below the street, where the crowds
continually flowed back and forth. I worked
with three Puerto Rican men who could not
speak English. I had no Spanish, and although
we understood each other well with regard to
the tasks at hand, sensing and adjusting to each
other's body movements in the extremely con-

</td></tr>
</table>

fined space in which we operated, I felt isolated with no one to talk to.
On my break I came out from behind the counter and passed the time
with two old black men who ran a shoeshine stand in a dark corner of
the corridor. It was a poor location, half hidden by columns, and they
didn't have much business. I would sit with my back against the wall
while they stood or moved around their ancient elevated stand, talking
to each other or to me, but always staring into the distance as they did so.

As the weeks went by I realized that they never looked at anything
in their immediate vicinity—not at me or their stand or anybody who
might come within ten or fifteen feet. They did not look at approaching
customers once they were inside the perimeter. Save for the instant it
took to discern the color of the shoes, they did not even look at what
they were doing while they worked, but rubbed in polish, brushed, and

559

Notice how Conroy uses considerable detail to create a scene he did not understand. After you read to the end of this story, ask yourself what Conroy accomplishes in this paragraph by using these details.

buffed by feel while looking over their shoulders, into the distance, as if awaiting the arrival of an important person. Of course there wasn't all that much distance in the underground station, but their behavior was so focused and consistent they seemed somehow to transcend the physical. A powerful mood was created, and I came almost to believe that these men could see through walls, through girders, and around corners to whatever hyperspace it was where whoever it was they were waiting and watching for would finally emerge. Their scattered talk was hip, elliptical, and hinted at mysteries beyond my white boy's ken, but it was the staring off, the long, steady staring off, that had me hypnotized. I left for a better job, with handshakes from both of them, without understanding what I had seen.

At last, ten years later, Conroy understands the scene he has just described. Think of an incident in your own life that you did not understand until some time later.

Perhaps ten years later, after playing jazz with   3
black musicians in various Harlem clubs, hanging out uptown with a few young artists and intellectuals, I began to learn from them something of the extraordinarily varied and complex riffs and rituals embraced by different people to help themselves get through life in the ghetto. Fantasy of all kinds—from playful to dangerous—was in the very air of Harlem. It was the spice of uptown life.

You may find an interesting comparison to Conroy's situation and "light bulb" experience in the descriptions by Malcolm X of learning to read, by Annie Dillard of the blind learning to see, or by William Rodman of coming to understand communication in another culture.

Only then did I understand the two shoeshine   4
men. They were trapped in a demeaning situation in a dark corner in an underground corridor in a filthy subway system. Their continuous staring off was a kind of statement, a kind of dance. Our bodies are here, went the statement, but our souls are receiving nourishment from distant sources only we can see. They were powerful magic dancers, sorcerers almost, and thirty-five years later I can still feel the pressure of their spell.

Garland's response, "Sixths," may have been a simple answer, or it may have been a deliberate teaching move. Where have you seen this style of teaching, which leaves a student in the dark until that "light bulb" experience occurs? Read Samuel Scudder's essay for a description of a similar experience.

The light bulb may appear over your head, is   5
what I'm saying, but it may be a while before it actually goes on. Early in my attempts to learn jazz piano, I used to listen to recordings of a fine player named Red Garland, whose music I admired. I couldn't quite figure out what he was doing with his left hand, however; the chords eluded me. I went uptown to an obscure club where he was playing with his trio, caught him on his break, and simply asked him. "Sixths," he said cheerfully. And then he went away.

I didn't know what to make of it. The basic   6

Conroy says he was trying to "fit the information into what he already knew," which is one of the most basic processes of understanding. Describe how this statement applies to your understanding of something in your life, from listening to a biology lecture to reading this essay.

This selection focuses on the ability to arrive at an understanding of a situation or at a solution to a problem. But are answers always possible? Can you think of examples of situations you still do not understand or questions you will never be able to answer? In her essay, Carol Bly addresses this difference between being able to solve problems and being able to ponder the unsolvable ones.

jazz chord is the seventh, which comes in various configurations, but it is what it is. I was a self-taught pianist, pretty shaky on theory and harmony, and when he said sixths I kept trying to fit the information into what I already knew, and it didn't fit. But it stuck in my mind—a tantalizing mystery.

A couple of years later, when I began playing with a bass player, I discovered more or less by accident that if the bass played the root and I played a sixth based on the fifth note of the scale, a very interesting chord involving both instruments emerged. Ordinarily, I suppose I would have skipped over the matter and not paid much attention, but I remembered Garland's remark and so I stopped and spent a week or two working out the voicings, and greatly strengthened my foundations as a player. I had remembered what I hadn't understood, you might say, until my life caught up with the information and the light bulb went on.

SAMUEL SCUDDER

Learning to See

Samuel Scudder (1837–1911) was born in Boston and graduated from Williams College and Harvard University. At Harvard, Scudder studied with the celebrated zoologist and geologist Louis Agassiz. Known for laying the foundation for descriptive biology and as the leading American opponent of Darwin, Agassiz made Harvard the center for natural history instruction and research during the mid-nineteenth century. Adopting the scientific methods of Agassiz, Scudder became known for the incredible detail with which he worked. Considered the most productive biologist of his time, he described 630 species of insects and named 1,144 species of fossil insects. *The Butterflies of the Eastern United States and Canada* (1888–1889), his best-known work, is the result of thirty years of research on butterflies. Other works include

Catalog of Scientific Serials of All Countries 1633–1876 (1879) and *Nomen-
clator zoologicus* (1882–1884). "Learning to See" was first published
anonymously in *Every Saturday*, April 4, 1874.

It was more than fifteen years ago that I entered the laboratory of   1
Professor Agassiz, and told him I had enrolled my name in the Scientific
School as a student of natural history. He asked me a few questions
about my object in coming, my antecedents generally, the mode in
which I afterwards proposed to use the knowledge I might acquire,
and, finally, whether I wished to study any special branch. To the latter
I replied that, while I wished to be well grounded in all departments of
zoology, I purposed to devote myself specially to insects.

"When do you wish to begin?" he asked.   2

"Now," I replied.   3

This seemed to please him, and with an energetic "Very well!" he   4
reached from a shelf a huge jar of specimens in yellow alcohol.

"Take this fish," said he, "and look at it; we call it a haemulon; by 5
and by I will ask what you have seen."

With that he left me, but in a moment returned with explicit in-   6
structions as to the care of the object entrusted to me.

"No man is fit to be a naturalist," said he, "who does not know   7
how to take care of specimens."

I was to keep the fish before me in a tin tray, and occasionally   8
moisten the surface with alcohol from the jar, always taking care to
replace the stopper tightly. Those were not the days of ground-glass
stoppers and elegantly shaped exhibition jars; all the old students will
recall the huge neckless glass bottles with their leaky, wax-besmeared
corks, half eaten by insects, and begrimed with cellar dust. Entomology
was a cleaner science than ichthyology, but the example of the Professor, who had unhesitatingly plunged to the bottom of the jar to produce
the fish, was infectious; and though this alcohol had a "very ancient
and fishlike smell,"[1] I really dared not show any aversion within these
sacred precincts, and treated the alcohol as though it were pure water.
Still I was conscious of a passing feeling of disappointment, for gazing
at a fish did not commend itself to an ardent entomologist. My friends
at home, too, were annoyed when they discovered that no amount of
eau-de-Cologne would drown the perfume which haunted me like a
shadow.

In ten minutes I had seen all that could be seen in that fish, and   9
started in search of the Professor—who had, however, left the Museum;
and when I returned, after lingering over some of the odd animals
stored in the upper apartment, my specimen was dry all over. I dashed
the fluid over the fish as if to resuscitate the beast from a fainting-fit,

1. Shakespeare, *The Tempest*, II, ii, 25.

and looked with anxiety for a return of the normal sloppy appearance. This little excitement over, nothing was to be done but to return to a steadfast gaze at my mute companion. Half an hour passed—an hour—another hour; the fish began to look loathsome. I turned it over and around; looked it in the face—ghastly; from behind, beneath, above, sideways, at a three-quarters' view—just as ghastly. I was in despair; at an early hour I concluded that lunch was necessary; so, with infinite relief, the fish was carefully replaced in the jar, and for an hour I was free.

On my return, I learned that Professor Agassiz had been at the Museum, but had gone, and would not return for several hours. My fellow-students were too busy to be disturbed by continued conversation. Slowly I drew forth that hideous fish, and with a feeling of desperation again looked at it. I might not use a magnifying-glass; instruments of all kinds were interdicted. My two hands, my two eyes, and the fish; it seemed a most limited field. I pushed my finger down its throat to feel how sharp the teeth were. I began to count the scales in the different rows, until I was convinced that that was nonsense. At last a happy thought struck me—I would draw the fish; and now with surprise I began to discover new features in the creature. Just then the Professor returned. 10

"That is right," said he; "a pencil is one of the best of eyes. I am glad to notice, too, that you keep your specimen wet, and your bottle corked." 11

With these encouraging words, he added: 12

"Well, what is it like?" 13

He listened attentively to my brief rehearsal of the structure of parts whose names were still unknown to me: the fringed gill-arches and movable operculum; the pores of the head, fleshy lips and lidless eyes; the lateral line, the spinous fins and forked tail; the compressed and arched body. When I had finished, he waited as if expecting more, and then, with an air of disappointment: 14

"You have not looked very carefully; why," he continued more earnestly, "you haven't even seen one of the most conspicuous features of the animal, which is as plainly before your eyes as the fish itself; look again, look again!" and he left me to my misery. 15

I was piqued; I was mortified. Still more of that wretched fish! But now I set myself to my task with a will, and discovered one new thing after another, until I saw how just the Professor's criticism had been. The afternoon passed quickly; and when, toward its close, the Professor inquired: 16

"Do you see it yet?" 17

"No," I replied, "I am certain I do not, but I see how little I saw before." 18

"That is next best," said he, earnestly, "but I won't hear you now; 19

put away your fish and go home; perhaps you will be ready with a better answer in the morning. I will examine you before you look at the fish."

This was disconcerting. Not only must I think of my fish all night, studying, without the object before me, what this unknown but most visible feature might be; but also, without reviewing my discoveries, I must give an exact account of them the next day. I had a bad memory; so I walked home by Charles River in a distracted state, with my two perplexities. [20]

The cordial greeting from the Professor the next morning was reassuring; here was a man who seemed to be quite as anxious as I that I should see for myself what he saw. [21]

"Do you perhaps mean," I asked, "that the fish has symmetrical sides with paired organs?" [22]

His thoroughly pleased "Of course! of course!" repaid the wakeful hours of the previous night. After he had discoursed most happily and enthusiastically—as he always did—upon the importance of this point, I ventured to ask what I should do next. [23]

"Oh, look at your fish!" he said, and left me again to my own devices. In a little more than an hour he returned, and heard my new catalogue. [24]

"That is good, that is good!" he repeated; "but that is not all; go on"; and so for three long days he placed that fish before my eyes, forbidding me to look at anything else, or to use any artificial aid. "Look, look, look," was his repeated injunction. [25]

This was the best entomological lesson I ever had—a lesson whose influence has extended to the details of every subsequent study; a legacy the Professor has left to me, as he has left it to many others, of inestimable value, which we could not buy, with which we cannot part. [26]

A year afterward, some of us were amusing ourselves with chalking outlandish beasts on the Museum blackboard. We drew prancing starfishes; frogs in mortal combat; hydra-headed worms; stately crawfishes, standing on their tails, bearing aloft umbrellas; and grotesque fishes with gaping mouths and staring eyes. The Professor came in shortly after, and was as amused as any at our experiments. He looked at the fishes. [27]

"Haemulons, every one of them," he said; "Mr. ——— drew them." [28]

True; and to this day, if I attempt a fish, I can draw nothing but haemulons. [29]

The fourth day, a second fish of the same group was placed beside the first, and I was bidden to point out the resemblances and differences between the two; another and another followed, until the entire family lay before me, and a whole legion of jars covered the table and surrounding shelves; the odor had become a pleasant perfume; and even [30] now, the sight of an old, six-inch, worm-eaten cork brings fragrant memories.

The whole group of haemulons was thus brought in review; and, whether engaged upon the dissection of the internal organs, the preparation and examination of the bony framework, or the description of the various parts, Agassiz's training in the method of observing facts and their orderly arrangement was ever accompanied by the urgent exhortation not to be content with them.   31

"Facts are stupid things," he would say, "until brought into connection with some general law."   32

At the end of eight months, it was almost with reluctance that I left these friends and turned to insects; but what I had gained by this outside experience has been of greater value than years of later investigation in my favorite groups.   33

ANNIE DILLARD

Seeing

Annie Dillard (1945–   ) first came into prominence as a writer with the publication of her Pulitzer Prize–winning *Pilgrim at Tinker Creek* (1974), and many readers continue to think of her as a solitary, mystical nature writer in the tradition of Henry David Thoreau. In 1987 she complicated this impression when she published *An American Childhood,* an often humorous memoir in which she describes her awakening to both the social and natural worlds. Both books reveal the intensity of her powers of observation, powers that continue to dominate her writing. At Rollins College in Virginia she majored in English and creative writing but also studied theology "because of the great beauty of it." Like all theologians, Dillard is concerned about questions of pain, death, communion, rebirth, and renewal. The keenness of Dillard's vision and her mystical nature are reflected in "Seeing," which is excerpted from *Pilgrim at Tinker Creek.*

I chanced on a wonderful book by Marius von Senden, called *Space and Sight.* When Western surgeons discovered how to perform safe cataract operations, they ranged across Europe and America operating on dozens of men and women of all ages who had been blinded by cataracts since birth. Von Senden collected accounts of such cases; the histories are fascinating. Many doctors had tested their patients' sense perceptions and ideas of space both before and after the operations. The vast majority of patients, of both sexes and all ages, had, in von Sen-   1 den's opinion, no idea of space whatsoever. Form, distance, and size were so many meaningless syllables. A patient "had no idea of depth, confusing it with roundness." Before the operation a doctor would give a blind patient a cube and a sphere; the patient would tongue it or feel it with his hands, and name it correctly. After the operation the doctor would show the same objects to the patient without letting him touch them; now he had no clue whatsoever what he was seeing. One patient called lemonade "square" because it pricked on his tongue as a square shape pricked on the touch of his hands. Of another postoperative patient, the doctor writes, "I have found in her no notion of size, for example, not even within the narrow limits which she might have encompassed with the aid of touch. Thus when I asked her to show me how big her mother was, she did not stretch out her hands, but set her two index-fingers a few inches apart." Other doctors reported their patients' own statements to similar effect. "The room he was in . . . he knew to be but part of the house, yet he could not conceive that the whole house could look bigger"; "Those who are blind from birth . . . have no real conception of height or distance. A house that is a mile away is thought of as nearby, but requiring the taking of a lot of steps. . . . The elevator that whizzes him up and down gives no more sense of vertical distance than does the train of horizontal."

For the newly sighted, vision is pure sensation unencumbered by   2
meaning: "The girl went through the experience that we all go through and forget, the moment we are born. She saw, but it did not mean anything but a lot of different kinds of brightness." Again, "I asked the patient what he could see; he answered that he saw an extensive field of light, in which everything appeared dull, confused, and in motion. He could not distinguish objects." Another patient saw "nothing but a confusion of forms and colours." When a newly sighted girl saw photographs and paintings, she asked, " 'Why do they put those dark marks all over them?' 'Those aren't dark marks,' her mother explained, 'those are shadows. That is one of the ways the eye knows that things have shape. If it were not for shadows many things would look flat.' 'Well, that's how things do look,' Joan answered. 'Everything looks flat with dark patches.' "

But it is the patients' concepts of space that are most revealing. One   3
patient, according to his doctor, "practiced his vision in a strange fashion; thus he takes off one of his boots, throws it some way off in front of him, and then attempts to gauge the distance at which it lies; he takes a few steps towards the boot and tries to grasp it; on failing to reach it, he moves on a step or two and gropes for the boot until he finally gets hold of it." "But even at this stage, after three weeks' experience of seeing," von Senden goes on, " 'space,' as he conceives it, ends with visual space, i.e., with colour-patches that happen to bound his view. He does not yet have the notion that a larger object (a chair) can

mask a smaller one (a dog), or that the latter can still be present even though it is not directly seen."

In general the newly sighted see the world as a dazzle of color- 4 patches. They are pleased by the sensation of color, and learn quickly to name the colors, but the rest of seeing is tormentingly difficult. Soon after his operation a patient "generally bumps into one of these colour-patches and observes them to be substantial, since they resist him as tactual objects do. In walking about it also strikes him—or can if he pays attention—that he is continually passing in between the colours he sees, that he can go past a visual object, that a part of it then steadily disappears from view; and that in spite of this, however he twists and turns—whether entering the room from the door, for example, or returning back to it—he always has a visual space in front of him. Thus he gradually comes to realize that there is also a space behind him, which he does not see."

The mental effort involved in these reasonings proves overwhelm- 5 ing for many patients. It oppresses them to realize, if they ever do at all, the tremendous size of the world, which they had previously conceived of as something touchingly manageable. It oppresses them to realize that they have been visible to people all along, perhaps unattractively so, without their knowledge or consent. A disheartening number of them refuse to use their new vision, continuing to go over objects with their tongues, and lapsing into apathy and despair. "The child can see, but will not make use of his sight. Only when pressed can he with difficulty be brought to look at objects in his neighbourhood; but more than a foot away it is impossible to bestir him to the necessary effort." Of a twenty-one-year-old girl, the doctor relates, "Her unfortunate father, who had hoped for so much from this operation, wrote that his daughter carefully shuts her eyes whenever she wishes to go about the house, especially when she comes to a staircase, and that she is never happier or more at ease than when, by closing her eyelids, she relapses into her former state of total blindness." A fifteen-year-old boy, who was also in love with a girl at the asylum for the blind, finally blurted out, "No, really, I can't stand it any more; I want to be sent back to the asylum again. If things aren't altered, I'll tear my eyes out."

Some do learn to see, especially the young ones. But it changes 6 their lives. One doctor comments on "the rapid and complete loss of that striking and wonderful serenity which is characteristic only of those who have never yet seen." A blind man who learns to see is ashamed of his old habits. He dresses up, grooms himself, and tries to make a good impression. While he was blind he was indifferent to objects unless they were edible; now, "a sifting of values sets in . . . his thoughts and wishes are mightily stirred and some few of the patients are thereby led into dissimulation, envy, theft and fraud."

On the other hand, many newly sighted people speak well of the 7 world, and teach us how dull is our own vision. To one patient, a human hand, unrecognized, is "something bright and then holes." Shown a bunch of grapes, a boy calls out, "It is dark, blue and shiny. . . . It isn't smooth, it has bumps and hollows." A little girl visits a garden. "She is greatly astonished, and can scarcely be persuaded to answer, stands speechless in front of the tree, which she only names on taking hold of it, and then as 'the tree with the lights on it.' " Some delight in their sight and give themselves over to the visual world. Of a patient just after her bandages were removed, her doctor writes, "The first things to attract her attention were her own hands; she looked at them very closely, moved them repeatedly to and fro, bent and stretched the fingers, and seemed greatly astonished at the sight." One girl was eager to tell her blind friend that "men do not really look like trees at all," and astounded to discover that her every visitor had an utterly different face. Finally, a twenty-two-year-old girl was dazzled by the world's brightness and kept her eyes shut for two weeks. When at the end of that time she opened her eyes again, she did not recognize any objects, but, "the more she now directed her gaze upon everything about her, the more it could be seen how an expression of gratification and as-tonishment overspread her features; she repeatedly exclaimed: 'Oh God! How beautiful!' "

I saw color-patches for weeks after I read this wonderful book. It 8 was summer; the peaches were ripe in the valley orchards. When I woke in the morning, color-patches wrapped round my eyes, intri-cately, leaving not one unfilled spot. All day long I walked among shifting color-patches that parted before me like the Red Sea and closed again in silence, transfigured, wherever I looked back. Some patches swelled and loomed, while others vanished utterly, and dark marks flitted at random over the whole dazzling sweep. But I couldn't sustain the illusion of flatness. I've been around for too long. Form is con-demned to an eternal danse macabre[1] with meaning: I couldn't unpeach the peaches. Nor can I remember ever having seen without understand-ing; the color-patches of infancy are lost. My brain then must have been smooth as any balloon. I'm told I reached for the moon; many babies do. But the color-patches of infancy swelled as meaning filled them; they arrayed themselves in solemn ranks down distances which unrolled and stretched before me like a plain. The moon rocketed away. I live now in a world of shadows that shape and distance color, a world where space makes a kind of terrible sense. What gnosticism[2] is this, and what physics? The fluttering patch I saw in my nursery window—

1. Dance of death.
2. Belief in the ability to transcend matter through faith, originating with the Gnostics of the early Christian era who believed Christ was noncorporeal.

silver and green and shape-shifting blue—is gone; a row of Lombardy poplars takes its place, mute, across the distant lawn. That humming oblong creature pale as light that stole along the walls of my room at night, stretching exhilaratingly around the corners, is gone, too, gone the night I ate of the bittersweet fruit, put two and two together and puckered forever my brain. Martin Buber[3] tells this tale: "Rabbi Mendel once boasted to his teacher Rabbi Elimelekh that evenings he saw the angel who rolls away the light before the darkness, and mornings the angel who rolls away the darkness before the light. 'Yes,' said Rabbi Elimelekh, 'in my youth I saw that too. Later on you don't see these things any more.' "

Why didn't someone hand those newly sighted people paints and brushes from the start, when they still didn't know what anything was? Then maybe we all could see color-patches too, the world unraveled from reason, Eden before Adam gave names. The scales would drop from my eyes; I'd see trees like men walking; I'd run down the road against all orders, hallooing and leaping. 9

Seeing is of course very much a matter of verbalization. Unless I call my attention to what passes before my eyes, I simply won't see it. It is, as Ruskin[4] says, "not merely unnoticed, but in the full, clear sense of the word, unseen." My eyes alone can't solve analogy tests using figures, the ones which show, with increasing elaborations, a big square, then a small square in a big square, then a big triangle, and expect me to find a small triangle in a big triangle. I have to say the words, describe what I'm seeing. If Tinker Mountain erupted, I'd be likely to notice. But if I want to notice the lesser cataclysms of valley life, I have to maintain in my head a running description of the present. It's not that I'm observant; it's just that I talk too much. Otherwise, especially in a strange place, I'll never know what's happening. Like a blind man at the ball game, I need a radio. 10

When I see this way I analyze and pry. I hurl over logs and roll away stones; I study the bank a square foot at a time, probing and tilting my head. Some days when a mist covers the mountains, when the muskrats won't show and the microscope's mirror shatters, I want to climb up the blank blue dome as a man would storm the inside of a circus tent, wildly, dangling, and with a steel knife claw a rent in the top, peep, and, if I must, fall. 11

But there is another kind of seeing that involves a letting go. When I see this way I sway transfixed and emptied. The difference between the two ways of seeing is the difference between walking with and 12

3. Austrian existential philosopher and Judaic scholar (1878–1965).
4. John Ruskin (1819–1900), a British art critic and essayist.

without a camera. When I walk with a camera, I walk from shot to shot, reading the light on a calibrated meter. When I walk without a camera, my own shutter opens, and the moment's light prints on my own silver gut. When I see this second way I am above all an unscrupulous observer.

It was sunny one evening last summer at Tinker Creek; the sun   13
was low in the sky, upstream. I was sitting on the sycamore log bridge with the sunset at my back, watching the shiners the size of minnows who were feeding over the muddy sand in skittery schools. Again and again, one fish, then another, turned for a split second across the current and flash! the sun shot out from its silver side. I couldn't watch for it. It was always just happening somewhere else, and it drew my vision just as it disappeared: flash, like a sudden dazzle of the thinnest blade, a sparking over a dun and olive ground at chance intervals from every direction. Then I noticed white specks, some sort of pale petals, small, floating from under my feet on the creek's surface, very slow and steady. So I blurred my eyes and gazed towards the brim of my hat and saw a new world. I saw the pale white circles roll up, roll up, like the world's turning, mute and perfect, and I saw the linear flashes, gleaming silver, like stars being born at random down a rolling scroll of time. Something broke and something opened. I filled up like a new wineskin. I breathed an air like light; I saw a light like water. I was the lip of a fountain the creek filled forever; I was ether, the leaf in the zephyr; I was flesh-flake, feather, bone.

When I see this way I see truly. As Thoreau says, I return to my   14
senses. I am the man who watches the baseball game in silence in an empty stadium. I see the game purely; I'm abstracted and dazed. When it's all over and the white-suited players lope off the green field to their shadowed dugouts, I leap to my feet; I cheer and cheer.

But I can't go out and try to see this way. I'll fail, I'll go mad. All   15
I can do is try to gag the commentator, to hush the noise of useless interior babble that keeps me from seeing just as surely as a newspaper dangled before my eyes. The effort is really a discipline requiring a lifetime of dedicated struggle; it marks the literature of saints and monks of every order East and West, under every rule and no rule, discalced[5] and shod. The world's spiritual geniuses seem to discover universally that the mind's muddy river, this ceaseless flow of trivia and trash, cannot be dammed, and that trying to dam it is a waste of effort that might lead to madness. Instead you must allow the muddy river to flow unheeded in the dim channels of consciousness; you raise your sights;

5. Barefooted, as monks often are.

you look along it, mildly, acknowledging its presence without interest and gazing beyond it into the realm of the real where subjects and objects act and rest purely, without utterance. "Launch into the deep," says Jacques Ellul,[6] "and you shall see."

The secret of seeing is, then, the pearl of great price. If I thought [16] he could teach me to find it and keep it forever I would stagger barefoot across a hundred deserts after any lunatic at all. But although the pearl may be found, it may not be sought. The literature of illumination reveals this above all: although it comes to those who wait for it, it is always, even to the most practiced and adept, a gift and a total surprise. I return from one walk knowing where the killdeer nests in the field by the creek and the hour the laurel blooms. I return from the same walk a day later scarcely knowing my own name. Litanies hum in my ears; my tongue flaps in my mouth Ailinon, alleluia![7] I cannot cause light; the most I can do is try to put myself in the path of its beam. It is possible, in deep space, to sail on solar wind. Light, be it particle or wave, has force: you rig a giant sail and go. The secret of seeing is to sail on solar wind. Hone and spread your spirit till you yourself are a sail, whetted, translucent, broadside to the merest puff.

When her doctor took her bandages off and led her into the garden, [17] the girl who was no longer blind saw "the tree with the lights in it." It was for this tree I searched through the peach orchards of summer, in the forests of fall and down winter and spring for years. Then one day I was walking along Tinker Creek thinking of nothing at all and I saw the tree with the lights in it. I saw the backyard cedar where the mourning doves roost charged and transfigured, each cell buzzing with flame. I stood on the grass with the lights in it, grass that was wholly fire, utterly focused and utterly dreamed. It was less like seeing than like being for the first time seen, knocked breathless by a powerful glance. The flood of fire abated, but I'm still spending the power. Gradually the lights went out in the cedar, the colors died, the cells unflamed and disappeared. I was still ringing. I had been my whole life a bell, and never knew it until at that moment I was lifted and struck. I have since only very rarely seen the tree with the lights in it. The vision comes and goes, mostly goes, but I live for it, for the moment when the mountains open and a new light roars in spate through the crack, and the mountains slam.

6. French writer on law, technology, ethics, and theology (1912–   ).
7. Dillard juxtaposes words suggesting an ancient Greek dirge and an ancient Hebrew hymn of praise or thanksgiving.

Learning to Read

Malcolm X (1925–1965) was born Malcolm Little in Omaha, Nebraska, the son of a Baptist minister who was brutally murdered by a
group of white supremacists who were enraged by his black separatist
views. After moving from town to town, the family settled in Detroit,
Michigan, where Malcolm dropped out of school and excelled at many
illicit activities that eventually earned him the name "Detroit Red." In
1946 he was arrested and sent to Charleston State Prison for robbery.
After being transferred to the Norfolk Prison Colony in 1948, Malcolm
met a convicted burglar, Bimbi, who encouraged him to "read books
with intellectual vitamins." During these years Malcolm also became
a follower of the Black Muslims and began corresponding with its
leader, Elijah Muhammad. After his release from prison in 1952, Malcolm became closely associated with Muhammad, but strife between
the two steadily increased. After touring Mecca, the birthplace of the
Muslim prophet Muhammad, Malcolm renounced his separatist views
and began advocating unity among all people. His break from the
Black Muslims proved deadly, however; and in 1965 he was shot and
killed during a speech he was giving in a Harlem ballroom. Since his
death, Malcolm X has been recognized as one of the foremost figures
in the African-American movement for equality. The following excerpt
is from *The Autobiography of Malcolm X* (1964).

I did write to Elijah Muhammad. He lived in Chicago at that time,   1
at 6116 South Michigan Avenue. At least twenty-five times I must have
written that first one-page letter to him, over and over. I was trying to
make it both legible and understandable. I practically couldn't read my
handwriting myself; it shames even to remember it. My spelling and
my grammar were as bad, if not worse. Anyway, as well as I could
express it, I said I had been told about him by my brothers and sisters,
and I apologized for my poor letter.

Mr. Muhammad sent me a typed reply. It had an all but electrical   2
effect upon me to see the signature of the "Messenger of Allah." After
he welcomed me into the "true knowledge," he gave me something to
think about. The black prisoner, he said, symbolized white society's
crime of keeping black men oppressed and deprived and ignorant, and
unable to get decent jobs, turning them into criminals.

He told me to have courage. He even enclosed some money for me,   3
a five-dollar bill. Mr. Muhammad sends money all over the country to
prison inmates who write to him, probably to this day.

Regularly my family wrote to me, "Turn to Allah . . . pray to the   4
East."

The hardest test I ever faced in my life was praying. You understand. 5
My comprehending, my believing the teachings of Mr. Muhammad had
only required my mind's saying to me, "That's right!" or "I never
thought of that."

But bending my knees to pray—that *act*—well, that took me a 6
week.

You know what my life had been. Picking a lock to rob someone's 7
house was the only way my knees had ever been bent before.

I had to force myself to bend my knees. And waves of shame and 8
embarrassment would force me back up.

For evil to bend its knees, admitting its guilt, to implore the forgive- 9
ness of God, is the hardest thing in the world. It's easy for me to see
and to say that now. But then, when I was the personification of evil,
I was going through it. Again, again, I would force myself back down
into the praying-to-Allah posture. When finally I was able to make
myself stay down—I didn't know what to say to Allah.

For the next years, I was the nearest thing to a hermit in the Norfolk 10
Prison Colony. I never have been more busy in my life. I still marvel
at how swiftly my previous life's thinking pattern slid away from me,
like snow off a roof. It is as though someone else I knew of had lived
by hustling and crime. I would be startled to catch myself thinking in
a remote way of my earlier self as another person.

The things I felt, I was pitifully unable to express in the one-page 11
letter that went every day to Mr. Elijah Muhammad. And I wrote at
least one more daily letter, replying to one of my brothers and sisters.
Every letter I received from them added something to my knowledge
of the teachings of Mr. Muhammad. I would sit for long periods and
study his photographs.

I've never been one for inaction. Everything I've ever felt strongly 12
about, I've done something about. I guess that's why, unable to do
anything else, I soon began writing to people I had known in the hustling world, such as Sammy the Pimp, John Hughes, the gambling
house owner, the thief Jumpsteady, and several dope peddlers. I wrote
them all about Allah and Islam and Mr. Elijah Muhammad. I had no
idea where most of them lived. I addressed their letters in care of the
Harlem or Roxbury bars and clubs where I'd known them.

I never got a single reply. The average hustler and criminal was too 13
uneducated to write a letter. I have known many slick, sharp-looking
hustlers, who would have you think they had an interest in Wall Street;
privately, they would get someone else to read a letter if they received
one. Besides, neither would I have replied to anyone writing me something as wild as "the white man is the devil."

What certainly went on the Harlem and Roxbury wires was that 14
Detroit Red was going crazy in stir, or else he was trying some hype to
shake up the warden's office.

During the years that I stayed in the Norfolk Prison Colony, never   15
did any official directly say anything to me about those letters, although,
of course, they all passed through the prison censorship. I'm sure, however, they monitored what I wrote to add to the files which every state
and federal prison keeps on the conversion of Negro inmates by the
teachings of Mr. Elijah Muhammad.

But at that time, I felt that the real reason was that the white man   16
knew that he was the devil.

Later on, I even wrote to the Mayor of Boston, to the Governor of   17
Massachusetts, and to Harry S. Truman. They never answered; they
probably never even saw my letters. I handscratched to them how the
white man's society was responsible for the black man's condition in
this wilderness of North America.

It was because of my letters that I happened to stumble upon start-   18
ing to acquire some kind of a homemade education.

I became increasingly frustrated at not being able to express what   19
I wanted to convey in letters that I wrote, especially those to Mr. Elijah
Muhammad. In the street, I had been the most articulate hustler out
there—I had commanded attention when I said something. But now,
trying to write simple English, I not only wasn't articulate, I wasn't
even functional. How would I sound writing in slang, the way I would
say it, something such as, "Look, daddy, let me pull your coat about a
cat, Elijah Muhammad—"

Many who today hear me somewhere in person, or on television,   20
or those who read something I've said, will think I went to school far
beyond the eighth grade. This impression is due entirely to my prison
studies.

It had really begun back in the Charlestown Prison, when Bimbi   21
first made me feel envy of his stock of knowledge. Bimbi had always
taken charge of any conversation he was in, and I had tried to emulate
him. But every book I picked up had few sentences which didn't contain
anywhere from one to nearly all of the words that might as well have
been in Chinese. When I just skipped those words, of course, I really
ended up with little idea of what the book said. So I had come to the
Norfolk Prison Colony still going through only book-reading motions.
Pretty soon, I would have quit even these motions, unless I had received
the motivation that I did.

I saw that the best thing I could do was get hold of a dictionary—to   22
study, to learn some words. I was lucky enough to reason also that I
should try to improve my penmanship. It was sad. I couldn't even write
in a straight line. It was both ideas together that moved me to request
a dictionary along with some tablets and pencils from the Norfolk Prison
Colony school.

I spent two days just riffling uncertainly through the dictionary's   23 pages. I'd never realized so many words existed! I didn't know *which* words I needed to learn. Finally, just to start some kind of action, I began copying.

In my slow, painstaking, ragged handwriting, I copied into my 24 tablet everything printed on that first page, down to the punctuation marks.

I believe it took me a day. Then, aloud, I read back, to myself, 25 everything I'd written on the tablet. Over and over, aloud, to myself, I read my own handwriting.

I woke up the next morning, thinking about those words— 26 immensely proud to realize that not only had I written so much at one time, but I'd written words that I never knew were in the world. Moreover, with a little effort, I also could remember what many of these words meant. I reviewed the words whose meanings I didn't remember. Funny thing, from the dictionary first page right now, that ''aardvark'' springs to my mind. The dictionary had a picture of it, a long-tailed, long-eared, burrowing African mammal, which lives off termites caught by sticking out its tongue as an anteater does for ants.

I was so fascinated that I went on—I copied the dictionary's next 27 page. And the same experience came when I studied that. With every succeeding page, I also learned of people and places and events from history. Actually the dictionary is like a miniature encyclopedia. Finally the dictionary's A section had filled a whole tablet—and I went on into the B's. That was the way I started copying what eventually became the entire dictionary. It went a lot faster after so much practice helped me to pick up handwriting speed. Between what I wrote in my tablet, and writing letters, during the rest of my time in prison I would guess I wrote a million words.

I suppose it was inevitable that as my word-base broadened, I could 28 for the first time pick up a book and read and now begin to understand what the book was saying. Anyone who has read a great deal can imagine the new world that opened. Let me tell you something: from then until I left that prison, in every free moment I had, if I was not reading in the library, I was reading on my bunk. You couldn't have gotten me out of books with a wedge. Between Mr. Muhammad's teachings, my correspondence, my visitors—usually Ella and Reginald[1]—and my reading of books, months passed without my even thinking about being imprisoned. In fact, up to then, I never had been so truly free in my life.

The Norfolk Prison Colony's library was in the school building. A 29 variety of classes was taught there by instructors who came from such

---

1. Ella is Malcolm's half-sister; Reginald is his brother.

places as Harvard and Boston universities. The weekly debates between inmate teams were also held in the school building. You would be astonished to know how worked up convict debaters and audiences would get over subjects like "Should Babies Be Fed Milk?"

Available on the prison library's shelves were books on just about 30 every general subject. Much of the big private collection that Parkhurst[2] had willed to the prison was still in crates and boxes in the back of the library—thousands of old books. Some of them looked ancient: covers faded, old-time parchment-looking binding. Parkhurst, I've mentioned, seemed to have been principally interested in history and religion. He had the money and the special interest to have a lot of books that you wouldn't have in general circulation. Any college library would have been lucky to get that collection.

As you can imagine, especially in a prison where there was heavy 31 emphasis on rehabilitation, an inmate was smiled upon if he demonstrated an unusually intense interest in books. There was a sizable number of well-read inmates, especially the popular debaters. Some were said by many to be practically walking encyclopedias. They were almost celebrities. No university would ask any student to devour literature as I did when this new world opened to me, of being able to read and *understand.*

I read more in my room than in the library itself. An inmate who 32 was known to read a lot could check out more than the permitted maximum number of books. I preferred reading in the total isolation of my own room.

When I had progressed to really serious reading, every night at 33 about ten P.M. I would be outraged with the "lights out." It always seemed to catch me right in the middle of something engrossing.

Fortunately, right outside my door was a corridor light that cast a 34 glow into my room. The glow was enough to read by, once my eyes adjusted to it. So when "lights out" came, I would sit on the floor where I could continue reading in that glow.

At one-hour intervals the night guards paced past every room. Each 35 time I heard the approaching footsteps, I jumped into bed and feigned sleep. And as soon as the guard passed, I got back out of bed onto the floor area of that light-glow, where I would read for another fifty-eight minutes—until the guard approached again. That went on until three or four every morning. Three or four hours of sleep a night was enough for me. Often in the years in the streets I had slept less than that.

2. Charles Henry Parkhurst (1842–1933): Presbyterian clergyman, reformer, and author who was the president of the Society for the Prevention of Crime in the 1890s.

ADRIENNE RICH

When We Dead Awaken: Writing as Re-Vision

Adrienne Rich (1929–   ) is one of the foremost poets of our time and one who has changed greatly over the course of her poetic career. Her first volume of poetry, *A Change of World* (1951), which won the Yale Series of Younger Poets award, was filled with formal, cautious verse that allowed her to handle her emotions, as she later said, with asbestos gloves. Twenty-two years later, her ninth volume, *Diving into the Wreck* (1973), won the National Book Award and contributed to a storm of controversy surrounding the author, who had become one of America's most influential and outspoken feminists. It is typical of Rich that she refused to accept the award as an individual but accepted it on behalf of women everywhere and contributed the stipend to charity. Rich continues to publish, lecture, and teach very actively. Her recent volumes include *Your Native Land, Your Life* (1986) and *Blood, Bread, and Poetry: Selected Prose 1979–1986* (1986). In *What Is Found There: Notebooks on Poetry and Politics* (1993), Rich weds her art with her activism, asserting, as she did in a recent interview, that "poetry expresses messages beyond the words it is contained in; it speaks our desires; it reminds us of what we lack, of our need, and of our hunger. It keeps us dissatisfied." "When We Dead Awaken" was first published in *College English* (October 1972) and is collected in *On Lies, Secrets, and Silence* (1979).

Ibsen's *When We Dead Awaken* is a play about the use that the male artist and thinker—in the process of creating culture as we know it—has made of women, in his life and in his work; and about a woman's slow struggling awakening to the use to which her life has been put. Bernard Shaw wrote in 1900 of this play:

> [Ibsen] shows us that no degradation ever devized or permitted is as disastrous as this degradation; that through it women can die into luxuries for men and yet can kill them; that men and women are becoming conscious of this; and that what remains to be seen as perhaps the most interesting of all imminent social developments is what will happen "when we dead awaken." [1]

It's exhilarating to be alive in a time of awakening consciousness; it can also be confusing, disorienting, and painful. This awakening of

1. G. B. Shaw, *The Quintessence of Ibsenism* (New York: Hill & Wang, 1922), p. 139.

dead or sleeping consciousness has already affected the lives of millions of women, even those who don't know it yet. It is also affecting the lives of men, even those who deny its claims upon them. The argument will go on whether an oppressive economic class system is responsible for the oppressive nature of male/female relations, or whether, in fact, patriarchy—the domination of males—is the original model of oppression on which all others are based. But in the last few years the women's movement has drawn inescapable and illuminating connections between our sexual lives and our political institutions. The sleepwalkers are coming awake, and for the first time this awakening has a collective reality; it is no longer such a lonely thing to open one's eyes.

Re-vision—the act of looking back, of seeing with fresh eyes, of   3
entering an old text from a new critical direction—is for women more than a chapter in cultural history: it is an act of survival. Until we can understand the assumptions in which we are drenched we cannot know ourselves. And this drive to self-knowledge, for women, is more than a search for identity: it is part of our refusal of the self-destructiveness of male-dominated society. A radical critique of literature, feminist in its impulse, would take the work first of all as a clue to how we live, how we have been living, how we have been led to imagine ourselves, how our language has trapped as well as liberated us, how the very act of naming has been till now a male prerogative, and how we can begin to see and name—and therefore live—afresh. A change in the concept of sexual identity is essential if we are not going to see the old political order reassert itself in every new revolution. We need to know the writing of the past, and know it differently than we have ever known it; not to pass on a tradition but to break its hold over us.

For writers, and at this moment for women writers in particular,   4
there is the challenge and promise of a whole new psychic geography to be explored. But there is also a difficult and dangerous walking on the ice, as we try to find language and images for a consciousness we are just coming into, and with little in the past to support us. I want to talk about some aspects of this difficulty and this danger.

Jane Harrison, the great classical anthropologist, wrote in 1914 in   5
a letter to her friend Gilbert Murray:

> By the by, about "Women," it has bothered me often—why do women never want to write poetry about Man as a sex—why is Woman a dream and a terror to man and not the other way around? . . . Is it mere convention and propriety, or something deeper?[2]

I think Jane Harrison's question cuts deep into the myth-making tradition, the romantic tradition; deep into what women and men have

---

2. J. G. Stewart, *Jane Ellen Harrison: A Portrait from Letters* (London: Merlin, 1959), p. 140.

been to each other; and deep into the psyche of the woman writer. Thinking about that question, I began thinking of the work of two twentieth-century women poets, Sylvia Plath and Diane Wakoski. It strikes me that in the work of both Man appears as, if not a dream, a fascination and a terror; and that the source of the fascination and the terror is, simply, Man's power—to dominate, tyrannize, choose, or reject the woman. The charisma of Man seems to come purely from his power over her and his control of the world by force, not from anything fertile or life-giving in him. And, in the work of both these poets, it is finally the woman's sense of *herself*—embattled, possessed—that gives the poetry its dynamic charge, its rhythms of struggle, need, will, and female energy. Until recently this female anger and this furious awareness of the Man's power over her were not available materials to the female poet, who tended to write of Love as the source of her suffering, and to view that victimization by Love as an almost inevitable fate. Or, like Marianne Moore and Elizabeth Bishop,[3] she kept sexuality at a measured and chiseled distance in her poems.

One answer to Jane Harrison's question has to be that historically   6 men and women have played very different parts in each others' lives. Where woman has been a luxury for man, and has served as the painter's model and the poet's muse, but also as comforter, nurse, cook, bearer of his seed, secretarial assistant, and copyist of manuscripts, man has played a quite different role for the female artist. Henry James repeats an incident which the writer Prosper Mérimée described, of how, while he was living with George Sand,

> he once opened his eyes, in the raw winter dawn, to see his companion, in a dressing-gown, on her knees before the domestic hearth, a candlestick beside her and a red *madras* round her head, making bravely, with her own hands the fire that was to enable her to sit down betimes to urgent pen and paper. The story represents him as having felt that the spectacle chilled his ardor and tried his taste; her appearance was unfortunate, her occupation an inconsequence, and her industry a reproof—the result of all which was a lively irritation and an early rupture.[4]

The specter of this kind of male judgment, along with the misnaming and thwarting of her needs by a culture controlled by males, has created problems for the woman writer: problems of contact with herself, problems of language and style, problems of energy and survival.

In rereading Virginia Woolf's *A Room of One's Own* (1929)[5] for the   7 first time in some years, I was astonished at the sense of effort, of

---

3. Marianne Moore (1887–1972) and Elizabeth Bishop (1911–1979) are two of the most prominent American poets of the twentieth century.
4. Henry James, "Notes on Novelists," in *Selected Literary Criticism of Henry James*, Morris Shapira, ed. (London: Heinemann, 1963), pp. 157–58.
5. Virginia Woolf: see "Professions for Women" (pp. 93–98).

pains taken, of dogged tentativeness, in the tone of that essay. And I recognized that tone. I had heard it often enough, in myself and in other women. It is the tone of a woman almost in touch with her anger, who is determined not to appear angry, who is *willing* herself to be calm, detached, and even charming in a roomful of men where things have been said which are attacks on her very integrity. Virginia Woolf is addressing an audience of women, but she is acutely conscious—as she always was—of being overheard by men: by Morgan and Lytton and Maynard Keynes[6] and for that matter by her father, Leslie Stephen.[7] She drew the language out into an exacerbated thread in her determination to have her own sensibility yet protect it from those masculine presences. Only at rare moments in that essay do you hear the passion in her voice; she was trying to sound as cool as Jane Austen, as Olympian as Shakespeare, because that is the way the men of the culture thought a writer should sound.

No male writer has written primarily or even largely for women, or with the sense of women's criticism as a consideration when he chooses his materials, his theme, his language. But to a lesser or greater extent, every woman writer has written for men even when, like Virginia Woolf, she was supposed to be addressing women. If we have come to the point when this balance might begin to change, when women can stop being haunted, not only by "convention and propriety" but by internalized fears of being and saying themselves, then it is an extraordinary moment for the woman writer—and reader.

I have hesitated to do what I am going to do now, which is to use myself as an illustration. For one thing, it's a lot easier and less dangerous to talk about other women writers. But there is something else. Like Virginia Woolf, I am aware of the women who are not with us here because they are washing the dishes and looking after the children. Nearly fifty years after she spoke, that fact remains largely unchanged. And I am thinking also of women whom she left out of the picture altogether—women who are washing other people's dishes and caring for other people's children, not to mention women who went on the streets last night in order to feed their children. We seem to be special

6. Novelist and essayist Edward Morgan Forster (1879–1970), biographer and essayist Lytton Strachey (1880–1932), and economist Maynard Keynes (1883–1946) were, along with Woolf, members of the Bloomsbury Group, a circle of English writers and intellectuals who met for several years at the beginning of this century in the Bloomsbury section of London.

7. *A.R., 1978:* This intuition of mine was corroborated when, early in 1978, I read the correspondence between Woolf and Dame Ethel Smyth (Henry W. and Albert A. Berg Collection, The New York Public Library, Astor, Lenox and Tilden Foundations); in a letter dated June 8, 1933, Woolf speaks of having kept her own personality out of *A Room of One's Own* lest she not be taken seriously: ". . . how personal, so will they say, rubbing their hands with glee, women always are; *I even hear them as I write.*" (Italics mine.)

women here, we have liked to think of ourselves as special, and we have known that men would tolerate, even romanticize us as special, as long as our words and actions didn't threaten their privilege of tolerating or rejecting us and our work according to *their* ideas of what a special woman ought to be. An important insight of the radical women's movement has been how divisive and how ultimately destructive is this myth of the special woman, who is also the token woman. Every one of us here in this room has had great luck—we are teachers, writers, academicians; our own gifts could not have been enough, for we all know women whose gifts are buried or aborted. Our struggles can have meaning and our privileges—however precarious under patriarchy—can be justified only if they can help to change the lives of women whose gifts—and whose very being—continue to be thwarted and silenced.

My own luck was being born white and middle-class into a house   10
full of books, with a father who encouraged me to read and write. So for about twenty years I wrote for a particular man, who criticized and praised me and made me feel I was indeed "special." The obverse side of this, of course, was that I tried for a long time to please him, or rather, not to displease him. And then of course there were other men— writers, teachers—the Man, who was not a terror or a dream but a literary master and a master in other ways less easy to acknowledge. And there were all those poems about women, written by men: it seemed to be a given that men wrote poems and women frequently inhabited them. These women were almost always beautiful, but threatened with the loss of beauty, the loss of youth—the fate worse than death. Or, they were beautiful and died young, like Lucy and Lenore.[8] Or, the woman was like Maud Gonne,[9] cruel and disastrously mistaken, and the poem reproached her because she had refused to become a luxury for the poet.

A lot is being said today about the influence that the myths and   11
images of women have on all of us who are products of culture. I think it has been a peculiar confusion to the girl or woman who tries to write because she is peculiarly susceptible to language. She goes to poetry or fiction looking for *her* way of being in the world, since she too has been putting words and images together; she is looking eagerly for guides, maps, possibilities; and over and over in the "words' masculine persuasive force" of literature she comes up against something that negates everything she is about: she meets the image of Woman in books writ-

8. Lucy, "a child of nature," is the idealized subject of William Wordsworth's "Lucy" poems (1799); Lenore is the beautiful maiden whose death is lamented in Edgar Allan Poe's poem "Lenore."
9. Maud Gonne (1866–1953): her beauty and activism in Irish politics inspired the poet W. B. Yeats, who, though she continually refused him, proposed to her several times.

ten by men. She finds a terror and a dream, she finds a beautiful pale face, she finds La Belle Dame Sans Merci, she finds Juliet or Tess or Salomé,[10] but precisely what she does not find is that absorbed, drudging, puzzled, sometimes inspired creature, herself, who sits at a desk trying to put words together.

So what does she do? What did I do? I read the older women poets with their peculiar keenness and ambivalence: Sappho, Christina Rossetti, Emily Dickinson, Elinor Wylie, Edna Millay, H.D. I discovered that the woman poet most admired at the time (by men) was Marianne Moore, who was maidenly, elegant, intellectual, discreet. But even in reading these women I was looking in them for the same things I had found in the poetry of men, because I wanted women poets to be the equals of men, and to be equal was still confused with sounding the same.

I know that my style was formed first by male poets: by the men I was reading as an undergraduate—Frost, Dylan Thomas, Donne, Auden, MacNiece, Stevens, Yeats. What I chiefly learned from them was craft.[11] But poems are like dreams: in them you put what you don't know you know. Looking back at poems I wrote before I was twenty-one, I'm startled because beneath the conscious craft are glimpses of the split I even then experienced between the girl who wrote poems, who defined herself in writing poems, and the girl who was to define herself by her relationships with men. "Aunt Jennifer's Tigers" (1951), written while I was a student, looks with deliberate detachment at this split.[12]

> *Aunt Jennifer's tigers stride across a screen,*
> *Bright topaz denizens of a world of green.*
> *They do not fear the men beneath the tree;*
> *They pace in sleek chivalric certainty.*
>
> *Aunt Jennifer's fingers fluttering through her wool*
> *Find even the ivory needle hard to pull.*
> *The massive weight of Uncle's wedding band*
> *Sits heavily upon Aunt Jennifer's hand.*

10. Rich's list defines women as destroyers or the destroyed: La Belle Dame Sans Merci (the lovely lady without pity) is the title character of an 1819 poem by John Keats that retells the myth of a mortal ravaged by his love for a supernatural *femme fatale;* Juliet is one of the star-crossed lovers of Shakespeare's 1595 play *Romeo and Juliet;* Tess is the doomed woman of Thomas Hardy's *Tess of the D'Urbervilles* (1891); and Salomé, from Oscar Wilde's 1894 play *Salomé,* demands the beheading of John the Baptist.

11. *A.R., 1978:* Yet I spent months, at sixteen, memorizing and writing imitations of Millay's sonnets; and in notebooks of that period I find what are obviously attempts to imitate Dickinson's metrics and verbal compression. I knew H.D. only through anthologized lyrics; her epic poetry was not then available to me.

12. *A.R., 1978:* Texts of poetry quoted herein can be found in A. R., *Poems Selected and New: 1950–1974* (New York: Norton, 1975).

> *When Aunt is dead, her terrified hands will lie*
> *Still ringed with ordeals she was mastered by.*
> *The tigers in the panel that she made*
> *Will go on striding, proud and unafraid.*

In writing this poem, composed and apparently cool as it is, I thought I was creating a portrait of an imaginary woman. But this woman suffers from the opposition of her imagination, worked out in tapestry, and her life-style, "ringed with ordeals she was mastered by." It was important to me that Aunt Jennifer was a person as distinct from myself as possible—distanced by the formalism of the poem, by its objective, observant tone—even by putting the woman in a different generation.

In those years formalism was part of the strategy—like asbestos [14] gloves, it allowed me to handle materials I couldn't pick up bare-handed. A later strategy was to use the persona of a man, as I did in "The Loser" (1958):

> *A man thinks of the woman he once loved: first, after her* [15]
> *wedding, and then nearly a decade later.*
>
> *I*
> *I kissed you, bride and lost, and went*
> *home from that bourgeois sacrament,*
> *your cheek still tasting cold upon*
> *my lips that gave you benison*
> *with all the swagger that they knew—*
> *as losers somehow learn to do.*
>
> *Your wedding made my eyes ache; soon*
> *the world would be worse off for one*
> *more golden apple dropped to ground*
> *without the least protesting sound,*
> *and you would windfall lie, and we*
> *forget your shimmer on the tree.*
>
> *Beauty is always wasted: if*
> *not Mignon's song sung to the deaf,*
> *at all events to the unmoved.*
> *A face like yours cannot be loved*
> *long or seriously enough.*
> *Almost, we seem to hold it off.*
>
> *II*
> *Well, you are tougher than I thought.*
> *Now when the wash with ice hangs taut*
> *this morning of St. Valentine,*
> *I see you strip the squeaking line,*
> *your body weighed against the load,*
> *and all my groans can do no good.*

Because you are still beautiful,
though squared and stiffened by the pull
of what nine windy years have done.
You have three daughters, lost a son.
I see all your intelligence
flung into that unwearied stance.

My envy is of no avail.
I turn my head and wish him well
who chafed your beauty into use
and lives forever in a house
lit by the friction of your mind.
You stagger in against the wind.

I finished college, published my first book by a fluke, as it seemed   16
to me, and broke off a love affair. I took a job, lived alone, went on
writing, fell in love. I was young, full of energy, and the book seemed
to mean that others agreed I was a poet. Because I was also determined
to prove that as a woman poet I could also have what was then defined
as a "full" woman's life, I plunged in my early twenties into marriage
and had three children before I was thirty. There was nothing overt in
the environment to warn me: these were the fifties, and in reaction to
the earlier wave of feminism, middle-class women were making careers
of domestic perfection, working to send their husbands through professional schools, then retiring to raise large families. People were moving
out to the suburbs, technology was going to be the answer to everything, even sex; the family was in its glory. Life was extremely private;
women were isolated from each other by the loyalties of marriage. I
have a sense that women didn't talk to each other much in the fifties—
not about their secret emptinesses, their frustrations. I went on trying
to write; my second book and first child appeared in the same month.
But by the time that book came out I was already dissatisfied with those
poems, which seemed to me mere exercises for poems I hadn't written.
The book was praised, however, for its "gracefulness"; I had a marriage
and a child. If there were doubts, if there were periods of null depression
or active despairing, these could only mean that I was ungrateful, insatiable, perhaps a monster.

About the time my third child was born, I felt that I had either to   17
consider myself a failed woman and a failed poet, or to try to find some
synthesis by which to understand what was happening to me. What
frightened me most was the sense of drift, of being pulled along on a
current which called itself my destiny, but in which I seemed to be
losing touch with whoever I had been, with the girl who had experienced her own will and energy almost ecstatically at times, walking
around a city or riding a train at night or typing in a student room. In

a poem about my grandmother I wrote (of myself): "A young girl, thought sleeping, is certified dead" ("Halfway"). I was writing very little, partly from fatigue, that female fatigue of suppressed anger and loss of contact with my own being; partly from the discontinuity of female life with its attention to small chores, errands, work that others constantly undo, small children's constant needs. What I did write was unconvincing to me; my anger and frustration were hard to acknowledge in or out of poems because in fact I cared a great deal about my husband and my children. Trying to look back and understand that time I have tried to analyze the real nature of the conflict. Most, if not all, human lives are full of fantasy—passive day-dreaming which need not be acted on. But to write poetry or fiction, or even to think well, is not to fantasize, or to put fantasies on paper. For a poem to coalesce, for a character or an action to take shape, there has to be an imaginative transformation of reality which is in no way passive. And a certain freedom of the mind is needed—freedom to press on, to enter the currents of your thought like a glider pilot, knowing that your motion can be sustained, that the buoyancy of your attention will not be suddenly snatched away. Moreover, if the imagination is to transcend and transform experience it has to question, to challenge, to conceive of alternatives, perhaps to the very life you are living at that moment. You have to be free to play around with the notion that day might be night, love might be hate; nothing can be too sacred for the imagination to turn into its opposite or to call experimentally by another name. For writing is re-naming. Now, to be maternally with small children all day in the old way, to be with a man in the old way of marriage, requires a holding-back, a putting-aside of that imaginative activity, and demands instead a kind of conservatism. I want to make it clear that I am *not* saying that in order to write well, or think well, it is necessary to become unavailable to others, or to become a devouring ego. This has been the myth of the masculine artist and thinker; and I do not accept it. But to be a female human being trying to fulfill traditional female functions in a traditional way *is* in direct conflict with the subversive function of the imagination. The word traditional is important here. There must be ways, and we will be finding out more and more about them, in which the energy of creation and the energy of relation can be united. But in those years I always felt the conflict as a failure of love in myself. I had thought I was choosing a full life: the life available to most men, in which sexuality, work, and parenthood could coexist. But I felt, at twenty-nine, guilt toward the people closest to me, and guilty toward my own being.

I wanted, then, more than anything, the one thing of which there was never enough: time to think, time to write. The fifties and early sixties were years of rapid revelations: the sit-ins and marches in the

South, the Bay of Pigs, the early antiwar movement,[13] raised large questions—questions for which the masculine world of the academy around
me seemed to have expert and fluent answers. But I needed to think
for myself—about pacifism and dissent and violence, about poetry and
society, and about my own relationship to all these things. For about
ten years I was reading in fierce snatches, scribbling in notebooks, writing poetry in fragments; I was looking desperately for clues, because if
there were no clues then I thought I might be insane. I wrote in a
notebook about this time:

> Paralyzed by the sense that there exists a mesh of relationships—e.g., be-
> tween my anger at the children, my sensual life, pacifism, sex (I mean sex in
> its broadest significance, not merely sexual desire)—an interconnectedness
> which, if I could see it, make it valid, would give me back myself, make it
> possible to function lucidly and passionately. Yet I grope in and out among
> these dark webs.

I think I began at this point to feel that politics was not something "out
there" but something "in here" and of the essence of my condition.

In the late fifties I was able to write, for the first time, directly about   19
experiencing myself as a woman. The poem was jotted in fragments
during children's naps, brief hours in a library, or at 3:00 A.M. after
rising with a wakeful child. I despaired of doing any continuous work
at this time. Yet I began to feel that my fragments and scraps had a
common consciousness and a common theme, one which I would have
been very unwilling to put on paper at an earlier time because I had
been taught that poetry should be "universal," which meant, of course,
nonfemale. Until then I had tried very much *not* to identify myself as a
female poet. Over two years I wrote a ten-part poem called "Snapshots
of a Daughter-in-Law" (1958–1960), in a longer looser mode than I'd
ever trusted myself with before. It was an extraordinary relief to write
that poem. It strikes me now as too literary, too dependent on allusion;
I hadn't found the courage yet to do without authorities, or even to
use the pronoun "I"—the woman in the poem is always "she." One
section of it, No. 2, concerns a woman who thinks she is going mad;
she is haunted by voices telling her to resist and rebel, voices which
she can hear but not obey.

> 2.
> *Banging the coffee-pot into the sink*
> *she hears the angels chiding, and looks out*
> *past the raked gardens to the sloppy sky.*
> *Only a week since They said:* Have no patience.

13. Sit-ins . . . antiwar movement: sit-ins and freedom marches were nonviolent ap-
proaches to the struggle for civil rights advocated by Martin Luther King, Jr.; in 1962 the
CIA ordered an invasion at the Cuban Bay of Pigs in a failed attempt to overthrow Fidel
Castro; and protesters opposed the involvement of the U.S. in the Vietnam War.

The next time it was: Be insatiable.
Then: Save yourself; others you cannot save.
Sometimes she's let the tapstream scald her arm,
a match burn to her thumbnail,

or held her hand above the kettle's snout
right in the woolly steam. They are probably angels,
since nothing hurts her anymore, except
each morning's grit blowing into her eyes.

The poem "Orion," written five years later, is a poem of reconnec-   20
tion with a part of myself I had felt I was losing—the active principle,
the energetic imagination, the "half-brother" whom I projected, as I
had for many years, into the constellation Orion. It's no accident that
the words "cold and egotistical" appear in this poem, and are applied
to myself.

Far back when I went zig-zagging
through tamarack pastures
you were my genius, you
my cast-iron Viking, my helmed
lion-heart king in prison.
Years later now you're young

my fierce half-brother, staring
down from that simplified west
your breast open, your belt dragged down
by an oldfashioned thing, a sword
the last bravado you won't give over
though it weighs you down as you stride

and the stars in it are dim
and maybe have stopped burning.
But you burn, and I know it;
as I throw back my head to take you in
an old transfusion happens again:
divine astronomy is nothing to it.

Indoors I bruise and blunder,
break faith, leave ill enough
alone, a dead child born in the dark.
Night cracks up over the chimney,
pieces of time, frozen geodes
come showering down in the grate.

A man reaches behind my eyes
and finds them empty
a woman's head turns away

from my head in the mirror
children are dying my death
and eating crumbs of my life.

Pity is not your forte.
Calmly you ache up there
pinned aloft in your crow's nest,
my speechless pirate!
You take it all for granted
and when I look you back

it's with a starlike eye
shooting its cold and egotistical spear
where it can do least damage.
Breathe deep! No hurt, no pardon
out here in the cold with you
you with your back to the wall.

The choice still seemed to be between "love"—womanly, maternal love, altruistic love—a love defined and ruled by the weight of an entire culture; and egotism—a force directed by men into creation, achievement, ambition, often at the expense of others, but justifiably so. For weren't they men, and wasn't that their destiny as womanly, selfless love was ours? We know now that the alternatives are false ones—that the word "love" is itself in need of re-vision.

There is a companion poem to "Orion," written three years later, [21] in which at last the woman in the poem and the woman writing the poem become the same person. It is called "Planetarium," and it was written after a visit to a real planetarium, where I read an account of the work of Caroline Herschel, the astronomer, who worked with her brother William, but whose name remained obscure, as his did not.

Thinking of Caroline Herschel, 1750–1848, astronomer, [22]
sister of William; and others

A woman in the shape of a monster
a monster in the shape of a woman
the skies are full of them

a woman   "in the snow
among the Clocks and instruments
or measuring the ground with poles"

in her 98 years to discover
8 comets

she whom the moon ruled
like us
levitating into the night sky
riding the polished lenses

Galaxies of women, there
doing penance for impetuousness
ribs chilled
in those spaces   of the mind

An eye,
*   "virile, precise and absolutely certain"*
*   from the mad webs of Uranisborg*

                    encountering the NOVA

every impulse of light exploding
from the core
as life flies out of us

         Tycho whispering at last
         "Let me not seem to have lived in vain"

What we see, we see
and seeing is changing

the light that shrivels a mountain
and leaves a man alive

Heartbeat of the pulsar
heart sweating through my body

The radio impulse
pouring in from Taurus

         I am bombarded yet   I stand

I have been standing all my life in the
direct path of a battery of signals
the most accurately transmitted most
untranslateable language in the universe
I am a galactic cloud so deep   so invo-
luted that a light wave could take 15
years to travel through me   And has
taken   I am an instrument in the shape
of a woman trying to translate pulsations
into images   for the relief of the body
and the reconstruction of the mind.

In closing I want to tell you about a dream I had last summer. I [23] dreamed I was asked to read my poetry at a mass women's meeting, but when I began to read, what came out were the lyrics of a blues song. I share this dream with you because it seemed to me to say something about the problems and the future of the woman writer, and probably of women in general. The awakening of consciousness is not like the crossing of a frontier—one step and you are in another country. Much of woman's poetry has been of the nature of the blues song: a cry of pain, of victimization, or a lyric of seduction.[14] And today, much poetry by women—and prose for that matter—is charged with anger. I think we need to go through that anger, and we will betray our own reality if we try, as Virginia Woolf was trying, for an objectivity, a detachment, that would make us sound more like Jane Austen or Shakespeare. We know more than Jane Austen or Shakespeare knew: more than Jane Austen because our lives are more complex, more than Shakespeare because we know more about the lives of women—Jane Austen and Virginia Woolf included.

Both the victimization and the anger experienced by women are   24 real, and have real sources, everywhere in the environment, built into society, language, the structures of thought. They will go on being tapped and explored by poets, among others. We can neither deny them, nor will we rest there. A new generation of women poets is already working out of the psychic energy released when women begin to move out towards what the feminist philosopher Mary Daly has described as the "new space" on the boundaries of patriarchy.[15] Women are speaking to and of women in these poems, out of a newly released courage to name, to love each other, to share risk and grief and celebration.

To the eye of a feminist, the work of Western male poets now   25 writing reveals a deep, fatalistic pessimism as to the possibilities of change, whether societal or personal, along with a familiar and thread-bare use of women (and nature) as redemptive on the one hand, threatening on the other; and a new tide of phallocentric sadism and overt woman-hating which matches the sexual brutality of recent films. "Political" poetry by men remains stranded amid the struggles for power among male groups; in condemning U.S. imperialism or the Chilean junta the poet can claim to speak for the oppressed while remaining, as male, part of a system of sexual oppression. The enemy is always outside the self, the struggle somewhere else. The mood of isolation, self-pity, and self-imitation that pervades "nonpolitical" poetry suggests that a profound change in masculine consciousness will have to precede any new male poetic—or other—inspiration. The creative energy of patriarchy is fast running out; what remains is its self-generating energy for destruction. As women, we have our work cut out for us.

14. *A.R., 1978:* When I dreamed that dream, was I wholly ignorant of the tradition of Bessie Smith and other women's blues lyrics which transcended victimization to sing of resistance and independence?

15. Mary Daly, *Beyond God the Father: Toward a Philosophy of Women's Liberation* (Boston: Beacon, 1973).

PATRICIA HAMPL

Memory and Imagination

Patricia Hampl (1946–   ), poet and memoirist, was born in St. Paul, Minnesota, to parents of Czech and Irish descent. She has published two volumes of poetry, *Woman Before an Aquarium* (1978) and *Resort and Other Poems* (1983), and a much-praised autobiography, *A Romantic Education,* winner of the Houghton Mifflin Literary Fellowship in 1981. "I suppose," she has said, "I write about all the things I had intended to leave behind, to grow out of, or deny: being a Midwesterner, a Catholic, a woman." In 1987 Hampl revisited her Midwestern experience by writing a fictional account of another Czech artist's experience, *Spillville,* which is about composer Antonín Dvořák's visit to a small Iowa town in 1893. In her most recent book, *Virgin Time: In Search of the Contemplative Life* (1992), she returns to her Catholic upbringing in an exploration of spirituality. Hampl wrote "Memory and Imagination" in 1986, especially for inclusion in *The Dolphin Reader.* In it you will find her argument for the political importance of writing about our own pasts.

When I was seven, my father, who played the violin on Sundays 1
with a nicely tortured flair which we considered artistic, led me by the hand down a long, unlit corridor in St. Luke's School basement, a sort of tunnel that ended in a room full of pianos. There many little girls and a single sad boy were playing truly tortured scales and arpeggios in a mash of troubled sound. My father gave me over to Sister Olive Marie, who did look remarkably like an olive.

Her oily face gleamed as if it had just been rolled out of a can and 2
laid on the white plate of her broad, spotless wimple. She was a small, plump woman; her body and the small window of her face seemed to interpret the entire alphabet of olive: her face was a sallow green olive placed upon the jumbo ripe olive of her black habit. I trusted her instantly and smiled, glad to have my hand placed in the hand of a woman who made sense, who provided the satisfaction of being what she was: an Olive who looked like an olive.

My father left me to discover the piano with Sister Olive Marie so 3
that one day I would join him in mutually tortured piano-violin duets for the edification of my mother and brother who sat at the table meditatively spooning in the last of their pineapple sherbet until their part was called for: they put down their spoons and clapped while we bowed, while the sweet ice in their bowls melted, while the music melted, and we all melted a little into each other for a moment.

But first Sister Olive must do her work. I was shown middle C, 4
which Sister seemed to think terribly important. I stared at middle

C and then glanced away for a second. When my eye returned, middle C was gone, its slim finger lost in the complicated grasp of the keyboard. Sister Olive struck it again, finding it with laughable ease. She emphasized the importance of middle C, its central position, a sort of North Star of sound. I remember thinking, "Middle C is the belly button of the piano," an insight whose originality and accuracy stunned me with pride. For the first time in my life I was astonished by metaphor. I hesitated to tell the kindly Olive for some reason; apparently I understood a true metaphor is a risky business, revealing of the self. In fact, I have never, until this moment of writing it down, told my first metaphor to anyone.

Sunlight flooded the room; the pianos, all black, gleamed. Sister 5 Olive, dressed in the colors of the keyboard, gleamed; middle C shimmered with meaning and I resolved never—never—to forget its location: it was the center of the world.

Then Sister Olive, who had had to show me middle C twice but 6 who seemed to have drawn no bad conclusions about me anyway, got up and went to the windows on the opposite wall. She pulled the shades down, one after the other. The sun was too bright, she said. She sneezed as she stood at the windows with the sun shedding its glare over her. She sneezed and sneezed, crazy little convulsive sneezes, one after another, as helpless as if she had the hiccups.

"The sun makes me sneeze," she said when the fit was over and 7 she was back at the piano. This was odd, too odd to grasp in the mind. I associated sneezing with colds, and colds with rain, fog, snow and bad weather. The sun, however, had caused Sister Olive to sneeze in this wild way, Sister Olive who gleamed benignly and who was so certain of the location of the center of the world. The universe wobbled a bit and became unreliable. Things were not, after all, necessarily what they seemed. Appearance deceived: here was the sun acting totally out of character, hurling this woman into sneezes, a woman so mild that she was named, so it seemed, for a bland object on a relish tray.

I was given a red book, the first Thompson book, and told to play 8 the first piece over and over at one of the black pianos where the other children were crashing away. This, I was told, was called practicing. It sounded alluringly adult, practicing. The piece itself consisted mainly of middle C, and I excelled, thrilled by my savvy at being able to locate that central note amidst the cunning camouflage of all the other white keys before me. Thrilled too by the shiny red book that gleamed, as the pianos did, as Sister Olive did, as my eager eyes probably did. I sat at the formidable machine of the piano and got to know middle C intimately, preparing to be as tortured as I could manage one day soon with my father's violin at my side.

But at the moment Mary Katherine Reilly was at my side, play- 9 ing something at least two or three lessons more sophisticated than my piece. I believe she even struck a chord. I glanced at her from the peasantry of single notes, shy, ready to pay homage. She turned toward me, stopped playing, and sized me up.

Sized me up and found a person ready to be dominated. With- 10
out introduction she said, "My grandfather invented the collapsible opera hat."

I nodded, I acquiesced, I was hers. With that little stroke it was 11
decided between us—that she should be the leader, and I the sidekick. My job was admiration. Even when she added, "But he didn't make a penny from it. He didn't have a patent"—even then, I knew and she knew that this was not an admission of powerlessness, but the easy candor of a master, of one who can afford a weakness or two.

With the clairvoyance of all fated relationships based on dominance 12
and submission, it was decided in advance: that when the time came for us to play duets, I should always play second piano, that I should spend my allowance to buy her the Twinkies she craved but was not allowed to have, that finally, I should let her copy from my test paper, and when confronted by our teacher, confess with convincing hysteria that it was I, I who had cheated, who had reached above myself to steal what clearly belonged to the rightful heir of the inventor of the collapsible opera hat. . . .

There must be a reason I remember that little story about my first 13
piano lesson. In fact, it isn't a story, just a moment, the beginning of what could perhaps become a story. For the memoirist, more than for the fiction writer, the story seems already *there,* already accomplished and fully achieved in history ("in reality," as we naively say). For the memoirist, the writing of the story is a matter of transcription.

That, anyway, is the myth. But no memoirist writes for long with- 14
out experiencing an unsettling disbelief about the reliability of memory, a hunch that memory is not, after all, *just* memory. I don't know why I remembered this fragment about my first piano lesson. I don't, for instance, have a single recollection of my first arithmetic lesson, the first time I studied Latin, the first time my grandmother tried to teach me to knit. Yet these things occurred too, and must have their stories.

It is the piano lesson that has trudged forward, clearing the haze of 15
forgetfulness, showing itself bright with detail more than thirty years after the event. I did not choose to remember the piano lesson. It was simply there, like a book that has always been on the shelf, whether I ever read it or not, the binding and title showing as I skim across the contents of my life. On the day I wrote this fragment I happened to take that memory, not some other, from the shelf and paged through it. I found more detail, more event, perhaps a little more entertainment than I had expected, but the memory itself was there from the start. Waiting for me.

Or was it? When I reread what I had written just after I finished it,   16
I realized that I had told a number of lies. I *think* it was my father who
took me the first time for my piano lesson—but maybe he only took
me to meet my teacher and there was no actual lesson that day. And
did I even know then that he played the violin—didn't he take up his
violin again much later, as a result of my piano playing, and not the
reverse? And is it even remotely accurate to describe as "tortured" the
musicianship of a man who began every day by belting out "Oh What
a Beautiful Morning" as he shaved?

More: Sister Olive Marie did sneeze in the sun, but was her name   17
Olive? As for her skin tone—I would have sworn it was olive-like; I
would have been willing to spend the better part of an afternoon trying
to write the exact description of imported Italian or Greek olive her face
suggested: I wanted to get it right. But now, were I to write that passage
over, it is her intense black eyebrows I would see, for suddenly they
seem the central fact of that face, some indicative mark of her serious
and patient nature. But the truth is, I don't remember the woman at
all. She's a sneeze in the sun and a finger touching middle C. That, at
least, is steady and clear.

Worse: I didn't have the Thompson book as my piano text. I'm   18
sure of that because I remember envying children who did have this
wonderful book with its pictures of children and animals printed on
the pages of music.

As for Mary Katherine Reilly. She didn't even go to grade school   19
with me (and her name isn't Mary Katherine Reilly—but I made that
change on purpose). I met her in Girl Scouts and only went to school
with her later, in high school. Our relationship was not really one of
leader and follower; I played first piano most of the time in duets. She
certainly never copied anything from a test paper of mine: she was a
better student, and cheating just wasn't a possibility with her. Though
her grandfather (or someone in her family) did invent the collapsible
opera hat and I remember that she was proud of that fact, she didn't
tell me this news as a deft move in a childish power play.

So, what was I doing in this brief memoir? Is it simply an example   20
of the curious relation a fiction writer has to the material of her own
life? Maybe. That may have some value in itself. But to tell the truth
(if anyone still believes me capable of telling the truth), I wasn't writing
fiction. I was writing memoir—or was trying to. My desire was to be
accurate. I wished to embody the myth of memoir: to write as an act
of dutiful transcription.

Yet clearly the work of writing narrative caused me to do something   21
very different from transcription. I am forced to admit that memoir is
not a matter of transcription, that memory itself is not a warehouse of
finished stories, not a static gallery of framed pictures. I must admit that
I invented. But why?

Two whys: why did I invent, and then, if a memoirist must inevitably invent rather than transcribe, why do I—why should anybody— write memoir at all?

I must respond to these impertinent questions because they, like the bumper sticker I saw the other day commanding all who read it to QUESTION AUTHORITY, challenge my authority as a memoirist and as a witness.

It still comes as a shock to realize that I don't write about what I know: I write in order to find out what I know. Is it possible to convey to a reader the enormous degree of blankness, confusion, hunch and uncertainty lurking in the act of writing? When I am the reader, not the writer, I too fall into the lovely illusion that the words before me (in a story by Mavis Gallant, an essay by Carol Bly, a memoir by M.F.K. Fisher), which *read* so inevitably, must also have been *written* exactly as they appear, rhythm and cadence, language and syntax, the powerful waves of the sentences laying themselves on the smooth beach of the page one after another faultlessly.

But here I sit before a yellow legal pad, and the long page of the preceding two paragraphs is a jumble of crossed-out lines, false starts, confused order. A mess. The mess of my mind trying to find out what it wants to say. This is a writer's frantic, grabby mind, not the poised mind of a reader ready to be edified or entertained.

I sometimes think of the reader as a cat, endlessly fastidious, capable, by turns, of mordant indifference and riveted attention, luxurious, recumbent, and ever poised. Whereas the writer is absolutely a dog, panting and moping, too eager for an affectionate scratch behind the ears, lunging frantically after any old stick thrown in the distance.

The blankness of a new page never fails to intrigue and terrify me. Sometimes, in fact, I think my habit of writing on long yellow sheets comes from an atavistic fear of the writer's stereotypic "blank white page." At least when I begin writing, my page isn't utterly blank; at least it has a wash of color on it, even if the absence of words must finally be faced on a yellow sheet as truly as on a blank white one. Well, we all have our ways of whistling in the dark.

If I approach writing from memory with the assumption that I know what I wish to say, I assume that intentionality is running the show. Things are not that simple. Or perhaps writing is even more profoundly simple, more telegraphic and immediate in its choices than the grating wheels and chugging engine of logic and rational intention. The heart, the guardian of intuition with its secret, often fearful intentions, is the boss. Its commands are what a writer obeys—often without knowing it. Or, I do.

That's why I'm a strong adherent of the first draft. And why it's worth pausing for a moment to consider what a first draft really is. By my lights, the piano lesson memoir is a first draft. That doesn't mean it exists here exactly as I first wrote it. I like to think I've cleaned it up from the first time I put it down on paper. I've cut some adjectives here, toned down the hyperbole there, smoothed a transition, cut a repetition—that sort of housekeeperly tidying-up. But the piece remains a first draft because I haven't yet gotten to know it, haven't given it a chance to tell me anything. For me, writing a first draft is a little like meeting someone for the first time. I come away with a wary acquaintanceship, but the real friendship (if any) and genuine intimacy—that's all down the road. Intimacy with a piece of writing, as with a person, comes from paying attention to the revelations it is capable of giving, not by imposing my own preconceived notions, no matter how well-intentioned they might be.

I try to let pretty much anything happen in a first draft. A careful 30 first draft is a failed first draft. That may be why there are so many inaccuracies in the piano lesson memoir: I didn't censor, I didn't judge. I kept moving. But I would not publish this piece as a memoir on its own in its present state. It isn't the "lies" in the piece that give me pause, though a reader has a right to expect a memoir to be as accurate as the writer's memory can make it. No, it isn't the lies themselves that makes the piano lesson memoir a first draft and therefore "unpublishable."

The real trouble: the piece hasn't yet found its subject; it isn't yet 31 about what it wants to be about. Note: what *it* wants, not what I want. The difference has to do with the relation a memoirist—any writer, in fact—has to unconscious or half-known intentions and impulses in composition.

Now that I have the fragment down on paper, I can read this little 32 piece as a mystery which drops clues to the riddle of my feelings, like a culprit who wishes to be apprehended. My narrative self (the culprit who has invented) wishes to be discovered by my reflective self, the self who wants to understand and make sense of a half-remembered story about a nun sneezing in the sun. . . .

We only store in memory images of value. The value may be lost 33 over the passage of time (I was baffled about why I remembered that sneezing nun, for example), but that's the implacable judgment of feeling: *this*, we say somewhere deep within us, is something I'm hanging on to. And of course, often we cleave to things because they possess heavy negative charges. Pain likes to be vivid.

Over time, the value (the feeling) and the stored memory (the im- 34 age) may become estranged. Memoir seeks a permanent home for feeling and image, a habitation where they can live together in harmony. Naturally, I've had a lot of experiences since I packed away that one from the basement of St. Luke's School; that piano lesson has been effaced by waves of feeling for other moments and episodes. I persist in believing the event has value—after all, I remember it—but in writing the memoir I did not simply relive the experience. Rather, I explored the mysterious relationship between all the images I could round up and the even more impacted feelings that caused me to store the images safely away in memory. Stalking the relationship, seeking the congruence between stored image and hidden emotion—that's the real job of memoir.

By writing about that first piano lesson, I've come to know things 35 I could not know otherwise. But I only know these things as a result of reading this first draft. While I was writing, I was following the images, letting the details fill the room of the page and use the furniture as they wished. I was their dutiful servant—or thought I was. In fact, I was the faithful retainer of my hidden feelings which were giving the commands.

I really did feel, for instance, that Mary Katherine Reilly was far 36 superior to me. She was smarter, funnier, more wonderful in every way—that's how I saw it. Our friendship (or she herself) did not require that I become her vassal, yet perhaps in my heart that was something I wanted; I wanted a way to express my feeling of admiration. I suppose I waited until this memoir to begin to find the way.

Just as, in the memoir, I finally possess that red Thompson book 37 with the barking dogs and bleating lambs and winsome children. I couldn't (and still can't) remember what my own music book was, so I grabbed the name and image of the one book I could remember. It was only in reviewing the piece after writing it that I saw my inaccuracy. In pondering this "lie," I came to see what I was up to: I was getting what I wanted. At last.

The truth of many circumstances and episodes in the past emerges 38 for the memoirist through details (the red music book, the fascination with a nun's name and gleaming face), but these details are not merely information, not flat facts. Such details are not allowed to lounge. They must work. Their work is the creation of symbol. But it's more accurate to call it the *recognition* of symbol. For meaning is not "attached" to the detail by the memoirist; meaning is revealed. That's why a first draft is important. Just as the first meeting (good or bad) with someone who later becomes the beloved is important and is often reviewed for signals, meanings, omens, and indications.

Now I can look at that music book and see it not only as "a detail," 39 but for what it is, how it *acts*. See it as the small red door leading straight into the dark room of my childhood longing and disappointment. That red book *becomes* the palpable evidence of that longing. In other words, it becomes symbol. There is no symbol, no life-of-the-spirit in the general or the abstract. Yet a writer wishes—indeed all of us wish—to speak about profound matters that are, like it or not, general and abstract. We wish to talk to each other about life and death, about love, despair, loss, and innocence. We sense that in order to live together we must learn to speak of peace, of history, of meaning and values. Those are a few.

We seek a means of exchange, a language which will renew these   40
ancient concerns and make them wholly and pulsingly ours. Instinctively, we go to our store of private images and associations for our authority to speak of these weighty issues. We find, in our details and broken and obscured images, the language of symbol. Here memory impulsively reaches out its arms and embraces imagination. That is the resort to invention. It isn't a lie, but an act of necessity, as the innate urge to locate personal truth always is.

All right. Invention is inevitable. But why write memoir? Why not   41
call it fiction and be done with all the hashing about, wondering where memory stops and imagination begins? And if memoir seeks to talk about "the big issues," about history and peace, death and love—why not leave these reflections to those with expert and scholarly knowledge? Why let the common or garden variety memoirist into the club? I'm thinking again of that bumper sticker: why Question Authority?

My answer, of course, is a memoirist's answer. Memoir must be   42
written because each of us must have a created version of the past. Created: that is, real, tangible, made of the stuff of a life lived in place and in history. And the down side of any created thing as well: we must live with a version that attaches us to our limitations, to the inevitable subjectivity of our points of view. We must acquiesce to our experience and our gift to transform experience into meaning and value. You tell me your story, I'll tell you my story.

If we refuse to do the work of creating this personal version of the   43
past, someone else will do it for us. That is a scary political fact. "The struggle of man against power," a character in Milan Kundera's novel *The Book of Laughter and Forgetting* says, "is the struggle of memory against forgetting." He refers to willful political forgetting, the habit of nations and those in power (Question Authority!) to deny the truth of memory in order to disarm moral and ethical power. It's an efficient way of controlling masses of people. It doesn't even require much bloodshed, as long as people are entirely willing to give over their personal memories. Whole histories can be rewritten. As Czeslaw Milosz said in his 1980 Nobel Prize lecture, the number of books published that seek to deny the existence of the Nazi death camps now exceeds one hundred.

What is remembered is what *becomes* reality. If we "forget" Ausch-   44
witz,[1] if we "forget" My Lai,[2] what then do we remember? And what

1. Polish site in World War II of the concentration camp Auschwitz-Birkenau, where more than a million prisoners, most of them Jews, were exterminated.
2. Incident in 1968 in which American troops massacred unarmed Vietnamese civilians, including women and children.

is the purpose of our remembering? If we think of memory naively, as a simple story, logged like a documentary in the archive of the mind, we miss its beauty but also its function. The beauty of memory rests in its talent for rendering detail, for paying homage to the senses, its capacity to love the particles of life, the richness and idiosyncrasy of our existence. The function of memory, on the other hand, is intensely personal and surprisingly political.

Our capacity to move forward as developing beings rests on a   45
healthy relation with the past. Psychotherapy, that widespread method of mental health, relies heavily on memory and on the ability to retrieve and organize images and events from the personal past. We carry our wounds and perhaps even worse, our capacity to wound, forward with us. If we learn not only to tell our stories but to listen to what our stories tell us—to write the first draft and then return for the second draft—we are doing the work of memoir.

Memoir is the intersection of narration and reflection, of storytelling   46
and essay-writing. It can present its story *and* reflect and consider the meaning of the story. It is a peculiarly open form, inviting broken and incomplete images, half-recollected fragments, all the mass (and mess) of detail. It offers to shape this confusion—and in shaping, of course it necessarily creates a work of art, not a legal document. But then, even legal documents are only valiant attempts to consign the truth, the whole truth and nothing but the truth to paper. Even they remain versions.

Locating touchstones—the red music book, the olive Olive, my   47
father's violin playing—is deeply satisfying. Who knows why? Perhaps we all sense that we can't grasp the whole truth and nothing but the truth of our experience. Just can't be done. What can be achieved, however, is a version of its swirling, changing wholeness. A memoirist must acquiesce to selectivity, like any artist. The version we dare to write is the only truth, the only relationship we can have with the past. Refuse to write your life and you have no life. At least, that is the stern view of the memoirist.

Personal history, logged in memory, is a sort of slide projector   48
flashing images on the wall of the mind. And there's precious little order to the slides in the rotating carousel. Beyond that confusion, who knows who is running the projector? A memoirist steps into this darkened room of flashing, unorganized images and stands blinking for a while. Maybe for a long while. But eventually, as with any attempt to tell a story, it is necessary to put something first, then something else. And so on, to the end. That's a first draft. Not necessarily the truth, not even *a* truth sometimes, but the first attempt to create a shape.

The first thing I usually notice at this stage of composition is the   49
appalling inaccuracy of the piece. Witness my first piano lesson draft. Invention is screamingly evident in what I intended to be transcription. But here's the further truth: I feel no shame. In fact, it's only now that

my interest in the piece truly quickens. For I can see what isn't there, what is shyly hugging the walls, hoping not to be seen. I see the filmy shape of the next draft. I see a more acute version of the episode or—this is more likely—an entirely new piece rising from the ashes of the first attempt.

The next draft of the piece would have to be a true re-vision, a new   50
seeing of the materials of the first draft. Nothing merely cosmetic will
do—no rouge buffing up the opening sentence, no glossy adjective to
lift a sagging line, nothing to attempt covering a patch of gray writing.
None of that. I can't say for sure, but my hunch is the revision would
lead me to more writing about my father (why was I so impressed by
that ancestral inventor of the collapsible opera hat? Did I feel I had
nothing as remarkable in my own background? Did this make me feel
inadequate?). I begin to think perhaps Sister Olive is less central to this
business than she is in this draft. She is meant to be a moment, not a
character.

And so I might proceed, if I were to undertake a new draft of the   51
memoir. I begin to feel a relationship developing between a former self
and me.

And, even more compelling, a relationship between an old world   52
and me. Some people think of autobiographical writing as the precious
occupation of a particularly self-absorbed person. Maybe, but I don't
buy that. True memoir is written in an attempt to find not only a self
but a world.

The self-absorption that seems to be the impetus and embar-   53
rassment of autobiography turns into (or perhaps always was) a hunger
for the world. Actually, it begins as hunger for *a* world, one gone or
lost, effaced by time or a more sudden brutality. But in the act of remembering, the personal environment expands, resonates beyond itself,
beyond its "subject," into the endless and tragic recollection that is
history.

We look at old family photographs in which we stand next to black,   54
boxy Fords and are wearing period costumes, and we do not gaze fascinated because there we are young again, or there we are standing, as
we never will again in life, next to our mother. We stare and drift
because there we are . . . historical. It is the dress, the black car that
dazzle us now and draw us beyond our mother's bright arms which
once caught us. We reach into the attractive impersonality of something
more significant than ourselves. We write memoir, in other words.
We accept the humble position of writing a version rather than "the
whole truth."

I suppose I write memoir because of the radiance of the past—it   55
draws me back and back to it. Not that the past is beautiful. In our
communal memoir, in history, the death camps *are* back there. In intimate life too, the record is usually pretty mixed. "I could tell you sto-

ries . . ." people say and drift off, meaning terrible things have happened to them.

But the past is radiant. It has the light of lived life. A memoirist 56 wishes to touch it. No one owns the past, though typically the first act of new political regimes, whether of the left or the right, is to attempt to re-write history, to grab the past and make it over so the end comes out right. So their power looks inevitable.

No one owns the past, but it is a grave error (another age would 57 have said a grave sin) not to inhabit memory. Sometimes I think it is all we really have. But that may be a trifle melodramatic. At any rate, memory possesses authority for the fearful self in a world where it is necessary to have authority in order to Question Authority.

There may be no more pressing intellectual need in our culture 58 than for people to become sophisticated about the function of memory. The political implications of the loss of memory are obvious. The authority of memory is a personal confirmation of selfhood. To write one's life is to live it twice, and the second living is both spiritual and historical, for a memoir reaches deep within the personality as it seeks its narrative form and also grasps the life-of-the-times as no political treatise can.

Our most ancient metaphor says life is a journey. Memoir is travel 59 writing, then, notes taken along the way, telling how things looked and what thoughts occurred. But I cannot think of the memoirist as a tourist. This is the traveller who goes on foot, living the journey, taking on mountains, enduring deserts, marveling at the lush green places. Moving through it all faithfully, not so much a survivor with a harrowing tale to tell as a pilgrim, seeking, wondering.

WILLIAM L. RODMAN

When Questions Are Answers

William L. Rodman (1943–   ) is a professor of anthropology at McMaster University in Hamilton, Ontario. Having taken his undergraduate degree from the University of Sydney, Rodman completed his Ph.D. at the University of Chicago in 1973. With his wife, Margaret, also a professional anthropologist, Rodman has conducted research in the South Pacific for over twenty years. A narrative account of their latest fieldwork, particularly the reaction of the local people to Margaret's contraction of malaria, is found in "To Die on Ambae: On the Possibility of Doing Field Work Forever" (*Anthropologica*, 1989). Rodman has also published articles on politics and law in Ambae, Vanuatu, and has edited (with Dorothy Counts) *Middlemen and Brokers in Oceania* (1982). His current teaching and research interests include interpretive anthropology, narrative in the human sciences, and witchcraft. "When Questions Are Answers" was published in *American Anthropologist* in June 1991.

AN INTRODUCTION

This is what I think happened, my reconstruction of an event that occurred over thirty years ago on a remote island in the South Pacific. What follows is a fiction, but it's as true a fiction as I can write on the basis of my own experience on the island and the information available to me. Minor details in my account might be incorrect but what is important is that today people on the island believe that the meeting between the anthropologist and the teenager took place, and that from that meeting they discovered the message of anthropology to the native peoples of the world. What I found, many years after the event, is that their interpretation of the message of anthropology had played a critical role in changing their way of life.

In the late 1950s, an anthropologist spent a few days as the guest of an Australian couple who maintained a trade store on the weather coast of Aoba, a northern island in the New Hebrides archipelago. The anthropologist had just completed ten months of fieldwork on the neighboring island of Pentecost; he was on his way home—Aoba was just a stopover, a place to wait for a boat that would take him to a place to wait for a plane back to North America.

At some point during the anthropologist's brief stay on the island, a young man named Andrew Namala walked down to the coast from his inland village.[1] He was a quiet young man, the brother of a schoolteacher but the son of a chief. He was close to his father, a man who had killed many pigs and gained high rank in the graded society (*hungwe*) before Church of Christ missionaries in the 1940s convinced their followers on the island to give up all customary activities. Andrew's father remained a traditional chief, for not even a missionary can strip a man of his rank in the graded society, but he was a nonpracticing chief, a chief in cultural exile who had become a proper Christian in the Church of Christ.

The day that Andrew walked down to the coast, the wife of the trader was tending store. She was a big, friendly woman, fluent in the local Pidgin English—Bislama—and knowledgeable about the personal

1. All names in this essay are pseudonyms. However, all the statements of the pseudonymous Ambaens (including Andrew Namala's story in the section entitled "Text") are translated versions of comments I tape-recorded in Bislama. [author's note]

lives of almost everyone who visited her store. She knew Andrew, and
she knew his father, too. One thing she knew about Andrew's father
was that the old chief was one of the few men in the Church of Christ
skilled in the art of sand drawing.

Sand drawings have an irresistible appeal for ethnographers. Copies 5
of the drawings can be found in the works of Codrington, Rivers, Dea-

Figure 1   Sand drawing entitled "The War-Club of the Spirits" (*Rungwe Bulana Tamate*), drawn by "Andrew Namala," Ambae Island, Vanuatu.

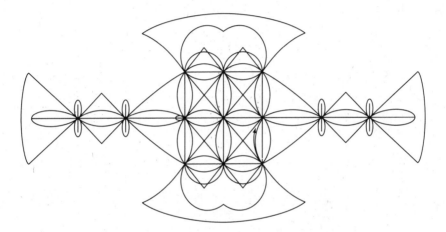

con, Layard, Harrisson, and almost every other ethnographer with an
interest in material culture who has worked in the northern New Hebrides.[2] (See Figure 1.) It's not hard to explain why the drawings have
attracted so much attention. They excite the basic ethnographic impulse
to record and preserve. The artist's medium is fine sand or dirt as soft
as talcum powder; if the artist is skillful, he creates a thing of beauty that
cannot last beyond a single afternoon. Sand drawings are symbolically
charged filigree that the wind blows away, myths in pictures that the
tide wipes clean. The trader's wife knew that the anthropologist had
collected some sand drawings on Pentecost, so she introduced him to
Andrew, the son of a local expert.

The anthropologist and the teenager went outside the trade store 6
to talk. It was hot in the store, and there were shade trees just out-

2. The man I call "Andrew Namala" drew the sand drawing represented in Figure 1.
The name of the sand drawing is "The War-Club of the Spirits" (*Rungwe Bulana Tamate*).
As much of a sand drawing as possible is drawn in one continuous line. I use the masculine pronoun in my description of the drawings because, on Ambae, the person who
works the sand drawings always is male. [author's note]

side—a wild mango, a rose apple, and some others. Moreover, there was a breeze off the sea.

At first, the anthropologist's questions concerned sand drawings, and then, when that subject ran dry, he asked the young man about a range of other topics—magic, supernatural power, subsistence techniques, the experiences of local people in World War II, and recent changes in patterns of nutrition, all topics on which he had collected information during his recent fieldwork. In a casual way, he seems to have been seeking information concerning Aoba that he could compare with data he gathered on Pentecost. Yet it's hard to consider the encounter an "interview." It wasn't planned; it lacked formality; from the anthropologist's point of view, it may even have lacked a sense of occasion. It was a way to pass the time before dinner, a pleasant way to decompress from fieldwork.

The anthropologist left Aoba a few days later. During the decades that were to follow, he never published anything that derived from his talk with the teenager. It's unlikely the conversation changed his life in any significant way.

To Andrew, however, the encounter *was* a meaningful event. It puzzled him. Who was the outsider? Why was he interested in the local way of life? What did his questions *mean*? In 1982, Andrew spoke to me of the interview as if it happened yesterday. As I listened, I found that most of the anthropologist's questions have an air of plausibility. I recognized them as legitimate questions for an ethnographer to ask, as questions I might ask someone in an unfamiliar locale.

Andrew's life was changed as a result of his encounter with the outsider and so, at least indirectly, was the way of life of the people with whom he lived. They included the 343 members of the Church of Christ in the Longana district of the island, now called Ambae, in the new Pacific nation that changed its name from "New Hebrides" to "Vanuatu" at the time of Independence in 1980 (see Figure 2). Andrew discovered an implicit pattern in the questions the anthropologist asked, and once the hidden meaning of the questions was revealed to him, the meeting took on new and deeper significance. Andrew's memory of his encounter with the anthropologist became instrumental knowledge, *used* knowledge, a key ideological justification for a profound change in the practice of a people's social affairs.

What follows here is primarily an account of how members of the Church of Christ on the island where I conduct fieldwork discovered the true meaning of anthropology and what that knowledge did to their lives. They shared their interpretation of the meaning of anthropology with me for a reason—because they wanted to teach me a lesson. So this is my story too, my explanation of how and why a group of chiefs on Ambae decided that the time had come to teach me the message of anthropology.

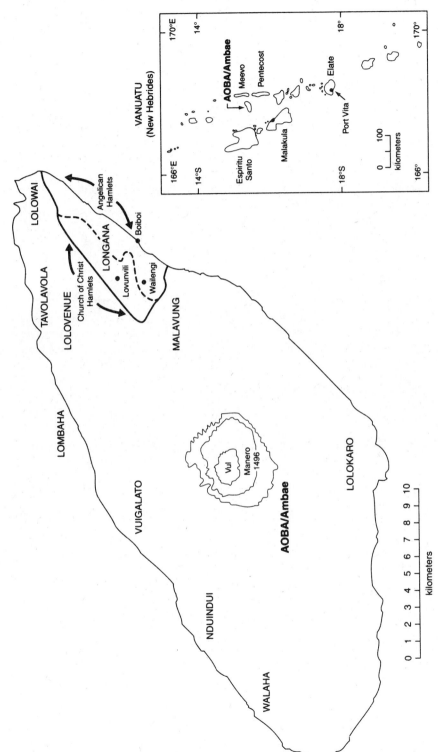

Figure 2

In 1982, early in my third term of fieldwork in the district of Lon-   12
gana on Ambae, a young man brought me a message from a friend
who lives in a hill village some distance away from the hamlet where
I stay on the island. The message was in Bislama and was handwritten
in pencil on part of a page torn from a school exercise book: "Come see
me Friday afternoon," the note said, and it was signed "Nicodemus." I
turned the scrap of paper over and scrawled "Friday's fine. See you
then," and gave it back to the messenger. I didn't add, but I felt, that
wild boars couldn't keep me away.

Nicodemus Wai (as anyone in Longana will tell you—and the   13
phrase never varies) is "different from other men." One way in which
he differs is that he talks differently: sometimes, even in private conversation, he sounds like he learned how to talk by listening to Churchill's
speeches on shortwave radio. He seems to think in rhetoric; his mind
pumps metaphors as naturally as water issues from a spring; his stories
have all the shadings of vivid dreams. But Nicodemus isn't just a
dreamer. He expresses himself in action as well as words. In the late
1960s, he became an early supporter of Jimmy Stevens, a.k.a. President
Moses, the charismatic descendant of a Tongan princess and a Scottish
seaman who founded a political movement with millenarian overtones
called "Na Griamel."[3] Na Griamel began on the island of Espiritu Santo,
30 miles across the sea from Aoba/Ambae. Partly through Nicodemus's
efforts, the entire population of the Church of Christ of the district of
Longana on Aoba became supporters of the movement. Then, in the
mid-1970s, Nicodemus became the voice of Radio Vanafo, Jimmy Stevens's illegal radio station, located deep in the Santo bush. In those
days, Nicodemus sometimes referred to himself as "a revolutionary
pussycat," "pussycat" being a reference not to his disposition but to his
ability to slip away from trouble unseen.

I had last seen Nicodemus in 1979. A year later, the Anglo-French   14
Condominium of the New Hebrides became the independent Republic
of Vanuatu. Achieving independence wasn't easy for the nationalists
who opposed British and French rule: two months before the date set
for independence, Jimmy Stevens led a rebellion against the central
government. When Vanuatu became a new nation, Na Griamel was
firmly in control of Espiritu Santo (known locally simply as "Santo"),
the largest island in the archipelago. Jimmy Stevens renamed Santo
"Vermarana" and declared the island independent of the rest of the
country. Since I had last seen Nicodemus, troops from Papua New
Guinea had smashed Na Griamel's radio transmitter, the Santo Rebel-

3. John Besant's (1984) *The Santo Rebellion: An Imperial Reckoning* provides a detailed
account of the career of Jimmy Stevens, Na Griamel, the Rebellion, and its aftermath.

lion had failed, and Jimmy Stevens had been tried and sentenced to prison, escaped, and attempted unsuccessfully to make a run for New Caledonia in a glass-bottomed boat he stole from a guided tour company in the capital, Port Vila.

Nicodemus and I lived in villages only a few miles apart, but we   15
seldom met because my hosts and his kin were political enemies who also belonged to rival religions. Longana runs about eight kilometers along a coastal track, which ends at a dry riverbed that marks one boundary of the district. There, the road turns and begins to rise abruptly for one-and-a-half kilometers into the foothills of the interior of the island. Two groups live in the district. The coastal population are Anglicans, followers of tradition, and supporters of the majority political party and the central government. They are the people with whom I have worked since my first fieldwork on the island in 1969. The 549 Anglicans live in scattered hamlets separate from those of the 343 members of the Church of Christ, all of whom live in the hills and most of whom at the time of independence were among the most loyal supporters of Jimmy Stevens and Na Griamel. Like most of the people with whom I was in daily contact, I seldom ventured into the Church of Christ area, and never without an invitation.

I heard from my Anglican adoptive kinsmen that Nicodemus had   16
been implicated in the theft of a large quantity of medical supplies from the Santo hospital during the Rebellion. I heard he had surrendered to police, been pardoned, found God, and started his own church, which lacked a name, the idea being that labels such as "Anglican" and "Church of Christ" only serve to create conflict and obscure the essential unity of Christians everywhere. I heard all these things as rumors and I badly wanted to see him: the "revolutionary pussycat" was leading one of the most interesting lives of anyone I knew.

On Friday, when I crested the hill that led into Nicodemus's village,   17
I saw him walking toward me, a big, broken-toothed smile on his face. I also saw something else, a sight to which I ascribed no particular significance at the time: Nicodemus's brother, Andrew Namala, sitting in front of the village's men's house in the company of a number of older men. Andrew was carving a *rungwe*, a traditional fighting-club that men of rank now use as a walking stick. He saw me, grinned, and waved. I waved back. He then returned to whittling and conversation with the other men.

I expected Nicodemus to take me to his house, a place where we   18
would not be disturbed. Instead, he directed me to a small house with walls of split and woven bamboo that stood on the edge of a clearing, about a hundred feet away from the men's house. He explained to me that it was a house the village had built for visitors; inside, it was cool and clean, a good place to talk.

Nicodemus and I seated ourselves on benches and faced each other   19

across a bare table. We chatted about our families as I set up my
tape recorder. I tested the microphone and then I asked him: "Have
you been back to Jimmy Stevens's headquarters on Santo since the
Rebellion?"

"Yes, just once," he replied in a thoughtful voice. "It used to be a   20
pretty place, but it's not anymore." His tone was that of a man evoking
memories within himself, trying to see the scene as it was. "The soldiers
ruined everything, the people's way of life, the gardens, everything. All
that's left there now is a French school." He paused and then took a
deep breath. "The reason I went back there is that an old friend of mine
had died. . . ." And at that instant the storyteller in Nicodemus took
over. He told me about the end of the Rebellion, about the dawn raid
on Jimmy Stevens's headquarters, about murders reported as accidents,
about the secret involvement of Americans belonging to the Phoenix
Foundation in the Rebellion. I found out why he had been accused of
the theft of the medical supplies and why he was never charged with
the crime. He told me the story of his surrender to the government
troops and why they let him go. He seemed to me much older than the
last time I had seen him, and he told me how tired he was of being a
"diver in deep waters"; now, he said, he had "come to the surface for
air." His only wish was to lead a quiet life, as a husband, as a father
to his five children, and as pastor to his flock in the Church-With-
No-Name.

The packed earth beneath my bare feet became cooler, and the   21
shadows within the house deepened. We had been talking for about
three hours when a boy scurried into the house, climbed into Nicodemus's lap and whispered in his ear. Nicodemus nodded and lowered
the boy to the ground. He slapped his hands on the table with an air
of finality: the spell was broken, the interview over. He rose in a way
that indicated he expected me to do the same. "Bill," he said, "the
chiefs are waiting for you. Your kava is ready."

Kava (*Piper mythysticum*) is a drug about which I feel profound   22
ambivalence. It is a bitter brew that everyone on Ambae admits tastes
awful: one of its several origin myths attributes its taste to the fact that
it first grew from the decaying vagina of a murdered woman. That myth
makes sense of why, today, Ambaen men hawk and spit after every
shell. It's also a powerful enough drug to alter perception in fundamental ways. Once I drank a shell so strong that everything I saw for the
next 20 minutes flickered, just like an old-time movie. Most often,
however, one or two draughts of kava merely numbs the tongue, eases
the mind, and generates companionship and goodwill among the drink-
ers. For a male fieldworker, accepting a host's invitation of kava is a
social necessity; it's better to accept and throw up than to refuse, however smilingly.

The men's house was filled. Every man of rank in the Church of   23

Christ area was there. Andrew Namala greeted me at the doorway, and
then I went from man to man, shaking hands in greeting, my body
bent slightly from the waist in a position of respect. In the center of the
clubhouse, there were five split coconut shells filled with kava. The
chief of highest rank in the men's house told me which shell of kava I
was to drink. He glanced around the men's house. "Thaddeus, you
come drink with us," he said. "You too, Sam . . . and you, Andrew."
He then took a twig and passed down the line of shells, dipping the
stick in the kava, raising it to his mouth and tasting it, and then moving
on to the next shell. I'd seen this done before, though not often, and
until I learned better I'd always assumed that the chief was testing the
kava for poison, symbolically if not actually. In fact, the trajectory
of the twig is from the chief's mouth to each cup, not the reverse:
the ritual is done so that guests will absorb some knowledge from
their host.

I drank my kava, stepped outside the men's house, spat, made other   24
terrible sounds, then came back inside, passed around a pack of Camels
and settled against a bamboo wall. It was strong stuff, and I began to
feel the hum and glow of the kava working on me. I smoked a cigarette,
pleasantly stoned, listening, watching as other men drank their shells
of kava.

When everyone in the men's house had downed a shell of kava,   25
the quality of sound in the room changed, became softer, quieter, and
someone began to tell a story. It was a few minutes before I realized
that I was listening to something more than idle men's house conversation. With some difficulty, I switched on my tape recorder. Andrew
squatted a few feet away, still working on his club in the semi-darkness.
There was a moment of silence as one story ended, then he began
to speak.

TEXT

"There was a man who came here shortly after World War II   26
ended." (He confers with others in the men's house about the visitor's
name. Someone suggests "Mr. Allen," but Andrew shakes his head and
continues.) "We don't remember his name but he came here to find
out about our sand drawings and about the messages we leave for each
other on the ground. Before he came here, he visited the island of
Pentecost, and then he arrived at Boi Boi, the landing down on the
coast. He stayed in the house of the trader who lived there—Mr.
Mueller.

"At that time, I was a young man, maybe seventeen or eighteen.   27
Sometimes, I would walk down to the coast to visit the Muellers' trade
store. One day, as I approached the store, Mrs. Mueller saw me coming,
and she yelled to me:

'Hey! Isn't your father the chief who knows about sand drawings?'   28
'Yes,' I said, 'and so do I.'   29
'Aww, you're just a kid; you don't know any sand drawings.'   30
'Oh yes I do,' I said . . . Now I remember! Mr. Jones! Mr. Jones   31
was his name. Mrs. Mueller introduced me to him.
'Do you know any sand drawings?' he asked me. 'A few,' I replied.   32
We went outside the store and sat down. Mr. Jones opened his   33
book and showed me a drawing.
'Do you know this one?' he asked, 'It's from Pentecost.'   34
'Yes,' I said, 'I know it.'   35
'What is it called?'   36
I told him.   37
He showed me another drawing. 'What's this one?'   38
'It's called fresh coconuts,' I said.   39
Altogether, Mr. Jones asked me if I knew four different drawings.   40
I knew each one.
'Enough,' he said. 'I want to ask you some questions. In the past,   41
did some men around here know how to make thunder?'
'Yes,' I said. 'They did.'   42
'What about now?'   43
'No longer.'   44
'O.K.,' he said, 'let me ask you about something else: in the past,   45
did some men around here know how to make earthquakes?'
'Yes,' I said. 'They did.'   46
'What about now?'   47
'No longer.'   48
'What about cyclones? Did men know how to make them?'   49
'Yes.'   50
'Now?'   51
'No.'   52
'Why do such men no longer exist?' he asked me.   53
Well, I didn't really know, so I just told him the first thing that   54
came to mind. I said: 'What happened was that the missionaries arrived.
They showed us the Bible and told us to leave our heathen ways. They
told us to burn or throw away our magical substances and to forget
about them.'
Then Mr. Jones asked me: 'Did you go to Santo during the war?'   55
'No,' I told him. 'I was too young. When the men of my village   56
returned from Santo, they told us: "It's over: the war has ended." '
'How do you think America managed to win the war?' he asked.   57
'I don't know,' I said.   58
'Do you drink tea?' asked Mr. Jones.   59
'Yes.'   60
'When you drink tea, do you eat anything?'   61
'Yes. Sometimes cabin biscuits, sometimes bread.'   62

'Do you like the taste of tea, biscuits, and bread?'   63

'Yes.'   64

'Fine,' said Mr. Jones. 'Do you eat rice?'   65

'Yes.'   66

'When you eat rice, do you eat any other food at the same time?'   67

'Sometimes meat, sometimes tinned fish.'   68

'Do you like the taste of rice, meat, and tinned fish?'   69

'Yes.'   70

'All right,' said Mr. Jones, 'I have another question: do you know   71
how to make a garden?'

'Yes.'   72

'Then tell me how you do it. What do you do when you want to   73
clear land?'

I showed him how I held my bush-knife and how I used the knife   74
to clear land.

It was then that I realized that he was teaching me a lesson, a   75
lesson about the value of traditional culture [*kastom*].

'Look,' he said, 'rain drives sunlight away. Night replaces day.   76
Think again about the reason why the Americans won the war. Have
you figured it out? I'll tell you. It's because the soldiers carried the Bible
with them. The Bible provides White men with their *kastom*. Why have
you people lost *your kastom*?'

My word! Then I understood.   77

I shared with Mr. Jones my knowledge of sand drawings and I   78
showed him the signs we write on the ground, the four main ones, the
one that tells your friends to wait for you, the one that says: 'I'm tired
of waiting—I've gone in this direction.' But I knew that there were
many other signs I didn't know, that nobody knew anymore.

Before Mr. Jones departed from the island, he told me he would   79
put the signs I had shown him into a book he would write after he
returned to America. 'I'll put the signs in a book,' he said, 'and then it
won't matter if I die or if you die. Even when we both are dead, the
signs will remain in the book for our children to see.'

You know, Bill, I think the kinds of things I've been talking about—   80
sand drawings, signs, that sort of thing—are the real *kastom* of Longana.
Lots of people who don't know much about *kastom* just talk about pigs.
Pigs, pigs, pigs. But pigs aren't the backbone of *kastom*. Pigs are just a
kind of money."

CONTEXT

Even at the time, bone-tired, the kava still working on my brain, I   81
had the feeling that Andrew was trying to tell me something of importance to him, something much more than merely an anecdote about
his encounter with a White man many years ago. When he finished

the story, he lapsed into silence, and returned to chip, chip, chipping away at his fighting-club. The light in the men's house was dim and fallow, the golden last light of late afternoon. Andrew worked on his club, his shoulders hunched, his face a dark and pensive mask. The time did not seem right to ask him questions. Soon, men seated in the shadows of the men's house returned to quiet conversation and then later we all went to another hill village where a mortuary feast was in progress. My "father"—old Mathias Tari—was there. We drank a shell of kava together, my second, his first, and waited for the bundles of food to come out of the earth oven. When we received our food, we set off down the hill toward home, the old man leading, me following behind, slipping, sliding, but somehow never quite falling.

Days passed, then weeks, and eventually I transcribed the tape of   82 my interview with Nicodemus. There, on the end of the last tape in the Nicodemus series, was Andrew Namala telling his story. This time, listening to him, I began to notice details—the way in which he knitted the segments of the narrative together, the progressions in the encounter between the anthropologist and the teenager, the apparent revelation at the climax of the story: "My word! Then I understood." But *what* had he understood? Why, then, did he share his knowledge willingly, even joyously, with the outsider? What was the lesson about *kastom* that he thought the anthropologist had taught him?

From these questions came others. I reflected on the occasion, and   83 I began to wonder about the context in which Andrew told me his story. The recounting of the tale had been truly a performance, and Andrew had played to a packed (men's) house: Why had so many chiefs gathered in his village on a work day, a Friday in the cool season? Then, too, there was the puzzle of why he had told me the story. Why in public? What was the significance of the last bit, the part he directed at me as if underlining the story's message: things like sand drawings are the backbone of *kastom* of Longana, pigs are not. Now *there's* an unorthodox view! When men speak of *kastom* in Longana, they mean pig-killing, rank-taking, the graded society (*hungwe*): I'd heard men use *kastom* as a synonym for "pig-killing" hundreds of times.[4] Andrew himself had been an important catalyst in the recent revival of pig-killing in the Church of Christ area in Longana. In 1979, I'd seen him take the second-highest rank, killing tusked boars in the midst of a thunderstorm, a man radiant with energy, in complete control of his body, his every movement clean and precise; Andrew's was the best of the many rank-takings I'd seen. That was then, three years ago, but now he was

---

4. Rodman inserts a note here citing other anthropological accounts of the graded society on Ambae. For economy's sake, we have deleted the citations. Those interested in this scholarly apparatus should consult the version of Rodman's article in *American Anthropologist*.

taking the line that "lots of people who don't know much about *kastom* just talk about pigs." Hell, everybody in Longana who engages in *kastom* talks about pigs. So what was he trying to tell me?

Some mysteries, if you dream on them enough and have enough   84 context, reveal themselves. It took me a while, but eventually I understood. The key to understanding Andrew's interpretation of his talk with the anthropologist (and also the key to the way in which he told me the story) is *qaltavalu*, literally "hidden talk," a form of communication based on a system of implicit meanings. People sometimes *qaltavalu* in everyday life; for example, a man may ask a woman for a plate of rice and not have food in mind at all. More commonly, it occurs as a rhetorical device in speeches: rival chiefs use *qaltavalu* against each other to devastating effect. "Hidden talk" is the process; shame is the product. *Qaltavalu* says to a rival: "Look, I am speaking about you in public, and *you* understand my meaning, even if everyone else does not. Shall I make my meaning explicit, or will you change your way of acting?" Or, perhaps, ". . . provide me with the support I need?" The threat of public exposure often is sanction (or blackmail) enough in a society in which people dread public humiliation.

Qaltavalu has a third use: it's one of the most important customary   85 techniques of instruction. Teachers on Ambae seldom state the obvious. Instead, they teach by parable, by indirection raised to the level of a fine art. They figure that a student is most apt to remember a lesson if he has to work to figure out what the lesson is.[5]

Andrew's encounter with the anthropologist made little sense to   86 the hill people in terms of their prior dealings with Europeans. By the 1950s, Longanans in the Church of Christ area had had limited experience with White people: in fact, most people's knowledge of Whites resulted exclusively from their contacts with the Australian trader and his wife (who were the only resident Whites in the district), missionaries, and very, *very* rarely, a government official. Longanan followers of the Church of Christ had heard missionaries preach against *kastom* as a mark of moral backwardness, as beliefs to be uprooted, substances to be destroyed, and behaviors to be transformed. In contrast to missionaries, traders and the occasional district agent didn't seem to regard *kastom*

5. Parallels to the Ambaean notion of *qaltavalu* can be found elsewhere in Oceania and in other parts of the world. Strathern, for example, discusses the "veiled speech" (*ik ek*) that Melpa of Highland New Guinea use in a number of contexts, including children's games, love songs, public argument and debate, and formal oratory. The Melpa also have a concept of "hidden truth" similar to that of Ambae. Unlike Ambae, however, Melpa figurative speech apparently is not used in education as a formal means for the transmission of knowledge. Outside Oceania, "hidden talk" as a pedagogical device sometimes occurs in places where a person's knowledge is supposed to grow in small increments, as among the Saramaka of Surinam, where old men teach their younger kinsmen in a style marked by ellipsis, concealment, and partial disclosure. [author's note]

as immoral, but they didn't take local traditions very seriously either: to them, *kastom* is play, a harmless set of activities that waste time and money.

In contrast to missionaries, traders, and district agents, the anthropologist clearly was interested in *kastom*. Andrew, the son of a chief, chose to interpret his meeting with the outsider in terms of a category of Ambaen culture, *qaltavalu*. What was the hidden meaning of the encounter? What was the anthropologist (cast in the role of "teacher") *really* saying? Viewed within the framework of ordinary conversation, the questions communicate little information. What, after all, does winning a war have to do with the taste of tea? But as *qaltavalu*—aiiyahhh!—patterns begin to emerge, and implicit links between the questions appear. Andrew puzzled over the meaning of the questions until they provided him with an answer to the problem of the anomalous White man. 87

He opens his narrative with the incident involving the trader's wife. He depicts her as *assuming* that members of the younger generation no longer know their own traditions. Andrew proves her wrong when he correctly identifies the Pentecost sand drawings. By so doing, he demonstrates to the anthropologist his interest in *kastom* and qualifies himself as a worthy recipient of the anthropologist's message. 88

The next section of the narrative consists of a set of questions that have in common the theme of lost power. The storyteller has the anthropologist establish an implicit relationship between lost power and the loss of tradition. The "teacher" is drawing his "student's" attention to the fact that, in the past, men possessed great supernatural powers: no one today knows how to make thunder, earthquakes, and cyclones. Then, abruptly, the anthropologist asks: "Why do such men no longer exist?" and Andrew, free-associating, is forced to confront the fact that missionaries were responsible for the loss of the knowledge and magical substances that had been the source of customary power. 89

The conversation appears to change course when the anthropologist asks Andrew: "Did you go to Santo during the war?" In fact, in his questions about World War II, Mr. Jones reveals his true intent, but not in an obvious way. "How do you think America managed to win the war?" is another question probing the theme of power. It's an extension of his previous questions, but Andrew doesn't catch the drift of his "teacher's" line of reasoning: "I don't know," he replies. 90

So Mr. Jones tries another tack: "Do you drink tea?" he asks. All the next set of questions concern diet. In a broader sense, however, the questions elicit information about change and the presence of foreign elements in Longana; Andrew is made to come face to face with his alienation from tradition. He is forced to admit he not only eats White people's food; he *likes* it. 91

All is not lost, however. Mr. Jones is a good teacher, a master of *qaltavalu*, so he nudges his student with yet another question: "Do you 92 know how to make a garden?" This most straightforward of questions, reconsidered as *qaltavalu*, is transformed into something like: "Do you remember the most fundamental traditional skill of all—how to make a living from the earth?" Andrew responds affirmatively. This allows the "teacher" to lead him in the direction of a reconsideration of his essential values. He asks Andrew to demonstrate the skills that bind him to the land. Andrew does so, and at last he understands that Mr. Jones is using customary means to make a point about *kastom*. But what *is* the point? Andrew still is not sure, so Mr. Jones steps out of character and makes his message explicit: in effect, he tells the young man that Americans are strong because their *kastom*, which can be found in the Bible, is powerful; Americans remain strong because they remain true to the traditional values associated with their own way of life. Missionaries deprived the islanders of indigenous *kastom*s and, as a result, people lost much of their power.

So what was the anthropologist's hidden message? What was the true meaning of the encounter and the questions he asked? The answer in the questions isn't hard to discover. The anthropologist made Andrew work toward an understanding that *kastom is* important: it is the way to power; those who lose their *kastom*s are powerless. By the end of the narrative, Andrew has discovered the "true" message of anthropology: anthropologists are an equal and opposing force in the world to certain kinds of missionaries. They are a counter to anti-*kastom* Christianity and those missionaries who urge people to abandon their traditional ways. The aim of anthropology is to teach all peoples to value their traditional ways.

The anthropologist's message to Andrew became Andrew's message to his people. At first, no one listened. For 15 years, he lived as an outsider in his own society, a man with a passionate concern for *kastom* in a Christian community that believed (with equal fervor) that *kastom* is anti-Christian. He learned from his father, and then, when his father died and there was no one else in the Church of Christ who could teach him *kastom*, he sought out chiefs in the Anglican sector of the district. It took courage to go to those chiefs. At that time, Anglicans and members of the Church of Christ regarded each other with mutual suspicion and hostility. He went to the chiefs, and he learned from them. Gradually, he became a master of tradition.

Then the times changed. In the 1970s, with the waning of colonialism, *kastom* became a symbol of national identity in the New Hebrides, a rallying cry of the pro-independence movement. The Anglicans in Longana all joined the Vanuaku Pati, which promoted *kastom* in the interests of national unity. Everyone in the Church of Christ joined Na Griamel, which claimed that the majority political party "pays only lip service to . . . customs, while Nagriamel made the respect for them a basic part of its party's philosophy." Not only politicians rode the pro-*kastom* bandwagon; missionaries with an eye to the future did too.

Church of Christ missionaries now maintained a cautious silence on matters of *kastom:* in the hill country of Longana, no one mistook the church's new attitude as one of approval or even tolerance; some men, however—and Andrew was one of them—thought that the church would no longer interfere in customary activities such as pig-killing and kava drinking. In this time of uncertainty, when men were still trying to interpret their changed circumstances, Andrew used the story of his meeting with the anthropologist as an ideological resource. He found a willing audience for its message. Men now were willing to listen to the idea that *kastom* is a path to power—nationally, locally, and personally. After a hiatus of forty years, members of the Church of Christ in Longana began to take rank again, and Andrew was one of the first. He started on the lowest level of the graded society (as was proper) and, within seven years, he had climbed to the second-highest rank.

I went to four pig-killings in the Church of Christ area in the late 1970s, when I spent 12 months in Longana. I went, but without much enthusiasm. I went mainly because people expected me to go, because if I stayed home it would have been an insult to the rank-taker and his sponsor. I had seen close to forty ranks taken in the Anglican area and I had written a Ph.D. dissertation on the topic. I had been there, done that, knew the moves, and wanted to get on to something else. What really interested me at the time was the fact that colonial authorities had withdrawn from participation in local legal affairs. People in Longana were beginning to codify their own laws and develop their own courts: that was what I wanted to study, not rank-taking. I stayed in the Anglican area of Longana, and I visited the Church of Christ mainly to see friends, like Nicodemus Wai, and to attend the occasional rank-taking.

When I next visited Longana, in 1982, I found that the pace of rank-taking in the Church of Christ had accelerated. Suddenly, *everybody* in the hills seemed to be killing pigs—grandfathers, church leaders, teenagers wearing Sony Walkman headsets. Pig-killing had become a fad, a craze, a way to wow your neighbors. Abuses were common: some men were skipping ranks, others were holding ceremonies with little or no preparation in the complex rituals. The first Church of Christ rank-taking I saw in 1982 was awful: the kid taking the rank clearly didn't know what he was doing, his resources were minimal, and the pigs died hard, screaming like babies. Andrew was one of the teenager's sponsors, a secondary sponsor without much say, and there was little he could do to improve the situation. At one point, he raced by the grassy hill where I was sitting and he yelled over his shoulder: "Hemia i kastom ya, be i kastom olbaot!" The phrase doesn't translate easily, but it means something like: "I guess this is *kastom*, but it's sure a mess!" It wasn't long after that ceremony that Nicodemus invited me to his village.

There's no doubt in my mind that Nicodemus's invitation was a   98
pretext, a way to get me to the village without arousing my suspicions,
and that Andrew told me the story of his encounter as a *qaltavalu*. In
fact, the *qaltavalu* was multi-leveled and complex.

In a sense, Andrew was trying to teach me the same lesson that   99
the anthropologist had taught him. He had seen me mainly in two
contexts: at rank-takings and in his brother's company. As far as he
could tell, I was interested in pigs and in certain kinds of radical change.
Somehow, I had lost the grand vision of anthropology: obviously, I
needed rerouting. He was saying to me: *kastom* is the true interest of
anthropology; there is much *kastom* you do not know; don't listen to
people who equate pigs with *kastom*; pigs are business, *kastom* is art,
and art endures.

He was shaming me, in a sense, but he was also flattering me,   100
trusting my local knowledge; a novice wouldn't catch the *qaltavalu*.
Writing this paper, it occurs to me that I wasn't the only target of his
qaltavalu that afternoon. Quite possibly, he had a larger purpose, an aim
rather more important than teaching an anthropologist the meaning of
anthropology. *Qaltavalu* is a subtle system of meaning, and Andrew was
a master of the form, and quite capable of sending a message to two
audiences at once. I think now that I was Andrew's pretext for aiming
a *qaltavalu* at the other men in the men's house. They—not me—were
his monster, his creation made of parts of the old culture, slugging back
kava as if there had never been years of abstinence, killing pigs with a
passion for prestige but without skill, without grace, with no respect.
They needed to slow down, to relearn the lesson that *kastom* is various
and subtle, a matter of the mind as well as public display. They too
needed to relearn the hidden message of anthropology that Mr. Jones
taught so many years ago.

CONCLUSIONS

I returned to Ambae in 1985, just in time to attend Andrew Na-   101
mala's mortuary feast. He died suddenly, of uncertain causes, precisely
100 days before I returned to the island. Some people—perhaps most—
attributed his death to sorcery. Indeed, there were men with knowledge
of magical spells who had a good motive to try to kill him. Andrew
was ambitious, much admired, much envied, and a master of *qaltavalu*.
If *qaltavalu* poses the question, then sometimes men in danger of public
humiliation find an answer in sorcery.[6]

---

6. Sorcery is part of *kastom*; it's the dark twin of benevolent magic, the magic that brings
gentle rains and cures the ill and makes pigs grow tusks as round as ridgepoles and as
big as a big-man's palm. You can't have the one without the possibility of the other.
[author's note]

At the mortuary feast, Andrew's widow asked me to photograph [102] his ceremonial regalia, which she laid out over his grave. There was the bustle in which I saw him kill pigs, the armbands he'd earned, the thick belt he'd made himself lined with cowrie shells, and also a traditional fighting-club, the one he'd been carving that afternoon in the clubhouse when he told me the *qaltavalu*. I stood there with my camera, and I was aware of his widow behind me, weeping softly and saying her dead husband's name over and over. Then I took the shot, and moved back to where the men were drinking kava.

That ends my narrative, and you may have realized that I, too, have [103] been engaging in *qaltavalu*, but my point is not what some may think, that we have lost our vision and should return to our roots and study "tradition." That was Andrew's *qaltavalu* to me, not my *qaltavalu* to you. My *qaltavalu* concerns our hidden talk to each other, in writing, in narratives buried in the text of our ethnographies. This essay presents a narrative explanation, "an account of the linkages among events as a process one seeks to explain." Embedded in the narrative is an allegory about several kinds of interpretive quest. The anthropologist I call "Mr. Jones" was "as much the question as the questioner." So was I, and so are all fieldworkers: the people we study study us, even in moments when we do not seek to study them. We are not just observers observed; we are interpreters interpreted. To figure out what the devil they think they are up to requires us to try to figure out what they think *we* are up to—our motivation, purposes, and (sometimes) the moral message we bring with us. This is an Other side to reflexivity, one crucial to understanding the dialogics of encounters in field research, and one that anthropologists have only begun to explore.[7]

7. Despite the growing interest in reflexive and dialogical perspectives in anthropology, anthropologists have devoted little attention to the Other's view of anthropology and the anthropological Self. Some notable exceptions to the general lack of consideration of the topic include Dumont, Dwyer, Feld, Stoller, and Page. Despite the efforts of such scholars, it still can reasonably be said that "rarely have we heard much of how the anthropologist was perceived by the people he or she studied, or of the impact that participating in anthropological research may have had on their lives." In a similar vein, Rosaldo points out that "anthropologists often talk about seeing things from the native point of view. . . . Yet we have given little thought to how members of other cultures conceive the translation of cultures." [author's note]

CAROL BLY

Growing Up Expressive

Carol Bly (1930–   ), although educated at a New England boarding
school and at Wellesley College, has spent most of her life in her home
state of Minnesota. She began writing in the 1970s, publishing several
essays in *Preview* and *Minnesota Monthly*. At the same time, she raised
four children, divorced her husband (poet Robert Bly), and gave much
of her time to civil and humanitarian activities. Bly was the humanities
consultant for the American Farm Project from 1978 to 1981 and since
1982 has been a consultant for the Land Stewardship Project; she has
also served on the Chamber of Commerce of Madison and on the
Board of Diocesan Publications for the Episcopal Church of Minnesota.
In addition to collaborating on essays (with Joe Paddock and Nancy
Paddock) for *Common Ground* (1981) and pamphlets such as *Soil and
Survival* (1985) for the Sierra Club, Bly published several of her own
essays in *Letters from the Country* (1981), from which "Growing Up
Expressive" comes. Recently, she has concentrated on her fiction, pub-
lishing two collections: *The Tomcat's Wife and Other Stories* (1992) and
Backbone: Short Stories (1994).

Love, death, the cruelty of power, and time's curve past the stars   1
are what children want to look at. For convenience's sake, let's say
these are the four most vitally touching things in life. Little children ask
questions about them with relish. Children, provided they are still little
enough, have no eye to doing any problem solving about love or death
or injustice or the universe; they are simply interested. I've noticed that
as we read aloud literature to them, about Baba Yaga, and Dr. Dolittle,
and Ivan and the Firebird, and Rat and Mole, children are not only
interested, they are prepared to be vitally touched by the great things
of life. If you like the phrase, they are what some people call "being as
a little child." Another way of looking at it is to say that in our minds
we have two kinds of receptivity to life going on all the time: first, being
vitally touched and enthusiastic (grateful, enraged, puzzled—but, at all
events, *moved*) and, second, having a will to solve problems.

Our gritty society wants and therefore deliberately trains problem   2
solvers, however, not mystics. We teach human beings to keep themselves conscious only of problems that *can* conceivably be solved. There
must be no hopeless causes. Now this means that some subjects, of
which death and sexual love come to mind straight off, should be kept
at as low a level of consciousness as possible. Both resist problem solving. A single-minded problem solver focuses his consciousness, of
course, on problems to be solved, but even he realizes there is a concentric, peripheral band of other material around the problems. This band

appears to him as "issues." He is not interested in these issues for
themselves; he sees them simply as impacting on the problems. He will
allow us to talk of love, death, injustice, and eternity—he may even
encourage us to do so because his group-dynamics training advises him
to let us have our say, thus dissipating our willfulness—but his heart
is circling, circling, looking for an opening to *wrap up* these "issues" so
he can return attention to discrete, solvable problems. For example, a
physician who has that mentality does not wish to be near dying patients very much. They are definitely not a solvable problem. If he is
wicked, he will regard them as a present issue with impact on a future
problem: then he will order experimentation done on them during their
last weeks with us. It means his ethic is toward the healing process
only, but not toward the dying person. His ethic is toward problem
solving, not toward wonder. He will feel quite conscientious while doing the experiments on the dying patient, because he feels he is saving
lives of future patients.

To return to little children for a second: they simply like to contem-   3
plate life and death. So our difficulty, in trying to educate adults so they
will be balanced but enthusiastic, is to keep both streams going—the
problem solving, which seems to be the mental genius of our species,
and the fearless contemplation of gigantic things, the spiritual genius of
our species.

The problem-solving mentality is inculcated no less in art and Eng-   4
lish classes than in mathematics and science. Its snake oil is hope of
success: by setting very small topics in front of people, for which it is
easy for them to see the goals, the problems, the solutions, their egos
are not threatened. They feel hopeful of being effective. Therefore, to
raise a generation of problem solvers, you encourage them to visit the
county offices (as our sixth-grade teachers do) and you lead them to
understand that this is citizenship. You carefully do not suggest that
citizenship also means comparatively complex and hopeless activities
like Amnesty International's pressure to get prisoners in far places released or at least no longer tortured. Small egos are threatened by huge,
perhaps insoluble problems. Therefore, one feeds the small ego confidence by setting before it dozens and dozens of very simple situations.
The ego is nourished by feeling it understands the relationship between
the county recorder's office and the county treasurer's office; in later
life, when young people find a couple of sticky places in county government, they will confidently work at smoothing them. How very different
an experience such problem solving is from having put before one the
spectacle of the United States' various stances and activities with respect
to germ warfare. Educators regularly steer off all interest in national
and international government to one side, constantly feeding our rural
young people on questions to which one can hope for answers on a
short timeline. We do not ask them to exercise that muscle which bears

the weight of vast considerations—such as cruelty in large govern-ments. By the time the average rural Minnesotan is eighteen, he or she expects to stay in cheerful places, devote some time to local government and civic work, and "win the little ones." Rural young people have a repertoire of pejorative language for hard causes: "opening that keg of worms," "no end to that once you get into it," "don't worry—you can't do anything about that from where you are," "we could go on about that forever!" They are right, of course: we could, and our species, at its most cultivated, does go on forever about love, death, power, time, the universe. But some of us, alas, have been conditioned by eighteen fashionably to despise those subjects because there are no im-mediate answers to all the questions they ask us.

The other way we negatively reinforce any philosophical bent in   5
children is to pretend we don't see the content in their artwork. We comment only on the technique, in somewhat the same way you can scarcely get a comment on rural preachers' sermon content: the re-sponse is always, He does a good (or bad) job of speaking. "Well, but what did he say?" "Oh, he talked really well. The man can preach!"

The way to devalue the content of a child's painting is to say,   6
"Wow, you sure can paint!" The average art teacher in Minnesota is at pains to find something to say to the third grader's painting of a space machine with complicated, presumably electronic equipment in it. Here is the drawing in words: A man is sitting at some controls. Outside his capsule, fire is flying from emission points on his ship toward another spaceship at right, hitting it. Explosions are coming out of its side and tail. What is an art teacher to do with this? Goodness knows. So he or she says, "My goodness, I can see there's a lot of action there!" It is said in a deliberately encouraging way but anyone can hear under the carefully supportive comment: "A lot of work going into nothing but more TV-inspired violence." One might as well have told the child, "Thank you for sharing."

I once attended a regional writers' group at which a young poet   7
wrote about his feelings of being a single parent and trying to keep his sanity as he cared for his children. In his poem, he raced up the stair-case, grabbed a gun, and shot the clock. When he finished reading it aloud to us, someone told him, "I certainly am glad you shared with us. I'd like to really thank you for sharing."

If we are truly serious about life we are going to have to stop   8
thanking people for sharing. It isn't enough response to whatever has been offered. It is half ingenuous, and sometimes it is insincere, and often it is patronizing. It is the *dictum excrementi*[1] of our decade.

I would like to keep in mind for a moment the art works described   9
above: the child's painting of a spaceship assaulting another spaceship,

1. The Latin translates roughly as "worthless expression."

and the harrowed father's racing up the staircase and shooting the clock. Here is a third. It is a twelve-year-old's theme for English class.

> They were their four days and nights before anyone found them. It was wet and cold down there. As little kids at the orphanage, they had been beaten every night until they could scarcely make it to bed. Now they were older. Duane and Ellen leaned together. "I love you forever," she told him. He asked her, "Even though my face is marked from getting scarlett fever and polio and small pox and newmonya and they wouldn't take decent care of me, not call the doctor or anything, so the marks will always be on me?" "You know I love you," Ellen told him. "You know that time they tortured me for information and I was there but I didn't talk and later I found out it was your uncle who did it. I didn't talk because I remembered the American flag." Just then they heard someone shout, "Anyone alive down there in this mess?" You see a bomb had gone off destroying a entire U.S.A. city where they lived. Duane had lived with his cruel uncle who took him out of the orphanage to get cheap labor and Ellen lived at a boardinghouse where there were rats that ate pages of her diary all the time. Now they both looked up and shouted "We're here!" A head appeared at the top of the well into which they had fallen or they would of been in 6,500 pieces like all the other men and ladies even pregnant ones and little kids in that town. Now this head called down, "Oh—a boy and a girl!" then the head explained it was going for a ladder and ropes and it ducked away and where it had been they saw the beginnings of stars for that night, the stars still milky in front of the bright blue because the sky wasn't dark enough yet to show them up good.

The English teacher will typically comment on this story by observing that the spelling is uneven, and adjectives get used as adverbs. In rural Minnesota (if not elsewhere) an English teacher can spend every class hour on adjectives used as adverbs: it is meat and potatoes to a nag. But when we discuss spelling, syntax, and adverbs, we are talking method, not content. The child notices that nothing is said of the story's *plot*. No one remarks on the *feelings* in it. Now if this happens every time a child hands in fiction or a poem, the child will realize by the time he reaches twelfth grade that meaning or feelings are not worth anything, that "mechanics" (note the term) are all that matter. [10]

It is rare for a public school English teacher to comment on a child's content unless the material is *factual*. Minnesota teachers encourage writing booklets about the state, themes on ecology and county government, on how Dad strikes the field each autumn, on how Mom avoids open-kettle canning because the USDA advises against it. In this way, our children are conditioned to regard writing as problem solving instead of contemplation, as routine thinking instead of imaginative inquiry. [11]

How can we manage it otherwise? [12]

I would like to suggest some questions we can ask children about their artwork which will encourage them to grow up into lovers, lobby [13] supporters, and Amnesty International members, instead of only township officers and annual protestors against daylight saving time. Let us gather all the elements of the three artworks presented in this Letter: the little boy's spaceship-war painting, the young divorced father's narrative poem, and the twelve-year-old girl's story of love in a well. We have a set of images before us, then:

> Man directing spaceship fire
> Another aircraft being obliterated
> Staircase, man shooting a clock; children
> Cruel orphanage
> Torture
> Last survivors of a decimated city

Let us, instead of lending the great sneer to these images, be respectful of them. It may help to pretend the painting is by Picasso, that Flaubert[2] wrote the father/clock scene, and that Tolstoy[3] wrote the well story. It helps to remember that Picasso felt the assault of historical events on us—like Guernica;[4] Flaubert, as skillfully as Dostoyevsky[5] and with less self-pity, was an observer of violent detail; and the Tolstoy who wrote *Resurrection* or the scene of Pierre's imprisonment in *War and Peace* would turn to the well/love story without qualm.   14

We know we would never say to Picasso, Flaubert, or Tolstoy, "Why don't you draw something you know about from everyday life? Why don't you write about something you know about? You say Anna was smashed beneath a train? Thank you for sharing!"   15

The fact is that a child's feelings about orphanages and torture and love are things that he does know about. They are psychic realities inside him, and when he draws them, he is drawing something from everyday life. Sometimes they are from his night life of dreaming, but in any event they are images of passion and he is drawing from his genuine if garbled experience. A few years ago there was a stupid movement to discourage children's reading of Grimms' fairy tales. Later, with a more sophisticated psychology, we learned that the stepmother who is hostile and overweening is a reality to all children; the cutting-off of the hero's right hand and replacing of it with a hand of silver is a reality to all children. Spaceships, witches' gingerbread houses, orphanages, being the last two people to survive on earth—all these are part of the inner landscape, something children know about. Therefore, in examin-   16

2. Gustave Flaubert (1821–1880), French author of such "realist" novels as *Madame Bovary*.
3. Leo Tolstoy (1828–1910), Russian novelist.
4. A Spanish fishing village whose bombing by fascist forces in 1937 inspired a painting by Pablo Picasso (1881–1973).
5. Feodor Dostoyevsky (1821–1881), Russian novelist.

ing their artwork, we need better sets of questions to ask them. Young people who are not repressed are going to lay their wild stuff in front of adults (hoping for comment of some kind, praise if possible) until the sands of life are run, so we had better try to be good at responding to them. And unless we want to raise drones suitable only for conveyor-belt shifts, we had better be at least half as enthusiastic as when they tell us, Mama, I got the mowing finished.

Here are some questions to ask our young artist. How much of that   17
electronic equipment is used for firepower and how much just to run the ship? After the other spaceship is blown up and the people in it are dead, what will this man do? Will he go home somewhere? Were the stars out that night? You said he'll go home to his parents. Did the other man have parents? How soon will that man's parents find out that his spaceship was destroyed? Could you draw in the stars? You said they were out—could you draw them into the picture some way? but don't ruin anything you've got in there now. Also, that wire you said ran to the solar plates, will you darken it so it shows better? Don't change it—just make it clearer. Yes—terrific! Can you see the planet where the other man would have returned to if he had lived till morning?

The young father's story: There is an obvious psychic complication   18
to this story: the violence in his shooting out the clock face is gratuitous, and the plea for attention on the part of the author directed at the reader is glaring: clock faces as psychological symbols are in the public domain. Anyone who tells a friend (or a group of strangers) I am going to shoot up a clock face at 11 P.M. is asking for psychological attention. In a civil world, to ask is to receive, so if we are civilized we have to pay attention and ask the young author: Why does the father in the story blast the clock? And, when he replies, we have to ask some more. If there was ever an instance in which it was O.K. to say, "Thanks for sharing," this is not it.

I should like to add that this will be especially difficult for rural   19
teachers because the traditional country way to treat any kind of mental problem is to stare it down. It didn't happen. I didn't hear that insane thing you just said, and you know you don't really hate your mother. What nice parent would shoot a clock? We uniformly do what Dr. Vaillant in *Adaptations to Life*[6] would call a denial adaptation. It takes a brave questioner when the young person brings in a crazy story.

The well/love story: Did you know there really are such orphanages?   20
There are orphanages where the children have to get up at four-thirty to work in the dairy, and the girls work hours and hours in the kitchens, and the children's growth is stunted. Did you make the girl so brave

---

6. A book published in 1977 by Dr. George E. Vaillant, studying the ways people succeed or fail in coping with various life changes.

on purpose? Were they a lucky couple or an unlucky couple, or is that the sort of a question you can't ask? You made a point of telling us they'd been through a lot of hardship. What would it have been like for them if they hadn't? Do you want to talk about what blew up the city? Did you imagine yourself in the well?

Those are not brilliant questions; they are simply respectful, because 21 the art works described are concerned with death by violence; cruelty by institutions; treachery by relations; bravery (or cowardice—either one is important); sexual love, either despite or encouraged by dreadful circumstances.

They are some of the subjects in *War and Peace,* in Dürer's[7] etchings, 22 paintings, and woodcuts, and in *Madame Bovary.*

It is a moot question in my mind which of two disciplines will be 23 the more useful in helping people stay vitally touched by the Great Things: psychology might do it—and English literature in high school might do it (instruction on the college level is generally so dutiful to methodology that it seems a lost cause to me. "How did D. H. Lawrence foreshadow this event?" and "What metaphors does Harold Rosenberg use in his discussion of Action Painting?" are the questions of technocrats, not preservers of spirit. It is as if we got home from church and the others said, "How was church?" "We had Eucharist," we tell them. "Well, how was it?" they ask. "Pretty good," we reply. "Bishop Anderson was there. He held the chalice eight inches above the rail so no one spilled, then he turned and wiped the chalice after each use so no germs were passed along. People who had already communed returned to their benches using the north aisle so there was no bottlenecking at the chancel.")

I don't think churches will be helpful in preserving the mystical 24 outlook as long as they see life and death as a *problem*—a problem of salvation—with a solution to be worked at. Churches have an axe to grind. They might take the father running up the staircase to be an impact subject: they would wish to use their program to solve his problem. Churchmen often appear to be companionable counselors, but the appearance is largely manner and habit. Under the manner, the clergyman's mindset is nearly always to see a disturbed or grieving person's imagery as *the issues.* From there, he swings into psychological problem solving.

I would like to commend this responsibility to our English teachers: 25 that they help our children preserve pity, happiness, and grief inside themselves. They can enhance those feelings by having young children both write and draw pictures. They can be very enthusiastic about the children's first drawings of death in the sky. Adults, particularly mature ones who have *not* got children in school at the moment, should make

7. Albrecht Dürer (1471–1528), German artist.

it clear that we expect this of English teachers and that we don't give a damn if LeRoy and Merv never in their lives get the sentence balance of past conditional and perfect subjunctive clauses right. We need to protect some of the Things Invisible inside LeRoy and Merv and the rest of us.

This is my last Letter from the Country. That is why it is so shrill. Gadflies are always looking out a chance to be shrill anyway, so I jumped to this one and have shouted my favorite hope: that we can educate children not to be problem solvers but to be madly expressive all their lives.

26

WILLIAM G. PERRY, JR.

Examsmanship and the Liberal Arts

William G. Perry, Jr. (1913–   ) served for many years with the Bureau of Study Counsel at Harvard University, where he advised students and studied the relation between education and the development of personality. "Examsmanship and the Liberal Arts" grew out of a five-year study in which Perry interviewed students to learn why some thrived in Harvard's intellectual climate and others of equal intelligence struggled unsuccessfully and unhappily. First published in *Examining at Harvard College* (1967), the essay suggests the general outline of Perry's answer: a university environment is essentially hostile to a simple black-and-white view of the world, and students who are willing to see the difficulty of finding *the* truth do better than their more rigid classmates. The essay, originally written for other members of the Harvard faculty, contrasts two epistemologies, or theories of knowledge—one based on what Perry calls "bull" and one based on what he calls "cow." A more complete account of these epistemologies and their importance in education can be found in Perry's book *Forms of Intellectual and Ethical Development in the College Years: A Scheme* (1970).

"But sir, I don't think I really deserve it, it was mostly bull, really." This disclaimer from a student whose examination we have awarded a straight "A" is wondrously depressing. Alfred North Whitehead invented its only possible rejoinder: "Yes sir, what you wrote is nonsense, utter nonsense. But ah! Sir! It's the right *kind* of nonsense!"

1

Bull, in this university, is customarily a source of laughter, or a problem in ethics. I shall step a little out of fashion to use the subject as a take-off point for a study in comparative epistemology. The phe-

2

nomenon of bull, in all the honor and opprobrium with which it is regarded by students and faculty, says something, I think, about our theories of knowledge. So too, the grades which we assign on examinations communicate to students what these theories may be.

We do not have to be out-and-out logical-positivists[1] to suppose   3 that we have something to learn about "what we think knowledge is" by having a good look at "what we do when we go about measuring it." We know the straight "A" examination when we see it, of course, and we have reason to hope that the student will understand why his work receives our recognition. He doesn't always. And those who receive lesser honor? Perhaps an understanding of certain anomalies in our customs of grading good bull will explain the students' confusion.

I must beg patience, then, both of the reader's humor and of his   4 morals. Not that I ask him to suspend his sense of humor but that I shall ask him to go beyond it. In a great university the picture of a bright student attempting to outwit his professor while his professor takes pride in not being outwitted is certainly ridiculous. I shall report just such a scene, for its implications bear upon my point. Its comedy need not present a serious obstacle to thought.

As for the ethics of bull, I must ask for a suspension of judgment.   5 I wish that students could suspend theirs. Unlike humor, moral commitment is hard to think beyond. Too early a moral judgment is precisely what stands between many able students and a liberal education. The stunning realization that the Harvard Faculty will often accept, as evidence of knowledge, the cerebrations of a student who has little data at his disposal, confronts every student with an ethical dilemma. For some it forms an academic focus for what used to be thought of as "adolescent disillusion." It is irrelevant that rumor inflates the phenomenon to mythical proportions. The students know that beneath the myth there remains a solid and haunting reality. The moral "bind" consequent on this awareness appears most poignantly in serious students who are reluctant to concede the competitive advantage to the bullster and who yet feel a deep personal shame when, having succumbed to "temptation," they themselves receive a high grade for work they consider "dishonest."

I have spent many hours with students caught in this unwelcome   6 bitterness. These hours lend an urgency to my theme. I have found that students have been able to come to terms with the ethical problem, to the extent that it is real, only after a refined study of the true nature of bull and its relation to "knowledge." I shall submit grounds for my suspicion that we can be found guilty of sharing the student's confusion of moral and epistemological issues.

---

1. Logical positivists like Bertrand Russell insist that philosophical speculation be tightly checked by reference to the "positive" data of experience. This position links them to the psychological behaviorists.

I

I present as my "premise," then, an amoral *fabliau*. Its hero-villain [7] is the Abominable Mr. Metzger '47. Since I celebrate his virtuosity, I regret giving him a pseudonym, but the peculiar style of his bravado requires me to honor also his modesty. Bull in pure form is rare; there is usually some contamination by data. The community has reason to be grateful to Mr. Metzger for having created an instance of laboratory purity, free from any adulteration by matter. The more credit is due him, I think, because his act was free from premeditation, deliberation, or hope of personal gain.

Mr. Metzger stood one rainy November day in the lobby of Memo- [8] rial Hall. A junior, concentrating in mathematics, he was fond of diverting himself by taking part in the drama, a penchant which may have had some influence on the events of the next hour. He was waiting to take part in a rehearsal in Sanders Theatre, but, as sometimes happens, no other players appeared. Perhaps the rehearsal had been canceled without his knowledge? He decided to wait another five minutes.

Students, meanwhile, were filing into the Great Hall opposite, and [9] taking seats at the testing tables. Spying a friend crossing the lobby toward the Great Hall's door, Metzger greeted him and extended appropriate condolences. He inquired, too, what course his friend was being tested in. "Oh, Soc. Sci. something-or-other." "What's it all about?"asked Metzger, and this, as Homer remarked of Patroclus, was the beginning of evil for him.

"It's about Modern Perspectives on Man and Society and All That," [10] said his friend. "Pretty interesting, really."

"Always wanted to take a course like that," said Metzger. "Any [11] good reading?"

"Yeah, great. There's this book"—his friend did not have time to [12] finish.

"Take your seats please" said a stern voice beside them. The idle [13] conversation had somehow taken the two friends to one of the tables in the Great Hall. Both students automatically obeyed; the proctor put blue books before them; another proctor presented them with copies of the printed hour-test.

Mr. Metzger remembered afterwards a brief misgiving that was sud- [14] denly overwhelmed by a surge of curiosity and puckish glee. He wrote "George Smith" on the blue book, opened it, and addressed the first question.

I must pause to exonerate the Management. The Faculty has a rule [15] that no student may attend an examination in a course in which he is not enrolled. To the wisdom of this rule the outcome of this deplorable story stands witness. The Registrar, charged with the enforcement of the rule, has developed an organization with procedures which are certainly the finest to be devised. In November, however, class rosters are still shaky, and on this particular day another student, named Smith, was absent. As for the culprit, we can reduce his guilt no further than to suppose that he was ignorant of the rule, or, in the face of the momentous challenge before him, forgetful.

We need not be distracted by Metzger's performance on the "objec- 16 tive" or "spot" questions on the test. His D on these sections can be explained by those versed in the theory of probability. Our interest focuses on the quality of his essay. It appears that when Metzger's friend picked up his own blue book a few days later, he found himself in company with a large proportion of his section in having received on the essay a C. When he quietly picked up "George Smith's" blue book to return it to Metzger, he observed that the grade for the essay was A. In the margin was a note in the section man's hand. It read "Excellent work. Could you have pinned these observations down a bit more closely? Compare . . . in . . . pp. . . ."

Such news could hardly be kept quiet. There was a leak, and the 17 whole scandal broke on the front page of Tuesday's *Crimson*. With the press Metzger was modest, as becomes a hero. He said that there had been nothing to it at all, really. The essay question had offered a choice of two books, Margaret Mead's *And Keep Your Powder Dry* or Geoffrey Gorer's *The American People*. Metzger reported that having read neither of them, he had chosen the second "because the title gave me some notion as to what the book might be about." On the test, two critical comments were offered on each book, one favorable, one unfavorable. The students were asked to "discuss." Metzger conceded that he had played safe in throwing his lot with the most laudatory of the two comments, "but I did not forget to be balanced."

I do not have Mr. Metzger's essay before me except in vivid mem- 18 ory. As I recall, he took his first cue from the name Geoffrey, and committed his strategy to the premise that Gorer was born into an "Anglo-Saxon" culture, probably English, but certainly "English speaking." Having heard that Margaret Mead was a social anthropologist, he inferred that Gorer was the same. He then entered upon his essay, centering his inquiry upon what he supposed might be the problems inherent in an anthropologist's observation of a culture which was his own, or nearly his own. Drawing in part from memories of table-talk on cultural relativity[2] and in part from creative logic, he rang changes on the relation of observer to observed, and assessed the kind and degree of objectivity which might accrue to an observer through training as an anthropologist. He concluded that the book in question did in

2. "An important part of Harvard's education takes place during meals in the Houses." An Official Publication. [author's note] Houses are dormitories for upper-division students.

fact contribute a considerable range of " 'objective', and even 'fresh'," insights into the nature of our culture. "At the same time," he warned, "these observations must be understood within the context of their generation by a person only partly freed from his embeddedness in the culture he is observing, and limited in his capacity to transcend those particular tendencies and biases which he has himself developed as a personality in his interaction with this culture since his birth. In this sense the book portrays as much the character of Geoffrey Gorer as it analyzes that of the American people." It is my regrettable duty to report that at this moment of triumph Mr. Metzger was carried away by the temptations of parody and added, "We are thus much the richer."

In any case, this was the essay for which Metzger received his honor grade and his public acclaim. He was now, of course, in serious trouble with the authorities.   19

I shall leave him for the moment to the mercy of the Administrative Board of Harvard College and turn the reader's attention to the section man who ascribed the grade. He was in much worse trouble. All the consternation in his immediate area of the Faculty and all the glee in other areas fell upon his unprotected head. I shall now undertake his defense.   20

I do so not simply because I was acquainted with him and feel a respect for his intelligence; I believe in the justice of his grade! Well, perhaps "justice" is the wrong word in a situation so manifestly absurd. This is more a case in "equity." That is, the grade is equitable if we accept other aspects of the situation which are equally absurd. My proposition is this: if we accept as valid those C grades which were accorded students who, like Metzger's friend, demonstrated a thorough familiarity with the details of the book without relating their critique to the methodological problems of social anthropology, then "George Smith" deserved not only the same, but better.   21

The reader may protest that the C's given to students who showed evidence only of diligence were indeed not valid and that both these students and "George Smith" should have received E's. To give the diligent E is of course not in accord with custom. I shall take up this matter later. For now, were I to allow the protest, I could only restate my thesis: that "George Smith's" E would, in a college of liberal arts, be properly a "better" E.   22

At this point I need a short-hand. It is a curious fact that there is no academic slang for the presentation of evidence of diligence alone. "Parroting" won't do; it is possible to "parrot" bull. I must beg the reader's pardon, and, for reasons almost too obvious to bear, suggest "cow."   23

Stated as nouns, the concepts look simple enough: 24

cow (pure): data, however relevant, without relevancies.
bull (pure): relevancies, however relevant, without data.

The reader can see all too clearly where this simplicity would lead. 25 I can assure him that I would not have imposed on him this way were I aiming to say that knowledge in this university is definable as some neuter compromise between cow and bull, some infertile hermaphrodite. This is precisely what many diligent students seem to believe: that what they must learn to do is to "find the right mean" between "amounts" of detail and "amounts" of generalities. Of course this is not the point at all. The problem is not quantitative, nor does its solution lie on a continuum between the particular and the general. Cow and bull are not poles of a single dimension. A clear notion of what they really are is essential to my inquiry, and for heuristic purposes I wish to observe them further in the celibate state.

When the pure concepts are translated into verbs, their complexities 26 become apparent in the assumptions and purposes of the students as they write:

> To cow (v. intrans.) or the act of cowing:
> To list data (or perform operations) without awareness of, or comment upon, the contexts, frames of reference, or points of observation which determine the origin, nature, and meaning of the data (or procedures). To write on the assumption that "a fact is a fact." To present evidence of hard work as a substitute for understanding, without any intent to deceive.

> To bull (v. intrans.) or the act of bulling:
> To discourse upon the contexts, frames of reference and points of observation which would determine the origin, nature, and meaning of data if one had any. To present evidence of an understanding of form in the hope that the reader may be deceived into supposing a familiarity with content.

At the level of conscious intent, it is evident that cowing is more 27 moral, or less immoral, than bulling. To speculate about unconscious intent would be either an injustice or a needless elaboration of my theme. It is enough that the impression left by cow is one of earnestness, diligence, and painful naiveté. The grader may feel disappointment or even irritation, but these feelings are usually balanced by pity, compassion, and a reluctance to hit a man when he's both down and moral. He may feel some challenge to his teaching, but none whatever to his one-ups-manship. He writes in the margin: "See me."

We are now in a position to understand the anomaly of custom: 28 As instructors, we always assign bull an E, *when we detect it;* whereas we usually give cow a C, *even though it is always obvious.*

After all, we did not ask to be confronted with a choice between 29 morals and understanding (or did we?). We evince a charming humanity, I think, in our decision to grade in favor of morals and pathos. "I simply *can't* give this student an E after he has *worked* so hard." At the same time we tacitly express our respect for the bullster's strength. We recognize a colleague. If he knows so well how to dish it out, we can be sure that he can also take it.

Of course it is just possible that we carry with us, perhaps from our   30
own school-days, an assumption that if a student is willing to work
hard and collect "good hard facts" he can always be taught to understand their relevance, whereas a student who has caught onto the forms
of relevance without working at all is a lost scholar.

But this is not in accord with our experience.   31

It is not in accord either, as far as I can see, with the stated values 32
of a liberal education. If a liberal education should teach students "how
to think," not only in their own fields but in fields outside their own—
that is, to understand "how the other fellow orders knowledge," then
bulling, even in its purest form, expresses an important part of what a
pluralist university holds dear, surely a more important part than the
collecting of "facts that are facts" which schoolboys learn to do. Here
then, good bull appears not as ignorance at all but as an aspect of
knowledge. It is both relevant and "true." In a university setting good
bull is therefore of more value than "facts," which, without a frame of
reference, are not even "true" at all.

Perhaps this value accounts for the final anomaly: as instructors,   33
we are inclined to reward bull highly, *where we do not detect its intent,*
to the consternation of the bullster's acquaintances. And often we do
not examine the matter too closely. After a long evening of reading
blue books full of cow, the sudden meeting with a student who at least
understands the problems of one's field provides a lift like a draught of
refreshing wine, and a strong disposition toward trust.

This was, then, the sense of confidence that came to our unfortu-   34
nate section man as he read "George Smith's" sympathetic considerations.

                                    II

In my own years of watching over students' shoulders as they work,   35
I have come to believe that this feeling of trust has a firmer basis than
the confidence generated by evidence of diligence alone. I believe that
the theory of a liberal education holds. Students who have dared to
understand man's real relation to his knowledge have shown themselves to be in a strong position to learn content rapidly and meaning-
fully, and to retain it. I have learned to be less concerned about the
education of a student who has come to understand the nature of man's
knowledge, even though he has not yet committed himself to hard
work, than I am about the education of the student who, after one or
two terms at Harvard, is working desperately hard and still believes that
collected "facts" constitute knowledge. The latter, when I try to explain
to him, too often understands me to be saying that he "doesn't *put in
enough generalities.*" Surely he has "put in *enough* facts."

I have come to see such quantitative statements as expressions of   36 an entire, coherent epistemology. In grammar school the student is taught that Columbus discovered America in 1492. The *more* such items he gets "right" on a given test the more he is credited with "knowing." From years of this sort of thing it is not unnatural to develop the conviction that knowledge consists of the accretion of hard facts by hard work.

The student learns that the more facts and procedures he can get   37 "right" in a given course, the better will be his grade. The more courses he takes, the more subjects he has "had," the more credits he accumulates, the more diplomas he will get, until, after graduate school, he will emerge with his doctorate, a member of the community of scholars.

The foundation of this entire life is the proposition that a fact is a   38 fact. The necessary correlate of this proposition is that a fact is either right or wrong. This implies that the standard against which the rightness or wrongness of a fact may be judged exists *someplace*— perhaps graven upon a tablet in a Platonic world outside and above *this* cave of tears. In grammar school it is evident that the tablets which enshrine the spelling of a word or the answer to an arithmetic problem are visible to my teacher who need only compare my offerings to it. In high school I observe that my English teachers disagree. This can only mean that the tablets in such matters as the goodness of a poem are distant and obscured by clouds. They surely exist. The pleasing of befuddled English teachers degenerates into assessing their prejudices, a game in which I have no protection against my competitors more glib of tongue. I respect only my science teachers, authorities who *really know.* Later I learn from them that "this is only what we think *now.*" But eventually, surely. . . . Into this epistemology of education, apparently shared by teachers in such terms as "credits," "semester hours" and "years of French," the student may invest his ideals, his drive, his competitiveness, his safety, his self-esteem, and even his love.

College raises other questions: by whose calendar is it proper to say   39 that Columbus discovered America in 1492? How, when, and by whom was the year 1 established in this calendar? What of other calendars? In view of the evidence for Leif Ericson's previous visit (and the American Indians), what historical ethnocentrism is suggested by the use of the word "discover" in this sentence? As for Leif Ericson, in accord with what assumptions do you order the evidence?

These questions and their answers are not "more" knowledge. They   40 are devastation. I do not need to elaborate upon the epistemology, or rather epistemologies, they imply. A fact has become at last "an observation or an operation performed in a frame of reference." A liberal education is founded in an awareness of frame of reference even in the most immediate and empirical examination of data. Its acquirement involves relinquishing hope of absolutes and of the protection they afford against doubt and the glib-tongued competitor. It demands an ever widening sophistication about systems of thought and observation.

It leads, not away from, but *through* the arts of gamesmanship to a new trust.

This trust is in the value and integrity of systems, their varied char- 41 acter, and the way their apparently incompatible metaphors enlighten, from complementary facets, the particulars of human experience. As one student said to me: "I used to be cynical about intellectual games. Now I want to know them thoroughly. You see I came to realize that it was only when I knew the rules of the game cold that I could tell whether what I was saying was tripe."

We too often think of the bullster as cynical. He can be, and not 42 always in a light-hearted way. We have failed to observe that there can lie behind cow the potential of a deeper and more dangerous despair. The moralism of sheer work and obedience can be an ethic that, unwilling to face a despair of its ends, glorifies its means. The implicit refusal to consider the relativity of both ends and means leaves the operator in an unconsidered proprietary absolutism. History bears witness that in the pinches this moral superiority has no recourse to negotiation, only to force.

A liberal education proposes that man's hope lies elsewhere: in the 43 negotiability that can arise from an understanding of the integrity of systems and of their origins in man's address to his universe. The prerequisite is the courage to accept such a definition of knowledge. From then on, of course, there is nothing incompatible between such an epistemology and hard work. Rather the contrary.

I can now at last let bull and cow get together. The reader knows 44 best how a productive wedding is arranged in his own field. This is the nuptial he celebrates with a straight A on examinations. The masculine context must embrace the feminine particular, though itself "born of woman." Such a union is knowledge itself, and it alone can generate new contexts and new data which can unite in their turn to form new knowledge.

In this happy setting we can congratulate in particular the Natural 45 Sciences, long thought to be barren ground to the bullster. I have indeed drawn my examples of bull from the Social Sciences, and by analogy from the Humanities. Essay-writing in these fields has long been thought to nurture the art of bull to its prime. I feel, however, that the Natural Sciences have no reason to feel slighted. It is perhaps no accident that Metzger was a mathematician. As part of my researches for this paper, furthermore, a student of considerable talent has recently honored me with an impressive analysis of the art of amassing "partial credits" on examinations in advanced physics. Though beyond me in some respects, his presentation confirmed my impression that instructors of Physics frequently honor on examinations operations structurally similar to those requisite in a good essay.

The very qualities that make the Natural Sciences fields of delight 46 for the eager gamesman have been essential to their marvelous fertility.

III

As priests of these mysteries, how can we make our rites more   47
precisely expressive? The student who merely cows robs himself, without knowing it, of his education and his soul. The student who only
bulls robs himself, as he knows full well, of the joys of inductive discovery—that is, of engagement. The introduction of frames of reference in
the new curricula of Mathematics and Physics in the schools is a hopeful
experiment. We do not know yet how much of these potent revelations
the very young can stand, but I suspect they may rejoice in them more
than we have supposed. I can't believe they have never wondered about
Leif Ericson and that word "discovered," or even about 1492. They
have simply been too wise to inquire.

Increasingly in recent years better students in the better high schools   48
and preparatory schools are being allowed to inquire. In fact they appear to be receiving both encouragement and training in their inquiry.
I have the evidence before me.

Each year for the past five years all freshmen entering Harvard and   49
Radcliffe have been asked in freshman week to "grade" two essays
answering an examination question in History. They are then asked to
give their reasons for their grades. One essay, filled with dates, is 99%
cow. The other, with hardly a date in it, is a good essay, easily mistaken
for bull. The "official" grades of these essays are, for the first (alas!) C
"because he has worked so hard," and for the second (soundly, I think)
B. Each year a larger majority of freshmen evaluate these essays as
would the majority of the faculty, and for the faculty's reasons, and
each year a smaller minority give the higher honor to the essay offering
data alone. Most interesting, a larger number of students each year,
while not overrating the second essay, award the first the straight E
appropriate to it in a college of liberal arts.

For us who must grade such students in a university, these develop-   50
ments imply a new urgency, did we not feel it already. Through our
grades we describe for the students, in the showdown, what we believe
about the nature of knowledge. The subtleties of bull are not peripheral
to our academic concerns. That they penetrate to the center of our care
is evident in our feelings when a student whose good work we have
awarded a high grade reveals to us that he does not feel he deserves it.
Whether he disqualifies himself because "there's too much bull in it,"
or worse because "I really don't think I've worked that hard," he presents a serious educational problem. Many students feel this sleaziness;
only a few reveal it to us.

We can hardly allow a mistaken sense of fraudulence to undermine   51
our students' achievements. We must lead students beyond their concept of bull so that they may honor relevancies that are really relevant.
We can willingly acknowledge that, in lieu of the date 1492, a consideration of calendars and of the word "discovered," may well be offered

with intent to deceive. We must insist that this does not make such considerations intrinsically immoral, and that, contrariwise, the date 1492 may be no substitute for them. Most of all, we must convey the impression that we grade understanding qua understanding. To be convincing, I suppose we must concede to ourselves in advance that a bright student's understanding is understanding even if he achieved it by osmosis rather than by hard work in our course.

These are delicate matters. As for cow, its complexities are not what   52
need concern us. Unlike good bull, it does not represent partial knowledge at all. It belongs to a different theory of knowledge entirely. In our theories of knowledge it represents total ignorance, or worse yet, a knowledge downright inimical to understanding. I even go so far as to propose that we award no more C's for cow. To do so is rarely, I feel, the act of mercy it seems. Mercy lies in clarity.

The reader may be afflicted by a lingering curiosity about the fate   53
of Mr. Metzger. I hasten to reassure him. The Administrative Board of Harvard College, whatever its satanic reputation, is a benign body. Its members, to be sure, were on the spot. They delighted in Metzger's exploit, but they were responsible to the Faculty's rule. The hero stood in danger of probation. The debate was painful. Suddenly one member, of a refined legalistic sensibility, observed that the rule applied specifically to "examinations" and that the occasion had been simply an hour-test. Mr. Metzger was merely "admonished."

GEORGE ORWELL

Politics and the English Language

George Orwell (1903–1950), a British writer born in India, was educated in England before serving with the Indian Imperial Police in Burma. Returning to Europe in 1927, Orwell soon plunged into a series of political and social investigations that led him to sympathize with Marxism. He lived with unemployed coal miners while he worked on *The Road to Wigan Pier* (1937) and fought with the Republican army in the Spanish Civil War before writing *Homage to Catalonia* (1938). Shortly afterward, however, Orwell's political views changed significantly as his concern about restrictions placed on individual freedom led him to reject the totalitarianism of the left as firmly as the totalitarianism of the right. Ineligible for military service in World War II, he worked tirelessly in the British Broadcasting Corporation's propaganda war in Asia. Orwell's fame in his own time was made largely by his novels—especially the satirical *Animal Farm* (1945) and the gloomy *1984* (1949), in which he portrayed a grim future ruled by mechanized language and thought. Orwell's long-lasting influence, however, has come from his nonfiction, collected in *Inside the Whale* (1940), *Dickens, Dali and Others* (1946), *Shooting an Elephant* (1950), and *Such, Such Were the Joys* (1953). "Politics and the English Language" was first published in *Horizon*, April 1946.

Most people who bother with the matter at all would admit that 1 the English language is in a bad way, but it is generally assumed that we cannot by conscious action do anything about it. Our civilization is decadent and our language—so the argument runs—must inevitably share in the general collapse. It follows that any struggle against the abuse of language is a sentimental archaism, like preferring candles to electric light or hansom cabs to aeroplanes. Underneath this lies the half-conscious belief that language is a natural growth and not an instrument which we shape for our own purposes.

Now, it is clear that the decline of a language must ultimately have 2 political and economic causes: it is not due simply to the bad influence of this or that individual writer. But an effect can become a cause, reinforcing the original cause and producing the same effect in an intensified form, and so on indefinitely. A man may take to drink because he feels himself to be a failure, and then fail all the more completely because he drinks. It is rather the same thing that is happening to the English language. It becomes ugly and inaccurate because our thoughts are foolish, but the slovenliness of our language makes it easier for us to have foolish thoughts. The point is that the process is reversible. Modern English, especially written English, is full of bad habits which spread by imitation and which can be avoided if one is willing to take the necessary trouble. If one gets rid of these habits one can think more clearly, and to think clearly is a necessary first step towards political regeneration: so that the fight against bad English is not frivolous and is not the exclusive concern of professional writers. I will come back to this presently, and I hope that by that time the meaning of what I have said here will have become clearer. Meanwhile, here are five specimens of the English language as it is now habitually written.

These five passages have not been picked out because they are 3 especially bad—I could have quoted far worse if I had chosen—but because they illustrate various of the mental vices from which we now suffer. They are a little below the average, but are fairly representative samples. I number them so that I can refer back to them when necessary:

> (1) I am not, indeed, sure whether it is not true to say that the Milton who once seemed not unlike a seventeenth-century Shelley had not become, out of an experience ever more bitter in each year, more alien [*sic*] to the founder of that Jesuit sect which nothing could induce him to tolerate.

> Professor Harold Laski (Essay in *Freedom of Expression*).

(2) Above all, we cannot play ducks and drakes with a native battery of idioms which prescribes such egregious collocations of vocables as the Basic *put up with* for *tolerate* or *put at a loss* for *bewilder*.

Professor Lancelot Hogben (*Interglossa*).

(3) On the one side we have the free personality: by definition it is not neurotic, for it has neither conflict nor dream. Its desires, such as they are, are transparent, for they are just what institutional approval keeps in the forefront of consciousness; another institutional pattern would alter their number and intensity; there is little in them that is natural, irreducible, or culturally dangerous. But *on the other side*, the social bond itself is nothing but the mutual reflection of these self-secure integrities. Recall the definition of love. Is not this the very picture of a small academic? Where is there a place in this hall of mirrors for either personality or fraternity?

Essay on psychology in *Politics* (New York).

(4) All the "best people" from the gentlemen's clubs, and all the frantic fascist captains, united in common hatred of Socialism and bestial horror of the rising tide of the mass revolutionary movement, have turned to acts of provocation, to foul incendiarism, to medieval legends of poisoned wells, to legalize their own destruction of proletarian organizations, and rouse the agitated petty-bourgeoisie to chauvinistic fervour on behalf of the fight against the revolutionary way out of the crisis.

Communist pamphlet.

(5) If a new spirit *is* to be infused into this old country, there is one thorny and contentious reform which must be tackled, and that is the humanization and galvanization of the B.B.C. Timidity here will bespeak cancer and atrophy of the soul. The heart of Britain may be sound and of strong beat, for instance, but the British lion's roar at present is like that of Bottom in Shakespeare's *Midsummer Night's Dream*—as gentle as any sucking dove. A virile new Britain cannot continue indefinitely to be traduced in the eyes or rather ears, of the world by the effete languors of Langham Place, brazenly masquerading as "standard English". When the Voice of Britain is heard at nine o'clock, better far and infinitely less ludicrous to hear aitches honestly dropped than the present priggish, inflated, inhibited, school-ma'amish arch braying of blameless bashful mewing maidens!

Letter in *Tribune*.

Each of these passages has faults of its own, but, quite apart from avoidable ugliness, two qualities are common to all of them. The first is staleness of imagery: the other is lack of precision. The writer either has a meaning and cannot express it, or he inadvertently says something else, or he is almost indifferent as to whether his words mean anything or not. This mixture of vagueness and sheer incompetence is the most marked characteristic of modern English prose, and especially of any kind of political writing. As soon as certain topics are raised, the concrete melts into the abstract and no one seems able to think of turns of speech that are not hackneyed: prose consists less and less of *words* chosen for the sake of their meaning, and more and more of *phrases* tacked together like the sections of a prefabricated hen-house. I list below, with notes and examples, various of the tricks by means of which the work of prose-construction is habitually dodged:

DYING METAPHORS

A newly invented metaphor assists thought by evoking a visual image, while on the other hand a metaphor which is technically "dead" (e.g. *iron resolution*) has in effect reverted to being an ordinary word and can generally be used without loss of vividness. But in between these two classes there is a huge dump of worn-out metaphors which have lost all evocative power and are merely used because they save people the trouble of inventing phrases for themselves. Examples are: *Ring the changes on, take up the cudgels for, toe the line, ride roughshod over, stand shoulder to shoulder with, play into the hands of, no axe to grind, grist to the mill, fishing in troubled waters, on the order of the day, Achilles' heel, swan song, hotbed.* Many of these are used without knowledge of their meaning (what is a "rift," for instance?), and incompatible metaphors are frequently mixed, a sure sign that the writer is not interested in what he is saying. Some metaphors now current have been twisted out of their original meaning without those who use them even being aware of the fact. For example, *toe the line* is sometimes written *tow the line*. Another example is *the hammer and the anvil*, now always used with the implication that the anvil gets the worst of it. In real life it is always the anvil that breaks the hammer, never the other way about: a writer who stopped to think what he was saying would be aware of this, and would avoid perverting the original phrase.

OPERATORS OR VERBAL FALSE LIMBS

These save the trouble of picking out appropriate verbs and nouns, and at the same time pad each sentence with extra syllables which give it an appearance of symmetry. Characteristic phrases are: *render inoperative, militate against, make contact with, be subjected to, give rise to, give grounds for, have the effect of, play a leading part (role) in, make itself felt, take effect, exhibit a tendency to, serve the purpose of, etc., etc.* The keynote is the elimination of simple verbs. Instead of being a single word, such as *break, stop, spoil, mend, kill,* a verb becomes a *phrase,* made up of a noun or adjective tacked on to some general-purposes verb such as *prove, serve, form, play, render.* In addition, the passive voice is wherever possible used in preference to the active, and noun constructions are used instead of gerunds (*by examination of* instead of *by examining*). The range of verbs is further cut down by means of the *-ize* and *de-* formation, and the banal statements are given an appearance of profundity by means of the *not un-* formation. Simple conjunctions and prepositions are replaced by such phrases as *with respect to, having regard to, the fact that, by dint of, in view of, in the interests of, on the hypothesis that;* and the ends of sentences are saved from anticlimax by such resounding commonplaces as *greatly to be desired, cannot be left out of account, a development to be expected in the near future, deserving of serious consideration, brought to a satisfactory conclusion,* and so on and so forth.

PRETENTIOUS DICTION

Words like *phenomenon, element, individual* (as noun), *objective, categorical, effective, virtual, basic, primary, promote, constitute, exhibit, exploit, utilize, eliminate, liquidate,* are used to dress up simple statements and give an air of scientific impartiality to biased judgments. Adjectives like *epoch-making, epic, historic, unforgettable, triumphant, age-old, inevitable, inexorable, veritable,* are used to dignify the sordid processes of international politics, while writing that aims at glorifying war usually takes on an archaic colour, its characteristic words being: *realm, throne, chariot, mailed fist, trident, sword, shield, buckler, banner, jackboot, clarion.* Foreign words and expressions such as *cul de sac, ancien régime, deus ex machina, mutatis mutandis, status quo, gleichschaltung, weltanschauung,* are used to give an air of culture and elegance. Except for the useful abbreviations *i.e., e.g.,* and *etc.,* there is no real need for any of the hundreds of foreign phrases now current in English. Bad writers, and especially scientific, political and sociological writers, are nearly always haunted by the notion that Latin or Greek words are grander than Saxon ones, and unnecessary words like *expedite, ameliorate, predict, extraneous, deracinated, clandestine, subaqueous* and hundreds of others constantly gain ground from their Anglo-Saxon opposite numbers.[1] The jargon peculiar to Marxist writing (*hyena, hangman, cannibal, petty bourgeois, these gentry, lacquey, flunkey, mad dog, White Guard,* etc.) consists largely of words and phrases translated from Russian, German or French; but the normal way of coining a new word is to use a Latin or Greek root with the appropriate affix and, where necessary, the *-ize* formation. It is often easier to make up words of this kind (*deregionalize, impermissible, extramarital, non-fragmentatory* and so forth) than to think

1. An interesting illustration of this is the way in which the English flower names which were in use till very recently are being ousted by Greek ones, *snapdragon* becoming *antirrhinum, forget-me-not* becoming *myosotis,* etc. It is hard to see any practical reason for this change of fashion: it is probably due to an instinctive turning-away from the more homely word and a vague feeling that the Greek word is scientific. [author's note]

up the English words that will cover one's meaning. The result, in general, is an increase in slovenliness and vagueness.

MEANINGLESS WORDS

In certain kinds of writing, particularly in art criticism and literary [8] criticism, it is normal to come across long passages which are almost completely lacking in meaning.[2] Words like *romantic, plastic, values, human, dead, sentimental, natural, vitality,* as used in art criticism, are strictly meaningless in the sense that they not only do not point to any discoverable object, but are hardly ever expected to do so by the reader. When one critic writes, "The outstanding feature of Mr. X's work is its living quality", while another writes, "The immediately striking thing about Mr. X's work is its peculiar deadness", the reader accepts this as a simple difference of opinion. If words like *black* and *white* were involved, instead of the jargon words *dead* and *living,* he would see at once that language was being used in an improper way. Many political words are similarly abused. The word *Fascism* has now no meaning except in so far as it signifies "something not desirable." The words *democracy, socialism, freedom, patriotic, realistic, justice,* have each of them several different meanings which cannot be reconciled with one another. In the case of a word like *democracy,* not only is there no agreed definition, but the attempt to make one is resisted from all sides. It is almost universally felt that when we call a country democratic we are praising it: consequently the defenders of every kind of régime claim that it is a democracy, and fear that they might have to stop using the word if it were tied down to any one meaning. Words of this kind are often used in a consciously dishonest way. That is, the person who uses them has his own private definition, but allows his hearer to think he means something quite different. Statements like *Marshal Pétain was a true patriot, The Soviet Press is the freest in the world, The Catholic Church is opposed to persecution,* are almost always made with intent to deceive. Other words used in variable meanings, in most cases more or less dishonestly, are: *class, totalitarian, science, progressive, reactionary, bourgeois, equality.*

Now that I have made this catalogue of swindles and perversions, [9] let me give another example of the kind of writing that they lead to. This time it must of its nature be an imaginary one. I am going to translate a passage of good English into modern English of the worst

---

2. Example: "Comfort's catholicity of perception and image, strangely Whitmanesque in range, almost the exact opposite in aesthetic compulsion, continues to evoke that trembling atmospheric accumulative hinting at a cruel, an inexorably serene timelessness . . . Wrey Gardiner scores by aiming at simple bull's-eyes with precision. Only they are not so simple, and through this contented sadness runs more than the surface bitter-sweet of resignation" (*Poetry Quarterly*). [author's note]

sort. Here is a well-known verse from *Ecclesiastes*:

> I returned and saw under the sun, that the race is not to the swift, nor the
> battle to the strong, neither yet bread to the wise, nor yet riches to men of
> understanding, nor yet favour to men of skill; but time and chance happen-
> eth to them all.

Here it is in modern English: 10

> Objective consideration of contemporary phenomena compels the conclu-
> sion that success or failure in competitive activities exhibits no tendency
> to be commensurate with innate capacity, but that a considerable element
> of the unpredictable must invariably be taken into account.

This is a parody, but not a very gross one. Exhibit (3), above, for   11
instance, contains several patches of the same kind of English. It will
be seen that I have not made a full translation. The beginning and
ending of the sentence follow the original meaning fairly closely, but
in the middle the concrete illustrations—race, battle, bread—dissolve
into the vague phrase "success or failure in competitive activities." This
had to be so, because no modern writer of the kind I am discussing—no
one capable of using phrases like "objective consideration of contemporary phenomena"—would ever tabulate his thoughts in that precise
and detailed way. The whole tendency of modern prose is away from
concreteness. Now analyse the two sentences a little more closely. The
first contains forty-nine words but only sixty syllables, and all its words
are those of everyday life. The second contains thirty-eight words of
ninety syllables: eighteen of its words are from Latin roots, and one
from Greek. The first sentence contains six vivid images, and only one
phrase ("time and chance") that could be called vague. The second
contains not a single fresh, arresting phrase, and in spite of its ninety
syllables it gives only a shortened version of the meaning contained in
the first. Yet without a doubt it is the second kind of sentence that is
gaining ground in modern English. I do not want to exaggerate. This
kind of writing is not yet universal, and outcrops of simplicity will occur
here and there in the worst-written page. Still, if you or I were told to
write a few lines on the uncertainty of human fortunes, we should
probably come much nearer to my imaginary sentence than to the one
from *Ecclesiastes*.

As I have tried to show, modern writing at its worst does not consist   12
in picking out words for the sake of their meaning and inventing images
in order to make the meaning clearer. It consists in gumming together
long strips of words which have already been set in order by someone
else, and making the results presentable by sheer humbug. The attraction of this way of writing is that it is easy. It is easier—even
quicker, once you have the habit—to say *In my opinion it is a not unjustifiable assumption that* than to say *I think*. If you use ready-made phrases,

you not only don't have to hunt about for words; you also don't have to bother with the rhythms of your sentences, since these phrases are generally so arranged as to be more or less euphonious. When you are composing in a hurry—when you are dictating to a stenographer, for instance, or making a public speech—it is natural to fall into a pretentious, Latinized style. Tags like *a consideration which we should do well to bear in mind* or *a conclusion to which all of us would readily assent* will save many a sentence from coming down with a bump. By using stale metaphors, similes and idioms, you save much mental effort, at the cost of leaving your meaning vague, not only for your reader but for yourself. This is the significance of mixed metaphors. The sole aim of a metaphor is to call up a visual image. When these images clash—as in *The Fascist octopus has sung its swan song, the jackboot is thrown into the melting pot*—it can be taken as certain that the writer is not seeing a mental image of the objects he is naming; in other words he is not really thinking. Look again at the examples I gave at the beginning of this essay. Professor Laski (1) uses five negatives in fifty-three words. One of these is superfluous, making nonsense of the whole passage, and in addition there is the slip *alien* for akin, making further nonsense, and several avoidable pieces of clumsiness which increase the general vagueness. Professor Hogben (2) plays ducks and drakes with a battery which is able to write prescriptions, and, while disapproving of the everyday phrase *put up with,* is unwilling to look *egregious* up in the dictionary and see what it means. (3), if one takes an uncharitable attitude towards it, is simply meaningless: probably one could work out its intended meaning by reading the whole of the article in which it occurs. In (4), the writer knows more or less what he wants to say, but an accumulation of stale phrases chokes him like tea leaves blocking a sink. In (5), words and meaning have almost parted company. People who write in this manner usually have a general emotional meaning— they dislike one thing and want to express solidarity with another—but they are not interested in the detail of what they are saying. A scrupulous writer, in every sentence that he writes, will ask himself at least four questions, thus: What am I trying to say? What words will express it? What image or idiom will make it clearer? Is this image fresh enough to have an effect? And he will probably ask himself two more: Could I put it more shortly? Have I said anything that is avoidably ugly? But you are not obliged to go to all this trouble: You can shirk it by simply throwing your mind open and letting the ready-made phrases come crowding in. They will construct your sentences for you—even think your thoughts for you, to a certain extent—and at need they will perform the important service of partially concealing your meaning even from yourself. It is at this point that the special connection between politics and the debasement of language becomes clear.

In our time it is broadly true that political writing is bad writing. 13

Where it is not true, it will generally be found that the writer is some kind of rebel, expressing his private opinions and not a "party line." Orthodoxy, of whatever colour, seems to demand a lifeless, imitative style. The political dialects to be found in pamphlets, leading articles, manifestos, White Papers and the speeches of under-secretaries do, of course, vary from party to party, but they are all alike in that one almost never finds in them a fresh, vivid, home-made turn of speech. When one watches some tired hack on the platform mechanically repeating the familiar phrases—*bestial atrocities, iron heel, bloodstained tyranny, free peoples of the world, stand shoulder to shoulder*—one often has a curious feeling that one is not watching a live human being but some kind of dummy: a feeling which suddenly becomes stronger at moments when the light catches the speaker's spectacles and turns them into blank discs which seem to have no eyes behind them. And this is not altogether fanciful. A speaker who uses that kind of phraseology has gone some distance towards turning himself into a machine. The appropriate noises are coming out of his larynx, but his brain is not involved as it would be if he were choosing his words for himself. If the speech he is making is one that he is accustomed to make over and over again, he may be almost unconscious of what he is saying, as one is when one utters the responses in church. And this reduced state of consciousness, if not indispensable, is at any rate favourable to political conformity.

In our time, political speech and writing are largely the defence of the indefensible. Things like the continuance of British rule in India, the Russian purges and deportations, the dropping of the atom bombs on Japan, can indeed be defended, but only by arguments which are too brutal for most people to face, and which do not square with the professed aims of political parties. Thus political language has to consist largely of euphemism, question-begging and sheer cloudy vagueness. Defenceless villages are bombarded from the air, the inhabitants driven out into the countryside, the cattle machine-gunned, the huts set on fire with incendiary bullets: this is called *pacification*. Millions of peasants are robbed of their farms and sent trudging along the roads with no more than they can carry: this is called *transfer of population* or *rectification of frontiers*. People are imprisoned for years without trial, or shot in the back of the neck or sent to die of scurvy in Arctic lumber camps: this is called *elimination of unreliable elements*. Such phraseology is needed if one wants to name things without calling up mental pictures of them. Consider for instance some comfortable English professor defending Russian totalitarianism. He cannot say outright, "I believe in killing off your opponents when you can get good results by doing so." Probably, therefore, he will say something like this:

"While freely conceding that the Soviet régime exhibits certain features which the humanitarian may be inclined to deplore, we must, I think, agree that a certain curtailment of the right to political opposition is an unavoidable concomitant of transitional periods, and that the rigours which the Russian people have been called upon to undergo have been amply justified in the sphere of concrete achievement."

The inflated style is itself a kind of euphemism. A mass of Latin words falls upon the facts like soft snow, blurring the outlines and covering up all the details. The great enemy of clear language is insincerity. When there is a gap between one's real and one's declared aims, one turns as it were instinctively to long words and exhausted idioms, like a cuttlefish squirting out ink. In our age there is no such thing as "keeping out of politics." All issues are political issues, and politics itself is a mass of lies, evasions, folly, hatred and schizophrenia. When the general atmosphere is bad, language must suffer. I should expect to find—this is a guess which I have not sufficient knowledge to verify—that the German, Russian and Italian languages have all deteriorated in the last ten or fifteen years, as a result of dictatorship.

But if thought corrupts language, language can also corrupt thought. A bad usage can spread by tradition and imitation, even among people who should and do know better. The debased language that I have been discussing is in some ways very convenient. Phrases like *a not unjustifiable assumption, leaves much to be desired, would serve no good purpose, a consideration which we should do well to bear in mind,* are a continuous temptation, a packet of aspirins always at one's elbow. Look back through this essay, and for certain you will find that I have again and again committed the very faults I am protesting against. By this morning's post I have received a pamphlet dealing with conditions in Germany. The author tells me that he "felt impelled" to write it. I open it at random, and here is almost the first sentence that I see: "(The Allies) have an opportunity not only of achieving a radical transformation of Germany's social and political structure in such a way as to avoid a nationalistic reaction in Germany itself, but at the same time of laying the foundations of a co-operative and unified Europe." You see, he "feels impelled" to write—feels, presumably, that he has something new to say—and yet his words, like cavalry horses answering the bugle, group themselves automatically into the familiar dreary pattern. This invasion of one's mind by ready-made phrases (*lay the foundations, achieve a radical transformation*) can only be prevented if one is constantly on guard against them, and every such phrase anesthetizes a portion of one's brain.

I said earlier that the decadence of our language is probably curable. Those who deny this would argue, if they produced an argument at all, that language merely reflects existing social conditions, and that we cannot influence its development by any direct tinkering with words and constructions. So far as the general tone or spirit of a language goes, this may be true, but it is not true in detail. Silly words and expressions have often disappeared, not through any evolutionary proc-

ess but owing to the conscious action of a minority. Two recent examples were *explore every avenue* and *leave no stone unturned,* which were
killed by the jeers of a few journalists. There is a long list of flyblown
metaphors which could similarly be got rid of if enough people would
interest themselves in the job; and it should also be possible to laugh
the *not un-* formation out of existence,[3] to reduce the amount of Latin
and Greek in the average sentence, to drive out foreign phrases and
strayed scientific words, and, in general, to make pretentiousness unfashionable. But all these are minor points. The defence of the English
language implies more than this, and perhaps it is best to start by saying
what it does *not* imply.

To begin with it has nothing to do with archaism, with the salvaging   19
of obsolete words and turns of speech, or with the setting up of a
"standard English" which must never be departed from. On the contrary, it is especially concerned with the scrapping of every word or
idiom which has outworn its usefulness. It has nothing to do with
correct grammar and syntax, which are of no importance so long as
one makes one's meaning clear, or with the avoidance of Americanisms,
or with having what is called a "good prose style." On the other hand
it is not concerned with fake simplicity and the attempt to make written
English colloquial. Nor does it even imply in every case preferring the
Saxon word to the Latin one, though it does imply using the fewest
and shortest words that will cover one's meaning. What is above all
needed is to let the meaning choose the word, and not the other way
about. In prose, the worst thing one can do with words is to surrender
to them. When you think of a concrete object, you think wordlessly,
and then, if you want to describe the thing you have been visualizing
you probably hunt about till you find the exact words that seem to fit.
When you think of something abstract you are more inclined to use
words from the start, and unless you make a conscious effort to prevent
it, the existing dialect will come rushing in and do the job for you, at
the expense of blurring or even changing your meaning. Probably it is
better to put off using words as long as possible and get one's meaning
as clear as one can through pictures or sensations. Afterwards one can
choose—not simply *accept*—the phrases that will best cover the meaning, and then switch round and decide what impression one's words
are likely to make on another person. This last effort of the mind cuts
out all stale or mixed images, all prefabricated phrases, needless repeti-
tions, and humbug and vagueness generally. But one can often be in
doubt about the effect of a word or a phrase, and one needs rules that

---

3. One can cure oneself of the *not un-* formation by memorizing this sentence: *A not
unblack dog was chasing a not unsmall rabbit across a not ungreen field.* [author's note]

one can rely on when instinct fails. I think the following rules will cover most cases:

(i) Never use a metaphor, simile or other figure of speech which you are used to seeing in print.

(ii) Never use a long word where a short one will do.

(iii) If it is possible to cut a word out, always cut it out.

(iv) Never use the passive where you can use the active.

(v) Never use a foreign phrase, a scientific word or a jargon word if you can think of an everyday English equivalent.

(vi) Break any of these rules sooner than say anything outright barbarous.

These rules sound elementary, and so they are, but they demand a deep change of attitude in anyone who has grown used to writing in the style now fashionable. One could keep all of them and still write bad English, but one could not write the kind of stuff that I quoted in those five specimens at the beginning of this article.

I have not here been considering the literary use of language, but merely language as an instrument for expressing and not for concealing or preventing thought. Stuart Chase and others have come near to claiming that all abstract words are meaningless, and have used this as a pretext for advocating a kind of political quietism. Since you don't know what Fascism is, how can you struggle against Fascism? One need not swallow such absurdities as this, but one ought to recognize that the present political chaos is connected with the decay of language, and that one can probably bring about some improvement by starting at the verbal end. If you simplify your English, you are freed from the worst follies of orthodoxy. You cannot speak any of the necessary dialects, and when you make a stupid remark its stupidity will be obvious, even to yourself. Political language—and with variations this is true of all political parties, from Conservatives to Anarchists—is designed to make lies sound truthful and murder respectable, and to give an appearance of solidity to pure wind. One cannot change this all in a moment, but one can at least change one's own habits, and from time to time one can even, if one jeers loudly enough, send some worn-out and useless phrase—some *jackboot, Achilles' heel, hotbed, melting pot, acid test, veritable inferno* or other lump of verbal refuse—into the dustbin where it belongs.

SUSAN GLASPELL

Trifles

Susan Glaspell (1882–1948) was born in Davenport, Iowa, the daughter of a feed dealer and an immigrant Irish woman. She took her B.A. from Drake University in Des Moines, Iowa, in 1899 and began her professional career by writing sentimental short stories for popular magazines. In 1915 she and her husband, George Cram Cook (a Harvard graduate from her hometown), joined Eugene O'Neill in founding the Provincetown Players, one of the most influential theater groups in U.S. history. Although she was from that point on identified as part of the literary avant-garde, her work continued to show her admiration for the pioneers who had settled the Midwest and especially for strong, capable farm women. Several of Glaspell's one-act plays were collected in *Plays* (1920). Among her full-length plays are *The Inheritors* (1921), *The Comic Artist* (1927), and *Alison's House* (1930), which won a Pulitzer Prize. Her novels include *Fidelity* (1915) and *Judd Rankin's Daughter* (1945). "Trifles," a one-act play produced by the Provincetown Players in 1916, is still a favorite of little theater groups.

Characters

GEORGE HENDERSON, *County Attorney*
HENRY PETERS, *Sheriff*
LEWIS HALE, *A Neighboring Farmer*

MRS. PETERS
MRS. HALE

SCENE

The kitchen in the now abandoned farmhouse of JOHN WRIGHT, *a gloomy kitchen, and left without having been put in order—unwashed pans under the sink, a loaf of bread outside the breadbox, a dish towel on the table—other signs of incompleted work. At the rear the outer door opens and the* SHERIFF *comes in followed by the* COUNTY ATTORNEY *and* HALE. *The* SHERIFF *and* HALE *are men in middle life, the* COUNTY ATTORNEY *is a young man; all are much bundled up and go at once to the stove. They are followed by two women—the* SHERIFF's *wife first; she is a slight wiry woman, a thin nervous face.* MRS. HALE *is larger and would ordinarily be called more comfortable looking, but she is disturbed now and looks fearfully about as she enters. The women have come in slowly, and stand close together near the door.*

COUNTY ATTORNEY. [*Rubbing his hands.*] This feels good. Come up to the fire, ladies.

MRS. PETERS. [*After taking a step forward.*] I'm not—cold.

SHERIFF. [*Unbuttoning his overcoat and stepping away from the stove as if to mark the beginning of official business.*] Now, Mr. Hale, before we move things about, you explain to Mr. Henderson just what you saw when you came here yesterday morning.

COUNTY ATTORNEY. By the way, has anything been moved? Are things just as you left them yesterday?

SHERIFF. [*Looking about.*] It's just the same. When it dropped below zero last night I thought I'd better send Frank out this morning to make a fire for us—no use getting pneumonia with a big case on, but I told him not to touch anything except the stove—and you know Frank.

COUNTY ATTORNEY. Somebody should have been left here yesterday.

SHERIFF. Oh—yesterday. When I had to send Frank to Morris Center for that man who went crazy—I want you to know I had my hands full yesterday, I knew you could get back from Omaha by today and as long as I went over everything here myself—

COUNTY ATTORNEY. Well, Mr. Hale, tell just what happened when you came here yesterday morning.

HALE. Harry and I had started to town with a load of potatoes. We came along the road from my place and as I got here I said, "I'm going to see if I can't get John Wright to go in with me on a party telephone." I spoke to Wright about it once before and he put me off, saying folks talked too much anyway, and all he asked was peace and quiet—I guess you know about how much he talked himself; but I thought maybe if I went to the house and talked about it before his wife, though I said to Harry that I didn't know as what his wife wanted made much difference to John—

COUNTY ATTORNEY. Let's talk about that later, Mr. Hale. I do want to talk about that, but tell now just what happened when you got to the house.

HALE. I didn't hear or see anything; I knocked at the door, and still it was all quiet inside. I knew they must be up, it was past eight o'clock. So I knocked again, and I thought I heard somebody say, "Come in." I wasn't sure, I'm not sure yet, but I opened the door—this door [*Indicating the door by which the two women are still standing*] and there in that rocker—[*Pointing to it.*] sat Mrs. Wright. [*They all look at the rocker.*]

COUNTY ATTORNEY. What—was she doing?

HALE. She was rockin' back and forth. She had her apron in her hand and was kind of—pleating it.

COUNTY ATTORNEY. And how did she—look?

HALE. Well, she looked queer.

COUNTY ATTORNEY. How do you mean—queer?

HALE. Well, as if she didn't know what she was going to do next. And kind of done up.

COUNTY ATTORNEY. How did she seem to feel about your coming?

HALE. Why, I don't think she minded—one way or other. She didn't pay much attention. I said, "How do, Mrs. Wright, it's cold, ain't it?" And she said, "Is it?"—and went on kind of pleating at her apron.

Well, I was surprised; she didn't ask me to come up to the stove, or to set down, but just sat there, not even looking at me, so I said, "I want to see John." And then she—laughed. I guess you would call it a laugh. I thought of Harry and the team outside, so I said a little sharp: "Can't I see John?" "No," she says, kind o' dull like. "Ain't he home?" says I. "Yes," says she, "he's home." "Then why can't I see him?" I asked her, out of patience. " 'Cause he's dead," says she. "*Dead?*" says I. She just nodded her head, not getting a bit excited, but rockin' back and forth. "Why—where is he?" says I, not knowing what to say. She just pointed upstairs—like that [*Himself pointing to the room above*]. I got up, with the idea of going up there. I walked from there to here—then I says, "Why, what did he die of?" "He died of a rope round his neck," says she, and just went on pleatin' at her apron. Well, I went out and called Harry. I thought I might—need help. We went upstairs and there he was lyin'—

COUNTY ATTORNEY. I think I'd rather have you go into that upstairs where   20
you can point it all out. Just go on now with the rest of the story.

HALE. Well, my first thought was to get that rope off. It looked . . . [*Stops, his face twitches.*] . . . but Harry, he went up to him, and he said, "No, he's dead all right, and we'd better not touch anything." So we went back down stairs. She was still sitting that same way. "Has anybody been notified?" I asked. "No," says she, unconcerned. "Who did this, Mrs. Wright?" said Harry. He said it businesslike—and she stopped pleatin' of her apron. "I don't know," she says. "You don't *know?*" says Harry. "No," says she. "Weren't you sleepin' in the bed with him?" says Harry. "Yes," says she, "but I was on the inside." "Somebody slipped a rope round his neck and strangled him and you didn't wake up?" says Harry. "I didn't wake up," she said after him. We must 'a looked as if we didn't see how that could be, for after a minute she said, "I sleep sound." Harry was going to ask her more questions but I said maybe we ought to let her tell her story first to the coroner, or the sheriff, so Harry went fast as he could to Rivers' place, where there's a telephone.

COUNTY ATTORNEY. And what did Mrs. Wright do when she knew that you had gone for the coroner?

HALE. She moved from that chair to this one over here [*Pointing to a small chair in the corner.*] and just sat there with her hands held together and looking down. I got a feeling that I ought to make some conversation, so I said I had come in to see if John wanted to put in a telephone, and at that she started to laugh, and then she stopped and looked at me—scared. [*The* COUNTY ATTORNEY, *who has had his notebook out, makes a note.*] I dunno, maybe it wasn't scared. I wouldn't like to say it was. Soon Harry got back, and then Dr. Lloyd came, and you, Mr. Peters, and so I guess that's all I know that you don't.

COUNTY ATTORNEY. [*Looking around.*] I guess we'll go upstairs first—and

then out to the barn and around there. [*To the* SHERIFF] You're convinced that there was nothing important here—nothing that would
point to any motive.

SHERIFF. Nothing here but kitchen things.

[*The* COUNTY ATTORNEY, *after again looking around the kitchen, opens the
door of a cupboard closet. He gets up on a chair and looks on a shelf. Pulls
his hand away, sticky.*]

COUNTY ATTORNEY. Here's a nice mess.

[*The women draw nearer.*]

MRS. PETERS. [*To the other woman.*] Oh, her fruit; it did freeze. [*To the*
COUNTY ATTORNEY] She worried about that when it turned so cold. She
said the fire'd go out and her jars would break.

SHERIFF. Well, can you beat the women! Held for murder and worryin'
about her preserves.

COUNTY ATTORNEY. I guess before we're through she may have something
more serious than preserves to worry about.

HALE. Well, women are used to worrying over trifles.

[*The two women move a little closer together.*]

COUNTY ATTORNEY. [*With the gallantry of a young politician.*] And yet, for
all their worries, what would we do without the ladies? [*The women
do not unbend. He goes to the sink, takes a dipperful of water from the
pail and pouring it into a basin, washes his hands. Starts to wipe them on
the roller towel, turns it for a cleaner place.*] Dirty towels! [*Kicks his foot
against the pans under the sink.*] Not much of a housekeeper, would
you say, ladies?

MRS. HALE. [*Stiffly.*] There's a great deal of work to be done on a farm.

COUNTY ATTORNEY. To be sure. And yet [*With a little bow to her*] I know
there are some Dickson county farmhouses which do not have such
roller towels.

[*He gives it a pull to expose its full length again.*]

MRS. HALE. Those towels get dirty awful quick. Men's hands aren't always as clean as they might be.

COUNTY ATTORNEY. Ah, loyal to your sex, I see. But you and Mrs. Wright
were neighbors. I suppose you were friends, too.

MRS. HALE. [*Shaking her head.*] I've not seen much of her of late years.
I've not been in this house—it's more than a year.

COUNTY ATTORNEY. And why was that? You didn't like her?

MRS. HALE. I liked her all well enough. Farmers' wives have their hands
full, Mr. Henderson. And then—

COUNTY ATTORNEY. Yes—?

MRS. HALE. [*Looking about.*] It never seemed a very cheerful place.

COUNTY ATTORNEY. No—it's not cheerful. I shouldn't say she had the
homemaking instinct.

MRS. HALE. Well, I don't know as Wright had, either.

COUNTY ATTORNEY. You mean that they didn't get on very well?

MRS. HALE. No, I don't mean anything. But I don't think a place'd be any cheerfuller for John Wright's being in it.

COUNTY ATTORNEY. I'd like to talk more of that a little later. I want to get   45
the lay of things upstairs now.

[*He goes to the left, where three steps lead to a stair door.*]

SHERIFF. I suppose anything Mrs. Peters does'll be all right. She was to take in some clothes for her, you know, and a few little things. We left in such a hurry yesterday.

COUNTY ATTORNEY. Yes, but I would like to see what you take, Mrs. Peters, and keep an eye out for anything that might be of use to us.

MRS. PETERS. Yes, Mr. Henderson.

[*The women listen to the men's steps on the stairs, then look about the kitchen.*]

MRS. HALE. I'd hate to have men coming into my kitchen, snooping around and criticising.

[*She arranges the pans under sink which the* COUNTY ATTORNEY *had shoved out of place.*]

MRS. PETERS. Of course it's no more than their duty.   50

MRS. HALE. Duty's all right, but I guess that deputy sheriff that came out to make the fire might have got a little of this on. [*Gives the roller towel a pull.*] Wish I'd thought of that sooner. Seems mean to talk about her for not having things slicked up when she had to come away in such a hurry.

MRS. PETERS. [*Who has gone to a small table in the left rear corner of the room, and lifted one end of a towel that covers a pan.*] She had bread set.

[*Stands still.*]

MRS. HALE. [*Eyes fixed on a loaf of bread beside the breadbox, which is on a low shelf at the other side of the room. Moves slowly toward it.*] She was going to put this in there. [*Picks up loaf, then abruptly drops it. In a manner of returning to familiar things.*] It's a shame about her fruit. I wonder if it's all gone. [*Gets up on the chair and looks.*] I think there's some here that's all right, Mrs. Peters. Yes—here; [*Holding it toward the window.*] this is cherries, too. [*Looking again.*] I declare I believe that's the only one. [*Gets down, bottle in her hand. Goes to the sink and wipes it off on the outside.*] She'll feel awful bad after all her hard work in the hot weather. I remember the afternoon I put up my cherries last summer.

[*She puts the bottle on the big kitchen table, center of the room. With a sigh, is about to sit down in the rocking-chair. Before she is seated realizes what chair it is; with a slow look at it, steps back. The chair which she has touched rocks back and forth.*]

MRS. PETERS. Well, I must get those things from the front room closet. [*She goes to the door at the right, but after looking into the other room, steps back.*] You coming with me, Mrs. Hale? You could help me carry them.

[*They go in the other room; reappear,* MRS. PETERS *carrying a dress and skirt,* MRS. HALE *following with a pair of shoes.*]

MRS. PETERS. My, it's cold in there.   55

[*She puts the clothes on the big table, and hurries to the stove.*]

MRS. HALE. [*Examining her skirt.*] Wright was close. I think maybe that's why she kept so much to herself. She didn't even belong to the Ladies Aid. I suppose she felt she couldn't do her part, and then you don't enjoy things when you feel shabby. She used to wear pretty clothes and be lively, when she was Minnie Foster, one of the town girls singing in the choir. But that—oh, that was thirty years ago. This all you was to take in?

MRS. PETERS. She said she wanted an apron. Funny thing to want, for there isn't much to get you dirty in jail, goodness knows. But I suppose just to make her feel more natural. She said they was in the top drawer in this cupboard. Yes, here. And then her little shawl that always hung behind the door. [*Opens stair door and looks.*] Yes, here it is.

[*Quickly shuts door leading upstairs.*]

MRS. HALE. [*Abruptly moving toward her.*] Mrs. Peters?

MRS. PETERS. Yes, Mrs. Hale?

MRS. HALE. Do you think she did it?   60

MRS. PETERS. [*In a frightened voice.*] Oh, I don't know.

MRS. HALE. Well, I don't think she did. Asking for an apron and her little shawl. Worrying about her fruit.

MRS. PETERS. [*Starts to speak, glances up, where footsteps are heard in the room above. In a low voice.*] Mr. Peters says it looks bad for her. Mr. Henderson is awful sarcastic in a speech and he'll make fun of her sayin' she didn't wake up.

MRS. HALE. Well, I guess John Wright didn't wake when they was slipping that rope under his neck.

MRS. PETERS. No, it's strange. It must have been done awful crafty and   65
still. They say it was such a—funny way to kill a man, rigging it all up like that.

MRS. HALE. That's just what Mr. Hale said. There was a gun in the house. He says that's what he can't understand.

MRS. PETERS. Mr. Henderson said coming out that what was needed for the case was a motive; something to show anger, or—sudden feeling.

MRS. HALE. [*Who is standing by the table.*] Well, I don't see any signs of anger around here. [*She puts her hand on the dish towel which lies on the table, stands looking down at table, one half of which is clean, the other half messy.*] It's wiped to here. [*Makes a move as if to finish work, then turns and looks at loaf of bread outside the breadbox. Drops towel. In that voice of coming back to familiar things.*] Wonder how they are finding things upstairs. I hope she had it a little more red-up up there. You know, it seems kind of *sneaking.* Locking her up in town and then coming out here and trying to get her own house to turn against her!

MRS. PETERS. But Mrs. Hale, the law is the law.

MRS. HALE. I s'pose 'tis. [*Unbuttoning her coat.*] Better loosen up your   70
things, Mrs. Peters. You won't feel them when you go out.

[MRS. PETERS *takes off her fur tippet, goes to hang it on hook at back of
room, stands looking at the under part of the small corner table.*]

MRS. PETERS. She was piecing a quilt.

[*She brings the large sewing basket and they look at the bright pieces.*]

MRS. HALE. It's log cabin pattern. Pretty, isn't it? I wonder if she was
goin' to quilt it or just knot it?

[*Footsteps have been heard coming down the stairs. The* SHERIFF *enters
followed by* HALE *and the* COUNTY ATTORNEY.]

SHERIFF. They wonder if she was going to quilt it or just knot it!

[*The men laugh; the women look abashed.*]

COUNTY ATTORNEY. [*Rubbing his hands over the stove.*] Frank's fire didn't
do much up there, did it? Well, let's go out to the barn and get that
cleared up.

[*The men go outside.*]

MRS. HALE. [*Resentfully.*] I don't know as there's anything so strange, our   75
takin' up our time with little things while we're waiting for them to
get the evidence. [*She sits down at the big table smoothing out a block
with decision.*] I don't see as it's anything to laugh about.

MRS. PETERS. [*Apologetically.*] Of course they've got awful important
things on their minds.

[*Pulls up a chair and joins* MRS. HALE *at the table.*]

MRS. HALE. [*Examining another block.*] Mrs. Peters, look at this one. Here,
this is the one she was working on, and look at the sewing! All the
rest of it has been so nice and even. And look at this! It's all over the
place! Why, it looks as if she didn't know what she was about!

[*After she has said this they look at each other, then start to glance back
at the door. After an instant* MRS. HALE *has pulled at a knot and ripped
the sewing.*]

MRS. PETERS. Oh, what are you doing, Mrs. Hale?

MRS. HALE. [*Mildly.*] Just pulling out a stitch or two that's not sewed
very good. [*Threading a needle.*] Bad sewing always made me fidgety.

MRS. PETERS. [*Nervously.*] I don't think we ought to touch things.   80

MRS. HALE. I'll just finish up this end. [*Suddenly stopping and leaning forward.*] Mrs. Peters?

MRS. PETERS. Yes, Mrs. Hale?

MRS. HALE. What do you suppose she was so nervous about?

MRS. PETERS. Oh—I don't know. I don't know as she was nervous. I
sometimes sew awful queer when I'm just tired. [MRS. HALE *starts to
say something, looks at* MRS. PETERS, *then goes on sewing.*] Well, I must
get these things wrapped up. They may be through sooner than we
think. [*Putting apron and other things together.*] I wonder where I can
find a piece of paper, and string.

MRS. HALE. In that cupboard, maybe. 85

MRS. PETERS. [*Looking in cupboard.*] Why, here's a birdcage. [*Holds it up.*] Did she have a bird, Mrs. Hale?

MRS. HALE. Why, I don't know whether she did or not—I've not been here for so long. There was a man around last year selling canaries cheap, but I don't know as she took one; maybe she did. She used to sing real pretty herself.

MRS. PETERS. [*Glancing around.*] Seems funny to think of a bird here. But she must have had one, or why would she have a cage? I wonder what happened to it.

MRS. HALE. I s'pose maybe the cat got it.

MRS. PETERS. No, she didn't have a cat. She's got that feeling some people 90 have about cats—being afraid of them. My cat got in her room and she was real upset and asked me to take it out.

MRS. HALE. My sister Bessie was like that. Queer, ain't it?

MRS. PETERS. [*Examining the cage.*] Why, look at this door. It's broke. One hinge is pulled apart.

MRS. HALE. [*Looking too.*] Looks as if someone must have been rough with it.

MRS. PETERS. Why, yes.

[*She brings the cage forward and puts it on the table.*]

MRS. HALE. I wish if they're going to find any evidence they'd be about 95 it. I don't like this place.

MRS. PETERS. But I'm awful glad you came with me, Mrs. Hale. It would be lonesome for me sitting here alone.

MRS. HALE. It would, wouldn't it? [*Dropping her sewing.*] But I tell you what I do wish, Mrs. Peters. I wish I had come over sometimes when *she* was here. I—[*Looking around the room.*]—wish I had.

MRS. PETERS. But of course you were awful busy. Mrs. Hale—your house and your children.

MRS. HALE. I could've come. I stayed away because it weren't cheerful— and that's why I ought to have come. I—I've never liked this place. Maybe because it's down in a hollow and you don't see the road. I dunno what it is but it's a lonesome place and always was. I wish I had come over to see Minnie Foster sometimes. I can see now—

[*Shakes her head.*]

MRS. PETERS. Well, you mustn't reproach yourself, Mrs. Hale. Somehow 100 we just don't see how it is with other folks until—something comes up.

MRS. HALE. Not having children makes less work—but it makes a quiet house, and Wright out to work all day, and no company when he did come in. Did you know John Wright, Mrs. Peters?

MRS. PETERS. Not to know him; I've seen him in town. They say he was a good man.

MRS. HALE. Yes—good; he didn't drink, and kept his word as well as most, I guess, and paid his debts. But he was a hard man, Mrs. Peters. Just to pass the time of day with him—[*Shivers.*] Like a raw wind that gets to the bone. [*Pauses, her eye falling on the cage.*] I should think she would 'a wanted a bird. But what do you suppose went with it?

MRS. PETERS. I don't know, unless it got sick and died.

[*She reaches over and swings the broken door, swings it again. Both women watch it.*]

MRS. HALE. You weren't raised round here, were you? [MRS. PETERS *shakes   105
her head.*] You didn't know—her?

MRS. PETERS. Not till they brought her yesterday.

MRS. HALE. She—come to think of it, she was kind of like a bird herself—real sweet and pretty, but kind of timid and—fluttery. How—she—did—change. [*Silence; then as if struck by a happy thought and relieved to get back to every day things.*] Tell you what, Mrs. Peters, why don't you take the quilt in with you? It might take up her mind.

MRS. PETERS. Why, I think that's a real nice idea, Mrs. Hale. There couldn't possibly be any objection to it, could there? Now, just what would I take? I wonder if her patches are in here—and her things.

[*They look in the sewing basket.*]

MRS. HALE. Here's some red. I expect this has got sewing things in it. [*Brings out a fancy box.*] What a pretty box. Looks like something somebody would give you. Maybe her scissors are in here. [*Opens box. Suddenly puts her hand to her nose.*] Why—[MRS. PETERS *bends nearer, then turns her face away.*] There's something wrapped up in this piece of silk.

MRS. PETERS. Why, this isn't her scissors.   110

MRS. HALE. [*Lifting the silk.*] Oh, Mrs. Peters—it's—

[MRS. PETERS *bends closer.*]

MRS. PETERS. It's the bird.

MRS. HALE. [*Jumping up.*] But, Mrs. Peters—look at it! Its neck! Look at its neck! It's all—other side ,to.

MRS. PETERS. Somebody—wrung—its—neck.

[*Their eyes meet. A look of growing comprehension, of horror. Steps are heard outside.* MRS. HALE *slips box under quilt pieces, and sinks into her chair. Enter* SHERIFF *and* COUNTY ATTORNEY. MRS. PETERS *rises.*]

COUNTY ATTORNEY. [*As one turning from serious things to little pleasantries.*]   115
Well, ladies, have you decided whether she was going to quilt it or knot it?

MRS. PETERS. We think she was going to—knot it.

COUNTY ATTORNEY. Well, that's interesting, I'm sure. [*Seeing the birdcage.*] Has the bird flown?

MRS. HALE. [*Putting more quilt pieces over the box.*] We think the—cat got it.

COUNTY ATTORNEY. [*Preoccupied.*] Is there a cat?

[MRS. HALE *glances in a quick covert way at* MRS. PETERS.]

MRS. PETERS. Well, not *now*. They're superstitious, you know. They leave. 120

COUNTY ATTORNEY. [*To* SHERIFF PETERS, *continuing an interrupted conversation.*] No sign at all of anyone having come from the outside. Their own rope. Now let's go up again and go over it piece by piece. [*They start upstairs.*] It would have to have been someone who knew just the—

[MRS. PETERS *sits down. The two women sit there not looking at one another, but as if peering into something and at the same time holding back. When they talk now it is in the manner of feeling their way over strange ground, as if afraid of what they are saying, but as if they can not help saying it.*]

MRS. HALE. She liked the bird. She was going to bury it in that pretty box.

MRS. PETERS. [*In a whisper.*] When I was a girl—my kitten—there was a boy took a hatchet, and before my eyes—and before I could get there—[*Covers her face an instant.*] If they hadn't held me back I would have—[*Catches herself, looks upstairs where steps are heard, falters weakly.*]—hurt him.

MRS. HALE. [*With a slow look around her.*] I wonder how it would seem never to have had any children around. [*Pause.*] No, Wright wouldn't like the bird—a thing that sang. She used to sing. He killed that, too.

MRS. PETERS. [*Moving uneasily.*] We don't know who killed the bird. 125

MRS. HALE. I knew John Wright.

MRS. PETERS. It was an awful thing was done in this house that night, Mrs. Hale. Killing a man while he slept, slipping a rope around his neck that choked the life out of him.

MRS. HALE. His neck. Choked the life out of him.

[*Her hand goes out and rests on the birdcage.*]

MRS. PETERS. [*With rising voice.*] We don't know who killed him. We don't *know*.

MRS. HALE. [*Her own feeling not interrupted.*] If there'd been years and years of nothing, then a bird to sing to you, it would be awful—still, after the bird was still. 130

MRS. PETERS. [*Something within her speaking.*] I know what stillness is. When we homesteaded in Dakota, and my first baby died—after he was two years old, and me with no other then—

MRS. HALE. [*Moving.*] How soon do you suppose they'll be through, looking for the evidence?

MRS. PETERS. I know what stillness is. [*Pulling herself back.*] The law has got to punish crime, Mrs. Hale.

MRS. HALE. [*Not as if answering that.*] I wish you'd seen Minnie Foster when she wore a white dress with blue ribbons and stood up there in the choir and sang. [*A look around the room.*] Oh, I *wish* I'd come over here once in a while! That was a crime! That was a crime! Who's going to punish that?

MRS. PETERS. [*Looking upstairs.*] We mustn't—take on. 135

MRS. HALE. I might have known she needed help! I know how things can be—for women. I tell you, it's queer, Mrs. Peters. We live close together and we live far apart. We all go through the same things—it's all just a different kind of the same thing. [*Brushes her eyes; noticing the bottle of fruit, reaches out for it.*] If I was you I wouldn't tell her her fruit was gone. Tell her it *ain't*. Tell her it's all right. Take this in to prove it to her. She—she may never know whether it was broke or not.

MRS. PETERS. [*Takes the bottle, looks about for something to wrap it in; takes petticoat from the clothes brought from the other room, very nervously begins winding this around the bottle. In a false voice.*] My, it's a good thing the men couldn't hear us. Wouldn't they just laugh! Getting all stirred up over a little thing like a—dead canary. As if that could have anything to do with—with—wouldn't they *laugh*!

[*The men are heard coming down stairs.*]

MRS. HALE. [*Under her breath.*] Maybe they would—maybe they wouldn't.

COUNTY ATTORNEY. No, Peters, it's all perfectly clear except a reason for doing it. But you know juries when it comes to women. If there was some definite thing. Something to show—something to make a story about—a thing that would connect up with this strange way of doing it—

[*The women's eyes meet for an instant. Enter* HALE *from outer door.*]

HALE. Well, I've got the team around. Pretty cold out there.   140

COUNTY ATTORNEY. I'm going to stay here a while by myself. [*To the* SHER-IFF.] You can send Frank out for me, can't you? I want to go over everything. I'm not satisfied that we can't do better.

SHERIFF. Do you want to see what Mrs. Peters is going to take in?

[*The* COUNTY ATTORNEY *goes to the table, picks up the apron, laughs.*]

COUNTY ATTORNEY. Oh, I guess they're not very dangerous things the ladies have picked out. [*Moves a few things about, disturbing the quilt pieces which cover the box. Steps back.*] No, Mrs. Peters doesn't need supervising. For that matter, a sheriff's wife is married to the law. Ever think of it that way, Mrs. Peters?

MRS. PETERS. Not—just that way.

SHERIFF. [*Chuckling.*] Married to the law. [*Moves toward the other room.*]   145
I just want you to come in here a minute, George. We ought to take a look at these windows.

COUNTY ATTORNEY. [*Scoffingly.*] Oh, windows!

SHERIFF. We'll be right out, Mr. Hale.

[HALE *goes outside. The* SHERIFF *follows the* COUNTY ATTORNEY *into the other room. Then* MRS. HALE *rises, hands tight together, looking intensely at* MRS. PETERS, *whose eyes make a slow turn, finally meeting* MRS. HALE'S. *A moment* MRS. HALE *holds her, then her own eyes point the way to where the box is concealed. Suddenly* MRS. PETERS *throws back quilt pieces and tries*

to put the box in the bag she is wearing. It is too big. She opens box, starts
to take bird out, cannot touch it, goes to pieces, stands there helpless. Sound
of a knob turning in the other room. MRS. HALE snatches the box and puts
it in the pocket of her big coat. Enter COUNTY ATTORNEY and SHERIFF.]

COUNTY ATTORNEY. [Facetiously.] Well, Henry, at least we found out that
she was not going to quilt it. She was going to—what is it you call
it, ladies?

MRS. HALE. [Her hand against her pocket.] We call it—knot it, Mr. Henderson.

CURTAIN

LI-YOUNG LEE

This Room and Everything in It

Li-Young Lee (1957–   ) is a Chinese American whose father was
once the personal physician to China's powerful leader, Mao Tse-tung.
After his father fell from favor and served two years as a political
prisoner, the family fled to Indonesia, where Lee was born. The family
lived in Hong Kong, Macau, and Japan before settling in America,
where Lee's father became a Presbyterian minister. Lee's relationship
with his father, who died in 1980, is the subject of much of his poetry.
Educated at the University of Arizona and the State University of New
York, Lee has taught at several institutions, including the University
of Iowa and Northwestern. He has received grants from the National
Endowment for the Arts and a Guggenheim fellowship. His first book
of poetry, *Rose*, was published in 1986; his second book, *The City in
Which I Love You* (1990), was the 1990 Lamont Poetry Selection of
the Academy of American Poets. In 1990 Lee traveled to China and
Indonesia to conduct research for *The Winged Seed* (1995), a book of
reminiscences. "This Room and Everything in It" is collected in *The
City in Which I Love You*.

Lie still now   1
while I prepare for my future,
certain hard days ahead,
when I'll need what I know so clearly this moment.

I am making use   2
of the one thing I learned
of all the things my father tried to teach me:
the art of memory.

I am letting this room
and everything in it
stand for my ideas about love
and its difficulties.   3

I'll let your love-cries,
those spacious notes
of a moment ago,
stand for distance.   4

Your scent,
that scent
of spice and a wound,
I'll let stand for mystery.   5

Your sunken belly
is the daily cup
of milk I drank
as a boy before morning prayer.   6

The sun on the face
of the wall
is God, the face
I can't see, my soul,   7

and so on, each thing
standing for a separate idea,
and those ideas forming the constellation
of my greater idea.
And one day, when I need
to tell myself something intelligent
about love,   8

I'll close my eyes
and recall this room and everything in it:
My body is estrangement.
This desire, perfection.
Your closed eyes my extinction.
Now I've forgotten my
idea. The book
on the windowsill, riffled by wind . . .
the even-numbered pages are
the past, the odd-
numbered pages, the future.
The sun is
God, your body is milk . . .   9

useless, useless . . .   10
your cries are song, my body's not me . . .
no good . . . my idea
has evaporated . . . your hair is time, your thighs are song . . .
it had something to do
with death . . . it had something
to do with love.

Appendix A: Sixteen Assignments Using The Dolphin Reader

The assignments below can be thought of as representatives of dozens of other possible assignments. If your instructor chooses to use them in their present form, notice that we have not specified length and format; check with her or him about such matters.

1. Among parents and also among experts in child-rearing, there is a constant tension between those who emphasize protecting the child from the dangers of the outside world and those who emphasize preparing the child for the realities of adult life. Using John Holt's "The Institution of Childhood" and Joy Overbeck's "Sex, Kids and the Slut Look" as sources, write an essay that describes this tension, then recommend to parents a strategy for balancing protection and preparation.

- You might want to concentrate on children of a particular age—twelve to fourteen, for example.
- Your own experiences and observations can provide you with a good deal of material, even if you elect not to mention yourself in the essay.
- The following essays in *The Dolphin Reader* include encounters between children and the adult world that might be useful as examples: Maya Angelou, "Momma"; Roger Wilkins, "Confessions of a Blue-Chip Black"; Adrienne Rich, "Split at the Root"; Katha Pollitt, "The Smurfette Principle"; Donald Hall, "Purpose, Blame, and Fire."
- You may want to do additional research by examining the book from which the Holt essay is excerpted, *Escape from Childhood,* as well as Neil Postman's *The Disappearance of Childhood,* and Michael Mitterauer's *A History of Youth.*

Your essay should be appropriate for inclusion in a magazine frequently read by parents—either a specialized publication like *Parenting* or a more generalized publication like *Redbook.* Look at these magazines to get a sense of the level of knowledge writers assume the audience to have and the ways that writers attempt to engage the reader's attention.

2. It is now generally acknowledged that children learn sex roles in the process of growing up: culture, more than biology, teaches girls feminine behavior and boys masculine behavior. If sex roles are not determined by genetics, then it would seem in principle that we are free to choose the roles we teach our children. Write an essay in which you describe the vision of masculinity and/or femininity you would like

your children to develop and in which you present a plan for developing it.

- If you wish, you may concentrate on the raising of either sons *or* daughters.
- Remember that your son or daughter will be living in a society that has already established (and sometimes conflicting) notions of masculinity and femininity. Be aware of the effect on all concerned of either accepting what the society offers or rejecting it.
- Particularly pertinent readings from *The Dolphin Reader* are Lois Gould's "X," Bernard Cooper's "A Clack of Tiny Sparks," Scott Russell Sanders's "Reasons of the Body," Alice Munro's "Boys and Girls," Sherwood Anderson's "Discovery of a Father," Katha Pollitt's "The Smurfette Principle," and Donald Hall's "Purpose, Blame, and Fire."

3. Perhaps because we live in a period when sex roles are changing dramatically, perceptions of masculinity and femininity have been the topic of many short articles in the press. *The New York Times,* for example, regularly publishes columns called "About Men" and "Hers," to which writers contribute essays about 1,500 words long, usually based on personal experience. Write an essay appropriate for such a column.

- For models see Noel Perrin's "The Androgynous Man," "Perri Klass's "Learning the Language," Stephen Harrigan's "Answering the Howl," and Katha Pollitt's "The Smurfette Principle," all of which were published in *The New York Times.* Note that three of the four deal directly with sex roles and that Klass's essay deals with them indirectly by presenting the perceptions of a woman entering what has been a man's profession.
- Note that the essay may be either humorous or serious.
- The essays in the *Femininity and Masculinity* unit should give you some ideas for writing. You may want to allude to one or more of these essays in your own. If you do, be sure to give information the reader may need about the author and the source, but *only* essential information. The newspaper reader doesn't need a scholarly citation.

You may want to consider submitting your essay to *The New York Times:* you will find an address for submissions on the Op-Ed page. Information about other potential places of publication can be found in *Writer's Market.*

4. Local newspapers, alumni magazines, company newsletters, and family archives often contain retrospective accounts of what life was

like in a particular community (a household, neighborhood, workplace, or school) at a particular time. Recall a community from your past and write an account of life there that would be of interest both to those who shared your experience and to those who did not but who have reason to be curious about it.

- The *Communities* unit and the *Insiders and Outsiders* unit include many essays that can serve as models for this type of writing, including Gretel Ehrlich's "Wyoming," Barry Lopez's "Manhattan, 1976," Meredith Maran's "Mean Streets," Karla F. C. Holloway's "The Thursday Ladies," Roger Wilkins's "Confessions of a Blue-Chip Black," and portions of Adrienne Rich's "Split at the Root."
- Remember that your readers are likely to be curious about how living in the community affected you (and so might have affected them).
- Pay particular attention to the forces that shape a community into a community: its peculiar rules and customs, its power structures and methods of control, its attitudes toward outsiders, the characteristic ways its members behave and talk.

Your instructor may ask you to specify (or invent) a place where your essay could be published and to describe the audience that would read it.

5. Political scientists often use the ancient Greek *polis*, or city-state, as a yardstick against which to measure modern communities. H.D.F. Kitto's chapter on the polis is so thorough in its description of the Greek model that after you read it, you should be in a position to do the same. Write an essay in which you compare a community you know to the Greek polis as Kitto describes it, demonstrating ways in which it is superior or inferior.

- Choose any size community you wish, but be alert to the implications of your choice. Comparing the U.S.A. to the Greek polis is possible and might lead to some interesting insights into the nature of American democracy. Comparing a given city or town to the polis is also possible and might lead to a fruitful discussion of the way that we interact with our neighbors. Comparing a family or school to a polis is a bit more far-fetched; it might be a springboard for ironic or humorous essays.
- Assume that your audience is educated enough to have some vague knowledge of what Greek democracy was like, but don't assume that they have read Kitto. You will have to provide them with a compressed picture of what a polis was.
- Make judgments. The comparison to the polis is a means to an

end, not an end in itself. It is a way of organizing and validating your impressions of the community, positive or negative.

Assume that you are writing for an audience with strong social and political interests. You might visualize your audience as the members of a political organization (e.g., Young Republicans or Young Democrats) or as a political science professor for whom you are writing an assigned essay.

6. It used to be said that America was an "assimilationist" or "melting pot" culture in which minorities were proud to blend into the "mainstream." Today, there is much more emphasis on diversity, and Americans often feel themselves torn between striving to assimilate or striving to build an identity as part of a culture outside the mainstream. The tension between assimilating and asserting a separate identity is most obvious in matters of race, religion, and gender, but anyone who feels like an outsider, including the disabled, the old, the poor, and (perhaps) the very rich, faces it. Write an essay in which you discuss a particular case of someone who feels this tension.

- You'll find the tension present in Roger Wilkins's "Confessions of a Blue-Chip Black," Terry Galloway's "I'm Listening as Hard as I Can," Naomi Wolf's "The Rites of Sisterhood," N. Scott Momaday's "The Way to Rainy Mountain," and Joseph Bruchac's "Turtle Meat."
- You may want to discuss your own difficulties with assimilation, or you may want to focus on the difficulties of someone else. If you focus on someone else, you will probably find an interview useful.
- Don't feel that your essay needs to take on deep grievances. Multicultural dilemmas are sometimes temporary (e.g., being the only woman in a calculus class) and sometimes even humorous (e.g., Dave Barry's "Lost in the Kitchen," which raises the question of whether men *can* assimilate with the human race).

Write your essay so that it would be publishable in a general-interest magazine like *Life* or in a magazine with a more political focus, like *The Nation* or *National Review*.

7. As the century approaches its end, we can expect people to look back with interest on the changes it has created in the human condition. Reading Thomas Alva Edison's "The Woman of the Future" and other essays and articles written around the turn of the century can give you a sense of the lives people lived a hundred years ago and their expectations about how those lives would change as inventions using the new technologies of electric and gasoline power came onto the market. Write

an essay in which you demonstrate ways that the century would have satisfied these writers' expectations and ways in which it would have surprised them or disappointed them.

- Consult such sources as *The Encyclopaedia Britannica* and *The McGraw-Hill Dictionary of Science and Technology* to establish the status of such inventions as the telephone and airplane at the turn of the century.
- To get a sense of what expectations were at the turn of the century, check such headings as "Telephone," "Electricity," and "Automobile" in volumes of *The Readers' Guide to Periodical Literature* that index magazines published from 1900 to 1910. Most college libraries will have back issues of such magazines as *Scientific American*, *The Atlantic Monthly*, and *Ladies' Home Journal* dating from this era.
- In order to make your essay manageable, focus on the impact of one invention or one class of inventions.
- Go to primary sources (the books, magazines, and newspapers of the time) to get a sense of how people reacted to technological changes as they evolved.

You may aim your essay at an audience particularly interested in technology, such as the subscribers to *Popular Mechanics*, or you may aim for a more general readership, like that of *Time*.

8. As more and more of human life is lived indoors or in outdoor settings (like the carefully manicured and pest-free suburban lawn) almost as carefully controlled as the indoors, accounts of times spent closer to nature become interesting in the same way that accounts of travels to exotic countries can be interesting. Write an essay in which you discuss an encounter with the natural world.

- Your encounter need not take place in the wilderness; any step away from your customary state of civilization may produce interesting material—even a weekend camping trip in a well-developed state park.
- Try to be a good travel writer, re-creating the sights, sounds, and smells of the place, particularly those you would not experience (or notice) in a more civilized setting.
- Report, too, on the logistics of your situation. How much "civilization" did you carry with you into nature, and how reliant were you on it?

Several essays and stories in *Nature and Civilization* and *Progress and Its Price* may stimulate your thinking for this essay, notably those by Diane Ackerman, Alice Walker, E. B. White, Harry Crews, Joseph Bruchac, and Carol Bly.

9. Many of the essays in *Nature and Civilization* directly or indirectly compare humans and animals, suggesting at times the surprises of our similarities, at times the vastness of our differences. Just how animal-like are humans? To answer this question, you must first define "nature" and "natural." While biologists often explain human behavior by looking for similar patterns in primates (to see what is "natural" behavior), in legal terms an act is "unnatural" if it falls outside of what is socially acceptable for human behavior. Defining human behavior in light of the animal world raises several possibilities for exploration: from how we understand everything from children to sexual behavior to the design of our work or school environment.

On the other hand, how human are animals? The more science tells us about the nature of animals, the more like us they seem to become, from the social networking we observe in an anthill to the language used by gorillas. Recently, an animal-rights activist claimed that "animal rights would become the civil rights issue of the twenty-first century," making the oppression of animals analogous to the treatment of slaves or the legal subordination of women. To what extent do animals deserve the same rights as human beings? Animal rights activists propose vegetarianism and the abolishing of animals in experimentation to the closing of zoos. Choose a position from the many suggested here, and argue for your own thesis about the nature of animals and/or humans or how they should be viewed. To get started, study the essays by Ackerman, Walker, Crews, Eiseley, and Hearne and the poem by Jarrell in order to create your own interpretation of our relationship to the animal world.

As you consider your audience, think of publications that favor a biological approach to defining human behavior as well as those opposed to linking us with animals, that prefer to set human beings apart not only physically but morally and spiritually as well. Consider, also, writing for an audience predisposed to disagree with your views.

10. Discussions between those who almost instinctively love modern technology and those who almost instinctively dislike it are sometimes foolish because the technology that affects our daily lives is so familiar that it is largely invisible to us. Write a paper in which you report on a thought experiment intended to make this technology more "visible." Conduct your thought experiment by recalling a segment of time from a recent day and listing the ways you were affected by technology that did not exist a hundred years ago, then ways that you were affected by technology that did not exist fifty years ago, then twenty-five, then ten. You may find that thirty minutes is a longer segment than you can manage.

- Consult such sources as *The Encyclopaedia Britannica* and *The McGraw-Hill Dictionary of Science and Technology* to establish the dates when devices came into use.

- Pay attention to *everything* that affected you at every moment: what you said, heard, felt, smelled, tasted, knew.
- Use your readings from *Progress and Its Price* and *Media* to give you some notions of what other writers have noticed about the good and bad effects of modern technology and communication on our lives.
- Leave your reader with a sense of what technology has gained for us or lost for us.

Make your essay appropriate for publication in a general-interest news-magazine or newspaper. The "My Turn" column in *Newsweek* could provide you with models.

11. The computer is conspicuously absent from "Technology and Democracy," Daniel Boorstin's survey of the social and psychological impacts of material progress, for the simple reason that computers were relatively rare (and very large and expensive) in 1972. Yet the general trends he discusses—the attenuation of experience, the decline of congregation, the rising sense of momentum, and the belief in solutions—might give us a method of analyzing the effects of the computer on our lives. Write an essay in which you extend Boorstin's analysis to cover the expansion of computer technology.

- If you play video games, use the Internet, or in any way use computers, your personal experience may help you write this essay.
- Since heavy users of computers tend to congregate on college campuses, it should be easy to supplement personal experience with interviews.

Your conclusions need not match Boorstin's. You may feel that the personal computer takes us in a direction he couldn't anticipate. Whatever your conclusions, consider writing your essay in a way that would make it publishable in *Omni, Byte,* or any of the many magazines that deal thoughtfully with the new technology.

12. Access to a videocassette recorder makes possible a kind of research not often done for college classes. With a VCR, you can study an individual program intensively, re-viewing scenes as a scholar rereads sections of a book. Or you can record a set of programs for purposes of comparison. Take advantage of this capability by writing an essay in which you scrutinize a program or set of programs (e.g., evening sitcoms) to show the attitudes it (or they) promote.

- Since children are more likely than adults to have their characters shaped by what they watch, you may want to focus on programming directed at them. You could study a Disney film, for instance, or a Saturday-morning cartoon show with its surrounding commercials. Katha Pollitt's "The Smurfette Principle" might give you some ideas for such an essay.

- David Bradley's "How TV Drew Our Family Together" focuses on the images of African-Americans that television brought into his home. Consider the possibility of doing a similar survey of today's images of African-Americans or any other group.
- Or you might focus on news and information sources that seem to be value-neutral. Neil Postman's "Now . . . This" can give you some ideas for such an essay. Comparing the way two networks (PBS versus CNN, for instance, or CNN versus NBC) cover the same event may produce an interesting essay on the question of whether there is such a thing as a neutral news source.

Write an essay that would appeal to readers of *TV Guide* or the entertainment section of your local newspaper.

13. The *Understanding* unit contains ten essays, a poem, and a play, all concerned with ways people get beyond superficial knowledge and achieve a deeper or clearer comprehension of the world. This type of comprehension is, of course, one of the great goals of a college education, but it is so difficult to define and measure that it sometimes gets lost in the day-to-day business of learning and being tested on "objective" material. Write an essay in which you try to clarify the meaning of *understanding* (as opposed to rote learning).

- Illustrate your definition(s) of understanding by referring to at least six of the selections in the unit.
- Present a view of understanding broad enough to be applied in the sciences, the humanities, the life outside academia.
- Present a view focused enough that someone who has read your essay could summarize your definition(s) of understanding in one hundred words or less.
- One way of approaching this assignment would be to develop a set of criteria that must be met before we can say that someone really understands something.

The content and tone of your essay should be appropriate for a mixed audience of college students and college teachers. A good way to get the tone right is to imagine that you are part of a committee of teachers and students who have been trying to clarify the college's mission for the twenty-first century. As part of this process, the committee is producing a booklet called *Understanding* to be distributed to faculty members, parents, students, and potential students. Your essay will be one of six included in the booklet.

14. Several of the writers of essays in *The Dolphin Reader* recall an episode that created a revolution in their thinking. Frank Conroy, for

instance, discusses events that gave him insight into the natures of jazz. Samuel Scudder tells us about an encounter that taught him to think as a biologist and William Rodman about one that taught him a lesson about anthropology. *The Dolphin Reader* contains similar "discovery" essays by Sherwood Anderson, Karla F. C. Holloway, George Orwell ("Shooting an Elephant"), Mary McCarthy, and Donald Hall. Write an essay in which you describe an event that spurred a revolution in your thinking.

15. Innumerable writers report that they learned their skill partly by intensively studying the work of a writer they admire. The purpose of this assignment is to give you an opportunity to do the same. Choose one writer represented in *The Dolphin Reader* whom you particularly admire. Starting with the information provided in the *Reader*, search out additional essays or stories by the writer. Using such sources as *Contemporary Authors, The Readers' Guide to Periodical Literature*, and computerized indexes, locate interviews with the writer and reviews of his or her work. Your reference librarian can be a great help to you with this assignment. As you prepare to write the paper, think about such questions as these:

- What is the relation between the writer's life and work?
- What constant themes unite various essays by the writer?
- What is the writer's purpose in writing?
- How does the writer establish a relationship with the reader? What is the nature of the relationship?
- What is the writer's tone? How does it vary from essay to essay or story to story?
- What are the salient features of the writer's style? Does the writer have more than one style?

The audience for your essay might be English teachers, in which case you might look at *English Journal* to get a sense of what a professional journal in the field is like. Or it might be writers or aspiring writers, in which case you might look at *Writer's Digest* or *The Writer*.

16. The editors of *The Dolphin Reader* want your help in their search for essays and stories. Write us a letter in which you recommend a selection for the next edition.

- To make the reasons for your recommendation clear, summarize the essay or story briefly and explain why you think its content would be appealing to college students.
- Quite independent of how entertaining readers might find the selection, explain how they would benefit by reading it or how others would benefit by their having read it.
- Explain what student writers can learn from the way that the

essay or story is written—what lesson(s) in style, organization, etc., a fledgling writer might learn from close study of the piece.

- If the selection is to fit into one of the existing units of the reader, tell what selection it should replace and why.
- If the selection doesn't fit into any of the existing units, describe a new unit into which it might fit.
- Give adequate bibliographic information to allow us to locate and read the selection.

Send your letter to:

Professor Carolyn Perry
English Department
Westminster College
Fulton, MO   65251

Be sure to include a return address so that we can respond with thanks and comments.

Appendix B: A Sampler of Style Exercises

That we all learn to write partly by reading is obvious, but to learn to read with a writer's eye is sometimes difficult. The set of style exercises that follow are intended to help you focus your attention on some stylistic features from our collected writers. Often they ask you to imitate the writer's style. Imitation has a less-than-glorious reputation in our nation of individualists, but we have the testimony of innumerable writers that close imitation of admirable prose can be a step toward developing a style as individual as a fingerprint. The key is first to try on another writer's style and then to set it aside or adapt it to your own.

When you imitate, do so phrase by phrase, trying to match the writer's rhythms exactly. If Thoreau gives you this:

> *I dug my cellar*
> > *in the side of a hill*
> > > *sloping to the south,*
> > > > *where a woodchuck had formerly dug his burrow*
> > > *down through sumach and blackberry roots,*
> > > *and the lowest strains of vegetation,*
> > > *six feet square by seven deep,*
> > > *to a fine sand*
> > > > *where potatoes would not freeze*
> > > > > *in any winter.*

You might respond with this:

> *She searched the drawer*
> > *at the bottom of the dresser*
> > > *stored in the attic,*
> > > > *where grandfather had always kept his mementos,*
> > > *down through clippings and theater tickets,*
> > > *many layers deep and hopelessly jumbled,*
> > > *to the dusty bottom*
> > > > *which no hand had touched*
> > > > > *for two generations.*

The imitation is rarely much good in its own right, but the process of imitating gives you a sense of how much thought and craft goes into the writer's work.

Once you get a sense of the stylistic options available to writers, you may find style exercises everywhere you look. The eighteen collected below are part of a larger collection available in the *Instructor's Resource Manual* for this book.

1. Annie Dillard, "Skin," page 33
   Dillard's Diction

Dillard's care in the choice of words is by now proverbial. To see it more clearly, examine the following passage from paragraphs 11–13 of "Skin." Without looking back at the original, try to determine which word in each set of brackets is Dillard's original choice. Be prepared to explain the merits of your choice in class discussion.

> The skin of my mother's face was smooth, fair, and tender; it took [marks/impressions] readily. She [slept/napped] on her side on the couch. Her face skin [pooled/gathered] on the low side; it [bunched/piled] up in the low corners of her deep-set eyes and [drew/hauled] down her lips and cheeks. How [plastic/flexible] was it? I pushed at a [puddle/wad] of it by her nose.
>   She [stirred/moved] and opened her eyes. I [stood/jumped] back.
>   She reminded me not to touch her face while she was sleeping. Anybody's face.
>   When she sat up, her cheek and brow bone [bore/sported] a red deep [gash/mark], the mark of the cushion's [reinforced seam/welting]. It was [stamped/textured] inside precisely with the upholstery's weave and [pattern/brocade].

2. Dave Barry, "Lost in the Kitchen," page 83
   Casual Style, Loose Sentences

Barry's casual style relies on frequent loose (cumulative) sentences that begin with a simple statement and then add on a series of modifying phrases and clauses that take the reader in unexpected directions. To appreciate how loose and casual the style is, combine the following short sentences (from paragraph 7) into one, without looking back at the original. Try to recapture the rambling effect of the original.

> I think most males rarely prepare food for others. They sometimes do. Then they have one specialty dish. In my case it is spaghetti. They prepare it maybe twice a year. It is a very elaborate production. They expect to be praised for it. It is as if they had developed a cure for heart disease, right there in the kitchen.

3. Virginia Woolf, "Professions for Women," page 93
   Examination of an Extended Metaphor

In paragraph 5 of "Professions for Women," Woolf uses the metaphor of a fisherman who hooks something unimaginably large to explain the situation of the female novelist whose imagination (likened to the minnow used as bait) runs up against "something about the body, about the passions." The metaphor is complex and worth thinking about. Try to recover the words for which capitalized words are substituted below. You may wish to work with your classmates.

> The image that comes to my mind when I think of this girl is the image of a WRITER lying sunk in dreams on the verge of a deep SUBJECT with a PEN held out over the PAPER. She was letting her imagination sweep unchecked round every NOOK and cranny of the world that lies RE-PRESSED in the depths of our unconscious being. Now came the experience, the experience that I believe to be far commoner with women writers than with men. The AGITATION raced through the girl's CONSCIOUS-NESS. Her imagination had rushed away. It had sought the SOURCES, the depths, the dark places where the STRONGEST EXPERIENCES slumber. And then there was a smash. There was an explosion. There was TURMOIL and confusion. The imagination had dashed itself against something hard.

4. N. Scott Momaday, "The Way to Rainy Mountain," page 178
   A Sentence with Parallel Subparts

Combine the following sentences into one, using one colon and three semicolons (as Momaday does in paragraph 10 of "The Way to Rainy Mountain"). The exercise should help sharpen your skills at parallel sentence construction. You will, of course, have to change wording slightly to combine the sentences.

> Now I can have her only in memory. I see my grandmother in the several postures. These were peculiar to her. I see her standing at the wood stove on a winter morning. I see her turning meat in a great iron skillet. I see her sitting at the south window. She is bent above her beadwork. I see her sitting there afterwards. Her vision had failed. She looked down for a very long time into the fold of her hands. I see her going out upon a cane. She went very slowly as she did when the weight of age came upon her. I see her praying.

5. H. D. F. Kitto, "The Polis," page 196
   A Memorable Analogy

In paragraph 6 of "The Polis," Kitto introduces a memorable analogy that shows his preference for the small Greek city-state rather than modern states "so big that they have to be referred to by their initials." With the help of a classmate, fill in the blanks, then discuss the effectiveness of the analogy: Is it precise? Does it clarify Kitto's attitude? Does it change the reader's attitude?

> The modern writer is sometimes heard to speak with splendid scorn of "those petty Greek states, with their interminable quarrels." Quite so; Plataea, Sicyon, Aegina and the rest are petty, compared with modern states. The ____ itself is petty, compared with ____—but then, the atmosphere of ____ is mainly ____, and that makes a difference. We do not like breathing ____—and the Greeks would not much have liked breathing the atmosphere of the vast modern State. They knew of one such, the Persian Empire—and thought it very suitable, for ____.

6. Adrienne Rich, "Split at the Root: An Essay on Jewish Identity,"
   page 251
   A Sentence with an Important Appositive

*Imitate the following sentence phrase by phrase, producing a sentence about
your own experience as an outsider (e.g., as the only male, female, Asian,
nerd, etc., in a group). The exercise should produce thoughts about weightier
matters than style.*

> *With enough excellence,*
> *you could presumably make it stop mattering*
>   *that you were Jewish;*
> *you could become the only Jew in the gentile world,*
>   *a Jew so "civilized,"*
>   *so far from "common,"*
>   *so attractively combining southern gentility*
>   *with European cultural values*
>   *that no one would ever confuse you*
>   *with the raw, "pushy" Jews of New York,*
>   *the "loud, hysterical" refugees from eastern Europe,*
>   *the "overdressed" Jews of the urban South.*

7. C. S. Lewis, "The Inner Ring," page 276
   A Periodic Sentence

*In paragraph 13 of "The Inner Ring," Lewis uses a long periodic sentence to
describe the insidious approach of the hint that leads a person to become a
scoundrel. Imitate his sentence, writing on a subject of your choice.*

> *Over a drink or a cup of coffee,*
> *disguised as a triviality*
>   *and*
> *sandwiched between two jokes,*
> *from the lips of a man, or woman,*
>   *whom you have recently been getting to know rather better*
>   *and*
>   *whom you hope to know better still—*
> *just at the moment when you are most anxious not to appear*
>   *crude,*
>   *or*
>   *naif,*
>   *or*
>   *a prig—*
>   *THE HINT WILL COME.*

8. Melissa Greene, "No Rms, Jungle Vu," page 328
   Multilevel Sentence Structure in a Paragraph

Paragraph 64 of "No Rms, Jungle Vu" comprises two back-to-back examples of well-structured longer sentences, one suspended, one cumulative. Imitate them with sentences on a subject of your choice.

> *The zoo-goer who emerges from the research literature—*
> > *benighted and happy-go-lucky,*
> > > *chomping his hot dog,*
> > > *holding his nose in the elephant house and*
> > > *scratching under his arm in the monkey house*
> > > > *to make his children laugh*
> *—is a walking anachronism.*
>
> *He is the creation of an outmoded institution—*
> > *the conventional zoo—*
> *in which the primate house, carnivore house,*
> *and reptile house,*
> > > *all lined with tile*
> > > *glow with an unreal greenish light*
> > > > *as if the halls were subterranean,*
> *and in which giraffes, zebras, and llamas*
> > *stand politely,*
> > > > *and as if on tiptoe,*
> > > > *on the neatly mown lawns of the moated exhibits.*

9. Annie Dillard, "The Fixed," page 344
   Precise Verbs and Verbals

In paragraph 8 of "The Fixed," Dillard describes a mantis laying eggs. The description uses a series of verbs and verb forms to show the abdomen's apparently separate life and intelligence. To appreciate how much can be suggested by verb forms, try to recall the words Dillard used instead of the generalized synonyms in capital letters.

> . . . I settled my nose an inch from that pulsing abdomen. It MOVED like a concertina, it MOVED like a bellows; it WENT, WORKING, over the BRIGHT, IRREGULAR surface of the egg case FEELING and TOUCHING, PUSHING and CORRECTING. It seemed to act so independently that I forgot the BREATHING brown stick at the other end. The bubble creature seemed to have two eyes, a frantic little brain, and two busy, soft hands. It looked like a hideous, harried mother PREPARING* a fat daughter for a beauty pageant, ADJUSTING* her, FUSSING over her, TOUCHING and REPAIRING and CLEANING and TOUCHING.

*In place of *preparing* and *adjusting*, Dillard uses participles formed of two words, like *giving up* (for surrendering) or *looking over* (for examining).

10. Jomo Kenyatta, "Gikuyu Industries," page 389
    Coherence in a Longer Paragraph

Many of Kenyatta's paragraphs are notably cohesive, filled with transitions and references that knit the sentences tightly together. Below are nine sentences that form paragraph 17. Their order has been scrambled. Unscramble them as best as you can; be prepared to explain your reasoning.

1. In the same manner the wife visits her women friends, requesting them to help in various ways.

2. During the feasting this group of men and women entertain themselves with traditional songs relating to teamwork.

3. Those who cannot take part in collecting building materials are asked to help in providing food and drink for the builders' feast, which is called *"iruga ria mwako."*

4. The man and his wife or wives receive their helpers joyfully and bid them to sit down and rest.

5. When a family is engaged in the work of building a hut or huts the help of neighbours and friends is necessary in order to expedite the work.

6. After all have arrived a feast is provided, consisting of a variety of food and drink.

7. On the day appointed many of these friends will turn up, bringing with them the required materials for building.

8. Before they part, a day is appointed when the actual building of a hut or huts will take place.

9. A man goes round asking his friends to help him, and at the same time telling them what kind of building materials he would like them to supply him with.

11. Alice Bloom, "On a Greek Holiday," page 457
    Use of Catalogues in a Description

*Bloom's style in "On a Greek Holiday" relies heavily on sentences that cata-
logue details and examples. Practice this style by imitating the sentence below
(from paragraph 3), describing a person you have seen. Hint: Mix literal and
metaphorical description as Bloom does.*

> The Greek woman is short and heavy, waistless,
>   and is wearing a black dress,
>   a black scarf pulled low around her eyes,
>   a black sweater,
>   thick black stockings,
>   black shoes.
> She is stupendously there,
>   black but for the walnut of her face,
>   in the white sun, against the white space.
> She looks, at once, as if she could do
>   everything she's ever done, anything needed,
>   and also at once, she gives off an emanation of
>   humor, powers, secrets, determinations, acts.
> She is moving straight ahead,
>   like a moving church,
>   a black peaked roof,
>   a hot black hat,
>   a dark tent,
>   like a doom,
>   a government,
>   a force for good and evil,
>   an ultimatum,
>   a determined animal.
> She probably can't read, or write;
> she may never in her life have left this island;
> but she is beautiful,
> she could crush you,
>   love you,
>   mend you,
>   deliver you of child or calf or lamb or illusion,
>   bleed a pig,
>   spear a fish,
>   wring a supper's neck,
>   till a field,
>   coax an egg into life.

12. Katha Pollitt, "The Smurfette Principle," page 485
     Cohesion and Coherence in a Paragraph

The following sentences can be rearranged to form paragraph 4 of Pollitt's essay. Attempt to put them in the "right" order; be prepared to explain your reasoning. What references and transitions hold the paragraph together? Compare the order you and your class prefer to Pollitt's order. How much "freedom" of order is there?

1. The message is clear.

2. In the worst cartoons—the ones that blend seamlessly into the animated cereal commercials—the female is usually a little-sister type, a bunny in a pink dress and hair ribbons who tags along with the adventurous bears and badgers.

3. Girls exist only in relation to boys.

4. Piggy, of "Muppet Babies," is a pint-size version of Miss Piggy, the camp glamour queen of the Muppet movies.

5. Contemporary shows are either essentially all-male, like "Garfield," or are organized on what I call the Smurfette principle: a group of male buddies will be accented by a lone female, stereotypically defined.

6. April, of the wildly popular "Teen-Age Mutant Ninja Turtles," functions as a girl Friday to a quartet of male superheroes.

7. Boys are the norm, girls the variation; boys are central, girls peripheral; boys are individuals, girls types.

8. Boys define the group, its story, and its code of values.

9. Thus, Kanga, the only female in "Winnie-the-Pooh," is a mother.

10. But the Smurfette principle rules the more carefully made shows, too.

13. Randall Jarrell, "A Sad Heart at the Supermarket," page 488
    A Two-Sentence Definition of a Way of Life

*Throughout "A Sad Heart at the Supermarket," Jarrell gives thumbnail
descriptions of a way of life that dismays him. The two sentences below (from
paragraph 7) form one such sketch, featuring parallel predicate verbs in the
first sentence and infinitives as subjects in the second. To practice Jarrell's style
while thinking about the issues he raises, imitate his sentences while writing
about a way of life very different from the consumer's.*

> *Everything about the knowledgeable consumer**
>> *looks like*
>> *or sounds like*
>> *or feels like*
>>> *money*
>>>> *and informed money at that.*
> *To live is*
>> *to consume,*
> *to understand life is*
>> *to know what to consume:*
> *he has learned to understand this,*
>> *so that his life is a series of choices*
>>> *—correct ones—*
>>>> *among the products and services of the world.*

**Note that we have omitted part of sentence 1.

14. Neil Postman, "Now . . . This," page 512
    A Periodic Sentence Moving from Cause to Effect

To practice writing a periodic sentence with parallel introductory phrases, imitate the following one from paragraph 3 of Postman's "Now . . . This."

> *In part because television*
> > *sells its time in seconds and minutes,*
> *in part because television*
> > *must use images rather than words,*
> *in part because its audience*
> > *can move freely to and from the television set,*
> *programs are structured so that*
> > *almost each eight-minute segment may stand*
> > > *as a complete event in itself.*

15. Patricia Hampl, "Memory and Imagination," page 591
    Contrasting Metaphors

In paragraph 26, Hampl uses contrasting metaphors to clarify her vision of the reader and the writer. To practice both her metaphorical technique and her syntax, imitate the passage, either developing your own vision of the reader and writer or developing a contrast between two other things that interest you. Remember that the quality of the metaphor is what counts: both its aptness and its interest.

> *I sometimes think of the reader as a cat,*
> > *endlessly fastidious,*
> > *capable, by turns,*
> > > *of mordant indifference and*
> > > > *riveted attention,*
> > *luxurious,*
> > *recumbent, and*
> > *ever poised.*
> *Whereas the writer is absolutely a dog,*
> > *panting and moping,*
> > *too eager*
> > > *for an affectionate scratch behind the ears,*
> > *lunging frantically*
> > > *after any old stick thrown in the distance.*

16. Carol Bly, "Growing Up Expressive," page 619
    An Extended Sentence-Combining Exercise

The following kernel sentences are culled from paragraph 16 of "Growing Up Expressive." Practice economy and coherence by combining them to form four to ten sentences. (Bly's original has six.) Your arrangement may require changes in order and wording. In square brackets are hints about Bly's wording.

1. A few years ago there was a stupid movement.
2. It was a movement to discourage children from reading a book.
3. The book was Grimms' fairy tales.
4. Later psychology became more sophisticated. [*with*]
5. We learned that a kind of stepmother is a reality to all children.
6. This kind of stepmother is hostile and overweening.
7. We learned that the cutting-off of a hand is a reality to all children.
8. The hand belongs to the hero.
9. It is his right hand.
10. It is replaced with another hand. [*-ing of*]
11. The other hand is made of silver.
12. There is an inner landscape. [Bly holds this till #17.]
13. Spaceships are part of it.
14. Witches' gingerbread houses are part of it.
15. Orphanages are part of it.
16. Being the last two people to survive on earth is part of it.
17. The inner landscape is something children know about. [—*all these*]
18. Therefore we need a better set of questions.
19. We need to ask children these questions.
20. We need to ask them when we are examining their artwork.
21. Some young people are going to lay their stuff in front of adults.
22. It is wild stuff.
23. These are young people who are not repressed. [*who*]
24. They will do this until the sands of life are run.
25. They are hoping for comment of some kind.
26. They are hoping for praise if possible.
27. We had better try to be good at responding to them. [*so*]
28. We are enthusiastic when they tell us something.
29. The something is "Mama, I've got the mowing done."
30. We had better be half as enthusiastic in another situation.
31. That situation is when they lay their stuff in front of us.
32. Otherwise we are acting as if we want to raise drones.
33. These drones are suitable only for conveyor-belt shifts.

17. William G. Perry, Jr., "Examsmanship and the Liberal Arts," page
    626
    "If . . . Then" and Other Qualifiers

*As a product of academic culture, Perry has developed a style that qualifies
and limits direct statements. In paragraph 32 of "Examsmanship and the
Liberal Arts," he states that "Bulling . . . expresses . . . what a pluralistic
university holds dear," but he spends another sixty words qualifying and
defining his terms. Try out the academic style by writing a parallel sentence
on a subject other than bulling. A concrete subject like basketball or hamburgers might get interesting results.*

> *If a liberal education should teach students "how to think,"*
>   *not only in their own fields*
>   *but in fields outside their own*
>   *—that is, to understand*
>   *"how the other fellow orders knowledge,"*
> *then BULLING,*
>   *even in its purest form,*
>   *EXPRESSES an important part of*
>   *WHAT A PLURALISTIC UNIVERSITY HOLDS DEAR,*
>   *surely a more important part*
>   *than the collecting of "facts that are facts"*
>   *which schoolboys learn to do.*

18. George Orwell, "Politics and the English Language," page 636
    Memorable Similes and Metaphors

*The similes and metaphors Orwell uses in "Politics and the English Lan-
guage" are remarkably vivid and memorable. To test how memorable, work
with other students in an attempt to fill in the blanks in the following passages.
Hints: think about a barnyard, tea, science fiction, weather, an octopus, and
a pain killer.*

> As soon as certain topics are raised, the concrete melts into the abstract
> and no one seems able to think of turns of speech that are not hackneyed:
> prose consists less and less of *words* chosen for the sake of their own mean-
> ing and more and more of *phrases* ＿＿ together like the ＿＿ ＿＿
> a ＿＿ ＿＿-＿＿ (paragraph 4).

> [T]he writer knows more or less what he wants to say, but an accumulation
> of stale phrases chokes him like ＿＿ ＿＿ ＿＿ a ＿＿ (paragraph 12).

"When one watches some tired hack on the platform mechanically repeating the familiar phrases . . . one often has a curious feeling that one is
not watching a live human being but some kind of _____: a feeling which
suddenly becomes stronger at moments when the light catches the
speaker's spectacles and turns them into _____ _____ which seem to have
no _____ behind them" (paragraph 13).

A mass of Latin words falls upon the facts like _____ _____, blurring the
outlines and covering up all the details (paragraph 16).

When there is a gap between one's real and one's declared aims, one turns
as it were instinctively to long words and exhausted idioms, like
a _____ _____ out _____ (paragraph 16).

Phrases like *a not unjustifiable assumption* . . . are a continuous temptation,
a _____ of _____ always at one's elbow (paragraph 17).

AUTHOR/

TITLE INDEX

ACKNOWLEDGMENTS

(continued from p. iv)

DIANE ACKERMAN: From *The Moon by Whale Light* by Diane Ackerman. Copyright © 1991 by Diane Ackerman. Reprinted by permission of Random House, Inc.

SHERWOOD ANDERSON: "Discovery of a Father" by Sherwood Anderson. Reprinted by permission of Harold Ober Associates Incorporated. Copyright 1939 by The Reader's Digest Association, Inc. Renewed © 1966 by Eleanor Copenhver Anderson.

MAYA ANGELOU: From *I Know Why the Caged Bird Sings* by Maya Angelou. Copyright © 1969 by Maya Angelou. Reprinted by permission of Random House, Inc.

TONI CADE BAMBARA: From *Gorilla, My Love* by Toni Cade Bambara. Copyright © 1972 by Toni Cade Bambara. Reprinted by permission of Random House, Inc.

DAVE BARRY: "Lost in the Kitchen" originally entitled, "Most Men Lost in Kitchen," Knight-Ridder Newspapers, May 2, 1986. Reprinted by permission of the author.

ALICE BLOOM: "On a Greek Holiday." Reprinted by permission from *The Hudson Review*, Vol. XXXVI, No. 3 (Autumn 1983). Copyright © 1983 by Alice Bloom.

CAROL BLY: "Growing Up Expressive" (pages 175–184) from *Letters from the Country* by Carol Bly. Copyright © 1973, 1974, 1975, 1977, 1978, 1979, 1981 by Carol Bly. Reprinted by permission of HarperCollins Publishers, Inc.

DANIEL J. BOORSTIN: "Technology and Democracy," Copyright, 1974, by Daniel J. Boorstin. From *Democracy and Its Discontents* (Random House, New York, 1974).

DAVID BRADLEY: "How TV Drew Our Family Together—In Spite of Its Messages," *TV Guide*, July 11, 1987. Copyright © 1987 by David Bradley. Reprinted with permission from *TV Guide* and the author. Reprinted by permission of the Wendy Weil Agency, Inc.

JENNIFER BRICE: Jennifer Brice, "My Mother's Body" from *American Nature Writing 1994*, selected by John A. Murray, published by Sierra Club Books. Reprinted by permission of the author.

GWENDOLYN BROOKS: "The Chicago Defender Sends a Man to Little Rock" by Gwendolyn Brooks from *Blacks*. Copyright © 1991, published by Third World Press, Chicago. Reprinted by permission of the author.

BRIGID BROPHY: "The Menace of Nature" from *Don't Ever Forget*. Copyright © 1966 by Brigid Brophy. All rights reserved. Reprinted by kind permission of the author.

JOSEPH BRUCHAC III: "Turtle Meat" by Joseph Bruchac, first published in *Earth Power Coming*, edited by Simon Ortiz, Navajo Community College Press.

PETER CAMERON: "Homework" from *One Way or Another* by Peter Cameron. Copyright © 1986 by Peter Cameron. Reprinted by permission of HarperCollins Publishers, Inc.

JOHN CHEEVER: "The Enormous Radio" from *The Stories of John Cheever* by John Cheever. Copyright © 1978 by John Cheever. Reprinted by permission of Alfred A. Knopf, Inc.

691

LI-YOUNG LEE: "This Room and Everything in It," copyright © 1990 by Li-Young Lee. Reprinted from *The City in Which I Love You,* by Li-Young Lee, with permission of BOAEditions, Ltd., 92 Park Ave., Brockport, NY 14420.

C. S. LEWIS: "The Inner Ring" from *Screwtape Proposes a Toast—and Other Pieces* by C. S. Lewis, reprinted by permission of HarperCollins Publishers Ltd.

LEWIS THOMAS: "Ponds," copyright © 1978 by Lewis Thomas. Originally appeared in *The New England Journal of Medicine,* from The Medusa and the Snail by Lewis Thomas. Used by permission of Viking Penguin, a division of Penguin Books USA Inc.

BARRY LOPEZ: "Manhattan, 1976" is the first of four sections in an essay called "Replacing Memory" which originally appeared in *The Georgia Review.* Copyright © 1993 by Barry Holstun Lopez. Reprinted by permission of Sterling Lord Literistic, Inc.

MEREDITH MARAN: From *What It's Like to Live Now* by Meredith Maran. Originally published in *The Utne Reader,* this essay was included in, "What It's Like to Live Now," by Meredith Maran. Copyright © 1995 by Meredith Maran. Used by permission of Bantam Books, a division of Bantam Doubleday Dell Publishing Group, Inc.

MARY MCCARTHY: "Names" from *Memories of a Catholic Girlhood,* copyright © 1957 and renewed 1985 by Mary McCarthy, reprinted by permission of Harcourt Brace & Company.

N. SCOTT MOMADAY: "The Way to Rainy Mountain" by N. Scott Momaday. First published in *The Reporter,* January 26, 1967. Reprinted by permission of the University of New Mexico Press.

ALICE MUNRO: "Boys and Girls" from *Dance of the Happy Shades,* © Alice Munro, 1968. Used by permission of McGraw-Hill Ryerson Limited, Canada.

GEORGE ORWELL: "Shooting an Elephant" from *Shooting an Elephant and Other Essays* by George Orwell, copyright 1950 by Sonia Brownell Orwell and renewed 1978 by Sonia Pitt-Rivers, reprinted by permission of Harcourt Brace & Company and the estate of the late Sonia Brownell Orwell and Martin Secker & Warburg.

GEORGE ORWELL: "Politics and the English Language" by George Orwell, copyright 1946 by Sonia Brownell Orwell and renewed 1974 by Sonia Orwell, reprinted from his volume of *Shooting an Elephant and Other Essays* by permission of Harcourt Brace & Company and the estate of the late Sonia Brownell Orwell and Martin Secker & Warburg.

JOY OVERBECK: "Sex, Kids and the Slut Look" from *Newsweek,* July 26, 1993, © 1993 by Joy Overbeck. All rights reserved. Reprinted by permission of the author.

NOEL PERRIN: "The Androgynous Man," *New York Times Magazine,* February 5, 1984. Copyright © 1984 by The New York Times Company. Reprinted by permission.

WILLIAM PERRY: "Examsmanship and the Liberal Arts" by William G. Perry, from *Examining in Harvard College.* Reprinted by permission of Harvard University Press.

KATHA POLLITT: "The Smurfette Principle" from *New York Times Magazine,* April 7, 1991, pp. 22–23. Copyright © 1991 by The New York Times Company. Reprinted by permission.

NEIL POSTMAN: "Now . . . This," from *Amusing Ourselves to Death* by Neil Postman.

Copyright © 1985 by Neil Postman. Used by permission of Viking Penguin, a division of Penguin Books USA Inc.

ADRIENNE RICH: "Split at the Root: An Essay on Jewish Identity," from *Nice Jewish Girls: A Lesbian Anthology* by Evelyn Torton Beck. Copyright © 1982, 1989 by Evelyn Torton Beck. Reprinted by permission of Beacon Press.

ADRIENNE RICH: "When We Dead Awaken: Writing as Re-Vision" is reprinted from *On Lies, Secrets, and Silence: Selected Prose 1966–1978* by Arienne Rich, by permission of W. W. Norton & Company, Inc. Copyright © 1979 by W. W. Norton & Company, Inc. "Aunt Jennifer's Tigers," "The Loser," "Orion," "Planetarium," and the lines from "Snapshots of a Daughter-in-Law" are reprinted from *Collected Early Poems: 1950–1970* by Adrienne Rich, by permission of W. W. Norton & Company, Inc. Copyright © 1993 by Adrienne Rich. Copyright © 1967, 1963, 1962, 1961, 1960, 1959, 1958, 1957, 1956, 1955, 1954, 1953, 1952, 1951 by Adrienne Rich. Copyright © 1984, 1975, 1971, 1969, 1966 by W. W. Norton & Company, Inc.

WILLIAM L. RODMAN: "When Questions Are Answers: The Message of Anthropology According to the People of Ambae." Reproduced by permission of the American Anthropological Association from *American Anthropologist* 93:2, June 1991. Not for further reproduction.

SCOTT RUSSELL SANDERS: From *The Secrets of the Universe* by Scott Russell Sanders. Copyright © 1991 by Scott Russell Sanders. Reprinted by permission of Beacon Press.

JULIET B. SCHOR: "The Constancy of Housewives' Hours" from *The Overworked American: The Unexpected Decline in Leisure* by Juliet Schor. Copyright © 1991 by BasicBooks, A Division of HarperCollins Publishers Inc. Reprinted by permission of BasicBooks, a division of HarperCollins Publishers, Inc.

GLORIA STEINEM: "Sex, Lies and Advertising," *Ms.* July/August 1990, pp. 18–28. Reprinted by permission of the author.

WYATT TOWNLEY: "A Plea for Video-Free Zones" from *Newsweek*, January 31, 1994, © 1994 Newsweek, Inc. All rights reserved. Reprinted by permission.

JUDY TROY: "The Way Things Will Be." Reprinted with permission of Scribner, an imprint of Simon & Schuster, Inc. from *Mourning Doves* by Judy Troy. Copyright © 1993 by Judy Troy. (Originally appeared in *The New Yorker*, October 15, 1990.)

JOHN UPDIKE: "Movie House" from *Telephone Poles and Other Poems* by John Updike. Copyright © 1963 by John Updike. Reprinted by permission of Alfred A. Knopf, Inc.

ALICE WALKER: "Am I Blue" from *Living by the Word: Selected Writings 1973–1987*, copyright © 1986 by Alice Walker, reprinted by permission of Harcourt Brace & Company.

VITA WALLACE: "Give Children the Vote," from *The Nation*, October 14, 1991. This article is reprinted from *The Nation* magazine. © The Nation Company, L.P.

E. B. WHITE: Drafts of "Notes and Comment" by E. B. White (final draft appearing in *The New Yorker*, July 26, 1969) are reprinted by permission of The Estate of E. B. White.

ROGER WILKINS: "Confessions of a Blue-Chip Black" by Roger Wilkins. Reprinted by permission of International Creative Management. Copyright © 1982 by Roger Wilkins.